D0997410

SELECT DOCUMENTS

OF

ENGLISH CONSTITUTIONAL HISTORY

THE MACMILLAN COMPANY
NEW YORK · BOSTON · CHICAGO · DALLAS
ATLANTA · SAN FRANCISCO

MACMILLAN & CO., LIMITED
LONDON · BOMBAY · CALCUTTA
MELBOURNE

THE MACMILLAN COMPANY
OF CANADA, LIMITED
TORONTO

Select Documents

of

English Constitutional History

EDITED BY

GEORGE BURTON ADAMS

PROFESSOR OF HISTORY IN YALE UNIVERSITY

AND

H. MORSE STEPHENS

PROFESSOR OF HISTORY IN CORNELL UNIVERSITY

New York

THE MACMILLAN COMPANY

LONDON: MACMILLAN & CO., LTD.

1935

PREFACE

THE pressure felt by two teachers of English history for a com-
prehensive volume of documents bearing on the development of
the English constitution has led to the compilation of this volume.
No source book for the illustration of English history yet published has met the needs of the student of constitutional history.
The excellent selections made by the late Bishop of Oxford, Mr.
G. W. Prothero, Mr. S. R. Gardiner, and Messrs. Gee and Hardy
only cover limited periods, or deal with one aspect of the subject.
Excellent as those selections are, they are too advanced or too
partial to be used in a college undergraduate course covering a
single year.   The University of Pennsylvania Reprints and the
Old South Leaflets contain too little material to illustrate a ful-
course of English constitutional history.   The editors have been
guided in the present selection by their practical experience in
undergraduate work, and it is hoped that it may meet the demands of similar courses of study in other colleges, and also
of courses pursued in some secondary and in many law schools.

Every teacher of history has his own ideas of the relative importance of documents, and this compilation cannot expect to
escape criticism either for its selections or for its omissions.
There was no difficulty in deciding upon the insertion of the most
famous documents, such as Magna Charta and the Bill of Rights,
but the selection of documents of lesser importance to form illus-
trations of the growth of constitutional customs and traditions
was of greater difficulty.   The editors have kept in mind in
making the selection that they were dealing with constitutional
and legal, and not with political, economic, and social questions,
and under this ruling many important documents, like the Grand

v

Remonstrance, were abbreviated, and others, like the Poor Laws and the Navigation Acts, were omitted altogether.

The feature of the earlier pages of this compilation which needs chiefly to be defended is the translation of the documents of the medieval period from Latin and Old French. It was only after long discussion and much hesitation that it was resolved to print translations rather than the originals. It was felt by the editors that although it might be indispensable for advanced students to use their documents in the original language, yet it was not possible to expect from large undergraduate classes sufficient training to enable all students in them to make ready use of the original documents. It was desired also to provide for the apparently growing demand for such material in secondary schools. Professor G. B. Adams, who is responsible for the selection and editing of the documents down to 1485, is responsible likewise for the translations of these documents, but in the case of statutes, the official translation in the *Statutes of the Realm* has been followed with only slight changes. Professor Adams does not presume that all the difficulties of translation have been here, for the first time, overcome, and he will be grateful to those who will call his attention to errors which have escaped him in spite of considerable pains to avoid them.

The problem with regard to the later documents after 1485 has been one of abridgment rather than of translation. The much greater length of the later documents made it impossible to print them in full, and Professor Morse Stephens is responsible for the abridgment as well as for the selection and editing of these later documents. It is as objectionable theoretically to abridge as to translate an original document, but as in the case of the translations the abridgments have been necessitated by practical considerations. A few of the most important documents have been printed in full, but most of them have been cut down in length, either by the omission of less important clauses or by inserting asterisks in the place of legal repetitions.

The most valuable feature of the three well-known volumes of selections made for the Oxford Clarendon Press by Bishop

Stubbs, Mr. Prothero, and Mr. Gardiner are the learned introductions to the documents they have edited. The editors of the
present selection did not feel it incumbent upon them to follow
this example, for their selection is intended to be used in class
along with some recognized text-book. The same consideration
which caused them to reject a general introduction explains also
the absence of special introductions to the different documents.
All that has been done is to give the date, a reference to the
original source, and occasionally to former reprints, and in the
case of documents earlier than 1485 to the pages in Stubbs's
Constitutional History where there is some discussion of the
document.

A few words should be given to the want of uniformity in
spelling and capitalization. As a general rule this reprint follows
the spelling and capitalization of the source from which the document is taken, as indicated at the head of each number. Some
of the later documents, such as 264, 265, and 266 preserve the
capitalization of the Acts of Parliament exactly as they were
printed; others follow the system used in earlier reprints; while
others again have been completely modernized. In all cases the
originals have been collated, but it was believed to be unnecessary
to return in every case to the original spelling and capitalization.

It only remains for the editors to express their great obligations
to their predecessors. Such a work as this could never have been
successfully undertaken had not the way been prepared by such
distinguished scholars as Bishop Stubbs, Mr. Prothero, and Mr.
Gardiner. Full credit has been given at the head of each number
when any document has been taken from the volumes edited by
these three historians, even although their reprints have been
carefully collated with the originals and occasional slips corrected.
It is hoped that one of the results of using this compilation with
undergraduate classes will be to attract attention to the interest
and importance of the study of documents, so that more advanced
students will turn to the more full and elaborate editions of these
distinguished scholars. Their three volumes, however, do not
cover the whole field. The *Select Charters and Other Illustra-*

tions of English Constitutional History, arranged and edited by William Stubbs, Bishop of Oxford, only reach to the death of Edward I in 1307 ; the *Select Statutes and Other Constitutional Documents*, edited by G. W. Prothero, concern the period from 1558 to 1625, the reigns of Elizabeth and James I; while the *Constitutional Documents of the Puritan Revolution*, selected and edited by Samuel Rawson Gardiner, deal with the period from 1625 to 1660. For the gaps which lie between these books considerable use has been made of the excellent collection of *Documents Illustrative of English Church History*, compiled by Henry Gee and W. J. Hardy, but for the most part documents not hitherto reprinted have been selected. In the period covered by Stubbs's *Select Charters* a number of documents not appearing in that collection have been included, especially such as illustrate the history of law.

Our thanks are due to Messrs. Gee and Hardy for permission to use a few of the translations in their *Documents Illustrative of English Church History*, and to Professor E. P. Cheyney for a similar permission to make use of translations appearing in the University of Pennsylvania *Translations and Reprints*. In both cases specific acknowledgment is made at the head of the translations borrowed. We desire to express our thanks also, for assistance rendered in getting this book into form for the press, to Professor G. M. Dutcher, Wesleyan University, Middletown, Connecticut.

GEORGE BURTON ADAMS.
H. MORSE STEPHENS.

OCTOBER 5, 1901.

CONTENTS

Contents

PAGE

HENRY IV

HENRY V

HENRY VI

Contents

Contents

Contents

Contents

Contents

ABBREVIATIONS

Bigelow Placita: Bigelow's Placita Anglo-Normannica.

Cheyney: Professor Cheyney in University of Pennsylvania Translations and Reprints.

G. & H.: Gee and Hardy's Documents Illustrative of English Church History

R. P.: Rolls of Parliament.

S. L: Statutes at Large.

S. R.: Statutes of the Realm.

Stubbs: Stubbs' Constitutional History.

Stubbs, S. C.: Stubbs' Select Charters.

English
Constitutional Documents

——◦◦∘◦∘◦——

1. Ordinance separating the Spiritual and Temporal Courts

(Date unknown. Latin text, Stubbs, *S. C.* 85. Translation, G. and H. 57.
1 Stubbs, 307.)

WILLIAM, by the grace of God king of the English, to R. Bainard, and G. de Magneville, and Peter de Valoines, and all my liege men of Essex, Hertfordshire and Middlesex greeting. Know ye and all my liege men resident in England, that I have by my common council, and by the advice of the archbishops, bishops, abbots and chief men of my realm, determined that the episcopal laws be mended as not having been kept properly nor according to the decrees of the sacred canons throughout the realm of England, even to my own times. Accordingly I command and charge you by royal authority that no bishop nor archdeacon do hereafter hold pleas of episcopal laws in the Hundred, nor bring a cause to the judgment of secular men which concerns the rule of souls. But whoever shall be impleaded by the episcopal laws for any cause or crime, let him come to the place which the bishop shall choose and name for this purpose, and there answer for his cause or crime, and not according to the Hundred but according to the canons and episcopal laws, and let him do right to God and his bishop. But if any one, being lifted up with pride, refuse to come to the bishop's court, let him be summoned three several times, and if by this means, even, he come not to obedience, let the authority of the king or sheriff be exerted ; and he who refuses to come to the bishop's judgment shall make good the bishop's law for every summons. This too I absolutely forbid that any sheriff, reeve or king's minister, or any other layman, do in any wise concern himself with the laws which belong to the bishop, or bring another man to judgment save in the

I

bishop's court. And let judgment nowhere be undergone but in the bishop's see or in that place which the bishop appoints for this purpose.

2. Writ for an Inquest of Lands at Ely

(1080.   Latin text, Bigelow's *Placita*, 24.   Translation by Editors.)

WILLIAM, king of the English, to Archbishop Lanfranc, and to Roger Count of Mortain, and to Godfrey Bishop of Coutances, greeting.

I order and direct you to assemble again all the shires which were present at the trial held concerning the lands of the church of Ely, before my consort went to Normandy the last time. With them, also, let there be those of my barons who had the right to be present and who were present at the aforesaid trial and who hold lands of the same church. When they have come together, let there be chosen some of those Englishmen who know how the lands of the said church were situated on the day that King Edward died, and what they say about it let them, thereupon, witness by an oath. This done, let there be restored to the church the lands which were in its demesne on the day of the death of Edward, excepting those which men claim that I have given to them. With regard to these, signify to me by letters which they are and who hold them. But let those who hold lands by service, which, without doubt, ought to be held from the church, make the best agreement they can with the abbot, and if they refuse, let the lands remain to the church. Let this also be done concerning those who hold sac and soc. Finally, order those men who hitherto by my order and direction have been accustomed to do it, to keep in repair the bridge at Ely.

3. Title of the Domesday Inquest for Ely

(1086.   Latin text, Stubbs, *S. C.* 86.   Translation by Editors.   1 Stubbs, 416.)

HERE is written down the inquest of lands, in what manner the king's barons have made inquisition, namely, by oath of the sheriff of the shire, and of all the barons and of their Frenchmen and of the whole hundred, of the priest, the reeve and six villeins of each vill. Next the name of the manor, who held it in the time of King Edward, who holds it now ; the number of hides ;

the number of plows on the demesne, the number of those of the
men ; the number of villeins ; the number of cotters ; the number
of serfs ; the number of freemen ; the number of sokemen ; the
amount of forest ; the amount of meadow ; the number of pastures ;
the number of mills ; the number of fishponds ; how much it has
been increased or diminished ; how much it was all worth then ;
and how much now ; how much each freeman and sokeman held
and holds there. All this three times over, namely, in the time of
King Edward, and when King William gave it, and as it now is,
and if more can be had than is had.

4. Typical Domesday Entries

(1086. Latin original. Translation by Editors. Specific references below.)

1. The same earl holds Hiham. Godwin held it. In the time
of King Edward there were two hides and a half, but it was assessed
at two hides, as they say, and now at two. There is land for
sixteen plows. In demesne is one, and thirty villeins and ten
borders with nineteen plows. There are six acres of meadow and
woods for two hogs. In the time of King Edward it was worth
100 shillings, now six pounds. It has been waste. (1 *Domesday*, 20, *a.*)

2. To the use of this manor the same Hugh claims three
messuages and a corner of a meadow and one virgate and five
acres of land against Turstin the chamberlain. Concerning this
the whole hundred bears testimony that his predecessors were
seised of it and holding it on the day on which King Edward was
alive and dead. (1 *Domesday*, 45, *a.*)

5. Writ applying Feudal Principles to the Church

(1095. Latin text, Round's *Feudal England*, 309. Translation by Editors.
1 Stubbs, 325.)

WILLIAM, King of the English, to all the French and English
who occupy freeholds from the bishopric of Worcester,
greeting.

Know ye that since the bishop has died, the honor has returned
into my possession. Now I will that you should give me from
your lands such relief as I have arranged [assessed] through my

barons.   Hugh de Lacy, twenty pounds ; Walter Punher, twenty pounds ;   *   *   *   Chipping, twenty shillings.

Witness : Ranulf the chaplain, and Eudes the steward, and Urso de Abetot.   If any one shall refuse to do this, Urso and Bernard shall seise their lands and money into my possession.

6. An Early Iter: The King *vs.* The Abbot of Tavistock

(1096.   Latin text, Bigelow's *Placita*, 69.   Translation by Editors.)

IN the year of the Lord's Incarnation the one thousand and ninty-sixth, and of the reign of William the Second of famous memory, the ninth, the said king sent at Quadragesima into Devonshire, Cornwall and Exeter, his lords Walklin the Bishop of Winchester, Ranulf the royal chaplain, William Capra, and Hardin Fitz-Belnold to examine royal pleas.   In which pleas, complaints have been made concerning a certain manor of the abbey of Tavistock, called Wulurunton, alleging and affirming that the said manor is wrongly held by the abbey of Tavistock and that on the contrary, it has always belonged of right to the royal demesne.   We denying their allegations and false charges, proved that in the judgment of many of our predecessors the said manor belonged of perpetual right to the abbey of Tavistock, without any dispute.   In which cause, together with the royal examiners of pleas above-mentioned, we besought the King of the English that, for the love of God and Saint Mary, he would grant that the aforesaid manor should belong to the abbey of Tavistock in perpetual right, without any question.   These very facts having been recited in the king's hearing, the king himself in granting our petition, and, for the sake of the souls of his father and mother, restoring in perpetuity to the abbey church of God and Saint Mary at Tavistock that manor, namely Wulurunton, made reply in these words :   *   *   *

7. Charter of Liberties of Henry I

(1100.   Latin text, Stubbs, *S. C.* 100.   Translation, Cheyney, 3.   1 Stubbs, 330.)

IN the year of the incarnation of the Lord, 1101, Henry, son of King William, after the death of his brother William, by the grace of God, king of the English, to all faithful, greeting :

1. Know that by the mercy of God, and by the common counsel of the barons of the whole kingdom of England, I have been crowned king of the same kingdom ; and because the kingdom has been oppressed by unjust exactions, I, from regard to God, and from the love which I have toward you, in the first place make the holy church of God free, so that I will neither sell nor place at rent, nor, when archbishop, or bishop, or abbot is dead, will I take anything from the domain of the church, or from its men, until a successor is installed into it. And all the evil customs by which the realm of England was unjustly oppressed will I take away, which evil customs I partly set down here.

2. If any one of my barons, or earls, or others who hold from me shall have died, his heir shall not redeem his land as he did in the time of my brother, but shall relieve it by a just and legitimate relief. Similarly also the men of my barons shall relieve their lands from their lords by a just and legitimate relief.

3. And if any one of the barons or other men of mine wishes to give his daughter in marriage, or his sister or niece or relation, he must speak with me about it, but I will neither take anything from him for this permission, nor forbid him to give her in marriage, unless he should wish to join her to my enemy. And if when a baron or other man of mine is dead, a daughter remains as his heir, I will give her in marriage according to the judgment of my barons, along with her land. And if when a man is dead his wife remains, and is without children, she shall have her dowry and right of marriage, and I will not give her to a husband except according to her will.

4. And if a wife has survived with children, she shall have her dowry and marriage portion, so long as she shall have kept her body legitimately, and I will not give her in marriage, except according to her will. And the guardian of the land and children shall be either the wife or another one of the relatives as shall seem to be most just. And I require that my barons should deal similarly with the sons and daughters or wives of their men.

5. The common tax on money which used to be taken through the cities and counties, which was not taken in the time of King Edward, I now forbid altogether henceforth to be taken. If any one shall have been seised, whether a moneyer or any other, with false money, strict justice shall be done for it.

6. All fines and all debts which were owed to my brother, I remit, except my rightful rents, and except those payments which had been agreed upon for the inheritances of others or for those things which more justly affected others. And if any one for his

own inheritance has stipulated anything, this I remit, and all reliefs which had been agreed upon for rightful inheritances.

7. And if any of my barons or men shall become feeble, however he himself shall give or arrange to give his money, I grant that it shall be so given. Moreover, if he himself, prevented by arms, or by weakness, shall not have bestowed his money, or arranged to bestow it, his wife or his children or parents, and his legitimate men shall divide it for his soul, as to them shall seem best.

8. If any of my barons or men shall have committed an offence he shall not give security to the extent of forfeiture of his money, as he did in the time of my father, or of my brother, but according to the measure of the offence so shall he pay, as he would have paid from the time of my father backward, in the time of my other predecessors; so that if he shall have been convicted of treachery or of crime, he shall pay as is just.

9. All murders moreover before that day in which I was crowned King, I pardon; and those which shall be done henceforth shall be punished justly according to the law of King Edward.

10. The forests, by the common agreement of my barons, I have retained in my own hand, as my father held them.

11. To those Knights who hold their land by the cuirass, I yield of my own gift the lands of their demesne ploughs free from all payments and from all labor, so that as they have thus been favored by such a great alleviation, so they may readily provide themselves with horses and arms for my service and for the defence of my kingdom.

12. A firm peace in my whole kingdom I establish and require to be kept from henceforth.

13. The law of King Edward I give to you again with those changes with which my father changed it by the counsel of his barons.

14. If any one has taken anything from my possessions since the death of King William, my brother, or from the possessions of any one, let the whole be immediately returned without alteration, and if any one shall have retained anything thence, he upon whom it is found will pay it heavily to me. Witnesses Maurice, bishop of London, and Gundulf, bishop, and William, bishop-elect, and Henry, earl, and Simon, earl, and Walter Giffard, and Robert de Montfort, and Roger Bigod, and Henry de Port, at London, when I was crowned.

8.   Writ concerning Lands at Stanton

(Date uncertain.   Latin text, *Chronicon Monasterii de Abingdon*, ii. 84.
Translation by Editors.)

HENRY, King of England, to Hugh of Buckland and William
sheriff of Oxfordshire, greeting.

Order on my behalf the men of your counties to declare the
whole truth concerning the three virgates of land which Rualcus
de Avranches claims, and if they belong to the manor of Stanton
which I gave to him, let him have possession ; but if not let the
abbey of Abingdon have possession.

Witness : Roger the chancellor.   By —— Basset ; at Cambridge.

9.   Writ concerning Lands at Caversham

(Date uncertain.   Latin text, *Chronicon Monasterii de Abingdon*, ii. 85.
Translation by Editors.)

HENRY, King of England, to Walter Giffard and Agnes his
mother, greeting.

I order that you render full justice to Faritius abbot of Abingdon concerning the land which Ralph of Caversham gave to
Abingdon by your permission, and of which the church was seised ;
and so do lest I hear from thence complaint of lack of justice.

Witness : Ranulf the chancellor, at Windsor.

10.   First Charter of Stephen

(1135.   Latin text, Stubbs, *S. C.* 119.   Translation, Cheyney, 5.   1 Stubbs, 346.)

STEPHEN, by the grace of God, king of the English, to the
justices, sheriffs, barons, and all his ministers and faithful,
French and English, greeting.

Know that I have conceded and by this my present charter confirmed to all my barons and men of England all the liberties and
good laws which Henry, King of the English, my uncle, gave and
conceded to them, and all the good laws and good customs which
they had in the time of King Edward, I concede to them.   Wherefore I wish and firmly command that they shall have and hold all
those good laws and liberties from me and my heirs, they and their
heirs, freely, quietly, and fully ; and I prohibit any one from bring·

ing any obstacle, or impediment, or diminution upon them in these matters on pain of forfeiture to me.

Witness William Martel, at London.

---------◆---------

11. Second Charter of Stephen

(1136.   Latin text, Stubbs, *S. C.* 120.   Translation, *Statutes of the Realm*
as in G. and H. 66.   1 Stubbs, 347.)

I STEPHEN, by the grace of God and the assent of the clergy and people elected king of the English, and consecrated by William, archbishop of Canterbury and legate of the Holy Roman Church, and confirmed by Innocent, pontiff of the Holy Roman See, from regard and love to God, do grant holy Church to be free and confirm due reverence to her.   I promise that I will not do nor allow any simony in the Church or in church affairs.   I permit and confirm justice and power over ecclesiastical persons and all clerks and their effects, and the distribution of ecclesiastical goods to be in the hands of the bishops.   The dignities of churches confirmed by their privileges, and their customs had of ancient continuance, I ordain and grant to remain inviolate.   All the possessions and holdings of churches which they had on that day when William the king, my grandfather, was alive and dead, I grant to them to be free and absolute without any appeal from claimants.   But if the Church shall hereafter seek to regain any of the things held or possessed before the death of the same king which the Church has no longer, I reserve them for my indulgence and dispensation for restoration and for consideration.   But I confirm whatever has been bestowed upon them since the death of this same king, by the liberality of kings or the gift of great men, by presentation or acquisition, or by any exchange of the faithful.   I promise that I will perform peace and justice in all things, and will maintain these for them as far as I can.   I reserve for myself the forests which William my grandfather, and William my uncle established and had.   All the others which King Henry further added I give back and grant to the churches and the kingdom without molestation.   If any bishop or abbot or other ecclesiastical person shall, before his death, reasonably devise or intend to devise his goods, I grant it to remain firm.   But if he shall be overtaken by death let the same devise take place with the advice of the Church for the health of his soul.   Moreover, whilst sees shall be without their proper pastors, these and all their possessions I will commit to the hand and custody of the clerks or good men of the same church, until a pastor be canonically appointed to succeed. I entirely abolish all exactions, and injuries, and miskennings wrongly introduced, whether by sheriffs or by any other. I will observe, and command and ordain to be observed, the good laws and ancient and just customs in murders and pleas and other causes. All these things I grant and confirm saving my royal and just dignity. Witness: W. Archbishop of Canterbury, Hugh Archbishop of Rouen, and Henry Bishop of Winchester, and Roger Bishop of Salisbury, and A. Bishop of Lincoln, and Nigel Bishop of Ely, and Everard Bishop of Norwich, and Simon Bishop of Worcester, and Bernard Bishop of Saint David's, and Owen Bishop of Evreux, Richard Bishop of Avranches, Robert Bishop of Hereford, John Bishop of Rochester, Athelwulf Bishop of Carlisle, and other lay signatories. At Oxford, in the year 1136 from the Lord's Incarnation, and the first of my reign.

———◆———

12. A Trial in the Curia Regis. Case of Abbot Walter *vs.* Gilbert de Baillol

(c. 1154. Latin text, Bigelow's *Placita*, 175. Translation by Editors.)

[" THE king grants his writ at the instance of Walter, abbot of Saint Martin, to John, earl of Eu, commanding him to do justice by the abbot against Gilbert de Baillol as to certain lands. The defendant evades the trial in various ways. Leave is finally obtained to bring the suit into the King's Court, but the king's presence cannot be obtained. The cause, though much litigated before the justiciars, comes to no satisfactory conclusion. The king's presence is at last obtained, and the trial proceeds." — BIGELOW.]

* * * Now therefore, since there was no longer opportunity for excuse, both parties appeared before the lord king, sitting in the seat of judgment. There stood forth in the midst one of the abbot's monks named Osmund, and a knight, Peter de Chriel, who, beginning at the beginning of the whole court proceedings, set forth in order before the king and his assessors, how the said land of Barnhorn had been partly given to the church of Saint Martin of Battle, and partly purchased, how afterwards it was taken away, and also how far progress had been made in the case, at the present so long since the beginning of the suit; adding also their complaint over the great and expensive delay of the affair,

and the constant and useless annoyance of the abbot and his party. Now since there was nothing in this statement of the case for prose-cution which could be successfully controverted, as the Curia Regis possessed testimony on every point; at the permission of the king, the deeds of purchase and of gift were read in the hearing of all, and also the charters of confirmation. Since the other party had little to answer to these, Gilbert de Baillol, that he might not seem to make no objection, answered that he had heard the reading of the deeds given by his predecessors, but he took occasion to note that no seals were affixed to them in attestation. Turning to him, that splendid and wise man Richard de Lucy, the brother of the said abbot, then the Justiciar of the lord king, inquired whether he had a seal. Upon his reply that he had a seal, the illustrious man smiled and said, "The old fashion was not for every little knight to have a seal, but it was customary for only kings and peo-ple of consequence to have them, and in the old times spite did not make men pettifoggers or sceptics." And when the said Gil-bert strove to cast doubt upon the confirmation by King Henry the elder, alleging that the abbot and monks were able to persuade the lord king not as a matter of justice but of favor, the lord king, taking the charter and seal of his grandfather King Henry into his own hands and turning to the said Gilbert, said, "By the eyes of God, if you can prove this charter false, it will be worth a thou-sand pounds to me in England." As he made little or no reply to these words, the king made this noteworthy remark, "If," said he, "the monks by means of a similar charter and confirmation were able to show that they had a right of this sort to the present place, to wit, Clarendon, which I chiefly love, there would be no just reply for me to make to save me from entirely surrendering it to them." The king, therefore, turning to the abbot and his party, said, "Go out, and having taken counsel, confer together to see if perchance there is anything upon which you wish to depend rather than upon this charter. Still I do not think you will seek at pres-ent any other proof." So the abbot and his party, withdrawing to take council concerning this, and recognizing that their charter sufficed for all proof, from the last words of the king in which he said, "I do not think you will seek at present any other proof," they returned into the presence of the king and his assessors, after holding the council, and asserted that they did not depend on others or seek other proof outside of the charter, that they claimed nothing more or less but the charter, but upon this they desired the judgment of the Curia Regis. As the other party had no reply to make inasmuch as it neither dared nor could assert that the charter was false because this could not be proved; by the unanimous consent of the whole court, judgment was given that, to the abbot and church of Saint Martin of Battle restitution should be made of everything which he demanded on the testimony of the charter. * * *

---

13. Constitutions of Clarendon

(1164. Latin text, Stubbs, *S. C.* 137. Translation, G. and H. 68. 1 Stubbs, 501)

IN the year 1164 from our Lord's Incarnation, the fourth of the pontificate of Alexander, the tenth of Henry II., most illustrious king of the English, in the presence of the same king, was made this remembrance or acknowledgment of a certain part of the customs, liberties, and dignities of his ancestors, that is of King Henry his grandfather, and of others, which ought to be observed and held in the realm. And owing to strifes and dissensions which had taken place between the clergy and justices of the lord the king and the barons of the realm, in respect of customs and dignities of the realm, this recognition was made before the archbishops and bishops and clergy, and the earls and barons and nobles of the realm. And these same customs recognized by the archbishops and bishops, and earls and barons, and by those of high rank and age in the realm, Thomas archbishop of Canterbury, and Roger archbishop of York, and Gilbert bishop of London, and Henry bishop of Winchester, and Nigel bishop of Ely, and William bishop of Norwich, and Robert bishop of Lincoln, and Hilary bishop of Chichester, and Jocelyn bishop of Salisbury, and Richard bishop of Chester, and Bartholomew bishop of Exeter, and Robert bishop of Hereford, and David bishop of Saint David's, and Roger elect of Worcester, conceded, and by word of mouth steadfastly promised on the word of truth, to the lord the king and his heirs, should be kept and observed in good faith and without evil intent, these being present: Robert earl of Leicester, Reginald earl of Cornwall, Conan earl of Brittany, John earl of Eu, Roger earl of Clare, earl Geoffrey de Mandeville, Hugh earl of Chester, William earl of Arundel, earl Patrick, William earl of Ferrers, Richard de Luci, Reginald de St. Valery, Roger Bigod, Reginald de Warenne, Richer de Aquila, William de Braose, Richard de Camville, Nigel de Mowbray, Simon de Beauchamp, Humphry de Bohun, Matthew de Hereford, Walter de Mayenne, Manser Biset the steward, William Malet, William de Courcy, Robert de Dunstanville, Jocelyn de Baillol, William de Lanvallei, William de Caisnet, Geoffrey de Vere, William de Hastings, Hugh de Moreville, Alan de Neville, Simon son of Peter, William Maudit the chamberlain, John Maudit, John Marshall, Peter de Mara, and many other mag· nates and nobles of the realm, as well clerical as lay.

Now of the acknowledged customs and dignities, of the realm a certain part is contained in the present document, of which part these are the chapters : —

1. If controversy shall arise between laymen, or clergy and lay- men, or clergy, regarding advowson and presentation to churches, let it be treated or concluded in the court of the lord the king.

2. Churches belonging to the fee of the lord the king cannot be granted in perpetuity without his own assent and grant.

3. Clerks cited and accused of any matter shall, when summoned by the king's justice, come into his own court to answer there con- cerning what it shall seem to the king's court should be answered there, and in the church court for what it shall seem should be answered there ; yet so that the king's justice shall send into the court of holy Church to see in what way the matter is there treated. And if the clerk be convicted, or shall confess, the Church must not any longer protect him.

4. Archbishops, bishops, and persons of the realm are not al- lowed to leave the kingdom without licence of the lord the king ; and if they do leave, they shall, if the king so please, give security that neither in going nor in staying, nor in returning, will they seek the ill or damage of the lord the king or realm.

5. Excommunicate persons are not to give pledge for the future, nor to take oath, but only to give security and pledge of abiding by the church's judgment that they may be absolved.

6. Laymen are not to be accused save by proper and legal ac- cusers and witnesses in the presence of the bishop, so that the archdeacon do not lose his right nor anything due to him thence. And if the accused be such that no one wills or dares to accuse them, the sheriff, when requested by the bishop, shall cause twelve lawful men from the neighborhood or the town to swear before the bishop that they will show the truth in the matter according to their conscience.

7. No one who holds of the king in chief, and none of his de- mesne officers are to be excommunicated, nor the lands of any one of them to be put under an interdict unless first the lord the king, if he be in the country, or his justiciar if he be outside the king- dom, be applied to, in order that he may do right for him ; and so that what shall appertain to the royal court be concluded there, and that what shall belong to the church court be sent to the same to be treated there.

8. In regard to appeals, if they shall occur, they must proceed from the archdeacon to the bishop, and from the bishop to the archbishop. And if the archbishop fail in showing justice, they must come at last to the lord the king, that by his command the dispute be concluded in the archbishop's court, so that it must not go further without the assent of the lord the king.

9. If a dispute shall arise between a clerk and a layman, or between a layman and a clerk, in respect of any tenement which the clerk wishes to bring to frank-almoign, but the layman to a lay fee, it shall be concluded by the consideration of the king's chief justice on the award of twelve lawful men, whether the tenement belong to frank-almoign or to lay fee, before the king's justiciar himself. And if the award be that it belongs to frank-almoign it shall be pleaded in the church court, but if to the lay fee, unless both claim under the same bishop or baron, it shall be pleaded in the king's court. But if both appeal concerning this fee to the same bishop or baron, it shall be pleaded in his own court, so that for making the award he who was first seised, lose not his seisin until the matter be settled by the plea.

10. If any one of a city, or castle, or borough, or a demesne manor of the lord the king, be cited by archdeacon or bishop for any offence for which he ought to answer them, and refuse to give satisfaction at their citations, it is well lawful to place him under interdict; but he must not be excommunicated before the chief officer of the lord the king of that town be applied to, in order that he may adjudge him to come for satisfaction. And if the king's officer fail in this, he shall be at the king's mercy, and thereafter the bishop shall be able to restrain the accused by ecclesiastical justice.

11. Archbishops, bishops, and all persons of the realm who hold of the king in chief, have their possessions from the lord the king as barony, and are answerable therefor to the king's justices and ministers, and follow and do all royal rights and customs, and like all other barons, have to be present at the trials of the court of the lord the king with the barons until it comes to a judgment of loss of limb, or death.

12. When an archbishopric or bishopric is vacant, or any abbey or priory of the king's demesne, it must be in his own hand, and from it he shall receive all revenues and rents as demesne. And when they come to provide for the church, the lord the king must cite the chief persons of the church, and the election must take place in the chapel of the lord the king himself, with the assent of the lord the king, and the advice of the persons of the realm

whom he shall have summoned to do this. And the person elected shall there do homage and fealty to the lord the king as to his liege lord for his life and limbs and earthly honor, saving his order, before he be consecrated.

13. If any of the nobles of the realm forcibly prevent the archbishop or bishop or archdeacon from doing justice in regard of himself or his people, the lord the king must bring them to justice. And if perchance any one should deforce the lord the king, the archbishops and bishops and archdeacons must judge him, so that he gives satisfaction to the lord the king.

14. The goods of those who are under forfeit of the king, no church or cemetery is to detain against the king's justice, because they belong to the king himself, whether they be found inside churches or outside.

15. Pleas of debt due under pledge of faith or without pledge of faith are to be in the king's justice.

16. Sons of villeins ought not to be ordained without the assent of the lord on whose land they are known to have been born.

Now the record of the aforesaid royal customs and dignities was made by the said archbishops and bishops, and earls and barons, and the nobles and elders of the realm, at Clarendon, on the fourth day before the purification of the Blessed Mary, ever Virgin, the lord Henry the king's son, with his father the lord the king being present there. There are moreover many other great customs and dignities of holy Mother Church and the lord the king and the barons of the realm, which are not contained in this writing. And let them be safe for holy Church and the lord the king and his heirs and the barons of the realm, and be inviolably observed.

---

14.   Assize of Clarendon

(**1166.**   Latin text, Stubbs, *S. C.* 143.   Translation, Cheyney, **22.**
1 Stubbs, 505, 662.)

HERE begins the Assize of Clarendon, made by King Henry II. with the assent of the archbishops, bishops, abbots, earls and barons of all England.

1. In the first place, the aforesaid King Henry, with the consent of all his barons, for the preservation of the peace and the keeping of justice, has enacted that inquiry should be made through the several counties and through the several hundreds, by twelve

of the most legal men of the hundred and by four of the most legal men of each vill, upon their oath that they will tell the truth, whether there is in their hundred or in their vill, any man who has been accused or publicly suspected of himself being a robber, or murderer, or thief, or of being a receiver of robbers, or murderers, or thieves, since the lord king has been king. And let the justices make this inquiry before themselves, and the sheriffs before themselves.

2. And let any one who has been found by the oath of the aforesaid, to have been accused or publicly suspected of having been a robber, or murderer, or thief, or a receiver of them, since the lord king has been king, be arrested and go to the ordeal of water and let him swear that he has not been a robber, or murderer, or thief, or receiver of them since the lord king has been king, to the value of five shillings, so far as he knows.

3. And if the lord of the man who has been arrested or his steward or his men shall have claimed him, with a pledge, within the third day after he has been seised, let him be given up and his chattels until he himself makes his law.

4. And when a robber, or murderer, or thief, or receiver of them shall have been seised through the above-mentioned oath, if the justices are not to come very soon into that county where they have been arrested, let the sheriffs send word to the nearest justice by some intelligent man that they have arrested such men, and the justices will send back word to the sheriffs where they wish that these should be brought before them ; and the sheriffs shall bring them before the justices ; and along with these they shall bring from the hundred and the vill where they have been arrested, two legal men to carry the record of the county and of the hundred as to why they were seised, and there before the justice let them make their law.

5. And in the case of those who have been arrested through the aforesaid oath of this assize, no one shall have court, or judgment, or chattels, except the lord king in his court before his justices, and the lord king shall have all their chattels. In the case of those, however, who have been arrested, otherwise than through this oath, let it be as it has been accustomed and ought to be.

6. And the sheriffs who have arrested them shall bring such before the justice without any other summons than they have from him. And when robbers, or murderers, or thieves, or receivers of them, who have been arrested through the oath or otherwise, are handed over to the sheriffs they also must receive them immediately without delay.

7. And in the several counties where there are no jails, let such be made in a borough or in some castle of the king, from the money of the king and from his forest, if one shall be near, or from some other neighboring forest, on the view of the servants of the king; in order that in them the sheriffs may be able to detain those who have been seised by the officials who are accustomed to do this or by their servants.

8. And the lord king moreover wills that all should come to the county courts to make this oath, so that no one shall remain behind because of any franchise which he has or court or jurisdiction which he had, but that they should come to the making of this oath.

9. And there is to be no one within a castle or without a castle, or even in the honor of Wallingford, who may forbid the sheriffs to enter into his court or his land for seeing to the frank-pledges and that all are under pledges; and let them be sent before the sheriffs under a free pledge.

10. And in cities and boroughs, let no one have men or receive them in his house or in his land or his soc, whom he does not take in hand that he will produce before the justice if they shall be required, or else let them be under a frankpledge.

11. And let there be none in a city or borough or in a castle or without or even in the honor of Wallingford who shall forbid the sheriffs to enter into his land or his jurisdiction to arrest those who have been charged or publicly suspected of being robbers or murderers or thieves or receivers of them, or outlaws, or persons charged concerning the forest; but he requires that they should aid them to capture these.

12. And if any one is captured who has in his possession the fruits of robbery or theft, if he is of bad reputation and has an evil testimony from the public, and has not a warrant, let him not have law. And if he shall not have been publicly suspected, on account of the possession which he has let him go to the water.

13. And if any one shall have acknowledged robbery or murder or theft or the reception of them in the presence of legal men or of the hundreds, and afterwards shall wish to deny it, he shall not have law.

14. The lord king wills moreover that those who make their law and shall be absolved by the law, if they are of very bad testimony, and publicly and disgracefully spoken ill of by the testimony of many and legal men, shall abjure the lands of the king, so that within eight days they shall go over the sea, unless the wind shall have detained them; and with the first wind which they shall have

afterward they shall go over the sea, and they shall not afterward return into England, except on the permission of the lord king; and then let them be outlawed if they return, and if they return they shall be seised as outlaws.

15. And the lord king forbids any vagabond, that is a wandering or an unknown man, to be sheltered anywhere except in a borough, and even there he shall be sheltered only one night, unless he shall be sick there, or his horse, so that he is able to show an evident excuse.

16. And if he shall have been there more than one night, let him be arrested and held until his lord shall come to give securities for him, or until he himself shall have secured pledges; and let him likewise be arrested who has sheltered him.

17. And if any sheriff shall have sent word to any other sheriff that men have fled from his county into another county, on account of robbery or murder or theft, or the reception of them, or for outlawry or for a charge concerning the forest of the king, let him arrest them. And even if he knows of himself or through others that such men have fled into his county, let him arrest them and hold them until he shall have secured pledges from them.

18. And let all sheriffs cause a list to be made of all fugitives who have fled from their counties; and let them do this in the presence of their county courts, and they will carry the written names of these before the justices when they come first before these, so that they may be sought through all England, and their chattels may be seised for the use of the king.

19. And the lord king wills that, from the time when the sheriffs have received the summons of the justices in eyre to appear before them with their county courts, they shall gather together their county courts and make inquiry for all who have recently come into their counties since this assize; and that they should send them away with pledges that they will be before the justices, or else keep them in custody until the justices come to them, and then they shall have them before the justices.

20. The lord king moreover prohibits monks and canons and all religious houses from receiving any one of the lesser people as a monk or canon or brother, until it is known of what reputation he is, unless he shall be sick unto death.

21. The lord king moreover forbids any one in all England to receive in his land or his jurisdiction or in a house under him any one of the sect of those renegades who have been excommunicated and branded at Oxford. And if any one shall have received them, he will be at the mercy of the lord king, and the

c

house in which they have been shall be carried outside the village
and burned.   And each sheriff will take this oath that he will
hold this, and will make all his servants swear this, and the
stewards of the barons, and all knights and free tenants of the
counties.

22. And the lord king wills that this assize shall be held in
his kingdom so long as it shall please him.

---

15. Inquest of the Sheriffs

(1170.   Latin text, Stubbs, *S. C.* 148.   Translation by Editors.   1 Stubbs, 510.)

IN the first place, the barons shall require bond and surety from
all the sheriffs who have been sheriffs since the lord king last
went over to Normandy, and from all who since that time have
been bailiffs or ministers of theirs who have held a bailiwick from
them and from all those who since that time have held the
hundreds of the barons which they have in the county whether
they hold them at a ferm or in custody; that on a day which
they shall set for them they will appear before the lord king to
do justice and to redress to him and to his men what they ought
to redress.   And if because of sickness the sheriffs shall be unable
to appear before them, let them send in their place persons to
answer for them, and let these give bond and surety sufficient
for the sheriffs and for themselves, that they will perform in the
presence of the lord king that which the sheriffs ought to perform
on the fixed day.

Afterwards they shall take an oath from all the barons and
knights and freemen of the county, that they will speak the truth
concerning that which shall be inquired of them on behalf of the
lord king, and that they will not conceal the truth for love of any
one, or for hatred, or for bribe or reward, or for fear or promise
or for any reason.

This shall be the manner of the inquest : —

I. In the first place let inquisition be made concerning the
sheriffs and their bailiffs what and how much they have received
from each hundred, and from each vill and from each man, since
the lord king went abroad, whence the land and the people have
been burdened ; and what they have received by a judgment of
the county or hundred, and what without a judgment, and what
they learn was taken by a judgment, let it be written down by

itself, and what without a judgment let it be written by itself; and concerning all exactions inquisition shall be made of the cause and the evidence.

II. Likewise let inquisition be made concerning the archbishops, bishops, earls and barons, and their stewards and officers, what and how much they have received from their lands, since the said term, from each of their hundreds, and from each of their vills, and from each of their men, by a judgment or without a judgment, and let them write down separately all these exactions and their causes and occasions.

III. And likewise let inquisition be made concerning those men who since that term have held in custody other bailiwicks from the lord king, whether of a bishopric, or of an abbey, or of a barony, or of any honor or escheat.

IV. And likewise let inquisition be made concerning the king's bailiffs who have travelled through his land to do the king's business, which has been assigned to them; and what they learn from this, let them write down.

V. Also concerning the chattels of those who fled because of the Assize of Clarendon and concerning the chattels of those who have been undone through that assize, let inquisition be made of what has been done and of what was obtained thence in each hundred and each vill, and let it be diligently and carefully written down. And likewise let inquisition be made whether any one has been unjustly accused under that assize for reward or promise or hatred or other unjust cause; and whether any accusation has been withdrawn or any accused person released for reward or promise or love and who received the reward for it, and likewise let this be written down.

VI. And let inquisition be made concerning the aids for marrying the king's daughter, what was obtained thence in each hundred and each vill, whether in payments or in remissions, and to whom this has been handed over and paid.

VII. And let inquisition be made of what and how much the foresters and their bailiffs and officers have received, since the said term, in their offices in whatever way they received it or under whatever circumstance, and whether they have remitted any of the rights of the king for reward or promise or for any friendship. And concerning forest offences; concerning those who have injured his forests and stags and hinds and other wild beasts; and what they learn, let them write down diligently; and whether the foresters or their bailiffs have arrested any one or attached any one by bond and surety or have accused any, and

afterwards have released them without trial on their own re-
sponsibility, and let inquisition be made concerning those who
have done these things and let it be written down.

VIII. And let all who have been accused of anything be placed
under bond and surety to appear before the lord king at a time
which shall be appointed for them, and to do right and to redress
to the king and to his men what they ought to redress, and let
those without sureties be held in custody.

IX. And inquisition shall be made whether the sheriffs or any
bailiffs have returned any of the things which they have taken or
whether they have made any peace with men since they heard
of the arrival of the lord king, to prevent any complaint from
thence reaching the lord king.

X. And let inquisition be made concerning amercements
whether any one has been released, for reward or love, from
what he had at first been amerced, and by whom this has been
done.

XI. And let inquisition be made concerning those who owe
homage to the lord king and have done it neither to him nor to
his son, and let them be written down.

XII. Concerning the demesnes of the lord king, let inquisition
be made whether the houses are enclosed with ditch and hedge,
and whether there are granaries there, and cow-sheds, and sheep-
folds and other buildings and stock, as the lord king ordered
before he went abroad.

XIII. And after they have been examined, my sheriffs and
officers shall employ themselves about my other affairs, and they
shall swear to attend lawfully to making the inquest throughout
the lands of the barons.

---

16. Assize of Northampton

(1176. Latin text, Stubbs, *S. C.* 150.   Translation by Editors.   1 Stubbs, 522.)

THESE are the assizes made at Clarendon and afterwards
revised at Northampton.

1. If any one shall have been accused before the justices of
the lord king of murder or theft or robbery or of harboring
men who do such things or of forgery or arson, by the oath of
twelve knights of the hundred, or if knights are not present, by
the oath of twelve freemen, lawful men, and by the oath of four

men from each vill of the hundred, he shall go to the ordeal of water, and if he is undone he shall lose one foot. And at Northampton it was added for rigorous justice that he shall likewise lose his right hand with his foot, and he shall abjure the realm and within forty days he shall leave the kingdom. And if he shall have been to the water whole he shall furnish sureties and remain in the kingdom, unless he has been accused of murder or other infamous felony by the community of the county and of the lawful knights of the country, of which if he has been accused in the said manner, although he has been to the water safely, nevertheless within forty days he shall depart from the realm, and take with him his chattels saving the rights of his lords, and at the mercy of the lord king he shall abjure the realm. Moreover this assize shall be in force from the time the assize was made at Clarendon continuously to this time and from now on as long as it shall please the lord king, in cases of murder and treason and arson and in all of the aforesaid cases except in petty thefts and robberies which have been committed in time of war, such as of horses, oxen and smaller things.

2. Item let no one either in borough or vill entertain in his house for more than one night any stranger for whom he refuses to be responsible, unless the hospitality has a reasonable excuse, which the master of the house shall declare to his neighbors. And when he leaves, let him depart in the presence of the neighbors and by day.

3. If any one has about him the fruits of murder or theft or robbery or forgery and confesses it or any other felony which he has committed, before the reeve of the hundred or borough and before lawful men, he cannot afterwards deny that crime before the justices. And likewise, if without such fruits in his possession, he shall confess anything of the sort before them, in like manner he cannot deny this before the justices.

4. Item if any freeholder dies let his heirs remain in such seisin as their father had of his fee on the day of his death, and let them have his chattels out of which they shall execute the will of the deceased : and afterwards they shall seek out their lord and pay him a relief and the other things which they ought to pay him from their fee. And if the heir is under age the lord of the fee shall receive his homage and may keep him in custody as long as is his right. The other lords if there are several shall receive his homage and he shall render to them what is right. And let the wife of the deceased have her dowry and the portion of his chattels which falls to her. And if the lord of the fee shall refuse the

heirs of the deceased the seisin of the said deceased which they claim, the justices of the lord king shall thereupon cause recognition to be made by twelve lawful men of what seisin the deceased had of it on the day of his death : and according to the recognition, restitution shall be made to his heirs. And if any one has done contrary to this and has been convicted of it let him remain at the king's mercy.

5. Item the king's justices shall cause a recognition to be made of dispossessions contrary to the Assize, since the lord king's coming to England next after the peace made between him and the king his son.

6. Item the justices shall receive oaths of fealty for the lord king from the first Sunday after Easter to the first Sunday after Pentecost from all, to wit, earls, barons, knights and freeholders, and also villeins, who wish to remain in the realm. And whoever refuses to take the oath of fealty, shall be arrested as an enemy of the lord king. The justices are also to give orders that all those who have not yet paid homage and allegiance to the lord king that, at a time which shall be named for them, they shall come and pay homage and allegiance to the king as liege lord.

7. Item the justices shall determine all pleas and rights pertaining to the lord king and to his crown, by writ of the lord king or of those who shall be in his place, in the matter of a half a knight's fee and under, unless the dispute is so great that it cannot be settled without the lord king, or such as the justices shall refer to him or to those who shall be in his place on account of their uncertainty. They shall take care according to their ability to act for the advantage of the lord king. They shall also hold assize in the case of wicked robbers and evil-doers of the land, in the counties through which they are about to go, which assize is by the advice of the king his son and of his men.

8. Item the justices shall see to it that those castles which were destroyed are completely destroyed and that those which ought to be destroyed are leveled to the ground. And unless they shall do this the lord king will have the judgment of his court upon them as upon those who hold in contempt his commands.

9. Item the justices shall make inquisition with regard to churches and lands and women who are in the gift of the lord king.

10. Item let the bailiffs of the lord king answer to the exchequer both for the returns from the assize and for all their acquisitions which they make in their bailiwicks ; those being excepted which pertain to the office of sheriff.

11. Item the justices shall make inquisition concerning the custody of castles both by whom and how much and where service ought to be made and let them report to the lord king.

12. Item a thief when he is arrested shall be handed over to the custody of the sheriff. And if the sheriff should be absent, he shall be taken to the nearest warden of a castle and he shall guard him till he delivers him to the sheriff.

13. Item the justices shall cause search to be made according to the custom of the land for those who have fled from the kingdom; and unless they are willing to return within the set time and stand trial in the court of the lord king, then let them be outlawed; and let the names of the outlaws be reported at Easter and at Michaelmas to the exchequer and from thence they shall be sent to the lord king.

17. Assize of Arms

(1181. Latin text, Stubbs, *S. C.* 154. Translation by Editors. 1 Stubbs, 632.)

ASSIZE concerning the bearing of arms in England.

1. Let whoever holds a knight's fee have a coat of mail and a helmet, a shield and a lance; and let every knight have as many coats of mail, and helmets, and shields, and lances as he has knight's fees in his demesne [that is, not subinfeudated, or held by knights under him].

2. Also, let every free layman who is worth sixteen marks in chattels or in revenue have a coat of mail and a helmet and a shield and a lance; also, let every free layman who is worth ten marks in chattels or revenue have a hauberk and a head-piece of iron and a lance.

3. Item let all burghers and the whole body of freemen have a doublet of mail and a head-piece of iron and a lance.

4. Moreover let each one of them swear that before the feast of Saint Hilary he will have these arms and that he will bear faith to the lord king Henry, namely the son of the empress Matilda, and that he will bear these arms in his service according to his order and for the protection of the lord king and of his realm. And let no one who has these arms sell them or pledge them or give them away, or in any other manner alienate them, neither let a lord in any manner take them away from his man, either by forfeiture, or by gift or as a pledge, or in any other manner.

5. If any one having these arms shall die, let his arms remain to his heir. But if the heir should be of such age that he could not use the arms if there should be need let the one who has him in custody likewise have the custody of his arms and let him find a man who can use arms in the service of the lord king until the heir is of such age that he can bear arms, and then let him have them.

6. Let every burgher who has more arms than he need have according to this assize sell them or give them away or otherwise alienate them to such a man as will keep them in the service of the lord king of England. And let none of them keep more arms than he is required to have according to this assize.

7. Item let no Jew keep a coat of mail or a hauberk in his possession, but let him sell it or give it away or otherwise dispose of it so that it shall remain in the service of the king.

8. Item let no one carry arms out of England except by the order of the lord king; neither let any one sell arms to any one who will carry them out of England.

9. Item let the justices cause oaths to be taken by lawful knights or other free and lawful men of the hundred or borough as many as they shall see fit, who shall have the value of chattels which makes it necessary for him to have a coat of mail and a helmet and a lance and a shield according as has been said; to wit, that one by one they will name to them all from their hundreds and neighborhoods and boroughs who have sixteen marks either in chattels or in revenue, and likewise those who have ten marks. And afterwards let the justices cause all those jurors and others to be registered; who have such an amount of chattels and revenues and what arms each ought to have according to the value of chattels or revenues, and afterwards in their presence, in the hearing of all those persons, let them cause that this assize concerning the having of arms be read and that they swear that they will have these arms according to the aforesaid value of chattels or revenue, and that they will hold them at the service of the lord king according to this said assize at the command and for the protection of the lord king Henry and of his realm. If indeed it should happen that any of those who ought to have these arms are not in the county at the time when the justices shall be in that county, the justices shall fix for him a time in another county, in their presence. And if he shall not have come to them in any county through which they shall go and he has not been in this land, a time shall be appointed for him at Westminster in the octaves of Saint Michael, that he shall be there to make his oath, as he values

his life and property.   And let it be commanded him that before the feast of the said Saint Hilary, he shall have arms according as it is required of him.

10. Item let the justices cause to be proclaimed throughout all the counties through which they shall go, that whoever has not these arms according as is aforesaid, the lord king shall have recourse to their persons and not at all to their land or chattels.

11. Item let no one swear concerning lawful and free men, who has not sixteen marks or ten marks in chattels.

12. Item let the justices order throughout all the counties that no one, as he values his life and property, shall buy or sell any ship to be taken away from England, and that no one shall export or cause to be exported from England, timber.   And the king commands that no one shall be received for the oath of arms except a freeman.

---

18.   Assize of the Forest or of Woodstock

(1184. Latin text, Stubbs, *S. C.* 157.   Translation by Editors.   1 Stubbs, 527

HERE begins the assize of the Forest of the lord Henry the king.

This is the assize of lord Henry the king, the son of Matilda, in England, concerning the forest and his venison, by the advice and assent of the archbishops, bishops and barons, earls and nobles of England, at Woodstock.

1. First he forbids that any one shall offend in regard to his venison or his forests in any respect : and he wills that no trust shall be put in the fact that hitherto he has had mercy because of their chattels upon those who had offended in regard to his venison and his forests.   For if any one hereafter shall offend and be convicted thereof, he wills that full justice be exacted as was done in the time of king Henry his grandfather.

2. Item he forbids that any one shall have bows or arrows, or hounds, or harriers in his forests unless he shall have as his warrantor the king or some one else who has the power to act as warrantor.

3. Item he forbids that any one shall give or sell anything to the wasting or destruction of his woods which are within the forest of king Henry : he grants fully that they may take from their woods what shall be necessary for them (*i.e.* firewood), with-out wasting, and this at the view of the royal forester.

4. Item he orders that all those who have woods within the bounds of the royal forest, shall place suitable foresters in their woods, for which foresters let those to whom the woods belong be sureties or find suitable sureties who can give redress if the foresters offend in regard to anything which pertains to the lord king. And those who, without the bounds of the forest visitation, have woods in which the venison of the lord king has peace [*i.e.* is under the protection of the law] shall have no forester unless they have sworn to the assize of the lord king, and to the peace of his venison, and to have some guardian for the keeping of his woods.

5. Item the lord king orders that his foresters shall take care concerning the forests of knights and others who have woods within the bounds of the royal forest, that the woods be not destroyed; for if in spite of this they shall have been destroyed, let those whose woods have been destroyed know well that redress will be exacted from their persons or their lands and not from another.

6. Item the lord king orders that all his foresters shall swear that according to their ability they will hold the assize of his forests as he made it; and that they will not annoy knights or other worthy men concerning anything which the lord king has granted to them in regard to their woods.

7. Item the king orders that in every county in which he has venison, twelve knights shall be appointed for guarding his vert and venison with the forest; and that four knights shall be appointed to agist his woods and to receive and keep his pasture rents; and the king forbids that any one shall agist his woods within the bounds of the forest before the king's own woods have been agisted, and the lord king's period for agisting the forest shall begin fifteen days before Michaelmas and shall last fifteen days after Michaelmas.

8. And the king orders that if his forester shall have demesne woods of the lord king in his custody, and those woods shall have been destroyed, and he can neither give nor allege a good reason for the destruction of the woods, the person of the forester himself and not something else shall be seized.

9. Item the king forbids that any clerk shall offend in regard to his venison or his forests: he especially orders his foresters that if they find them offending, they shall not hesitate to lay hands upon them to seise and arrest them, and the king himself will fully warrant them.

10. Item the king orders that his essarts new and old shall be

inspected [every third year], and his purprestures and wastes of the
forest and that each be recorded by itself.

11. Item the king orders that the [archbishops, bishops] earls
and barons and knights and freeholders and all men shall come
at the summons of his master forester if they wish to avoid being
at the mercy of the lord king, to try the forest pleas of the lord
king and to transact his other business in county court.

12. At Woodstock the king orders that from whoever has
offended in regard to his forests for the first time, good sureties
shall be taken ; and if he shall offend a second time, likewise ; but
if he shall offend a third time, for the third offence no other sureties
shall be taken from him, nor anything else except the very person
of the offender.

[13. Item he orders that every man of twelve years of age,
remaining within the hunting reserve, and clerks holding a lay fief
shall take oath to keep his peace.

14. Item he orders that the lawing of mastiffs shall be performed wherever his wild animals have peace or are accustomed
to have it.

15. Item he orders that no tanner or bleacher of hides shall
dwell in his forests outside of a borough.

16. Item the king orders that no one for the future shall chase
in any manner to capture wild animals by night within or without
the forest, wherever his wild animals frequent or are accustomed
to have peace, under penalty of imprisonment for one year and
of paying a fine or ransom at the king's pleasure, and that no one,
under the same penalty, shall make any obstruction living or dead
against his wild animals in his forests and woods or in other places
disafforested by himself or his predecessors.]

------◆------

19.   Ordinance of the Saladin Tithe

(1188. Latin text, Stubbs, *S. C.* 160. Translation by Editors. 1 Stubbs, 627.)

1. THIS year each one shall give in alms a tenth of his revenues
and movables, with the exception of the arms and horses and
clothing of the knights, and likewise with the exception of the
horses and books and clothing and vestments and articles required in divine service of whatever sort of the clerks, and of the
precious stones of both clerks and laymen.

2. Moreover this money shall be collected in each parish in

the presence of the parish priest and the arch-priest, and one Knight-Templar and one Knight-Hospitaller, and a servant of the lord king and the king's clerk, and a servant of the baron and his clerk, and a clerk of the bishops ; excommunication having been pronounced previously by the archbishops, bishops and arch-priests each one in every parish upon any one who does not rightfully give the aforesaid tenth in the presence and cognizance of those who ought to be present, as has been said.   And if any one, to their knowledge shall have given less than he ought, four or six lawful men shall be chosen from the parish, who upon oath shall declare what amount he ought to have declared ; and then this sum shall be added to the smaller amount he had given.

3. But clerks and knights who shall have taken the cross shall not pay this tithe except for their own property and demesnes : and whatever their vassals ought to pay shall be collected for their use by the aforesaid and the whole shall be paid over to them.

4. Moreover the bishops by their letters in each parish of their dioceses shall cause proclamation to be made on the day of the Nativity and of Saint Stephen and of Saint John that each one shall get together at his home the prescribed tenth before the Purification of the Blessed Virgin, and on the following day and thereafter in the presence of the aforesaid at the place to which he has been summoned each man shall make payment.

---

20. Writ Præcipe

(Latin text, Glanville, *Tractatus de legibus et consuetudinibus regni Angliæ,* I. c. 6. Translation by Editors. Digby, *Real Property,* Fifth Edition, 73.)

THE king to the sheriff, greeting.
Command A. that, lawfully and without delay, he restore to B. one hide of land, in such a town from which the said B. complains that the aforesaid A. is keeping him by force, and if he does not do it, summon him by good summoners, to be before me or my justices, on the morrow after the octave of Easter in such a place, to show cause wherefore he has not done it ; and have there the summoners and this writ.

Witness : Ranulph de Glanville, at Clarendon.

21. Form of Proceeding on the Judicial Visitation

(1194. Latin text, Stubbs, *S. C.* 259. Translation, Riley, *The Annals of Roger de Hoveden*, ii. 334, with slight changes. 1 Stubbs, 543.)

Form of Proceeding in the Pleas of the Crown

IN the first place, four knights are to be chosen from out of the whole county, who, upon their oaths, are to chose two lawful knights of every hundred and wapentake, and these two are to chose upon their oath ten knights of every hundred or wapentake, or, if there shall not be knights sufficient, free and lawful men, in order that these twelve may together make inquisition on each of the following heads in every hundred or wapentake.

Heads of the Pleas of the Crown

1. Of the pleas of the crown, both new and old, and all those which have not yet been concluded before the justiciaries of our lord the king.

2. Item of all recognizances and all pleas which have been summoned before the justiciaries, by writ of the king or of the chief justice, or which have been sent before them from the supreme court of the king.

3. Item of escheats, what these are now, and what these have been, since the king set out on his expedition to the land of Jerusalem ; and what were at that time in the king's hands, and whether they are now in his hands or not ; and of all escheats of our lord king, if they have been taken out of his hands, how, and by whom, and into whose hands they have come, and of what kind, and if any person has had any profits from the same, and what, and what was the value thereof, and what is the present value ; and if there is any escheat, which belongs to our lord the king, which is not at present in his hands.

4. Item of churches which are in the gift of our lord the king.

5. Item of wardships of children, which belong to our lord the king.

6. Item of marriages of maidens, or of widows, which belong to our lord the king.

7. Item of malefactors, and their harborers and abettors.

8. Item of forgers.

9. Item of murderers of the Jews, who they are, and of the pledges of Jews so slain, their chattels, lands, debts, and writings

and who has the same ; and how much each person owes them, and what pledges they had, and who holds the same, and how much they are worth, and who has the profits thereof, and what they are ; all the pledges and the debts of the Jews so slain are to be seised for the king ; and those who were present at the murder of the Jews, who have not made a composition thereon with our lord the king, or with his justiciaries, are to be arrested and are not to be liberated except by our lord the king, or his justiciaries.

10. Item of all aids given for the ransom of our lord the king, how much each person promised, and how much he has paid, and how much is still due from him.

11. Item of the adherents of earl John, and such of them as have made a composition with our lord the king, and such as have not.

12. Item of the chattels of earl John or his adherents, which have not been converted to the use of our lord the king ; and how much the sheriffs and their bailiffs have received ; and who has given any thing contrary to the ancient customs of the kingdom.

13. Item of all the lands of earl John, of his demesnes, and wards, and escheats, and his gifts, and for what reason the same were given, and all the gifts of earl John are to be seised for our lord the king, except those which have been confirmed by the king.

14. Item of the debts and fines which are due to earl John, and for what causes ; and all the same are to be demanded on behalf of our lord the king.

15. Item of usurers, and of the chattels of such of them as are dead.

16. Item of wines sold contrary to the assize, and of false measures for wine as also for other things.

17. Item of such crusaders as have died before setting out for the land of Jerusalem ; and who possesses their chattels, and what they are, and how many.

18. Item of grand assizes, which are of lands a hundred shillings in value or less.

19. Item of defaults.

20. Also in every county there are to be three knights chosen, and one clerk, who are to be keepers of the pleas of the crown.

21. And no sheriff is to be justice in his shrievalty, nor yet in any county which he has held since the first coronation of our lord the king.

22. Also all the cities, and boroughs, and demesne lands of our lord the king are to be talliaged.

23. Also, the said justices, together with the bailiffs of William of the Church of Saint Mary, Geoffrey Fitz-Peter, William de Chimelli, William Bruere, Hugh Bardolph, and of the sheriff of each place, are to cause the knights mentioned on the roll to be summoned in their respective counties, to appear at a time and place which they shall signify to them, and to make them swear in their presence that they will use all their lawful endeavors to restore the lands and escheats belonging to our lord the king, and to value the same to the advantage of our lord the king, and not through hatred, favor or regard for any person, to omit so to do. And the said knights before named shall, upon their oath, make choice of twelve lawful knights, or free and lawful men, if knights shall not be found for the purpose, in the different parts of each county on the circuit of the said justices itinerant, as shall seem expedient; who shall, in like manner, make oath that they will use all their lawful endeavors to restore, and to value and establish the rights of wardship and escheat in those parts, and will give their counsel and assistance to advantage the king therein, as before mentioned. The said jurors shall also, upon oath, choose from free men as many and such as they shall think necessary for the performance of the aforesaid business of our lord the king as to escheats and wardships, in such manner as may be best done for the advantage of our lord the king. It is also to be known, that the said wardships and escheats shall be made good out of the revenues arising therefrom up to the feast of Michaelmas, as also from the revenues at that time due; and, if they shall not suffice, then the deficiency shall be supplied by a toll of our lord the king: it being understood that those who hold the said wardships and escheats to farm shall, at the feast of Saint Michael, answer for the same, and thenceforward for the improvements as well. And as for those who shall hold the said wardships and escheats to farm, our lord the king shall give them warranty for the same from year to year until the termination thereof; so that, although our lord the king should give any of them to any person, the farmer shall still hold his farm till the end of the year, by paying to him to whom our lord the king shall have so given it, the rent which shall be due to the king for the same until the end of the year. The rights of justice of the escheat, however, which he shall have so given shall remain with our lord the king, unless our lord the king shall have given them by name. The farmer, when he shall have given up his farm, is to have all his stock which he shall have placed upon the farm, and all his property over and above the property of the king there, freely and without diminution. They

shall also have letters patent of our lord the archbishop, containing the tenor of the charter of our lord the king made relative thereto.

Most diligent enquiry shall also be made what is the rental assessed upon each manor in the demesne, and the value of all other assessments in the said manors, and how many carrucates there are, and how much they are each worth, not estimating them at a fixed value of twenty shillings only, but, according as the land is good or bad, whether the value is likely to increase or decrease. Those persons who shall take these farms shall stock their farms, as already said, according to the above named value from the revenues of the escheats and wardships. Enquiry is also to be made with how many oxen and plough horses each carrucate ought to be stocked ; and how many and what amount of stock each manor is able to support and the result thereof is then to be openly and distinctly reduced to writing. The price set upon a bull shall be four shillings, and upon a cow the same, upon a plough-horse the same, upon a sheep with fine wool ten pence, upon a sheep with coarse wool six pence, upon a sow twelve pence, and upon a boar twelve pence ; and when the farmers give up their farms they shall be answerable in the aforesaid sums, or in animals payable for the same, at the option of the farmers ; and when all the aforesaid stock shall be placed thereon and duly valued, they shall all be enrolled openly and distinctly, and the register thereof shall be deposited in the exchequer. From this assize are to be excepted bishoprics and abbeys, and lands of barons who are nearly of age.

Also let enquiry be made, by the oath of the parties aforesaid, as to all wardships and escheats which are not in the hands of our lord the king, and they are to be taken possession of by our lord the king, and dealt with as other lands and escheats.

24. Heads concerning the Jews.

All debts and pledges of Jews are to be enrolled, as also their lands, houses, rents, and possessions. Any Jew who shall make concealment of any one of these things, shall forfeit to our lord the king his body, as also the thing concealed, and all his possessions and all his chattels ; and no Jew shall ever be allowed to recover what he has so concealed. Also, let six or seven places be appointed at which they shall make their loans, and let two lawful Christians and two lawful Jews and two lawful scribes be appointed, and in their presence, and in that of the clerks of William of the Church of Saint Mary and of William de Chimelli, let such loans be made, and let a deed describing the loan be made, after the manner of an indenture. One part is to remain in the hands of the Jew, sealed with his seal to whom the money is paid, while the other part is to remain in the common chest; on which there are to be three locks; whereof the two Christians are to keep one key, the two Jews another, and the clerks of William of the Church of Saint Mary and of Master William de Chimelli, the third; as also three seals, those who have the keys setting thereon their seals. The clerks also of the two Williams aforesaid are to have a register containing copies of all the deeds, and as the deeds are altered so shall the register be altered. For each deed shall be paid three pence; a moiety thereof by the Jew and a moiety by him to whom the money is lent; of which the two scribes are to have two pence, and the keeper of the register the third: and, for the future, no loan shall be made, no payment made to Jews, no alteration of the deeds, except in presence of the persons aforenamed, or the major part of them, if all shall be unable to be present. The said two Christians also are to have a register of receipts for payments made henceforth to Jews, and the two Jews are to have one, and the keeper of the register one. Also, every Jew shall make oath on his roll [of the Law] that he will cause all his debts, pledges, rents, and all his property and possessions to be enrolled, and that, as above stated, he will not conceal anything; and that, if he shall be able to learn that any one has concealed anything, he will secretly disclose the same to the judges sent to them, and that forgers of deeds and clippers of money, when he shall know of such persons, he will give information against, and detect the same, and the like with regard to the deeds so forged.

25. Also, the inquisition which was to be made relative to the exactions and seizures made by all bailiffs of the king, as well by the justices as by the sheriffs, constables, and foresters and their servants, since the time of the first coronation of our lord king Richard, and why such seizures were made, and by whom; and relative to all the chattels, gifts, and promises made on the occasion of seizure of the lands of earl John and his supporters; and who received the same, and what, and how much, was deferred by command of Hubert, archbishop of Canterbury, the king's chief justice.

22. The Coronation of John

(May, 1199.   Latin text, Stubbs, *S. C.* 270.   Translation, Giles's *Roger of Wendover's Flowers of History*, ii. 180, slightly altered.   1 Stubbs, 553.)

JOHN duke of Normandy came over into England, and landed at Shoreham on the 25th of May; on the day after, which was the eve of our Lord's ascension, he went to London to be crowned there.   On his arrival therefore, the archbishops, bishops, earls, barons, and all others, whose duty it was to be present at his coronation, assembled together.   The archbishop, standing in the midst, addressed them thus, "Hear, all of you, and be it known that no one has an antecedent right to succeed another in the kingdom, unless he shall have been unanimously elected, under the guidance of the Holy Spirit, on account of the superior merits of his character, after the example of Saul the first anointed king, whom the Lord set over his people, not as the son of a king, nor as born of royal ancestry.   In the same manner, after Saul came David, son of Jesse.   Saul was chosen because he was a brave man, and suited for the royal dignity: David, because he was holy and humble.   Thus those who excel in vigor are elevated to kingly dignity.   But, if any relative of a deceased king excel others in merit, all should the more readily and zealously consent to his election.   We have said this to maintain the cause of earl John, who is here present, brother of our illustrious king Richard, lately deceased without heirs of his body, and as the said earl John is prudent, active, and indubitably noble, we have, under God's Holy Spirit, unanimously elected him for his merits and his royal blood."   Now the archbishop was a man of bold character and a support to the kingdom by his steadiness and incomparable wisdom, no one, therefore, dared to dispute what he said, as knowing that he had good cause for what he did.   Earl John and all who were present acquiesced, and they unanimously elected the earl, crying out, "God save the king."   Archbishop Hubert was afterwards asked why he acted in this manner, to which he replied that he had foreseen, and had been informed and assured by revelations that John would one day or other bring the kingdom into great confusion, and that he might not have free hand to do this he determined that he should owe his elevation to election and not to hereditary right.   Moreover the archbishop placed the crown on his head, and anointed him king, in the church of the chief of the apostles, at Westminster,

on the 27th of May ; Philip, bishop of Durham, made an appeal
to prevent this coronation taking place in the absence of Geoffrey
archbishop of York, but did not obtain his wish.   At this coronation king John bound himself by a triple oath, namely, to love
Holy Church and its ordained priests, and to preserve it harmless
from the attacks of evil designers, and to do away with bad laws,
substituting good ones in their stead, and to see justice rightly
administered throughout England.   He was afterwards adjured
by the same archbishop on behalf of God, and strictly forbidden
to presume to accept this honor, unless he purposed in his mind,
to fulfil in deed, what he had sworn to ; in reply to this the king
promised that, by God's assistance, he would in all good faith
keep the oath which he had made.   On the following day, after
he had received the homage and fealty of his subjects, he went
to Saint Alban's, the proto-martyr of England, to pray ; and so,
making but a very short stay in England, he with the advice of
the nobles duly settled everything that required his attention.

---

23. Writ for the Assessment of the Thirteenth

(February, 1207.   Latin text, Stubbs, *S. C.* 283.   Translation by Editors.
1 Stubbs, 620.)

THE king to all, etc.   Be it known that by the common
advice and assent of our council at Oxford it was provided,
for the defence of our realm and the recovery of our right, and
granted that every layman in all England, of whomsoever he may
hold, who has rents and chattels in England, should give us in aid
from every mark of his annual revenue, twelve pence, and from
every mark's worth of every sort of movable chattels which he had
on the octave of the Purification of the Blessed Virgin, that is at
the time of the council, twelve pence, and thus in proportion more
or less.   And all the stewards and bailiffs of earls and barons, shall
take oath before our justices of the value of the rents and movable
chattels of their lords and likewise concerning their own.   And
every man except the earls and barons shall take oath concerning
his own rents and chattels, according as our justices despatched
for this purpose shall see to be best suited to our advantage.
And if any one shall have been convicted of removing his chattels
fraudulently to avoid our profit, or of concealing them in any
place, or of putting them in the power of any one else, or of
appraising them at less than their value, all his chattels shall be

seised for our use free of claims, and he himself shall be put in our prison until he shall be liberated by us. Moreover, let every hundred in your county be recorded by itself and each parish in every hundred by itself, so that our justices may know how to answer for every vill by itself. Moreover, when our justices shall have made the assessment of this aid of ours in any hundred, city, or vill, they shall immediately cause copy to be made from their rolls of all the particulars of the aid assessed, and shall hand over to the sheriff for the collection of the aid noted in each roll from fortnight to fortnight, with all speed, and our justices shall keep their own rolls safely in their possession until they bring them to us. It is also decreed that all our clerks, and all our justices and their clerks, and all who shall busy themselves in any of this work, shall swear that they will do this work faithfully and with all their might, as it has been set forth, and that for nothing will they neglect this. Moreover, we command, upon penalties of life and limb, that every good penny of lawful weight, although it is not new, shall be accepted both for our use and for that of all others in our realm. Moreover, for assessing this aid in your county we send, in our stead, Robert of Berkeley, Richard of Mucegros, William of Falaise, Master R. of Gloucester, Walter of Aura, Adam Fitz-Nigel, etc. And we bid you to be just as attentive to them in this as to ourselves.

Witness myself at Northampton, the seventeenth day of February.

---

24. Recognitions, Assizes, and the Jury

(Latin originals, Delisle, *Recueil de Jugements de l'Echiquier de Normandie.* Translation by Editors. Date and reference in each case. Though the first three cases are from Normandy, the usage is exactly the same as in England, and they are earlier than the Magna Carta. The last two are from Maitland's *Bracton's Note Book.*)

1. EUSTACE CALLOT, under age, asked seisin of the land of his father, that is of the manor of R., of which his father was seised in the year and day on which he died, of which Richard Callot his uncle was disseising him. A recognition was made concerning this by legal men and they swore that Robert Callot, his father, was seised of it at some time, but they did not know whether he was seised of it on the day on which he died or not. And so it was judged that he who was holding should hold, and that the right should remain between them. Afterwards the said

Eustace asked a recognition whether his father was seised of the said manor when he married his mother or not. But his uncle, who was holding that manor, asked the judgment of the king's court whether there ought to be taken another recognition concerning this than that which the said Eustace had had of the seisin of his father. But the bailiff pointed this out to lord Walter the chamberlain at Rouen. But lord Walter was unwilling to make judgment upon it at Rouen, but he postponed it to the exchequer of the lord king at Falaise, and when judgment was to be made upon it there, it was said and testified by many that the mother of the said Eustace asked the whole of the said manor in dower in the court of the lord king, and that she had by agreement in the court of the lord king a third part of that manor in dower. And so it was judged that the said Eustace as protector of that dower should have two parts of that manor. (p. 13, 1209.)

2. Recognition [recordatio] between Matthew le V. and Andrew de O. by [13 names] who say that they were at a certain assize at Grandmesnil and saw and heard that a certain inquiry by oath [jury] was made there between the same Matthew and the same Andrew concerning a certain land of the fee of Grandmesnil, and of the seisin of W. de A., uncle of the said Matthew. Ten men of those who made the inquiry by oath said that they never saw the said W. have seisin of the said land, but always they saw the father of the same Andrew and the same Andrew seised of that land. Two other men of those who made the inquiry by oath said that they knew nothing about it. And so the seisin of that land was judged in that assize to the same Andrew, and it was judged in that assize that the plea remained between them. It is judged that the same Andrew have seisin of that land, and the said Matthew in mercy for a false claim. (p. 27, 1212.)

3. *Darrien Presentment.* — It is judged that Alan de Av. have seisin of the presentation of the church of Av., since Henry de Al. who disseised the same Alan of this is unwilling to submit to a recognition according to the usages and customs of Normandy as to who presented the last parson deceased to that church, and the same Henry is in mercy. (p. 33, 1213.)

4. *Novel Disseisin.* — The assize came to inquire [recognitura] if Robert chaplain of Owresby unjustly etc. disseised Helena of Crosholm of her free tenement in Norton after etc. And R. came not nor was found and so the assize was taken by default. The jurors say he disseised her because R. made to reap in the land of the same Helena and to carry off. And so it was judged that Helena recover her seisin and R. be in mercy. (Case 1204, III., p. 217.)

5. *Mort d'Ancestor.* — The assize came to inquire if Simon son of Thomas, father of Richard son of Simon who is under age, was seised in his demesne and of fee of half a virgate of land with appurtenances in Brinton on the day on which he died, etc., and if etc. which land Gunnora of Brinton held, who came and called Richard of Brinton to warrant it, who came and warranted it to her and said . . . And since Richard is under age it was judged that he is not able to answer to this and so the assize proceeds. The jurors say that the said Simon died so seised as the writ says and that Richard is next heir of that same land which Gunnora held, concerning which she called to warrant the said Richard, whether there was more or less than half a virgate there. (Case 42, II., p. 39.)

---

25. John's Concession of the Kingdom to the Pope

(May, 1213. Latin text, Stubbs, *S. C.* 284. Translation, G. and H. 75.
1 Stubbs, 560.)

JOHN, by the grace of God king of England, lord of Ireland, duke of Normandy and Aquitaine, earl of Anjou, to all the faithful in Christ who shall inspect this present charter, greeting. We will it to be known by all of you by this our charter, confirmed by our seal, that we, having offended God and our mother the holy Church in many things, and being on that account known to need the divine mercy, and unable to make any worthy offering for the performance of due satisfaction to God and the Church, unless we humble ourselves and our realms — we, willing to humble ourselves for him who humbled himself for us even to death, by the inspiration of the Holy Spirit's grace under no compulsion of force or of fear, but of our good and free will, and by the common consent of our barons, offer and freely grant to God and His holy apostles Peter and Paul, and the holy Roman Church, our mother, and to our lord the Pope Innocent and his catholic successors, the whole realm of England and the whole realm of Ireland with all their rights and appurtenances, for the remission of our sins and those of all our race, as well quick as dead ; and from now receiving back and holding these as a feudal dependant, from God and the Roman Church, in the presence of the prudent man Pandulf, subdeacon and familiar of the lord the pope, do and swear fealty for them to the aforesaid our lord the

Pope Innocent and his catholic successors and the Roman Church, according to the form written below, and will do liege homage to the same lord the Pope in his presence if we shall be able to be present before him; binding our successors and heirs by our wife, for ever, that in like manner to the supreme pontiff for the time being, and to the Roman Church, they should pay fealty and acknowledge homage without contradiction. Moreover, in proof of this our perpetual obligation and grant, we will and establish that from the proper and special revenues of our realms aforesaid, for all service and custom that we should render for ourselves, saving in all respects the penny of blessed Peter, the Roman Church receive 1000 marks sterling each year, to wit at the feast of Saint Michael 500 marks, and at Easter 500 marks; 700 to wit for the realm of England, and 300 for the realm of Ireland; saving to us and our heirs, our rights, liberties, and royalties. All which, as aforesaid, we willing them to be perpetually ratified and confirmed, bind ourselves and successors not to contravene. And if we or any of our successors shall presume to attempt this, whoever he be, unless he come to amendment after due admonition, let him forfeit right to the kingdom, and let this charter of obligation and grant on our part remain in force for ever.

The Oath of Fealty

I, John, by the grace of God king of England and lord of Ireland, from this hour forward will be faithful to God and the blessed Peter and the Roman Church, and my lord the Pope Innocent and his successors following in catholic manner: I will not be party, in deed, word, consent, or counsel, to their losing life or limb or being unjustly imprisoned. Their damage, if I am aware of it, I will prevent, and will have removed if I can; or else, as soon as I can, I will signify it, or will tell such persons as I shall believe will tell them certainly. Any counsel they intrust to me, immediately or by their messengers or their letter, I will keep secret, and will consciously disclose to no one to their damage. The patrimony of blessed Peter, and specially the realm of England and the realm of Ireland, I will aid to hold and defend against all men to my ability. So help me God and these holy gospels. Witness myself at the house of the Knights of the Temple near Dover, in the presence of the lord H. Archbishop of Dublin; . . . Warren, son of Gerald. The 15th day of May in the 14th year of our reign.

26.   Writ of Summons

(May, 1213.   Latin text, Stubbs, *S. C.* 276.   Translation, Giles, *Roger of Wendover's Flowers of History*, ii.   274.   1 Stubbs, 565.)

THE next day the king sent letters to all the sheriffs of the kingdom, ordering them to send four liege men from each town in their demesnes, together with the warden, to Saint Alban's on the fourth of August, that through them and his other agents he might make inquiries about the losses and confiscated property of each of the bishops, and how much was due to each.

27.   Writ of Summons to a Great Council

(November, 1213.   Latin text, Stubbs, *S. C.* 287.   Translation by Editors, 1 Stubbs, 567, 609.)

THE king to the sheriff of Oxfordshire, greeting.   We direct you to cause all the knights of your bailiwick, who have been summoned to appear before me at Oxford on All Saints' Day, to come in fifteen days with their arms ; but all the barons to come in like manner unarmed : and that you cause four discreet men of your county to meet us there at the same time to consult with us about the affairs of our realm.

Witness myself at Witney, the seventh day of November.

Similar writs were directed to all the sheriffs.

28.   Grant of Freedom of Election to Churches

(November, 1214.   Latin text, Stubbs, *S. C.* 288.   Translation, G. and H. 77.   1 Stubbs, 568.)

Charter of King John for Free Elections in all England

JOHN, by the grace of God, king of England, lord of Ireland, duke of Normandy and Aquitaine, earl of Anjou, to the archbishops, bishops, earls, barons, knights, bailiffs, and to all who shall see or hear these letters, greeting.   Since by the grace of God, of the mere and free will of both parties, there is full agreement concerning damages and losses in the time of the interdict, between us and our venerable fathers Stephen, archbishop of Canterbury, primate of all England, and Cardinal of the Holy Roman Church and Bishops William of London, Eustace of Ely, Giles of Hereford, Joscelin of Bath and Glastonbury, and Hugh of Lincoln — we wish not only to make satisfaction to them, as far as in God we can, but also to make sound and beneficial provision for all the Church of England forever ; and so whatsoever custom has been hitherto observed in the English Church, in our own times and those of our predecessors, and whatsoever right we have claimed for ourselves hitherto in the elections of any prelates, we have at their own petition, for the health of our soul and the souls of our predecessors and successors kings of England, freely of our mere and spontaneous will, with the common consent of our barons, granted and constituted, and by this our present charter have confirmed : that henceforth in all and singular the churches and monasteries, cathedral and conventual, of all our kingdom of England, the elections of all prelates, whatsoever, greater or less, be free forever, saving to ourselves and our heirs the custody of vacant churches and monasteries which belong to us. We promise also that we will neither hinder nor suffer nor procure to be hindered by our ministers that in all and singular the churches and monasteries mentioned, after the prelacies are vacant, the electors should, whenever they will, freely set a pastor over them, yet so that leave to elect be first asked of us and our heirs, which we will not deny nor defer. And if by chance, which God forbid, we should deny or defer, let the electors, none the less, proceed to make canonical election ; and likewise, after the election is concluded, let our assent be demanded, which in like manner we will not deny, unless we put forth some reasonable excuse and lawfully prove it, by reason of which we should not consent. Wherefore we will and firmly forbid that when churches or monasteries are vacant, any one in anything proceed or presume to proceed in opposition to this our charter. But if any do ever at any time proceed in opposition to it, let him incur the curse of Almighty God and our own. These being witnesses : Peter, bishop of Winchester, . . . William of Huntingfield. Given by the hand of Master Richard de Marisco, our Chancellor, at the new Temple in London, on the 21st day of November in the 16th year of our reign.

29. Great Charter of Liberties

(June, 1215. Latin text, Stubbs, *S. C.* 296. Translation, Cheyney, **6.** I Stubbs, 569.)

JOHN, by the grace of God, king of England, lord of Ireland, duke of Normandy and Aquitaine, count of Anjou, to the archbishops, bishops, abbots, earls, barons, justiciars, foresters, sheriffs, reeves, servants, and all bailiffs and his faithful people greeting. Know that by the suggestion of God and for the good of our soul and those of all our predecessors and of our heirs, to the honor of God and the exaltation of holy church, and the improvement of our kingdom, by the advice of our venerable fathers Stephen, archbishop of Canterbury, primate of all England and Cardinal of the Holy Roman Church, Henry, archbishop of Dublin, William of London, Peter of Winchester, Joscelyn of Bath and Glastonbury, Hugh of Lincoln, Walter of Worcester, William of Coventry, and Benedict of Rochester, bishops; of Master Pandulf, subdeacon and member of the household of the lord Pope, of Brother Aymeric, master of the Knights of the Temple in England; and of the noblemen William Marshall, earl of Pembroke, William, earl of Salisbury, William, earl Warren, William, earl of Arundel, Alan of Galloway, constable of Scotland, Warren Fitz-Gerald, Peter Fitz-Herbert, Hubert de Burgh, seneschal of Poitou, Hugh de Nevil, Matthew Fitz-Herbert, Thomas Bassett, Alan Bassett, Philip d'Albini, Robert de Ropesle, John Marshall, John Fitz-Hugh, and others of our faithful.

1. In the first place we have granted to God, and by this our present charter confirmed, for us and our heirs forever, that the English church shall be free, and shall hold its rights entire and its liberties uninjured; and we will that it thus be observed; which is shown by this, that the freedom of elections, which is considered to be most important and especially necessary to the English church, we, of our pure and spontaneous will, granted, and by our charter confirmed, before the contest between us and our barons had arisen; and obtained a confirmation of it by the lord Pope Innocent III.; which we will observe and which we will shall be observed in good faith by our heirs forever.

We have granted moreover to all free men of our kingdom for us and our heirs forever all the liberties written below, to be had and holden by themselves and their heirs from us and our heirs.

2. If any of our earls or barons, or others holding from us in chief by military service shall have died, and when he has died

his heir shall be of full age and owe relief, he shall have his inheritance by the ancient relief; that is to say, the heir or heirs of an earl for the whole barony of an earl a hundred pounds; the heir or heirs of a baron for a whole barony a hundred pounds; the heir or heirs of a knight, for a whole knight's fee, a hundred shillings at most; and who owes less let him give less according to the ancient custom of fiefs.

3. If moreover the heir of any one of such shall be under age, and shall be in wardship, when he comes of age he shall have his inheritance without relief and without a fine.

4. The custodian of the land of such a minor heir shall not take from the land of the heir any except reasonable products, reasonable customary payments, and reasonable services, and this without destruction or waste of men or of property; and if we shall have committed the custody of the land of any such a one to the sheriff or to any other who is to be responsible to us for its proceeds, and that man shall have caused destruction or waste from his custody we will recover damages from him, and the land shall be committed to two legal and discreet men of that fief, who shall be responsible for its proceeds to us or to him to whom we have assigned them; and if we shall have given or sold to any one the custody of any such land, and he has caused destruction or waste there, he shall lose that custody, and it shall be handed over to two legal and discreet men of that fief who shall be in like manner responsible to us as is said above.

5. The custodian moreover, so long as he shall have the custody of the land, must keep up the houses, parks, warrens, fish ponds, mills, and other things pertaining to the land, from the proceeds of the land itself; and he must return to the heir, when he has come to full age, all his land, furnished with ploughs and implements of husbandry according as the time of wainage requires and as the proceeds of the land are able reasonably to sustain.

6. Heirs shall be married without disparity, so nevertheless that before the marriage is contracted, it shall be announced to the relatives by blood of the heir himself.

7. A widow, after the death of her husband, shall have her marriage portion and her inheritance immediately and without obstruction, nor shall she give anything for her dowry or for her marriage portion, or for her inheritance which inheritance her husband and she held on the day of the death of her husband; and she may remain in the house of her husband for forty days after his death, within which time her dowry shall be assigned to her.

8. No widow shall be compelled to marry so long as she prefers to live without a husband, provided she gives security that she will not marry without our consent, if she holds from us, or without the consent of her lord from whom she holds, if she holds from another.

9. Neither we nor our bailiffs will seise any land or rent, for any debt, so long as the chattels of the debtor are sufficient for the payment of the debt ; nor shall the pledges of a debtor be distrained so long as the principal debtor himself has enough for the payment of the debt ; and if the principal debtor fails in the payment of the debt, not having the wherewithal to pay it, the pledges shall be responsible for the debt ; and if they wish, they shall have the lands and the rents of the debtor until they shall have been satisfied for the debt which they have before paid for him, unless the principal debtor shall have shown himself to be quit in that respect towards those pledges.

10. If any one has taken anything from the Jews, by way of a loan, more or less, and dies before that debt is paid, the debt shall not draw interest so long as the heir is under age, from whomsoever he holds ; and if that debt falls into our hands, we will take nothing except the chattel contained in the agreement.

11. And if any one dies leaving a debt owing to the Jews, his wife shall have her dowry, and shall pay nothing of that debt ; and if there remain minor children of the dead man, necessaries shall be provided for them corresponding to the holding of the dead man ; and from the remainder shall be paid the debt, saving the service of the lords. In the same way debts are to be treated which are owed to others than the Jews.

12. No scutage or aid shall be imposed in our kingdom except by the common council of our kingdom, except for the ransoming of our body, for the making of our oldest son a knight, and for once marrying our oldest daughter, and for these purposes it shall be only a reasonable aid ; in the same way it shall be done concerning the aids of the city of London.

13. And the city of London shall have all its ancient liberties and free customs, as well by land as by water. Moreover, we will and grant that all other cities and boroughs and villages and ports shall have all their liberties and free customs.

14. And for holding a common council of the kingdom concerning the assessment of an aid otherwise than in the three cases mentioned above, or concerning the assessment of a scutage we shall cause to be summoned the archbishops, bishops, abbots, earls, and greater barons by our letters individually ; and besides we shall

cause to be summoned generally, by our sheriffs and bailiffs all those who hold from us in chief, for a certain day, that is at the end of forty days at least, and for a certain place; and in all the letters of that summons, we will express the cause of the summons, and when the summons has thus been given the business shall proceed on the appointed day, on the advice of those who shall be present, even if not all of those who were summoned have come.

15. We will not grant to any one, moreover, that he shall take an aid from his free men, except for ransoming his body, for making his oldest son a knight, and for once marrying his oldest daughter; and for these purposes only a reasonable aid shall be taken.

16. No one shall be compelled to perform any greater service for a knight's fee, or for any other free tenement than is owed from it.

17. The common pleas shall not follow our court, but shall be held in some certain place.

18. The recognition of *novel disseisin, mort d'ancestor,* and *darrein presentment* shall be held only in their own counties and in this manner: we, or if we are outside of the kingdom our principal justiciar, will send two justiciars through each county four times a year, who with four knights of each county, elected by the county, shall hold in the county, and on the day and in the place of the county court, the aforesaid assizes of the county.

19. And if the aforesaid assizes cannot be held within the day of the county court, a sufficient number of knights and free-holders shall remain from those who were present at the county court on that day to give the judgments, according as the business is more or less.

20. A free man shall not be fined for a small offence, except in proportion to the measure of the offence; and for a great offence he shall be fined in proportion to the magnitude of the offence, saving his freehold; and a merchant in the same way, saving his merchandise; and the villain shall be fined in the same way, saving his wainage, if he shall be at our mercy; and none of the above fines shall be imposed except by the oaths of honest men of the neighborhood.

21. Earls and barons shall only be fined by their peers, and only in proportion to their offence.

22. A clergyma shall be fined, like those before mentioned, only in proportion to his lay holding, and not according to the extent of his ecclesiastical benefice.

23. No vill or man shall be compelled to make bridges over the rivers except those which ought to do it of old and rightfully.

24. No sheriff, constable, coroners, or other bailiffs of ours shall hold pleas of our crown.

25. All counties, hundreds, wapentakes, and trithings shall be at the ancient rents and without any increase, excepting our demesne manors.

26. If any person holding a lay fief from us shall die, and our sheriff or bailiff shall show our letters-patent of our summons concerning a debt which the deceased owed to us, it shall be lawful for our sheriff or bailiff to attach and levy on the chattels of the deceased found on his lay fief, to the value of that debt, in the view of legal men, so nevertheless that nothing be removed thence until the clear debt to us shall be paid ; and the remainder shall be left to the executors for the fulfilment of the will of the deceased ; and if nothing is owed to us by him, all the chattels shall go to the deceased, saving to his wife and children their reasonable shares.

27. If any free man dies intestate, his chattels shall be distributed by the hands of his near relatives and friends, under the oversight of the church, saving to each one the debts which the deceased owed to him.

28. No constable or other bailiff of ours shall take any one's grain or other chattels, without immediately paying for them in money, unless he is able to obtain a postponement at the goodwill of the seller.

29. No constable shall require any knight to give money in place of his ward of a castle if he is willing to furnish that ward in his own person or through another honest man, if he himself is not able to do it for a reasonable cause ; and if we shall lead or send him into the army he shall be free from ward in proportion to the amount of time during which he has been in the army through us.

30. No sheriff or bailiff of ours or any one else shall take horses or wagons of any free man for carrying purposes except on the permission of that free man.

31. Neither we nor our bailiffs will take the wood of another man for castles, or for anything else which we are doing, except by the permission of him to whom the wood belongs.

32. We will not hold the lands of those convicted of a felony for more than a year and a day, after which the lands shall be returned to the lords of the fiefs.

33. All the fish-weirs in the Thames and the Medway, and throughout all England shall be done away with, except those on the coast.

34. The writ which is called *præcipe* shall not be given for the future to any one concerning any tenement by which a free man can lose his court.

35. There shall be one measure of wine throughout our whole kingdom, and one measure of ale, and one measure of grain, that is the London quarter, and one width of dyed cloth and of russets and of halbergets, that is two ells within the selvages ; of weights, moreover it shall be as of measures.

36. Nothing shall henceforth be given or taken for a writ of inquisition concerning life or limbs, but it shall be given freely and not denied.

37. If any one holds from us by fee farm or by socage or by burgage, and from another he holds land by military service, we will not have the guardianship of the heir or of his land which is of the fief of another, on account of that fee farm, or socage, or burgage ; nor will we have the custody of that fee farm, or socage, or burgage, unless that fee farm itself owes military service. We will not have the guardianship of the heir or of the land of any one, which he holds from another by military service on account of any petty serjeanty which he holds from us by the service of paying to us knives or arrows, or things of that kind.

38. No bailiff for the future shall put any one to his law on his simple affirmation, without credible witnesses brought for this purpose.

39. No free man shall be taken or imprisoned or dispossessed, or outlawed, or banished, or in any way destroyed, nor will we go upon him, nor send upon him, except by the legal judgment of his peers or by the law of the land.

40. To no one will we sell, to no one will we deny, or delay right or justice.

41. All merchants shall be safe and secure in going out from England and coming into England and in remaining and going through England, as well by land as by water, for buying and selling, free from all evil tolls, by the ancient and rightful customs, except in time of war, and if they are of a land at war with us ; and if such are found in our land at the beginning of war, they shall be attached without injury to their bodies or goods, until it shall be known from us or from our principal justiciar in what way the merchants of our land are treated who shall be then found in the country which is at war with us ; and if ours are safe there, the others shall be safe in our land.

42. It is allowed henceforth to any one to go out from our kingdom, and to return, safely and securely, by land and by water,

saving their fidelity to us, except in time of war for some short time, for the common good of the kingdom ; excepting persons imprisoned and outlawed according to the law of the realm, and people of a land at war with us, and merchants, of whom it shall be done as is before said.

43. If any one holds from any escheat, as from the honor of Wallingford, or Nottingham, or Boulogne, or Lancaster, or from other escheats which are in our hands and are baronies, and he dies, his heir shall not give any other relief, nor do to us any other service than he would do to the baron, if that barony was in the hands of the baron ; and we will hold it in the same way as the baron held it.

44. Men who dwell outside the forest shall not henceforth come before our justiciars of the forest, on common summons, unless they are in a plea of, or pledges for any person or persons who are arrested on account of the forest.

45. We will not make justiciars, constables, sheriffs or bailiffs except of such as know the law of the realm and are well inclined to observe it.

46. All barons who have founded abbeys for which they have charters of kings of England, or ancient tenure, shall have their custody when they have become vacant, as they ought to have.

47. All forests which have been afforested in our time shall be disafforested immediately ; and so it shall be concerning river banks which in our time have been fenced in.

48. All the bad customs concerning forests and warrens and concerning foresters and warreners, sheriffs and their servants, river banks and their guardians shall be inquired into immediately in each county by twelve sworn knights of the same county, who shall be elected by the honest men of the same county, and within forty days after the inquisition has been made, they shall be entirely destroyed by them, never to be restored, provided that we be first informed of it, or our justiciar, if we are not in England.

49. We will give back immediately all hostages and charters which have been liberated to us by Englishmen as security for peace or for faithful service.

50. We will remove absolutely from their bailiwicks the relatives of Gerard de Athyes, so that for the future they shall have no bailiwick in England ; Engelard de Cygony, Andrew, Peter and Gyon de Chancelles, Gyon de Cygony, Geoffrey de Martin and his brothers, Philip Mark and his brothers, and Geoffrey his nephew and their whole retinue.

51. And immediately after the reëstablishment of peace we

will remove from the kingdom all foreign-born soldiers, cross-bow men, serjeants, and mercenaries who have come with horses and arms for the injury of the realm.

52. If any one shall have been dispossessed or removed by us without legal judgment of his peers, from his lands, castles, franchises, or his right we will restore them to him immediately ; and if contention arises about this, then it shall be done according to the judgment of the twenty-five barons, of whom mention is made below concerning the security of the peace. Concerning all those things, however, from which any one has been removed or of which he has been deprived without legal judgment of his peers by King Henry our father, or by King Richard our brother, which we have in our hand, or which others hold, and which it is our duty to guarantee, we shall have respite till the usual term of crusaders ; excepting those things about which the suit has been begun or the inquisition made by our writ before our assumption of the cross ; when, however, we shall return from our journey or if by chance we desist from the journey, we will immediately show full justice in regard to them.

53. We shall, moreover, have the same respite and in the same manner about showing justice in regard to the forests which are to be disafforested or to remain forests, which Henry our father or Richard our brother made into forests; and concerning the custody of lands which are in the fief of another, custody of which we have until now had on account of a fief which any one has held from us by military service ; and concerning the abbeys which have been founded in fiefs of others than ourselves, in which the lord of the fee has asserted for himself a right ; and when we return or if we should desist from our journey we will immediately show full justice to those complaining in regard to them.

54. No one shall be seised nor imprisoned on the appeal of a woman concerning the death of any one except her husband.

55. All fines which have been imposed unjustly and against the law of the land, and all penalties imposed unjustly and against the law of the land are altogether excused, or will be on the judgment of the twenty-five barons of whom mention is made below in connection with the security of the peace, or on the judgment of the majority of them, along with the aforesaid Stephen, archbishop of Canterbury, if he is able to be present, and others whom he may wish to call for this purpose along with him. And if he should not be able to be present, nevertheless the business shall go on without him, provided that if any one or more of the aforesaid twenty-five barons are in a similar suit they should be removed as

far as this particular judgment goes, and others who shall be chosen and put upon oath, by the remainder of the twenty-five shall be substituted for them for this purpose.

56. If we have dispossessed or removed any Welshmen from their lands, or franchises, or other things, without legal judgment of their peers, in England, or in Wales, they shall be immediately returned to them ; and if a dispute shall have arisen over this, then it shall be settled in the borderland by judgment of their peers, concerning holdings of England according to the law of England, concerning holdings of Wales according to the law of Wales, and concerning holdings of the borderland according to the law of the borderland. The Welsh shall do the same to us and ours.

57. Concerning all those things, however, from which any one of the Welsh shall have been removed or dispossessed without legal judgment of his peers, by King Henry our father, or King Richard our brother, which we hold in our hands, or which others hold, and we are bound to warrant to them, we shall have respite till the usual period of crusaders, those being excepted about which suit was begun or inquisition made by our command before our assumption of the cross. When, however, we shall return or if by chance we shall desist from our journey, we will show full justice to them immediately, according to the laws of the Welsh and the aforesaid parts.

58. We will give back the son of Lewellyn immediately, and all the hostages from Wales and the charters which had been liberated to us as a security for peace.

59. We will act toward Alexander, king of the Scots, concerning the return of his sisters and his hostages, and concerning his franchises and his right, according to the manner in which we shall act toward our other barons of England, unless it ought to be otherwise by the charters which we hold from William his father, formerly king of the Scots, and this shall be by the judgment of his peers in our court.

60. Moreover, all those customs and franchises mentioned above which we have conceded in our kingdom, and which are to be fulfilled, as far as pertains to us, in respect to our men ; all men of our kingdom as well clergy as laymen, shall observe as far as pertains to them, in respect to their men.

61. Since, moreover, for the sake of God, and for the improvement of our kingdom, and for the better quieting of the hostility sprung up lately between us and our barons, we have made all these concessions ; wishing them to enjoy these in a complete and firm stability forever, we make and concede to them the security

described below ; that is to say, that they shall elect twenty-five barons of the kingdom, whom they will, who ought with all their power to observe, hold, and cause to be observed, the peace and liberties which we have conceded to them, and by this our present charter confirmed to them ; in this manner, that if we or our justiciar, or our bailiffs, or any one of our servants shall have done wrong in any way toward any one, or shall have transgressed any of the articles of peace or security ; and the wrong shall have been shown to four barons of the aforesaid twenty-five barons, let those four barons come to us or to our justiciar, if we are out of the kingdom, laying before us the transgression, and let them ask that we cause that transgression to be corrected without delay. And if we shall not have corrected the transgression or, if we shall be out of the kingdom, if our justiciar shall not have corrected it within a period of forty days, counting from the time in which it has been shown to us or to our justiciar, if we are out of the kingdom ; the aforesaid four barons shall refer the matter to the remainder of the twenty-five barons, and let these twenty-five barons with the whole community of the country distress and injure us in every way they can; that is to say by the seizure of our castles, lands, possessions, and in such other ways as they can until it shall have been corrected according to their judgment, saving our person and that of our queen, and those of our children ; and when the correction has been made, let them devote themselves to us as they did before. And let whoever in the country wishes take an oath that in all the above-mentioned measures he will obey the orders of the aforesaid twenty-five barons, and that he will injure us as far as he is able with them, and we give permission to swear publicly and freely to each one who wishes to swear, and no one will we ever forbid to swear. All those, moreover, in the country who of themselves and their own will are unwilling to take an oath to the twenty-five barons as to distressing and injuring us along with them, we will compel to take the oath by our mandate, as before said. And if any one of the twenty-five barons shall have died or departed from the land or shall in any other way be prevented from taking the above-mentioned action, let the remainder of the aforesaid twenty-five barons choose another in his place, according to their judgment, who shall take an oath in the same way as the others. In all those things, moreover, which are committed to those five and twenty barons to carry out, if perhaps the twenty-five are present, and some disagreement arises among them about something, or if any of them when they have been summoned are not willing or are not able to be present, let that be considered valid and firm which the greater part of those who are present arrange or command, just as if the whole twenty-five had agreed in this ; and let the aforesaid twenty-five swear that they will observe faithfully all the things which are said above, and with all their ability cause them to be observed.   And we will obtain nothing from any one, either by ourselves or by another by which any of these concessions and liberties shall be revoked or diminished ; and if any such thing shall have been obtained, let it be invalid and void, and we will never use it by ourselves or by another.

62. And all ill-will, grudges, and anger sprung up between us and our men, clergy and laymen, from the time of the dispute, we have fully renounced and pardoned to all.   Moreover, all transgressions committed on account of this dispute, from Easter in the sixteenth year of our reign till the restoration of peace, we have fully remitted to all, clergy and laymen, and as far as pertains to us, fully pardoned.   And moreover we have caused to be made for them testimonial letters-patent of lord Stephen, archbishop of Canterbury, lord Henry, archbishop of Dublin, and of the aforesaid bishops and of Master Pandulf, in respect to that security and the concessions named above.

63. Wherefore we will and firmly command that the Church of England shall be free, and that the men in our kingdom shall have and hold all the aforesaid liberties, rights and concessions, well and peacefully, freely and quietly, fully and completely, for themselves and their heirs, from us and our heirs, in all things and places, forever, as before said.   It has been sworn, moreover, as well on our part as on the part of the barons, that all these things spoken of above shall be observed in good faith and without any evil intent.   Witness the above named and many others. Given by our hand in the meadow which is called Runnymede, between Windsor and Staines, on the fifteenth day of June, in the seventeenth year of our reign.

---

30. Writ for the Collection of a Carrucage

(August, 1220.   Latin text, Stubbs, *S. C.* 352.   Translation by Editors.
2 Stubbs, 36.)

THE king to the sheriff of Northamptonshire, Greeting.
     Know ye that, on account of our great need and the very urgent pressure of our debts and likewise for the protection of our territory of Poitou, all the magnates and subjects of our whole

realm have granted to us collectively and voluntarily a gift to be made to us, to wit, from each carrucate as it was defined on the morrow of the feast of the Blessed John the Baptist last part, in the fourth year of our reign, two shillings are to be collected by your own hand and the hands of two of the more lawful knights of your country; who shall be chosen to do this, by the will and counsel of all of the county in full county court. And therefore we bid you and firmly and strictly enjoin you that, after the convocation of the full court of your county, by the will and consent of those of the county, you cause to be chosen two of the more lawful knights of the whole county who shall best know how, wish and be able to attend to this business to our advantage, and when these have been associated with you, you shall immediately cause this gift to be assessed throughout your whole bailiwick and collected from each carrucate, as aforesaid, excepting the demesnes of the archbishops, bishops, and their villeins, and excepting the demesnes of the order of the Cistercians and Premonstratensians. And you shall see to it that you know how to make answer to us strictly and openly, on the morrow of Michaelmas next coming, at London, how many carrucates there are in your bailiwick from which we ought to have this gift; and the money coming from thence you shall cause to be safely collected by the hands of the aforesaid two knights and by your own hand, and that money you shall cause to be brought to London on the aforesaid day under your seal and the seals of the aforesaid two knights, and you shall have it deposited safely in the New Temple until it shall have been arranged what ought to be done with it; and you, as you value your life and property, busy yourself in this, lest afterwards, by occasion of malfeasance done by you and the aforesaid knights in the inquisition and collection, we should have to make diligent inquisition by faithful subjects sent from our court, to the serious confusion of yourself and of those who shall have been associated with you in the making of the aforesaid inquisition and collection.

Witness, etc., at Oxford, the ninth day of August.

31. Writ for the Assembling of the County Court before the Judges Itinerant

(April, 1231.　Latin text, Stubbs, *S. C.* 358.　Translation by Editors.
2 Stubbs, 214.)

THE king to the sheriff of Yorkshire, Greeting.

Summon by good summoners all archbishops, bishops, abbots, priors, earls, barons, knights, and all freeholders from your bailiwick, from each vill four lawful men and the reeve, and from each borough twelve lawful burgesses, throughout your whole bailiwick, and all others who are accustomed and ought to appear before the justices itinerant, that they be present at York on the octave of Trinity Sunday in the fifteenth year of our reign, before our beloved and faithful S. de Segrave, Ralph Fitz-Robert, Brian Fitz-Alan, William of Lisle, Robert of Lexington, Master Robert of Shardelawe, and William of London, whom we have appointed our justices, to hear and perform our commands.　Also, at that time, cause to be brought before the said justices all pleas of the crown which have not been tried, and those which have arisen since our justices last went on circuit in those parts, and all attachments concerning those pleas, and all the assizes and all the pleas which are set down for the first assize of the justices, with the writs of the assizes and pleas, so that those assizes and pleas shall not be omitted, on account of any default of yours or of your summons.　Also cause it to be proclaimed and made known throughout your whole bailiwick that all the assizes and all the pleas which were appointed a term for a hearing and have not been brought to an end before our justices at Westminster, or before our justices who last went on circuit in your county to hear all pleas, or before the justices sent thither to hold assizes of novel disseisin and of jail-delivery, shall at that time come before our aforesaid justices at York, in the same status in which they have remained by our order, or by the order of our aforesaid justices itinerant or our justices of the bench.　Summon also all those who have been sheriffs since the last circuit of the aforesaid justices in those parts that they be present at that time and place before our aforesaid justices, with the writs concerning the assizes and the pleas which they received during their term of office, to answer for their term as they ought to answer before the justices itinerant.　And have there the summons and this writ.

Witness Hubert de Burgh, etc., at Westminster, the twentieth day of April.

32. Writ for the Collection of Scutage

(July, 1235. Latin text, Stubbs, *S. C.* 364. Translation by Editors. 2 Stubbs, 52.)

THE king to the sheriff of Somersetshire, Greeting.
Know that the earls and barons and all others of our whole realm of England, of their own free will and not as a precedent, have granted us an effectual aid to promote our great undertakings. Wherefore provision was made by their advice that we should have from each knight's fee which is held from us in chief, and from the wardships, as well from a new feoffment as from an old one, two marks to furnish us the aforesaid aid, of which they made provision to give us one moiety at Michaelmas in the nineteenth year of our reign, and the other moiety at Easter in our twentieth year. They also made provision that the said scutage should be collected by the hands of their bailiffs in each county and paid by the hands of the same to two knights whom we have designated in each county for conveying it to our exchequer in London, and delivering it there to our treasurer and our chamberlains; and therefore we order that, at the command of all the earls and barons and all others who hold from us in chief, in the aforesaid bailiwick, in the aforesaid manner, and without delay, you shall make distraint upon all the knights and freeholders who hold from them by knight service in your bailiwick for the paying to their bailiffs from each knight's fee and wardship two marks to render us the aforesaid aid at the aforesaid times, and for the delivery of it to John of Aura and Henry of Meriet whom we have appointed for this purpose in your county, as aforesaid etc.
Witness myself at Westminster, the seventeenth of July in the nineteenth year, etc.

———◆———

33. Writ of Summons for Two Knights of the Shire to grant an Aid

(February, 1254. Latin text, Stubbs, *S. C.* 376. Translation by Editors. 2 Stubbs, 69, 232.)

FORM directed to all the magnates and sheriffs of England.
The king to the sheriff of Bedfordshire and Buckinghamshire, Greeting.
Since the earls and barons and other magnates of our realm

have faithfully promised us that they will be in London in three weeks from next Easter, furnished with horses and arms and well equipped to go without any delay to Portsmouth, to come over to Gascony to us, to aid us against the king of Castile who intends to invade our territory of Gascony with a strong force, next summer, we have ordered you to constrain to this all those in your bailiwick who hold lands worth twenty pounds a year from us in chief, or from others who are under age and in our wardship; we straitly command you, that besides all those aforesaid, you cause to come before our council at Westminster on the fifteenth day after Easter next, four lawful and discreet knights from the said counties whom the said counties shall have chosen for this purpose, in place of all and singular of the said counties, that is, two from one county and two from the other, who together with the knights from the other counties whom we have had summoned for the same day, shall arrange what aid they are willing to pay us in our need. And you yourself carefully set forth to the knights and others of the said counties, our need and how urgent is our business, and effectually persuade them to pay us an aid sufficient for the time being; so that the aforesaid four knights at the aforesaid time shall be able to give definite answer concerning the said aid to the aforesaid council, for each of the said counties. We also give you an absolute command that all dues to us in your bailiwick which are in arrears, and ought to be paid to our exchequer before Easter next, or which ought to be paid to the exchequer at the aforesaid Easter, you shall have at the aforesaid exchequer on the fifteenth day after the aforesaid Easter, and you are to know that unless you have the aforesaid debts then and there, we shall not only cause you to be placed under arrest but we shall also cause those dues to be collected from your lands and tenements to your exceeding loss.

Witness Eleanor the queen and Richard earl of Cornwall, at Windsor, the eleventh day of February.

----

34.   Provisions of Oxford

(Summer of 1258.   Text, Latin and French, Stubbs, *S. C.* 387.   Translation of Latin by Editors, of French as in Stubbs, *S. C.* 393.   2 Stubbs, 76.)

Provision made at Oxford

IT is provided that from each county there shall be chosen four discreet and lawful knights, who on each day when the county court is held, shall meet to hear all complaints made by the sheriffs or bailiffs or any one else against all persons whatsoever, concerning all trespasses whatsoever, and to make the attachments which belong to the said complaints before the next coming of the chief justice into those parts. Also they shall take sufficient sureties from the plaintiff to prosecute and from the defendant to appear for trial before the aforesaid justice at his next coming. And that the aforesaid four knights shall cause enrollment to be made of all the aforesaid complaints, with their attachments in proper order and sequence, that is, each hundred separately and by itself. So that the aforesaid justice at his next coming shall be able to hear and bring to an end the aforesaid complaints, one by one from each hundred. And they shall make known to the sheriff that all the hundredmen and their bailiffs shall be made to appear before the said justice, at his next coming, at a time and place which he shall have announced to them ; so that each hundredman shall cause all plaintiffs and defendants from his bailiwick to appear in succession according as the said justice shall have called to trial from the said hundred ; and also so many and such knights as well as free and lawful men from his bailiwick by whom the truth of the matter can best be established, in such manner that all shall not be troubled together and at the same time, but as many shall appear as can be tried and brought to an end in one day.

Likewise it is provided that no knight of the aforesaid counties, shall be excused by writ of the lord king that he be not placed upon juries and assizes, nor be quit with respect to this provision thus made for the common advantage of the whole realm.

Those elected from the Party of the Lord King

The lord bishop of London, the lord bishop-elect of Winchester, the lord Henry son of the king of Germany, the lord John earl of Warenne, the lord Guy of Lusignan, the lord William of Valence, the lord John earl of Warwick, the lord John Mansel, friar John of Darlington, the abbot of Westminster, the lord Henry of Wengham.

Those elected from the Party of the Earls and Barons

The lord bishop of Worcester, the lord Simon earl of Leicester, the lord Richard earl of Gloucester, the lord Humphrey earl of Hereford, the lord Roger Marshall, the lord Roger of Mortimer, the lord John Fitz-Geoffrey, the lord Hugh Bigot, the lord Rich-

ard de Gray, the lord William Bardulf, the lord Peter de Montfort,
the lord Hugh le Despenser.

And if it happens that any one of these cannot be present,
through necessity, the rest of these shall choose whom they will,
to wit, the other necessary in the place of the one absent, in order
to transact this business.

This the Commonalty of England swore at Oxford

We, so and so, make known to all men, that we have sworn
upon the holy Gospels, and are held together by such oath, and
promise in good faith, that each one of us and we all together will
mutually aid each other, both ourselves and those belonging to us,
against all people, doing right and taking nothing that we cannot
without doing mischief, saving faith to the king and the crown.
And we promise under the same oath, none of us will henceforth
take land or movables by which this oath can be disturbed or in
any ways impaired.   And if any one acts against this, we will hold
him as a mortal enemy.

This is the Oath to the Twenty-four

Each swore on the holy Gospels, that he to the honor of God,
and to his faith to the king, and to the profit of the realm, will
ordain and treat with the aforesaid sworn persons upon the reformation and amendment of the state of the realm.   And that he
will not fail for gift, nor for promise, for love, nor for hate, nor for
fear of any one, nor for gain, nor for loss, loyally to do according
to the tenor of the letter which the king and his son have together
given for this.

This the Chief Justice of England swor

He swears that he will well and loyally according to his power
do that which belongs to the justiciar of right to hold, to all persons, to the profit of the king and the kingdom, according to the
provision made and to be made by the twenty-four, and by the
counsel of the king and the great men of the land, who shall swear
in these things to aid and support him.

This the Chancellor of England swore

That he will seal no writ, excepting writs of course, without the
commandment of the king and of his council who shall be present.

Nor shall he seal a gift of a great wardship, or of a great (   )[1] nor of escheats, without the assent of the great council or of the major part. And that he will seal nothing which may be contrary to the ordinance which is made and shall be made by the twenty-four, or by the major part. And that he will keep no fee otherwise than what is given to the others. And he shall be given a companion in the form which the council shall provide.

This is the Oath which the Guardians of the King's Castles made

That they will keep the castles of the king loyally and in good faith for the use of the king and of his heirs; and that they will give them up to the king or to his heirs, and to none other, and by his counsel and in no other manner, to wit, by honest men of the land elected as his council, or by the major part. And this form by writ lasts for twelve years. And from that time forward by this settlement and this oath they shall not be hindered so that they cannot freely give them up to the king and his heirs.

These are those who are sworn of the King's Council

The archbishop of Canterbury, the bishop of Worcester, the earl of Leicester, the earl of Gloucester, the earl Marshall, Peter of Savoy, the earl of Albemarle, the earl of Warwick, the earl of Hereford, John Mansel, John Fitz-Geoffrey, Peter de Montfort, Richard de Gray, Roger of Mortimer, James of Aldithley.

The twelve on the king's side have elected out of the twelve on that of the commonalty the earl Roger the Marshall, and Hugh Bigot.

And the party of commonalty have elected out of the twelve who are on the king's side the earl of Warwick and John Mansel.

And these four have power to elect the council of the king, and when they have elected them, they shall present them to the twenty-four; and there, where the greater part of these agree, it shall be held.

These are the Twelve who are elected by the Barons to treat at the Three Parliaments by Year with the King's Council for all the Commonalty of the Land of the Common Need

The bishop of London, the earl of Winchester, the earl of Hereford, Philip Basset, John of Balliol, John of Verdun, John de

---

[1] A blank space in the manuscript.

Gray, Roger of Sumery, Roger de Monthaut, Hugh le Despenser, Thomas of Gresley, Giles d'Argentine.

These are the Twenty-four appointed by the Commonalty to treat of Aid to the King

The bishop of Worcester, the bishop of London, the bishop of Salisbury, the earl of Leicester, the earl of Gloucester, the earl Marshall, Peter of Savoy, the earl of Hereford, the earl of Albe-marle, the earl of Winchester, the earl of Oxford, John Fitz-Geoffrey, John de Gray, John of Balliol, Roger of Mortimer, Roger de Monthaut, Roger of Sumery, Peter de Monfort, Thomas of Gresley, Fulk of Kerston, Giles d'Argentine, John Kyriel, Philip Basset, Giles of Erdinton.

And if any one of these cannot or will not serve, those who shall be there have power to elect another in his place.

Of the State of Holy Church

Be it remembered that the state of the holy church be amended by the twenty-four elected to reform the state of the realm of England, when they shall see place and time, according to the power which they have respecting it by the letter of the king of England.

Of the Chief Justice

Moreover, that a justice be appointed, one or two, and what power he shall have, and that he be only for a year. So that at the end of the year, he answer concerning his time before the king and his council and before him who shall follow him.

Of the Treasurer, and of the Exchequer

The like of the treasurer. That he too give account at the end of the year. And other good persons are to be placed at the exchequer according to the direction of the aforesaid twenty-four. And there let all the issues of the land come, and in no part else-where. And let that which shall be seen to require amendment, be amended.

Of the Chancellor

The like of the chancellor. That he at the end of the year answer concerning his time. And that he seal nothing out of course by the sole will of the king. But that he do it by the council which shall be around the king.

Of the Power of the Justice and Bailiffs

The chief justice has power to amend the wrongs done by all the other justices and bailiffs, and earls, and barons, and all other people, according to the law and justice of the land, and in fit places, and that the justice take nothing unless it be presents of bread and wine, and such things, to wit, meat and drink, as have been used to be brought to the tables of the chief men for the day. And let this same thing be understood of all the king's councillors and all his bailiffs. And that no bailiff by occasion of plea or of his office, take any fee in his own hand, or through the agency of another in any manner. And if he is convicted, that he be punished, and he who gives likewise. And if it be fitting, that the king give to his justiciar and his people who serve him, so that they have no occasion to take any thing from elsewhere.

Of the Sheriffs

Let there be provided as sheriffs, loyal people, and substantial men, and land tenants ; so that in each county there be a vavasour of the same county as sheriff, to treat the people of the county well, loyally, and rightfully. And that he take no fee, and that he be sheriff only for a year together ; and that in the year he give up his accounts at the exchequer and answer for his time. And that the king grant unto him out of his own, according to his contribution, so that he can guard the county rightfully. And that he take no fee, neither he nor his bailiffs. And if they be convicted let them be punished.

Be it remembered that such amendment is to be applied to the Jewry, and to the wardens of the Jewry, that the oath as to the same may be kept.

Of the Escheators

Let good escheators be appointed ; and that they take nothing of the effects of the dead, of such lands as ought to be in the king's hand. Also that the escheators have free administration of the goods until they shall have done the king's will, if they owe him debts. And that, according to the form of the Charter of liberty. And that inquiry be made into the wrongs done which the escheators have done there aforetime, and amendment be made of such and such. Nor let tallage on any thing else be taken, excepting such as ought to be according to the Charter of liberty.

Let the Charter of liberty be kept firmly.

Of the Exchange of London

Be it remembered to amend the exchange of London, and the city of London, and all the other cities of the king which have gone to shame and destruction by the tallages and other oppressions.

Of the Place of Reception of the King and Queen

Be it remembered to amend the hostelry of the king and the queen.

Of the Parliaments, how Many shall be held by Year, and in what Manner

It is to be remembered that the twenty-four have ordained that there be three parliaments a year. The first at the octave of Saint Michael. The second the morrow of Candlemas. The third the first day of June, to wit, three weeks before Saint John. To these three parliaments the elected councillors of the king shall come, even if they are not sent for, to see the state of the realm, and to treat of the common wants of the kingdom, and of the king in like manner. And other times in like manner when occasion shall be, by the king's command.

So it is to be remembered that the commonalty elect twelve honest men, who shall come at the parliaments and other times when occasion shall be, when the king or his council shall send for them to treat of the wants of the king and of the kingdom. And that the commonalty shall hold as established that which these twelve shall do. And that shall be done to spare the cost of the commonalty.

There shall be fifteen named by these four, to wit, by the earl Marshall, the earl of Warwick, Hugh Bigot, and John Mansel, who are elected by the twenty-four to name the aforesaid fifteen, who shall be the king's council. And they shall be confirmed by the aforesaid twenty-four, or by the major part of them. And they shall have power to counsel the king in good faith concerning the government of the realm and all things which appertain to the king or to the kingdom; and to amend and redress all things which they shall see require to be redressed and amended. And over the chief justice and over all other people. And if they cannot all be present, that which the majority shall do shall be firm and established. [The names of the principal castles of the king, and of those who have them in keeping, follow in the Ms.]

35.   The Provisions of the Barons or of Westminster

(October, 1259.   Latin text and translation, 1 S. R. 8, Stubbs, S. C. 401.
2 Stubbs, 83.)

IN the year of the Incarnation of our Lord, one thousand two
hundred and fifty-nine, and the forty-third year of the reign of
king Henry the son of king John, there being assembled at Westminster in the fifteenth of Saint Michael, our said lord the king
and his great men, by the common counsel and consent of the
said king and great men, the underwritten provisions were made
by the same king and great men, and were published in the
manner following.

1. Of doing suits, unto the courts of the great men and others
the lords of these courts, it is provided and with full consent
ordained, that no man who hath been infeoffed by deed shall be
distrained from henceforth to do suit unto the court of his lord,
unless he be specially bounden to do suit by the form of his deed :
except those whose ancestors or who themselves have used to do
such suit, before the first voyage of the said lord the king into
Brittany ; from the time whereof there have passed twenty-nine
years and a half at the time of making this ordinance ; and in like
manner no man infeoffed without deed from the time of the Conquest, or by other ancient feoffment, shall be distrained to do such
suit ; unless he or his ancestors have used to do the same, before
the first voyage of the said lord the king into Brittany.

2. And if any inheritance wherefrom only one suit was due,
shall descend unto many heirs, as parceners thereof, he that hath
the elder's share of that inheritance shall do one suit for himself
and his coparceners ; and his coparceners shall contribute after
their shares, to the doing of that suit.   And in like manner if
many shall have been infeoffed of any inheritance wherefrom one
suit were due, the lord of that fee shall have but one suit therefrom ; nor can he exact more than one suit from the said inheritance, as it hath been used to be done before.   And if the persons
infeoffed have no warrantor or mean who ought to acquit them
thereof, then all of them shall contribute after their shares, to the
doing of that suit.

3. And if it happen that the lords of courts do distrain their
tenants for such suit, contrary to this provision, then upon the
complaint of those tenants they shall be attached to appear in the

king's court at a short day to answer therefore; and they shall
have but one essoin if they be within the realm; and the cattle
or other distresses taken upon this occasion shall be delivered
to the plaintiff forthwith, and shall remain delivered until the plea
between them be ended.   And if the lords of the courts who have
made such distresses, shall not appear at the day whereto they
were attached, or shall not keep the day given to them upon the
essoin, then the sheriff shall be commanded to cause them to
come upon another day; at which day if they come not, the
sheriff shall be commanded to distrain them by all that they possess within his bailiwick, so that he shall answer to the king for
the issues, and to have their bodies by a certain day to be prefixed, so that if they should not come upon that day, the party
plaintiff may go thence without day; and the cattle or other distresses shall remain delivered until those lords shall recover that
suit by award of the court of our lord the king; and in the mean
time such distresses shall cease : saving to the lords of the courts
their right to recover those suits in form of law, when they will
sue therefore.   And when the lords of the courts shall appear to
answer unto the plaintiffs for such distresses, if they be thereupon
convicted, then by the award of the court, the plaintiffs shall
recover against them their damages, which they have sustained
by occasion of the aforesaid distress.   And in like manner, if tenants, after this act, do withdraw from their lords their suits which
they ought to do, and which before the time of the aforesaid
voyage and hitherto they have used to do, the lords of the courts
shall obtain justice to recover their suits, together with their damages, by the same process and dispatch, in respect of appointment
of days and awarding of distresses, like as the tenants do recover
their damages.   And this matter of recovering damages must be
understood of the withdrawings done to themselves, and not of the
withdrawings done to their predecessors : nevertheless the lords
of the courts shall not recover seisin of such suits against their
tenants by default; as that hath not been the custom hitherto.
And concerning the suits that were withdrawn before the time
of the aforesaid voyage, let the common law have its course, as it
hath used to have before.

4. Concerning the sheriff's turn, it is provided that archbishops,
bishops, abbots, priors, earls, barons, shall not be obliged to come
thither, nor any men of religion, or women, unless their presence
be specially required ; but the turn shall be holden as it was wont
to be in the times of our lord the king's predecessors.   And where
any do hold tenements in divers hundreds, they shall not be obliged

to come to such turn except in the bailiwicks where they shall dwell : and the turns shall be holden according to the form of the king's Great Charter, and as they were wont to be holden in the times of king John and king Richard.

5. It is also provided that neither in the circuit of justicers, nor in the county and hundred courts, nor in the courts baron, shall fines be taken from any from henceforth for fair pleading, nor for not being troubled on that account.

6. In the plea of dower that is called *Unde nihil habet*, from henceforth there shall be given four days in the year at least, and more if it may be conveniently done.

7. In assizes of darrein presentment, and in the plea of *Quare impedit* of churches vacant, the day shall be given from fifteen days to fifteen days, or from three weeks to three weeks, according as the place may be far or near. And in the plea of *Quare impedit*, if the disturber come not at the first day for which he shall have been summoned, nor cast an essoin, then he shall be attached unto another day, on which day if he come not nor cast an essoin, he shall be distrained by the great distress above mentioned. And if he come not then, upon his default the bishop shall be written to, that the claim of the disturber shall not obstruct the plaintiff for that term ; saving unto the disturber his right at another time, when he will sue therefore.

8. Concerning charters of exemption and privilege, that the purchasers shall not be impanelled in assizes, juries, or recognitions, it is provided, that if their oath should be so necessary, that without it justice could not be administered, as in the great assize and perambulations, and where they may have been named as witnesses in charters, or writings of covenants, or in attaints or other like cases, they shall be compelled to swear ; saving unto them at another time their aforesaid privilege and exemption.

9. If any heir should be under age after the death of his ancestor, and his lord have the wardship of his lands, if that lord will not render unto the said heir his lands when he cometh to lawful age, without plea, the heir shall recover his land as from the death of his ancestor, together with the damages that he shall have sustained by that withholding from the time of his coming to lawful age ; and if an heir at the time of his ancestor's death be of full age, and such heir, apparent and known to be the heir, be found in the inheritance, his chief lord shall not put him out, nor take or remove any thing therefrom, but shall take simple seisin only for the acknowledgment of his seigniory.

F

10. And if a chief lord do maliciously keep such an heir out of the possession, whereby it behoveth him to proceed by an action of mort d'ancestor or cosinage, then he shall recover his damages, as in the action of novel disseisin.

11. No man from thenceforth shall be permitted, for any manner of cause, to make distresses out of his fee, nor in the king's or common highway, except our lord the king and his officers.

12. It is also provided, that where land that is holden in socage is in the custody of an heir's kinsfolk, because the heirs were within age, those guardians cannot make waste or sale or any despoiling in that inheritance, but shall keep it safely for the use of the heir: so that when he shall come to age, they shall answer unto him by a lawful account for the issues of the said inheritance; saving unto those guardians their reasonable expenses. Neither can the said guardians give or sell the marriage of the said heir, but for the benefit of the heir himself.

13. No escheator, or commissioner, or justice, especially assigned to take any assizes, or to hear and determine any complaints, shall from henceforth have authority to amerce for default of the common summons, except the chief justice or justices in eyre in their circuits.

14. It shall not be lawful for men of religion to enter into any man's fee, without the license of the chief lord of whom the fee is immediately holden.

15. Concerning essoins it is provided, that in the county or hundred courts, or courts baron, or elsewhere, no man shall be obliged to swear for the warranting of his essoin.

16. None but the king from henceforth shall hold plea in his court of a false judgment given in the court of his tenants; because such pleas do especially belong to the king's crown and dignity.

17. It is provided also, that if any man's cattle be taken and unjustly detained, the sheriff after complaint thereof made unto him, may deliver them, without let or gainsaying of him who took the said cattle, if they were taken without liberties, and if such cattle should be taken within liberties, and the bailiffs of the liberties will not deliver them, then the sheriff, for the default of the said bailiffs, shall cause them to be delivered.

18. No man from henceforth shall distrain his free tenants to answer for their freehold, nor for any matters pertaining to their freehold, without the king's writ; nor shall cause his free tenants to swear against their will: for none can do this without a precept of the king.

19. It is provided also, that if bailiffs who are bounden to render account unto their lords shall withdraw themselves, and have no lands or tenements whereby they may be distrained, then they shall be attached by their bodies, so that the sheriffs in whose bailiwicks they shall be found, shall cause them to come to the rendering of their account.

20. Also farmers during their farms, shall not make waste, or sale, or exile, in woods, houses, men, or in any thing else belonging to the tenements which they have to farm ; unless they have a special grant in the writing of their covenant, making mention that they may do so.   And if they do, and be convicted thereof, they shall restore damages in full.

21. The justices in eyre from henceforth shall not amerce the township in their circuit, because all that are twelve years old do not appear before the sheriffs and coroners upon inquests for the death of man, or other things pertaining to the crown ; so that from those townships there come enough for the making of such inquests fully.

22. The fine of murder from henceforth shall not be adjudged before the justices, where it hath been adjudged to be misfortune only : but the fine of murder shall hold place upon those slain feloniously, and not otherwise.

23. It is moreover provided, that no man who is vouched to warranty before the justices in eyre, in a plea of land or tenement, shall from henceforth be amerced because he was not present, save on the first day of the coming of the justices : but if the vouchee be within the county, then the sheriff shall be enjoined to cause him to come within the third or fourth day, according to the distance of the places, as it was wont to be in the circuit of the justices : and if he dwell without the county, then he shall have a reasonable summons of fifteen days at the least, according to the discretion of the justices and the common law.

24. If any clerk should be arrested for any crime or charge that toucheth the crown, and afterwards by the king's precept, be let to bail, or be replevied, so that those to whom he is let to bail should have him before the justices, from henceforth they to whom he hath been let to bail, or his other pledges shall not be amerced, if they have his body before the justices, although he will not or cannot make answer before them by reason of the privilege of clergy.

36. Confirmation of the Charters

(March, 1265.   Latin text, Stubbs, *S. C.* 416.   Translation by Editors.
2 Stubbs, 94.)

THE king to all the people of the county of York, Greeting.
* * * We will and expressly agree that, if we or the said
Edward our son shall have presumed to go in any way contrary —
may it be far from us — to the said ordinance, or our provision,
or oath, or to disturb the peace and tranquillity of our realm, or
to molest, by reason of their former acts in the time of the late
disturbance and war, any one of the aforesaid, or of the party of
the aforesaid whom we have defied, or do or procure the doing
of injury to any of them, it shall be lawful for every one in our
realm to rise against us and to use all the ways and means they
can to hinder us; to which we will that each and every one shall
henceforth be bound by our command, notwithstanding the fealty
and homage which he has sworn to us; so that they shall in no
way give attention to us, but that they shall do everything which
aims at our injury and shall in no way be bound to us, until that
in which we have transgressed and offenced shall have been by a
fitting satisfaction brought again into due state, according to the
form of the ordinance of the aforesaid, and of our provision or
oath; this having been done let them be obedient to us as they
were before. * * *

Witness myself at Westminster, the fourteenth day of March,
in the forty-ninth year of our reign.

———◆———

37. The Statutes of Westminster; the First

(1275.   French text and translation, 1 *S. R.* 26, Stubbs, *S C.* 450.
2 Stubbs, 113.)

THESE be the acts of king Edward, son to king Henry, made
at Westminster at his first parliament general after his coronation, on the Monday of Easter Utas, the third year of his reign,
by his council and by the assent of archbishops, bishops, abbots,
priors, earls, barons, and the commonalty of the realm, being
thither summoned : because * * * ; the king hath ordained and
established these acts underwritten, which he intendeth to be necessary and profitable unto the whole realm.

*   *   *   *   *   *   *   *   *

5. And because elections ought to be free, the king commandeth upon great forfeiture, that no man by force of arms, nor by malice, or menacing, shall disturb any to make free election.

*   *   *   *   *   *   *   *   *

36. Forasmuch as before this time, reasonable aid to make one's son knight, or to marry his daughter, was never put in certain, nor how much should be taken, nor at what time, whereby some levied unreasonable aid, and more often than seemed necessary, whereby the people were sore grieved ; it is provided, that from henceforth of a whole knight's fee there be taken but twenty shillings, and of twenty-pound land holden in socage, twenty shillings ; and of more, more ; and of less, less ; after the rate. And that none shall levy such aid to make his son knight, until his son be fifteen years of age, nor to marry his daughter, until she be of the age of seven years. And of that there shall be made mention in the king's writ, formed on the same, when any will demand it. And if it happen that the father, after that he hath levied such aid of his tenants, die before he hath married his daughter, the executors of the father shall be bound to the daughter, for so much as the father received for the aid. And if the father's goods be not sufficient, his heir shall be charged therewith unto the daughter.

*   *   *   *   *   *   *   *   *

------------◆------------

38. Grant of Customs on Wool, Woolfells, and Leather

(May, 1275. Latin text, Stubbs, *S. C.* 451. Translation by Editors. 2 Stubbs, 113, 550.)

WILLIAM of Valence, earl of Pembroke, to all the faithful in Christ to whom the present writ shall come, Greeting in the Lord.

Since the archbishops, bishops, and other prelates of the realm of England, and the earls, barons, and we and the communities of the said realm, at the instance and request of the merchants, have for many reasons, unanimously granted to the great prince and lord, our well-beloved lord Edward, by the grace of God, the illustrious king of England, for us and our heirs, a half mark from each sack of wool, and a half mark from each three hundred woolfells, which make a sack, and one mark from each last of leather, exported from the realm of England and the land of Wales, to be collected henceforth in each and every port of England and Wales, as well within liberties as without; we, at the request and instance of the aforesaid merchants, do grant, for ourselves and our heirs, that the same lord the king and his heirs in each and every one of our ports in Ireland, both within our liberties and without, shall have a half mark from each sack of wool, and a half mark from each three hundred woolfells, which make a sack, and one mark from each last of leather, exported from the land of Ireland, to be collected by the hand of the wardens and bailiffs of the said king, saving to us the forfeiture of those who, without licence and warrant of the said lord the king, by his letters patent signed by his seal for this provided, shall have presumed to carry out of Ireland wool, woolfells, or leather of this sort, through our fiefs where we have liberties. From which the aforesaid lord the king and his heirs shall receive and have the half mark from the wool and woolfells and the mark from the lasts of leather in the form aforesaid; nevertheless so that in each of our ports where the writs of the aforesaid lord the king do not run, two of the more discreet and faithful men of those ports shall be chosen who, upon oath, until the merchants of the aforesaid wool, woolfells, and leather shall have his warrant for it under the seal of the lord the king for this provided, shall faithfully collect the customs from the wool, woolfells, and leather, seized in the said ports, and shall receive them for the use of the said lord the king and shall answer to him for them.

In testimony whereof, we have set our seal to the present writ. Given in the general parliament of the aforesaid lord the king, at Westminster on Sunday the feast of Saint Dunstan the bishop, in the third year of the reign of the said king.

---

39.   Writ for Distraint of Knighthood

(June, 1278.   Latin text, Stubbs, *S. C.* 457.   Translation by Editors.
2 Stubbs, 115, 221, 294.)

THE king to the sheriff of Gloucestershire, Greeting.
We order and straitly enjoin you, that, without delay, you distrain all those in your bailiwick who have twenty pound lands or a whole knight's fee worth twenty pounds a year, and who hold from us in chief and ought to be knights and are not; that before the feast of the Lord's nativity next coming or at the same feast, they receive the insignia of knighthood from us: also, without

delay, distrain all those from your bailiwick who have twenty
pound lands or a whole knight's fee worth twenty pounds a year,
from whomsoever they hold, and ought to be knights and are not,
that they receive insignia of the same sort at the same feast or
before : so that you receive from the same good and sufficient
security for it, and cause the names of all of them to be written
down in a roll upon the attestation of two lawful knights of the
aforesaid county, and to be transmitted to us, without delay, under
your seal and the seals of the two knights.   And we will you to
know that we will make prompt visitation upon your action in the
execution of this order of ours, and thereupon we shall cause suitable remedy to be made for it.

Witness the king at Westminster, the twenty-sixth day of June.

40.   Statute of Mortmain or De Religiosis

(November, 1279.   Latin text, 1 *S. R.* 51, Stubbs, *S. C.* 458.   Translation,
1 *S. R.* 51, G. and H. 81.   2 Stubbs, 117.)

THE king to his justices of the bench, Greeting.
Where of late it was provided, that religious men should
not enter into the fees of any without licence and will of the chief
lords, of whom such fees be holden immediately ; and notwithstanding such religious men have since entered as well into their
own fees, as into the fees of other men, appropriating and buying
them, and sometimes receiving them of the gift of others, whereby
the services that are due of such fees, and which at the beginning were provided for defence of the realm, are wrongfully withdrawn, and the chief lords do lose their escheats of the same : we
therefore, to the profit of our realm, intending to provide convenient remedy, by the advice of our prelates, earls, barons, and
other our subjects, being of our council, have provided, established,
and ordained, that no person, religious or other, whatsoever he be,
presume to buy or sell, or under the color of gift or lease, or by
reason of any other title, whatsoever it be, to receive of any man,
or by any other craft or device to appropriate to himself any lands
or tenements under pain of forfeiture of the same whereby such
lands or tenements may any wise come into mortmain.   We have
provided also, that if any person, religious or other, do presume
in any manner either by craft or device to offend against this
statute, it shall be lawful to us and other chief lords of the fee

immediate to enter into the land so alienated, within a year from the time of the alienation, and to hold it in fee and inheritance. And if the chief lord immediate be negligent, and will not enter into such fee within the year, then it shall be lawful to the next chief lord immediate of the same fee to enter into the same fee within half a year next following, and to hold it as before is said ; and so every lord immediate may enter into such fee if the next lord be negligent in entering into the same fee, as is aforesaid. And if all the chief lords of such fees, being of full age, within the four seas, and out of prison, be negligent or slack in this behalf, for the space of one year, we, immediately after the year accomplished, from the time that such purchases, gifts, or appropriations hap to be made, shall take such lands or tenements into our hand, and shall infeoff other therein by certain services to be done for the same to us for the defence of our realm ; saving to the chief lords of the same fees their wards and escheats, and other things to them belonging, and the services for the same, due and accustomed.   And therefore we command you, that you cause the aforesaid statute to be read before you, and from henceforth to be kept firmly and observed.

Witness myself at Westminster the fifteenth day of November, the seventh year of our reign.

---

41.   The Statute of Merchants, or of Acton Burnell

(October, 1283.   French text and translation, 1 *S. R.* 53.   2 Stubbs, 121.)

FORASMUCH as merchants, which heretofore have lent their goods to divers persons, be greatly impoverished, because there is no speedy law provided for them to have recovery of their debts at the day of payment assigned ; and by reason hereof many merchants do refrain to come into this realm with their merchandises, to the damage as well of the merchants, as of the whole realm ; the king by himself and his council hath ordained and established, that the merchant which will be sure of his debt, shall cause his debtor to come before the mayor of London, or of York, or Bristol, and before the mayor and a clerk, which the king shall appoint for the same, for to acknowledge the debt and the day of payment ; and the recognizance shall be entered into a roll with the hand of the said clerk, which shall be known.   Moreover, the

said clerk shall make with his own hand a bill obligatory, whereunto the seal of the debtor shall be put, with the king's seal, that
shall be provided for the same purpose, the which seal shall remain
in the keeping of the mayor and clerk aforesaid : and if the debtor
doth not pay at the day to him limited, the creditor may come
before the said mayor and clerk with his bill obligatory ; and if it
be found by the roll, and by the bill, that the debt was acknowledged, and that the day of payment is expired, the mayor shall
incontinent cause the movables of the debtor to be sold, as far as
the debt doth amount, by the appraising of honest men, as also
chattels, and burgages devisable, until the whole sum of the debt ;
and the money, without delay, shall be paid to the creditor. And
if the mayor can find no buyer, he shall cause the movables to be
delivered to the creditor at a reasonable price, as much as doth
amount to the sum of the debt : and in allowance of his debt : and
the king's seal shall be put unto the sale and deliverance of the
burgages devisable for a perpetual witness.   And if the debtor
have no movables within the jurisdiction of the mayor, whereupon
the debt may be levied, but hath some otherwhere within the
realm, then shall the mayor send the recognizance, made before
him and the clerk aforesaid, unto the chancellor, under the seal
aforesaid ; and the chancellor shall direct a writ unto the sheriff,
in whose bailiwick the movables of the debtor be, and the sheriff
shall cause the creditor to be satisfied in such form as it is prescribed that the mayor should have done in case that the movables of the debtor had been within his power ; and let them that
shall appraise the movable goods, to be delivered unto the creditor,
take good heed that they do set a just and reasonable price upon
them ; for if they do set an over high price for favor borne to the
debtor, and to the damage of the creditor, then shall the thing so
appraised be delivered unto themselves at such price as they have
limited, and they shall be forthwith answerable unto the creditor
for his debt.   And if the debtor will say, that his movable goods
were delivered or sold for less than they were worth, yet shall he
have no remedy thereby ; forasmuch as the mayor or the sheriff
hath sold the movable goods lawfully to him that offered most ;
for he may blame himself, that before the day of the suit he had
it in his power to have sold his movable goods, and to have levied
the money with his own hand, and yet he would not.   And if the
debtor have no movables whereupon the debt may be levied, then
shall his body be taken where it may be found, and kept in prison
until that he have made agreement, or his friends for him ; and if
he have not of his own wherewith he may sustain himself in prison,

the creditor shall find him bread and water, to the end that he die not in prison for default of sustenance, the which costs the debtor shall recompense him with his debt, before that he be let out of prison. And if the creditor be a merchant stranger, he shall remain at the costs of the debtor for so long time as he shall be suing for the levying of his debt, until the day that the movable goods of the debtor be sold or delivered unto him. And if the creditor do not content himself with the debtor alone for the surety of his payment, by reason whereof pledges or mainpernors be founden, then those pledges or mainpernors shall come before the mayor and clerk abovesaid, and shall bind themselves by writings and recognizances, as afore is said of the debtor. And in like manner if the debt be not paid at the day limited, such execution shall be awarded against the pledges or mainpernors, as before is said of the debtor; provided nevertheless, that so long as the debt may be fully taken and levied of the goods movable of the debtor, the mainpernors or pledges shall be without damage: notwithstanding, for default of movable goods of the debtor, the creditor shall have his recovery against the mainpernors or pledges, in such manner and form as before is limited against the principal debtor.

And to defray the charge of the aforesaid clerk, the king shall take out of every pound one penny. This ordinance and act the king willeth to be holden from henceforth throughout all his realm of England, among all persons whosoever they may be, who shall freely choose to make such recognizance; except Jews, to whom this statute extendeth not.

And by this statute a writ of debt shall not be abated. And the chancellor, barons of the exchequer, justices of the one bench and of the other, and justices errants, shall not be estopped to take recognizances of debts of those who shall choose so to do before them; but the execution of recognizances before them shall not be made according to the form aforesaid, but according to law, usage, and manner heretofore used.

Given at Acton Burnell, the twelfth day of October in the eleventh year of our reign.

42.   The Statutes of Westminster; the Second

(June, 1285.   Latin text and translation, 1 *S. R.* 71.   2 Stubbs, 122.   Clause I.,
here given, is known as *De donis conditionalibus.*)

* * * OUR lord the king in his parliament, after the feast of Easter, holden the thirteenth year of his reign at Westminster, * * * did provide certain acts, as shall appear here following.

First, Concerning lands that many times are given upon condition, that is to wit, where any giveth his land to any man and his wife, and to the heirs begotten of the bodies of the same man and his wife, with such condition expressed that if the same man and his wife die without heir of their bodies between them begotten, the land so given shall revert to the giver or his heir: In case also where one giveth lands in free marriage, which gift hath a condition annexed, though it be not expressed in the deed of gift, which is this, that if the husband and wife die without heir of their bodies begotten, the land so given shall revert to the giver or his heir: in case also where one giveth land to another, and the heirs of his body issuing; it seemed very hard, and yet seemeth to the givers and their heirs, that their will being expressed in the gift, was not heretofore, nor yet is observed: for in all the cases aforesaid, after issue begotten and born between them, to whom the lands were given under such condition, heretofore such feoffees had power to aliene the land so given, and to disherit their issue of the land, contrary to the minds of the givers, and contrary to the form expressed in the gift: and further, when the issue of such feoffee is failing, the land so given ought to return to the giver, or his heir, by form of the gift expressed in the deed though the issue, if any were, had died: yet by the deed and feoffment of them, to whom land was so given upon condition, the donors have heretofore been barred of their reversion, which was directly repugnant to the form of the gift: wherefore our lord the king, perceiving how necessary and expedient it should be to provide remedy in the aforesaid cases, hath ordained, that the will of the giver, according to the form in the deed of gift manifestly expressed, shall be from henceforth observed; so that they to whom the land was given under such condition, shall have no power to aliene the land so given, but that it shall remain unto the issue of them to whom it was given after their death, or unto the giver or his heirs, if issue fail either by reason that there is no issue at all, or if any issue be, it fail by death, the heir of such issue failing.   Neither shall the second husband of any such woman, from henceforth, have any thing in the land so given upon condition, after the death of his wife, by the law of England, nor the issue of the second husband and wife shall succeed in the inheritance, but immediately after the death of the husband and wife, to whom the land was so given, it shall return to their issue, or to the giver, or his heir, as before is said. * * *   And it is to wit that this statute shall hold place touching alienation of land contrary to the form of the gift hereafter to be made, and shall not extend to gifts made before.   And if a fine be levied hereafter upon such lands, it shall be void in the law; neither shall the heirs, or such as the reversion belongeth unto, though if they be of full age, within England, and out of prison, need to make their claim. * * *

XXIV.   *   *   *   *   *   *   *   *   *

And whensoever from henceforth it shall fortune in the chancery, that in one case a writ is found, and in like case falling under like law, and requiring like remedy, is found none, the clerks of the chancery shall agree in making the writ, or shall adjourn the plaintiffs until the next parliament and write the cases in which they cannot agree, and refer them to the next parliament, and by consent of men learned in the law, a writ shall be made, lest it might happen hereafter that the court should long time fail to minister justice unto complainants.

*   *   *   *   *   *   *   *   *

43. The Statute of Winchester

(October, 1285.   French text and translation, 1 S. R. 96, Stubbs, S. C. 470–472.   2 Stubbs, 122, 219.)

1. FORASMUCH as from day to day, robberies, murders, and arsons be more often used than they have been heretofore, and felons cannot be attainted by the oath of jurors which had rather suffer felonies done to strangers to pass without pain, than to indite the offenders of whom great part be people of the same country, or at least if the offenders be of another country the receivers be of places near; and they do the same because an oath is not put unto jurors; nor upon the country where such felonies were done as to the restitution of damages, hitherto no

pain hath been limited for their concealment and laches; our lord the king, for to abate the power of felons, hath established a pain in this case, so that from henceforth, for fear of the pain more than for fear of any oath, they shall not spare any nor conceal any felonies; and doth command that cries be solemnly made in all counties, hundreds, markets, fairs, and all other places where great resort of people is, so that none shall excuse himself by ignorance, that from henceforth every country be so well kept that immediately upon such robberies and felonies committed fresh suits shall be made from town to town and from country to country.

2. Likewise when need requires, inquests shall be made in towns by him that is lord of the town, and after in the hundred and in the franchise and in the county, and sometimes in two, three, or four counties, in case when felonies shall be committed in the marches of shires, so that the offenders may be attainted. And if the country will not answer for such manner of offenders, the pain shall be such, that every country, that is to wit, the people dwelling in the country, shall be answerable for the robberies done and also the damages: so that the whole hundred where the robbery shall be done, with the franchises being within the precinct of the same hundred, shall be answerable for the robberies done. And if the robbery be done in the division of two hundreds, both the hundreds and the franchises within them shall be answerable; and after that the felony or robbery is done, the country shall have no longer space than forty days, within which forty days it shall behoove them to agree for the robbery or offence, or else that they will answer for the bodies of the offenders.

3. And forasmuch as the king will not that his people should be suddenly impoverished by reason of this penalty, that seemeth very hard to many, the king granteth that it shall not be incurred immediately, but it shall be respited until Easter next following, within which time the king may see how the country will order themselves, and whether such felonies and robberies do cease. After which term let them all be assured that the aforesaid penalty shall run generally; that is to say, every country, that is to wit, the people in the country, shall be answerable for felonies and robberies done among them.

4. And for the more surety of the country, the king hath commanded that in great towns being walled, the gates shall be closed from the sun-setting until the sun-rising; and that no man do lodge in suburbs, nor in the edges of the town, except in the day-time, nor yet in the day-time, unless his host will answer for him; and the bailiffs of towns every week, or at the least every fifteenth

day, shall make inquiry of all persons being lodged in the suburbs or the edges of the towns ; and if they do find any that have received or lodged in any other way people of whom there may be suspicion that they are against the peace, the bailiffs shall do right therein. And the king commandeth, that from henceforth all watches be made as it hath been used in times past, that is to wit, from the day of the Ascension unto the day of Saint Michael, in every city by six men at every gate ; in every borough, by twelve men ; in every town, by six or four, according to the number of the inhabitants of the town, and they shall keep the watch continually all night from the sun-setting unto the sun-rising. And if any stranger do pass by them he shall be arrested until morning ; and if no suspicion be found he shall go quit ; and if they find cause of suspicion, they shall forthwith deliver him to the sheriff, and the sheriff shall receive him without delay, and shall keep him safely, until he be delivered in due manner. And if they will not obey the arrest, they shall levy hue and cry upon them, and such as keep the watch shall follow them with all the town and the towns near, with hue and cry from town to town, until that they be taken and delivered to the sheriff as before is said ; and for the arrestments of such strangers none shall be punished.

5. And further, it is commanded that highways leading from one market town to another shall be enlarged, whereas woods, hedges, or dykes be, so that there be neither dyke, underwood, nor bush whereby a man may lurk to do hurt, near to the way, within two hundred foot of the one side and two hundred foot on the other side ; so that this statute shall not extend unto oaks, nor unto great trees, so as it shall be clear underneath. And if by default of the lord that will not abate the dyke, underwood, or bushes, in the manner aforesaid, any robberies be done therein, the lord shall be answerable for the felony ; and if murder be done the lord shall make a fine at the king's pleasure. And if the lord be not able to fell the underwoods, the country shall aid him therein. And the king willeth that in his demesne lands and woods, within his forest and without, the ways shall be enlarged as before is said. And if perchance a park be near to the highway, it is requisite that the lord shall minish his park so that there be a border of two hundred foot near the highway, as before is said, or that he make such a wall, dyke, or hedge that offenders may not pass, nor return to do evil.

6. And further it is commanded that every man have in his house harness for to keep the peace after the ancient assize ; that is to

say, every man between fifteen years of age and sixty years, shall be assessed and sworn to armor according to the quantity of their lands and goods; that is to wit, for fifteen pounds lands, and goods of forty marks, an hauberke, an helm of iron, a lance, a knife, and a horse; and for ten pounds of lands, and twenty marks goods, an hauberke, an helme of iron, a lance, and a knife; and for five pound lands, a doublet, an helme of iron, a lance, and a knife; and from forty shillings of land and more up to one hundred shillings, a lance, a bow and arrows, and a knife; and he that hath less than forty shillings yearly shall be sworn to *falces, gisarmes,* knives, and other small arms; and he that hath less than twenty marks in goods, shall have swords, knives, and other small arms; and all other that may shall have bows and arrows out of the forest, and in the forest bows and pilets. And that view of armor be made every year two times. And in every hundred and franchise two constables shall be chosen to make the view of armor; and the constables aforesaid shall present before justices assigned, when they shall come into the country, such defaults as they shall have found about armor, and of suits, and of watches, and of highways; and also shall present all such as do lodge strangers in uplandish towns, for whom they will not answer. And the justices assigned shall present at every parliament unto the king such defaults as they shall find, and the king shall provide remedy therein. And from henceforth let the sheriffs take good heed, and bailiffs within franchises and without, greater or lesser, that have any bailiwick or forestry in fee or otherwise, that they shall follow the cry with the country, as they are able, having horses and armor so to do; and if there be any that do not, the defaults shall be presented by the constables to the justices assigned, and after by them to the king; and the king will provide remedy as before is said. And the king commandeth and forbiddeth that from henceforth neither fairs nor markets be kept in churchyards, for the honor of the church.

Given at Winchester, the eighth of October, in the thirteenth year of the reign of the king.

44. The Statute of Circumspecte Agatis

(c. 1285. Latin text and translation, 1 *S. R.* 101. Translation G. and H. 83, is followed here. 2 Stubbs, 123. This so-called statute seems to be the combination of the writ *Circumspecte Agatis,* which forms the first paragraph, and another document of uncertain date. The statute occurs in various forms and with various readings in the different manuscripts and printed copies ; which have been collated to form the texts cited above.)

THE king to such and such judges, Greeting.

See that ye act circumspectly in the matter touching the bishop of Norwich and his clergy, in not punishing them if they shall hold pleas in the court Christian concerning those things which are merely spiritual, to wit : — concerning corrections which prelates inflict for deadly sin, to wit, for fornication, adultery, and such like, for which, sometimes corporal punishment is inflicted, and sometimes pecuniary, especially if a freeman be convicted of such things.

Item if a prelate impose a penalty for not enclosing a churchyard, leaving the church uncovered or without proper ornament, in which cases no other than a pecuniary fine can be inflicted.

Item if a rector demand the greater or the lesser tithe, provided the fourth part of any church be not demanded.

Item if a rector demand a mortuary in places where a mortuary has been usually given.

Item if a prelate of any church demand a pension from the rector as due to him : — all such demands are to be made in the ecclesiastical court.

Concerning laying violent hands on a clerk, and in case of defamation, it has been granted formerly that pleas thereof may be held in the court Christian, provided money be not demanded ; but proceedings may be taken for the correction of the sin ; and likewise for breach of faith. In all these cases the ecclesiastical judge has to take cognizance, the king's prohibition notwithstanding, although it be put forward.

Wherefore laymen generally obtain a prohibition for tithes, oblations, mortuaries, redemptions of penances, laying violent hands on a clerk or a lay-brother, and in case of defamation, in which cases proceedings are taken to exact canonical punishment.

The lord the king made answer to these articles, that in tithes, obventions, oblations, and mortuaries, when proceedings are taken, as is aforesaid, there is no place for prohibition. And if a clerk or religious person shall sell for money to any one his tithes stored ın the barn, or being elsewhere, and be impleaded in the court Christian, the royal prohibition has place, for by reason of sales, spiritual things are temporal, and then tithes pass into chattels.

Item if dispute arise concerning the right of tithes, having its origin in the right of patronage, and the quantity of these tithes exceeds the fourth part of the church, the king's prohibition has place.

Item if a prelate impose pecuniary penalty on any one for sin, and demand the money, the king's prohibition has place, if the money is exacted before prelates.

Item if any one shall lay violent hands on a clerk, amends must be made for a breach of the peace of the lord the king, before the king, and for excommunication before the bishop ; and if corporal penalty be imposed which, if the defendant will, he may redeem by giving money to the prelate or person injured, neither in such cases is there place for prohibition.

In defamations of freemen let the prelates correct, the king's prohibition notwithstanding, although it be tendered.

———◆———

45. The Statutes of Westminster ; the Third : Quia Emptores

(July, 1290.   Latin text, 1 *S. R.* 106, Stubbs, *S. C.* 478.   Translation, 1 *S. R.* 106.   2 Stubbs, 126, 259.)

1. FORASMUCH as purchasers of lands and tenements of the fees of great men and others, have many times heretofore entered into their fees, to the prejudice of the lords, to which purchasers the freeholders of such great men and others have sold their lands and tenements to be holden in fee to them and their heirs of their feoffers, and not of the chief lords of the fees, whereby the same chief lords have many times lost their escheats, marriages, and wardships of lands and tenements belonging to their fees ; which thing seemed very hard and extreme unto those great men and other lords, and moreover in this case manifest disheritance : our lord the king, in his parliament at Westminster after Easter, the eighteenth year of his reign, that is to wit, in the quinzime of Saint John the Baptist, at the instance of the great men of the realm, granted, provided, and ordained, that from henceforth it shall be lawful to every freeman to sell at his own pleasure his lands and tenements, or part of them ; so that the feoffee shall

G

hold the same lands or tenements of the same chief lord, and by the same services and customs as his feoffor held before.

2. And if he shall sell any part of such lands or tenements to any, the feoffee shall immediately hold it of the chief lord, and shall be forthwith charged with the services, for so much as pertaineth, or ought to pertain to the said chief lord for the same parcel, according to the quantity of the land or tenement sold. And so in this case the same part of the service shall cease to be taken by the chief lord by the hands of the feoffor, from the time that the feoffee ought to be attendant and answerable to the same chief lord, according to the quantity of the land or tenement sold, for the parcel of the service so due.

3. And it is to be understood, that by the said sales or purchases of lands or tenements, or any parcels of them, such lands or tenements shall in no wise come into mortmain, either in part or in whole, neither by policy nor craft, contrary to the form of the statute made thereupon of late. And it is to wit, that this statute extendeth but only to lands sold to be holden in fee simple ; and that it extendeth to the time coming ; and it shall begin to take effect at the feast of Saint Andrew the apostle next coming.

------

46. Writs of Summons to Parliament

(30 September – 3 October, 1295. Latin text, Stubbs, *S. C.* 484. Translation, Cheyney, 33. 2 Stubbs, 133, 209, 211, 235.)

Summons of the Clergy

THE King to the venerable father in Christ Robert, by the same grace archbishop of Canterbury, primate of all England, greeting. As a most just law, established by the careful providence of sacred princes, exhorts and decrees that what affects all, by all should be approved, so also, very evidently should common danger be met by means provided in common. You know sufficiently well, and it is now, as we believe, divulged through all regions of the world, how the king of France fraudulently and craftily deprives us of our land of Gascony, by withholding it unjustly from us. Now, however, not satisfied with the before-mentioned fraud and injustice, having gathered together for the conquest of our kingdom a very great fleet, and an abounding multitude of warriors, with which he has made a hostile attack on our kingdom and the inhabitants of the same kingdom, he now proposes to destroy the English language altogether from the earth, if his power should correspond to the detestable proposition of the contemplated injustice, which God forbid. Because, therefore, darts seen beforehand do less injury, and your interest especially, as that of the rest of the citizens of the same realm, is concerned in this affair, we command you, strictly enjoining you in the fidelity and love in which you are bound to us, that on the Lord's day next after the feast of St. Martin, in the approaching winter, you be present in person at Westminster; citing beforehand [præmunientes] the dean and chapter of your church, the archdeacons and all the clergy of your diocese, causing the same dean and archdeacons in their own persons, and the said chapter by one suitable proctor, and the said clergy by two, to be present along with you, having full and sufficient power from the same chapter and clergy, to consider, ordain and provide, along with us and with the rest of the prelates and principal men and other inhabitants of our kingdom, how the dangers and threatened evils of this kind are to be met. Witness the king at Wangham, the thirtieth day of September.

Identical summons were sent out to the two archbishops and eighteen bishops, and, with the omission of the last paragraph, to seventy abbots.

Summons of the Barons

The king to his beloved and faithful relative, Edmund, Earl of Cornwall, greeting. Because we wish to have a consultation and meeting with you and with the rest of the principal men of our kingdom, as to provision for remedies against the dangers which in these days are threatening our whole kingdom; we command you, strictly enjoining you in the fidelity and love in which you are bound to us, that on the Lord's day next after the feast of St. Martin, in the approaching winter, you be present in person at Westminster, for considering, ordaining and doing along with us and with the prelates, and the rest of the principal men and other inhabitants of our kingdom, as may be necessary for meeting dangers of this kind.

Witness the king at Canterbury, the first of October.

Similar summons were sent to seven earls and forty-one barons.

Summons of Representatives of the Counties and Boroughs

The king to the sheriff of Northamptonshire. Since we intend to have a consultation and meeting with the earls, barons and other principal men of our kingdom with regard to providing remedies against the dangers which are in these days threatening the same kingdom ; and on that account have commanded them to be with us on the Lord's day next after the feast of St. Martin in the approaching winter, at Westminster, to consider, ordain, and do as may be necessary for the avoidance of these dangers ; we strictly require you to cause two knights from the aforesaid county, two citizens from each city in the same county, and two burgesses from each borough, of those who are especially discreet and capable of laboring, to be elected without delay, and to cause them to come to us at the aforesaid time and place.

Moreover, the said knights are to have full and sufficient power for themselves and for the community of the aforesaid county, and the said citizens and burgesses for themselves and the communities of the aforesaid cities and boroughs separately, then and there for doing what shall then be ordained according to the common counsel in the premises ; so that the aforesaid business shall not remain unfinished in any way for defect of this power. And you shall have there the names of the knights, citizens and burgesses and this writ.

Witness the king at Canterbury on the third day of October.

Identical summons were sent to the sheriffs of each county.

---

47. The Bull " Clericis Laicos "

(February, 1296. Latin text, Rymer's *Fœdera*, i. 836. Translation, G. and H. 87. 2 Stubbs, 135.)

BONIFACE bishop, servant of the servants of God, for the perpetual memory of the matter. That laymen have been very hostile to clerks antiquity relates, which too the experiences of the present times manifestly declare, whilst not content with their own bounds they strive for the forbidden and loose the reins for things unlawful. Nor do they prudently consider how power over clerks or ecclesiastical persons or goods is forbidden them : they impose heavy burdens on the prelates of the churches and ecclesiastical persons regular and secular, and tax them, and impose collections : they exact and demand from the same the half, tithe, or twentieth, or any other portion or proportion of their revenues or goods ; and in many ways they essay to bring them under slavery, and subject them to their authority. And, as we sadly relate, some prelates of the churches and ecclesiastical persons, alarmed where there should be no alarm, seeking transient peace, fearing more to offend the temporal majesty than the eternal, acquiesce in such abuses, not so much rashly as improvidently, authority or licence of the Apostolic See not having been obtained. We therefore desirous of preventing such wicked actions, do, with apostolic authority decree, with the advice of our brethren, that whatsoever prelates and ecclesiastical persons, religious or secular, of whatsoever orders, condition or standing, shall pay or promise or agree to pay to lay persons collections or taxes for the tithe, twentieth, or hundredth of their own rents, or goods, or those of the churches, or any other portion, proportion, or quantity of the same rents, or goods, at their own estimate or value, under the name of aid, loan, relief, subsidy, or gift, or by any other title, manner, or pretext demanded, without the authority of the same see.

And also whatsoever emperors, kings, or princes, dukes, earls, or barons, powers, captains, or officials, or rectors, by whatsoever names they are reputed, of cities, castles, or any places whatsoever, wheresoever situate, and all others of whatsoever rank, pre-eminence or state, who shall impose, exact, or receive the things aforesaid, or arrest, seise, or presume to occupy things anywhere deposited in holy buildings, or to command them to be arrested, seised, or occupied, or receive them when occupied, seised, or arrested, and also all who knowingly give aid, counsel, or favor, openly or secretly, in the things aforesaid, by this same should incur sentence of excommunication. Universities, too, which may have been to blame in these matters, we subject to ecclesiastical interdict.

The prelates and ecclesiastical persons above mentioned we strictly command, in virtue of their obedience, and under pain of deposition, that they in no wise acquiesce in such things without express licence of the said see, and that they pay nothing under pretext of any obligation, promise, and acknowledgement whatsoever, made so far, or in progress heretofore, and before such constitution, prohibition, or order come to their notice, and that the seculars aforesaid do not in any wise receive it, and if they do pay, or the aforesaid, let them fall under sentence of excommunication by the very deed.

Moreover let no one be absolved from the aforesaid sentences of excommunication and interdict, save at the moment of death, without authority and special licence of the Apostolic See, inasmuch as it is part of our intention that such a terrible abuse of secular powers should not in any wise pass under dissimulation, any privileges whatsoever notwithstanding, in whatsoever tenors, forms or modes, or arrangement of words, conceded to emperors, kings and the others aforesaid ; against which premises aforesaid we will that aid be given by no one, and by no persons in any respect.

Let it then be lawful to none at all to infringe this page of our constitution, prohibition, or order, or to gainsay it by any rash attempt ; and if any one presume to attempt this, let him know that he will incur the indignation of Almighty God, and of his blessed apostles Peter and Paul.

Given at Rome in Saint Peter's on the twenty-fourth of February in the second year of our pontificate.

---

48. Confirmatio Cartarum

(October, 1297.   French text and translation, 1 *S. R.* 123, Stubbs, *S. C.* 494–496. 2 Stubbs, 146.)

EDWARD, by the grace of God, king of England, lord of Ireland, and duke of Guyenne, to all those that these present letters shall hear or see, Greeting.

1. Know ye that we to the honor of God, and of holy Church, and to the profit of our realm, have granted for us and our heirs, that the great Charter of Liberties, and the Charter of the Forest, which were made by common assent of all the realm, in the time of king Henry our father, shall be kept in every point without breach. And we will that the same charters shall be sent under our seal, as well to our justices of the forest, as to others, and to all sheriffs of shires, and to all our other officers, and to all our cities throughout the realm, together with our writs, in the which it shall be contained, that they cause the foresaid charters to be published, and to declare to the people that we have confirmed them in all points ; and to our justices, sheriffs, mayors, and other ministers, which under us and by us have the laws of our land to guide, that they shall allow the same charters in all their points, in pleas before them, and in judgments ; that is to wit, the Great Charter as the common law, and the Charter of the Forest according to the Assize of the forest, for the wealth of our realm.

2. And we will, that if any judgment be given from henceforth contrary to the points of the charters aforesaid by the justices, or by any other our ministers that hold plea before them against the points of the charters, it shall be undone and holden for nought.

3. And we will, that the same charters be sent, under our seal, to cathedral churches throughout our realm, there to remain, and shall be read before the people two times by the year.

4. And that all archbishops and bishops shall pronounce the sentence of great excommunication against all those that by deed, aid, or counsel do contrary to the foresaid charters, or that in any point break or undo them. And that the said curses be twice a year denounced and published by the prelates aforesaid. And if the same prelates, bishops, or any of them be remiss in the denunciation of the said sentences, the archbishops of Canterbury and York for the time being, as is fitting, shall compel and distrain them to make that denunciation in form aforesaid.

5. And for so much as divers people of our realm are in fear, that the aids and tasks which they have given to us beforetime towards our wars and other business, of their own grant and good will, howsoever they were made, might turn to a bondage to them and their heirs, because they might be at another time found in the rolls, and so likewise the prises taken throughout the realm by our ministers in our name ; we have granted for us and our heirs, that we shall not draw such aids, tasks, nor prises into a custom, for any thing that hath been done heretofore, or that may be found by roll or in any other manner.

6. Moreover we have granted for us and our heirs as well to archbishops, bishops, abbots, priors, and other folk of holy Church, as also to earls, barons, and to all the commonalty of the land, that for no business from henceforth we shall take of our realm such manner of aids, tasks, nor prises, but by the common assent of all the realm, and for the common profit thereof, saving the ancient aids and prises due and accustomed.

And for so much as the more part of the commonalty of the realm find themselves sore grieved with the maletote of wools, that is to wit, a toll of forty shillings for every sack of wool, and have made petition to us to release the same ; we at their requests have clearly released it, and have granted that we will not take such thing nor any other without their common assent and good will ; saving to us and our heirs the custom of wools, skins, and leather, granted before by the commonalty aforesaid. In witness of which things we have caused these our letters to be made patents.

Witness Edward our son at London the tenth day of October, the five and twentieth year of our reign.

And be it remembered that this same charter, in the same terms, word for word, was sealed in Flanders under the king's great seal, that is to say, at Ghent the fifth day of November in the twenty-fifth year of the reign of our aforesaid lord the king, and sent into England.

———◆———

49. De Tallagio non Concedendo

(**1297.**   Latin text, 1 *S. R.* 125, Stubbs, *S. C.* 497.   Translation, 1 *S. R.* 125.
2 Stubbs, 148, 545.)

1. No tallage or aid shall be laid or levied by us or our heirs in our realm, without the good will and assent of the archbishops, bishops, earls, barons, knights, burgesses, and other freemen of our realm.

2. No officer of ours, or of our heirs, shall take corn, wool, leather, or any other goods, of any manner of person, without the good will and assent of the party to whom the goods belonged.

3. Nothing from henceforth shall be taken in the name or by occasion of maletote.

4. We will and grant for us and our heirs, that all clerks and laymen of our land shall have all their laws, liberties, and free customs, as largely and wholly as they have used to have the same at any time when they had them best and most fully ; and if any statutes have been made by us or our ancestors, or any customs brought in contrary to them, or any manner of article contained in this present charter, we will and grant, that such manner of statutes and customs shall be void and frustrate for evermore.

5. Moreover, we have pardoned Humphrey Bohun earl of Hereford and Essex, constable of England, Roger Bigod, earl of Norfolk and Suffolk, marshal of England, and other earls, barons, knights, esquires, and namely John of Ferrers, with all other being of their fellowship, confederacy, and bond, and also to all other that hold twenty pound land in our realm, whether they hold of us in chief, or of other, that were appointed at a day certain to pass over with us into Flanders, the rancor and ill-will which for the aforesaid causes we conceived against them, and all other offences, if any, that they have done against us or ours unto the making of this present charter.

6. And for the more assurance of this thing, we will and grant, for ourselves and our heirs, that all archbishops and bishops for ever in their cathedral churches, this present charter being first read, shall excommunicate, and publicly in the several parish churches of their dioceses, shall cause to be excommunicated, or

to be declared excommunicated twice in the year, all those that willingly do or procure to be done any thing contrary to the tenor, force, and effect of this present charter in any point and article. In witness of which thing we have set our seal to this present charter, together with the seals of the archbishops, bishops, earls, barons, and others which voluntarily have sworn that, as much as in them is, they shall observe the tenor of this present charter in all causes and articles, and shall extend their faithful aid to the keeping thereof forever.

50. The Statute of Carlisle

(March, 1307.   Latin text and translation, 1 *S. R.* 150.   G. and H. 92.
2 Stubbs, 163.)

OF late it came to the knowledge of our lord the king, by the grievous complaint of the honorable persons, lords, and other noblemen of his realm, that whereas monasteries, priories, and other religious houses were founded to the honor and glory of God, and the advancement of the holy Church, by the king and his progenitors, and by the said noblemen and their ancestors, and a very great portion of lands and tenements have been given by them to the said monasteries, priories, and houses, and the religious men serving God in them, to the intent that clerks and laymen might be admitted in such monasteries, priories, and religious houses, according to their sufficient ability, and that sick and feeble men might be maintained, hospitality, almsgiving, and other charitable deeds might be exercised and done in them for the souls of the said founders and their heirs ; the abbots, priors, and governors of the said houses, and certain aliens their superiors, as the abbots and priors of the Cluniacs, Cistercians, and Premonstratensians, and of the orders of Saint Augustine, and Saint Benedict, and many more of other religion and order, have newly appointed to be made, and at their own pleasure ordained divers unwonted, heavy, and intolerable tallages, payments, and impositions upon every of the said monasteries and houses in subjection unto them in England, Ireland, Scotland, and Wales, without the privity of our lord the king and his nobility, contrary to the laws and customs of the said realm ; and thereby the number of religious persons, and other servants in the said houses and religious places being oppressed by such tallages, payments, and impositions, the service of God is diminished ; alms are withheld from the poor, the sick, and feeble, the healths of the living and the souls of the dead be miserably defrauded, hospitality, almsgiving, and other godly deeds do cease ; and so that which in times past was charitably given to godly uses, and to the increase of the service of God, is now converted to an evil tax ; by permission whereof besides those things which are before mentioned, there groweth great scandal to the people, and infinite losses are well known to have ensued, and are still like to ensue, to the disheritance of the founders of the said houses and their heirs, unless speedy and sufficient remedy be provided to redress so many and grievous detriments : wherefore our foresaid lord the king, considering that it would be very prejudicial to him and his people if he should any longer suffer so great losses and injuries to be winked at, and therefore being willing to maintain and defend the monasteries, priories, and other religious houses and places erected in his kingdom, and in all lands subject to his dominion, according to the will and pious wishes of their founders, and from henceforth to provide sufficient remedy to reform such oppressions, as he is bound, by the counsel of his earls, barons, great men, and other nobles and of the commons of his kingdom in his parliament holden at Westminster, on the Sunday next after the feast of Saint Matthias the apostle, in the three and thirtieth year of his reign, did ordain and enact :

2. "That no abbot, prior, master, warden, or other religious person, of whatsoever condition, state or religion he be, being under the king's power or jurisdiction, shall by himself, or by merchants or others, secretly or openly, by any art or device, carry or send, or by any means cause to be sent, any tax imposed by the abbots, priors, masters, or wardens of religious houses or places, their superiors, or in any way assessed among themselves, out of his kingdom and his dominion, under the name of a rent, tallage, tribute, or any kind of imposition, or otherwise in the name of exchange, sale, loan or other contract howsoever it may be termed ; neither shall depart into any other country for visitation, or upon any other color, by that means to carry the goods of their monasteries and houses out of the kingdom and dominion aforesaid. And if any will presume to offend this present statute, he shall be grievously punished according to the quality of his offence, and according to his contempt of the king's prohibition.

3. "Moreover our foresaid lord the king doth inhibit all and singular abbots, priors, masters, and governors of religious houses and places, being aliens, to whose authority, subjection, and obedience the houses of the same orders in his kingdom and

dominion be subject, that they do not at any time hereafter impose, or by any means assess any tallages, payments, impositions,
tributes, or other burdens whatsoever, upon the monasteries,
priories, or other religious houses in subjection unto them as is
aforesaid ; and that upon forfeiture of all that they have in their
power, and can forfeit in future."

4. And further, our lord the king hath ordained and established
that the abbots of the orders of Cistercians and Premonstratensians, and other religious orders, whose seal hath heretofore been
used to remain only in the custody of the abbot, and not of the
convent, shall hereafter have a common seal, and shall deposit the
same in the custody of the prior of the monastery or house, and
four of the most worthy and discreet men of the convent of the
same house, to be laid up in safe keeping under the private seal
of the abbot of the same house ; so that the abbot, or superior of
the house which he doth govern, shall by no means be able of
himself to establish any contract or obligation, as heretofore he
hath used to. And if it fortune hereafter, that writings obligatory
of donations, purchases, sales, alienations, or of any other contracts,
be found sealed with any other seal than such a common seal kept
as is aforesaid, they shall be adjudged void and of no force in law.
But it is not the meaning of our lord the king to exclude the
abbots, priors, and other religious, aliens, by the ordinances and
statutes aforesaid, from executing their office of visitation in his
kingdom and dominion ; but they may visit at their pleasures, by
themselves or others, the monasteries and other places in his kingdom and dominion in subjection unto them, according to the duty
of their office, in those things only that belong to regular observation and the discipline of their order. Provided, that they which
shall execute this office of visitation, shall carry, or cause to be
carried out of his kingdom and dominion, none of the goods or
things of such monasteries, priories, and houses, saving only their
reasonable and competent charges.

And though the publication and open notice of the ordinances
and statutes aforesaid was stayed in suspense, for certain causes,
since the last parliament, until this present parliament holden at
Carlisle in the octaves of Saint Hilary, in the five and thirtieth year
of the reign of the same king Edward, and to the intent that they
might proceed with greater deliberation and advice; our lord the
king, after full conference and debate had with his earls, barons,
nobles, and other great men and the commons of his kingdom,
touching the premises, by their whole consent and agreement hath
ordained and enacted, that the ordinances and statutes aforesaid

under the manner, form, and conditions aforesaid, from the first
day of May next ensuing, shall henceforward be inviolably observed
and available for ever, and the offenders of them shall thenceforth
be subjected to the pains prescribed.

————◆————

51. The New Ordinances

(October, 1311. French text and translation, 1 *S. R.* 157. 2 Stubbs, 344.
The original ordinances form the first six articles of the New Ordinances.)

EDWARD by the grace of God, king of England, lord of Ireland, and duke of Aquitaine, to all to whom these letters shall
come, Greeting.   Know ye that whereas on the sixteenth day of
March, in the third year of our reign, to the honor of God, and for
the weal of us and of our realm, we did grant of our free will by
our letters patent to the prelates, earls, and barons of our said
realm, that they might choose certain persons of the prelates, earls,
and barons, whom they should see fit to call unto them ; and we
did also grant, by the same letters, to those who should be chosen,
whosoever they should be, by the said prelates, earls, and barons,
full power to order the state of our household, and of our realm before mentioned, * * * : and the honorable father in God Robert,
by the grace of God archbishop of Canterbury, primate of all England, the bishops, earls, and barons thereunto chosen, by virtue
of our said letters, have ordained upon the said matters in the
form which followeth :

Forasmuch as by bad and deceitfull counsel our lord the king
and all his subjects, are dishonored in all lands ; and moreover the
crown hath been in many points abased and dismembered, and his
lands of Gascony, Ireland, and Scotland on the point of being lost,
if God do not give amendment ; and his realm of England upon
the point of rising, on account of oppressions, prises, and destruc-
tions ; the which things being known and shown, our lord the king,
of his free will hath granted to the prelates, earls, and barons, and
to the other good people of his realm, that certain persons should be
chosen to order and establish the state of his household and of his
realm, as more fully appears by the commission of our lord the king
thereof made : Wherefore we, Robert, by the grace of God archbishop of Canterbury, primate of all England, the bishops, earls,
and barons chosen by virtue of the said commission, do ordain, to

the honor of God and of holy Church, and to the honor of the
king and of his realm, in the manner which followeth :

* * * * * * * * *

4. Moreover, it is ordained, that the customs of the realm be
kept and received by people of the realm, and not by aliens; and
that the issues and profits of the same customs, together with all
other issues and profits of the realm arising from any matters
whatsoever, shall come entirely to the king's exchequer, and by
the treasurer and the chamberlains shall be delivered, to maintain the household of the king, and otherwise to his profit, so that
the king may live of his own, without taking prises other than
those anciently due and accustomed; and all others shall cease.

* * * * * * * * *

9. Forasmuch as the king ought not to undertake deed of war
against any one, nor to go out of his realm, but by common
assent of his baronage, for the many perils that may happen to
him and his realm, we do ordain, that the king henceforth shall
not go out of his realm, nor undertake against any one deed of
war, without the common assent of his baronage, and that in parliament. And if he otherwise do, and upon such enterprise cause
to be summoned his service, such summons shall be for none;
and if it happen that the king undertake deed of war against any
one, or go out of the realm, with the assent of his said baronage,
and it be necessary that he appoint a guardian in his realm, then
he shall appoint him with the common assent of his baronage,
and that in parliament.

* * * * * * * * *

11. Also, new customs have been levied, and the old enhanced,
as upon wools, cloths, wines, *avoir de pois*, and other things,
whereby the merchants come more seldom, and bring fewer good
into the land, and the foreign merchants abide longer than they
were wont to do, by which abiding things become more dear than
they were wont to be, to the damage of the king and his people;
we do ordain, that all manner of customs and imposts levied
since the coronation of king Edward, son of king Henry, be
entirely put out, and altogether extinguished for ever, notwithstanding the charter which the said king Edward made to the
merchants aliens, because the same was made contrary to the
Great Charter and the franchise of the city of London, and without the assent of the baronage; and if any, of whatsoever condition he be, do take or levy any thing beyond the ancient

customs due and rightful, or make disturbance, whereby the merchants cannot of their goods do their will, and therof be attainted, there shall be awarded to the plaintiffs their damages, having regard to the purchase, to the suit, to the costs and losses which they shall have had, and to the violation of the Great Charter; and the trespasser shall be imprisoned according to the quantity of the trespass, and according to the discretion of the justices, and he shall never be in the king's service; saving nevertheless to the king the customs of wools, woolfells, and leather; that is to say, for each sack of wool, half a mark, and for three hundred woolfells, half a mark, and for a last of leather, one mark, if the goods be liable thereto: and henceforth merchants strangers shall come, abide, and go according to the ancient customs, and according to that which of old they were wont to do.

*　　*　　*　　*　　*　　*　　*　　*　　*

14. And forasmuch as many evils have come to pass by such counsellors and such ministers, we do ordain that the king do make the chancellor, chief justice of the one bench and the other, the treasurer, the chancellor and chief baron of the exchequer, the steward of his household, the keeper of his wardrobe, and comptroller and a fit clerk to keep the privy seal, a chief keeper of the forests on this side of Trent, and another on the other side of Trent, and also an escheator on this side of Trent and another on the other side of Trent, and the chief clerk of the king in the common bench, by the counsel and assent of his baronage, and that in parliament; and if it happen by any chance, that it be expedient to appoint any of the said ministers before there be a parliament, then the king shall appoint thereto by the good counsel which he shall have near him, until the parliament.　And so it shall henceforth be done of such ministers when need shall be.

*　　*　　*　　*　　*　　*　　*　　*　　*

17. Moreover we do ordain, that the sheriffs be from henceforth appointed by the chancellor, the treasurer, and the others of the council who shall be present; and if the chancellor be not present, they shall be appointed by the treasurer and barons of the exchequer, and by the justices of the bench, and that such be appointed and made who are fit and sufficient and who have lands and tenements whereof they can answer to the king and to the people for their deeds, and that no other than such be appointed, and that they have their commission under the great seal.

*　　*　　*　　*　　*　　*　　*　　*　　*

29. * * * : We do ordain, that the king shall hold a parliament once in the year, or twice, if need be, and that in a convenient place: * * *

*   *   *   *   *   *   *   *   *

32. Forasmuch as the law of the land and common right are often delayed, by letters issued under the king's privy seal, to the great grievance of the people, we do ordain, that from henceforth the law of the land and common right be not delayed nor disturbed by letters of the said seal; and if any thing be done in any of the places of the court of our lord the king, or elsewhere, by such letters issued under the privy seal against right or the law of the land, it shall avail nothing, and be holden for none.

*   *   *   *   *   *   *   *   *

* * * Given at London, the fifth day of October, in the fifth year of our reign.

————◆————

52. Articuli Cleri

(November, 1316. Latin text and translation, 1 *S. R.* 171. 2 Stubbs, 356.)

THE king to all to whom, &c., Greeting.
  Understand ye, that whereas * * * : and of late in our parliament holden at Lincoln, the ninth year of our reign, we caused the articles underwritten, with certain answers made to some of them heretofore, to be rehearsed before our council, and made certain answers to be corrected; and to the residue of the articles underwritten, answers were made by us and our council; of which said articles, with the answers of the same, the tenors here ensue.

*   *   *   *   *   *   *   *   *

6. Also if any cause or matter, the knowledge whereof belongeth to a court spiritual, and shall be definitively determined before a spiritual judge, so that it pass into a judgment, nor was not in suspense by an appeal; and after, if upon the same thing a question is moved before a temporal judge between the same parties, and it be proved by witness or instruments, such an exception is not to be admitted in a temporal court.   The answer.   When any one case upon different grounds, is debated before judges spiritual and temporal, as above appeareth upon the case of laying violent hands on a clerk, they say, that notwithstanding

the spiritual judgment, the king's court shall discuss the same matter according as it may seem expedient to that court.

7. Also the king's letter is used to be directed unto ordinaries, that have wrapped those that be in subjection unto them in the sentence of excommunication, that they should absolve them by a certain day, or else that they do appear, and show wherefore they have excommunicated them: the answer. The king decreeth, that hereafter no such letters shall be suffered to go forth, but in case where it is found that the king's liberty is prejudiced by the excommunication.

* * * * * * * * *

Witness the king at York, the twenty-fourth day of November, in the tenth year of the reign of king Edward, the son of king Edward.

---◆---

53. Revocation of the New Ordinances

(May, 1322. French text and translation, 1 *S. R.* 189. 2 Stubbs, 369.)

WHEREAS our lord king Edward, son of king Edward, on the sixteenth day of March in the third year of his reign, to the honor of God, and for the weal of himself and his realm, did grant unto the prelates, earls, and barons of his realm, that they might choose certain persons of the prelates, earls, and barons, and of other lawful men whom they should deem sufficient to be called unto them, for the ordaining and establishing the estate of the household of our said lord the king, and of his realm according to right and reason, and in such manner that their ordinances should be made to the honor of God, and to the honor and profit of holy Church, and to the honor of the said king, and to his profit and to the profit of his people, according to right and reason, and to the oath which our said lord the king made at his coronation: and the archbishop of Canterbury, primate of all England, the bishop, earls, and barons thereunto chosen, did make certain ordinances which begin thus:

"Edward by the grace of God, king of England, lord of Ireland, and duke of Aquitaine, to all to whom these letters shall come, Greeting. Know ye that whereas on the sixteenth day of March in the third year of our reign, to the honor of God, &c." and which end thus, "Given at London the fifth day of October in the fifth year of our reign."

The which ordinances our said lord the king, at his parliament at York, in three weeks from Easter in the fifteenth year of his reign, did, by the prelates, earls, and barons, among whom were the more part of the said Ordainers who were then living, and by the commonalty of his realm, there by his command assembled, cause to be rehearsed and examined: and forasmuch as upon that examination it was found, in the said parliament, that by the matters so ordained the royal power of our said lord the king was restrained in divers things, contrary to what ought to be, to the blemishing of his royal sovereignty, and against the estate of the crown; and also, forasmuch as, in time past, by such ordinances and provisions, made by subjects against the royal power of the ancestors of our lord the king, troubles and wars have happened in the realm, whereby the land hath been in peril, it is accorded and established, at the said parliament, by our lord the king, and by the said prelates, earls, and barons, and the whole commonalty of the realm, at this parliament assembled, that all the things, by the said ordainers ordained and contained in the said ordinances, shall from henceforth for the time to come cease and shall lose their name, force, virtue, and effect for ever; the statutes and establishments duly made by our lord the king and his ancestors, before the said ordinances, abiding in their force: and that forever hereafter, all manner of ordinances or provisions, made by the subjects of our lord the king or of his heirs, by any power or authority whatsoever, concerning the royal power of our lord the king or of his heirs, or against the estate of our said lord the king or of his heirs, or against the estate of the crown, shall be void and of no avail or force whatever; but the matters which are to be established for the estate of our lord the king and of his heirs, and for the estate of the realm and of the people, shall be treated, accorded and established in parliaments, by our lord the king, and by the assent of the prelates, earls, and barons, and the commonalty of the realm; according as it hath been heretofore accustomed.

H

54. Statute concerning the Lands of the Templars

(March, 1324.   Latin text and translation, 1 *S. R.* 194.)

* * * WHEREUPON, the greater part of the king's council, as well the justices as other lay persons being
assembled together, the said justices affirmed precisely, that our
lord the king, and other lords of the fees aforesaid, might well
and lawfully, by the laws of the realm, retain the foresaid lands
as their escheats, in regard of the ceasing and dissolution of the
order aforesaid: but because the lands and tenements aforesaid
were given to the brethren of the said order for the defence of
Christians, * * * ; it seemed good to our lord the king, the noblemen, and others assembled in the same parliament, for the health
of their souls, * * *, that the foresaid lands and tenements, * * *,
and all other things pertaining thereunto, * * *, shall be assigned
and delivered to other men of most holy religion; * * * : and
thereupon in the same parliament it is agreed, ordained and
established for law to continue for ever in this behalf, that neither
our lord the king, nor any other lords of the fees aforesaid, or
any other person, hath title or right to retain the foresaid lands
and tenements, with the appurtenances or any part thereof, in
the name of escheat, or by any other means, or hereafter to challenge the same lands in respect of the ceasing or dissolution of
the foresaid military order of Templars, whereof the brethren of
the same order were seised in their demesnes as of fee, at the
time of ceasing and dissolution aforesaid; * * * : it is agreed and
enacted in the said parliament * * * that all the lands, tenements, lordships, fees, churches, advowsons of churches, and
liberties, with all things to them any way belonging, which were
the said Templar's at the time of their ceasing and dissolution,
shall be assigned and delivered to the foresaid Order of the Hospital, and to the prior and brethren of the same Hospital, to
remain to them and their successors forever: * * *

55. Articles of Accusation against Edward II

(January, 1327. French text, Twysden's *Historiae Anglicanae Scriptores Decem*, 2765. Translation by Editors. 2 Stubbs, 379.)

IT has been decided that prince Edward, the eldest son of the king shall have the government of the realm and shall be crowned king, for the following reasons:

1. First, because the king is incompetent to govern in person. For throughout his reign he has been controlled and governed by others who have given him evil counsel, to his own dishonor and to the destruction of holy Church and of all his people, without his being willing to see or understand what is good or evil or to make amendment, or his being willing to do as was required by the great and wise men of his realm, or to allow amendment to be made.

2. Item, throughout his reign he has not been willing to listen to good counsel nor to adopt it nor to give himself to the good government of his realm, but he has always given himself up to unseemly works and occupations, neglecting to satisfy the needs of his realm.

3. Item, through the lack of good government he has lost the realm of Scotland and other territories and lordships in Gascony and Ireland which his father left him in peace, and he has lost the friendship of the king of France and of many other great men.

4. Item, by his pride and obstinacy and by evil counsel he has destroyed holy Church and imprisoned some of the persons of holy Church and brought distress upon others and also many great and noble men of his land he has put to a shameful death, imprisoned, exiled, and disinherited.

5. Item, wherein he was bound by his oath to do justice to all, he has not willed to do it, for his own profit and his greed and that of the evil councillors who have been about him, nor has he kept the other points of his oath which he made at his coronation, as he was bound to do.

6. Item, he has stripped his realm, and done all that he could to ruin his realm and his people, and what is worse, by his cruelty and lack of character he has shown himself incorrigible without hope of amendment, which things are so notorious that they cannot be denied.

56. Statute of Northampton

(June, 1328.   French text and translation, 1 *S. R.* 257.   2 Stubbs, 390, 613.)

2. ITEM, whereas offenders have been greatly encouraged, because that charters of pardon have been so easily granted in times past, of manslaughters, robberies, felonies, and other trespasses against the peace; it is ordained and enacted, that such charter shall not be granted, but only where the king may do it by his oath, that is to say, where a man slayeth another in his own defence, or by misfortune: * * *

*   *   *   *   *   *   *   *   *

12. Item, whereas all the counties in England were in old time assessed to a certain ferm, and then were all the hundreds and wapentakes in the sheriff's hands rated to this ferm; and after were approvers sent into divers counties, which did increase the ferms of some hundreds and wapentakes; and after, the kings at divers times have granted to many men part of the same hundreds and wapentakes for the old ferms only; and now late the sheriffs be wholly charged of the increase, which amounteth to a great sum, to the great hurt of the people, and disherison of the sheriffs and their heirs: it is ordained, that the hundreds and wapentakes let to ferm by the king that now is, be it for term of life or otherwise, which were sometime annexed to the ferms of the counties where the sheriffs be charged, shall be joined again to the counties; and that the sheriffs and their heirs have allowance for the time that is past; and that from henceforth such hundreds and wapentakes shall not be given nor severed from the counties.

———◆———

57. Statute concerning Justices and Sheriffs

(1330.   French text and translation, 1 *S. R.* 261.   2 Stubbs, 286, 391.)

*   *   *   *   *   *   *   *   *

2. ITEM, it is ordained, that good and discreet persons, other than of the places, if they may be found sufficient, shall be assigned in all the shires of England, to take assizes, juries, and certifications, and to deliver the jails; and that the said justices shall take the assizes, juries, and certifications, and deliver the jails, at the least three times a year, and mo: ʾ

often, if need be; also there shall be assigned good and lawful men in every county to keep the peace; and in the said assignments, mention shall be made that such as shall be indicted or taken by the said keepers of the peace, shall not be let to mainprise [bail] by the sheriffs, nor by none other ministers, if they be not mainpernable by the law; nor that such as shall be indicted, shall not be delivered but at the common law.   And the justices assigned to deliver the jails shall have power to deliver the same jails of those that shall be indicted before the keepers of the peace; and that the said keepers shall send their indictments before the justices, and they shall have power to enquire of sheriffs, jailers, and others, in whose ward such indicted persons shall be, if they make deliverance, or let to mainprise any so indicted, which be not mainpernable, and to punish the said sheriffs, jailers, and others, if they do anything against this act.

*   *   *   *   *   *   *   *   *

13. Item, because divers charters of pardon have been granted of felonies, robberies, and manslaughters, against the form of the statute lately made at Northampton, containing that no man should have such charters out of the parliament, whereby such misdoers have been the more bold to offend; it is enacted, that from henceforth the same statute shall be kept and maintained in all points.

14. Item, it is accorded that a parliament shall be holden every year once, or more often if need be.

15. Item, because sheriffs have before this time let hundreds and wapentakes in their bailiwicks to so high ferm, that the bailiff cannot levy the said ferm, without doing extortion and duress to the people; it is ordained, that the sheriffs shall from henceforth let their hundreds and wapentakes for the old ferm, and not above; and that the justices assigned shall have power to enquire of the said sheriffs, and punish them that shall be found offending against this statute.

58. Presentment of Englishry Abolished and Grant of a Subsidy

(April, 1340.   First statute of 14 Edward III.   French text and translation, *S. R.* 281.   2 Stubbs, 401.)

TO the honor of God and of holy Church, by the assent of the prelates, earls, barons, and other, assembled at the parliament holden at Westminster the Wednesday next after Mid-Lent, in the fourteenth year of the reign of our lord king Edward the Third of England, and the first year of his reign of France; the king for the peace and quietness of his people, as well great as small, doth grant and establish the things underwritten, which he wills to be holden and kept in all points perpetually to endure.

*   *   *   *   *   *   *   *   *

4. Item, because many mischiefs have happened in divers counties of England, which had no knowledge of presentment of Englishry, whereby the commons of the counties were often amerced before the justices in eyre, to the great mischief of the people; it is assented, that from henceforth no justice errant shall put in any article or opposition, presentment of Englishry against the commons of the counties, nor against any of them; but that Englishry and presentment of the same, be wholly out and void forever, so that no person by this cause may be from henceforth impeached.

*   *   *   *   *   *   *   *   *

20. Item, for the grants, releases, and pardons of the debts, chattels of felons and fugitives, and many other things and good establishments above written, which the king hath granted to the prelates, earls, barons, and all the commons of his realm, for the ease of them perpetually to endure, the said prelates, earls, barons, and all the commons of the realm, willing of one assent and good will, having regard to the will that the king their liege lord hath towards them, and to the great travail that he hath made and sustained as well in his wars of Scotland, as against the parts of France, and other places, and to the good will which he hath to travail to keep his realm, and maintain his wars, and to purchase his rights: they have granted to him the ninth lamb, the ninth fleece, and the ninth sheaf, to be taken by two years then next to come.   And of cities and boroughs the very ninth

part of all their goods and chattels, to be taken and levied by lawful and reasonable tax by the same two years, in aid of the good keeping of this realm, as well by land as by sea, and of his wars, as well against the parts of Scotland, as against the parts of France, Gascony, and elsewhere.   And in right of merchants foreign, which dwell not in the cities nor boroughs, and also of other people that dwell in forests and wastes, and all others that live not of their tillage, or their store of sheep, by the good advice of them which shall be deputed taxers, they shall be set lawfully at the value to the fifteenth, without being unreasonably charged; and it is not the intent of the king, nor of other great men, nor the commons, that by this grant made to the king of fifteenths, the poor cotiers, nor other that live of their bodily travail, shall be comprised within the tax of the said fifteenths, but shall be discharged by the advice of them which be deputed taxers, and of the great men which be deputed surveyors.

21. Item, though the commons of the realm did pray the king, that he would by assent of the parliament grant and establish, that never should be taken more custom of a sack of wool than half a mark, nor of lead, nor tin, leather, nor woolfells, but the old custom: nevertheless the king prayed the prelates, earls, barons, and all the commonalty, for the great business which he hath now in hand as they well know, that they would grant to him some aid upon the wools, leather, woolfells, and other merchandises, to endure for a small season; whereupon deliberation had, the said prelates, earls, barons, and commons of his realm, hath granted to him forty shillings to be taken of every sack of wool, and forty shillings of every three hundred woolfells, and forty shillings of every last of leather, and other merchandises that pass beyond the sea, after the rate; and to begin at the feast of Easter, in the fourteenth year of his reign, and to endure till the feast of Pentecost, then next following, and from that feast till the feast of Pentecost then next ensuing in a whole year. And for this grant, the king by the assent of the prelates, earls, barons, and all others assembled in parliament, hath granted, that from the feast of Pentecost, that cometh in a year, he nor his heirs shall not demand, assess, nor take, nor suffer to be taken more custom of a sack of wool of any Englishman, but half a mark of custom only; and upon the woolfells and leather the old custom; and the sack ought to contain twenty-six stones, and every stone fourteen pounds. * * *   And this establishment lawfully, to be holden and kept, the king hath promised in the presence of the prelates, earls, barons, and others in his parlia-

ment, no more to charge, set, or assess, upon the custom, but in the manner as afore is said.   In the same manner the prelates, earls, and barons have promised lawfully, as much as in them is, that they shall procure the king, as much as they may, to hold the same; and that they shall in no wise assent to the contrary, if it be not by assent of the prelates, earls, barons, and commons of the realm, and that in full parliament.   And for the more greater surety, and to give cause to all to eschew to counsel to the contrary of this point established, the prelates have promised to give sentence upon all them that come against the same in any point.

59. Unauthorized Charges and Taxes Abolished

(April, 1340.   Second statute of 14 Edward III.   French text and translation, 1 *S. R.* 289.   2 Stubbs, 402.)

EDWARD, by the grace of God, king of England and of France, and lord of Ireland, to all to whom these letters shall come, Greeting.

1. Know ye, that whereas the prelates, earls, barons, and commons of our realm of England, in our present parliament holden at Westminster the Wednesday next after the Sunday of Middle Lent, the fourteenth year of our reign of England, and the first of France, have granted to us of their good gree and good will, in aid of the speed of our great business which we have to do, as well on this side the sea as beyond, the ninth sheaf, the ninth fleece, and the ninth lamb, to be taken by two years next coming after the making of the same, and the citizens of cities and the burgesses of boroughs, the very ninth part of all their goods; and the foreign merchants, and others which live not of tillage, nor of store of sheep, the fifteenth of their goods lawfully to the value: we, willing to provide for the indemnity of the said prelates, earls, barons, and others of the commonalty, and also of the citizens, burgesses, and merchants aforesaid, will and grant for us and our heirs, to the same prelates, earls, barons and commons, citizens, burgesses and merchants, that the same grant which is so chargeable, shall not another time be had forth in example, nor fall to their prejudice in time to come, nor that they be from henceforth charged nor grieved to make common aid, or to sustain charge, if it be not by the common assent of

the prelates, earls, barons, and other great men, and commons
of our said realm of England, and that in the parliament; and
that all the profits rising from the said aid, and of the wards and
marriages, customs and escheats, and other profits rising of the
said realm of England, shall be put and spent upon the maintenance of the safeguard of our said realm of England, and of
our wars in Scotland, France, and Gascony, and in no places
elsewhere during the said wars.

*   *   *   *   *   *   *   *

60. England not to be Subject to the King as King of France

(April, 1340.   Third statute of 14 Edward III.   French text and translation, 1 *S. R.* 292.   2 Stubbs, 402.)

THE king to all to whom these letters shall come, Greeting:
Know ye, that whereas some people do think, that by
reason that the realm of France is devolved to us as right heir of
the same, and forasmuch as we be king of France, our realm of
England should be put in subjection of the king and of the realm
of France in time to come; we, * * * will and grant and establish for us, and for our heirs and successors, by assent of the prelates, earls, barons, and commons * * * that * * * our said realm
of England, nor the people of the same, of what estate or condition they be, shall not in any time to come be put into subjection nor in obeisance of us, nor of our heirs nor successors as
kings of France; * * *

61. Inquiry into Accounts

(May, 1341.   French text, 2 *R. P.* 128, 130.   Translation by Editors.
2 Stubbs, 409.)

12. ITEM, the great men and commons of the land pray, for
the common profit of the king and of themselves, that certain
persons be deputed by commission to audit the accounts of all
those who have received the wool of our said lord, or other
aids granted to him; and also of those who have received and
paid out his money, as well beyond the seas as in the realm from

the commencement of his war until now; and that the rolls and other remembrances, obligations, and other things made abroad be delivered into the chancery, to be enrolled and recorded, just as was wont to be done heretofore.

38. Item, as to the second article, that is to say, of auditing accounts of those who have received the wool of the king, and other aids, etc. It is the king's pleasure that this be done by good men deputed for the purpose, with the addition that the treasurer and the chief baron be of the number: and that it be done concerning this as it was heretofore ordained; and that the lords be chosen in this parliament. And also that all rolls, remembrances, and obligations made beyond the sea, be delivered into the chancery.

---

62. An Act to secure the Rights of Peers and Others, and to secure the Responsibility of the King's Ministers

(May, 1341. French text and translation, 1 *S. R.* 295. 2 Stubbs, 409.)

* * * * * * * * *

1. FIRST, it is accorded and assented, that the franchise of holy Church, and the Great Charter, and the Charter of the Forest, and the other statutes made by our sovereign lord the king and his progenitors, peers, and the commons of the land, for the common profit of the people, be firmly kept and maintained in all points. And if anything be from henceforth made against the Great Charter, and the Charter of the Forest it shall be declared in the next parliament, and by the peers of the realm it shall be duly redressed. And if any, of what condition he be, do any thing to the contrary, he shall stand to the judgment of the peers in the next parliament, and so from parliament to parliament, as well of franchises used, as of them which shall be now granted; and that the franchises granted by our sovereign lord the king, or his progenitors, to holy Church, to the peers of the land, to the city of London and to other cities and boroughs, and to them of the five ports, and to the commons of the land, and all their franchises and free customs shall be maintained in all points, without any thing doing to the contrary. And that the writs demanded to have allowance of charters, of franchises and customs, charters of pardons, of debts, and of all other things

granted by the king, and by his progenitors before this time, be freely granted without disturbance before all manner justices, or other ministers where it needeth to have allowance, and they shall be made quit at the exchequer, or elsewhere.

2. Item, whereas before this time the peers of the land have been arrested and imprisoned, and their temporalties, lands and tenements, goods and chattels, asseised in the king's hands, and some put to death without judgment of their peers: it is accorded and assented that no peer of the land, officer or other, because of his office, nor of things touching his office, nor by other cause shall be brought in judgment to lose his temporalties, lands, tenements, goods and chattels, nor to be arrested, nor imprisoned, outlawed, exiled, nor forejudged, nor put to answer, nor to be judged, but by award of the said peers in the parliament. Saving always to our sovereign lord the king, and his heirs in other cases the laws rightfully used, and by due process, and saved also the suit of the parties. And if perchance any peer will, of his agreement, elsewhere answer or be judged, but in the parliament, that the same shall not turn in prejudice of the other peers, nor of himself in any other case; except if any of the peers be sheriff or fermer of fee, or hath been officer, or hath received money, or other chattels of the king, because of which office or receipt he is bound to account, that the same shall account by himself or by his attorney in places accustomed; so that the pardons before this time made in the parliament, shall stand in their force.

3. Item, because that the points of the Great Charter be blemished in divers manners, and less well holden than they ought to be, to the great peril and slander of the king, and damage of his people especially inasmuch as clerks, peers of the land, and other free men be arrested and imprisoned, and ousted of their goods and chattels, who were not appealed nor endited, nor suit of the party against them affirmed: it is accorded and assented, that from henceforth such things shall not be done. And if any minister of the king, or other person, of what condition he be, do or come against any point of the Great Charter, or other statutes, or the laws of the land, he shall answer in the parliament, as well at the king's suit, as at the suit of the party, where no remedy nor punishment was ordained before this time, as far forth where it was done by commission or commandment of the king, as of his own authority, notwithstanding the ordinance made before this time at Northampton, which by assent of the king, the prelates, earls, barons, and the commonalty of the

land, in this present parliament is repealed and utterly annulled. And that the chancellor, treasurer, barons, and chancellor of the exchequer, the justices of the one bench and of the other, justices assigned in the country, steward and chamberlain of the king's house, keeper of the privy seal, treasurer of the wardrobe, controllers, and they that be chief deputed to abide nigh the king's son duke of Cornwall, shall be now sworn in this parliament, and so from henceforth at all times that they shall be put in office, to keep and maintain the privileges and franchises of holy Church, and the points of the Great Charter, and the Charter of the Forest, and all other statutes, without breaking any point.

4. Item, it is assented, that if any of the officers aforesaid, or controllers, or chief clerk in the common bench, or in the king's bench, by death or by other cause be ousted of his office, that our sovereign lord the king, by the accord of the great men, which shall be found most nighest in the country, which he shall take towards him, and by the good counsel which he shall have about him, shall put another convenient in the said office; who shall be sworn after the form aforesaid. And that in every parliament, at the third day of the same parliament, the king shall take in his hands the offices of all the ministers aforesaid, and so shall they abide four or five days; except the offices of justices of the one place or the other, justices assigned, barons of the exchequer; so always that they and all other ministers be put to answer to every complaint; and if default be found in any of the said ministers, by complaint or other manner, and of that he be attainted in parliament, he shall be punished by judgment of the peers, and put out of his office, and another convenient put in his place. And upon the same our sovereign lord the king shall do to be pronounced and made execution without delay according to the judgment of the said peers in the parliament.

*   *   *   *   *   *   *   *   *

63. Revocation of the Preceding Statute

(October, 1341.   Latin text and translation, 1 *S. R.* 297.   2 Stubbs, 410.)

THE king to the sheriff of Lincoln, Greeting.   Whereas at our parliament summoned at Westminster in the quinzime of Easter last past, certain articles expressly contrary to the laws and customs of our realm of England, and to our prerogatives and rights royal were pretended to be granted by us by the manner of a statute; we, considering how that by the bond of our oath we be tied to the observance and defence of such laws, customs, rights, and prerogatives, and providently willing to revoke and call again such things to a due state, which be so improvidently done, upon conference and treatise thereupon had with the earls, barons, and other wise men of our said realm, and because we never consented to the making of the said pretended statute, but as then it behoved us, we dissimulated in the premises, protests being before made for the revoking of the said statute, if indeed it should proceed, to eschew the dangers which by the denying of the same we feared to come, forasmuch as the said parliament otherwise had been, without dispatching anything, in discord dissolved, and so our earnest business had likely been ruinated, which God prohibit, and the said pretended statute we permitted then to be sealed: it seemed to the said earls, barons, and other wise men, that since the said statute did not of our free will proceed, the same should be void, and ought not to have the name nor strength of a statute; and therefore by their counsel and assent we have decreed the said statute to be void, and the same, in so far as it proceeded of deed, we have agreed to be annulled; willing nevertheless, that the articles contained in the said pretended statute which by other of our statutes, or of our progenitors kings of England, have been approved, shall, according to the form of the said statutes in every point, as convenient is, be observed; and the same we do, only to the conservation and reintegration of the rights of our crown, as we be bound, and not that we should in any wise grieve or oppress our subjects, whom we desire to rule by lenity and gentleness. And therefore we do command thee, that all these things thou cause to be openly proclaimed in such places within thy bailiwick where thou shalt see expedient. Witness myself at Westminster the first day of October, the fifteenth year of our reign.

By the king himself and his council.

------

64. An Act regulating the Coinage

(May, 1343. French text and translation, 1 *S. R.* 299. 2 Stubbs, 413.)

ITEM, it is accorded to make money of good sterling in England of the weight and alloy of the ancient sterling, which shall be current in England between the great men and commons

of the land, and the which shall not be carried out of the realm
of England in any manner, nor for any cause whatsoever; and in
case that the Flemings will make good money of silver groats or
other, according in alloy with good sterling, that such money
shall be current in England between merchant and merchant, and
others who of their own accord will receive the same; so that no
silver be carried out ot the realm.

*   *   *   *   *   *   *   *   *

65. Attempts to Tax though the Merchants resisted

(May, 1343.   French text, 2 *R. P.* 140.   Translation by Editors.
2 Stubbs, 412.)

28. ITEM, that the maletote of wool remain at half a mark
as was used in the time of the king's progenitors and as it was
granted by statute during the king's own reign.   And seeing
that the merchants of themselves have granted, without the assent of the commons, a subsidy of forty shillings on each sack
of wool besides the lawful maletote of half a mark, you will, if it
is your pleasure, have regard that it is all to the charge and to
the mischief of your commons.   Wherefore, if it is your pleasure, you will not suffer this mischief, but you will rather amend it
at this parliament, for it is against reason, that the commons
should be charged of their goods by the merchants.

The intent of our lord the king is not to charge the commons
with the subsidy which the merchants have granted him, nor may
it be regarded as a charge on the commons.   Particularly inasmuch as the commons have put a certain price upon the wool
throughout the counties; which price the king wills to continue,
and that within this price no wool shall be bought upon forfeiture
of the same wool in the hands of the merchants who purchased
the same.

66. Grant of a Subsidy for Two Years

(June, 1344.   French text and translation, 1 *S. R.* 300.   2 Stubbs, 414.)

IT is to be remembered, that at the parliament holden at Westminster, the Monday next after the utas of the Holy Trinity,
the year of reign of our sovereign lord the king that now is of

England the eighteenth and of France the fifth, among othei things many things were showed in full parliament, which were attempted by the party adversary to our sovereign lord the king, of France, against the truce lately taken in Britain, betwixt our said sovereign lord the king and his said adversary; and how that his said adversary enforceth himself as much as he may, to destroy our said sovereign lord the king, and his allies, subjects, lands, and places, and the tongue of England; and that was prayed by our said sovereign lord the king of the prelates, great men and commons, that they would give him such counsel and aid, as should be expedient in so great necessity: And the said prelates, great men and commons, taking good deliberation and advice, and openly seeing the subversion of the land of England, and the king's great business, which God defend, if hasty remedy be not provided, have counselled jointly and severally, and prayed with great instance our sovereign lord the king, that he would make him as strong as he might to pass the sea, in assurance of the aid of God and of his good quarrel, effectually this time to make an end of his wars, or by way of peace or else by force; and that nor for letters, words, nor fair promises, he shall let his passage, till he see the effect of his business; and for this cause the said great men do grant, to pass and to adventure them with him. And the said commons do grant to him, for the same cause upon a certain form two fifteenths of the commonalty, and two tenths of the cities and boroughs, to be levied in manner as the last fifteenth granted to him was levied, and not in other manner; and to be paid by two years, at the feasts of All Saints, and of Easter next following, for the first year; and in case that our sovereign lord the king doth pass the sea, to pay at the same terms a fifteenth and a tenth of the second year, and not in other manner; so that the money levied of the same, be dispended in the business showed to them in this parliament, by the advice of the great men thereto assigned, and that the aids beyond Trent, be put in defence of the North. And our said sovereign lord the king, for this cause, and in the ease of the said commons, and of all his faithful subjects of England, by the assent of the prelates, great men, and commons, hath granted of his good grace these things underwritten:

*   *   *   *   *   *   *   *   *

67. A Grant of the Clergy for Three Years

(July, 1344.   Latin text and translation, 1 *S. R.* 302.   2 Stubbs, 414.)

*   *   *   *   *   *   *   *   *

FIRST, whereas many things have been attempted, by the party our adversary of France, against the truce late taken in Britain, betwixt us and him, and how that he enforceth himself, as much as he may, to destroy us, and our allies, subjects, lands, and places, and the tongue of England: And thereupon we prayed the prelates, great men, and commons, that they should give us such counsel and aid as there should be need of in so great extremity and the said prelates, great men and commons, having thereof good deliberation and advice, and seeing openly the subversion of the land of England, and of our great business, which God defend, if speedy remedy be not provided; have counselled jointly and severally, and with great instance prayed us, that in assurance of the aid of God, and our good quarrel we should make us as strong by all the good means that we might, at this time to finish our wars; and that for letters, words, nor fair promises, we should not let our passage, till we did see the effect of our business: and for this cause, the great men aforesaid granted to pass, and to adventure themselves with us; and the said prelates and procurators of the clergy, have granted to us for the same cause, a triennial tenth, to be paid at certain days, that is to say, of the province of Canterbury, at the feasts of the Purification of our Lady, and of Saint Barnabas the apostle: and of the province of York, at the feasts of Saint Luke, and the Nativity of Saint John Baptist.   And we for this cause, in maintenance of the estate of holy Church, and in ease of the said prelates, and all the clergy of England, by assent of the great men, and of the commons, do grant of our good grace the things underwritten; that is to say, that no archbishop nor bishop shall be impeached before our justices because of crime, unless we especially do command them, till another remedy be thereof ordained.

*   *   *   *   *   *   *   *   *

68. Grant on Conditions

(April, 1348. French text, 2 *R. P.* 200. Translation by Editors.
2 Stubbs, 417, 606.)

4. * * * NEVERTHELESS, provided that the aid now granted
by the said commons be in no manner turned into wool neither
by loan, nor by valuation, nor in other manner be levied
nor more hastily, than in the form in which it be granted,
and that in the meantime the circuits of the justices, as well
of the forest as of common pleas and general inquisitions,
cease throughout the land; that the aid be levied, and that
the subsidy granted of forty shillings on each sack of wool
cease at the end of three years, which will be now at Michaelmas next coming, and that henceforth no such grant be
made by the merchants, inasmuch as it is only to the grievance
and charge of the commons, and not of the merchants who buy
the wool at so much the less. And also, that henceforth no
imposition, tallage, nor charge by loan, nor of any other sort
whatsoever, be put by the privy council of our lord the king without their grant and assent in parliament: and also, that two prelates, two lords, and two justices in this present parliament be
assigned to hear and examine all the petitions previously put forward in the last parliament by the commons which have not yet
been answered; and with them the petitions now set forth, in the
presence of four or six of the commons chosen by them for this
special purpose, so that the said petitions be answered reasonably in the present parliament, and of those which have been
previously answered in full, that the answers be in force without
change. And also that the merchants who have evilly deceived
our lord the king, and have been extortionate toward his people
in the matter of the twenty thousand sacks of wool of loan
granted by the commons to our said lord, be put to answer before
the justices having power to hear and determine throughout the
counties of England, and that no release nor charter of pardon be allowed them. And that the said justices make inquisition of the false money which ruins the people. And that David
Bruce, William Douglas and the other chieftains of Scotland be
in no manner released neither for ransom nor on parole. And
also that our lord the king restore to the commons the twenty
thousand sacks of wool in time past taken from the commons by
loan and that the aid for the marrying of the daughter of our

I

lord the king cease in the meantime. And that there be no Marshalsea in England, save the Marshalsea of our lord the king, or of the guardian of England when our lord the king shall be out of England, upon these conditions above named and not otherwise. And also, provided that the said conditions be entered on the roll of parliament as a matter of record, so that there can be remedy if anything to the contrary is attempted in time to come. Thus, the said poor commons, to their very great mischief, grant to our lord the king three fifteenths to be levied for three years commencing at Michaelmas next coming; so that each of the three years one fifteenth and no more be levied, at two terms of the year, at Michaelmas and at Easter, in equal portions. And that the said aid be assigned and kept solely for the war of our lord the king and in no manner for the payment of former debts. And also, if, by the grace of God, peace or long truce be made in the meantime, that the fifteenth for the last of the three years be not levied; but of that fifteenth the grant shall lose its force completely. And that letters patent of these conditions, and of the manner of this grant be made under the great seal to all the counties of England, without paying anything therefor. And that the said patents make mention of the great necessity of our lord the king, which has arisen since the last parliament. And also in case of war with Scotland that the aid granted north of the Trent be turned to the conduct of that war and in defense of that part of the country, as before this time has been done.

---

69. An Ordinance concerning Laborers and Servants

(June, 1349.   Latin text and translation, 1 *S. R.* 307.   2 Stubbs, 420, 428, 476.)

THE king to the sheriff of Kent, Greeting. Because a great part of the people, and especially of workmen and servants, late died of the pestilence, many seeing the necessity of masters, and great scarcity of servants, will not serve unless they may receive excessive wages, and some rather willing to beg in idleness, than by labor to get their living; we, considering the grievous incommodities, which of the lack especially of ploughmen and such laborers may hereafter come, have upon deliberation and treaty with the prelates and the nobles, and learned men assisting us, of their mutual counsel ordained:

1. That every man and woman of our realm of England, of what condition he be, free or bond, able in body, and within the age of three score years, not living in merchandise, nor exercising any craft, nor having of his own whereof he may live, nor proper land, about whose tillage he may himself occupy, and not serving any other, if he be required to serve in convenient service, his estate considered, he shall be bounden to serve him which shall so him require; and take only the wages, livery, meed, or salary, which were accustomed to be given in the places where he oweth to serve, the twentieth year of our reign of England, or five or six other common years next before. Provided always, that the lords be preferred before others in their bondmen or their land tenants, so in their service to be retained: so that nevertheless the said lords shall retain no more than be necessary for them; and if any such man or woman, being so required to serve, will not do the same, that proved by two true men before the sheriff, bailiff, lord, or constable of the town where the same shall happen to be done, he shall anon be taken by them, or any of them, and committed to the next jail, there to remain under strait keeping, till he find surety to serve in the form aforesaid.

* * * * * * * * *

5. Item, that sadlers, skinners, whitetawers, cordwainers, tailors, smiths, carpenters, masons, tilers, boatmen, carters, and all other artificers and workmen, shall not take for their labor and workmanship above the same that was wont to be paid to such persons the said twentieth year, and other common years next before, as afore is said, in the place where they shall happen to work; and if any man take more, he shall be committed to the next jail, in manner as afore is said.

6. Item, that butchers, fishmongers, hostelers, brewers, bakers, pulters, and all other sellers of all manner of victual, shall be bound to sell the same victual for a reasonable price, having respect to the price that such victual be sold at in the places adjoining, so that the same sellers have moderate gains, and not excessive, reasonably to be required according to the distance of the place from whence the said victuals be carried; * * *

* * * * * * * * *

70. Statute of Laborers

(February, 1351.   French text and translation, 1 *S. R.* 311.   2 Stubbs, 428, 476.)

WHEREAS late against the malice of servants, which were idle, and not willing to serve after the pestilence, without taking excessive wages, it was ordained by our lord the king, and by assent of the prelates, nobles, and other of his council, that such manner of servants, as well men as women, should be bound to serve, receiving salary and wages, accustomed in places where they ought to serve in the twentieth year of the reign of the king that now is, or five or six years before; and that the same servants refusing to serve in such manner, should be punished by imprisonment of their bodies, as in the said statute is more plainly contained: whereupon commissions were made to divers people in every county to inquire and punish all them which offend against the same: and now forasmuch as it is given the king to understand in this present parliament, by the petition of the commonalty, that the said servants having no regard to the said ordinance, but to their ease and singular covetise, do withdraw themselves to serve great men and others, unless they have livery and wages to the double or treble of that they were wont to take the said twentieth year, and before, to the great damage of the great men, and impoverishing of all the said commonalty, whereof the said commonalty prayeth remedy: wherefore in the said parliament, by the assent of the said prelates, earls, barons, and other great men, and of the same commonalty there assembled, to refrain the malice of the said servants, be ordained and established the things underwritten, that is to wit:

* * * * * * * * *

5. Item, that the said stewards, bailiffs, and constables of the said towns, be sworn before the same justices, to inquire diligently by all the good ways they may, of all them that come against this ordinance, and to certify the same justices of their names at all times, when they shall come into the country to make their sessions; so that the same justices on certificate of the same stewards, bailiffs, and constables, of the names of the rebels, shall cause them to be attached by their body, to be before the said justices, to answer of such contempts, so that they make fine and ransom to the king, in case they be attainted; and moreover to be commanded to prison, there to remain till they have

found surety, to serve, and take, and do their work, and to sell things vendible in the manner aforesaid; and in case that any of them come against his oath, and be thereof attainted, he shall have imprisonment of forty days; and if he be another time convict, he shall have imprisonment of a quarter of a year, so that at every time that he offendeth and is convict, he shall have double pain: * * *

    *   *   *   *   *   *   *   *   *

7. Item, that the said justices make their sessions in all the counties of England at the least four times a year, that is to say, at the feast of the Annunciation of our Lady, Saint Margaret, Saint Michael, and Saint Nicholas; and also at all times that shall need, according to the discretion of the said justices; * * *

---

71. Statute of Provisors of Benefices

(February, 1351.   French text and translation, 1 *S. R.* 316.   2 Stubbs, 430, 3 Stubbs, 324.)

WHEREAS late in the parliament of good memory of Edward king of England, grandfather to our lord the king that now is, the five and thirtieth year of his reign, holden at Carlisle, the petition being heard, which was offered unto the said grandfather and his council in his said parliament, by the commonalty of the said realm, containing, that whereas the holy Church of England was founded in the estate of prelacy, within the realm of England, by the said grandfather and his progenitors, and the earls, barons, and other nobles of his said realm, and their ancestors, to inform them and the people of the law of God, and to make hospitalities, alms, and other works of charity, in the places where the churches were founded, for the souls of the founders, their heirs, and all Christians; and certain possessions, as well in fees, lands, rents, as in advowsons, which do extend to a great value, were assigned by the said founders to the prelates and other people of the holy Church of the said realm, to sustain the same charge, and especially of the possessions which were assigned to archbishops, bishops, abbots, priors, religious, and all other people of holy Church, by the kings of the said realm, earls, barons, and other great men of his realm; the same kings, earls, barons, and other nobles, as lords and advowees, have had and ought to have the custody of such voidances [vacancies], and the presentments and the collations of the benefices being of such prelacies: and the said kings in times past were wont to have the greatest part of their council, for the safeguard of the realm when they had need, of such prelates and clerks so advanced; the pope of Rome, accroaching to him the seignories of such possessions and benefices doth give and grant the same benefices to aliens which did never dwell in England, and to cardinals, which might not dwell here, and to others as well aliens as denizens, as if he had been patron or advowee of the said dignities and benefices, as he was not of right by the law of England; whereby if they should be suffered, there should scarcely be any benefice within a short time in the said realm, but that it should be in the hands of aliens and by virtue of such provisions, against the good will and disposition of the founders of the same benefices; and so the elections of arch-bishops, bishops, and other religious should fail, and the alms, hospitalities, and other works of charity, which should be done in the said places, should be withdrawn, the said grandfather, and other lay-patrons, in the time of such voidances, should lose their presentments, the said council should perish, and goods without number should be carried out of the realm, in annulling of the estate of the holy Church of England, and disherison of the said grandfather, and the earls, barons, and other nobles, and in offence and destruction of the laws and rights of his realm, and to the great damage of his people, and in subversion of all the estate of his said realm, and against the good disposition and will of the first founders: by the assent of the earls, barons, and other nobles and of all the said commonalty, at their instances and requests, the damage and grievances afore considered, in the said full parliament it was provided, ordained, and established, that the said oppressions, grievances, and damages in the same realm from henceforth should not be suffered in any manner. And now it is showed to our lord the king in this present parliament holden at Westminster, at the utas of the Purification of our Lady, the five and twentieth year of his reign of England, and of France the twelfth, by the grievous complaints of all the commons of his realm, that the grievances and mischiefs afore-said do daily abound, to the greater damage and destruction of all this realm more than ever were before, namely, that now of late our Holy Father the pope by procurement of clerks and other wise, hath reserved, and doth daily reserve to his collation generally and especially, as well archbishoprics, bishoprics, abbeys, and priories, as all other dignities and other benefices of England, which be of the advowry of people of holy Church,

and doth give the same as well to aliens as to denizens, and
taketh of all such benefices the first fruits, and many other profits,
and a great part of the treasure of the said realm is carried
away and dispended out of the realm, by the purchasers of such
graces; and also by such privy reservations many clerks advanced
in this realm by their true patrons, which have peaceably holden
their advancements by long time be suddenly put out: whereupon
the said commons have prayed, our said lord the king, that since
the right of the crown of England, and the law of the said realm
is such, that upon the mischiefs and damages which happen to
his realm, he ought, and is bound by his oath, with the accord of
his people in his parliament, thereof to make remedy and law,
for the voiding of the mischiefs and damages which thereof
ensue, that it may please him therefor to ordain remedy:

Our lord the king seeing the mischiefs and damage before
mentioned, and having regard to the said statute made in the
time of his said grandfather, and to the causes contained in the
same; which statute holdeth always his force, and was never
defeated nor annulled in any point, and by so much as he is
bounden by his oath to cause the same to be kept as the law of
his realm, though that by sufferance and negligence it hath been
since attempted to the contrary; also having regard to the grievous complaints made to him by his people in divers his parliaments holden heretofore, willing to ordain remedy for the great
damages and mischiefs which have happened and daily do happen
to the Church of England by the said cause, by the assent of all
the great men and the commonalty of the said realm to the honor
of God, and the profit of the said Church of England, and of all
his realm, hath ordained and established, that the free elections
of archbishops, bishops, and all other dignities and benefices
elective in England, shall hold from henceforth in the manner
as they were granted by the king's progenitors, and founded by
the ancestors of other lords.   And that all prelates and other
people of holy Church, which have advowsons of any benefices of
the king's gift, or of any of his progenitors, or of other lords and
donors, to do divine services, and other charges thereof ordained,
shall have their collations and presentments freely to the same, in
the manner as they were enfeoffed by their donors.   And in case
that reservation, collation, or provision be made by the court of
Rome, of any archbishopric, bishopric, dignity, or other benefice, in disturbance of the elections, collations, or presentations
aforenamed that at the same time of the voidance, when such
reservations, collations, and provisions shall take effect, our lord

the king and his heirs shall have and enjoy for the same time the collations to the archbishoprics, bishoprics, and other dignities elective, which be of his advowry, such as his progenitors had, before that free election was granted, seeing that the elections were first granted by the king's progenitors upon a certain form and condition, as to demand licence of the king to choose, and after the election to have his royal assent, and not in other manner; which conditions not kept, the thing ought by reason to resort to its first nature. And if any such reservation, provision, or collation be made of any house of religion of the king's advowry, in disturbance of free election, our sovereign lord the king and its heirs, shall have for that time the collation to give this dignity to a convenient person. And in case that collation, reservation, or provision be made by the court of Rome of any church, prebend, or other benefices, which be of the advowry of people of holy Church, whereof the king is advowee paramount immediate, that at the same time of the voidance, at which time the collation, reservation or provision should take effect as afore is said, the king and his heirs shall thereof have the presentment or collation for that time; and so from time to time, when soever such people of holy Church shall be disturbed of their presentments or collations by such reservations, collations, or provisions, as afore is said; saving to them the right of their advowsons and their presentments, when no collation or provision of the court of Rome is thereof made, or where that the said people of holy Church shall or will to the same benefices present or make collation; and that their presentees may enjoy the effect of their collations or presentments: and in the same manner every other lord, of what condition that he be, shall have the collations or presentments to the houses of religion which be of his advowry and other benefices of holy Church which be pertaining to the same houses. And if such advowees do not present to such benefices within the half year after such voidances, nor the bishop of the place do not give the same by lapse of time within a month after half a year, that then the king shall have thereof the presentments and collations as he hath of other of his own advowry. And in case that the presentees of the king, or the presentees of other patrons of holy Church or of their advowees, or they to whom the king, or such patrons or advowees aforesaid, have given benefices pertaining to their presentments or collations, be disturbed by such provisors, so that they may not have possession of such benefices by virtue of the presentments or collations to them made, or that they which be in pos-

session of such benefices be impeached upon their said possessions
by such provisors; then the said provisors, their procurators,
executors, and notaries, shall be attached by their body, and
brought in to answer; and if they be convict, they shall abide in
prison without being let to mainprise, or bail, or otherwise
delivered, till that they have made fine and ransom to the king
at his will, and satisfaction to the party that shall feel himself
grieved. And nevertheless before that they be delivered, they
shall make full renunciation, and find sufficient surety that they
shall not attempt such things in time to come, nor sue any
process by them, nor by other, against any man in the court of
Rome, nor in any part elsewhere, for any such imprisonments
or renunciations, nor any other thing depending of them.

*   *   *   *   *   *   *   *   *

72. The Statute of Treasons

(March, 1352.   French text and translation, 1 *S. R.* 319.   2 Stubbs, 431.)

*   *   *   *   *   *   *   *   *

2. ITEM, whereas divers opinions have been before this time
what case should be adjudged treason, and what not; the king,
at the request of the lords and of the commons, hath made a
declaration in the manner as hereafter followeth, that is to say;
when a man doth compass or imagine the death of our lord the
king, or of our lady his wife, or of their eldest son and heir; or
if a man do violate the king's wife, or the king's eldest daughter unmarried, or the wife of the king's eldest son and heir;
or if a man do levy war against our lord the king in his realm,
or be adherent to the king's enemies in his realm, giving to them
aid and comfort in the realm, or elsewhere, and thereof be proveably attainted of open deed by people of their condition: and if
a man counterfeit the king's great or privy seal, or his money;
and if a man bring false money into this realm, counterfeit to the
money of England, as the money called lushburgh, or other, like
to the said money of England, knowing the money to be false, to
merchandise or make payment in deceit of our said lord the king
and of his people; and if a man slay the chancellor, treasurer, or
the king's justices of the one bench or the other, justices in eyre,
or justices of assize, and all other justices assigned to hear and
determine, being in their places, doing their offices: and it is to

be understood, that in the cases above rehearsed, that ought to be judged treason which extends to our lord the king, and his royal majesty: and of such treason the forfeiture of the escheats pertaineth to our sovereign lord, as well of the lands and tenements holden of other, as of himself: and moreover there is another manner of treason, that is to say, when a servant slayeth his master, or a wife her husband, or when a man secular or religious slayeth his prelate, to whom he oweth faith and obedience: and such manner of treason giveth forfeiture of escheats to every lord of his own fee: and because that many other like cases of treason may happen in time to come, which a man cannot think or declare at this present time; it is accorded, that if any other case, supposed treason, which is not above specified, doth happen of new, before any justices, the justices shall tarry without any going to judgment of the treason, till the case be showed before the king in his parliament, and it be declared, whether it ought to be judged treason or else felony. And if perchance any man of this realm ride armed openly or secretly with men of arms against any other, to slay him, or rob him, or take him, or retain him till he hath made fine or ransom for to have his deliverance, it is not the mind of the king nor his council, that in such case it shall be judged treason, but shall be judged felony or trespass, according to the laws of the land of old time used, and according as the case requireth. * * *

  * * * * * * * * *

 22. Item, because that some do purchase in the court of Rome provisions, to have abbeys and priories in England, in destruction of the realm, and of holy religion; it is accorded, that every man that purchaseth such provisions of abbeys or priories, that he and his executors and procurators, which do sue and make execution of such provisions, shall be out of the king's protection; and that a man may do with them as of enemies of our sovereign lord the king and his realm; and he that offendeth against such provisors in body or in goods, or in other possessions, shall be excused against all people, and shall never be impeached nor grieved for the same at any man's suit.

  * * * * * * * * *

73. Statute of Præmunire

(September, 1353.   French text and translation, 1 *S. R.* 329.   **2 Stubbs**
430, 3 Stubbs, 341.)

*   *   *   *   *   *   *   *   *

1. FIRST, because it is showed to our lord the king, by the
grievous and clamorous complaints of the great men and commons aforesaid, how that divers of the people be, and have
been drawn out of the realm to answer of things, whereof the
cognizance pertaineth to the king's court; and also that the
judgments given in the same court be impeached in the court of
another, in prejudice and disherison of our lord the king, and of
his crown, and of all the people of his said realm, and to the
undoing and destruction of the common law of the same realm
at all times used: whereupon, good deliberation had with the
great men and other of his said council, it is assented and accorded
by our lord the king, and the great men and commons aforesaid,
that all the people of the king's liegeance of what condition that
they be, which shall draw any out of the realm in plea, whereof
the cognizance pertaineth to the king's court, or of things whereof
judgments be given in the king's court, or which do sue in the
court of another, to defeat or impeach the judgments given in the
king's court, shall have a day containing the space of two months,
by warning to be made to them in the place where the possessions
be, which be in debate, or otherwise where they have lands or
other possessions, by the sheriffs, or others the king's ministers,
to appear before the king and his council, or in his chancery, or
before the king's justices in his places of the one bench or the
other, or before other the king's justices which to the same shall
be deputed, to answer in their proper persons to the king, of the
contempt done in this behalf; and if they come not at the said
day in their proper person to be at the law, they, their procurators, attorneys, executors, notaries, and maintainors, shall from
that day forth be put out of the king's protection, and their lands,
goods, and chattels forfeit to the king, and their bodies, wheresoever they may be found, shall be taken and imprisoned, and
ransomed at the king's will; and upon the same a writ shall be
made to take them by their bodies, and to seise their lands,
goods, and possessions into the king's hands; and if it be
returned that they be not found, they shall be put in exigent, and
outlawed.

Provided always, that at what time they come before they be outlawed, and will yield them to the king's prison to be justified by the law, and to receive that which the court shall award in this behalf, that they shall be thereto received; the forfeiture of the lands, goods, and chattels abiding in their force, if they do not yield them within the said two months, as afore is said.

*   *   *   *   *   *   *   *   *

---

74. Ordinance of the Staples

(September, 1353.   French text and translation, 1 *S. R.* 332.   2 Stubbs, 431.)

EDWARD by the grace of God king of England and of France, and lord of Ireland, to all our sheriffs, mayors, bailiffs, ministers, and other our faithful people to whom these present letters shall come, Greeting: Whereas, good deliberation had with the prelates, dukes, earls, barons and knights of the counties, that is to say of every county, one for all the county, and of the commons of cities and boroughs of our realm of England, summoned to our great council, holden at Westminster the Monday next after the feast of Saint Matthew the apostle, the seven and twentieth year of our reign of England, and of France the fourteenth, for the damage which hath notoriously come as well to us and to the great men, as to our people of our realm of England, and of our lands of Wales and Ireland, because that the staple of wools, leather and woolfells of our said realm and lands have been holden out of our said realm and lands, and also for the great profits which should come to the said realm and lands if the staple were holden within the same, and not elsewhere; to the honor of God, and in relief of our realm and lands aforesaid and for to eschew the perils that may happen of the contrary in time to come, by the counsel and common assent of the said prelates, dukes, earls, and barons, knights and commons aforesaid, we have ordained and established the things under-written, that is to say:

1.   First, that the staple of wools, leather, woolfells, and lead. growing or coming forth within our said realm and lands, shall be perpetually holden at the places underwritten; that is to say, for England at Newcastle-upon-Tyne, York, Lincoln, Norwich, Westminster, Canterbury, Chichester, Winchester, Exeter, and Bristol; for Wales, at Carmaerthen; and for Ireland, at Dublin,

Waterford, Cork, and Drogheda, and not elsewhere: and that all the said wools, as well old as new, woolfells, leather and lead, which shall be carried out of the said realm and lands, shall be first brought to the said staples, and there the said wool and lead, betwixt merchant and merchant, or merchant and others, shall be lawfully weighed by the standard; and that every sack and sarpler of the same wools so weighed, be sealed under the seal of the mayor of the staple; and that all the wools so weighed and sealed at the staple of York, Lincoln, Norwich, Westminster, Canterbury, and Winchester, and also leather, woolfells, and lead which shall come there, the customs of the staple thereof paid, shall be witnessed by bill, sealed with the seal of the mayor of the staple, and brought to the ports underwritten, that is to say; from York to Hull, from Lincoln to Saint Botolf, from Norwich to Great Yarmouth, from Westminster to London, from Canterbury to Sandwich, and from Winchester to Southampton; and there the said wools and lead shall be another time weighed by our customers assigned in the same ports; and all the wool and lead brought to the said ports of Newcastle, Chichester, Exeter, Bristol, Carmaerthen, Dublin, Waterford, Cork, and Drogheda, where the other staples be holden, shall be but once weighed by the standard betwixt merchant and merchant, or merchant and other, in presence of our customers there; and an indenture shall be made betwixt the mayor of the staple being in the port of the sea, and our customers there, of all the wools and lead so weighed, and also of all the leather and woolfells which shall come to the said staples to pass there: and the same wools and lead, and also the leather and woolfells customed and cocketed, and the customs thereof duly paid to our said customers in all these said ports, that is to say, of denizens for the time that they have passed, half a mark of a sack of wool, half a mark of three hundred woolfells, a mark of a last of leather, and of aliens ten shillings of a sack of wool, ten shillings of three hundred woolfells, and twenty shillings of a last of leather, and three pence of every twenty shillings of lead, then the said merchandises shall be carried by merchants strangers which have bought the same, and not by Englishmen, Welshmen, nor Irishmen, to the parts beyond the sea out of the said realm and lands, to what parts it shall please the said merchants strangers: and that the said mayor and customers shall delay no man willingly for gain; nor for such cause, nor in other manner, shall any take of any person to do that which pertaineth to their office, upon pain of imprisonment, and to pay the party the double of that which they have so taken, and also of that which the party shall be endamaged because of such taking or delay, and moreover be ransomed at our will, but shall hold them content of that which they did take in certain to do their office: and that the mayor of the staple and customers take an oath of all the merchants which so shall pass with wools, leather, woolfells and lead that they shall hold no staple beyond the sea, of the same merchandises.

2. Item, * * * we have ordained and established, that all merchants strangers, which be not of our enmity, of what land or nation that they be, may safely and surely under our protection and safe-conduct come and dwell in our said realm and lands where they will, and from thence return with their ships, wares and all manner of merchandises, and freely sell their merchandises at the staple and elsewhere within the same realm and lands, to any that will buy them, paying the customs thereof due. * * *

* * * * * * * * *

75. Protest of Parliament against Legislation by Ordinance

(October, 1353.   French text, 2 *R. P.* 253.   Translation by Editors.
2 Stubbs, 429.)

42. ITEM, because many articles touching the estate of the king and the common profit of his realm were accorded and granted by him, the prelates, great men, and commons of his land, at the council now held; the said commons pray that the said articles be recited at the next parliament, and entered in the roll in the same parliament; to such intent that the ordinances and accords made in councils be not of record, as if they had been made by common parliament.

As to the tenth article, it is the king's pleasure that all the ordinances made of the staple be published and proclaimed in each county of England and in each place where the staples are, to the end that they be firmly kept.   And at the next parliament, for greater surety, that they be rehearsed and put on the roll of parliament.

76. Certain Ordinances confirmed by Parliament

(May, 1354.   French text, 2 *R. P.* 257.   Translation by Editors.   2 Stubbs, 429.)

16. AND so the said commons prayed in this parliament, that the ordinances of the staple and all the other ordinances made at the last council held at Westminster the Monday after the feast of Saint Matthew the apostle last past, which they had considered with good deliberation and counsel and which seemed to them good and profitable for our lord the king and all his people, be affirmed in this parliament and held for a statute to endure forever.   To which prayer the king and all the great men unanimously agreed, as at all times, that if anything is to be added it shall be added, or if anything is to be repealed it shall be repealed in parliament, whenever it shall be necessary, and in no other manner.

---

77. An Act concerning Justices of the Peace

(February, 1361.   French text and translation, 1 *S. R.* 364.   2 Stubbs, 286.)

*   *   *   *   *   *   *   *   *

1. FIRST, that in every county of England shall be assigned for the keeping of the peace, one lord, and with him three or four of the most worthy in the county, with some learned in the law, and they shall have power to restrain the offenders, rioters, and all other barrators, and to pursue, arrest, take, and chastise them according their trespass or offence; and to cause them to be imprisoned and duly punished according to the law and customs of the realm, and according to that which to them shall seem best to do by their discretions and good advisement; and also to inform them, and to inquire of all those that have been pillors and robbers in the parts beyond the sea, and be now come again, and go wandering, and will not labor as they were wont in times past; and to take and arrest all those that they may find by indictment, or by suspicion, and to put them in prison; and to take of all them that be not of good fame, where they shall be found, sufficient surety and mainprise of their good

behavior towards the king and his people, and the other duly to
punish; to the intent that the people be not by such rioters or
rebels troubled nor endamaged, nor the peace blemished, nor
merchants nor other passing by the highways of the realm disturbed, nor put in fear by peril which might happen of such
offenders; and also to hear and determine at the king's suit all
manner of felonies and trepasses done in the same county according to the laws and customs aforesaid; and that writs of oyer and
determiner be granted according to the statutes thereof made, and
that the justices which shall be thereto assigned be named by the
court, and not by the party.   And the king will, that all general
inquiries before this time granted within any seignories, for the
mischiefs and oppressions which have been done to the people
by such inquiries, shall cease utterly and be repealed: and that
fines, which are to be made before justices for a trespass done by
any person, be reasonable and just, having regard to the quantity
of the trespass, and the causes for which they may be made.

*   *   *   *   *   *   *   *   *

———◆———

78. Purveyance, English to be used in the Courts, etc.

(November, 1362.   French text and translation, 1 *S. R.* 371.   2 Stubbs, 434.)

*   *   *   *   *   *   *   *   *

2. ITEM, for the grievous complaint which hath been made
of purveyors of victuals of the houses of the king, the queen,
their eldest son, and of other lords and ladies of the realm,
the king of his own will, without motion of the great men or
commons, hath granted and ordained in ease of his people,
that from henceforth no man of the said realm shall have any
taking, but only himself and the queen his companion; and
moreover, of the assent aforesaid, it is ordained and established,
that upon such purveyances from henceforth to be made for the
houses of the king and the queen, ready payment shall be made
in hand, that is to say, the price for which such victuals be sold
commonly in the markets about: * * *

*   *   *   *   *   *   *   *   *

11. Item, the king by the assent aforesaid having regard to the
great subsidy that the commons have granted now in this parlia·

ment, of wools, leather, and woolfells to be taken for three years, wills and grants that after the said term passed, nothing be taken nor demanded of the said commons, but only the ancient custom of half a mark; nor that this grant now made, or which hath been made in times past, shall not be had in example nor charge of the said commons in time to come: and that the merchants denizens may pass with their wools as well as the foreigns, without being restrained; and that no subsidy, nor other charge, be set nor granted upon the wools, by the merchants nor by none other from henceforth, without the assent of the parliament.

12. Item, that in the commissions of justices of the peace, and of laborers, express mention be made, that the same justices make their sessions four times by the year, that is to say, one session within the utas of the Epiphany, the second within the second week of Mid-Lent, the third betwixt the feasts of Pentecost and of Saint John Baptist, the fourth within the eight days of Saint Michael.

*   *   *   *   *   *   *   *   *

15. Item, because it is often showed to the king by the prelates dukes earls, barons, and all the commonalty, of the great mischiefs which have happened to divers of the realm, because the laws, customs, and statutes of this realm be not commonly known in the same realm, for that they be pleaded, showed, and judged in the French tongue, which is much unknown in the said realm; so that the people which do implead, or be impleaded, in the king's court, and in the courts of other have no knowledge nor understanding of that which is said for them or against them by their sergeants and other pleaders; and that reasonably the said laws and customs shall be the more soon learned and known, and better understood in the tongue used in the said realm, and by so much every man of the said realm may the better govern himself without offending of the law, and the better keep, save, and defend his heritage and possessions; and in divers regions and countries where the king, the nobles, and other of the said realm have been, good governance and full right is done to every person, because that their laws and customs be learned and used in the tongue of the country: the king, desiring the good governance and tranquillity of his people, and to put out and eschew the harms and mischiefs which do or may happen in this behalf by the occasions aforesaid, hath ordained and established by the assent aforesaid, that all pleas which shall be pleaded in his court whatsoever, before any of his justices whatsoever, or in his other

K

places, or before any of his other ministers whatsoever, or in the courts and places of any other lords whatsoever within the realm, shall be pleaded, showed, defended, answered, debated, and judged in the English tongue, and that they be entered and inrolled in Latin; and that the laws and customs of the same realm, terms, and processes, be holden and kept as they be and have been before this time; and that by the ancient terms and form of pleaders no man be prejudiced, so that the matter of the action be fully showed in the declaration and in the writ: and it is accorded by the assent aforesaid, that this ordinance and statute of pleading begin and hold place at the fifteenth of Saint Hilary next coming.

79. Refusal of Tribute to the Pope

(May, 1366. French text, 2 *R. P.* 290. Translation by Editors. 2 Stubbs, 435.)

7. * * * HE (the chancellor) told them how the king had heard that the pope, by force of an agreement which he said that king John had made with the pope, to do him homage for the realm of England and the land of Ireland, and that by reason of the said homage, he ought to pay each year forever a thousand marks, is minded to institute process against the king and his realm for the said service and to recover the tribute. Wherefore the king prayed the said prelates, dukes, earls, and barons for their advice and good council, as to what he should do in case the pope should proceed against him or his said realm for that cause. And the prelates asked the king to allow them to take counsel by themselves alone and to answer on the morrow. On the said morrow, first the prelates by themselves, and then the other dukes, earls, barons, and great men answered and said, that neither the said king John, nor any other could put himself nor his realm nor his people in such subjection, without their assent and accord. And the commons having been questioned upon this and having taken counsel answered in like manner. * * *

80. Lawyers and Sheriffs excluded from Parliament

(November, 1372.   French text and translation, 1 *S. R.* 394.   2 Stubbs, 445.)

WHEREAS men of the law who follow divers businesses in the king's courts on behalf of private persons, with whom they are, do procure and cause to be brought into parliament many petitions in the name of the commons, which in no wise relate to them, but only the private persons with whom they are engaged; also sheriffs who are common officers for the people, and ought to be abiding in their office, for the doing right to every one, are named, and have heretofore been and returned to parliament knights of the shires, by the same sheriffs; it is accorded and assented in this parliament, that hereafter no man of the law following business in the king's court, nor any sheriff for the time that he is sheriff, be returned nor accepted knights of the shires; nor that they who are men of the law and sheriffs now returned to parliament have any wages; but the king willeth that knights and sergeants of the most worthy of the county be hereafter returned knights in parliament; and that they be elected in full county.

---

81. Grant of Tunnage and Poundage, by Citizens and Burgesses alone

(November, 1372.   French text, 2 *R. P.* 310.   Translation by Editors.
2 Stubbs, 444, 557.)

14. AND after this leave was given to the knights of the shires to depart and to sue out their writs for their expenses.   And so they departed.

15. But the citizen and burgesses who had come to the said parliament, were commanded to tarry for certain reasons, which citizens and burgesses, the next day after, having assembled before the prince and others, prelates and great men, in a chamber near the white chamber, it was shown to them, how the year before, grant had been made for a certain term for the safe and sure conduct of the ships and merchandises coming to this land by sea and passing from it, a subsidy, that is to say, on each tun of wine coming into this land, two shillings, and of each pound

of merchandise of what sort soever, both that entering and that leaving, six pence, which term is already past. That they in consideration of the perils and mischiefs which might come to their ships and merchandises at the hands of enemies on the sea, should will to grant such a subsidy to endure for a year, for the said reasons. Which subsidy they granted to the king to take and to levy in the manner in which it was taken and levied in the year last past. And so they departed.

———◆———

82. Impeachment of Richard Lyons

(May, 1376. French text, 2 *R. P.* 323. Translation by Editors. 2 Stubbs, 451, 593.)

17. FIRST, Richard Lyons, merchant of London, was impeached and accused by the said commons of many deceptions, extortions, and other crimes committed by him against the king our lord, and against his people as well during the time when he was in attendance upon the household and council of the king as also during the time when he was farmer of the subsidies and customs of the king. And especially because the said Richard, by covenant made between him and certain of the privy council of our lord the king to secure their own profit and advantage thereof, has procured the making of many patents and writs of licence for carrying great quantities of wool, woolfells, and other merchandises to places outside of the staple of Calais, contrary to the ordinances and prohibitions made before this time in parliament, to the damage of the same staple of Calais and of the revenue there, to the great damage of the king and of the realm of England and to the ruin of the city of Calais aforesaid. And also, because he has put and procured to be put upon the wool, woolfells, and other merchandises, certain new impositions without the assent of parliament, and he has levied and collected those impositions largely for his own use and for the use of those about the king who are of the said covenant, without the oversight or witness of any comptroller, and without his being charged by record or otherwise except at his will, but he alone is sole treasurer and receiver, and the high treasurer of the realm does not interfere at all. And it is commonly said that he takes in certain from a parcel ten shillings, and from other parcels twelve pence, from each sack etc., which

amounts to a vast sum for all the time that he has been receiver and treasurer thereof, as is aforesaid. And likewise of another new imposition of four pence made and put by him upon each pound of coin sent abroad by Lombards and other merchants, in the way of exchange, by his own authority and without warrant or assent of parliament, or otherwise. And this same imposition of four pence on the pound, a great portion collected and held for the use of the king, he pays our lord the king nothing thereof. And also of various loans made for the use of the king without necessary cause: and especially of one loan which was recently made in London of twenty thousand marks, for which twenty thousand marks our lord the king was obliged to repay thirty thousand marks; and this by the advice of the said Richard, and of other privy councillors about the king, who had agreed with the creditors to receive part of the profit, and to be partners secretly in the said loan: to which loan the said Richard furnished his own money and afterwards gained by way of usury from the king his lord, of whose council he had formerly been a member, a great quantity of coin to the great damage and deception of the king. And also of many other extortions, frauds, deceptions, oppressions, champerties, and maintenances, committed against our lord the king and against his people, in every part of the realm, as well during the time that the said Richard was farmer of the subsidies and customs of the king throughout the realm, and thus acted toward him and his council, and treasurer or receiver of the said new impositions, as at other times, by taking upon himself notoriously the royal power in all the said things, which would have been a horrible matter to rehearse in full. And also in that when the king our lord was debtor of record for many great sums of money to various persons, the said Richard by the assent of other privy councillors about the king, of his said covenant, made bargains in many such debts, some at one time for the tenth penny and at another time for the twentieth or the hundredth penny, and obtained the payment of the entire debt by the king. And also by his subtleties of this sort, and for his personal profit, both the king our lord and the said debtors were foully deceived; and especially the prior of Saint John of Jerusalem in England, to whom the king was debtor for a certain sum, and the said Richard had thereof four marks out of every twenty as brokerage, for obtaining for the prior the payment of the balance. And at another time of the lord le Despenser, to whom the king was also debtor; and the said Richard obtained from him, in the same manner another large sum of money. And also, of many others, to the great deception, slander, and degradation of the king and of his court.

18. To which the said Richard, being present in parliament, replied, that as to the loan made to the king of the twenty thousand marks aforesaid, he was entirely free from any blame. And further he said that he had thereof neither profit nor gain, nor did he furnish anything to the loan aforesaid, in money, nor in anything else: and this he was ready to prove by all the reasonable means that might be demanded. And as to the said imposition of ten shillings and of twelve pence on the sack of wool etc., and of four pence on the pound of coin he could not clearly excuse himself of having also levied and collected them and of taking thereof a portion for himself that is to say, twelve pence from each sack of wool, etc. But this he did, he said, at the express command of our lord the king and at the prayer and with the consent of the merchants who asked for such licences. And as to the residue of those impositions, he had caused them to be entirely delivered to the receiver of the chamber of the king and had accounted therefor fully in the said chamber. And the said Richard was told that for it he ought to produce the warrant under the authority of which he had done the said things. But no warrant nor authorization was produced in parliament under the seal of the king, nor otherwise; save only that he said, that he had commandment therefor from the king himself and from his council to do it. And upon this, testimony was given openly in parliament, that our lord the king had said expressly the day before to certain lords here present in parliament, that he did not know how nor in what manner he had entered into such an office with regard to him; and furthermore, he did not recognize him as his officer. And as to the other articles the said Richard made no answer; but he said that if he had committed offence or done wrong in any wise, he placed himself at the mercy of the king our lord.

19. Thereupon the said Richard was ordered to prison during the king's pleasure; and to be put to fine and ransom, according to the amount and heinousness of his offence: and that he lose his liberty of the city of London, and that he never hold office of the king nor enter the council nor the palace of the king. And accordingly, the said Richard was afterwards brought before the lords of parliament, and there he was told that it seemed to the lords that his evil deeds were so great and heinous that he could not make adequate satisfaction for them. And at once the said Richard placed at the mercy of the king, his person, his lands,

tenements, goods, and chattels; and there willed and granted that his person, lands, goods, and chattels should be at the mercy of the king to ordain and to do therewith as was his pleasure: requesting the king to grant him his life, if it were his pleasure; and if that were not his pleasure, that he should do with him and his, his entire will. Wherefore it is also adjudged that all his lands, tenements, goods, and chattels be seised into the hands of the king, and that his person remain in prison, during the king's pleasure. And as to the extortions committed by the said Richard or his deputies during the time that he was farmer of the said subsidies or custom, as is above said, it is ordained in parliament, that good inquisition be made by proper persons in all the ports of England.

---

83. Grant of a Poll Tax, and Petition for special Treasurers

(February, 1377. French text, 2 *R. P.* 364. Translation by Editors.
2 Stubbs, 459.)

19. THE noble lords and commons assembled in this parliament perceiving clearly the great charges and the very grievous and insupportable expenses which our lord the king makes and still must needs make more and more every day, as well, that is to say in the maintenance of the war and the defense of the realm of England, as otherwise, of their common assent and free will, have granted to our said lord the king in maintenance of his said wars, four pence to be taken of the goods of each person of the said realm, as well males as females, above the age of fourteen years. Excepting only genuine mendicants without fraud. Praying most humbly to their said liege lord that it will please him to excuse them because they are not now able to grant a greater subsidy: for, they would have been most willing to do this, if it had not been that they had been so impoverished in the past, as well by great losses on the sea, as otherwise by bad years which had befallen them so that they are not able to do more at present.

20. And also the said commons pray that it may please our lord the king to name two earls and two barons, of those who shall seem to him best, who shall be guardians and treasurers as well of this subsidy now granted and of the subsidy which the clergy

of England is yet to grant to the king our lord, as of the subsidy of wool, leather, and woolfells granted in the last parliament: and that these four earls and barons be sworn in their presence that whatever is received by them of the said subsidies shall be wholly expended for the said wars and for no other work; and that the high treasurer of England shall receive nothing of it and shall not meddle in it in any manner.

———◆———

84. Persons appointed to supervise Expenditures

(1377.   French original, 3 *R. P.* 7.   Translation by Editors.   2 Stubbs, 465, 597.)

27.   ITEM, the lords and commons of the realm of England, perceiving clearly the great peril of the realm, that it is on the point of being lost, if God does not give a remedy for it most speedily, amid the great wars which are waged against it and quite openly on either side as well by land as by sea, of which there is more to be feared than ever before: And therefore in aid of the expenditures which must be made for the conduct of the war of the realm in resisting so many enemies and for the aid and rescue of the realm aforesaid, for the aid of our lord they now of their free will grant to the said king our lord, two fifteenths outside the cities and boroughs, and two tenths within the said cities and boroughs, to be levied on their goods; * * * And humbly praying their liege lord and the other lords of parliament, that as well of these moneys as of the money of the tenths now to be granted by the clergy of England and also of the moneys arising from the subsidies of wools, certain suitable persons shall be appointed by the king to be treasurers or guardians to such effect that these moneys shall be entirely applied to the expenses of the war and to nothing else in any way.   And be it remembered that this request was granted them by the king, saving to the king entirely his old duty of half a mark from citizens and ten shillings from foreigners due on each sack of wool exported from the realm, etc.   And thereupon our lord the king appointed William Walworth and John Philipot, merchants of London, to be guardians of the said sums for the use aforesaid, and to render faithful account of their receipts and expenditures in such manner as shall be ordained by our lord the king and his said great council in reasonable manner.   And thereupon, by commandment of our said lord the king, the said William and John

accepted their charge and they took oath and swore in the presence of the king himself in full parliament to do this faithfully.
Saving always to the king, that he should be repaid first for the
sum expended by him and paid for this last expedition by sea,
which amounts to more than fifteen thousand pounds sterling, for
which the king is still debtor to his creditors.

———◆———

85. Account of Expenditures required by Parliament

(1378. French original, 3 *R. P.* 35. Translation by Editors. 2 Stubbs,
467, 598.)

20. AND thereupon the commons, after considerable deliberation, make request once more to our lord the king that it
may please him to communicate to his said commons how and
in what manner were expended the said great sums thus given
and granted for the said war; and that proper order should
be made, that if it should so happen that any lord or any other
person engaged for the last expedition or anywhere else had a
smaller number of men to his credit than he had engaged to have
with him and had received wages and money of the king, that
surplus money over and above the wages of the men shown should
be repaid to our said lord the king to be used for the war, in discharge, therefore of the commons aforesaid. And they also
make request that it may please our lord the king to grant that
the commons shall be informed of the names of those who are to
be the great officers of the realm and of those who are to be
councilors to our lord the king and governors of his person,
inasmuch as he is thus of tender age, for the ensuing year, according to the manner at other times ordained in parliament.

21. To which answer was made by the said Monsieur Richard
at the said commandment that it had never been known that, of
a subsidy or other grant made to the king in parliament or out of
parliament by the commons, an account had afterwards been rendered to the commons or to any one else except to the king and
his officers; nevertheless that our said lord the king wills and
commands, for the satisfaction of his commons, of his own
motion, without doing it of right or by constraint of the said
request now made to him, that the said William Walworth here
present together with certain other persons of the council of our

lord the king assigned thereto by the king, shall clearly set forth
to you in writing the receipts and expenditures made therefor, on
this agreement, that this shall not in future be considered a precedent or an inference that this should have been done otherwise
than by the personal volition and command alone of our said
lord the king as has been said.   And as to the surplus of the
wages received over and above the men shown, you shall know
that this belongs to our said lord the king and his ministers of
the exchequer and to no one else; and those of the exchequer
should not pay any attention to such matters nor should they keep
any record of these things, but that the greatest lord of England
should do it.

And as to the said officers and councillors, our said lord the
king by the advice of the lords has chosen the said officers, and
his councillors shall be of such as shall please him, as soon as he
shall be able to attend to it; of which names you shall be duly
informed, if it please the king.

*   *   *   *   *   *   *   *   *

86. The King orders Accounts submitted to Parliament

(1379.   French original, 3 *R. P.* 56.   Translation by Editors.   2 Stubbs,
468, 698.)

7. AND that you [Parliament] may be fully informed of the
real nature of the said necessary expenditures made and to be
made, the treasurers for the said war shall be present and shall
appear, at such an hour as pleases you, to show you clearly
in writing their receipts and expenditures made since the
last parliament, and the amounts due, with the other necessary
expenditures above mentioned, to be made for the march of
Calais, at Cherbourg, at Brest, in the marches of Scotland, in
Ireland, and elsewhere.   And our lord the king wills that, if any-
one in the realm shall feel aggrieved at anything done to him
wrongly and contrary to the law, which cannot be remedied without parliament, he shall bring forward his petition in the matter
in parliament, and for receiving, trying, and examining such
bills, our said lord the king has made assignment of certain prelates, lords, justices, and clerks, in the form and manner which
follows: and he wills and commands that full justice shall be

done and ordained in this parliament to all men, as well to the
least as to the greatest; and that this present parliament shall continue from day to day until the king our lord shall give you his
leave and license to depart.

12. These are the names of the prelates and lords appointed to
examine the estate of the king, at the request of the commons;
that is to say, the archbishop of Canterbury, the bishop of London, the bishop of Rochester, the Earl of March, the earl of
Warwick, the earl of Stafford, the Lord Latimer, Guy de Brienne,
or John Cobham, and Roger Beauchamp. First, to examine the
revenues accruing from the subsidy of wools received since the
last feast of St. Michael and which probably will be received
before the coming feast of St. Michael. Item, to examine as
well all the revenues of the realm received since the said time,
also the revenues of the alien priors and the ancient maletote
of wools, the vacancies of the bishoprics and abbeys, and all
other profits whatsoever, and those which will probably be
received and levied before the said feast of St. Michael, both
by the hands of the treasurer of war as the collector and of the
hanaper of the chancery and all other offices whatsoever of our
lord the king. Item, to examine what manner of fees or wages
were used to be taken by the grand and petty officers of the
king in the time of King Edward, the grandfather of our lord
who now is. Item, to examine what annuities granted by our
lord the king, the said grandfather, and by the prince, whom
God assoil, were paid. Item, to examine the properties of the
royal grandfather, that is to say, where they have gone and into
whose hands, and what persons were paid in discharge of the
alms of the said grandfather; and what part thereof remains for
the use of our lord the king; and what has become of the rest.
And that those who have the distribution thereof be held to
account by the said lords, and whether they have come to the
profit of the king in discharge of his people, or not. Item, to
look over and examine the sum of the expenses of the household
of our lord the king, calling before them the officers of the aforesaid household, the better to inform themselves. Item, the wardships, marriages, forfeitures and escheats. Item, the revenues
of Calais, and the other castles and fortresses, the other revenues
of the war by sea and by land. Item, the revenues of Bordeaux,
that is to say, of wine and money, and other such profits. Item,
the subsidy of cloths, that is to say, the cloth with the seal
eighteen pence. Item, the profits from the possessions of the
rebellious cardinals. Item, to see to it that those who have taken

wages for the war be made to give account of them and to answer
for that which remains in their hands. Item, of the moneys
called Roman pence, which amounts to a great sum, and of the
arrears of many years. And be it remembered that the said lords
appointed have themselves the command of the king in parliament to enter, that is to say, altogether or three of them at least,
of whom one should be of each rank, the places and offices of the
king which shall be necessary for this matter, with the officers or
guardians of the same, and to examine together with the said
officers the rolls, accounts, and whatsoever other things touch
upon this matter, and to do and accomplish as much as is said
above and to report distinctly to our said lord the king and to
his council what they shall have done or found, with their best
advice on this matter. And our lord the king wills and commands all his officers and ministers of the said places to show to
the said lords appointed, or three of them, the rolls, accounts,
tallies, and whatsoever other evidences touch this matter and to
attend them in the manner before said as much and as often as
they shall be required by the said lords or any of them.

---

87. The Poll-tax of 1379

(1379. French original.   3 R. P. 57.   Translation by Editors.
2 Stubbs, 468.)

13. ITEM, the lords and commons of the realm of England
sitting in this parliament grant for themselves and for all the
commons of England the subsidy of wools, leather, and woolfells; and another subsidy, to be taken of the goods of certain
persons in the realm, under a certain form and manner em-
bodied in a schedule made thereof and delivered before parliament, the tenor of which follows word for word :

The lords and commons of the realm of England considering
the great needs of the said realm and the malice of the enemies
in France and elsewhere, desiring the great recovery of the said
realm and the destruction of the said enemies, * * * grant, that
if the mark on the sack of wools and the six pence on the pound
which were granted at the last parliament held at Gloucester, be
excused and annulled at present, the subsidy of wools to last for
one entire year after the feast of St. Michael next to come; that
is to say, on each sack as much as was granted before the said

parliament of Gloucester, and a sum of money to be levied upon divers persons of the realm in the following manner, as well within the royal franchises as without; that is to say,

14. The Duke of Lancaster and the Duke of Brittany,

each one	10 marks
Item, each earl of England	4 pounds
Item, each widowed countess in England, the same as the earls .	4 pounds
Item, each baron and banneret, or knight of equal wealth . . .	40 *s.*
Item, each widowed baroness shall pay as the baron and each widow of a knight as the knight	40 *s.*
Item, each bachelor and each esquire who by the statute ought to be knight	20 *s.*
Item, each widowed lady, wife of a bachelor or esquire, according to her condition	20 *s.*
Item, each esquire of less estate	6 *s.* 8 *d.*
Item, each widow of such an esquire or merchant of sufficient means	6 *s.* 8 *d.*
Item, each esquire possessing neither land nor rent, nor castles, who is in service, or under arms	3 *s.* 4 *d.*
Item, the chief prior of the Hospital of St. John, as a baron . .	40 *s.*
Item, each commander of this Order of England, as a bachelor .	20 *s.*
Item, each other brother knight of the said Order . . .	13 *s.* 4 *d.*
Item, all the other brothers of the said Order, each as an esquire without possessions	3 *s.* 4 *d.*
15. Item, each justice, as well of one bench as of the other, and those who have been justices of the same benches, and the chief baron of the exchequer, each	100 *s.*
Item, each sergeant and greater apprentice of the law . . .	40 *s.*
Item, other apprentices who follow the law, each . . .	20 *s.*
Item, all the other apprentices of less estate, and attorneys, each .	6 *s.* 8 *d.*
16. Item, the mayor of London pays as an earl	4 pounds
Item, the aldermen of London, each as a baron	40 *s.*
Item, all the mayors of the large towns of England, each as a baron .	40 *s.*
Item, the other mayors of the other small towns, according to the condition of their estate	{ 20 *s.*, 10 *s.*, or 1/2 mark
And all the aldermen of the large towns, and the great merchants of the realm, pay as bachelors	20 *s.*
Item, other merchants of sufficient means	13 *s.* 4 *d.*
Item, all the lesser merchants and artificers who have profit of the land, according to the condition of their estate	{ 6 *s.* 8 *d.*, 3 *s.* 4 *d.*, 2 *s.*, 12 *d.* or *k.*

Item, each sergeant and franklin of the country, according to his estate . . . .
$\begin{cases} 6 s.\,8\,d. \\ 40\,d. \end{cases}$

Item, the farmers of the manors, benefices, and granges, merchants of cattle and of other small merchandise, according to their estate . . . .
$\begin{cases} 1/2 \text{ mark,} \\ 40\,d.,\,2\,s., \\ \text{or } 12\,d. \end{cases}$

17. Item, all the advocates, notaries, and married solicitors pay as sergeants of the law, apprentices of the law, and attorneys, each according to his estate . . . . . .
$\begin{cases} 40\,s., \\ 20\,s.,\,\text{or} \\ 1/2 \text{ mark} \end{cases}$

Item, married pardoners, and summoners, each according to his estate . . . .
$\begin{cases} 3 s.\,4\,d., \\ 2\,s.,\,\text{or} \\ 12\,d. \end{cases}$

Item, all the hostlers who do not belong to the estate of merchant, each according to his estate . . . . . .
$\begin{cases} 40\,d., \\ 2\,s.,\,\text{or} \\ 12\,d. \end{cases}$

Item, each married man, for himself and his wife, who do not belong to the above named estates, above the age of sixteen, except veritable beggars . . . .   4 d.

And each single man and woman of such condition and above the said age . . . .   4 d.

Item, each foreign merchant, of whatsoever estate he may be, pays according to his condition as the other residents. And these payments above named shall be levied from no person except in the place where he is living and nowhere else. And be it remembered, that the sums above named which are not definitely determined shall be fixed at the discretion of the assessors and controllers appointed for this purpose. And that the collectors of this subsidy above named fix the days of their payment at the feast of St. John the Baptist next to come and at the feast of St. Peter ad vincula next ensuing after that.

———◆———

88. The Poll-tax of 1380

(1380. French original, 3 R. P. 90. no. 15.   Translation by Editors.
2 Stubbs, 470.)

15. FIRST, the lords and commons have agreed that there shall be given for the needs aforesaid, by each layman of the realm within the franchise or without, as well by the males as

by the females, of whatsoever estate or condition they may be, who have passed the age of fifteen years, three groats, except the very beggars, who shall be charged nothing. Saving always that the levy be made in such order and form that each layman shall be charged fairly according to his condition and in the following manner: that is to say, that for the whole sum assessed in each town the wealthy according to their condition shall aid the poorer; provided that the most wealthy shall not pay above the sum of sixty groats for himself and his wife, and no person less than one groat for himself and his wife: and that no person be charged to pay except in that place where he and his wife and children live or in the place where he lives in service. And that all artificers, laborers, servants, and other laymen as also all servants whatsoever living with prelates and lords temporal, abbots, priors of collegiate churches, clerks of the chancery, and in the common bench, the king's bench, the exchequer, the receipt and with all other officers, knights, esquires, merchants, citizens, burgesses, and with all other persons, that each of them be assessed and taxed according to the condition of his estate and in the said form. And that commissions be given to a sufficient number of persons, as well in the counties as in cities and boroughs, to be collectors and controllers of the sum aforesaid: and that they shall take an oath to discharge their duties well and loyally. And it is not the intention of the said commons to make this present grant for anything except only the sustenance of the earl of Buckingham and the other lords and men in his company in parts of Brittany and for the defense of the realm and safe-guard of the sea. And that this present grant should not be made nor taken in the form nor after the manner of any levy of groats before this time, but should be levied solely on persons now living; provided the two divisions of the said payment be made on the fifteenth of St. Hilary next to come, and the third part at the Feast of Pentecost next ensuing thereafter: provided always that no one of the knights, citizens, and burgesses who have come to this present parliament be made collector or controller of the sums aforesaid. And that it pleases our lord the king and his council to ordain for the said levy, as well of the servants of the household of our lord the king as of the other lords in the realm, that they should be evenly charged, according to the purport of this grant.

And the commons pray, that during the war justices in eyre and of trailbaston shall not go on circuit among the said poor commons, but that the justice of the peace hold their courts according to the tenure of their commission.

And the commons grant to our lord the king the subsidy on wools to last till the Feast of St. Martin next to come.

————◆————

89. Merchants to use English Ships only. Charters granted the Peasants Annulled

(May, 1382.   French text and translation, 2 *S. R.* 17.   2 Stubbs, 482.)

*   *   *   *   *   *   *   *   *

3. ITEM, to increase the navy of England, which is now greatly diminished: it is assented and accorded, that none of the king's liege people do from henceforth ship any merchandise in going out or coming within the realm of England, anywhere, but only in ships of the king's liegeance; and every person of the said liegeance, which * * * do ship and merchandise in any other ships * * * shall forfeit to the king all his merchandises shipped in other vessels, wheresoever they be found hereafter, or the value of the same; * * *

*   *   *   *   *   *   *   *   *

6. Item, it is ordained, that all manner manumissions, obligations, releases, and other bonds made by compulsion, duress, and menace, in the time of this last rumor and riot against the laws of the land, and good faith, shall be wholly quashed, annulled and holden for void; and they that have done to be made, or do yet withhold such manumissions, obligations, releases, bonds, and other deeds so made by duress, shall be sent before the king and his council, thereof to answer there of their deed, and further shall be constrained to make delivery and restitution of the said deeds to them that made the same against their good will, with the copies of the same, if perchance they have thereof made any before, another time to use or renew the effect of the same if they may.   And likewise it is accorded, that all entries made in lands or tenements, and also all feoffments made in the time of the same rumor by compulsion and menace, or otherwise with force of people, against the law, shall be void, and holden for none.   And the king straitly defendeth to all manner of people, upon pain of as much as they may forfeit against him in body and goods, that none from henceforth make nor begin again, in any way, such riot and rumor, nor other like.

And if any the same do, and that duly proved, it shall be done of him as of a traitor to the king and to his said realm.

*   *   *   *   *   *   *   *   *

8. Item, touching the charters, releases, obligations, and other deeds and muniments, burnt, destroyed, or otherwise eloined in the same rumor, it is assented, that they which thereof feel them grieved, shall put their petitions distinctly made upon their matters specially before the king and his council, betwixt this and the Nativity of Saint John Baptist next coming at the furthest, and there make sufficient proof of the said muniments so lost, and of the form and tenor of the same; and that done, such remedy shall thereof be provided for them at every man's complaint, as best shall seem in the case, saving the law.

*   *   *   *   *   *   *   *   *

90. An Act against Heretical Preaching

(May, 1382.   French text and translation, 2 *S. R.* 23.   2 Stubbs, 487.)

*   *   *   *   *   *   *   *   *

5. ITEM, forasmuch as it is openly known, that there be divers evil persons within the realm, going from county to county, and from town to town, in certain habits under dissimulation of great holiness, and without the licence of our holy father the pope, or of the ordinaries of the places or other sufficient authority, do preach daily, not only in churches and churchyards, but also in markets, fairs, and other open places, where a great congregation of people is, divers sermons containing heresies and notorious errors, to the great emblemishing of the Christian faith, and destruction of the laws, and of the estate of holy Church, to the great peril of the souls of the people, and of all the realm of England, as more plainly is found and sufficiently proved before the reverend father in God the archbishop of Canterbury, and the bishops and other prelates, and masters of divinity, and doctors of canon and of civil law, and a great part of the clergy of the said realm specially assembled for this cause; which persons do also preach divers matters of slander, to engender discord and dissension betwixt divers estates of the said realm, as well spiritual as temporal, in exciting of the people, to the great peril of all the realm: which preachers cited or summoned before the ordinaries of the places, there to answer of

L

that whereof they be impeached, will not obey to their summons and commandments, nor care not for their monitions, nor censures of the holy Church, but expressly despise them, and moreover by their subtil words do draw and beguile the people to hear their sermons, and to maintain them in their errors by strong hand and by great routs: it is ordained in this present parliament, that the king's commissions be directed to the sheriffs and other ministers of our sovereign lord the king, or other sufficient persons after and according to the certifications of the prelates thereof to be made in the chancery from time to time, to arrest all such preachers, and also their fautors, maintainers, and abettors, and to hold them in arrest and strong prison, till they will justify them according to the law and reason of holy Church: And the king will and commandeth, that the chancellor make such commission at all times, that he by the prelates or any of them shall be certified and thereof required, as is aforesaid.

---

91. An Act to reform the Administration of Justice

(June, 1385.   Latin text and translation, 2 *S. R.* 36.   2 Stubbs, 640.)

TO the honor of God, and at the request of the commonalty of the realm of England made to our lord the king in his parliament holden at Westminster in the morrow of Saint Martin, the eighth year of his reign; the same our lord the king of the assent of the prelates, great men, and commons aforesaid, hath caused to be made in the same parliament, a certain statute for the common profit of the said realm, and especially for the good and just governance, and due execution of the common law, in the form following.

1. First, it is accorded and statuted, that holy Church have all her liberties; and that the Great Charter, and the Charter of the Forest, the Statutes of purveyors and laborers, and all other statutes and ordinances heretofore made and not repealed, shall be holden and observed, and put in due execution according to the form and effect of the same.

2. Item, it is accorded and statuted, that no man of law shall be from henceforth justice of assizes, or of the common deliverance of jails in his own country; and that the chief justice of the common bench be assigned amongst others to take such

assizes, and deliver jails ; but as to the chief justice of the king's bench, it shall be as for the most part of an hundred years last past was wont to be done.

3. Item, whereas late in the time of the noble king Edward, grandfather of our sovereign lord the king that now is, it was ordained, that justices, as long as they should be in the office of justices, should not take fee nor robe of any except of the king, and that they should not take gift nor reward by them nor yet by other, privily nor openly, of any man which should have anything to do afore them in any wise, except meat and drink, of small value; and that they should not give counsel to any great or small in things or affairs, where the king is party, or which in any wise touch the king, upon a certain pain contained in the said ordinance: and in the same manner it is ordained of the barons of the exchequer, as in the said ordinance is more plainly contained; and the said ordinance being rehearsed in the parliament, it is accorded and statuted, that no justice of the king's bench nor of the common bench, nor none of the barons of the exchequer, as long as they shall be in the office of justice or barons, shall take from henceforth by himself or other, privily or openly, robe, fee, pension, gift, nor reward, of any but of the king, nor entertainment of any, except entertainment of meat and drink, which shall be of no great value. And that from henceforth they shall give no counsel to any, great or small, in things or affairs, wherein the king is party, or which in any wise touch the king, and that they be not of any man's counsel in any cause, plea, or quarrel, hanging the plea before them or in other of the king's great courts or places, upon pain of loss of their office, and making to the king fine and ransom.

*   *   *   *   *   *   *   *   *

5. * * * ; it is accorded and statuted, that all pleas and suits touching the common law, and which ought to be examined and discussed at the common law, shall not be hereafter drawn or holden by any means before the said constable and marshal, but that the court of the same constable and marshal shall have that which belongeth to the same court, * * *

92. An Act regarding Fugitive Villeins

(December, 1385.   French text and translation, 2 *S. R.* 38.)

*   *   *   *   *   *   *   *   *

2. ITEM, whereas divers villeins and neifs, as well of great lords as of other people, as well spiritual as temporal, do flee into cities, towns, and places enfranchised, as the city of London, and other like, and feign divers suits against their lords, to the intent to make them free by the answer of their lords: it is accorded and assented, that the lords nor other, shall not be forbarred of their villeins, because of their answer in the law.

*   *   *   *   *   *   *   *   *

———◆———

93. Articles of Impeachment against Suffolk

(1386.   French original.   3 *R. P.* 216.   Translation by Editors.
2 Stubbs, 497.)

IN this parliament, all the commons with one accord, assembled unanimously and came before the king, prelates and lords, in the chambers of parliament, complaining grievously of Michael de la Pole, earl of Suffolk, late chancellor of England, then present and accused him by word of mouth in the following manner, to wit:

6. First, that the said earl, being chancellor and sworn to promote the king's welfare, purchased from our lord the king lands, tenements, and rents, of great value as appears by record in the rolls of the chancery, contrary to his oath, whereas he had not deserved so much considering the great need of the king and of the realm: and besides this, because the said earl was chancellor at the time of the said purchase, the said lands and tenements were appraised at a less value than they were worth per year by a great sum, in deceit of the king.

Item, whereas nine lords were appointed at the last parliament to inspect and examine the estate of the king and the realm, and to give their advice as to how it could be best improved and brought under a better government and order; and on this inspection made and the report made to the king both by word of mouth and in writing, the said late chancellor had said in full parliament, that the said advice and ordinance ought to be put into due execution; and this was not done, and it was the fault of himself as he was then chief officer.

Item, whereas the tax was granted by the commons at the last parliament to be expended in a certain manner demanded by the commons and assented to by the king and lords, and not at all otherwise, the moneys arising therefrom were expended in another manner, so that the sea was not guarded in the manner which had been ordained; because of which many mischances had befallen the realm and very probably would in the future, and this because of the neglect of the said late chancellor.

Item, whereas a certain Tideman of Limburgh, who had for himself and heirs as the gift of the grandfather of the king fifty pounds yearly on the customs duties of Kingston on Hull which Tideman forfeited to the king, and also the payment of the said annual fifty pounds had been discontinued for twenty or thirty years, the said late chancellor knowing this, purchased from him and from the heirs of the said Tideman the said annual fifty pounds and brought it about that the king confirmed the said purchase, whereas the king should have had the profit.

Item, whereas the chief master of St. Antony is a schismatic, and for this reason the king should have the profit which belongs to him in the kingdom of England, the said late chancellor, who should have promoted and secured the profit of the king, leased the said profit of the king for twenty marks per year and took thereof for his own especial use very nearly one thousand marks, and at the time when the master of St. Antony who is now in England should have had possession and delivery of the said profit, he was not able to have it until he and two persons with him had bound themselves by an acknowledgement in the chancery and by bonds in the sum of £3,000 to pay annually to the said late chancellor and to John his son one hundred pounds per year, for the term of both their lives.

Item, that in the time of the said late chancellor were granted and made divers charters and patents of murders, treasons, felonies, erasures of the rolls, sale of the laws, and in particular, since the beginning of this parliament, was made and sealed a charter of certain franchises granted to the castle of Dover, in disherison of the crown and the subversion of all the offices and courts of the king and of his laws.

Item, whereas ordinance was made at the last parliament for the town of Ghent providing that ten thousand marks should be paid as ransom and for this ransom three thousand marks should be expended; because of the default and neglect of the said late chancellor the said town was lost; notwithstanding that the ten thousand marks had been paid and the said three thousand marks expended for the ransom, as has been said.

On all these articles the said commons demand the judgment of parliament.

---

94. Threat to depose Richard II

(1386. Latin original. Knighton's chronicle, Rolls Series, II. 219. Translation by Editors. 2 Stubbs, 497.)

YET one other thing remains of our message for us to announce to you on the part of your people. For they have it from an old statute, and in fact not very long ago put into force, which is to be regretted, that if the king from any malignant design or foolish contumacy or contempt or wanton wilfulness or in any irregular way should alienate himself from his people, and should not be willing to be governed and regulated by the laws, statutes and laudable ordinances of the realm with the wholesome advice of the lords and peers of the realm, but should headily and wantonly by his own mad designs work out his own private purpose, then it should be lawful for them with the common assent and consent of the people of the realm to depose the king himself from the royal throne and to elevate to the royal throne in his place some near kinsman of the royal line.

---

95. The Second Statute of Provisors

(May, 1390. French text and translation, 2 S. R. 68. 2 Stubbs, 430, 508, 612, 3 Stubbs, 309, 324, 338.)

2. ITEM, whereas the noble king Edward, grandfather to our lord the king that now is, at his parliament holden at Westminster, at the utas of the purification of our Lady, the five and twentieth year of his reign, caused to be rehearsed the statute made at Carlisle in the time of his grandfather king Edward, son of king Henry, touching the estate of the holy Church of England; the said grandfather of the king that now is, by the assent of the great men of his realm, being in the same parliament,

holden the said five and twentieth year, to the honor of God and
of holy Church, and of all his realm, did ordain and establish,
that the free elections of archbishoprics, bishoprics, and all other
dignities and benefices elective in England, should hold from
thenceforth in the manner as they were granted by his progenitors,
and by the ancestors of other lords founders; and that all prelates and other people of holy Church, which had advowsons of
any benefices of the gift of the king, or of his progenitors, or of
other lords and donors, should freely have their collations and
presentments; and thereupon a certain punishment was ordained
in the same statute for them which accept any benefice or dignity
contrary to the said statute made at Westminster the said twenty-
fifth year, as afore is said; which statute our lord the king hath
caused to be recited in this present parliament at the request of
his commons in the same parliament, the tenor whereof is such
as hereafter followeth: * * *

* * * * * * * * *

And further more our lord the king that now is, of the assent
of the great men of his realm being in this present parliament,
hath ordained and established, that for all archbishoprics, bishoprics, and other dignities and benefices elective, and all other
benefices of holy Church, which began to be void in deed the
twenty-ninth day of January, the thirteenth year of the reign of
our lord king Richard that now is, or after, or which shall be
void in time to come within the realm of England, the said
statute made the said twenty-fifth year shall be firmly holden forever, and put in due execution from time to time in all manner
of points; and if any do accept of a benefice of holy Church
contrary to this statute, and that duly proved, and be beyond the
sea, he shall abide exiled and banished out of the realm forever
and his lands and tenements, goods and chattels shall be forfeit
to the king; and if he be within the realm, he shall be also exiled
and banished as afore is said, and shall incur the same forfeiture,
and take his way, so that he be out of the realm in six weeks next
after such acceptation; and if any receive any such person banished coming from beyond the sea, or being within the realm
after the said six weeks, knowing thereof, he shall be also exiled
and banished, and incur such forfeiture as afore is said; and
that their procurators, notaries, executors, and summoners have
the pain and forfeiture aforesaid.   Provided nevertheless, that
all they to whom our holy father the pope, or his predecessors,
have provided any archbishopric, bishopric, or other dignity, or

benefices elective, or other benefices of holy Church, of the patronage of people of holy Church, in respect of any voidance before the said twenty-ninth day of January, and thereof were in actual possession before the same twenty-ninth day, shall have and enjoy the said archbishoprics, bishoprics, dignities, and other benefices peaceably for their lives, notwithstanding the statutes and ordinance aforesaid.   And if the king send by letter or in other manner to the court of Rome, at the entreaty of any person, or if any other send or sue to the same court, whereby anything is done contrary to this statute, touching any archbish-opric, bishopric, dignity, or other benefice of holy Church within the said realm, if he that maketh such motion or suit be a prel-ate of holy Church, he shall pay to the king the value of his tem-poralties of one year; and if he be a temporal lord, he shall pay to the king the value of his lands and possessions not moveable of one year; and if he be another person of a more mean estate, he shall pay to the king the value of the benefice for which suit is made, and shall be imprisoned one year.   And it is the intent of this statute, that of all dignities and benefices of holy Church, which were void indeed the said twenty-ninth day of January, which be given, or to which it is provided by the pope before the same twenty-ninth day, that they to whom such gifts or pro-visions be made, may freely of such gifts and provisions sue execution without offence of this statute: provided always, that of no dignity or benefice which was full the said twenty-ninth day of January, no man because of any collation, gift, reserva-tion, and provision, or other grace papal, not executed before the said twenty-ninth day, shall not sue thereof execution, upon the pains and forfeitures contained in this present statute.

3. Item, it is ordained and established, that if any man bring or send within the realm, or the king's power, any summons, sentences, or excommunications against any person, of what condition that he be, for the cause of the moving, making assent, or execution of the said statute of provisors, he shall be taken, arrested, and put in prison, and forfeit all his lands and tene-ments, goods and chattels forever, and incur the pain of life and of member.   And if any prelate make execution of such summons, sentences, or excommunications, that his temporalties be taken and abide in the king's hands, till due redress and cor-rection be thereof made.   And if any person of less estate than a prelate, of what condition that he be, make such execution, he shall be taken, arrested, and put in prison, and have imprisonment, and make fine and ransom by the discretion of the king's council.

96. Statute of Maintenance and Liveries

(May, 1390.   French text and translation, 2 *S. R.* 74.   2 Stubbs, 509,
640, 3 Stubbs, 549.)

THE king to the sheriff of Kent, Greeting.
Whereas by the laws and customs of our realm, which we
are bound, by the oath made at our coronation, to preserve, all
our lieges within the same realm, as well poor as rich, ought
freely to sue, defend, receive and have justice and right, and the
accomplishment and execution thereof, in any our courts whatsoever and elsewhere, without being disturbed or oppressed by
maintenance, menace, or in any other manner; and now so it is,
that in many of our parliaments heretofore holden, and namely,
in the parliaments last holden at Cambridge and Westminster,
grievous complaint and great clamor hath been made unto us, as
well by the lords spiritual and temporal as by the commons of
our said realm, of great and outrageous oppressions and maintenances made to the damage of us and of our people, in divers
parts of the same realm, by divers maintainors, instigators, barrators, procurors, and embraceors of quarrels and inquests in the
country, whereof many are the more encouraged and bold in their
maintenance and evil deeds aforesaid, because that they be of
the retinue of lords and others of our said realm, with fees,
robes, and other liveries, called liveries of company; We have
ordained and straitly forbidden, by the advice of our great council, that no prelate, nor other man of holy Church, nor bachelor,
nor esquire, nor other of less estate, give any manner of such
livery called livery of company; and that no duke, earl, baron,
or banneret give such livery of company to knight or esquire, if
he be not retained with him for the term of his life for peace and
for war, by indenture, without fraud or evil device, or unless he
be a domestic and familiar abiding in his household; nor to any
valet called yeoman archer, nor to other of less estate than esquire,
if he be not, in like manner, a familiar abiding in his household.
And that all lords spiritual and temporal, and all others of what
condition or estate they be, shall utterly oust all such maintainors,
instigators, barrators, procurors, and embraceors of quarrels and
inquests from their fees, robes, and all manner of liveries, and
from their service, company, and retainer, without receiving
any such on their retainer, in any manner, in time to come ; and
that no lord spiritual nor temporal, nor any other, that hath or

shall have people of his retinue, shall suffer any that belong to
him, to be a maintainor, instigator, barrator, procuror, or embraceor of quarrels and inquests in the country, in any manner,
but shall put them away from his service and retinue, as afore is
said, as soon as it can be discovered; and that if any lord do oust
any such maintainor, instigator, barrator, procuror, or embraceor
from his company for this cause, that then no other lord do retain
or receive him of his retinue nor of his company in any manner;
and that none of our lieges, great nor small, of what condition or
estate he be, whether he be of the retinue of any lord, or other
person whatever who belongeth not to any retinue, shall not undertake any quarrel other than his own, nor shall maintain it, by
himself nor by other, privily nor openly; and that all those who
use and wear such livery called livery of company, contrary to
this our ordinance, shall leave them off altogether within ten
days after the proclamation of this same ordinance, without using
or wearing them any more afterwards; and that this our ordinance
be held and firmly kept, and duly executed, in all points, as well
by those who have or shall have people of their retinue, as by all
other persons, in that which to them belongeth touching the same
ordinance, upon pain of imprisonment, fine, and ransom, or of
being punished in other manner, according as shall be advised by
us and our council: wherefore we command and charge you that
incontinently, upon sight hereof, you cause to be published and
proclaimed this our ordinance in cities, boroughs, market towns,
and other public places within your bailiwick, as well within franchise as without, and do cause the same to be holden and duly
executed in all points.

Given under our great seal at Westminster, the twelfth day of
May.

By the king himself and the council.

Like writs are directed to the several sheriffs throughout
England.

97. Conveyances to the Uses of Religious Houses and other Corporations forbidden, etc.

(February, 1392. French text and translation, 2 *S. R.* 78. 2 Stubbs, 509, 638.)

* * * * * * * * *

3. ITEM, * * * It is declared, ordained and established
that of all manner of contracts, pleas, and quarrels, and all other

things rising within the bodies of counties, as well by land, as by water, * * * and also wreck of the sea, shall be tried determined, discussed, and remedied by the laws of the land, and not before nor by the admiral, nor his lieutenant in any wise. Nevertheless, of the death of a man, and of a mayhem done in great ships, being and hovering in the main stream of great rivers, only beneath the bridges of the same rivers most next to the sea, and in none other places of the same rivers, the admiral shall have cognizance, and also to arrest ships in the great fleets for the great voyages of the king and of the realm; saving always to the king all manner of forfeitures and profits thereof coming; and he shall have also jurisdiction upon the said fleets, during the said voyages only : saving always to the lords, cities, and boroughs their liberties and franchises.

5. Item, whereas it is contained in the statute *de religiosis*, * * * and now of late by subtile imagination, and by art, and device, some religious persons, parsons, vicars, and other spiritual persons, have entered in divers lands and tenements, which be adjoining to the churches, and of the same, by sufferance and assent of the tenants, have made churchyards, and by bulls of the bishop of Rome have caused the same to be dedicated and hallowed, and in them do make continually parochial burying without licence of the king and of the chief lords; therefore it is declared in this parliament, that this is manifestly within the compass of the said statute. And moreover it is agreed and assented, that all they that be possessed by feoffment, or by any other manner, to the use of religious people, or other spiritual persons, of lands and tenements, fees, advowsons, or any manner other possessions whatsoever, to amortise them, and whereof the said religious and spiritual persons take the profits, that betwixt this and the feast of Saint Michael next coming, they shall cause them to be amortised by the licence of the king and of the lords, or else that they shall sell and aliene them to some other use between this and the said feast, upon pain to be forfeited to the king, and to the lords, according to the form of the said statute of religious, as lands purchased by religious people : and that from henceforth no such purchase be made, so that such religious or other spiritual person take thereof the profits, as afore is said, upon pain aforesaid; and that this same statute extend and be observed of all lands, tenements, fees, advowsons, and other possessions, purchased or to be purchased to the use of guilds or fraternities. And moreover it is assented, because mayors, bailiffs, and commons of cities, boroughs, and other towns which

have a perpetual commonalty, and others which have offices perpetual be as perpetual as people of religion, that from henceforth
they shall not purchase to them, and to their commons or office,
upon the pain contained in the said statute *de religiosis;* * * *

    *   *   *   *   *   *   *   *   *

12. Item, * * * it is agreed and assented, that from henceforth
none of the king's subjects be compelled, neither by any mean
constrained, to come nor to appear before the council of any lord
or lady, to answer for his freehold, nor any for anything touching
his freehold, nor for any other thing, real or personal, that belongeth to the law of the land in any manner: and if any find himself
grieved in time to come, contrary to this ordinance and agreement, he may complain to the chancellor for the time being, and
he shall give him remedy.

98. The Second Statute of Praemunire

(May, 1393.   16 Richard II. c. 5.   French text and translation, 2 *S. R.*
84. 2 Stubbs, 435, 509, 3 Stubbs, 341, 363.)

5. ITEM, whereas the commons of the realm in this present
parliament have showed to our redoubted lord the king, grievously complaining, that whereas the said our lord the king,
and all his liege people, ought of right, and of old time were
wont to sue in the king's court, to recover their presentments to
churches, prebends, and other benefices of holy Church, to the
which they had right to present, the cognizance of the plea of
which suit belongeth only to the king's court of the old right of
his crown, used and approved in the time of all his progenitors
kings of England; and when judgment shall be given in the same
court upon such a plea and suit, the archbishops, bishops, and
other spiritual persons which have institution of such benefices
within their jurisdiction, be bound, and have made execution of
such judgments by the king's commandments of all the time
aforesaid without interruption, for another, lay-person, may not
make such execution, and also be bound of right to make execution of many other of the king's commandments, of which right
the crown of England hath been peaceably seised, as well in the
time of our said lord the king that now is, as in the time of all
his progenitors till this day: but now of late divers processes be
made by the holy father the pope and censures of excommunication upon certain bishops of England, because they have made

execution of such commandments, to the open disherison of the
said crown, and destruction of the regalty of our said lord the
king, his law, and all his realm, if remedy be not provided: and
also it is said, and a common clamor is made, that the said father
the pope hath ordained and purposed to translate some prelates
of the same realm, some out of the realm, and some from one
bishopric into another within the same realm, without the king's
assent and knowledge, and without the assent of the prelates,
which so shall be translated, which prelates be much profitable
and necessary to our said lord the king, and to all his realm; by
which translations, if they should be suffered, the statutes of the
realm should be defeated and made void; and his said liege sages
of his council, without his assent, and against his will, carried
away and gotten out of his realm, and the substance and treasure
of the realm shall be carried away, and so the realm destitute as
well of council as of substance, to the final destruction of the
same realm; and so the crown of England, which hath been so
free at all times, that it hath been in subjection to no realm, but
immediately subject to God in all things touching the regalty of
the same crown, and to none other, should be submitted to the
pope, and the laws and statutes of the realm by him defeated and
avoided at his will, in perpetual destruction of the sovereignty of
the king our lord, his crown, his regalty, and of all his realm,
which God defend: and moreover, the commons aforesaid say,
that the said things so attempted be clearly against the king's
crown and his regalty, used and approved of the time of all his
progenitors; wherefore they and all the liege commons of the
same realm will stand with our said lord the king, and his said
crown, and his regalty, in the cases aforesaid, and in all other
cases attempted against him, his crown, and his regalty in all
points, to live and to die; and moreover they pray the king, and
him require by way of justice, that he would examine all the
lords in the parliament, as well spiritual as temporal severally,
and all the states of the parliament, how they think of the cases
aforesaid, which be so openly against the king's crown, and in
derogation of his regalty, and how they will stand in the same
cases with our lord the king, in upholding the rights of the said
crown and regalty: Whereupon the lords temporal so demanded,
have answered every one by himself, that the cases aforesaid be
clearly in derogation of the king's crown, and of his regalty, as it
is well known, and hath been of a long time known, and that they
will stand with the same crown and regalty in these cases specially,
and in all other cases which shall be attempted against the same

crown and regalty in all points, with all their power: and moreover it was demanded of the lords spiritual there being, and the
procurators of others being absent, their advice and will in all
these cases; which lords, that is to say, the archbishops, bishops,
and other prelates, being in the said parliament severally examined, making protestations, that it is not their mind to say, nor
affirm, that our holy father the pope may not excommunicate
bishops, nor that he may make translation of prelates after law
of holy Church, answered and said, that if any execution of processes made in the king's court, as before, be made by any, and
censures of excommunications be made against any bishops of
England, or any other of the king's liege people, for that they
have made execution of such commandments, and that if any
executions of such translations be made of any prelates of the
same realm, which lords be very profitable and necessary to our
said lord the king and to his said realm, or that his sage men of
his council, without his assent, and against his will, be removed
and carried out of the realm, so that the substance and treasure
of the realm may be consumed, that the same is against the king
and his crown, as it is contained in the petition before named:
and likewise the same procurators, every one by himself examined upon the said matters, have answered and said in the same,
and for their lords, as the said bishops have said and answered,
and that the said lords spiritual will and ought to stand with the
king in these cases lawfully in maintaining of his crown, and in
all other cases touching his crown and his regalty, as they be
bound by their liegeance: whereupon our said lord the king, by
the assent aforesaid, and at the request of his said commons,
hath ordained and established, that if any purchase or pursue, or
cause to be purchased or pursued in the court of Rome, or elsewhere, any such translations, processes, and sentences of excommunications, bulls, instruments, or any other things whatsoever,
which touch the king our lord, against him, his crown, and his
regalty, or his realm, as is aforesaid, and they which bring them
within the realm, or them receive, or make thereof notification
or any other execution whatsoever within the same realm or without, that they, their notaries, procurators, maintainors, abettors,
fautors, and counsellors, shall be put out of the king's protection, and their lands and tenements, goods and chattels, forfeit
to our lord the king; and that they be attached by their bodies,
if they may be found, and brought before the king and his council, there to answer to the cases aforesaid, or that process be
made against them by *præmunire facias*, in manner as it is

ordained in other statutes of provisors, and other which do sue
in the court of another in derogation of the regalty of our lord
the king.

———————◆———————

99. New Definition of Treason

(September, 1397.   French text and translation, 2 *S. R.* 94.   2 Stubbs,
520, 3 Stubbs, 537.)

*   *   *   *   *   *   *   *   *

3. ITEM, it is ordained and stablished, that every **man,**
which compasseth or purposeth the death of the king, **or**
to depose him, or to render up his liege homage, or he **that**
raiseth people and rideth against the king to make war within his
realm, and of that be duly attainted and judged in the parliament, shall be judged as a traitor of high treason against the
crown; and he for him and his heirs shall forfeit all the lands,
tenements and possessions, liberties and all other hereditaments,
which he hath or any other hath to his use, or had the day of the
treason done, as well in fee tail as in fee simple, to the king and
his heirs, as well such lands holden of other as of himself forever;
and also such possession as other have to his use. *   *   *

*   *   *   *   *   *   *   *   *

———————◆———————

100. Delegation of Powers by Parliament of Shrewsbury

(1398.   French original, 3 *R. P.* 368, No. 74.   Translation by Editors.
2 Stubbs, 522.)

ITEM, the same Thursday, the commons prayed the king, as
they had divers petitions before them both for special persons and others, neither read nor answered, and also several other
matters and affairs which had been moved in the presence of the
king, which, because of the shortness of the time, could not well
be satisfactorily determined at present: That it should please the
king to give full power to certain lords, and to other persons
whom it should please him, to examine, answer, and determine
the said petitions and the matters and affairs aforesaid and all
the dependencies of the same.   To which prayer the king assented.
And thereupon, with the authority and assent of parliament, were

ordained and appointed John duke of Lancaster, Edmond duke of York, Edward duke of Albemarle, Thomas duke of Surrey, John duke of Exeter, John marquis of Dorset, Roger earl of March, John earl of Salisbury, Henry earl of Northumberland, Thomas earl of Gloucester, Thomas earl of Worcester, and Thomas earl of Wiltshire, or six of them; John Bussey, Henry Green, John Russell, Richard Chelmswick, Robert Teye, and John Golafre, knights coming for the parliament, or three of them, to examine, answer, and plainly determine both all the said petitions and the matters contained in them, and all other matter and affairs moved in the presence of the king and all the dependences of the same not determined, according as it seemed best to them by their good advice and discretion in this matter by authority of the said parliament.

———◆———

101. Grant of Subsidy for Life to Richard II by Parliament of Shrewsbury

(1398.   French original, 3 *R. P.* 368, No. 75.   Translation by Editors.
2 Stubbs, 522.)

ITEM, the same day, the commons of the realm, with assent of the lords spiritual and temporal, granted to the king the subsidy of wools, leather, and woolfells for the term of his life, and one fifteenth, and tenth, and half a fifteenth and half a tenth, in the following manner and form.

To the reverence of God and of Holy Church, and for the good and peace of the realm, and for the full affection and complete confidence which the commons of the realm have in our very redoubtable lord the king, the said commons with the assent of the lords spiritual and temporal, at the parliament summoned and commenced at Westminster and adjourned to Shrewsbury, have granted to our said lord the king the subsidy of wools, leather, and woolfells leaving the kingdom which the king takes at present, to have during the life of our said lord the king. And also six shillings, eight pence on the sack of wool and of leather, and woolfells, to be levied from foreigners over and above that accustomed to be paid for a sack of wool before this time: On protest that this grant be not considered either a precedent or example in the time of the succeeding kings of England in time to come. And also, for the great love and full affection which our said lord the king has for his said commons, the said

commons with assent of the lords spiritual and temporal, have
granted to our said lord the king one entire fifteenth and tenth,
and one half-fifteenth and half-tenth, to be levied on the people
in the manner customary before this time, to the terms underwritten: that is to say, one half-fifteenth and half-tenth, in the
month of St. Michael next to come, and another half-fifteenth
and half-tenth, on the fifteenth of Easter then next ensuing; and
another half-fifteenth and half-tenth on the fifteenth of St.
Michael thereafter next ensuing.

102. Resignation of Richard II

(1399.   Latin original, 3 R. P. 416.   Translation by Editors.   2 Stubbs,
528, 529, 3 Stubbs, 14, 528.)

IN God's name, Amen.   I, Richard, by the grace of God, king
of England and France, and lord of Ireland, absolve all archbishops and bishops of the said kingdoms and lordships, and all
other prelates whatsoever of secular or regular churches of whatsoever dignity, rank, state, or condition they may be, and dukes,
marquises, earls, barons, knights, vassals, and vavassors and all
my liege men, clerical or secular by whatsoever name they are
known, from the oath of fealty and homage and all others whatsoever made to me and from every bond of allegiance, royalty
and lordship with which they have been or are bound by oath to
me, or bound in any other way whatsoever; and these and their
heirs and successors in perpetuity from these bonds and oaths and
all other bonds whatsoever, I relieve, free, and excuse; absolved,
excused and freed as far as pertains to my person, I release them
from every performance of their oath which could follow from
their promises or from any of them; and all royal dignity and
majesty and royalty and also the lordship and power in the said
realms and lordship; and my other lordships and possessions or
whatsoever others belong to me in any way, under whatsoever
name they are known, which are in the aforesaid realms and
lordships or elsewhere; and all right and color of right, and
title, possessions, and lordship which I have ever had, still have
or shall be able to have in any way, in these or any of them, or
to these with their rights and everything pertaining to them or
dependent upon them in any way whatsoever; from these or any
of them; and also the command, government, and administration of such realms and lordships; and all and every kind of

M

absolute and mixed sovereignty and jurisdiction in these realms and lordships belonging to me or to belong to me; the name and honor and royal right and title of king, freely, voluntarily, unequivocally, and absolutely, and in the best fashion, wise, and form possible, in these writings I renounce, and resign as a whole, and release in word and deed, and yield my place in them, and retire from them forever.

Saving to my successors, kings of England, in the realms and lordships and all other premises in perpetuity, the rights belonging or to belong to them, in them or in any of them, I confess, acknowledge, consider, and truly judge from sure knowledge that I in the rule and government of the said realms and lordships and all pertaining to them have been and am wholly insufficient and useless, and because of my notorious deserts am not unworthy to be deposed. And I swear on these holy gospels touched bodily by me that I will never contravene these premises of renunciation, resignation, demise and surrender, nor will I impugn them in any way, in deed or in word by myself or by another or others, or as far as in me lies permit them to be contravened or impugned publicly or secretly, but I will hold this renunciation, resignation, demise, and surrender unalterable and acceptable and I will keep it firmly and observe it in whole and in every part; so may God help me and these holy scriptures of God. I, Richard, the aforesaid king, subscribe myself with my own hand.

----◆----

103. Deposition of Richard II and Election of Henry IV

(1399.   Latin and English original, 3 R. P. 422.   Translation by Editors.
2 Stubbs, 528, 531, 3 Stubbs, 13, 14.)

51. AND since it seemed to all these estates, after they had made examination separately and also together, that these crimes and shortcomings were sufficient and notorious enough for the deposition of the said king, having considered his confession concerning his own insufficiency and the other things contained in the said renunciation and surrender openly set forth, all the abovesaid estates unanimously agreed that for these abundant reasons they should proceed to the deposition of the said king, for the greater safety and tranquillity of the people and for the security of the realm.

Then the aforesaid estate unanimously and amicably appointed certain commissioners, namely the bishop of St. Asaph, the abbot of Glastonbury, the earl of Gloucester, the lord of Berkeley, Thomas Erpingham and Thomas Gray, knights, and Wm. Thirning, justice, and then publicly deputed them to carry out the sentence of such deposition and to depose the said king Richard from all the dignity, majesty and honor of a king, in the place of and with the name and authority of all the aforesaid estates, as had been observed in like cases of the ancient custom of the realm. And thereupon the said commissioners, taking upon themselves the burden of such a commission and seating themselves before the said royal throne as the tribunal, some deliberation having been held previously respecting these things, brought the sentence of deposition reduced to writing, in the place of and with the name and authority of the aforesaid and they had the said sentence of the will and command of the commissioners, read and delivered by the said bishop of St. Asaph, their fellow commissioner and colleague, in the following words:

52. In the name of God, Amen. We, John bishop of St. Asaph, John abbot of Glastonbury, Thomas earl of Gloucester, Thomas lord Berkeley, Thomas Erpingham and Thomas Gray, knights, and William Thirning, justice, for the peers and nobles of the realm of England spiritual and temporal, and for the commons of the realm, representing all the estates of this realm, commissioners specially deputed for the writings below, seated before the tribunal, after having considered the very many perjuries, and the cruelty, and many other crimes of the said Richard, which he has committed and perpetrated in respect to his rule in the above mentioned realms and lordship throughout the time of his rule and having openly and publicly proposed, shown, and declared them in the presence of the said estates; which have been and are so public, notorious, plainly manifest, and famous that none have been able or are able to be concealed by subterfuge; and also by the confession of the aforesaid Richard who acknowledges and considers and truly judges from his own sure knowledge that he has been and is utterly insufficient and useless in the rule and government of the aforesaid realms and lordship and those things pertaining to them, and on account of his notorious deserts is not unworthy to be deposed, which was set forth previously by Richard himself, and published according to his will and command in the presence of the said estates, and by them made known and explained to the public, and diligent deliberation having previously been held concerning

these and all things involved in this business in the presence of the aforesaid estates and by us, in the representation, name and authority committed to us in the matter, for abundant reason and as a precaution for the rule and government of the said realms and lordship and the rights pertaining to them, we pronounce, decree, and declare that Richard himself has been and is useless, incapable, utterly insufficient and unworthy; and because of the circumstances stated above and in consequence of them we pronounce, decree and declare him worthy to be deposed from all royal dignity and honor, if any dignity and honor of this sort remain to him, and by a like precaution, we depose him by our definite sentence in all and each of these writings. To the lords, archbishops, bishops and prelates, dukes, marquisses, earls, knights, vassals and vavassors, and other men of the said realms and lordship, and of other places subject to the said realms and lordship, their subjects and liegemen whomsoever, it is expressly forbidden that any one of them should in any way submit or attend to the said Richard as if he were king or lord of the aforesaid realms and lordship.

53. Moreover in addition the said estates wishing that nothing should be lacking which can be and ought to be required concerning these circumstances set down above, after having considered separately, appointed the same persons formerly nominated commissioners to be their procurators jointly and separately, to bear and to restore to the said king Richard the homage and fealty formerly rendered to him and to announce all the circumstances touching this deposition and renunciation, if it should be necessary. And immediately, as it was evident from the circumstances set down above and their occasion that the realm of England with its appurtenances was vacant, the aforesaid Henry duke of Lancaster rising from his place, and standing erect so that he might be able to be well seen by the people and protecting himself humbly with the sign of the cross on his forehead and breast, after first calling upon the name of Christ, claimed the aforesaid English realm inasmuch as it was vacant, together with the crown and all its parts and appurtenances in his mother tongue in this form of words:

In the name of the Father, Son, and Holy Ghost, I, Henry of Lancaster, challenge this realm of England and the crown with all the members and the appurtenances, as I that am descended by right line of the blood coming from the good lord king Henry III, and through that right, that God of his grace hath sent me with help of my kin and of my friends to recover it: the

which realm was in point to be undone for default of governance
and undoing of the good laws.

54. After the lord spiritual and temporal and all the estates
there present had considered this demand and claim singly and
jointly what was to be judged concerning that demand and claim,
the said estate with all the people, without any difficulty or
delay, unanimously agreed that the aforesaid duke should reign
over them. And as soon as the said king had showed to the
estates of the realm the signet of king Richard, delivered to him
as a token of good will as is clearly set forth, the aforesaid archbishop, taking the said king Henry by his right hand, led him
to the aforesaid royal throne. And after the said king on bended
knees before the said throne had prayed for a short time, the
said archbishop of Canterbury, joining to himself the aforesaid
archbishop of York, took the said king and caused him to sit on
the aforesaid royal throne, while the people applauded vigorously
with excessive joy.

———◆———

104. Act for the Security of the Subject and in Repeal of the Acts of the Parliament of Shrewsbury

(October, 1399.   French text and translation, 2 *S. R.* 111.   3 Stubbs, 19.)

HENRY, by the grace of God, king of England, and of France,
and lord of Ireland, to the laud and honor of God, and
reverence of Holy Church, for to nourish unity, peace, and concord in all parts within the realm of England, and for the redress
and recovery of the same realm, which now of late hath been
dangerously put to great ruin, mischief, and desolation; of the
assent of the prelates, dukes, earls, and barons, and at the instance
and special request of the commons of the same realm, assembled
at his parliament holden at Westminster in the feast of St. Faith
the Virgin, the first year of his reign, hath caused to be ordained,
and established certain ordinances and statutes in form as hereafter followeth.

1. First, that Holy Church have and enjoy all her rights,
liberties, and franchises, entirely and without inblemishing:
and that the great charter, and the charter of the forest, and
other good ordinances and statutes made in the time of his noble
progenitors, and not repealed, be firmly holden and kept in all
points: and that the peace within this realm be holden and kept,

so that all his lawful liege people and subjects may from hence-forth safely and peaceably go, come, and dwell, according to the laws and usages of the same realm; and that good justice and even right be done to every person.

2. Item, that no lord spiritual nor temporal nor other person, of what estate or condition that he be, which came with our sovereign lord the king that now is into the realm of England, nor none other persons, whatsoever they be, then dwelling within the same realm, and which came to the king in aid of him to pursue them that were against the good intent of our sovereign lord the king and the common profit of the realm, in which pursuit Richard late king of England the second after the conquest was pursued, taken, and put in ward, and yet remaineth in ward, be impeached, grieved nor vexed, in person nor in goods, in the king's court nor in the court of none other for the pursuit of the said king, taking and withholding of his body, nor for the pursuit of any other, taking of persons and chattels or of the death of a man, or any other thing done in the said pursuit, from the day that the said king that now is arrived, till the day of the coronation of our said sovereign lord king Henry. And the intent of the king is not that offenders, which committed trespasses or other offences out of the said pursuit without special warrant shall be aided or have any advantage of this statute; but that they be thereof answerable at the common law.

3. Item, whereas the Monday next after the feast of the Exaltation of the Holy Cross, the xxi year of the reign of the said late King Richard, a parliament was summoned and holden at Westminster, and from thence adjourned to Shrewsbury, at which town a certain power was committed by authority of the parliament, to certain persons to proceed upon certain articles and matters comprised in the roll of the parliament thereof made, as by the same roll may appear, in which parliament, and also by authority foresaid, divers statutes, judgments, ordinances, and stablishments were made, ordained, and given erroneously and right sorrowfully; in great disherison and final destruction and undoing of many honorable lords and other liege people of the realm, and of their heirs forever: our sovereign lord the king, considering the great mischiefs aforesaid, by the advice and assent of all the lords spiritual and temporal, and of all the commonalty, hath judged the said parliament, holden the said xxi year, and the authority thereof given, as afore is said, with all the circumstances and dependents thereupon to be of no force nor value: and that the same parliament, with the authority afore-

said, and all the circumstances and dependents thereupon, be wholly reversed, revoked, voided, undone, repealed, and annulled forever.

*　*　*　*　*　*　*　*　*

105. Haxey's Case

(1399. French original, 3 *R. P.* 434, No. 104. Translation by Editors. 2 Stubbs, 516, 624.)

ITEM, as at the parliament held at Westminster on the day of St. Vincent, in the twentieth year of King Richard, for the honor and profit of the said king and all the realm. Thomas Haxey, clerk, presented a bill to the commons of the said parliament; for which bill, by the wish of the said king, the said Thomas was adjudged a traitor, and forfeited all that he had, contrary to the right and the custom which had been used before in parliament, in destruction of the customs of the commons. May it please our very gracious lord the king in this present parliament to amend that judgment and make it void as erroneous; and to reinstate the said Thomas fully in his rank, estate, goods, and chattels, ferms, annuities, pensions, lands, tenements, rents, office, advowsons, and possessions whatsoever with their appurtenances and that he be able to enter upon the aforesaid ferms, annuities, lands, tenements, rents, office, advowsons, and possessions and to hold them as he held them the day of the drawing up of the said bill: even the judgment or any declaration by this cause, gift. or grant of these goods, chattels, ferms, annuities, pensions, lands, tenements, rents, offices, advowsons, and possessions, or of any of them, to any other person made in any way since the said judgment notwithstanding. As well in fulfillment of the right as for the saving of the liberties of the said commons.

The king wills, by the advice and assent of all the lords spiritual and temporal, that the judgment rendered against Thomas Haxey, clerk, in the parliament held at Westminster in the twentieth year of the late king Richard, be wholly annulled, reversed, repealed and made void and held of no force or effect; and that the said Thomas be reinstated in his name and reputation, and made and held an able person such as he was before the said judgment was rendered — as in the record made thereof and enrolled before in this roll of parliament as appears more at length.

106.   The Statute "De Haeretico"

(1401.   Latin text and translation, 2 *S. R.* 125.   3 Stubbs, 33, 369.)

*   *   *   *   *   *   *   *   *

15. ITEM, whereas it is showed to our sovereign lord the king on the behalf of the prelates and clergy of his realm of England in this present parliament, that although the catholic faith builded upon Christ, and by his apostles and the holy church sufficiently determined, declared, and approved, hath been hitherto by good and holy and most noble progenitors and predecessors of our sovereign lord the king in the said realm amongst all the realms of the world, most devoutly observed, and the church of England by his said most noble progenitors and ancestors, to the honor of God and of the whole realm aforesaid, laudably endowed, and in her rights and liberties sustained, without that that the same faith or the said church was hurt or grievously oppressed, or else perturbed by any perverse doctrine or wicked heretical or erroneous opinions; yet nevertheless divers false and perverse people of a certain new sect, of the said faith, of the sacraments of the church, and the authority of the same damnably thinking, and against the law of God and of the church usurping the office of preaching, do perversely and maliciously in divers places within the said realm under the color of dissembled holiness, preach and teach these days openly and privily divers new doctrines, and wicked heretical and erroneous opinions, contrary to the same faith and blessed determinations of the holy church; and of such sect and wicked doctrine and opinions, they make unlawful conventicles and confederacies, they hold and exercise schools, they make and write books, they do wickedly instruct and inform people, and as much as they may excite and stir them to sedition and insurrection, and maketh great strife and division among the people, and other enormities horrible to be heard daily do perpetrate and commit, in subversion of the said catholic faith and doctrine of the holy church, in diminution of divine worship, and also in destruction of the estates, rights and liberties of the said church of England; by which sect and wicked and false preachings, doctrines, and opinions of the said false and perverse people, not only most greatest peril of the souls, but also many more other hurts, slanders, and perils, which God prohibit, might come to this realm, unless it be the more plentifully and speedily holpen by the

king's majesty in this behalf; especially since the diocesans of
the said realm cannot by their jurisdiction spiritual, without aid
of the said royal majesty, sufficiently correct the said false and
perverse people, nor refrain their malice, because the said false
and perverse people do go from diocese to diocese, and will not
appear before the said diocesans, but the same diocesans and
their jurisdiction spiritual, and the keys of the church with the
censures of the same, do utterly contemn and despise; and so
their wicked preachings and doctrines doth from day to day
continue and exercise, to the utter destruction of all order and
rule of right and reason.   Upon which novelties and excesses
above rehearsed, the prelates and clergy aforesaid, and also the
commons of the said realm being in the same parliament, have
prayed our sovereign lord the king, that his royal highness would
vouchsafe in the said parliament to provide a convenient remedy;
the same our sovereign lord the king graciously considering the
premises, and also the laudable steps of his said most noble progenitors and ancestors, for the conservation of the said catholic
faith, and sustentation of the said divine worship, and also the
safeguard of the estate, rights, and liberties of the said church of
England, to the laud of God, and merit of our said sovereign
lord the king, and prosperity and honor of all his said realm,
and for the eschewing of such dissensions, divisions, hurts,
slanders, and perils, in time to come, and that this wicked sect,
preachings, doctrines and opinions should from henceforth cease
and be utterly destroyed, by the assent of the great lords and
noble persons of the same realm, being in the said parliament,
hath granted, stablished, and ordained, from henceforth firmly
to be observed, that none within the said realm, or any other
dominions, subject to his royal majesty, presume to preach
openly or privily, without the license of the diocesan of the same
place first required and obtained, curates in their own churches,
and persons hitherto privileged, and other of the canon law
granted, only except; nor that none from henceforth anything
preach, hold, teach, or instruct openly or privily, or make or
write any book contrary to the catholic faith or determination of
the holy church, nor of such sect and wicked doctrines and opinions shall make any conventicles, or in any wise hold or exercise
schools; and also that none from henceforth in any wise favor
such preacher, or maker of any such and like conventicles, or
person holding or exercising schools, or making or writing such
books, or so teaching, informing, or exciting the people, nor any
of them maintain or any wise sustain; and that all and singular

having such books or any writings of such wicked doctrine and opinions, shall really with effect deliver or cause to be delivered all such books and writings to the diocesan of the same place within forty days from the time of the proclamation of this ordinance and statute. And if any person or persons, of whatsoever sex, estate, or condition that he or they be, from henceforth do or attempt against the said royal ordinance and statute aforesaid in the premises or in any of them, or such books in the form aforesaid do not deliver, then the diocesan of the same place in his diocese, such person or persons in this behalf defamed or evidently suspected, and every of them, may by the authority of the said ordinance and statute cause to be arrested, and under safe custody in his prisons to be detained, till he or they of the articles laid to him or them in this behalf, do canonically purge him or themselves, or else such wicked sect, preachings, doctrines, and heretical and erroneous opinions do adjure, according as the laws of the church do demand and require : so that the said diocesan by himself or his commissaries do openly and judicially proceed against such persons so arrested, and remaining under his safe custody to all effect of the law, and determine that same business according to the canonical decrees within three months after the said arrest, any lawful impediment ceasing. And if any person in any case above expressed, be before the diocesan of the place or his commissaries canonically convict, then the same diocesan may cause to be kept in his prison the said persons so convict for the manner of his default, and after the quality of the offense according and as long as to his discretion shall seem expedient; and moreover to put the same person to pay to our sovereign lord the king a pecuniary fine; except in cases where he, according to the canonical decrees, ought to be left to the secular court, according as the same fine shall seem competent to the diocesan, for the manner and quality of the offense; in which case the same diocesan shall be bound to certify the king of the same fine in his exchequer by his letters patents sealed with his seal, to the effect that such fine by the king's authority may be required and levied to his use of the goods of the same person so convict. And if any person within the said realm and dominions, upon the said wicked preachings, doctrines, opinions, schools, and heretical and erroneous informations, or any of them, be before the diocesan of the same place or his commissaries convict by sentence, and the same wicked sect, preachings, doctrines, and opinions, schools and informations, do refuse duly to adjure, or by the diocesan of the same

place or his commissaries, after the abjuration made by the same
person be pronounced relapsed, so that according to the holy
canons he ought to be left to the secular court, whereupon credence shall be given to the diocesan of the same place, or to his
commissaries in this behalf, then the sheriff of the county of the
same place, and mayor and sheriffs or sheriff, or mayor and bailiffs of the city, town and borough of the same county next to the
same diocesan or the said commissaries, shall be personally present in preferring of such sentences, by the same diocesan or his
commissaries against such persons, and every of them, when they
by the same diocesan or his commissaries shall be required; and
they the same persons and every of them, after such sentence
promulgate, shall receive, and them before the people in an high
place cause to be burnt; that such punishment may strike in fear
to the minds of other, whereby no such wicked doctrine and
heretical and erroneous opinions, nor their authors and fautors in
the said realm and dominions against the catholic faith, Christian
law, and determination of the holy church, which God prohibit,
be sustained or in any wise suffer: in which all and singular the
premises concerning the said ordinance and statute, the sheriffs,
mayors and bailiffs of the said counties, cities, boroughs, and
towns, shall be attending, aiding and supporting to the said
diocesans and their commissaries.

*   *   *   *   *   *   *   *   *

———◆———

107. Sir Arnold Savage asks for the Privileges of Parliament

(1401.   French original, 3 *R. P.* 455, No. 8.   Translation by Editors.
3 Stubbs, 29.)

SATURDAY, the twenty-second of January, the commons of
the realm presented to the king Sir Arnold Savage as their
speaker and procurator in parliament whom the king kindly
accepted.   And then the said Sir Arnold humbly requested the
king, that he might make protestation, that, if he should say anything through ignorance, negligence or in any other way which
was not agreed to by his companions or which should be displeas-
ing to the king, or too little through lack of wisdom, or too
much through folly or ignorance that the king would excuse him
therefor, and that it might be corrected and amended by his said

companions: and that the said commons should have their liberty
in parliament as they had had before this time; and that this
protestation should be recorded in the roll of parliament; which
protestation seemed honest and reasonable to the king and he
agreed to it.   And after that, the said Sir Arnold, in order to
have in memory the pronouncement of parliament which was
pronounced by the said Sir Wm. Thirning on his own authority,
declared in substance before the king and his lords in parliament
the reasons for the summons of the said parliament, to his knowledge clearly and briefly.   And besides, he prayed our said lord the
king on the part of the said commons that on the matters brought
before the said commons in this present parliament they should
have good advice and deliberation without being suddenly called
upon to reply to the most important matters at the end of parliament, as had been done before this time.   To which reply was
made by the king through the earl of Worcester that it was not
the intention of the king to follow this order of action and that
he did not imagine any such subtlety, also that they should have
good advice and deliberation from time to time as the need
demanded.

---

108. Members excused for Matters spoken in Parliament

(1401.   French original, 3 *R. P.* 456, No. 11.   Translation by Editors.
3 Stubbs, 30.)

ITEM, on the same day the said commons showed to our lord
the king how on certain matters moved among them, it might
happen in the future that certain of their companions, out of
complaisance to the king, and for their own advancement, should
recount to our said lord the king such matters before they had
been determined and discussed or agreed upon among the commons, by reason of which the said lord our king might be grievously moved against the said commons or some of them; wherefore
they most humbly pray our lord the king, not to receive any such
person to recount such matters nor to give him hearing nor any
faith nor credence to such a person.   To which answer was made
by the king that it was his will that the said commons should
have deliberation and advice, to discuss and treat of all matters
among themselves, in order to bring them to a better end and
conclusion, in so far as they know how, for the welfare and honor

of himself and of all his realm.   And that he would not hear any
such person or give him credence, before such matters had been
shown to the king, by the advice and with the assent of all the
commons, according to the purport of their said prayer.

---

109. Responses to the Petitions of the Commons

(1401.   French original, 3 *R. P.* 458, No. 23.   Translation by Editors.
3 Stubbs, 30.)

ITEM, the same Saturday, the said commons pointed out to our
said lord the king, that, as in divers parliaments before this
time, their common petitions had not been answered before they
had made their grant of some aid or subsidy to our lord the king;
therefore they prayed our said lord the king that for the great
convenience and comfort of the said commons it should please
our lord the king to grant to the said commons that they should
be able to learn the responses to their said petitions before any
such grant was made.   To which response was made that on this
matter the king wished to confer with the lords of parliament and
to do in regard to it what it should seem best to do with the
advice of the said lords.   And then afterwards, that is to say on
the last day of the parliament, response was made that this
manner of deed had not been seen nor used in the time of any
of his ancestors or predecessors, that they should have any response
to their petitions or knowledge of the same before they had taken
up and completed all the other business of parliament, be it to
make any grant or otherwise.   And therefore the king did not
wish in any way to change the good customs and usages made
and used in former times.

---

110. Act to regulate the Succession

(1406.   French text and translation, 2 *S. R.* 151.   3 Stubbs, 58.)

*   *   *   *   *   *   *   *   *

2. ITEM, at the request and of the assent of the said lords
and commons, in the said parliament, it is ordained and
established, that the inheritance of the crown, and of the
realms of England and France, and of all the other dominions of

our said lord the king beyond the sea, with all the appurtenances, shall be settled and remain in the person of the same our lord the king, and in the heirs of his body begotten; and especially at the request and of the assent aforesaid, it is ordained and established, pronounced, decreed, and declared, that the lord the prince Henry eldest son to our said lord the king, be heir apparent to the same our lord the king, to succeed him in the said crown, realms and dominions, to have them with all the appurtenances after the decease of the same our lord the king, to him and his heirs of his body begotten; and if he die without heir of his body begotten, then all the said crown, realms and dominions, with all the appurtenances, shall remain to the Lord Thomas, second son of our said lord the king, and to the heirs of his body begotten; and if he die without issue of his body, that then all the said crown, realms and dominions, with all the appurtenances, shall remain to the Lord John, the third son of our said lord the king, and to the heirs of his body begotten; and if he die without heir of his body begotten, that then all the foresaid crown, realms and dominions, with all the appurte- nances, shall remain to the Lord Humphrey, the fourth son of our said lord the king, and the heirs of his body begotten.

* * * * * * * * *

---

111. The Manner of electing Knights of the Shire

(1406. French and Latin text and translation, 2 *S. R.* 156. 3 Stubbs, 58, 264, 417.)

* * * * * * * * *

15. ITEM, our lord the king, at the grievous complaint of his commons of the undue election of the knights of counties for the parliament, which be sometime made of affection of sheriffs, and otherwise against the form of the writs directed to the sheriff, to the great slander of the counties, and hindrance of the business of the commonalty of the said county; our sov- ereign lord the king, willing therein to provide remedy, by the assent of the lords spiritual and temporal, and of all the com- monalty of the realm in this present parliament, hath ordained and established, that from henceforth the elections of such knights shall be made in the form as followeth; that is to say, that

at the next county [court], to be holden after the delivery of the
writ of the parliament, proclamation shall be made in the full
county of the day and place of the parliament, and that all they
that be there present, as well suitors duly summoned for the same
cause, as other, shall attend to the election of their knights for
the parliament; and then in the full county they shall proceed
to the election freely and indifferently, notwithstanding any
request or commandment to the contrary; and after that they be
chosen, the names of the persons so chosen, be they present or
absent, shall be written in an indenture under the seals of all
them that did choose them, and tacked to the same writ of the
parliament; which indenture, so sealed and tacked, shall be
holden for the sheriff's return of the said writ, touching the
knights of the shires.   And that in the writs of the parliament to
be made hereafter, this clause shall be put: and thy election in
thy full county made, distinctly and openly, under thy seal and
the seals of those who were present at that election, to us in our
chancery, at the day and place in the writ contained, certify
without delay.

*   *   *   *   *   *   *   *   *

112. Commons to originate Money Bills

(1407.   French original, 3 *R. P.* 611.   Translation by Editors.   3 Stubbs, 62.)

21. ITEM, on Friday, the second day of December, which
was the last day of parliament, the commons came before the
king and the lords in parliament and there by command of
the king a schedule of indemnity for a certain dispute between
the lords and commons was read; and thereupon it was commanded by our said lord the king, that the said schedule be
recorded in the roll of parliament; of which schedule the tenor
was as follows. — Be it remembered that on Monday the twenty-
first day of November, the king our sovereign lord being in the
council room within the abbey of Gloucester, there being in his
presence the lords spiritual and temporal assembled at this present parliament, there was a discussion among them on the state
of the realm and the defence of the same in order to resist the
malice of the enemies who on every coast seemed to be harassing
the said realm and the faithful subjects of the same, and no man
would be able to resist that malice, if for the safe-guard and

defence of the said realm, our sovereign lord the king aforesaid had not some notable aid and subsidy granted to him in this present parliament. And thereupon it was demanded of the aforesaid lords by way of question, what aid would be sufficient and needful in this case? To which demand and question the said lords made response severally that considering the necessity of the king on one side and the poverty of his people on the other, a less aid would not suffice than one tenth and a half from the cities and boroughs, and one fifteenth and a half from other laymen. And besides, to grant a prolongation of the subsidy on wools, leather, and woolfells, and three shillings on the ton, and twelve pence in the pound, from the feast of St. Michael next coming till the feast of St. Michael in two years then next ensuing. Whereupon, by command of the king our said lord, word was sent to the commons of this present parliament to send before our said lord the king and the said lords a certain number of the members of their company, to hear and to report to their companions that which they should have in command of our lord the king aforesaid. And thereupon the said commons sent to the presence of the king our said lord and the said lords twelve of their companions; to whom, by command of our said lord the king the question aforesaid was declared and the response of the aforesaid lords severally given to it. Which response, it was the will of our said lord the king, they should report to the rest of their companions; also that they should see to it that they conformed most nearly to the purpose of the lords abovesaid. Which report having been made to the said commons, they were greatly disturbed, saying and affirming that this was in great prejudice and derogation of their liberties; and when our said lord the king heard of this, not wishing that anything should be done at present or in time to come, which could in any way turn against the liberty of the estate, for which they were come to parliament, nor against the liberty of the lords aforesaid, willed and granted and declared, with the advice and assent of the said lords, in the following manner. That is to say, that it is lawful for the lords to discuss among themselves assembled in this present parliament, and in every other in time to come, in the absence of the king, concerning the estate of the realm and the remedy needful to it. And that in like manner it is lawful for the commons, on their part, to discuss together concerning the state and remedy aforesaid. Provided always, that the lords on their part and the commons on theirs, make no report to our said lord the king of any grant granted by the commons, and agreed to by the lords,

nor of the negotiations of the said grant, before the said lords and
commons shall be of one assent and of one accord in the matter,
and then in the manner and form customary, that is to say by the
mouth of the speaker of the said commons for the time being, to
the end that the said lords and commons should have the agreement of our said lord the king.   Besides this our said lord the
king wills with the assent of the lords aforesaid that the negotiations had as aforesaid in this present parliament neither be
treated as an example in time to come, nor be turned to the
prejudice or derogation of the liberty of the estate, for which
the said commons were now come together, neither in this present parliament nor in any other in time to come.   But wills that
the said and all other estates be as free as they had been before.

------

113. Act restraining Abuses by the Sheriffs in Election Returns

(**1410.**   French text and translation, 2 *S. R.* 162.   3 Stubbs, 67, 420.)

*   *   *   *   *   *   *   *   *

1. FIRST, whereas in the parliament holden at Westminster,
the seventh year of the reign of our said lord the king, there
was ordained and established, by a statute for the preservation of the liberties and franchises of the election of the
knights of the shire used through the realm, a certain form
and manner of the election of such knights, as in the said statute
more fully is contained; and forasmuch as in the same statute no
penalty was ordained or limited in special upon the sheriffs of
the counties, if they make any returns to the contrary of the
same statute; it is ordained and stablished, that the justices
assigned to take assizes, shall have power to inquire in their
sessions of assizes of such returns made; and if it be found by
inquest, and due examination before the same justices, that any
such sheriff hath made, or hereafter make, any return contrary
to the tenor of the said statute, that then the same sheriff shall
incur the penalty of one hundred pounds to be paid to our said
lord the king; and moreover, that the knights of the counties so
unduly returned, shall lose their wages of the parliament, of old
time accustomed.

*   *   *   *   *   *   *   *   *

N

114. Grant of Subsidy, and Tunnage and Poundage

(1413.   French original, 4 *R. P.* 6.   Translation by Editors.
3 Stubbs, 79.)

17. To the honor of God and for the great love and affection which your poor commons of your realm of England have for you, our very excellent lord, the king, for the good of the kingdom and good governance in time to come, your aforementioned poor commons with the assent of the lords spiritual and temporal, the ninth day of June, the first year of your reign, in your parliament held at Westminster, grant to you, our sovereign lord, for the defence of your realm of England, the subsidy of wools, leather and woolfells, to be levied from the coming feast of St. Michael in the entire four years next ensuing, in the form which follows.   That is to say from resident merchants, on each sack of wool 43*s.* 4*d.* and on each 240 woolfells 43*s.* 4*d.* and on each last of leather 100*s.* going out of the realm.   And from the alien merchants, on each sack of wool 50*s.* and on each 240 woolfells 50*s.* and on each last of leather 106*s.* 8*d.* passing out of the realm.   And likewise your aforementioned poor commons with the consent aforementioned, for the safeguard of the sea grant to you our very excellent lord, 3*s.* on each tun of wine coming into the said realm, and passing out from it, except the tuns of wine taken at the price for your use. And also the aforementioned commons with the consent aforementioned grant to you for the said safeguard of the sea, 12*d.* in the pound of every kind of merchandise coming into the said realm and passing out of it, except wools, hides and woolfells. And except every kind of grain, flour and dried fish and cattle coming into the said realm.   And except ale which is carried out of the realm to supply your city of Calais by people of the cities of Baldesey, Falkenham, and Alderton on the Gosford and others as they are charged since the conquest of the said city of Calais. To take and receive the same 3*s.* on each tun of wine and 12*d.* in the pound, from the feast of St. Michael next to come to the feast of St. Michael the entire year ensuing.   Upon the condition that the merchants resident and alien coming into the realm of England with their merchandise be well and honestly treated and demeaned with their merchandise on paying the said subsidy of 12*d.* in the pound of their merchandise according

to the value that the merchandise costs abroad, and that they be
believed on their oath or by their letters.   And if the said merchants be found false, that they pay the double subsidy on that
which has not paid customs duty, without other forfeiture or new
payments, as they were treated and demeaned in the time of your
father, whom God assoil, and of your noble progenitors kings of
England, without oppression or extortion done to the merchants
aforementioned.   And that the citizens and burgesses shall be
treated in pursuing and making their fines to have their liberties
and franchises, as they were treated in the time of your father,
whom God assoil, and of your noble progenitors kings of England.   And besides this your said commons having regard to
the East March and West March of Scotland, and the marches
of Wales and the land of Ireland and the marches of Calais and
the land of Guienne, and the safeguard of the sea, by the entire
reliance which your said poor commons have in you, our very
sovereign lord, and to the intent that, with the aid of God,
by your gracious and good government in time to come the said
commons have good hope of being discharged of all such subsidies and tunnage and poundage, and taxes and tallages in time
to come, with the consent aforementioned, for the defence of the
realm and safeguard of the sea grant to you our very gracious
lord an entire fifteenth and an entire tenth to be levied from laymen in the accustomed manner.   That is to say, a half at the
feast of St. Martin in the winter next coming, and the other half
at the feast of Easter next ensuing.   Upon the condition that
the sea be well and sufficiently guarded for the safety of the navy
and the merchandise of the merchants of the realm of England.
Protesting, that your said commons be not held nor bound to
the wars of the said marches of Scotland, nor of the land of
Ireland, nor of the marches of Wales, nor of the marches of
Calais, nor the land of Guienne, nor for the safeguard of the sea
by any grant in time to come.

---

115. Residence required of Knights of the Shire and of their Electors

(1413.   French text and translation, 2 *S. R.* 170.   3 Stubbs, 80, 438.)

*   *   *   *   *   *   *   *   *

1. FIRST, that the statutes made, concerning the election
of the knights of the shires to come to the parliament, be holden

and kept in all points; adjoining to the same, that the knights of the shires which from henceforth shall be chosen in every shire, be not chosen unless they be resident within the shires where they shall be chosen, the day of the date of the writ of the summons of the parliament; and that the knights and esquires, and others which shall be choosers of those knights of the shires, be also resident within the same shires, in manner and form as is aforesaid. And moreover it is ordained and established, that the citizens and burgesses of the cities and boroughs be chosen men, citizens and burgesses resident, dwelling and free in the same cities and boroughs, and no other in any wise.

*   *   *   *   *   *   *   *   *

116. Confiscation of the Alien Priories

(1414.   French original, 4 *R. P.* 22, No. 21.   Translation by Editors. 3 Stubbs, 84.)

ITEM, the commons pray that in case final peace be made between you our sovereign lord and your adversary of France in time to come, and thereupon all the possessions of the alien priories in England should be restored to the chief religious houses abroad to which all those possessions belong, damage and loss would fall upon your said realm and on your people of the same realm by the great ferms and revenues of money which from year to year forever after would be paid in from the possessions to the chief houses aforesaid to the great impoverishment of your same realm in that respect which God forbid: May it please your very noble and very gracious lordship to consider, that at the commencement of the said war between the said realms, your lieges, of all the possessions which they then had of gifts from your noble progenitors in the parts abroad within the jurisdiction of France by judgment rendered in that same realm were forever ousted and disherited. And therefore to graciously decree in this parliament with the assent of your lords both spiritual and temporal that all the possessions of the alien priories in England shall remain in your hands to you and to your heirs forever to the intent that divine services in the places aforementioned shall be more duly held by English people in time to come than they have been before this time in these places by French people. Except the possessions of the alien conventual priors and of the priors who are inducted and instituted. And

except all the alien possessions given by the gracious lord
the king your father whom God assoil to the master and college
of Fotheringay and to his successors of the foundation of our
said lord the king your father and of the foundation of Edward
duke of York, any peace to be made notwithstanding, together
with all kinds of franchises and liberties granted by our said
lord the king your father to the said master and college and its
successors and confirmed by you, * * * saving the services
owing to the lords of English sees, if any there are, notwithstanding that the same grant made by our said lord the king your
father to the said master and college and his successors should
be extended only during the war between your very sovereign
lord and your adversary of France, and saving also to each of
your lieges as well spiritual as temporal the estate and possession which they have at present in any of such alien possessions,
purchased or to purchase, in perpetuity or for life or for a term
of years, from the chief religious houses abroad by the licence of
our lord the king your very noble father, whom God assail,
or of king Edward the Third your great grandfather, or of king
Richard the Second since the conquest, or by your gracious gift,
grant, confirmation or licence had at present in such case.   Paying and supporting all the charges, pensions, annuities and provisions granted to any of your lieges by you or by any of your
noble progenitors to be taken from the possessions or alien
priories aforementioned.

REPLY

The king wills it, and also that the said master and college of
Fotheringay have an exemplification of the king under his great
seal of the present petition for their greatest security in this
respect and with the assent of the lords spiritual and temporal
sitting in this present parliament.

---

117. King agrees not to alter the Petitions of the Commons

(1414.   French and English original, 4 R. P. 22, No. 22.   Translation
by Editors.   3 Stubbs, 84, 269.)

ITEM, be it remembered, that the commons delivered to the
king our very sovereign lord, in this present parliament a
petition, of which the tenor follows word for word.

Our sovereign lord, your humble and true lieges that have come for the commons of your land, trusting in your great justice that as it hath been ever their liberty and freedom that there should no statute or law be made unless they gave thereto their assent, considering that the commons of your land, the which is and ever hath been, a member of your parliament, have been as well assenters as petitioners, that from this time forth, by complaint of the commons of any mischief, asking remedy by mouth of their speaker for the commons or else by written petition, that there never be any law made thereupon and engrossed as statute and law, neither by addition or by diminution, by no manner of term or terms, the which should change the sentence and the intent asked by the speaker by mouth, or the petitions aforesaid given in writing by the manner aforesaid, without the assent of the foresaid commons. Considering our sovereign lord that it is not in any wise the intent of your commons if it be so that they ask you by speaking or by writing, two things or three or as many as pleases them; but that ever it stand in the freedom of your Highness to grant which of those that please you and to refuse the rest.

REPLY

The king by his especial grace granteth that from henceforth nothing be enacted to the petitions of his commons that be contrary to their asking whereby they should be bound without their assent; saving always to our liege lord his prerogative to grant and deny what him list of their petitions and askings aforesaid.

118. Grant of a Subsidy and Tunnage and Poundage for Life

(1415.   French original, 4 *R. P.* 63, No. 5.   Translation by the Editors. 3 Stubbs, 88.)

THE commons of the realm assembled in this present parliament, considering that the king our sovereign lord, to the honor of God and to avoid the effusion of Christian blood, has made to his adversary of France, divers requests to have his heritage returned to him, according to right and justice, and although there has been much negotiation as well on this side of the sea as on the other, at great cost to our sovereign lord the king; nevertheless, the king our said sovereign lord, has not obtained by means of these requests and negotiations his said heritage nor any notable parts of it.   And therefore the king our said sovereign lord though with the revenue of his realm and of the grant of the subsidy, granted to him before, he did not have the means to pursue his claim by way of deed, nevertheless hoping in God that he should see himself sustained and supported in his just quarrel, our said lord the king of his good courage has lately undertaken a voyage abroad, pledging his jewels to obtain money and in his own person has gone and arrived before the town of Harfleur and there besieged it with such force that he has taken and obtained it and holds it at present and to guard the same city he has placed there certain lords and many others, men at arms and archers, to his great cost and expense, and having made such ordinance for the safeguard of the said town, our said lord the king of his excellent courage with few people, regard being had to the might of France, went from the town of Harfleur by land towards the marches of Calais, where on his road many dukes, counts and other lords with the might of the realm of France in very great numbers met and fought him until God by His grace gave the victory to the king our said lord, to the honor and exaltation of the crown, of its good fame, and to the special comfort of his loyal lieges and to the fear of all his enemies and probably to the perpetual profit of all his realm, to the honor and reverence of God, and for the great affection and entire love that the commons of the realm of England have for our said sovereign lord the king, with the assent of the lords spiritual and temporal assembled in the parliament held at Westminster the Monday next after the feast of All Saints the year of the reign of our said sovereign lord the king, third, grant to the same sovereign lord the king, the 12th day of November, in the same parliament for the defence of the realm, the subsidy on wool, leather and woolfells to be raised from the merchants denizens, for the subsidy of each sack of wool 43s. 4d., and of each 240 woolfells 43s. 4d. and on each last of leather 100s. and from the alien merchants, on each sack of wool 60s. and on each 240 woolfells, 60s. and on each last of leather 106s. 8d. to take and receive from the feast of St. Michael next to come for all the life of our said lord the king to be disposed and used according to his very gracious wish and discretion, for the defence aforesaid, provided always that no grant be made to any one by our said sovereign lord the king by his letters patent for life or for a term of years of the subsidy aforementioned nor part of it.   And if any such grant be made it will be void and held for null and that this grant be not taken as an example by the kings of England in time to come.

[There follows a grant of tunnage and poundage in terms nearly identical with those of No. 114, but for the king's life.]

———◆———

119. Government during the Minority of Henry VI

(1422.   Latin, French, and English original, 4 *R. P.* 174.   Translation by Editors.   3 Stubbs, 100.   No. 33 illustrates parliamentary procedure.)

24. BE it remembered that on the twenty-seventh day of this parliament, the tender state of our most revered lord king Henry the Sixth after the conquest was considered, that he himself cannot personally decide in these days in respect to the protection and defence of his English realm and English church. The said lord king, fully confident of the prudence and diligence of his very dear uncles, John duke of Bedford, and Humphrey duke of Gloucester, and with the assent and advice of the lords spiritual and temporal, in the present parliament, and also with the assent of the commons of the English realm in the same parliament, has ordained and appointed his said uncle, duke of Bedford, now in foreign parts, protector and defender of his realm and the aforesaid English church and chief counsellor of his lord the king and that the duke shall be made and nominated protector and defender of his realm and chief counsellor of the king himself after he shall have returned to England and shall have come into the presence of the aforesaid lord the king and from that time as long as he shall remain in the said realm and as long as it shall be pleasing to our said lord the king.   And further, our lord the king, with the aforesaid assent and advice, has ordained and appointed in the absence of his aforesaid uncle the duke of Bedford, his aforesaid uncle the duke of Gloucester now in his realm of England, protector and defender of his realm and the English church and chief counsellor of the said lord the king; and that the same duke of Gloucester be made and nominated protector and defender of the said English realm and church and chief counsellor of the said lord the king as long as it shall be pleasing to the king; * * *

*   *   *   *   *   *   *   *   *

25. Be it remembered that when our lord king as well with the assent and advice of the lords spiritual and temporal as with the assent of the commons of the realm of England in the present parliament, by his letters patent, ordained and appointed his very dear uncle John duke of Bedford, now in foreign parts, protector and defender of the said realm and church of England, and also his principal counsellor, * * * and also in like manner the said lord the king, with the aforesaid assent and advice had ordained and appointed in the absence of his very dear uncle, the aforesaid duke of Bedford, Humphrey duke of Gloucester, now present in the said realm, the protector and defender of the aforesaid realm and church, and his principal counsellor: the aforesaid lord the king, considering the various labors which it will be necessary for the said dukes to endure on the occasions set forth above, and wishing therefore that their persons be attended with honors and gracious favors, with the aforesaid assent and advice, wills, concedes and ordains, that the said duke of Bedford, as often and whenever he shall assume the aforesaid burden and shall truly take it upon himself and occupy himself with it, and the said duke of Gloucester, as often and whenever he himself shall take upon himself and shall administer that burden, shall be able when the offices of forester, parker, and keeper of the warrens are vacant in the realm of England and the parts of Wales, pertaining to the donation of the said lord the king as of his crown, to dispose of these offices under the following form, to wit; that whenever any of the said offices shall happen to be vacant in the future,. either of the said dukes holding and exercising the burden of the business of protection and defence, shall be able to nominate a suitable person to the said office and under his signet, as custodian of the private seal of the said lord the king, for the time being, shall be able to certify it; * * *   Item, the said lord king, by the advice, consent, and for the cause aforesaid, has willed, granted and ordained that each of the aforesaid dukes, for the time during which he shall hold and exercise the burden of the protection and defence aforesaid, shall be able to nominate suitable persons to any parish churches from the value of twenty marks to the value of thirty marks inclusive, and also to all the prebends in the king's chapels in the donation of the lord king, under the right of the crown, when they shall be vacant, with the exception of the deanships in the king's chapels of this sort, * * *   Other offices, prebends, and benefices not specified above, and the aforesaid deanships, belonging to the donation or presentation of the lord king, are,

belong and appertain to the disposition of the said lord king, with the advice of the said protector and defender for the time being and of the rest of the lords of the council of the said lord king, from time to time, when they shall be vacant; except the benefices whose disposition belongs to the chancellor of England by virtue of his office and to the treasurer of England by virtue of his office.

26. Be it said, that after the king our sovereign lord, with the assent and advice of the lords spiritual and temporal in this parliament and also with that of the commons of England assembled in the same, had ordered and constituted the powerful prince Humphrey duke of Gloucester his uncle, protector and defender of the realm and church of England, and his principal councillor in the absence of the excellent prince John duke of Bedford, * * * at the request of the said commons, certain persons of estate as well spiritual as temporal were with the advice and assent of all the lords aforesaid, named and elected as councillors assistant to the government, the names of which persons, written in a small schedule and read openly in this parliament, follow:

The duke of Gloucester, the archbishop of Canterbury, the bishop of London, the bishop of Winchester, the bishop of Norwich, the bishop of Worcester, the duke of Exeter, the earl of March, the earl of Warwick, the earl Marshall, the earl of Northumberland, the earl of Westmoreland, the lord Fitz Hugh, Ralph Cromwell, Walter Hungerford, John Tiptoft, Walter Beauchamp.

27. And be it said also, that the same persons who were named and elected councillors assistant, since that nomination and election have condescended to undertake such assistance to the government, in the manner and form contained in a schedule of paper written in English, containing as well all their names, as also five especial articles delivered in this same parliament, by the same persons named councillors assistant, the tenor of which schedule follows.

28. The which lords above said have condescended to take it upon them in the manner and form that follows. First, forasmuch as execution of law and keeping of the peace stand much in justices of the peace, sheriffs and escheators, [and] the profits of the king and the revenues of the realm be greatly increased or reduced to nothing by customers, comptrollers, weighers, searchers and all such other officers, therefore the same lords will and desire that such officers and all others be made by advice and nomination of the said lords saving always and reserving to

my lords of Bedford and of Gloucester all that belongeth to them by a special act made in parliament; and to the bishop of Winchester what hath been granted him by our sovereign lord that last was, on whose soul God have mercy, and confirmed by authority of parliament.

29. Item, that all manner of wards, marriages, ferms and other incidents that belong to the crown, when they fall in, be let, sold, and disposed by the said lords of the council, and that indifferently at the falling in, without favor or any manner of partiality or fraud.

30. Item, that if anything be done or enacted by council, six, or four at least, officers of the said council be present; and in all great matters that shall pass by council, that all be present or at any rate the greater part; and if it be such matter that the king hath been accustomed to be consulted upon, that then the said lords do not proceed therein without the advice of my lords of Bedford, or of Gloucester.

31. Item, forasmuch as the two chamberlains of the exchequer, have been ordered of old time to control the receipts and the payments in any wise made, the lords desire, that the treasurer of England for the time being, and either of the chamberlains, have a key of that that should come into the receipt, and that they be sworn before my lord of Gloucester, and all the lords of the council, that for no friendship shall they make any man privy, but the lords of the council, to what the king hath within his treasury.

32. Item, that the clerk of the council be charged and sworn to truly enact, and write daily, the names of all the lords that are present from time to time, to see what, how, and by whom, anything passeth.

33. And thereupon, the said articles having been read in parliament, before the aforementioned lords, and well understood by them, were fully assented to and accorded by them; the said schedule of paper was by certain of my honorable lords of parliament on the part of the king and all the lords of parliament sent and delivered to the aforesaid commons in order to be informed of their intent thereupon. Whereupon afterwards the said commons apprised of this, and by the report of many reverend and honorable lords made in the said parliament, on the part of the said commons, thanked the aforesaid lords, and [voted] that they were well content with all the contents of the said schedule, with this that to the first article of the said five articles should be added a clause, as a proviso, which the said lords, reporters of

the said commons, delivered on their part in parliament, in a schedule of parchment written in French, and the tenor of which follows here.

Provided always that the lords and other persons and officers, who have estate and authority, either by inheritance or for life or otherwise, to make and constitute by virtue of their offices, officers, deputies and ministers, which belong to them by right, and as annexed to them and to their offices, of old time accustomed and used, shall not be restrained nor prejudiced in that which belongs to them, by color of this ordinance or appointment.

To which schedule of parchment and the contents of the same, read before the said lords in parliament, were the same lords agreed and fully assented.

120. Definition of the Powers of the Duke of Gloucester as Protector

(1428. English original, 4 *R. P.* 326, No. 25. 3 Stubbs, 109.)

HIGH and mighty prince, my lord of Gloucester, we lords spiritual and temporal, assembled by the command of the king our sovereign lord in this his present parliament, be well remembered how, that soon after the beginning of this parliament, it liked you to move unto us and to say, that you were the protector and defender of this land, and so named and called; willing therefore and desiring to know of us, what authority and power belonged to you, the which desire you likewise repeated the third day of this present month of March, saying that we must well consider matters of parliament in your absence, but that we should not conclude without you; affirming also that you would not in any wise come into the house accustomed for the king and the lords of parliament, until the time that you knew what your authority and your power were therein. And for so much and to the end, that you have no cause to absent yourself from this said parliament for lack of our answer to your said desire, we lords abovesaid call to mind, how that in the first parliament held by the king our sovereign lord that now is, at Westminster, you desired to have had the government of this land, affirming that it belonged to you by right, as well as by means of your birth, as by the last will of the king that was, your brother, whom God assoil, alleging for you such grounds and motives as it was

thought in your discretion made for your intent. Whereupon
the lords spiritual and temporal assembled in parliament, among
whom were your uncles, the bishop of Winchester who now liveth,
and the duke of Exeter, and your cousin earl of March that are
gone to God, and of Warwick, and others in great number that
now live, had great and long deliberation and advice, searched
precedents of the government of the land in similar times and
cases, when kings of this land have been of tender age, took also
information of the laws of the land, of such persons as are not-
ably learned therein, and finally found your said desire not caused
nor grounded in precedent, nor in the law of the land; the
which the king that is dead might not in his life, nor by his last
will nor otherwise alter, change nor abrogate, without the assent
of the three estates, nor commit or grant to any person, government or rule of this land longer than he lived; but on the other
hand, the said lords found your said desire not according with
the laws of this land, and against the right and freedom of the
estates of the same land. How be it, be it not thought, that any
such thing wittingly proceeded of your intent. And nevertheless
to keep peace and tranquility, and to the intent to ease and
appease you, it was advised and appointed by the authority of the
king, the three estates of this land assenting that you in the
absence of my lord, your brother of Bedford, should be chief of
the king's council, and devised therefore unto you a name different from the other councillors, not the name of tutor, lieutenant, governor, nor of regent nor any name that should import
authority of government of the land, but the name of protector
and defender, the which importeth a personal duty of attendance
to the actual defence of the land, as well against enemies without,
if the case required, as against rebels within if any there should
be, which God forbid; granting you therewith certain power,
which is specified and contained in an act of the said parliament, to endure as long as it pleaseth the king. In which if the
intent of the said estates had been, that you should have had more
power or authority, more would have been expressed therein; to
which appointment, ordinance and act, you thereto agreed as
for your person, making nevertheless protestation, that it was not
your intent in any wise to derogate or do prejudice unto my
lord your brother of Bedford by your said agreement, as toward
any right that he would pretend or claim in the government of
this land, and as toward any pre-eminence that you might have
or belong to you as chief of the council, it is plainly declared
in the said acts and articles, subscribed by my said lord of Bed

ford, by yourself, and the other lords of the council. But as in parliament to which you are called upon your faith and allegiance as duke of Gloucester, as other lords are and not otherwise, we know no power nor authority that you have, other than you as duke of Gloucester should have, the king being in parliament, at years of most discretion; we marvelling with all our hearts, that considering the open declaration of authority and power belonging to my lord of Bedford, and to you in his absence, and also to the king's council, subscribed purely and simply by my said lord of Bedford, and by you, that you should in any wise be stirred or moved not to content you therewith, or to pretend you any other: especially considering that the king, blessed be our Lord, is since the time of the said power granted unto you, much advanced and grown in person, in wit and understanding, and likely with the grace of God to occupy his own royal power within a few years. And forasmuch considering the things and causes above said, and many others that would be too long to write, we lords aforesaid, pray, exhort and require you, to content you with the power abovesaid and declared, with which my lord your brother of Bedford, the king's eldest uncle, contented him; and that you do not desire, will nor use any larger power: giving you this that is above written, for our answer to your aforesaid demand, which we will dwell and abide with, without variance or change. * * *

———◆———

121. Electors of Knights of the Shire must be Forty Shilling Freeholders

(1429. French text and translations, 2 *S. R.* 243. 3 Stubbs, 114, 265.)

* * * * * * * * *

7. ITEM, whereas the elections of knights of shires chosen to come to the parliaments of the king, in many counties of England, have now of late been made by very great, and excessive number of people dwelling within the same counties of the which most part was by people of small substance, or of no value, whereof every of them pretended a voice equivalent, as to such elections to be made, with the most worthy knights and esquires dwelling within the same counties; whereby manslaughters, riots, batteries, and divisions among the gentlemen and other people of the same counties, shall very likely rise and

be, unless convenient remedy be provided in this behalf: our lord the king, considering the premises, hath provided, and ordained by authority of this present parliament, that the knights of the shires to be chosen within the same realm of England to come to the parliaments hereafter to be holden, shall be chosen in every county, by people dwelling and resident in the same, whereof every one of them shall have free tenement to the value of forty shillings by the year at the least above all charges; and that they which shall be so chosen shall be dwelling and resident within the same counties; and such as have the greatest number of them that may expend forty shillings by year and above, as afore is said, shall be returned by the sheriffs of every county, knights for the parliament, by indentures sealed betwixt the said sheriffs and the said choosers so to be made; and every sheriff of England shall have power, by the said authority, to examine upon the holy evangelists every such chooser, how much he may expend by the year: and if any sheriff return knights to come to the parliament contrary to this ordinance, that the justices of assizes in their sessions of assizes shall have power by the authority aforesaid, thereof to inquire; and if by inquest the same be found before the same justices, and the sheriff thereof be duly attainted, that then the said sheriff shall incur the pain of an hundred pounds to be paid to our lord the king, and also that he have imprisonment by a year, without being let to bail or mainprise; and that the knights for the parliament returned contrary to the said ordinance shall lose their wages. Provided always, that he which cannot expend forty shillings by year as afore is said shall in no wise be chooser of the knights for the parliament; and that in every writ that shall hereafter go forth to the sheriffs to choose knights for the parliament, mention be made of the said ordinances.

* * * * * * * * *

122. Larke's Case: Privileges of Member's Servants

(1429. French original, 4 *R. P.* 357, No. 57. Translation by Editors. 3 Stubbs, 514.)

THE commons pray that as one William Larke, servant to Wm. Milrede, coming to your court of the present parliament for the city of London, in the service of the said Wm.

Milrede then sitting, through the subtle imagination and con-
jecture of one Margery Janyns was arrested in the court of
pipoudrez of the abbot of Westminster, by his officers there, and
removed from there to your common bench by writ of *corpus
cum causa* at the suit of the said Margery, and by the justices of
your said bench commanded to Fleet prison and there detained
in prison till the present, by the force of a judgment given
against the said Wm. Larke in your said bench by your said justices, both because the said Wm. Larke was condemned at the
suit of the said Margery in your said bench in an action of trespass, to the damage of 208 £ 6s. 8d. before the day of the summoning of this present parliament, and for fine to make to you
because the trespasser was found with force and arms. May it
please Your Royal Majesty to consider that the said Wm. Larke,
at the time of the said arrest, was in the service of the said Wm.
Milrede, supposing truly by the privilege of your court of parliament to be free of all arrest during your said court, except for
treason, felony or surety of the peace; to order by the authority
of the same parliament, that the said Wm. Larke may be delivered out of your said prison of Fleet, the said condemnation,
judgment and execution or anything depending hereupon against
him or upon him notwithstanding. Saving at all times to the
said Margery and to her executors, their execution outside of
the said judgment against the said Wm. Larke, after the end of
the said parliament, and also to grant, by the authority aforementioned, that no one of your said lieges, that is to say, lords,
knights from your counties, citizens, burgesses, in your parliaments to come, their servants or familiars, be at all arrested nor
detained in prison during the time of your parliament, except for
treason, felony, or surety of the peace as was said before.

RESPONSE

The king, by the advice of the lords spiritual and temporal and
at the special request of the commons, sitting in this present
parliament, and also with the consent of the counsel of Margery
Janyns named in this petition, wills and grants by the authority
of the said parliament, that Wm. Larke named in the said petition, be delivered immediately out of Fleet prison. And that
the said Margery, after the end of this parliament, have her execution of the judgment which she has against the said William,
in the common bench, as it is contained in the same petition,
in the same form that it should have had if the said judgment

had never been executed.   And that the judges of the said bench
give to the said Margery, after the end of this parliament, execution of the said judgment, by *capias ad satisfaciendum*, and by
exigent; and likewise issue processes from our lord the king, for
his fine regarding the said William, by *capias* and *exigent*, as
they should have done, if the said William had never been taken
nor imprisoned, by cause of the said judgment.   And besides
the king wills, by the authority of the same parliament, that the
chancellor of England for the time being, from the end of the
said parliament, make commissions to different persons assigned
at discretion, to take the said William and to deliver him to the
keeper of the Fleet, who is held to receive and guard him, until
satisfaction shall be given to the aforesaid Margery, of the sum
to recover from him by the aforementioned judgment, and
to the king, of that which belongs to him in the case.   And that
the said deliverance to the said keeper, have the same effect for
the said Margery, as would execution for her made by *capias ad
satisfaciendum*, any variance through the said petition or the
indorsement of the same, and the record of the same recovery,
or any other thing notwithstanding, and as to the rest of the
petition: the king will consider.

---

123. Act against Smuggling

(1437.   French text and translation, 2 *S. R.* 294.)

*   *   *   *   *   *   *   *

8. ITEM, our sovereign lord the king, to remove and eschew
the great unlawfulness and damage, which daily is to him done,
in withholding the customs and subsidies, and to the staple
of Calais in hindering of the sale of wool and woolfells, by
such which do ship their wools and woolfells in divers secret
ports and creeks, and other suspect places within this realm,
stealing, bringing, and carrying away the same, not customed
to divers parts beyond the sea, and not to Calais; hath ordained by the authority aforesaid, that from henceforth no
manner of person shall ship nor cause to be shipped wools, woolfells, nor other merchandises pertaining to the staple, in no place
within this realm, but all only at the keys and wharfs being in
the ports assigned by statute, where the kings weights and his
beam be set.   And that every master of the ships and vessels, in

o

the which such wool and woolfells and merchandises be put, shall find sufficient surety to the customers of the ports, where they do ship, to carry the said wool and woolfells and merchandises to the staple of Calais, and to bring a certification from thence, that he hath so done. Saving always to the merchants of Genoa, Venice, Tuscany, Lombardy, Florence, and Catalonia, and to the burgesses of Berwick, the liberties to them granted by statute heretofore.

———◆———

124. Against Abuse in Appointment of Justices of the Peace

(1439. French text and translation, 2 S. R. 309.)

* * * * * * * * *

11. ITEM, whereas by statutes made in the time of the king's noble progenitors, it was ordained, that in every county of England justices should be assigned of the most worthy of the same counties, to keep the peace, and to do other things, as in the same statutes fully is contained; which statutes notwithstanding, now of late in many counties of England, a greater number have been deputed and assigned, than before this time were wont to be, whereof some be of small substance, by whom the people will not be governed nor ruled, and some for their necessity do great extortion and oppression upon the people, whereof great inconveniences be likely to rise daily if the king thereof do not provide remedy: the king willing against such inconveniences to provide remedy, hath ordained and established, by authority aforesaid, that no justice of peace within the realm of England, in any county, shall be assigned or deputed, if he have not lands and tenements to the value of XX pounds by year; and if any be ordained hereafter to be justice of peace in any county, which hath not lands and tenements to the value aforesaid, that he thereof shall notify the chancellor of England for the time being, which shall put another sufficient in his place; and if he give not the said notification as before, within a month after that he hath notice of such commission, or if he sit, or make any warrant or precept by force of such commission, he shall incur the penalty of XX pounds and nevertheless be put out of the commission as before and the king shall have one half of the said penalty, and he that will sue for the king, the other half; and he that will so sue for the king, and for himself, shall have an action to demand

the same penalty by writ of debt at the common law. Provided always, that this ordinance shall not extend to cities, towns, or boroughs, which be counties incorporate of themselves; nor to cities, towns, or boroughs which have justices of peace of persons dwelling in the same by commission or grant of the king, or of his progenitors: provided also, that if there be not sufficient persons having lands and tenements to the value aforesaid, learned in the law, and of good governance, within any such county, that the chancellor of England for the time being shall have power to put other discreet persons learned in the law, in such commissions, though they have not lands and tenements to the value aforesaid, by his discretion.

* * * * * * * * *

---

125. Qualifications of Knights of the Shire

(1445. French text and translation, 2 *S. R.* 342. 3 Stubbs, 265, 427.)

* * * * * * * * *

14. * * * So that the knights of the shire for the parliament thereafter to be chosen, shall be notable knights of the same counties for the which they shall so be chosen, or otherwise such notable esquires, gentlemen of birth of the same counties, as shall be able to be knights; and no man to be such knight which standeth in the degree of a yeoman and under.

* * * * * * * * *

---

126. Attainder of John Cade

(1450. French text and translation, 2 *S. R.* 357.)

* * * * * * * * *

1. FIRST, whereas the false traitor John Cade, naming himself John Mortimer, late called Captain of Kent, the viii day of July, the xxviii year of the reign of our said sovereign lord the king at Southwark, in the county of Surrey, and the ix day of July, the aforesaid year at Dertford and Rochester in the county of Kent, also at the town of Rochester aforesaid, and elsewhere, the x and xi day of July then next ensuing, within the realm of England, falsely and traitorously imagined the king's death,

destruction and subversion of this realm, in gathering and levying a great number of the king's people, and them exciting to make insurrection against the king, falsely and traitorously in the places aforesaid, and at the times before recited, against the king's royalty, crown, and dignity; and there and then made and levied war falsely and traitorously against the king and his highness; and howbeit though he be dead and mischieved, yet by the law of the land not punished: our said sovereign lord the king considering the premises, to put such traitors in doubt so to do in time coming, and for salvation of himself and of his realm, by advice of his lords spiritual and temporal in the said parliament assembled, and at the request of his commons, hath ordained by the authority of the said parliament, that he shall be of these treasons attainted; and that by the same authority he shall forfeit to the king all his goods, lands and tenements, rents and possessions, which he had the said eighth day of July, or after, and his blood corrupt, and disabled forever, and to be called a false traitor within the said realm forever.

*   *   *   *   *   *   *   *   *

127. Privilege of Members from Arrest: Clerk's Case

(1460.   Latin and English original, 5 *R. P.* 374.   Translation by Editors.
3 Stubbs, 515.)

9. ITEM, a certain other petition was presented to our said lord the king, in the said parliament, through the said commons, according to the tenor which follows:

To the king our sovereign lord, pray the commons, forasmuch that great delay hath been in this parliament, by this that Walter Clerk, burgess of Chippenham in the shire of Wiltes, which came by your high commandment to this your present parliament, and attended to the same in the house for the commons accustomed, the freedom of which commons so called, hath ever afore this time been and ought to be, that the same commons have free coming, going, and their abiding; against which freedom, the said Walter was, after his said coming, and during this your present parliament, arrested at your suit, for a fine to be made to your Highness, and imprisoned in the counter of London, and from thence removed into your exchequer, and then committed into your prison of Fleet, as well for xl pounds in which he was condemned to your Highness, and also for xx marks, in which he was condemned to Robert Basset, in an action of trespass, and also for xx pounds in which he was condemned to John Payne, in an action of maintenance, and for the fines due to your Highness in the same condemnation; and since that committing, the said Walter was outlawed at the suit of the said John Payne, and for that and other premises, in the same prison of Fleet is retained, against the liberties and freedoms used, had and enjoyed afore this time by your said commons.

Please it your Highness, in eschewing the said delay caused by the premises, by the advice and assent of the lords spiritual and temporal in this present parliament assembled, and by authority of the same, to ordain and establish, that your chancellor of England have power to direct your writ or writs, to the warden of the said prison of Fleet, commanding him by the same, to have the said Walter before him without delay, and then to dismiss him at large, and to discharge the said warden of him, of and for every of the premises, so that the said Walter may attend daily of this your parliament, as his duty is to do. And that by the said authority, neither your said chancellor, warden of Fleet, nor any other person nor persons, in any wise be hurt, endamaged nor grieved, because of the said dismissing at large of the said Walter. Saving alway, as well to you, sovereign lord, your execution of your said xl pounds, and of your said fine, and all your other interest in that party, as to the said Robert Basset, and John Payne, and each of them, their execution in the premises, after the dissolving of this your present parliament, the said arrest of the said Walter, and the said committing and prisoning of him to ward notwithstanding, as fully and effectually, as if the same Walter at any time for any of the premises never had been arrested, nor committed to ward. Saving also to your said commons called now to this your parliament, and their successors, their whole liberties, franchises and privileges, in as ample form and manner, as your said commons at any time before this day have had, used and enjoyed, and ought to have, use and enjoy, this present act and petition in any wise notwithstanding.

Which said petition having been read, heard, and fully understood in the said parliament, by the advice and assent of the lords spiritual and temporal being in the said parliament, and at the request of the said commons, response was made to the same in the following form: The king wills it.

128. Recognition of the Duke of York as Heir to the Throne

(1460.   English original, 5 *R. P.* 375.   3 Stubbs, 190.)

10. MEMORANDUM, that the xvi day of October, the ix day of this present parliament, the council of the right high and mighty prince Richard duke of York, brought into the parliament chamber a writing, containing the claim and title of the right, that the said duke pretended unto the crowns of England and of France, and lordship of Ireland, and the same writing delivered to the right reverend father in God George bishop of Exeter, chancellor of England, desiring him that the same writing might be opened to the lords spiritual and temporal assembled in this present parliament, and that the said duke might have brief and expedient answer thereof: whereupon the said chancellor opened and showed the said desire to the lords spiritual and temporal, asking the question of them, whether they would the said writing should be openly read before them or no.   To the which question it was answered and agreed by all the said lords: inasmuch as every person high and low, suing to this high court of parliament, of right must be heard, and his desire and petition understood, that the said writing should be read and heard, not to be answered without the king's commandment, forasmuch as the matter is so high, and of so great weight and poise   Which writing there then was read; the tenor whereof followeth, in these words:

*   *   *   *   *   *   *   *   *

18. Item, the Saturday, the xvii day of this present parliament, it was showed unto the lords spiritual and temporal being in this present parliament, by the mouth of the said chancellor, that the said duke of York called busily to have hasty and speedy answer of such matters as touched his title abovesaid; and how that forasmuch as it is thought by all the lords, that the title of the said duke cannot be defeated, and eschewing of the great inconveniencies that may ensue, a means was found to save the king's honor and estate, and to appease the said duke, if he would; which is this: that the king shall keep the crowns, and his estate and royal dignity, during his life; and the said duke and his heirs to succeed him in the same: exhorting and stirring all the said lords, that if any of them could find any other or better means, that it might be showed.   Whereupon, sad and

ripe communication in this matter had, it was concluded and agreed by all the said lords; that since it was so, that the title of the said duke of York cannot be defeated, and in eschewing the great inconveniencies that might ensue, to take the means above rehearsed, the oaths that the said lords had made unto the king's Highness at Coventry, and other places saved, and their consciences therein cleared. And over that, it was agreed by the said lords, that the said means should be opened and declared to the king's Highness. And forthwith they went to the king, where he was in his chamber within his palace of Westminster. And in their going out of the parliament chamber, the said chancellor asked of the said lords, that since it was so, that the said means should be opened by his mouth to the king's good grace, if they would abide by him howsoever that the king took the matter; and they all answered and said yea.

All these premises thus showed and opened to the king's Highness, he, inspired with the grace of the Holy Ghost, and in eschewing of effusion of Christian blood, by good and sad deliberation and advice had with all his lords spiritual and temporal, condescended to accord to be made between him and the said duke, and to be authorized by the authority of this present parliament. The tenor of which accord hereafter ensueth, in manner and form following:

19. Blessed be Jesus, in whose hand and bounty resteth and is the peace and unity betwixt princes, and the weal of every realm, through whose direction agreed it is, appointed and accorded as followeth, betwixt the most high and most mighty prince King Henry the Sixth, king of England and of France, and lord of Ireland, on the one part, and the right high and mighty prince Richard Plantagenet duke of York, on the other part, upon certain matters of variance moved betwixt them, and in especial upon the claim and title unto the crowns of England and of France, and royal power, estate, and dignity, appertaining to the same, and lordship of Ireland, opened, showed and declared by the said duke, before all the lords spiritual and temporal being in this present parliament: the said agreement, appointment and accord, to be authorized by the same parliament.

*   *   *   *   *   *   *   *   *

20. The said title nevertheless notwithstanding, and without prejudice of the same, the said Richard duke of York, tenderly desiring the weal, rest and prosperity of this land, and to set apart all that might be trouble to the same; and considering the

possession of the said king Henry the Sixth, and that he hath for his time been named, taken and reputed king of England and of France, and lord of Ireland; is content, agreed and consenteth, that he be had, reputed and taken, king of England and of France, with the royal estate, dignity and pre-eminence belonging thereto, and lord of Ireland, during his life natural; and for that time, the said duke without hurt or prejudice of his said right and title, shall take, worship and honor him for his sovereign lord.

21. Item, the said Richard duke of York, shall promise and bind him by his solemn oath, in manner and form as followeth:

In the name of God, Amen. I Richard duke of York, promise and swear by the faith and truth that I owe to almighty God, that I shall never do, consent, procure or stir, directly or indirectly, privily or openly, nor as much as in me is and shall be, suffer to be done, consented, procured or stirred, anything that may be or tend to the abridgement of the natural life of king Henry the Sixth, or to the hurt or diminishing of his reign or royal dignity, by violence or any other wise, against his freedom and liberty; but that if any person or persons, would do or presume anything to the contrary, I shall with all my power and might withstand it, and make it to be withstood as far as my power will stretch thereunto; so help me God, and these holy evangelists.

Item, Edward earl of March, and Edmund earl of Rutland, the sons of the said Richard duke of York, shall make like oath.

22. Item, it is accorded, appointed and agreed, that the said Richard duke of York, enjoy, be entitled, called and reputed from henceforth, very and rightful heir to the crowns, royal estate, dignity and lordship abovesaid; and after the disease of the said king Henry, or when he will lay from him the said crowns, estate, dignity and lordship, the said duke and his heirs, shall immediately succeed to the said crowns, royal estate, dignity and lordship.

*   *   *   *   *   *   *   *   *

24. Item, if any person or persons, imagine or compass the death of the said duke, and thereof proveably be attaint of open deed done by folks of their condition, that it be deemed and adjudged high treason.

25. Item, for the more establishing of the said accord, it is appointed and consented, that the lords spiritual and temporal being in this present parliament, shall make oaths to accept, take, worship and repute, the said Richard duke of York, and

his said heirs, as above is rehearsed; and keep, observe and strengthen as much as appertaineth unto them, all the things abovesaid, and resist to their power all them that will presume the contrary, according to their estates and degrees.

26. Item, the said Richard duke of York, earls of March and Rutland, shall promise and make oath, to help, aid and defend the said lords, and every of them, against all those that will quarrel, or anything attempt against the said lords, or any of them; by occasion of agreement or consenting to the said accord, or assistance giving to the said duke and earls, or any of them.

Item, it is agreed and appointed, that this accord, and every article hereof, be opened and notified by the king's letters patents or otherwise, at such times and places, and in manner, as it shall be thought expedient to the said Richard duke of York, with the advice of the lords of the king's council.

27. The king, understanding certainly the said title of the said Richard duke of York, just, lawful, true and sufficient, by the advice and assent of the lords spiritual and temporal, and commons, in this parliament assembled, and by authority of the same parliament, declareth, approveth, ratifieth, confirmeth and accepteth the said title, just, good, lawful and true, and thereunto giveth his assent and agreement, of his free will and liberty. And over that, by the said advice and authority declareth, entitleth, calleth, establisheth, affirmeth and reputeth the said Richard duke of York, very, true and rightful heir to the crowns, royal estate, and dignity of the realms of England and of France, and of the lordship of Ireland aforesaid; and that according to the worship and reverence that thereto belongeth, he be taken, accepted and reputed, in worship and reverence, by all the estates of the said realm of England, and of all his subjects hereof: saving and ordaining by the same authority, the king to have the said crowns, realms, royal estate, dignity and pre-eminence of the same, and the said lordship of Ireland, during his life natural. And furthermore, by the same advice and authority, willeth, consenteth and agreeth, that after his disease, or when it shall please his Highness to lay from him the said crowns, estate, dignity and lordship, or thereof ceaseth: the said Richard duke of York and his heirs, shall immediately succeed him in the said crowns, royal estate, dignity and lordship, and them then have and enjoy, any act of parliament, statute, ordinance, or other thing to the contrary made, or interruption or discontinuance of possession, notwithstanding. And moreover, by the said advice and authority, stablisheth, granteth, confirmeth, approveth, ratifieth

and accepteth the said accord, and all things therein contained, and thereunto freely and absolutely assenteth and agreeth.

And by the same advice and authority, ordaineth and establisheth, that if any person or persons, imagine or compass the death of the said duke, and thereof proveably be attaint of open deed done by folks of their condition, that it be deemed and adjudged high treason.

28. And furthermore ordaineth, granteth and stablisheth, by the said advice and authority, that all statutes, ordinances and acts of parliament, made in the time of the said king Henry the Fourth, by the which he and the heirs of his body coming, or Henry late king of England the Fifth, the son and heir of the said king Henry the Fourth, and the heirs of the body of the same king Henry the Fifth coming, were or be inheritable to the said crowns and realms, or to the heritage or enheritement of the same, be annulled, repelled, revoked, dampned, cancelled, void, and of no force or effect: * * *

* * * * * * * * *

---

129. Act declaring Valid Acts of Lancastrian Kings

(1461. French text and translation, 2 *S. R.* 380. 3 Stubbs, 201.)

EDWARD, by the grace of God king of England and of France, and lord of Ireland, the fourth after the conquest: to the honor of God and of Holy Church, to nourish peace, unity, and concord within his realm of England, which he most entirely desireth, by the advice and assent of the lords spiritual and temporal of the same realm, and at the special request of the commons of his said realm come and assembled at his first parliament holden at Westminster upon the fourth day of November, in the first year of his reign, and by authority of the same parliament, hath caused to be ordained and established certain statutes, declarations, and ordinances, in manner and form following.

1. First, that in eschewing of ambiguities, doubts, and diversities of opinions, which may rise, ensue, or be taken of and upon acts judicial, and exemplifications of the same, made or had in the time or times of Henry the Fourth, Henry the Fifth his son, and Henry the Sixth his son, late kings of England successively,

in deed and not of right; our said lord the king, by the advice and assent of the lords spiritual and temporal, and at the request of the said commons in the said parliament assembled, and by authority of the same, hath declared, established, and enacted in the said parliament, that all fines, and final concords, levied or made of any lands, tenements, possessions, rents, inheritances, or other things, and all acts judicial, recoveries, and processes, determined or commenced, not revoked, reversed nor annulled, made or had in any court or courts of record, or any court or courts holden in any of the times of the pretensed reigns of any of the said late kings, in deed and not in right, other than by authority of any parliament holden in any of their times, and exemplifications of the said fines, acts judicial, and recoveries, out of any of the said parliaments, and every of them, shall be of all such force, virtue, and effect, as if the said fines, final concords, acts, recoveries, processes, and other the premises, had or made out of any of the said parliaments, and exemplifications of the same, had been commenced, sued, had or determined in the time of any king lawfully reigning in this realm, and obtaining the crown of the same by just title.

And also that all letters patents made by any of the pretensed kings to any person or persons, of creation, insignicion or erection of any of them, to any estate, dignity or pre-eminence, shall be to the said person or persons, and to such of their heirs which be contained in the same letters patents, of such force, avail and effect, as touching such creation, insignicion or erection, as if the same letters patents had been made or granted to any of them by any king lawfully reigning in this realm and obtaining the crown of the same by just title; and that they being so created, insigned or erected, shall have new grants of the king of their annuities for the maintenance of their estates, as hath been of old time accustomed; except such persons, and every of them, whom our sovereign lord the king reputeth and holdeth for his rebels or enemies.

*   *   *   *   *   *   *   *   *

130. Treaty of Commerce with Burgundy

(November, 1467. French original, 11 Rymer, 592–594, 598. Translation by Editors. This treaty was renewed with some modifications 12 July, 1478, 2 January, 1487, and 24 February, 1496 (12 Rymer, 578). This last is known as the *Intercursus Magnus*.)

FIRST, that all merchants as well of the realm of England, of Ireland, and of Calais, as the merchants of the duchy, county and country of Brabant, of Flanders, the town and lordship of Mechlin and the other countries of our said cousin the duke, be they merchants of wools, leathers, of provisions or of any other merchandise, their factors and servants shall be able to travel securely by land, on foot, on horseback or otherwise and in passing in and beyond the waters of Gravelines and of Calais to Brabant, Flanders, Mechlin and other countries above mentioned, and from Brabant, Flanders, Mechlin and the other countries above mentioned to Calais, together with the goods and merchandise, to take their way between the sea and the castles of Mark and of Oye and to trade one with the other in all kinds of merchandise, provisions and other things, * * * except armor, artillery, cannon, powder, and other things made similarly and for hostile purposes.

And that the said merchants, their factors and servants shall be able, each of them to whom it shall be necessary, to buy and to have provisions freely of those of the other part, and to carry them by land in and beyond the waters aforesaid, one to the other; that is to say, those of England and the rest of the country of England (by which we mean Ireland and Calais) in to Flanders to Mechlin, and the other aforesaid countries; and those of Brabant, of Flanders, of Mechlin and aforesaid countries to Calais; to travel by the way aforesaid, without any hindrance, disturbance or prohibition whatsoever, for this cause neither incurring any penalty nor being held to blame in any manner by the lords of one part or the other or by their justices, officers or subjects.

Item, that all merchants of England, Ireland and Calais, be they merchants of wools, leathers, of provisions or of any other merchandise whatsoever, their factors and servants, masters of ships and sailors, shall be able to travel by sea, to pass, to repass, to hold intercourse with, to enter, be, and dwell safely in the said duchy, county, and countries of Brabant, Flanders, the lordship and town of Mechlin, and the other countries aforesaid, and within the ports and harbors of the same with all their goods, merchandise, and ships, and to trade with all the merchants of Brabant, of Flanders, and of Mechlin, and of all the said countries and whatsoever other merchants, their factors and servants in all kinds of merchandise, as well foods as other kinds (except armor * * * for hostile purposes) and to depart with their said ships, goods, merchandise, and whatsoever else, being able to bring them back and to return in safety:

And that likewise all merchants of the said countries and lordships of Brabant, Flanders, Mechlin, and other aforesaid countries, be they merchants of wools * * * shall be able * * * to dwell securely in the kingdom of England, in Ireland, and in Calais and within the ports and harbors of the same kingdom, country, and town, authorized by the king (that is to say, in the ports and harbors where customs officials and other officers are ordered to watch and wait for the entrance and exit of ships and merchandise, and not in others) with their goods and merchandise and ships and to trade with all the English merchants and others and their factors and servants in all kinds of merchandise, as well foods as other kinds (except the said armor * * *) and to carry into the aforesaid ports in England, Ireland and Calais their own goods, provisions and others, and the goods of the other aforesaid countries and lordships of Brabant, of Flanders, of Mechlin and the other aforesaid places, and to depart and return safely with all their said goods, merchandise and ships:

And also that the said merchants, their factors and servants shall be able, each of them to whom it shall be necessary, to buy and to have provisions freely of those of the other country and to carry them by sea one to the other * * * without being held to blame because they have so done, by the lords of one side or the other, nor by their officers; nor shall harm be done, or hindrance or disturbance made, by those of the part of England to the merchants of Brabant, Flanders, Mechlin, and aforesaid places, nor also by those of the aforesaid parts of Brabant, Flanders, Mechlin and other countries aforesaid to the merchants of the countries of England by violence, by reason of war and pillage, made or to be made, nor otherwise in any way for whatsoever cause; respecting and paying, as regards the merchants of England, of Ireland and of Calais, in the countries of Brabant, Flanders, Mechlin, and other aforesaid countries for the merchandise which they shall carry over and bring back; and likewise as regards the merchants of Brabant, Flanders, Mechlin, and aforesaid countries in the said realm and countries of England, Ireland and Calais, for the merchandise which they shall carry over there and bring back, the customs, tolls, and duties due and customary when merchandise has had course in time past between the realms and countries aforesaid included in present agreement, without being constrained to other duties.

And in respect to the merchants of one side or the other, touching the merchandise which they shall bring over and carry back each on his part, they shall pay the tolls and duties at the ordinance of their prince and lord according to that which is customary in their country.

And by this it is not intended to prejudice the prince or lord of one country or another from levying in those countries and lordships such tolls and duties, with respect to his subjects, as shall seem good to him.

Except this, that the said merchants, of one side or the other, their factors and servants, masters of ships and sailors, to whom it shall be lawful to have with them in their ships armor and artillery, for the preservation and safety of themselves and their goods, in travelling by sea, and to take the same with them into whatsoever ports at which they arrive, shall upon leaving their said ships leave behind such armor in their said ships or vessels; except knives, a dagger, or a sword, which they shall be able to carry, if it seem good to them, to their inns, where they shall be bound to leave their said swords.

At all times, the prince of one part or the other shall be able, for a reasonable cause, such as the need or high price of food, to make restriction as regards such kinds of food as shall seem necessary to him for his own welfare and that of his subjects, this present agreement not preventing.

And if it should happen that any ships, by the fortune of the sea or the pursuit of enemies, should be constrained to take refuge in any ports or harbors in England which are not authorized as has been said, in such a case they shall be able to be and enter safely in the said ports and harbors, without being able (being at the said harbors and ports) to lade, to stow, or to unlade any commodities, foods, merchandise, or other things.

Item, that the said merchants of England, their factors and servants, masters of ships and sailors, shall be able to hold intercourse with and dwell securely in the countries of Brabant, Flanders, Mechlin, and the aforesaid countries, and in the ports and harbors of the same countries, with their goods, ships, and any merchandises whatsoever, provisions and other things.

And likewise the merchants of Brabant, Flanders, Mechlin, and the other countries aforesaid and their factors and servants, masters of ships and sailors shall be able to be, to hold intercourse with, and to dwell safely in the kingdom of England, in Ireland, and at Calais, and in the ports and harbors of England, Ireland, and Calais aforesaid, without any misdeed being done or any hindrance or disturbance made by those of Brabant, Flanders, Mechlin and the aforesaid places nor by any others whatsoever (of whatsoever nation or country they may be) to the merchants of the country of England nor by those of that country of England or any others whatsoever to the merchants of Brabant, Flanders, Mechlin and the aforesaid countries, nor to their factors, servants, masters of ships, and sailors, of one part or the other, by violence, by reason of war, pillage, or robbery done or to be done, nor otherwise in any manner; provided that the merchants of any other country whatsoever be safe with all their goods and ships at the said countries of Brabant, Flanders, Mechlin, and other aforesaid countries, and in the ports and harbors of the said countries of Flanders, without any misdeed done or hindrance or disturbance made to them by those of the part of England; nor damage done or hindrance made in body or goods or in any possible manner by those of the other said countries to those of the part of England, their factors, servants, and goods, being in the said countries of Brabant, Flanders, the lordship and town of Mechlin, and in the other countries abovenamed, and in the ports and harbors of the same: * * *

Given in the city of Brussels, the twenty-fourth day of November, the year of grace one thousand four hundred and sixty-seven.

---

131. Confirmation of Richard's Title

(1484.   English original, 6 *R. P.* 241.   3 Stubbs, 235.)

* * * * * * * * *

BESIDES this we consider, how that ye be the undoubted son and heir of Richard late duke of York, very inheritor to the said crown and dignity royal, and as in right king of England, by way of inheritance; and that at this time, the premises duly considered, there is none other person living but ye only, that by right may claim the said crown and dignity royal, by way of inheritance, and how that ye be born within this land; by reason whereof, as we deem in our minds, ye be more naturally inclined to the prosperity and common weal of the same; and all the three estates of the land have, and may have, more certain knowledge of your birth and filiation abovesaid. We consider also, the great wit, prudence, justice, princely courage, and the memorable and laudable acts in divers battles, which we by experience know ye heretofore have done, for the salvation and defense of this same realm; and also the great noblesse and excellence of your birth and blood, as of him that is descended of the three most royal houses in Christendom, that is to say, England, France, and Spain.

Wherefore, these premises by us diligently considered, we desiring effectually the peace, tranquility, and public weal of this land, and the reduction of the same to the ancient honorable estate and prosperity, and having in your great prudence, justice, princely courage, and excellent virtue, singular confidence, have chosen in all that that in us is, and by this our writing choose you, high and mighty prince, into our king and sovereign lord &c., to whom we know for certain it appertaineth of inheritance so to be chosen. And hereupon we humbly desire, pray, and require your said noble grace, that according to this election of us the three estates of this land, as by your true inheritance, ye will accept and take upon you the said crown and royal dignity, with all things thereunto annexed and appertaining, as to you of right belonging, as well by inheritance as by lawful election: and, in case you so do, we promise to serve and to assist your Highness, as true and faithful subjects and liegemen, and to live and die with you in this matter, and every other just quarrel. For certainly we be determined, rather to aventure and commit us to the peril of our lives and jeopardy of death, than to live in such thraldom and bondage as we have lived long time heretofore, oppressed and injured by extortions and new impositions, against the laws of God and man, and the liberty, old police, and laws of this realm, wherein every Englishman is inherited. Our Lord God, King of all kings, by whose infinite goodness and eternal providence all things be principally governed in this world, lighten your soul, and grant you grace to do, as well in this matter as in all other, all that that may be according to his will and pleasure, and to the common and public weal of this land; so that, after great clouds, troubles, storms and tempests, the sun of justice and of grace may shine upon us, to the comfort and gladness of all true Englishmen.

Albeit that the right, title, and estate, which our sovereign lord
the king Richard the Third, hath to and in the crown and royal
dignity of this realm of England, with all things thereunto within
the same realm, and without it, united, annexed and appertaining,
be just and lawful, as grounded upon the laws of God and of
nature, and also upon the ancient laws and laudable customs of
this said realm, and so taken and reputed by all such persons
as are learned in the abovesaid laws and customs.   Yet nevertheless, forasmuch as it is considered, that the most part of the
people of this land is not sufficiently learned in the abovesaid laws
and customs, whereby the truth and right in this behalf of likelihood may be hid, and not clearly known to all the people, and
thereupon put in doubt and question.   And besides this, how that
the court of parliament is of such authority, and the people of
this land of such nature and disposition, as experience teacheth,
that manifestation and declaration of any truth or right, made
by the three estates of this realm assembled in parliament, and
by authority of the same, maketh, before all other things, most
faith and certainty; and, quieting men's minds, removeth the
occasion of all doubts and seditious language.   Therefore, at the
request, and by assent of the three estates of this realm, that is
to say, the lords spiritual and temporal, and commons of this
land, assembled in this present parliament, by authority of the
same, be it pronounced, decreed, and declared, that our said
sovereign lord the king was, and is, very and undoubted king
of this realm of England, with all things thereunto within the
same realm, and without it, united, annexed and appertaining,
as well by right of consanguinity and inheritance, as by lawful
election, consecration, and coronation.   And besides this, that,
at the request, and by the assent and authority abovesaid, be it
ordained, enacted and established, that the said crown and royal
dignity of this realm, and the inheritance of the same, and other
things thereunto within this same realm, or without it, united,
annexed, and now appertaining, rest and abide in the person of
our said sovereign lord the king, during his life, and, after his
disease, in his heirs of his body begotten.   And in especial, at
the request, and by assent and authority abovesaid, be it ordained, enacted, established, pronounced, decreed, and declared,
that the high and excellent prince Edward, son of our said sovereign lord the king, be heir apparent of the same our sovereign
lord the king, to succeed to him in the abovesaid crown and
royal dignity, with all things as is aforesaid thereunto united,
annexed and appertaining; to have them after the disease of

P

our said sovereign lord the king, to him and to his heirs of his body lawfully begotten.

*   *   *   *   *   *   *   *   *

132. Grant of Subsidy

(1484.   English original, 6 *R. P.* 238.   3 Stubbs, 236.)

SO the worship of God.   We your poor commons by your high commandment come to this your present parliament, for the shires, cities and boroughs of this your noble realm, by the assent of all the lords spiritual and temporal in this your present parliament assembled, grant by this present indenture to you, our sovereign lord, for the defense of this your said realm, and in especial for the safeguard and keeping of the sea, a subsidy called tonnage, to be taken in manner and form following; that is to say, iii shillings of every ton of wine coming into this your said realm, and of every ton of sweet wine coming into the same your realm, by any foreign merchant, as well by the merchants of Hanse and of Almain, as of any other foreign merchant, iii shillings, over the said iii shillings afore granted: to have and to perceive yearly the said subsidy, from the first day of this present parliament, for term of your natural life.   And over that, we your said commons, by the assent aforesaid, grant to you, our said sovereign lord, for the safeguard and keeping of the sea, another subsidy called poundage; that is to say, of all manner merchandises of every merchant denizen and alien, as well of the merchants of Hanse and of Almain, as of any other foreign merchant, carried out of this your said realm or brought into the same by way of merchandise, of the value of every xx*s.*, xii*d.*; except tin, whereof the merchants strangers to pay for subsidy, of the value of every xx*s.*, ii*s.*; and the merchants denizens, xii*d.*; and all such manner merchandises of every merchant denizen, to be valued after that they cost at the first buying or *achate*, by their oaths, or of their servants buyers of the said merchandises in their absence, or by their letters, the which the same merchants have of such buying from their factors; all manner of woolen cloth made and wrought within this your realm, by any merchant denizen not born alien, to be carried out of the same realm within the time of this grant, all manner wools, woolfells and hides, going out of the same, and every manner of corn, flour, all manner of fresh fish, bestial, and wine, into this your realm coming, ale, and all manner victual going out of this your said realm for the victualing of your town of Calais, and of the marches there under your obeyance, out of this grant always except: to have and to receive yearly the said subsidy of poundage, from the said first day of this present parliament, during your natural life; except afore except. And if any concealment be found in the merchants of the duty aforesaid, that they for such concealment pay thereof only the double subsidy, without any other hurt of forfeiture in that behalf; and that these grants be not taken in ensample to the kings of England in time to come. And that it may please your Highness, that as well merchants denizens, as strangers, coming into this your said realm with their merchandises, be well and honestly entreated and demeaned in their subsidies and all other things, and that the said merchants be entreated and demeaned as they were in the time of your noble progenitors, without oppression to be done to the merchants aforesaid, by the treasurer of England for the time being, customers, controllers, searchers, or any other your officers, paying their subsidies abovesaid. And that the said subsidies and every parcel of them, be employed and applied for the safeguard and keeping of the sea, and defense of this your said realm, in manner and form as it is before rehearsed. And over that, we your said poor commons, by the assent aforesaid, grant to you, our said sovereign lord, for the great affection and true humble hearts that we have to your Highness, for the defense of this your noble realm, a subsidy of wools, woolfells and hides, to be paid and levied in manner and form that followeth; that is to say, of every merchant denizen, for the subsidy of every sack of wool, xxxiii*s*. iiii*d*., and of every ccxl woolfells, xxxiii*s*. iiii*d*., and of every last of hides lxvi*s*. viii*d*.; to have and to receive the said subsidy, from the said first day of this present parliament, for term of your life: and of every merchant stranger, not born your liegeman, as well those that be made denizens, as hereafter shall be made by your letters patents or otherwise, as of other merchants strangers, of every sack of wool, lxvi*s*. viii*d*., and of every ccxl woolfells, lxvi*s*. viii*d*., and of every last of hides, lxxiii*s*. iiii*d*., going out of this your said realm; to have and to receive the said subsidies of the merchandises of the said aliens, from the said first day of this present parliament, during your natural life: the one half of all the said subsidies, by the merchants denizens to be paid at the end of six months next after the going out of the merchandises, and the other half at the end of six months

then next following, for to dispose and ordain after your right
gracious will and discretion for the defense abovesaid. * ﹡ *

﹡   ﹡   ﹡   ﹡   ﹡   ﹡   ﹡   ﹡   ﹡

133. An Act to free Subjects from
Benevolences

(**1484.**   French text and translation, 2 *S. R.* 478.   3 Stubbs, 219, 237.)

2. THE king remembering how the commons of this his realm
by new and unlawful inventions and inordinate covetousness,
against the law of this realm, have been put to great thraldom
and importable charges and exactions, and in especial by a new
imposition named a benevolence, whereby divers years the subjects and commons of this land against their wills and freedom
have paid great sums of money to their almost utter destruction;
for divers and many worshipful men of this realm by occasion
thereof were compelled by necessity to break up their households
and to live in great penury and wretchedness, their debts unpaid
and their children unpreferred, and such memorials as they had
ordained to be done for the wealth of their souls were made void
and annulled, to the great displeasure of God and to the destruction of this realm; therefore the king will it be ordained, by
the advice and assent of his lords spiritual and temporal and
the commons of this present parliament assembled, and by the
authority of the same, that his subjects and the commonalty of
this his realm from henceforth in no wise be charged by none
such charge or imposition called benevolence, nor by such like
charge; and that such exactions called benevolences, afore this
time taken be taken for no example to make such or any like
charge of any his said subjects of this realm hereafter, but it be
dampned and annulled forever.

134. Recognition of the Title of Henry VII

(1485.   1 Henry VII. c. 1.   2 S. R. 499.)

HENRY, by the grace of God, king of England and of France, and lord of Ireland, at the parliament holden at Westminster the seventh day of November, in the first year of the reign of King Henry, the seventh after the conquest.

To the pleasure of Almighty God, the wealth, prosperity and surety of this realm of England, to the singular comfort of all the king's subjects of the same and in avoiding of all ambiguities and questions, with the assent of the lords spiritual and temporal, and at the request of the commons, it is ordained, established and enacted by authority of this present parliament, that the inheritances of the crowns of the realms of England and of France, with all the permanence and royal dignity to the same pertaining, and all other seigniuriez to the king belonging beyond the sea with the appurtenances thereto in any wise due or pertaining, be, rest, remain and abide in the most royal person of our now sovereign lord King Henry the VIIth and in the heirs of his body lawfully coming, perpetually with the grace of God so to endure and in none other.

———◆———

135. An Act against bringing in of Gascony Wine, except in English, Irish, or Welshmen's Ships

(1485.   1 Henry VII. c. 8.   2 S. R. 502.)

ITEM, in the said parliament it was called to remembrance of the great minishing and decay that hath been now of late time of the navy within this realm of England, and idleness of the mariners within the same, by the which this noble realm within short process of time, without reformation be had therein, shall not be of habilite and power to defend itself: wherefore at the prayer of the said commons, the king our sovereign lord, by the advice of the lords spiritual and temporal, in this said present parliament assembled, and by authority of the same, it is enacted, ordained and established, that no manner person of what degree or condition that he be of, buy nor sell within this said realm,

Ireland, Wales, Calais or the marches thereof, or Berwick, from
the feast of Michaelmas next now coming, any manner of wines of
the growing of the duchy of Guyenne or of Gascony, but such as
shall be aventured and brought in an English, Irish or Welshman's
ship or ships, and the mariners of the same English, Irish or
Welshmen for the more part, or men of Calais or of the marches
of the same ; and that upon pain of forfeiture of the same wines
so bought or sold contrary to this act, the one half of that forfeiture to be to the king our sovereign lord and that other half
to the finder of that forfeiture : this act and ordinance to endure
betwixt this and the next parliament, saving alway to the king his
prerogative.

———◆———

136.   Establishment of the Court of Star Chamber

(1487.   3 Henry VII. c. 1.   2 S. R. 509.   This text revised from "The Statutes of Henry VII., printed by Caxton in 1489," ed. Rae.)

FIRST, the king our sovereign lord remembereth how by unlawful maintenances, giving of liveries, signs and tokens, and
retainders by indentures, promises, oaths, writings, or otherwise
embraceries of his subjects, untrue demeanings of sheriffs in
making of panels and other untrue returns, by taking of money by
juries, by great riots and unlawful assemblies, the policy and good
rule of this realm is almost subdued, and for the none punishing
of these inconveniences and by occasion of the premises nothing or little can be found by inquiry, whereby the laws of the
land in execution may take little effect, to the increase of murders, robberies, perjuries, and unsureties of all men living and
losses of their lands and goods, to the great displeasure of Almighty
God ; therefore it is ordained for reformation of the premises by
the authority of the said parliament, that the chancellor and treasurer of England for the time being and keeper of the king's privy
seal, or two of them, calling to him a bishop and a temporal lord
of the king's most honourable council, and the two chief justices
of the king's bench and common pleas for the time being, or
other two justices in their absence, upon bill or information put to
the said chancellor for the king, or any other, against any person
for any misbehaving before rehearsed, have authority to call
before them by writ or privy seal the said misdoers, and them and
other by their discretions by whom the truth may be known to

examine, and such as they find therein defective to punish them after their demerits, after the form and effect of statutes thereof made, in like manner and form as they should and ought to be punished if they were thereof convict after the due order of the law.

* * * * * * * * *

137. Allegiance to a De Facto King not Treason

(1495. 11 Henry VII. c. 1. 2 S. R. 568.)

THE king our sovereign lord, calling to his remembrance the duty of allegiance of his subjects of this his realm, and that they by reason of the same are bound to serve their prince and sovereign lord for the time being in his wars for the defence of him and the land against every rebellion, power and might reared against him, and with him to enter and abide in service in battle if the case so require ; and that for the same service what fortune ever fall by chance in the same battle against the mind and weal of the prince, as in this land some time past hath been seen, that it is not reasonable, but against all laws, reason, and good conscience that the said subjects going with their sovereign lord in wars, attending upon him in his person or being in other places by his commandment within this land or without, anything should lose or forfeit for doing their true duty and service of allegiance : it be therefore ordained, enacted and established by the king our sovereign lord by the advice and assent of the lords spiritual and temporal and the commons in this present parliament assembled, and by authority of the same, that from henceforth no manner of person nor persons, whatsoever he or they be, that attend upon the king and sovereign lord of this land for the time being in his person and do him true and faithful service of allegiance in the same, or be in other places by his commandment, in his wars within this land or without, that for the said deed and true duty of allegiance he or they be in no wise convict or attaint of high treason nor of other offences for that cause by act of parliament or otherwise by any process of law, whereby he or any of them shall lose or forfeit life, lands, tenements, rents, possessions, hereditaments, goods, chattels or any other things, but to be for that deed and service utterly discharged of any vexation, trouble

or loss ; and if any act or acts or other process of the law hereafter thereupon for the same happen to be made contrary to this
ordinance, that then that act or acts or other process of the law
whatsoever they shall be, stand and be utterly void.

II. Provided alway that no person nor persons shall take any
benefit or advantage by this act which shall hereafter decline from
his or their said allegiance.

---

138. An Act against Unlawful Retainers and Liveries

(150¾.   19 Henry VII. c. 14.   2 S. R. 658.)

THE king our sovereign lord calleth to his remembrance that
where before this time divers statutes, for punishment of
such persons that give or receive liveries, or that retain any person or persons or be retained with any person or persons, with
divers pains and forfeitures in the same statutes comprised, have
been made and established, and that notwithstanding divers persons have taken upon them some to give and some to receive
liveries and to retain and be retained contrary to the form of the
said statutes, and little or nothing is or has been done for the
punishment of the offenders in that behalf, wherefore our sovereign lord the king by the advice of the lords spiritual and temporal and of the commons of his realm in this parliament being
and by the authority of the same, hath ordained, established and
enacted, that all his statutes and ordinances before this time made
against such as make unlawful retainers, and such as be so retained,
or that give or receive livery, be plainly observed and kept and
put in due execution.

II. And over that our said sovereign lord and king ordaineth,
establisheth and enacteth by the said authority, that no person of
what estate or degree or condition he be, by himself or any other
for him by his commandment or agreement or assent, privily or
openly give any livery or sign, or retain any person other than
such as he giveth household wages unto without fraud or colour, or
that he be his manual servant or his officer or man learned in one
law or in the other, by any writing, oath, promise, livery, sign,
badge, token, or in any other manner or wise unlawfully retain ;
and if any do the contrary that then he run and fall in the pain
and forfeiture for every such livery and sign, badge or token c. s.

and the taker and accepter of every such livery, badge, token, or sign to forfeit and pay for every such livery and sign, badge, or token so accepted c. s., and for every month that he useth or keepeth such livery or sign, badge or token after that he hath taken or accepted the same to forfeit and pay c. s., and every person that by oath, writing or promise, or in any other wise unlawfully retain privily or openly, and also every such person that so is retained, to forfeit and pay for every such time c. s., and as well every person that so retaineth as every person that is so retained to forfeit and pay for every month that such retainer is continued c. s.   And that every person that before the making of this act by livery, sign, token, writing, badge, oath, promise or otherwise unlawfully hath retained any person, or by reason thereof is retained at the time of making of this act, contrary to the premises, that as well every of them that keepeth any person so in retainer as every person that so is and continueth so retained shall forfeit to the king for every month, from the feast underwritten, that such retainer is continued, c. s.

*　*　*　*　*　*　*　*　*

VI.   Moreover the king our sovereign lord by the advice, assent and authority aforesaid, hath ordained, established, and enacted, that every person that will sue or complain before the chancellor of England or the keeper of the king's great seal in the star chamber, or before the king in his bench, or before the king and his council attending upon his most royal person wheresoever he be, so that there be three of the same council at the least, of the which two shall be lords spiritual or temporal, against any person or persons offending or doing against the form of this ordinance or any other of the premises, be admitted by their discretion to give information, and every such informer so admitted shall be received to sue upon the said matter by information, and that he be received and admitted to give such information or informations before the said chancellor or keeper of the seal in the star chamber or before the king in his bench or before the king and his council aforesaid against as many such offenders as the person that so shall inform will or shall name ; and that upon the same all such persons be called by writ, subpoena, privy seal or otherwise, and the said chancellor or keeper of the seal or the king in his bench or the said council to have power to examine all persons defendants and every of them, as well by oath as otherwise, and to adjudge him or them convict or attaint as well by such examination as otherwise in such penalties as is aforesaid as the case shall require ; and also shall charge by judgment in the same such person or persons so convict or attaint to the person, plaintiff or informer in all costs therein had, by the discretion of him or them before whom he shall be so attainted or convicted ; and also the same party, plaintiff or informer shall have such reasonable reward of that that by his complaint shall grow to the king as shall be thought reasonable by the discretion of the said chancellor or keeper of the great seal, justices or council.

* * * * * * * * *

139.   Reversal of Attainders

(150¾.   19 Henry VII. c. 28.   2 *S. R.* 669.)

THE king our sovereign lord, considering that divers and many persons, whereof some of them and some of their ancestors were and be attainted of high treason for divers offences by them committed and done against their natural duty of their allegiance, make and have made instant and diligent pursuit in their most humble wise to His Highness of his mercy and pity to have the said attainders reversed and the same persons so attainted to be severally restored, that is to say Humphrey Stafford son to Humphrey Stafford esquire, John Baynton son to Robert Baynton late of Fallesdon in the county of Wiltes, Robert Ratclyff son to John Ratclyff knight, late Lord Fytzwalter, Thomas Mountforde son and heir to Simon Mountforde knight, Thomas Wyndham son to John Wyndham knight, Thomas Tyrrell son to James Tyrrell knight, John Charleton son to Richard Charleton knight, Charles Clyfforde son and heir to Jane sister and heir to Thomas Courteney late Earl of Devonshire, John Malory of Lynchebarowe in the county of Northampton gentleman ; the king's Highness of his especial grace, mercy and pity, being sorry for any such untruth and fall of any of his subjects in such case, is therefore inclined to hear and speed reasonably the said petitioners, so if there were convenient time and space in this present parliament, as yet is not, for the great and weighty matters concerning the common weal of this land treated in the same, and that the said parliament draweth so near to the end, and that after the same His Highness is not minded for the ease of his subjects without great, necessary and urgent causes of long time to call and summon a new parliament, by which long tract of time the said suitors and petitioners

were and should be discomforted and in despair of expedition of
their suits, petitions and causes, unless convenient remedy for
them were purveyed in this behalf: wherefore and in consideration of the premises the king's Highness is agreed and contented
that it be enacted by the lords spiritual and temporal and the commons in this present parliament assembled and by authority of the
same, that the king's Highness, from henceforth during his life,
shall have plain and full authority and power by his letters patent
under his great seal, to reverse, annull, repeal and avoid all the
attainders of the said persons and every of them and the heirs
of every of them, and of all other persons and the heirs of such
persons and every of them as have been attainted of high treason
by act of parliament or by the common law, at any time from the
xxii day of August the first year of his most noble reign to the first day
of this present parliament ; and also of all persons attainted in and
by this present parliament ; and also of all other persons attainted
of treason at any time during the reign of King Richard the Third
as well by the course and order of the common law as by the
authority of parliament or otherwise : and furthermore the king's
Grace by his letters patents under his said great seal to have full
authority and power to restore the same persons so attainted and
their heirs and every of them and to enable them in name, blood
and inheritance as if the said attainders or any of them had never
been had nor made ; and that the said letters patent rehearsing
the said reversal, repeal, annullation and avoydance of the said
acts of attainder or any of them, and the restitutions and enable-
ments of the said persons or any of them, and the inheritance contained in any of the king's said letters patent at any time hereafter
to be made according to the effect of this act, be as good, effectual
and available in the law to every of the same persons to whom
they shall be made according to the effect, tenor, purports, grants
and words in the same so made according to the effect of this
act, as if the same matters, words, tenors, and purports, contained in any of the said letters patent so made, were fully enacted,
established and authorized by authority of parliament.

II. Provided alway that all persons that have or hold any
honours, castles, lordships, manors, lands, tenements, fees, offices,
annuities, fermes, rent charges, liberties, franchises, or other hereditaments or possessions, by the king's letters patent, privy seal,
placard or bills assigned, in fee simple, fee tail or for term of life
or of years or at will, or by letters patent made by King Edward
the IVth, shall have, hold and enjoy to them, their heirs and assignees, against such persons as so hereafter shall be restored and

their heirs and assignees and against all other to their use and against none other persons, all the same honours, castles, manors, lordships, lands, tenements, fees, offices, rents and other premises, after the form, tenor and effect of the same letters patent, privy seal, placard or bills assigned, as if this act or any such restitution to them had never been had or made.

——◆——

140. Grant of Two Aids

(150¾.   19 Henry VII. c. 32.   2 S. R. 675.)

FORASMUCH as the king our sovereign lord is rightfully entitled to have two reasonable aids according to the laws of this land, the one aid for the making knight of the right noble prince his first begotten son Arthur late Prince of Wales deceased whose soul God pardon, and the other aid for the marriage of the right noble princess his first begotten daughter Margaret now married unto the king of Scots; and also that His Highness hath sustained and borne great and inestimable charges for the defense of this his realm, and for a firm and perpetual peace with the realm of Scotland and many other countries and regions, to the great weal, comfort and quietness of all his subjects; the commons in this present parliament assembled, considering the premises, and that if the same aids should be either of them levied and had by reason of their tenures according to the ancient laws of this land, should be to them doubtful, uncertain and great inquietness for the search and non knowledge of their several tenures and of their lands chargeable to the same, have made humble petition unto His Highness graciously to accept and take of them the sum of xl M^l li. as well in recompense and satisfaction of the said two aids, as for the said great and inestimable charges which His Grace hath sustained and borne as is aforesaid, to the weal, surety and comfort perpetual of them, their heirs and successors; upon the which petition and offer so made His Grace benignly considering the good and loving mind of his subjects and to eschew and avoid the great vexations, troubles and unquietness which to them should have ensued if the said aids were levied, received and taken after the ancient laws and form, as the said commons in their said petition have considered, and also calling to his most noble remembrance the good and acceptable services that the nobles of this realm and other his faithful and true subjects of the same in their own personages and otherwise have done to His Grace, and thereby sustained manifold costs and charges to his great honour and pleasure, and also to the common weal of this his realm, of his mere motion and abundant grace, and for the tender zeal and love that His Highness beareth to his said nobles and subjects, hath remitted, pardoned and released, and by this present act doth remit, pardon and release unto his said nobles and all his said subjects in any wise chargeable or contributory to the said aids or either of them or any part of them, and to their heirs, executors and successors, all his right, title and interest which His Grace hath or in any wise may or ought to have by reason of the said two aids or either of them ; and also His Grace holdeth him right well pleased with the said loving offer and grant of his subjects by them so made for his great and inestimable costs and charges by His Highness borne and sustained as is above said ; and over this of his more ample grace and pity, that the poor people of his commons of this his land should not in any wise be contributory or chargeable to any part of the said sum of xl M^l li. but to be thereof discharged, hath pardoned, remitted and released the sum of x M. li., parcel of the said sum of xl M. li., and is content to accept and take of them the sum of xxx M. li. only in full recompense and satisfaction of and for all the premises ; which sum of xxx M. li. it is enacted, ordained and established by the authority of this present parliament to be ordered, assessed, levied, paid, and had after the manner and form ensuing that is to say : that every shire within this realm shall bear and pay such sums of money assessed upon every of the said shires as here under in this act particularly it doth appear ; and that the cities and boroughs, towns and places, being within every shire, not by themselves accountable in the king's exchequer for xv ^{mes} and x ^{mes}, be chargeable with the said shires to the satisfaction and payment of the said sum of xxx M^l li. ; and all cities, boroughs and towns, not contributory nor chargeable with shires and accountable by themselves in the said exchequer for any xv ^{me} and xme, shall be charged toward the contenting and satisfaction of the said sum of xxx M^l li. with like and such sums of money as also hereunder in this act particularly it doth appear ; and that to the payment of the said sum of xxx M^l li ; every person or persons having lands or tenements or other hereditaments or possessions, in lands or tenements in fee simple, fee tail, freehold at will after the custom of the manor, ward, execution or ancient demesne, within any of the said cities, shires, towns or boroughs to the yearly value of xx^{ti} s. of free charter land or of xxvi s. viii d. of land holden at will above all charges, whereof they or any of them be seised or possessed or any other person or persons to the use of them or any of them, and not therewith chargeable with spiritual dismes, or any person or persons having goods or chattels to their proper use to the value of x marcs and above, not accounting their cattle for their plough nor their necessary stuff and implements of household, shall for the same be chargeable for the payment of the said sum of xxx M¹ li.; and none other persons of less substance in lands and goods; and that such x marcs of goods shall be seised and chargeable with like and equal sums rateable at xx s. of freehold or xxvi s. viii d. of copyhold in every shire, city and borough and in no other form : which sum of xxx M¹ li. to be levied in the said shires shall be ordered and assessed by the discretion of the commissioners in this act named, before the feast of Saint Michael the Archangel next coming, or four of them at the least, calling to them other discreet persons dwelling within the said shires such as they shall think necessary which shall give unto them their advice and assistance for the execution of the premises ; and in every of the said cities, boroughs and towns which are accountable by themselves in the exchequer as is aforesaid for the levying of such sums as they shall be chargeable with for the said sum of xxx M¹ li. to be ordered and assessed by the mayors, justices of peace, sheriffs, bailiffs and other head officers of the same cities, boroughs or towns or four of them at the least, calling to them other discreet persons dwelling within the said cities, boroughs and towns as they shall think necessary which shall give to them their advice and assistance for execution of the premises ; and that all persons be charged and bound by the said ordering and assessing according to the effect of the same, the said sum of xxx M¹ li. to be paid to our said sovereign lord the king in this exchequer by the collectors to be assigned for the gathering and collection of the same at the feast of Saint Andrew next coming ; and the said sums of the said xxx M¹ li. in form afore rehearsed or ordered and assessed, as well the said commissioners in the said shires or four of them at the least, as in the said cities and boroughs or four of them at the least, shall name collectors for the levy of the same, and certify under their seals the names of the said collectors into the king's exchequer before the feast of All Saints next coming ; and that the collectors to be named and assigned to gather and levy the said sum of xxx M¹ li. shall have full authority and power, after eight days next ensuing the said assessing, to levy and gather the same and for non payment thereof to distrain, take, apprise indifferently and sell as much of the goods and chattels of every person within the shires, cities or boroughs where they shall be collectors as shall serve for the payment of such sum or sums of money which every of them shall be ordered and assessed to pay, not charging any person but only for the sum upon him assessed ; and for non payment of any sum of money ordered and assessed in form aforesaid on every person that it shall be lawful to the said collectors to distrain, take and apprise indifferently and sell as much of the said goods and chattels of the farmers and tenants of any of the same persons so assessed not paying as shall serve for the payment of such sums of money as shall upon the said persons not making payment be ordered or assessed ; and that no person or persons be distrained or his goods or chattels taken for any sum upon him ordered or assessed, but after such rate and in such towns, cities, boroughs and places where his lands or his goods be for the which he is assessed ; also that the said commissioners in every shire or four of them at the least, shall by writing indented under their seals deliver to the collectors of the said sum of xxx M^l li. within eight days next after the said assessing, the names and sums of every person which they shall be appointed and limited to gather by the said writing.

*   *   *   *   *   *   *   *   *

141. Benefit of Clergy denied to Murderers

(1512.   4 Henry VIII. c. 2.   3 *S. R.* 49.)

WHEREAS robberies, murders and felonies daily increase more and more, and are committed and done in more heinous, open and detestable wise than hath been often seen in times past, and the persons so offending little regard the punishment thereof by the course of the common law nor by reason of any statute heretofore made, but bear them bold of their clergy and imagining and pleading of feigned and untrue foreign pleas triable in foreign counties to the intent to be removed from place to place by colourable and untrue suggestions, and for to be untruely acquit by favor, might and corruption so that they live in manner without fear or dread ; for reformation whereof and for the common wealth of this realm and for to put the said murderers, felons and offenders in more fear and dread so to offend ; be it ordained, established and enacted by the king our sovereign lord, the lords

spiritual and temporal and the commons in this present parliament assembled and by the authority of the same, that all person
or persons hereafter committing murder or felony in any church,
chapel or hallowed place, or of and upon malice prepense rob or
murder any person or persons in the king's highway, or else rob
or murder any person in his house the owner or dweller of the
house, his wife, child or servant then being therein and put in
fear or dread by the same, that such person or persons so offending be not from henceforth admitted to his or their clergy, such
as are within holy orders only except.

*   *   *   *   *   *   *   *   *

142. Act in Strode's Case

(1512.   4 Henry VIII. c. 8.   3 S. R. 53.)

*   *   *   *   *   *   *   *   *

II. * * *   AND over that be it enacted by the said authority
that all suits, accusations, condemnations, executions, fines, amerciaments, punishments, corrections, grievances, charges and impositions put or had or hereafter to be put or had unto or upon the
said Richard [Strode] and to every other of the person or persons
afore specified, that now be of this present parliament or that of
any parliament hereafter shall be, for any bill speaking, reasoning
or declaring of any matter or matters concerning the parliament
to be convened and treated of, be utterly void and of none effect.
And over that be it enacted by the said authority that if the said
Richard Strode or any of all the said other person or persons
hereafter be vexed, troubled or otherwise charged for any causes
as is afore said, that then he or they and every of them so vexed
or troubled of and for the same to have action upon the case
against every such person or persons so vexing or troubling any
contrary to this ordinance and provision, in the which action the
party grieved shall recover treble damages and costs, and that no
protection, essoin, nor wager of law in the said action in any wise
be admitted nor received.

*   *   *   *   *   *   *   *   *

143. Resumption of Royal Grants

(151⅘.   6 Henry VIII. c. 25.   3 *S. R.* 153.)

TO the king our sovereign lord,
     Pray and in the most humble wise beseech your Highness
your humble subjects the commons in this present parliament by
your high commandment assembled, that where the most noble
and Christian princes king Henry the VIth, king Edward the IIIrd
and the most famous and renowned prince of most worthy memory king Henry the VIIth your father, whom God pardon, and
other your noble progenitors have kept as honourable estates, as
well in their own persons as in their households and other their
charges, as well in defence of this your realm as in defence of the
towns of Calais, Guyenne, Hammes, Berwick and the marches of
the same, and other charges of this your realm of the only revenues
thereof, as hath done any king or Christian prince in any other
Christian region, not only to the great honour of the same but also
to the great ease, rest and quietness of the people of the same,
which caused all other lands and realms to have this your realm
in great renown, dread and fear and your said progenitors to be
dreaded of all outward nations ; and so it is most dread sovereign
lord that the revenues of your lands and other things being in your
hands and possession are so greatly minished, by reason of the
manifold gifts, grants and releases passed from your Highness since
the beginning of your most noble reign hitherto, that the residue
thereof now remaining in your hands and possession in no wise
sufficeth nor can suffice to bear and sustain your great charges,
which daily increase as well by reason of your wars now being in
hand against your ancient enemies the Scots as of your great
charges in keeping and defence of your city of Tournay late by
your Grace victoriously conquered, and which of very necessity
must be maintained and borne as accordeth to your princely estate
and honour of your Highness and surety of your humble subjects
and of your realm : in consideration whereof may it please your
Highness by the advice and assent of the lords spiritual and temporal in this present parliament assembled and by authority of the
same, for the conservation and maintaining of your most royal
estate and other charges above rehearsed, to the pleasure of God
and for your own honour and surety and also for the universal weal,
ease, rest and surety of this your realm and land, and for the minishing and lessening of the charges and burden of your said poor

Q

commons and subjects of the same which your Grace oweth to prefer and specially regard before the favour of any particular persons or earthly things; to take, seise, resume and have in your hands from the feast of Easter next coming all and singular those and such annuities granted to any person or persons by your Highness by your letters patents, * * *

———◆———

144. The Conditional Restraint of Annates

(1532.   23 Henry VIII. c. 20.   3 *S. R.* 385.   The whole act reprinted in **G.** and H. 178–186.)

FORASMUCH as it is well perceived, by long-approved experience, that great and inestimable sums of money have been daily conveyed out of this realm, to the impoverishment of the same ; and specially such sums of money as the pope's holiness, his predecessors, and the Court of Rome, by long time have heretofore taken of all and singular those spiritual persons which have been named, elected, presented, or postulated to be archbishops or bishops within this realm of England, under the title of annates, otherwise called first-fruits: which annates, or first-fruits, heretofore have been taken of every archbishopric, or bishopric, within this realm, by restraint of the pope's bulls, for confirmations, elections, admissions, postulations, provisions, collations, dispositions, institutions, installations, investitures, orders, holy benedictions, palls, or other things requisite and necessary to the attaining of those their promotions ; and have been compelled to pay, before they could attain the same, great sums of money, before they might receive any part of the fruits of the said archbishopric, or bishopric, whereunto they were named, elected, presented, or postulated ; by occasion whereof, not only the treasure of this realm has been greatly conveyed out of the same, but also it has happened many times, by occasion of death, unto such archbishops, and bishops, so newly promoted, within two or three years after his or their consecration, that his or their friends, by whom he or they have been holpen to advance and make payment of the said annates, or first-fruits, have been thereby utterly undone and impoverished :

II. And for because the said annates have risen, grown, and increased, by an uncharitable custom, grounded upon no just or good title, and the payments thereof obtained by restraint of bulls, until the same annates, or first-fruits, have been paid, or surety made for the same; which declares the said payments to be exacted, and taken by constraint, against all equity and justice:

III. The noblemen, therefore, of the realm, and the wise, sage, politic commons of the same, assembled in this present Parliament, considering that the Court of Rome ceases not to tax, take, and exact the said great sums of money, under the title of annates, or first-fruits, as is aforesaid, to the great damage of the said prelates and this realm; which annates or first-fruits, were first suffered to be taken within the same realm, for the only defence of Christian people against the infidels, and now they be claimed and demanded as mere duty, only for lucre, against all right and conscience: insomuch that it is evidently known, that there has passed out of this realm unto the Court of Rome, since the second year of the reign of the most noble prince of famous memory, King Henry VII., unto this present time, under the name of annates, or first-fruits, paid for the expedition of bulls of archbishoprics and bishoprics, the sum of eight hundred thousand ducats, amounting in sterling money, at the least, to eight score thousand pounds, besides other great and intolerable sums which have yearly been conveyed to the said Court of Rome, by many other ways and means, to the great impoverishment of this realm:

IV. And albeit that our said sovereign the king, and all his natural subjects, as well spiritual as temporal, be as obedient, devout, catholic, and humble children of God and Holy Church, as any people be within any realm christened; yet the said exactions of annates, or first-fruits, be so intolerable and importable to this realm, that it is considered and declared, by the whole body of this realm now represented by all the estates of the same assembled in this present Parliament, that the king's highness before Almighty God is bound, as by the duty of a good Christian prince, for the conservation and preservation of the good estate and commonwealth of this his realm, to do all that in him is to obviate, repress, and redress the said abuses and exactions of annates, or first-fruits: and because that divers prelates of this realm be now in extreme age, and in other debilities of their bodies, so that of likelihood bodily death in short time shall or may succeed unto them; by reason whereof great sums of money shall shortly after their deaths be conveyed unto the Court of Rome, for the unreasonable and uncharitable causes abovesaid, to the universal damage, prejudice, and impoverishment of this realm, if speedy remedy be not in due time provided:

V. It is therefore ordained, established, and enacted, by authority of this present Parliament, that the unlawful payments of annates, or first-fruits, and all manner contributions for the same, for any archbishopric or bishopric, or for any bulls hereafter to be obtained from the Court of Rome, to or for the aforesaid purpose and intent, shall from henceforth utterly cease, and no such hereafter to be paid for any archbishopric, or bishopric, within this realm, other or otherwise than hereafter in this present Act is declared; and that no manner person nor persons hereafter to be named, elected, presented, or postulated to any archbishopric, or bishopric, within this realm, shall pay the said annates, or first-fruits, for the said archbishopric, or bishopric, nor any other manner of sum or sums of money, pensions, or annuities for the same, or for any other like exaction, or cause, upon pain to forfeit to our said sovereign lord the king, his heirs and successors, all manner his goods and chattels for ever, and all the temporal lands and possessions of the same archbishopric, or bishopric, during the time that he or they which shall offend, contrary to this present Act, shall have, possess, or enjoy the archbishopric, or bishopric, wherefore he shall so offend contrary to the form aforesaid.

*   *   *   *   *   *   *   *   *

XII. And if that upon the aforesaid reasonable, amicable, and charitable ways and means, by the king's highness to be experimented, moved, or compounded, or otherwise approved, it shall and may appear, or be seen unto his grace, that this realm shall be continually burdened and charged with this, and such other intolerable exactions and demands, as heretofore it hath been; and that thereupon, for continuance of the same, our said holy father the pope, or any of his successors, or the Court of Rome, will, or do, or cause to be done at any time hereafter, so as is above rehearsed, unjustly, uncharitably, and unreasonably, vex, inquiet, molest, trouble, or grieve our said sovereign lord, his heirs or successors, kings of England, or any of his or their spiritual or lay subjects, or this his realm, by excommunication, excommengement, interdiction, or by any other process, censures, compulsories, ways or means:

XIII. Be it enacted by the authority aforesaid, that the king's highness, his heirs and successors, kings of England, and all his spiritual and lay subjects of the same, without any scruples of conscience, shall and may lawfully, to the honour of Almighty God, the increase and continuance of virtue and good example within this realm, the said censures, excommunications, interdictions, compulsories, or any of them notwithstanding, minister, or cause to be ministered, throughout this said realm, and all other the dominions or territories belonging or appertaining thereunto, all and all manner of sacraments, sacramentals, ceremonies, or other divine service of Holy Church, or any other thing or things necessary for the health of the soul of mankind, as they heretofore at any time or times have been virtuously used or accustomed to do within the same; and that no manner such censures, excommunications, interdictions, or any other process or compulsories, shall be by any of the prelates, or other spiritual fathers of this region, nor by any of their ministers or substitutes, at any time or times hereafter published, executed, nor divulged, nor suffered to be published, executed, or divulged in any manner of wise.

XIV. Be it remembered that on the 9th day of July, in the 25th year of the reign of King Henry, the same lord the king, by his letters patent, sealed under his great seal, ratified and confirmed the aforesaid Act, and gave to that Act his royal assent.

———◆———

145. Act in Restraint of Appeals

(1533. 24 Henry VIII. c. 12. 3 S. R. 427. The whole act reprinted in G. and H. 187–195.)

WHERE by divers sundry old authentic histories and chronicles, it is manifestly declared and expressed, that this realm of England is an empire, and so hath been accepted in the world, governed by one supreme head and king, having the dignity and royal estate of the imperial crown of the same, unto whom a body politic, compact of all sorts and degrees of people, divided in terms, and by names of spiritualty and temporalty, be bounden and ought to bear, next to God, a natural and humble obedience: he being also institute and furnished, by the goodness and sufferance of Almighty God, with plenary, whole, and entire power, pre-eminence, authority, prerogative and jurisdiction, to render and yield justice, and final determination to all manner of folk, residents, or subjects within this his realm, in all causes, matters, debates, and contentions, happening to occur, insurge, or begin within the limits thereof, without restraint, or provocation to any foreign princes or potentates of the world; the body spiritual whereof having power, when any cause of the law divine happened to come in question, or of spiritual learning, then it was declared, interpreted, and showed by that part of the said body politic, called the spiritualty, now being usually called the

English Church, which always hath been reputed, and also found of that sort, that both for knowledge, integrity, and sufficiency of number, it hath been always thought, and is also at this hour, sufficient and meet of itself, without the intermeddling of any exterior person or persons, to declare and determine all such doubts, and to administer all such offices and duties, as to their rooms spiritual doth appertain ; for the due administration whereof, and to keep them from corruption and sinister affection, the king's most noble progenitors, and the antecessors of the nobles of this realm, have sufficiently endowed the said Church, both with honour and possessions ; and the laws temporal, for trial of property of lands and goods, and for the conservation of the people of this realm in unity and peace, without rapine or spoil, was and yet is administered, adjudged, and executed by sundry judges and ministers of the other part of the said body politic, called the temporalty ; and both their authorities and jurisdictions do conjoin together in the due administration of justice, the one to help the other.

II. And whereas the king, his most noble progenitors, and the nobility and commons of this said realm, at divers and sundry parliaments, as well as in the time of King Edward I., Edward III., Richard II., Henry IV., and other noble kings of this realm, made sundry ordinances, laws, statutes, and provisions for the entire and sure conservation of the prerogatives, liberties, and pre-eminences of the said imperial crown of this realm, and of the jurisdiction spiritual and temporal of the same, to keep it from the annoyance as well of the see of Rome, as from the authority of other foreign potentates, attempting the diminution or violation thereof, as often, and from time to time, as any such annoyance or attempt might be known or espied ;

And notwithstanding the said good statutes and ordinances made in the time of the king's most noble progenitors, in preservation of the authority and prerogative of the said imperial crown, as is aforesaid ; yet nevertheless since the making of the said good statutes and ordinances, divers and sundry inconveniences and dangers, not provided for plainly by the said former acts, statutes, and ordinances, have arisen and sprung by reason of appeals sued out of this realm to the see of Rome, in causes testamentary, causes of matrimony and divorces, right of tithes, oblations and obventions, not only to the great inquietation, vexation, trouble, cost and charges of the king's highness, and many of his subjects and residents in this his realm, but also to the great delay and let to the true and speedy determination of the said causes, for so much as the parties appealing to the said Court of Rome most commonly do the same for the delay of justice ;

And forasmuch as the great distance of way is so far out of this realm, so that the necessary proofs, nor the true knowledge of the cause, can neither there be so well known, nor the witnesses there so well examined, as within this realm, so that the parties grieved by means of the said appeals be most times without remedy :

In consideration whereof the king's highness, his nobles and commons, considering the great enormities, dangers, long delays and hurts, that as well to his highness, as to his said nobles, subjects, commons, and residents of this his realm, in the said causes testamentary, causes of matrimony and divorces, tithes, oblations and obventions, do daily ensue, does therefore by his royal assent, and by the assent of the lords spiritual and temporal, and the commons, in this present parliament assembled, and by authority of the same, enact, establish, and ordain, that all causes testamentary, causes of matrimony and divorces, rights of tithes, oblations and obventions (the knowledge whereof by the goodness of princes of this realm, and by the laws and customs of the same, appertaineth to the spiritual jurisdiction of this realm) already commenced, moved, depending, being, happening, or hereafter coming in contention, debate, or question within this realm, or within any the king's dominions, or marches of the same, or elsewhere, whether they concern the king our sovereign lord, his heirs and successors, or any other subjects or residents within the same, of what degree soever they be, shall be from henceforth heard, examined, discussed, clearly, finally, and definitively adjudged and determined within the king's jurisdiction and authority, and not elsewhere, in such courts spiritual and temporal of the same, as the natures, conditions, and qualities of the causes and matters aforesaid in contention, or hereafter happening in contention, shall require, without having any respect to any custom, use, or sufferance, in hindrance, let, or prejudice of the same, or to any other thing used or suffered to the contrary thereof by any other manner of person or persons in any manner of wise ; any foreign inhibitions, appeals, sentences, summons, citations, suspensions, interdictions, excommunications, restraints, judgments, or any other process or impediments, of what natures, names, qualities, or conditions soever they be, from the see of Rome, or any other foreign courts or potentates of the world, or from and out of this realm, or any other the king's dominions, or marches of the same, to the see of Rome, or to any other foreign courts or potentates, to the let or impediment thereof in any wise notwithstanding.

And that it shall be lawful to the king our sovereign lord, and to his heirs and successors, and to all other subjects or residents within this realm, or within any the king's dominions, or marches of the same, notwithstanding that hereafter it should happen any excommengement, excommunications, interdictions, citations, or any other censures, or foreign process out of any outward parts, to be fulminate, promulged, declared, or put in execution within this said realm, or in any other place or places, for any of the causes before rehearsed, in prejudice, derogation, or contempt of this said Act, and the very true meaning and execution thereof, may and shall nevertheless as well pursue, execute, have, and enjoy the effects, profits, benefits, and commodities of all such processes, sentences, judgments, and determinations done, or hereafter to be done, in any of the said courts spiritual or temporal, as the cases shall require, within the limits, power, and authority of this the king's said realm, and dominions and marches of the same, and those only, and none other to take place, and to be firmly observed and obeyed within the same.

* * * * * * * * *

X. And if it shall happen any person or persons hereafter to pursue or provoke any appeal contrary to the effect of this Act, or refuse to obey, execute, and observe all things comprised within the same, concerning the said appeals, provocations, and other foreign processes to be sued out of this realm, for any the causes aforesaid, that then every such person or persons so doing, refusing, or offending contrary to the true meaning of this Act, their procurers, fautors, advocates, counsellors, and abettors, and every of them, shall incur into the pains, forfeitures, and penalties ordained and provided in the said statute made in the said sixteenth year of King Richard II., and with like process to be made against the said offenders, as in the same statute made in the said sixteenth year more plainly appeareth.

---

146. Ecclesiastical Appointments Act

(1534.   25 Henry VIII. c. 20.   3 *S. R.* 462.   The whole act, "The Absolute Restraint of Annates, Election of Bishops, and Letters Missive Act," reprinted in G. and H. 201–209.)

* * * * * * * * *

IV. AND furthermore be it ordained and established by the authority aforesaid, that at every avoidance of every archbishopric

or bishopric within this realm, or in any other the king's dominions, the king our sovereign lord, his heirs and successors, may
grant to the prior and convent, or the dean and chapter of the
cathedral churches or monasteries where the see of such archbishopric or bishopric shall happen to be void, a licence under the
great seal, as of old time has been accustomed, to proceed to
election of an archbishop or bishop of the see so being void, with
a letter missive, containing the name of the person which they
shall elect and choose : by virtue of which licence the said dean
and chapter, or prior and convent, to whom any such licence and
letters missive shall be directed, shall with all speed and celerity
in due form elect and choose the same person named in the said
letters missive, to the dignity and office of the archbishopric or
bishopric so being void, and none other.

And if they do defer or delay their election above twelve days
next after such licence and letters missive to them delivered,
that then for every such default the king's highness, his heirs and
successors, at their liberty and pleasure shall nominate and present, by their letters patent under their great seal, such a person to
the said office and dignity so being void, as they shall think able
and convenient for the same.

And that every such nomination and presentment to be made
by the king's highness, his heirs and successors, if it be to the
office and dignity of a bishop, shall be made to the archbishop
and metropolitan of the province where the see of the same
bishopric is void, if the see of the said archbishopric be then full,
and not void ; and if it be void, then to be made to such archbishop or metropolitan within this realm, or in any the king's
dominions, as shall please the king's highness, his heirs or successors : and if any such nomination or presentment shall happen
to be made for default of such election to the dignity or office of
any archbishop, then the king's highness, his heirs and successors,
by his letters patent under his great seal, shall nominate and
present such person, as they will dispose to have the said office
and dignity of archbishopric being void, to one such archbishop
and two such bishops, or else to four such bishops within this
realm, or in any of the king's dominions, as shall be assigned by
our said sovereign lord, his heirs or successors.

V. And be it further enacted by the authority aforesaid, that
whensoever any such presentment or nomination shall be made by
the king's highness, his heirs or successors, by virtue and authority
of this Act, and according to the tenor of the same ; that then every
archbishop and bishop, to whose hands any such presentment and

nomination shall be directed, shall with all speed and celerity invest and consecrate the person nominate and presented by the king's highness, his heirs or successors, to the office and dignity that such person shall be so presented unto, and give and use to him pall, and all other benedictions, ceremonies, and things requisite for the same, without suing, procuring, or obtaining hereafter any bulls or other things at the see of Rome, for any such office or dignity in any behalf.

And if the said dean and chapter, or prior and convent, after such licence and letters missive to them directed, within the said twelve days do elect and choose the said person mentioned in the said letters missive, according to the request of the king's highness, his heirs or successors, thereof to be made by the said letters missive in that behalf, then their election shall stand good and effectual to all intents.

* * * * * * * * *

VII. And be it further enacted by the authority aforesaid, that if the prior and convent of any monastery, or dean and chapter of any cathedral church, where the see of any archbishop or bishop is, within any of the king's dominions, after such licence as is afore rehearsed, shall be delivered to them, proceed not to election, and signify the same according to the tenor of this Act, within the space of twenty days next after such licence shall come to their hands; or else if any archbishop or bishop, within any the king's dominions, after any such election, nomination, or presentation shall be signified unto them by the king's letters patent, shall refuse, and do not confirm, invest, and consecrate with all due circumstance as is aforesaid, every such person as shall be so elected, nominate, or presented, and to them signified as is above mentioned, within twenty days next after the king's letters patent of such signification or presentation shall come to their hands; or else if any of them, or any other person or persons, admit, maintain, allow, obey, do or execute any censures, excommunications, interdictions, inhibitions, or any other process or act, of what nature, name, or quality soever it be, to the contrary, or let of due execution of this Act; that then every prior and particular person of his convent, and every dean and particular person of the chapter, and every archbishop and bishop, and all other persons, so offending and doing contrary to this Act, or any part thereof, and their aiders, counsellors, and abetters, shall run into the dangers, pains, and penalties of the Statute of the Provision and Præmunire, made in the five-and-twentieth year of the reign of King Edward III., and in the sixteenth year of King Richard II.

———◆———

147. The First Act of Succession

(1534.   25 Henry VIII. c. 22.   3 S. R. 471.   The whole act reprinted in G. and H. 232–243.)

IN their most humble wise shown unto your majesty your most humble and obedient subjects, the lords spiritual and temporal and the commons in this present Parliament assembled, that since it is the natural inclination of every man gladly and willingly to provide for the surety of both his title and succession, although it touch only his private cause ; we therefore, most rightful and dreadful sovereign lord, reckon ourselves much more bound to beseech and instant your highness (although we doubt not of your princely heart and wisdom, mixed with a natural affection to the same) to foresee and provide for the perfect surety of both you, and of your most lawful succession and heirs, upon which dependeth all our joy and wealth, in whom also is united and knit the only mere true inheritance and title of this realm, without any contradiction ;

Wherefore we your said most humble and obedient subjects, in this present Parliament assembled, calling to our remembrance the great divisions which in times past have been in this realm, by reason of several titles pretended to the imperial crown of the same, which sometimes, and for the most part ensued, by occasion of ambiguity and doubts, then not so perfectly declared, but that men might, upon froward intents, expound them to every man's sinister appetite and affection, after their sense, contrary to the right legality of the succession and posterity of the lawful kings and emperors of this realm ; whereof hath ensued great effusion and destruction of man's blood, as well of a great number of the nobles, as of other the subjects, and especially inheritors in the same ; and the greatest occasion thereof hath been because no perfect and substantial provision by law hath been made within this realm of itself, when doubts and questions have been moved and proponed, of the certainty and legality of the succession and posterity of the crown ; by reason whereof the Bishop of Rome and See Apostolic, contrary to the great and inviolable grants of jurisdictions given by God immediately to emperors, kings and princes, in succession to their heirs, has presumed, in times past,

to invest who should please them, to inherit in other men's kingdoms and dominions, which thing we, your most humble subjects,
both spiritual and temporal, do utterly abhor and detest ; and sometimes other foreign princes and potentates of sundry degrees,
minding rather dissension and discord to continue in the realm, to
the utter desolation thereof, than charity, equity, or unity, have
many times supported wrong titles, whereby they might the more
easily and facilely aspire to the superiority of the same ; the continuance and sufferance whereof, deeply considered and pondered,
were too dangerous and perilous to be suffered any longer within
this realm, and too much contrary to the unity, peace, and tranquillity of the same, being greatly reproachable and dishonourable
to the whole realm :

II. In consideration whereof, your said most humble and obedient subjects, the nobles and commons of this realm, calling
further to their remembrance that the good unity, peace, and
wealth of this realm, and the succession of the subjects of the
same, most especially and principally above all worldly things
consists and rests in the certainty and surety of the procreation
and posterity of your highness, in whose most royal person, at this
present time, is no manner of doubt nor question ; do therefore
most humbly beseech your highness, that it may please your
majesty, that it may be enacted by your highness, with the assent
of the lords spiritual and temporal, and the commons, in this
present Parliament assembled, and by the authority of the same,
that the marriage heretofore solemnized between your highness
and the Lady Katherine, being before lawful wife to Prince
Arthur, your elder brother, which by him was carnally known, as
doth duly appear by sufficient proof in a lawful process had and
made before Thomas, by the sufferance of God, now archbishop
of Canterbury and metropolitan and primate of all this realm,
shall be, by authority of this present Parliament, definitively,
clearly, and absolutely declared, deemed, and adjudged to be
against the laws of Almighty God, and also accepted, reputed,
and taken of no value nor effect, but utterly void and annulled, and
the separation thereof, made by the said archbishop, shall be
good and effectual to all intents and purposes ; any licence, dispensation, or any other act or acts going afore, or ensuing the
same, or to the contrary thereof, in any wise notwithstanding ; and
that every such licence, dispensation, act or acts, thing or things
heretofore had, made, done, or to be done to the contrary thereof, shall be void and of none effect ; and that the said Lady
Katherine shall be from henceforth called and reputed only dow-

ager to Prince Arthur, and not queen of this realm ; and that the lawful matrimony had and solemnized between your highness and your most dear and entirely beloved wife Queen Anne shall be established, and taken for undoubtful, true, sincere, and perfect ever hereafter, according to the just judgment of the said Thomas, archbishop of Canterbury, metropolitan and primate of all this realm, whose grounds of judgment have been confirmed, as well by the whole clergy of this realm in both the Convocations, and by both the universities thereof, as by the universities of Bologna, Padua, Paris, Orleans, Toulouse, Angers, and divers others, and also by the private writings of many right excellent well-learned men ; which grounds so confirmed, and judgment of the said archbishop ensuing the same, together with your marriage solemnized between your highness and your said lawful wife Queen Anne, we your said subjects, both spiritual and temporal, do purely, plainly, constantly, and firmly accept, approve, and ratify for good and consonant to the laws of Almighty God, without error or default, most humbly beseeching your majesty, that it may be so established for ever by your most gracious and royal assent.

*   *   *   *   *   *   *   *   *

VI. And also be it enacted by authority aforesaid, that all the issue had and procreated, or hereafter to be had and procreated, between your highness and your said most dear and entirely beloved wife Queen Anne, shall be your lawful children, and be inheritable, and inherit, according to the course of inheritance and laws of this realm, the imperial crown of the same, with all dignities, honours, pre-eminences, prerogatives, authorities, and jurisdictions to the same annexed or belonging, in as large and ample manner as your highness at this present time has the same as king of this realm ; the inheritance thereof to be and remain to your said children and right heirs in manner and form as hereafter shall be declared, that is to say :

VII. First the said imperial crown, and other the premises, shall be to your majesty, and to your heirs of your body lawfully begotten, that is to say : to the first son of your body, between your highness and your said lawful wife, Queen Anne, begotten, and to the heirs of the body of the same first son lawfully begotten, and for default of such heirs, then to the second son of your body and of the body of the said Queen Anne begotten, and to the heirs of the body of the said second son lawfully begotten, and so to every son of your body and of the body of the said Queen Anne begotten, and to the heirs of the body of every such son begotten, according to the course of inheritance in that behalf; and if it shall happen your said dear and entirely beloved wife Queen Anne to decease without issue male of the body of your highness to be begotten (which God defend), then the same imperial crown, and all other the premises, to be to your majesty, as is aforesaid, and to the son and heir male of your body lawfully begotten, and to the heirs of the body of the same son and heir male lawfully begotten; and for default of such issue, then to your second son of your body lawfully begotten, and to the heirs of the body of the same second son lawfully begotten, and so from son and heir male to son and heir male, and to the heirs of the several bodies of every such son and heir male to be begotten, according to the course of inheritance, in like manner and form as is above said.

And for default of such sons of your body begotten, and of the heirs of the several bodies of such sons lawfully begotten, that then the said imperial crown, and other the premises, shall be to the issue female between your majesty and your said most dear and entirely beloved wife, Queen Anne, begotten, that is to say: first to the eldest issue female, which is the Lady Elizabeth, now princess, and to the heirs of her body lawfully begotten, and for default of such issue, then to the second issue female, and to the heirs of her body lawfully begotten, and so from issue female to issue female, and to the heirs of their bodies one after another, by course of inheritance, according to their ages, as the crown of England has been accustomed, and ought to go, in cases where there be heirs female to the same; and for default of such issue, then the said imperial crown, and all other the premises, shall be in the right heirs of your highness for ever.

* * * * * * * * *

XIII. And for the more sure establishment of the succession of your most royal majesty, according to the tenor and form of this Act, be it further enacted by authority aforesaid, that as well all the nobles of your realm spiritual and temporal, as all other your subjects now living and being, or which hereafter shall be, at their full ages, by the commandment of your majesty or of your heirs, at all times hereafter from time to time, when it shall please your highness or your heirs to appoint, shall make a corporal oath in the presence of your highness or your heirs, or before such others as your majesty or your heirs will depute for the same, that they shall truly, firmly, and constantly, without fraud or guile, observe, fulfil, maintain, defend, and keep, to their cunning, wit, and uttermost of their powers, the whole effects and contents of this present Act. And that all manner your subjects, as well spiritual as temporal, suing livery, restitutions, or *ouster le main* out of the hands of your highness or of your heirs, or doing any fealty to your highness or to your heirs, by reason of tenure of their lands, shall swear a like corporal oath, that they and every of them, without fraud or guile, to their cunning, wit, and uttermost of their powers, shall truly, firmly, and constantly observe, fulfil, maintain, defend, and keep the effects and contents contained and specified in this Act, or in any part thereof; and that they, nor any of them, shall hereafter have any liveries, *ouster le main*, or restitution out of your hands, nor out of the hands of your heirs, till they have made the said corporal oath in form above rehearsed. And if any person or persons, being commanded by authority of this Act to make the said oath afore limited, obstinately refuse that to do, in contempt of this Act, that then every such person so doing, to be taken and accepted for offender in misprision of high treason ; and that every such refusal shall be deemed and adjudged misprision of high treason ; and the offender therein to suffer such pains and imprisonment, losses and forfeitures, and also lose privileges of sanctuaries, in like manner and form as is above mentioned for the misprisions of treasons afore limited by this Act.

*   *   *   *   *   *   *   *   *

148. Act of Supremacy of Henry VIII

(1534.   26 Henry VIII. c. 1.   3 *S. R.* 492.   G. and H. 243-244.)

ALBEIT the king's majesty justly and rightfully is and ought to be the supreme head of the Church of England, and so is recognized by the clergy of this realm in their Convocations, yet nevertheless for corroboration and confirmation thereof, and for increase of virtue in Christ's religion within this realm of England, and to repress and extirp all errors, heresies, and other enormities and abuses heretofore used in the same : be it enacted by authority of this present Parliament, that the king our sovereign lord, his heirs and successors, kings of this realm, shall be taken, accepted, and reputed the only supreme head in earth of the Church of England, called *Anglicana Ecclesia;* and shall have and enjoy, annexed and united to the imperial crown of this realm, as well the title and style thereof, as all honours, dignities, pre-eminences, jurisdictions, privileges, authorities, immunities, profits, and commodities to the said dignity of supreme head of the same Church belonging and appertaining; and that our said sovereign lord, his heirs and successors, kings of this realm, shall have full power and authority from time to time to visit, repress, redress, reform, order, correct, restrain, and amend all such errors, heresies, abuses, offences, contempts, and enormities, whatsoever they be, which by any manner spiritual authority or jurisdiction ought or may lawfully be reformed, repressed, ordered, redressed, corrected, restrained, or amended, most to the pleasure of Almighty God, the increase of virtue in Christ's religion, and for the conservation of the peace, unity, and tranquillity of this realm; any usage, custom, foreign law, foreign authority, prescription, or any other thing or things to the contrary hereof notwithstanding.

---

149. The Treasons Act

(1534. 26 Henry VIII. c. 13. 3 *S. R.* 508. G. and H. 247-250.)

FORASMUCH as it is most necessary, both for common policy and duty of subjects, above all things to prohibit, provide, restrain, and extinct all manner of shameful slanders, perils, or imminent danger or dangers, which might grow, happen, or rise to their sovereign lord the king, the queen, or their heirs, which when they be heard, seen, or understood, cannot be but odible, and also abhorred of all those sorts that be true and loving subjects, if in any point they may do, or shall touch the king, his queen, their heirs or successors, upon which dependeth the whole unity and universal weal of this realm, without providing wherefore too great a scope of unreasonable liberty should be given to all cankered and traitorous hearts, willers and workers of the same; and also the king's loving subjects should not declare unto their sovereign lord now being, which unto them has been, and is most entirely both beloved and esteemed, their undoubted sincerity and truth.

II. Be it therefore enacted by the assent and consent of our sovereign lord the king, and the lords spiritual and temporal, and commons in this present Parliament assembled, and by the authority of the same, that if any person or persons, after the first day of February next coming, do maliciously wish, will, or desire, by words or writing, or by craft imagine, invent, practise, or attempt any bodily harm to be done or committed to the king's most royal person, the queen's, or their heirs apparent, or to deprive them or any of them of their dignity, title, or name of their royal estates, or slanderously and maliciously publish and pronounce, by express writing or words, that the king our sovereign lord should be heretic, schismatic, tyrant, infidel or usurper of the crown, or rebelliously do detain, keep, or withhold from our said sovereign lord, his heirs or successors, any of his or their castles fortresses, fortalices, or holds within this realm, or in any other the king's dominions or marches, or rebelliously detain, keep, or withhold from the king's said highness, his heirs or successors, any of his or their ships, ordnances, artillery, or other munitions or fortifications of war, and do not humbly render and give up to our said sovereign lord, his heirs or successors, or to such persons as shall be deputed by them, such castles, fortresses, fortalices, holds, ships, ordnances, artillery, and other munitions and fortifications of war, rebelliously kept or detained, within six days next after they shall be commanded by our said sovereign lord, his heirs or successors, by open proclamation under the great seal :

That then every such person and persons so offending in any the premises, after the said first day of February, their aiders, counsellors, consenters, and abettors, being thereof lawfully convicted according to the laws and customs of this realm, shall be adjudged traitors, and that every such offence in any the premises, that shall be committed or done after the said first day of February, shall be reputed, accepted, and adjudged high treason, and the offenders therein and their aiders, consenters, counsellors, and abettors, being lawfully convicted of any such offence as is aforesaid, shall have and suffer such pains of death and other penalties, as is limited and accustomed in cases of high treason.

III. And to the intent that all treasons should be the more dread, hated and detested to be done by any person or persons, and also because it is a great boldness and an occasion to ill-disposed persons, to adventure and embrace their malicious intents and enterprises, which all true subjects ought to study to eschew : be it therefore enacted by the authority aforesaid, that none offender in any kinds of high treasons whatsoever they be, their aiders, consenters, counsellors, nor abettors, shall be admitted to have the benefit or privilege of any manner of sanctuary, considering that matters of treasons touch so nigh both the surety of the king our sovereign lord's person, and his heirs and successors.

IV. And over that, be it enacted by authority aforesaid, that if any of the king's subjects, denizens or other, do commit or prac-

R

tise out of the limits of this realm, in any outward parts, any such offences, which by this Act are made, or heretofore have been made treason, that then such treasons, whatsoever they be, or wheresoever they shall happen so to be done or committed, shall be inquired and presented by the oaths of twelve good and lawful men, upon good and probable evidence and witness, in such shire and county of this realm, and before such persons as it shall please the king's highness to appoint by commission under his great seal, in like manner and form as treasons committed within this realm have been used to be inquired of and presented ; and that upon every indictment and presentment found and made of any such treasons, and certified into the King's Bench, like process and other circumstance shall be there had and made against the offenders, as if the same treasons, so presented, had been lawfully found to be done and committed within the limits of this realm. And that all process of outlawry hereafter to be made and had within this realm against any offenders in treason, being resident or inhabited out of the limits of this realm, or in any of the parts beyond the sea, at the time of the outlawry pronounced against them, shall be as good and as effectual in the law to all intents and purposes, as if such offenders had been resident and dwelling within this realm at the time of such process awarded, and outlawry pronounced.

V. And be it further enacted by authority aforesaid, that every offender and offenders, being hereafter lawfully convicted of any manner of high treasons, by presentment, confession, verdict or process of outlawry, according to the due course and custom of the common laws of this realm, shall lose and forfeit to the king's highness, his heirs and successors, all such lands, tenements, and hereditaments, which any such offender or offenders shall have of any estate of inheritance in use or possession, by any right, title, or means, within this realm of England, or elsewhere, within any of the king's dominions, at the time of any such treason committed, or any time after ; saving to every person and persons, their heirs and successors (other than the offenders in any treasons, their heirs and successors, and such person and persons as claim to any their uses,) all such rights, titles, interests, possessions, leases, rents, offices, and other profits, which they shall have at the day of committing such treasons, or any time afore, in as large and ample manner as if this Act had never been had nor made.

150. Act for the Dissolution of the Lesser Monasteries

(1536. 27 Henry VIII. c. 28. 3 *S. R.* 575. The whole act reprinted in G. and H. 257–268.)

FORASMUCH as manifest sin, vicious, carnal and abominable living is daily used and committed among the little and small abbeys, priories, and other religious houses of monks, canons, and nuns, where the congregation of such religious persons is under the number of twelve persons, whereby the governors of such religious houses, and their convent, spoil, destroy, consume, and utterly waste, as well their churches, monasteries, priories, principal houses, farms, granges, lands, tenements, and hereditaments, as the ornaments of their churches, and their goods and chattels, to the high displeasure of Almighty God, slander of good religion, and to the great infamy of the king's highness and the realm, if redress should not be had thereof. And albeit that many continual visitations hath been heretofore had, by the space of two hundred years and more, for an honest and charitable reformation of such unthrifty, carnal, and abominable living, yet nevertheless little or none amendment is hitherto had, but their vicious living shamelessly increases and augments, and by a cursed custom so rooted and infected, that a great multitude of the religious persons in such small houses do rather choose to rove abroad in apostasy, than to conform themselves to the observation of good religion ; so that without such small houses be utterly suppressed, and the religious persons therein committed to great and honourable monasteries of religion in this realm, where they may be compelled to live religiously, for reformation of their lives, there can else be no redress nor reformation in that behalf :

In consideration whereof, the king's most royal majesty — being supreme head on earth, under God, of the Church of England, daily studying and devising the increase, advancement, and exaltation of true doctrine and virtue in the said Church, to the only glory and honour of God, and the total extirping and destruction of vice and sin, having knowledge that the premises be true, as well by the accounts of his late visitations, as by sundry credible informations, considering also that divers and great solemn monasteries of this realm, wherein (thanks be to God) religion is right well kept and observed, be destitute of such full numbers of religious persons, as they ought and may keep — has thought good that a plain declaration should be made of the premises, as well to the lords spiritual and temporal, as to other his loving subjects, the commons, in this present Parliament assembled : whereupon the said lords and commons, by a great deliberation, finally be resolved, that it is and shall be much more to the pleasure of Almighty God, and for the honour of this his realm, that the possessions of such small religious houses, now being spent, spoiled, and wasted for increase and maintenance of sin, should be used and committed to better uses, and the unthrifty religious persons, so spending the same, to be compelled to reform their lives : and thereupon most humbly desire the king's highness that it may be enacted by authority of this present Parliament, that his majesty shall have and enjoy to him and to his heirs for ever, all and singular such monasteries, priories, and other religious houses of monks, canons, and nuns, of what kinds or diversities of habits, rules, or order soever they be called or named, which have not in lands, tenements, rents, tithes, portions, and other hereditaments, above the clear yearly value of two hundred pounds. And in like manner shall have and enjoy all the sites and circuits of every such religious houses, and all and singular the manors, granges, meases, lands, tenements, rents, reversions, services, tithes, pensions, portions, churches, chapels, advowsons, patronages, annuities, rights, entries, conditions, and other hereditaments appertaining or belonging to every such monastery, priory, or other religious house, not having, as is aforesaid, above the said clear yearly value of two hundred pounds, in as large and ample manner as the abbots, priors, abbesses, prioresses, or other governors of such monasteries, priories, and other religious houses now have, or ought to have the same in the right of their houses. And that also his highness shall have to him and to his heirs all and singular such monasteries, abbeys, and priories, which at any time within one year next before the making of this Act have been given and granted to his majesty by any abbot, prior, abbess, or prioress, under their convent seals, or that otherwise, have been suppressed or dissolved, and all and singular the manors, lands, tenements, rents, services, reversions, tithes, pensions, portions, churches, chapels, advowsons, patronages, rights, entries, conditions, and all other interests and hereditaments to the same monasteries, abbeys, and priories, or to any of them appertaining or belonging ; to have and to hold all and singular the premises, with all their rights, profits, jurisdictions, and commodities, unto the king's majesty, and his heirs and assigns for ever, to do and use therewith his and their own wills, to the pleasure of Almighty God, and to the honour and profit of this realm.

*   *   *   *   *   *   *   *   *

IX. And be it further enacted, ordained, and established by authority aforesaid, that all and singular persons, bodies politic and corporate, to whom the king's majesty, his heirs and successors, hereafter shall give, grant, let, or demise any site or precinct, with the houses thereupon builded, together with the demesnes of any monasteries, priories, or other religious houses, that shall be dissolved or given to the king's highness by this Act, and the heirs, successors, executors, and assigns of every such person, body politic and corporate, shall be bound by authority of this Act, under the penalties hereafter ensuing, to keep, or cause to be kept, an honest continual house and household in the same site or precinct, and to occupy yearly as much of the same demesnes in ploughing and tillage of husbandry, that is to say, as much of the said demesnes which hath been commonly used to be kept in tillage by the governors, abbots, or priors of the same houses, monasteries, or priories, or by their farmer or farmers occupying the same within the time of twenty years next before this Act.

X. And if any person or persons, bodies politic or corporate, that shall be bounden by this Act, do not keep an honest household of husbandry and tillage, in manner and form as is aforesaid, that then he or they so offending shall forfeit to the king's highness for every month so offending six pounds thirteen shillings and fourpence, to be recovered to his use in any of his courts of record.

XI. And over that it is enacted by authority aforesaid, that all justices of peace, in every shire where any such offence shall be committed or done, contrary to the true meaning and intent of this present Act, shall, in every quarter and general sessions within the limits of their commission, inquire of the premises, and shall have full power and authority to hear and determine the same, and to tax and assess no less fine for every the said offences, than is afore limited for the same offences, and the estreats thereof to be made and certified into the king's exchequer, according and at such time and form as other estreats of fines, issues, and amerciaments are made by the same justices.

151. The King at Twenty-four may repeal Acts of Parliament passed during his Minority

(1536.   28 Henry VIII. c. 17.   3 *S. R.* 673.)

FORASMUCH as laws and statutes may happen hereafter to be made within this realm at parliaments held at such times as the kings of the same shall happen to be within age, having small knowledge and experience of their affairs, to the great hindrance and derogation of the imperial crown of this realm, and to the universal damage of the common wealth of the subjects of the same : be it therefore enacted by authority of this present parliament, that if the imperial crown of this realm, after the decease of the king's most royal majesty, whose life our Lord long preserve, descend, come or remain to the heirs of our said sovereign lord or to any person to be limited by his highness, as of very right it must and ought to do according to the laws of this realm established for the same, the said heirs or such person being within the age of twenty-four years, and that then any act or acts of parliament shall happen to be made and established, in any parliament that then shall be held before such heir or heirs, person or persons then being in possession of the said crown shall be of their full ages of twenty-four years, that then every such heir or heirs of our said sovereign lord, or such persons so possessed of the crown and being within the same age of twenty-four years, shall have full power and authority at all times, after they shall come to their said full ages of twenty-four years, by their letters patent under the great seal of England, to revoke, annul and repeal all and singular such acts made and established by their royal assents, in any parliament held during the time that they were within their said age of twenty-four years ; their royal assents had to the same during the time that they were within the said age of twenty-four years or any act or acts hereafter to be made to the contrary thereof notwithstanding.

II. And be it also enacted by authority aforesaid that every such repeal, annullation and revocation of any act or acts, that shall be made and established in any parliament held before the time that such heirs or person possessed of the crown shall be of the said age of twenty-four years, shall be as good and effectual to all intents and purposes as though it had been done by authority of parliament.

152. The Lex Regia

(1539. 31 Henry VIII. c. 8. 3 S. R. 726.)

FORASMUCH as the king's most royal majesty for divers considerations, by the advice of his council, hath heretofore set forth divers and sundry his grace's proclamations, as well for and concerning divers and sundry articles of Christ's religion, as for an unity and concord to be had amongst the loving and obedient subjects of this his realm and other his dominions, and also concerning the advancement of his commonwealth and good quiet of his people, which nevertheless divers and many froward, wilful and obstinate persons have wilfully contemned and broken, not considering what a king by his royal power may do, and for lack of a direct statute and law to coarct offenders to obey the said proclamations, which, being still suffered, should not only encourage offenders to the disobedience of the precepts and laws of Almighty God, but also be too much to the great dishonour of the king's most royal majesty, who may full ill bear it, and also give too great heart and boldness to all malefactors and offenders; considering also that sudden causes and occasions fortune many times which do require speedy remedies, and that by abiding for a parliament in the mean time might happen great prejudice to ensue to the realm; and weighing also that His Majesty (which by the kingly and regal power given him by God may do many things in such cases) should not be driven to extend the liberty and supremacy of his regal power and dignity by wilfulness of froward subjects; it is therefore thought in manner more than necessary that the king's highness of this realm for the time being with the advice of his honourable council should make and set forth proclamations, for the good and politic order and governance of this his realm of England, Wales and other his dominions from time to time for the defence of his regal dignity and the advancement of his commonwealth and good quiet of his people, as the cases of necessity shall require, and that an ordinary law should be provided by the assent of his majesty and parliament, for the due punishment, correction and reformation of such offences and disobediences; be it therefore enacted by the authority of this present parliament, with the king's majesty, the lords spiritual and temporal and the commons' assent, that always the king for the time being with the advice of his honourable council, whose names hereafter followeth, may set forth at all times by proclamations, under such penalties and pains and of such sort as to his highness and his said honourable council shall seem necessary and requisite ; and that those same shall be obeyed, observed and kept as though they were made by act of parliament for the time in them limited, unless the king's highness dispense with them or any of them under his great seal.

II. Provided always that the words, meaning and intent of this act be not understood, interpreted, construed or extended, that by virtue of it any of the king's liege people, of what estate, degree or condition soever he or they be, bodies politic or corporate, their heirs or successors, should have any of his or their inheritance, lawful possessions, offices, liberties, privileges, franchises, goods or chattels taken from them or any of them, nor by virtue of the said act suffer any pains of death, other than shall be hereafter in this act declared, nor that by any proclamation to be made by virtue of this act, any acts, common laws standing at this present time in strength and force, nor yet any lawful or laudable customs of this realm or any of them, shall be infringed, broken or subverted : and especially all those acts standing this hour in force which have been made in the king's highness' time ; but that every such person and persons, bodies politic and corporate, their heirs and successors and the heirs and successors of every of them, their inheritances, lawful possessions, offices, liberties, privileges, franchises, goods and chattels shall stand and be in the same state and condition, to every respect and purpose, as if this act or proviso had never been had or made ; except such forfeitures, pains and penalties as in this act and in every proclamation which shall be declared and expressed ; and except such persons which shall offend any proclamation to be made by the king's highness, his heirs or successors for and concerning any kind of heresies against the Christian religion.

III. Furthermore be it enacted by the authority of this present parliament, that to the intent the king's subjects should not be ignorant of his proclamations every sheriff or other officer and minister to whom any such proclamation shall be directed by the king's writ under his great seal, shall proclaim or cause the same to be proclaimed within fourteen days after the receipt thereof in four several market towns if there be so many or else in six other towns or villages within the limits of their authority ; and they to cause the said proclamations to be fixed and set up openly upon places convenient in every such town, place or village, upon pain and penalty of such sum and sums of money or imprisonment of body as shall be contained in the said proclamation or proclamations.

IV. And be it further enacted by the authority aforesaid, that if any person or persons, of what estate, degree or condition soever he or they be, which at any time hereafter do wilfully offend and break or obstinately not observe and keep any such proclamation or any article therein contained which shall proceed from the king's majesty by the advice of his council as is aforesaid, that then all and every such offender or offenders, being thereof, within one half year next after his or their offence committed, accused and thereof within eighteen months next after the same offence so committed convicted by confession or lawful witness and proofs before the archbishop of Canterbury metropolitan, the chancellor of England, the lord treasurer of England, the lord president of the king's most honourable council, the lord privy seal, the great chamberlain of England, lord admiral, lord steward or grand master, lord chamberlain of the king's most honourable household, two other bishops being of the king's council, such as his grace shall appoint for the same, the secretary, the treasurer and comptroller of the king's most honourable household, the master of the horse, the two chief judges and the master of the rolls for the time being, the chancellor of the augmentations, the chancellor of the duchy, the chief baron of the exchequer, the two general surveyors, the chancellor of the exchequer, the under treasurer of the same, the treasurer of the king's chamber for the time being, in the star chamber at Westminster or elsewhere, or at the least before the half of the number afore rehearsed, of which number the lord chancellor, the lord treasurer, the lord president of the king's most honourable council, the lord privy seal, the chamberlain of England, the lord admiral, the two chief judges for the time being or two of them shall be two, shall lose and pay such penalties, forfeitures of sums of money, to be levied of his or their land, tenants, goods and chattels to the king's use, and also suffer such imprisonment of his body, as shall be expressed, mentioned and declared in any such proclamation or proclamations which such offender or offenders shall offend and break or not observe and keep, contrary to this act as is aforesaid ; and that execution shall be had, done and made against every such offender and offenders with the addition of the names or surnames, towns or counties, mystery or occupation of the said offenders, by such order, process, ways and means and after such manner, form and condition as by the king's highness and the said council shall be devised and thought most convenient for example of such offenders : provided alway that none offender, which shall offend contrary to the form of any such proclamations, shall incur the danger and penalty thereof, except such proclamation or proclamations be had, done or made in such shire or county where the offender hath or shall dwell or be most conversant within a year before.

V. And be it further enacted by the authority aforesaid, that the lord chancellor, the lord privy seal and either of them, with the assent of six of the afore named, shall have power and authority by their discretions, upon every information to be given to them or either of them touching the premises, to cause process to be made against all and singular such offenders by writs under the king's great seal or under his grace's privy seal in form following, that is to say ; first by proclamation under a pain or a penalty by the discretion of the aforesaid councillors appointed for the awarding of process, and if he appear not to the same without a lawful excuse, then the said councillors to award out another proclamation upon allegation of the same offender, for the due examination, trial and conviction of every such person and persons as shall offend contrary to this act, for the due execution to be had of and for the same in manner and form as is above remembered ; except it be within the liberty of the county palatine of the duchy of Lancaster ; and in case it so be, then to pass by the chancellor of the king's duchy of Lancaster under the seal of the said duchy, with the assent of six at the least of the aforenamed councillors.

*   *   *   *   *   *   *   *   *

VIII. And be it further enacted, that if it happen our said sovereign lord the king to decease (whose life God long preserve) before such time as that person which shall be his next heir or successor to the imperial crown of this realm, shall accomplish and come to the age of eighteen years, that then all and singular proclamations which shall be in any wise made and set forth into any part of this realm or other the king's dominions by virtue of this act, within the aforesaid years of the said next heir or successor, shall be set forth in the successor's name then being king, and shall import or bear underwritten the full names of such of the king's honourable council then being as shall be the devisors or setters forth of the same which shall be in this case the whole number afore rehearsed, or at least the more part of them, or else the proclamations to be void and of none effect.

*   *   *   *   *   *   *   *   *

153. Act for the Dissolution of the Greater Monasteries

(1539. 31 Henry VIII. c. 13. 3 *S. R.* 733. The whole act reprinted in G. and H. 281–303.)

WHERE divers and sundry abbots, priors, abbesses, prioresses, and other ecclesiastical governors and governesses of divers monasteries, abbacies, priories, nunneries, colleges, hospitals, houses of friars, and other religious and ecclesiastical houses and places within this our sovereign lord the king's realm of England and Wales, of their own free and voluntary minds, good wills and assents, without constraint, coarction, or compulsion of any manner of person or persons, since the fourth day of February, the twenty-seventh year of the reign of our now most dread sovereign lord, by the due order and course of the common laws of this his realm of England, and by their sufficient writings of record, under their convent and common seals, have severally given, granted, and by the same their writings severally confirmed all their said monasteries, abbacies, priories, nunneries, colleges, hospitals, houses of friars, and other religious and ecclesiastical houses and places, and all their sites, circuits, and precincts of the same, and all and singular their manors, lordships, granges, meases, lands, tenements, meadows, pastures, rents, reversions, services, woods, tithes, pensions, portions, churches, chapels, advowsons, patronages, annuities, rights, entries, conditions, commons, leets, courts, liberties, privileges, and franchises appertaining or in any wise belonging to any such monastery, abbacy, priory, nunnery, college, hospital, house of friars, and other religious and ecclesiastical houses and places, or to any of them, by whatsoever name or corporation they or any of them were then named or called, and of what order, habit, religion, or other kind or quality soever they or any of them then were reputed, known, or taken; to have and to hold all the said monasteries, abbacies, priories, nunneries, colleges, hospitals, houses of friars, and other religious and ecclesiastical houses and places, sites, circuits, precincts, manors, lands, tenements, meadows, pastures, rents, reversions, services, and all other the premises, to our said sovereign lord, his heirs and successors for ever, and the same their said monasteries, abbacies, priories, nunneries, colleges, hospitals, houses of friars, and other religious and ecclesiastical houses and places, sites, circuits, precincts, manors, lordships, granges, meases, lands, tenements, meadows, pastures, rents, reversions, services, and other the premises, voluntarily, as is aforesaid, have renounced, left, and forsaken, and every of them has renounced, left, and forsaken :

II. Be it therefore enacted by the king our sovereign lord, and the lords spiritual and temporal, and the commons, in this present Parliament assembled, and by authority of the same, that the king our sovereign lord shall have, hold, possess, and enjoy to him, his heirs and successors for ever, all and singular such late monasteries, abbacies, priories, nunneries, colleges, hospitals, houses of friars, and other religious and ecclesiastical houses and places, of what kinds, natures, qualities, or diversities of habits, rules, professions, or orders they, or any of them, were named, known, or called, which since the said fourth day of February, the twenty-seventh year of the reign of our said sovereign lord, have been dissolved, suppressed, renounced, relinquished, forfeited, given up, or by any other mean come to his highness ; and by the same authority, and in like manner, shall have, hold, possess, and enjoy all the sites, circuits, precincts, manors, lordships, granges, meases, lands, tenements, meadows, pastures, rents, reversions, services, woods, tithes, pensions, portions, parsonages appropri-ated, vicarages, churches, chapels, advowsons, nominations, patron-ages, annuities, rights, interests, entries, conditions, commons, leets, courts, liberties, privileges, franchises, and other whatsoever hereditaments, which appertained or belonged to the said late monasteries, abbacies, priories, nunneries, colleges, hospitals, houses of friars, and other religious or ecclesiastical houses and places, or to any of them, in as large and ample manner and form as the late abbots, priors, abbesses, prioresses, and other ecclesiastical governors and governesses of such late monasteries, abbacies, priories, nunneries, colleges, hospitals, houses of friars, and other religious and ecclesiastical houses and places, had, held, or occupied, or of right ought to have had, holden, or occu-pied, in the rights of their said late monasteries, abbacies, priories, nunneries, colleges, hospitals, houses of friars, or other religious or ecclesiastical houses or places, at the time of the said dissolu-tion, suppression, renouncing, relinquishing, forfeiting, giving up, or by any other manner of means coming of the same to the king's highness since the fourth day of February above specified.

*　*　*　*　*　*　*　*　*

154. The Six Articles Act

(1539. 31 Henry VIII. c. 14. 3 S. R. 739. The whole act reprinted in
G. and H. 303-319.)

WHERE the king's most excellent majesty is, by God's law, supreme head immediately under Him of this whole Church and congregation of England, intending the conservation of the same Church and congregation in a true, sincere, and uniform doctrine of Christ's religion, calling also to his blessed and most gracious remembrance as well the great and quiet assurance, prosperous increase, and other innumerable commodities, which have ever ensued, come, and followed, of concord, agreement, and unity in opinions, as also the manifold perils, dangers, and inconveniences which have heretofore, in many places and regions, grown, sprung, and arisen, of the diversities of minds and opinions, especially of matters of Christian religion, and therefore desiring that such a unity might and should be charitably established in all things touching and concerning the same, as the same, so being established, might chiefly be to the honour of Almighty God, the very Author and Fountain of all true unity and sincere concord, and consequently redound to the common wealth of this his highness's most noble realm, and of all his loving subjects, and other residents and inhabitants of or in the same; has therefore caused and commanded this his most High Court of Parliament, for sundry and many urgent causes and considerations, to be at this time summoned, and also a synod and Convocation of all the archbishops, bishops, and other learned men of the clergy of this his realm, to be in like manner assembled.

II. And forasmuch as in the said Parliament, synod, and Convocation, there were certain Articles, matters, and questions proponed and set forth touching Christian religion, that is to say:

First, whether in the most blessed Sacrament of the Altar remaineth, after the consecration, the substance of bread and wine, or no.

Secondly, whether it be necessary by God's law that all men should be communicate with both kinds, or no.

Thirdly, whether priests, that is to say, men dedicate to God by priesthood, may, by the law of God, marry after, or no.

Fourthly, whether vow of chastity or widowhood, made to God advisedly by man or woman, be, by the law of God, to be observed, or no.

Fifthly, whether private masses stand with the law of God, and be to be used and continued in the Church and congregation of England, as things whereby good Christian people may and do receive both godly consolation and wholesome benefits, or no.

Sixthly, whether auricular confession is necessary to be retained, continued, used, and frequented in the Church, or no.

III. The king's most royal majesty, most prudently pondering and considering, that by occasion of variable and sundry opinions and judgments of the said Articles, great discord and variance has arisen, as well amongst the clergy of this his realm, as amongst a great number of vulgar people, his loving subjects of the same, and being in a full hope and trust that a full and perfect resolution of the said Articles should make a perfect concord and unity generally amongst all his loving and obedient subjects, of his most excellent goodness not only commanded that the said Articles should deliberately and advisedly, by his said archbishops, bishops, and other learned men of his clergy, be debated, argued, and reasoned, and their opinions therein to be understood, declared, and known, but also most graciously vouchsafed, in his own princely person, to descend and come into his said High Court of Parliament and council, and there, like a prince of most high prudence and no less learning, opened and declared many things of high learning and great knowledge, touching the said Articles, matters, and questions, for a unity to be had in the same ; whereupon, after a great and long, deliberate, and advised disputation and consultation had and made concerning the said Articles, as well by the consent of the king's highness, as by the assent of the lords spiritual and temporal, and other learned men of his clergy in their Convocation, and by the consent of the commons in this present Parliament assembled, it was and is finally resolved, accorded, and agreed in manner and form following, that is to say :

First, that in the most blessed Sacrament of the Altar, by the strength and efficacy of Christ's mighty word (it being spoken by the priest), is present really, under the form of bread and wine, the natural body and blood of our Saviour Jesus Christ, conceived of the Virgin Mary ; and that after the consecration there remaineth no substance of bread or wine, nor any other substance, but the substance of Christ, God and man.

Secondly, that communion in both kinds is not necessary *ad salutem*, by the law of God, to all persons ; and that it is to be believed, and not doubted of, but that in the flesh, under the form of bread, is the very blood ; and with the blood, under the form of wine, is the very flesh; as well apart, as though they were both together.

Thirdly, that priests after the order of priesthood received, as afore, may not marry, by the law of God.

Fourthly, that vows of chastity or widowhood, by man or woman made to God advisedly, ought to be observed by the law of God; and that it exempts them from other liberties of Christian people, which without that they might enjoy.

Fifthly, that it is meet and necessary that private masses be continued and admitted in this the king's English Church and congregation, as whereby good Christian people, ordering themselves accordingly, do receive both godly and goodly consolations and benefits; and it is agreeable also to God's law.

Sixthly, that auricular confession is expedient and necessary to be retained and continued, used and frequented in the Church of God.

IV. For the which most godly study, pain, and travail of his majesty, and determination and resolution of the premises, his most humble and obedient subjects, the lords spiritual and temporal, and the commons, in this present Parliament assembled, not only render and give unto his highness their most high and hearty thanks, and think themselves most bound to pray for the long continuance of his grace's most royal estate, but also being desirous that his most godly enterprise may be well accomplished, and brought to a full end and perfection, and so established that the same might be to the honour of God, and after, to the common quiet, unity, and concord to be had in the whole body of this realm for ever, most humbly beseech his royal majesty, that the resolution and determination above written of the said Articles may be established, and perpetually perfected, by authority of this present Parliament:

V. It is therefore ordained and enacted by the king our sovereign lord, the lords spiritual and temporal, and the commons, in this present Parliament assembled, and by the authority of the same, that if any person or persons within this realm of England, or any other the king's dominions, after the twelfth day of July next coming, by word, writing, imprinting, ciphering, or in any other wise do publish, preach, teach, say, affirm, declare, dispute, argue, or hold any opinion, that in the blessed Sacrament of the Altar, under form of bread and wine (after the consecration thereof), there is not present really the natural body and blood of our Saviour Jesus Christ, conceived of the Virgin Mary, or that after the said consecration there remaineth any substance of bread or wine, or any other substance, but the substance of Christ, God and man, or after the time abovesaid publish, preach, teach, say, affirm, declare, dispute, argue, or hold opinion that in the flesh, under form of bread, is not the very blood of Christ ; or that with the blood, under form of wine, is not the very flesh of Christ, as well apart as though they were both together ; or by any of the means abovesaid, or otherwise, preach, teach, declare, or affirm the said Sacrament to be of other substance than is abovesaid ; or by any means contemn, deprave, or despise the said blessed Sacrament : that then every such person and persons so offending, their aiders, comforters, counsellors, consenters, and abettors therein, being thereof convicted in form underwritten, by the authority abovesaid, shall be deemed and adjudged heretics. And that every such offence shall be adjudged manifest heresy, and that every such offender and offenders shall therefor have and suffer judgment, execution, pain, and pains of death by way of burning, without any abjuration, clergy, or sanctuary to be therefor permitted, had, allowed, admitted, or suffered ; and also shall therefor forfeit and lose to the king's highness, his heirs and successors, all his or their honours, manors, castles, lands, tenements, rents, reversions, services, possessions, and all other his or their hereditaments, goods and chattels, terms and freeholds, whatsoever they be, which any such offender or offenders shall have at the time of any such offence or offences committed or done, or at any time after, as in cases of high treason.

VI. And furthermore be it enacted, by the authority of this present Parliament, that if any person or persons, after the said twelfth day of July, preach in any sermon or collation openly made to the king's people, or teach in any common school or to other congregation of people, or being called before such judges and according to such form of the law as hereafter shall be declared, do obstinately affirm, uphold, maintain, or defend that the communion of the said blessed Sacrament in both kinds, that is to say, in form of bread and also of wine, is necessary for the health of man's soul, to be given or ministered, or ought or should be given or ministered to any person in both kinds, or that it is necessary so to be received or taken by any person other than by priests being at Mass and consecrating the same ; or that any man, after the order of priesthood received as aforesaid, may marry or may contract matrimony ; or that any man or woman which advisedly has vowed or professed, or shall vow or profess, chastity or widowhood, may marry or may contract matrimony ; or that private masses be not lawful or not laudable, or should not be celebrated, had, nor used in this realm, nor be not agreeable to the laws of God; or that auricular confession is not expedient and necessary to be retained and continued, used and frequented, in the Church of God; or if any priest, after the said twelfth day of July, or any other man or woman which advisedly has vowed, or after the said day advisedly do vow chastity or widowhood, do actually marry or contract matrimony with any person : that then all and every person and persons so preaching, teaching, obstinately affirming, upholding, maintaining, or defending, or making marriage or contract of matrimony, as is above specified, be and shall be, by authority above written, deemed and adjudged a felon and felons; and that every offender in the same, being therefor duly convicted or attainted by the laws underwritten, shall therefore suffer pains of death, as in cases of felony, without any benefit of clergy or privilege of church or sanctuary to him or her to be allowed in that behalf, and shall forfeit all his or her lands and goods, as in cases of felony, and that it shall be lawful to the patron or patrons of any manner of benefice which any such offender at the time of his said conviction or attainder had, to present one other incumbent thereunto, as if the same person so convicted or attainted had been bodily deceased.

VII. Also be it enacted by the authority aforesaid, that if any person or persons, after the said twelfth day of July, by word, writing, printing, ciphering, or otherwise than is above rehearsed, publish, declare, or hold opinion that the said communion of the blessed Sacrament in both kinds aforesaid is necessary for the health of man's soul to be given or ministered in both kinds, and so ought or should be given and ministered to any person, or ought or should be so in both kinds received or taken by any person other than by priests being at Mass and consecrating the same as is aforesaid, or that any man after the order of priesthood received as is aforesaid, may marry or may make contract of matrimony, or that any man or woman which advisedly has made or shall make a vow to God of chastity or widowhood, may marry or may make contract of matrimony, or that private masses be not lawful or not laudable, or should not be celebrated, had, nor used, nor be agreeable to the laws of God, or that auricular confession is not expedient and necessary to be retained and continued, used and frequented, in the Church of God; every person, being for every such offence duly convicted or attainted by the laws underwritten, shall forfeit and lose to the king, our sovereign lord, all his goods and chattels for ever, and also the profits of all his lands, tenements, annuities, fees, and offices during his life, and all his

s

benefices and spiritual promotions shall be utterly void, and also shall suffer imprisonment of his body at the will and pleasure of our said sovereign lord the king; and if any such person or persons, being once convicted of any the offences mentioned in this article as is abovesaid, do afterwards eftsoons offend in any of the same, and be thereof accused, indicted, or presented and convicted again by the authority of the laws underwritten, that then every such person and persons so being twice convicted and attainted of the said offences, or of any of them, shall be adjudged a felon and felons, and shall suffer judgment, execution, and pains of death, loss and forfeiture of lands and goods, as in cases of felony, without any privilege of clergy or sanctuary to be in any wise permitted, admitted, or allowed in that behalf.

VIII. Be it further enacted by the authority abovesaid, that if any person, which is or has been a priest, before this present Parliament or during the time of session of the same has married and has made any contract of matrimony with any woman, or that any man or woman, which before the making of this Act advisedly has vowed chastity or widowhood, before this present Parliament or during the session of the same has married or contracted matrimony with any person; that then every such marriage and contract of matrimony shall be utterly void and of none effect, and that the ordinaries, within whose diocese or jurisdiction the person or persons so married or contracted is or be resident or abiding, shall from time to time make separation and divorces of the said marriages and contracts.

*   *   *   *   *   *   *   *   *

X. And be it further enacted by authority abovesaid, that if any person or persons at any time hereafter contemn or contemptuously refuse, deny, or abstain to be confessed at the time commonly accustomed within this realm and Church of England, or contemn or contemptuously refuse, deny, or abstain to receive the holy and blessed Sacrament abovesaid at the time commonly used and accustomed for the same, that then every such offender, being thereof duly convicted or attainted by the laws underwritten, shall suffer such imprisonment and make such fine and ransom to the king our sovereign lord and his heirs, as by his highness or by his or their council, shall be ordered and adjudged in that behalf. And if any such offender or offenders, at any time or times after the said conviction or attainder so had, do eftsoons contemn or contemptuously refuse, deny, or abstain to be confessed or to be communicate in manner and form above written, and be

thereof duly convicted or attainted by the laws underwritten, that
then every such offence shall be deemed and adjudged felony, and
the offender or offenders therein shall suffer pains of death, and
lose and forfeit all his and their goods, lands, and tenements as
in cases of felony.

＊　＊　＊　＊　＊　＊　＊　＊　＊

XXI. And it is also enacted by the authority abovesaid, that
the said commissioners and every of them shall, from time to time,
have full power and authority, by virtue of this Act, to take into
his or their keeping [or] possession all and all manner of books
which be and have been, or hereafter shall be, set forth, read, or
declared within this realm, or other the king's dominions, wherein
is or be contained or comprised any clause, article, matter, or
sentence repugnant or contrary to the tenor, form, or effect of this
present Act, or any of the articles contained in the same.   And the
said commissioners, or three of them at the least, to burn or otherwise destroy the said books, or any part of them, as unto the said
commissioners, or unto three of them at the least, shall be thought
expedient by their discretions.

＊　＊　＊　＊　＊　＊　＊　＊　＊

———◆———

155. The Attainder of Queen Katherine Howard

(1542.   33 Henry VIII. c. 21.   3 S. R. 857.)

IN their most humble wise beseech your most royal Majesty the
lords spiritual and temporal and all other your most loving
and obedient subjects the commons of this your most high court
of parliament assembled ; that where, besides any man's expectation, such chance hath happened, by Mistress Katherine Howard
which Your Highness took to your wife, both to Your Majesty
chiefly and so consequently to us all that the like we think hath
scarce been seen, the likelihoods and appearances being so far contrary to that which by evident and due proof is now found true ;

＊　＊　＊　＊　＊　＊　＊　＊　＊

of and for which treasons being manifestly and plainly proved, as
well by the confession of the said queen and other the said parties
as by divers other witnesses and proofs, the said Francis Dereham

and Thomas Culpepper having been lawfully and truly and according to the laws of the realm convicted and attainted, and the said queen and Jane, lady Rochford, be lawfully indicted, insomuch that Thomas Culpepper and Francis Dereham have justly suffered therefor pains of death according to their merits as by the records thereof more plainly at large may appear ; it may therefore please Your Highness of your most excellent and accustomed goodness, and for the entire love, favour and hearty affection that Your Majesty hath always heretofore borne and yet beareth to the commonwealth of this your realm of England, and for the conservation of your most excellent Highness and posterity, and of the good peace, unity and rest of us your most bounden and obedient subjects, to grant and assent, at the most humble desire and petition of your loving and obedient subjects the lords spiritual and temporal and the commons in this present parliament assembled, that this their lawful indictment and attainders of such as have lately suffered may be approved by the authority of this present parliament : and that it may be enacted that the said queen Katherine and Jane, lady Rochford, for their said abominable and detestable treasons by them and every of them most abominably and traitorously committed and done against Your Majesty and this your realm, shall be by the authority of this present parliament convicted and attainted of high treason ; and that the same queen Katherine and Jane, lady Rochford, and either of them shall have and suffer pains of death, loss of goods, chattels, debts, farms and all other things as in cases of high treason by the laws of this your realm hath been accustomed granted and given to the crown : and also that the said queen Katherine, Jane, lady Rochford, Thomas Culpepper, and Francis Dereham, and every of them, shall lose and forfeit to Your Highness and to your heirs all such right, title, interest, use and possession, which they or any of them had the twenty-fifth day of August in the thirty-third year of your reign or any time since, of, in or to all such their honours, manors, meases, lands, tenements, rents, reversions, remainders, uses, possessions, offices, rights, conditions and all other their hereditaments of what names, natures or qualities soever they be ; and that all such rights, title, interest, use and possession, which they or any of them had or of right ought to have the said twenty-fifth day of August or any time since, of, in or to the same honours, castles, manors, meases, lands, tenements, rents, reversions, remainders, uses, possessions, offices, rights, commodities, and hereditaments, by the authority aforesaid shall be deemed vested and judged to be in the actual and real possession of Your Majesty, without any office or inquisition thereof hereafter to be taken or found according to the common laws of this your realm.

*   *   *   *   *   *   *   *   *

---

156. Ferrers' Case

(1543. 3 Holinshed's Chronicle, 824–826.)

IN the Lent season, whilst the parliament yet continued, one George Ferrers, gentleman, servant to the king, being elected a burgess for the town of Plymouth in the county of Devonshire, in going to the parliament house, was arrested in London by a process out of the king's bench, at the suit of one White, for the sum of two hundred marks or thereabouts, wherein he was late afore condemned, as a surety for the debt of one Weldon of Salisbury: which arrest being signified to Sir Thomas Moyle, knight, then speaker of the parliament, and to the knights and burgesses there, order was taken, that the sergeant of the parliament, called St. John, should forthwith repair to the Compter in Bread Street (whither the said Ferrers was carried) and there demand delivery of the prisoner.

The sergeant (as he had in charge) went to the Compter, and declared to the clerks there what he had in commandment. But they and other officers of the city were so far from obeying the said commandment, as after many stout words they forcibly resisted the said sergeant.* * * The sheriffs of London, called Rowland Hill and Henry Suckliffe, came thither, to whom the sergeant complained of this injury, and required of them the delivery of the said burgess, as afore. But they, bearing with their officers, made little account either of his complaint or of his message, rejecting the same contemptuously.* * *

The sergeant thus hardly entreated, made return to the parliament house, and finding the speaker, and all the burgesses set in their places, declared unto them the whole case as it fell, who took the same in so ill part, that they altogether (of whom there were not a few, as well of the king's privy council, as also of his privy chamber) would sit no longer without their burgess, but rose up wholly, and repaired to the upper house, where the whole case was declared by the mouth of the speaker, before Sir Thomas Audley, knight, then lord chancellor of England, and all the lords and judges there assembled, who, judging the contempt to be very great, referred the punishment thereof to the order of the commons house. They returning to their places again, upon new debate of the case, took order, that their sergeant should eftsoons repair to the sheriff of London, and require delivery of the said burgess, without any writ or warrant had for the same, but only as afore.

And yet the lord chancellor offered there to grant a writ, which they of the commons house refused, being in a clear opinion, that all commandments and other acts [of] proceeding from the nether house, were to be done and executed by their sergeant without writ, only by show of his mace, which was his warrant. But before the sergeant's return into London, the sheriffs having intelligence how heinously the matter was taken, became somewhat more mild, so as upon the said second demand, they delivered the prisoner without any denial. But the sergeant having then further in commandment from those of the nether house, charged the said sheriffs to appear personally on the morrow, by eight of the clock before the speaker in the nether house, and to bring thither the clerks of the Compter, and such officers as were parties to the said affray, and in like manner to take into his custody the said White, which wittingly procured the said arrest, in contempt of the privilege of the parliament.

Which commandment being done by the said sergeant accordingly, on the morrow the two sheriffs, with one of the clerks of the Compter (which was the chief occasion of the said affray) together with the said White, appeared in the commons house, where the speaker charging them with their contempt and misdemeanour aforesaid, they were compelled to make immediate answer, without being admitted to any counsel. Albeit, Sir Roger Cholmeley, then recorder of London, and other of the counsel of the city there present, offered to speak in the cause, which were all put to silence, and none suffered to speak, but the parties themselves: whereupon, in conclusion, the said sheriffs and the same White were committed to the Tower of London, and the said clerk (which was the occasion of the affray) to a place there called Little Ease, and the officer of London which did the arrest, called Taylor, with four other officers, to Newgate, where they remained from the eighth and twentieth until the thirtieth of March, and then they were delivered, not without humble suit made by the mayor of London and other their friends.

And for so much as the said Ferrers being in execution upon a condemnation of debt, and set at large by privilege of parliament, was not by law to be brought again into execution, and so the party without remedy for his debt, as well against him as his principal debtor; after long debate of the same by the space of nine or ten days together, at last they resolved upon an act of parliament to be made, and to revive the execution of the said debt against the said Weldon which was principal debtor, and to discharge the said Ferrers. But before this came to pass, the commons house was divided upon the question : howbeit in conclusion, the act passed for the said Ferrers, won by fourteen voices.

The king then being advertised of all this proceeding, called immediately before him the lord chancellor of England and his judges, with the speaker of the parliament, and other of the gravest persons of the nether house, to whom he declared his opinion to this effect. First commending their wisdoms in maintaining the privileges of their house (which he would not have to be infringed in any point) he alleged that he being head of the parliament, and attending in his own person upon the business thereof, ought in reason to have privilege for him and all his servants attending there upon him. So that if the said Ferrers had been no burgess, but only his servant, yet in respect thereof he was to have the privilege as well as any other.

For I understand (quoth he) that you not only for your own persons, but also for your necessary servants, even to your cooks and housekeepers, enjoy the said privilege ; insomuch as my lord chancellor here present hath informed us, that he being speaker of the parliament, the cook of the Temple was arrested in London, and in execution upon a statute of the staple. And forsomuch as the said cook, during all the parliament, served the speaker in that office, he was taken out of execution, by the privilege of the parliament. And further we be informed by our judges, that we at no time stand so highly in our estate royal, as in the time of parliament, wherein we as head, and you as members, are conjoined and knit together into one body politic, so as whatsoever offense or injury (during that time) is offered to the meanest member of the house, is to be judged as done against our person, and the whole court of parliament. Which prerogative of the court is so great (as our learned counsel informeth us) as all acts and processes coming out of any other inferior courts must for the time cease and give place to the highest.

* * * * * * * * *

Whereupon Sir Edward Montacute, lord chief justice, very gravely told his opinion, confirming by divers reasons all that the king had said, which was assented unto by all the residue, none speaking to the contrary. The act indeed passed not the higher house, for the lords had not time to consider of it, by reason of the dissolution of the parliament, the feast of Easter then approaching. Because this case hath been diversely reported, and is commonly alleged as a precedent for the privilege of the parliament; I have endeavoured myself to learn the truth thereof, and so set it forth with the whole circumstance at large according to their instructions, who ought best both to know and remember it.

* * * * * * * * *

157. Act Fixing the Succession

(1544. 35 Henry VIII. c. 1. 3 *S. R.* 955.)

WHERE in the parliament held at Westminster the eighth day of June in the twenty-eighth year of the reign of our most dread sovereign lord King Henry the Eighth an act was had and made for the establishment of the succession of the imperial crown of this realm of England, by which act among divers other things it was enacted, that the imperial crown of this realm with all dignities, honours, preeminences, prerogatives, authorities and jurisdictions to the same annexed or belonging should be to the king's majesty and his heirs of his body lawfully begotten, that is to say, to the first son of his body between His Highness and his then lawful wife Queen Jane, now deceased, begotten, and to the heirs of the body of the same first son lawfully begotten, and for default of such heirs, then to the second son of His Highness' body and of the body of the said Queen Jane begotten, and to the heirs of the body of the same second son begotten, with divers other limitations of the estates, conveyance and remainders of the said imperial crown and other the premises: and it was also enacted further by the said statute, that for lack of issue of our said sovereign lord the king's body lawfully begotten, that then His Highness should and might give, will, limit, assign, appoint or dispose the said imperial crown and other the premises to what person or persons, and give the same person or persons such estate in the same, as it should please His Majesty by his gracious letters patents under the great seal, or by his last will in writing signed with his most gracious hand; as by the same act among divers other things therein contained more at large it doth appear:

since the making of which act, the king's majesty hath one only
issue of his body lawfully begotten betwixt His Highness and his
said late wife Queen Jane, the noble and excellent prince, Prince
Edward, whom Almighty God long preserve; and also His
Majesty hath now of late, since the death of the said Queen Jane,
taken to his wife the most virtuous and gracious Lady Katherine,
now queen of England, late wife of John Neville, knight, Lord
Latimer deceased, by whom as yet His Majesty hath none issue,
but may have full well when it shall please God; and forasmuch
as our said most dread sovereign lord the king, upon good and
just grounds and causes, intendeth by God's grace to make a voyage royal in His Majesty's most royal person into the realm of
France, against his ancient enemy the French king; His Highness
most prudently and wisely considering and calling to his remembrance how this realm standeth at this present time in the case of
succession, and poising and weighing further with himself the
great trust and confidence that his loving subjects have had and
have in him, putting in his hands wholly the order and declaration of the succession of this realm; recognizing and acknowledg-
ing also that it is in the only pleasure and will of Almighty God how
long His Highness or his said entirely beloved son, Prince Edward, shall live, and whether the said prince shall have heirs of his
body lawfully begotten or not, or whether His Highness shall have
heirs begotten and procreated between His Majesty and his said
most dear and entirely beloved wife Queen Katherine that now is,
or any lawful heirs and issues hereafter of his own body begotten
by any other his lawful wife; and albeit that the king's most
excellent majesty, for default of such heirs as be inheritable by
the said act, might by the authority of the said act, give and dispose the said imperial crown and other the premises by his letters
patents under his great seal, or by his last will in writing signed
with his most gracious hand, to any person or persons of such
estate therein as should please His Highness to limit and appoint;
yet to the intent that His Majesty's disposition and mind therein
should be openly declared and manifestly known and notified, as
well to the lords spiritual and temporal as to all other his loving
and obedient subjects of this his realm, to the intent that their
assent and consent might appear to concur with thus far as followeth of His Majesty's declaration in this behalf; His Majesty therefore thinketh convenient afore his departure beyond the seas,
that it be enacted by His Highness with the assent of the lords
spiritual and temporal and the commons in this present parliament assembled and by authority of the same, and therefore be it

enacted by the authority aforesaid, that in case it shall happen the king's majesty and the said excellent prince his yet only son Prince Edward and heir apparent, to decease without heir of either of their bodies lawfully begotten (as God defend) so that there be no such heir male or female of any of their two bodies, to have and inherit the said imperial crown and other his dominions, according and in such manner and form as in the aforesaid act and now in this is declared, that then the said imperial crown and all other the premises shall be to the Lady Mary, the king's Highness' daughter, and to the heirs of the body of the same Lady Mary lawfully begotten, with such conditions as by His Highness shall be limited by his letters patents under his great seal, or by His Majesty's last will in writing signed with his gracious hand ; and for default of such issue the said imperial crown and other the premises shall be to the Lady Elizabeth, the king's second daughter, and to the heirs of the body of the said Lady Elizabeth lawfully begotten, with such conditions as by His Highness shall be limited by his letters patents under his great seal, or by His Majesty's last will in writing signed with his gracious hand ; anything in the said act made in the said twenty-eighth year of our said sovereign lord to the contrary of this act notwithstanding.

*   *   *   *   *   *   *   *   *

IV. Provided alway, that if the said Lady Mary do not keep and perform such conditions as shall be limited and appointed to her said estate in the said imperial crown and other the premises as is aforesaid, and the said Lady Elizabeth being then dead without any heir of her body lawfully begotten, that then and from thenceforth for lack of heirs of the several bodies of the king's majesty and the said lord prince lawfully begotten, the said imperial crown and other the premises shall be, come and remain to such person and persons and of such estate and estates as the king's highness by his letters patents sealed under his great seal, or by his last will in writing signed with His Majesty's hand shall limit and appoint.

V. Provided always and be it enacted by authority aforesaid, that in case the king's majesty do not declare and limit by his letters patents or by his last will in form as is aforesaid any condition to the estates and interests afore limited to the said Lady Mary and Lady Elizabeth, nor to the estate or interest of any of them, that then every such of the said Lady Mary and Lady Elizabeth, to whose estate or interest no condition shall be limited by the king's majesty in form aforesaid, shall have and enjoy such interest, estate and remainder in the said imperial crown and other the premises as is before limited by this act, without any manner of condition ; anything in this present act to the contrary thereof notwithstanding.

VI. And forasmuch as it standeth in the only pleasure and will of Almighty God, whether the king's majesty shall have any heirs begotten and procreated between His Highness and his said most entirely beloved wife Queen Katherine, or by any other his lawful wife, or whether the said Prince Edward shall have issue of his body lawfully begotten, or whether the Lady Mary and Lady Elizabeth or any of them shall have any issue of any of their several bodies lawfully begotten, and if such heirs should fail (which God defend) and no provision made in the king's life who should rule and govern this realm for lack of such heirs as in this present act is afore mentioned, that then this realm after the king's transitory life and for lack of such heirs, should be destitute of a lawful governor to order, rule and govern the same ; be it therefore enacted by the authority of this present parliament, that the king's Highness shall have full power and authority to give, dispose, appoint, assign, declare and limit, by his gracious letters patents under his great seal, or else by His Highness' last will made in writing and signed with his most gracious hand, at his only pleasure from time to time hereafter, the imperial crown of this realm and all other the premises, to be, remain, succeed and come, after his decease and for lack of lawful heirs of either of the bodies of the king's Highness and Prince Edward begotten, and also for lack of lawful heirs of the bodies of the said Lady Mary and Lady Elizabeth to be procreated and begotten as is afore limited in this act, to such person or persons in remainder or reversion as shall please His Highness, and according to such estate and after such manner and form, fashion, order or condition as shall be expressed, declared, named and limited in His Highness' letters patents, or by his last will in writing signed with his most gracious hand as is afore said ; anything contained in this present act or in the said former act to the contrary thereof in any wise notwithstanding.

* * * * * * * * *

158. Act concerning Treasons committed out of the Realm

(1544.   35 Henry VIII. c. 2.   3 *S. R.* 958.)

FORASMUCH as some doubts and questions have been moved, that certain kinds of treasons, misprisions and concealments of treasons, done, perpetrated or committed out of the king's majesty's realm of England and other His Grace's dominions, cannot nor may by the common laws of this realm be inquired of, heard and determined within this his said realm of England ; for a plain remedy, order and declaration therein to be had and made, be it enacted by authority of this present parliament, that all manner of offences being already made or declared, or hereafter to be made or declared by any the laws and statutes of this realm, to be treasons, misprisions of treasons or concealments of treasons, and done, perpetrated or committed or hereafter to be done, perpetrated or committed by any person or persons out of this realm of England, shall be from henceforth inquired of, heard and determined before the king's justices of his bench for pleas to be held before himself, by good and lawful men of the same shire where the said bench shall sit and be kept, or else before such commissioners and in such shire of the realm as shall be assigned by the king's majesty's commission, and by good and lawful men of the same shire; in like manner and form to all intents and purposes as if such treasons, misprisions of treasons or concealments of treasons had been done, perpetrated and committed within the same shire where they shall be so inquired of, heard and determined as is aforesaid.

II. Provided always that if any the peers of this realm shall happen to be indicted of any such treason or other offences aforesaid by authority of this act, that then after such indictment they shall have their trial by their peers in such like manner and form as hath heretofore been accustomed.

159. Act for the Dissolution of Chantries

(1547. 1 Edward VI. c. 14. 4 *S. R.* 24. The whole act reprinted in G. and H. 328–357.)

THE king's most loving subjects, the Lords spiritual and temporal, and the Commons, in this present Parliament assembled, considering that a great part of superstition and errors in Christian religion has been brought into the minds and estimations of men, by reason of the ignorance of their very true and perfect salvation through the death of Jesus Christ, and by devising and phantasying vain opinions of purgatory and masses satisfactory to be done for them which be departed, the which doctrine and vain opinion by nothing more is maintained and upholden, than by the abuse of trentals, chantries, and other provisions made for the continuance of the said blindness and ignorance ; and further considering and understanding, that the alteration, change, and amendment of the same, and converting to good and godly uses, as in erecting of grammar schools to the education of youth in virtue and godliness, the further augmenting of the universities, and better provision for the poor and needy, cannot, in this present Parliament, be provided and conveniently done, nor cannot nor ought to have any other manner person to be committed, than to the king's highness, whose majesty, with and by the advice of his highness's most prudent council, can and will most wisely and beneficially, both for the honour of God and the weal of this his majesty's realm, order, alter, convert, and dispose the same ;

*   *   *   *   *   *   *   *   *

IX. And furthermore be it ordained and enacted by the authority aforesaid, that the king our sovereign lord shall, from the said feast of Easter next coming, have and enjoy to him, his heirs and successors for ever, all fraternities, brotherhoods, and guilds, being within the realm of England and Wales, and other the king's dominions ; and all manors, lands, tenements, and other hereditaments belonging to them or any of them — other than such corporations, guilds, fraternities, companies, and fellowships of mysteries or crafts, and the manors, lands, tenements, and other hereditaments pertaining to the said corporations, guilds, fraternities, companies, and fellowships of mysteries or crafts above mentioned — and shall by virtue of this Act be judged and deemed in the actual and real possession of our said sovereign lord the king, his heirs and successors, from the said feast of Easter next coming, for ever, without any inquisition or office thereof to be had or found.

*   *   *   *   *   *   *   *   *

XI. And also that the same commissioners, or two of them at the least, by virtue of this Act and of the commission to them directed, shall have full power and authority to assign, and shall appoint (in every such place where guild, fraternity, [or] the priest or incumbent of any chantry *in esse*, the first day of this present Parliament, by the foundation ordinance or the first institution thereof, should or ought to have kept a grammar school or a preacher, and so has done since the feast of St. Michael the Archangel last past) lands, tenements, and other hereditaments of every such chantry, guild, and fraternity to remain and continue in succession to a schoolmaster or preacher for ever, for and toward the keeping of a grammar school or preaching, and for such godly intents and purposes, and in such manner and form, as the same commissioners, or two of them at the least, shall assign or appoint.

And also to make and ordain a vicar to have perpetuity for ever in every parish church, the first day of this present Parliament, being a college, free chapel, or chantry, or appropriated, annexed, or united to any college, free chapel, or chantry, that shall come to the king's hands by virtue of this Act, and to endow every such vicar sufficiently, having respect to his cure and charge; the same endowment to be to every such vicar, and to his successors for ever, without any other licence or grant of the king, the bishop, or other officers of the diocese.

And also the said commissioners, or two of them at the least, shall have authority by force of this Act, to assign in every great town or parish, where they shall think necessary to have more priests than one, for the ministering of the sacraments within the same town or parish, lands and tenements belonging to any chantry, chapel, or stipendiary priests, being within the same town or parish the first day of this present Parliament, to be to such person and persons as the said commissioners, or two of them at the least, shall assign or appoint to continue in succession for ever, for and towards the sufficient finding and maintenance of one or more priests within the same town or parish, as by the said commissioners, or two of them, shall be thought necessary or convenient; and as well to make ordinances and rules concerning the service, use, and demeanour of every such priest and schoolmaster, as is aforesaid, to be appointed, as also by what name or names he and they shall from henceforth be named and called.

*   *   *   *   *   *   *   *   *

XIX. Provided always, and be it ordained and enacted by the authority aforesaid, that this Act, or any article, clause, or matter contained in the same, shall not in any wise extend to any college, hostel, or hall being within either of the Universities of Cambridge and Oxford; nor to any chantry founded in any of the colleges, hostels, or halls being in the same Universities; nor to the free chapel of St. George the Martyr, situate in the castle of Windsor; nor to the college called St. Mary's College of Winchester beside Winchester, of the foundation of Bishop Wykeham; nor to the college of Eton; nor to the parish church commonly called the Chapel in the Sea in Newton, within the isle of Ely, in the county of Cambridge; nor to any manors, lands, tenements, or heredita-ments to them or any of them pertaining or belonging; nor to any chapel made or ordained for the ease of the people dwelling dis-tant from the parish church, or such like chapel whereunto no more lands or tenements than the churchyard or a little house or close does belong or pertain; nor to any cathedral church or college where a bishop's see is, within this realm of England or in Wales, nor to the manors, lands, tenements, or other heredita-ments of any of them, other than to such chantries, obits, lights, and lamps, or any of them, as at any time within five years next before the beginning of this present Parliament have been had, used, or maintained within the said cathedral churches, or within any of them, or of the issues, revenues, or profits of any of the said cathedral churches, to which chantries, obits, lights, and lamps it is enacted by the authority aforesaid that this Act shall extend.

*   *   *   *   *   *   *   *   *

XXXIV. Provided also, and be it enacted by the authority afore-said, that this present Act, nor anything therein contained, shall in any wise extend or be prejudicial or hurtful to the general cor-poration of any city, borough, or town within this realm, or any other king's dominions, nor shall extend to any the lands or hereditaments of them or any of them; anything herein contained to the contrary in any wise notwithstanding.

*   *   *   *   *   *   *   *   *

160. First Act of Uniformity of Edward VI

(1549. 2 & 3 Edward VI. c. 1. 4 *S. R.* 37. G. and H. 358–366.)

WHERE of long time there has been had in this realm of England and in Wales divers forms of common prayer, commonly called the service of the Church; that is to say, the Use of Sarum, of York, of Bangor, and of Lincoln; and besides the same now of late much more divers and sundry forms and fashions have been used in the cathedral and parish churches of England and Wales, as well concerning the Matins or Morning Prayer and the Evensong, as also concerning the Holy Communion, commonly called the Mass, with divers and sundry rites and ceremonies concerning the same, and in the administration of other sacraments of the Church: and as the doers and executors of the said rites and ceremonies, in other form than of late years they have been used, were pleased therewith, so others, not using the same rites and ceremonies, were thereby greatly offended;

And albeit the king's majesty, with the advice of his most entirely beloved uncle, the lord protector, and other of his highness's council, has heretofore divers times essayed to stay innovations or new rites concerning the premises; yet the same has not had such good success as his highness required in that behalf:

Whereupon his highness by the most prudent advice aforesaid, being pleased to bear with the frailty and weakness of his subjects in that behalf, of his great clemency has not been only content to abstain from punishment of those that have offended in that behalf, for that his highness taketh that they did it of a good zeal; but also to the intent a uniform quiet and godly order should be had concerning the premises, has appointed the Archbishop of Canterbury, and certain of the most learned and discreet bishops, and other learned men of this realm, to consider and ponder the premises; and thereupon having as well eye and respect to the most sincere and pure Christian religion taught by the Scripture, as to the usages in the primitive Church, should draw and make one convenient and meet order, rite, and fashion of common and open prayer and administration of the sacraments, to be had and used in his majesty's realm of England and in Wales; the which at this time, by the aid of the Holy Ghost, with one uniform agreement is of them concluded, set forth, and delivered to his highness, to his great comfort and quietness of mind, in a book entitled, 'The Book of the Common Prayer and Administration of the Sacraments, and other Rites and Ceremonies of the Church, after the Use of the Church of England' :

Wherefore the lords spiritual and temporal, and the commons, in this present parliament assembled, considering as well the most godly travail of the king's highness, of the lord protector, and of other his highness's council, in gathering and collecting the said archbishop, bishops, and learned men together, as the godly prayers, orders, rites, and ceremonies in the said book mentioned, and the considerations of altering those things which be altered and retaining those things which be retained in the said book, but also the honour of God and great quietness, which by the grace of God shall ensue upon the one and uniform rite and order in such common prayer and rites and external ceremonies to be used throughout England and in Wales, at Calais and the marches of the same, do give to his highness most hearty and lowly thanks for the same ; and humbly pray, that it may be ordained and enacted by his majesty, with the assent of the lords and commons in this present parliament assembled, and by the authority of the same, that all and singular person and persons that have offended concerning the premises, other than such person and persons as now be and remain in ward in the Tower of London, or in the Fleet, may be pardoned thereof; and that all and singular ministers in any cathedral or parish church or other place within this realm of England, Wales, Calais, and the marches of the same, or other the king's dominions, shall, from and after the feast of Pentecost next coming, be bound to say and use the Matins, Evensong, celebration of the Lord's Supper, commonly called the Mass, and administration of each of the sacraments, and all their common and open prayer, in such order and form as is mentioned in the same book, and none other or otherwise.

And albeit that the same be so godly and good, that they give occasion to every honest and conformable man most willingly to embrace them, yet lest any obstinate person who willingly would disturb so godly order and quiet in this realm should not go unpunished, that it may also be ordained and enacted by the authority aforesaid, that if any manner of parson, vicar, or other whatsoever minister, that ought or should sing or say common prayer mentioned in the said book, or minister the sacraments, shall after the said feast of Pentecost next coming refuse to use the said common prayers, or to minister the sacraments in such cathedral or parish church or other places as he should use or minister the same, in such order and form as they be mentioned and set forth in the

T

said book; or shall use, wilfully and obstinately standing in the
same, any other rite, ceremony, order, form, or manner of Mass
openly or privily, or Matins, Evensong, administration of the sacraments, or other open prayer than is mentioned and set forth in
the said book (open prayer in and throughout this Act, is meant
that prayer which is for other to come unto or hear either in common churches or private chapels or oratories, commonly called the
service of the Church) ; or shall preach, declare, or speak anything in the derogation or depraving of the said book, or anything
therein contained, or of any part thereof; and shall be thereof lawfully convicted according to the laws of this realm, by verdict of
twelve men, or by his own confession, or by the notorious evidence
of the fact : — shall lose and forfeit to the king's highness, his heirs
and successors, for his first offence, the profit of such one of his
spiritual benefices or promotions as it shall please the king's highness to assign or appoint, coming and arising in one whole year
next after his conviction : and also that the same person so convicted shall for the same offence suffer imprisonment by the space
of six months, without bail or mainprize : and if any such person
once convicted of any offence concerning the premises, shall after
his first conviction again offend and be thereof in form aforesaid
lawfully convicted, that then the same person shall for his second
offence suffer imprisonment by the space of one whole year, and
also shall therefore be deprived *ipso facto* of all his spiritual promotions; and that it shall be lawful to all patrons, donors, and
grantees of all and singular the same spiritual promotions, to present to the same any other able clerk, in like manner and form as
though the party so offending were dead : and that if any such
person or persons, after he shall be twice convicted in form aforesaid, shall offend against any of the premises the third time, and
shall be thereof in form aforesaid lawfully convicted, that then the
person so offending and convicted the third time shall suffer imprisonment during his life.

And if the person that shall offend and be convicted in form
aforesaid concerning any of the premises, shall not be beneficed
nor have any spiritual promotion, that then the same person so
offending and convicted shall for the first offence suffer imprisonment during six months, without bail or mainprize : and if any
such person not having any spiritual promotion, after his first conviction shall again offend in anything concerning the premises, and
shall in form aforesaid be thereof lawfully convicted, that then the
same person shall for his second offence suffer imprisonment during
his life.

II. And it is ordained and enacted by the authority abovesaid, that if any person or persons whatsoever, after the said feast of Pentecost next coming, shall in any interludes, plays, songs, rhymes, or by other open words declare or speak anything in the derogation, depraving, or despising of the same book or of anything therein contained, or any part thereof; or shall by open fact, deed, or by open threatenings, compel or cause, or otherwise procure or maintain any parson, vicar, or other minister in any cathedral or parish church, or in any chapel or other place, to sing or say any common and open prayer, or to minister any sacrament otherwise or in any other manner or form than is mentioned in the said book ; or that by any of the said means shall unlawfully interrupt or let any parson, vicar, or other ministers in any cathedral or parish church, chapel, or any other place, to sing or say common and open prayer, or to minister the sacraments, or any of them, in any such manner and form as is mentioned in the said book ; that then every person being thereof lawfully convicted in form abovesaid, shall forfeit to the king our sovereign lord, his heirs and successors, for the first offence ten pounds. And if any person or persons, being once convicted of any such offence, again offend against any of the premises, and shall in form aforesaid be thereof lawfully convicted, that then the same persons so offending and convicted shall for the second offence forfeit to the king our sovereign lord, his heirs and successors, twenty pounds ; and if any person after he, in form aforesaid, shall have been twice convicted of any offence concerning any of the premises, shall offend the third time, and be thereof in form abovesaid lawfully convicted, that then every person so offending and convicted shall for his third offence forfeit to our sovereign lord the king all his goods and chattels, and shall suffer imprisonment during his life : and if any person or persons, that for his first offence concerning the premises shall be convicted in form aforesaid, do not pay the sum to be paid by virtue of his conviction, in such manner and form as the same ought to be paid, within six weeks next after his conviction, that then every person so convicted, and so not paying the same, shall for the same first offence, instead of the said ten pounds, suffer imprisonment by the space of three months without bail or mainprize. And if any person or persons, that for his second offence concerning the premises shall be convicted in form aforesaid, do not pay the sum to be paid by virtue of his conviction, in such manner and form as the same ought to be paid, within six weeks next after his said second conviction, that then every person so convicted, and not so paying the same, shall for the same second offence, instead of the said twenty pounds, suffer imprisonment during six months without bail or mainprize.

III. And it is ordained and enacted by the authority aforesaid, that all and every justices of *oyer* and *terminer*, or justices of assize, shall have full power and authority in every of their open and general sessions to inquire, hear, and determine all and all manner of offences that shall be committed or done contrary to any article contained in this present Act, within the limits of the commission to them directed, and to make process for the execution of the same, as they may do against any person being indicted before them of trespass, or lawfully convicted thereof.

IV. Provided always, and be it enacted by the authority aforesaid, that all and every archbishop and bishop shall or may at all time and times at his liberty and pleasure join and associate himself, by virtue of this Act, to the said justices of *oyer* and *terminer*, or to the said justices of assize, at every of the said open and general sessions to be holden in any place within his diocese, for and to the inquiry, hearing, and determining of the offences aforesaid.

V. Provided always, that it shall be lawful to any man that understands the Greek, Latin, and Hebrew tongue, or other strange tongue, to say and have the said prayers, heretofore specified, of Matins and Evensong in Latin, or any such other tongue, saying the same privately, as they do understand ;

VI. And for the further encouraging of learning in the tongues in the Universities of Cambridge and Oxford, to use and exercise in their common and open prayer in their chapels (being no parish churches) or other places of prayer, the Matins, Evensong, Litany, and all other prayers (the Holy Communion, commonly called the Mass, excepted) prescribed in the said book, in Greek, Latin, or Hebrew ; anything in this present Act to the contrary notwithstanding.

VII. Provided also, that it shall be lawful for all men, as well in churches, chapels, oratories, or other places, to use openly any psalm or prayer taken out of the Bible, at any due time, not letting or omitting thereby the service or any part thereof mentioned in the said book.

VIII. Provided also, and be it enacted by the authority aforesaid, that the books concerning the said services shall at the costs and charges of the parishioners of every parish and cathedral church be attained and gotten before the feast of Pentecost next following, or before ; and that all such parish and cathedral churches, or other places where the said books shall be attained and gotten before the said feast of Pentecost, shall within three weeks next after the said books so attained and gotten use the said service, and put the same in use according to this Act.

IX. And be it further enacted by the authority aforesaid, that no person or persons shall be at any time hereafter impeached or otherwise molested of or for any of the offences above mentioned, hereafter to be committed or done contrary to this Act, unless he or they so offending be thereof indicted at the next general sessions to be holden before any such of the justices of *oyer* and *terminer* or justices of assize, next after any offence committed or done contrary to the tenor of this Act.

X. Provided always, and be it ordained and enacted by the authority aforesaid, that all and singular lords in the Parliament, for the third offence above mentioned, shall be tried by their peers.

XI. Provided also, and be it ordained and enacted by the authority aforesaid, that the Mayor of London, and all other mayors, bailiffs, and other head officers of all and singular cities, boroughs, and towns corporate within this realm, Wales, Calais, and the marches of the same, to the which justices of assize do not commonly repair, shall have full power and authority by virtue of this Act to inquire, hear, and determine the offences abovesaid, and every of them yearly, within fifteen days after the feasts of Easter and St. Michael the Archangel, in like manner and form as justices of assize and *oyer* and *terminer* may do.

XII. Provided always, and be it ordained and enacted by the authority aforesaid, that all and singular archbishops and bishops, and every of their chancellors, commissaries, archdeacons, and other ordinaries, having any peculiar ecclesiastical jurisdiction, shall have full power and authority by virtue of this Act, as well to inquire in their visitations, synods, and elsewhere within their jurisdiction, [or] at any other time or place, to take accusations and informations of all and every the things above mentioned, done, committed, or perpetrated, within the limits of their jurisdiction and authority, and to punish the same by admonition, excommunication, sequestration, or deprivation, and other censures and process, in like form as heretofore has been used in like cases by the king's ecclesiastical laws.

XIII. Provided always, and be it enacted, that whatsoever person offending in the premises shall for the first offence receive punishment of the ordinary, having a testimonial thereof under the said ordinary's seal, shall not for the same offence again be summoned before the justices ; and likewise receiving for the said first offence punishment by the justices, he shall not for the same

offence again receive punishment of the ordinary; anything contained in this Act to the contrary notwithstanding.

———◆———

161. First Mention of Lords Lieutenant

(1550.   3 & 4 Edward VI. c. 5.   4 S. R. 107.)

*   *   *   *   *   *   *   *   *

XIII. PROVIDED always and it is enacted by the authority abovesaid, that if the king shall by his letters patents make any lieutenant in any county or counties of this realm, for the suppressing
of any commotion, rebellion or unlawful assembly, that then as
well all justices of peace of every such county and the sheriffs and
sheriff of the same, as all mayors, bailiffs and other head officers
and all inhabitants and subjects of any county, city, borough or
town corporate within every such county, shall upon the declaration of the said letters patents and request made be bound to
give attendance upon the same lieutenant to suppress any commotion, rebellion or unlawful assembly, unless he or they being so
required have any reasonable excuse for his not attendance, upon
pain of imprisonment for one whole year.

*   *   *   *   *   *   *   *   *

———◆———

162. Second Act of Uniformity of Edward VI

(1552.   5 & 6 Edward VI. c. 1.   4 S. R. 130.   G. and H. 369–372.)

WHERE there has been a very godly order set forth by the
authority of Parliament, for common prayer and administration of the sacraments to be used in the mother tongue within
the Church of England, agreeable to the word of God and the
primitive Church, very comfortable to all good people desiring to
live in Christian conversation, and most profitable to the estate of
this realm, upon the which the mercy, favour, and blessing of
Almighty God is in no wise so readily and plenteously poured as
by common prayers, due using of the sacraments, and often
preaching of [the] gospel, with the devotion of the hearers :
    And yet this notwithstanding, a great number of people in
divers parts of this realm, following their own sensuality, and

living either without knowledge or due fear of God, do wilfully and damnably before Almighty God abstain and refuse to come to their parish churches and other places where common prayer, administration of the sacraments, and preaching of the word of God, is used upon the Sundays, and other days ordained to be holy days.

II. For reformation hereof, be it enacted by the king our sovereign lord, with the assent of the Lords and Commons in this present Parliament assembled, and by the authority of the same, that from and after the feast of All Saints next coming, all and every person and persons inhabiting within this realm, or any other the king's majesty's dominions, shall diligently and faithfully (having no lawful or reasonable excuse to be absent) endeavour themselves to resort to their parish church or chapel accustomed, or upon reasonable let thereof, to some usual place where common prayer and such service of God shall be used in such time of let, upon every Sunday, and other days ordained and used to be kept as holy days, and then and there to abide orderly and soberly during the time of the common prayer, preachings, or other service of God there to be used and ministered, upon pain of punishment by the censures of the Church.

III. And for the due execution hereof, the king's most excellent majesty, the Lords temporal, and all the Commons in this present [Parliament] assembled, do in God's name earnestly require and charge all the archbishops, bishops, and other ordinaries, that they shall endeavour themselves to the uttermost of their knowledge, that the due and true execution thereof may be had throughout their dioceses and charges, as they will answer before God for such evils and plagues wherewith Almighty God may justly punish His people for neglecting this good and wholesome law.

IV. And for their authority in this behalf, be it further likewise enacted by the authority aforesaid, that all and singular the same archbishops, bishops, and all other their officers exercising ecclesiastical jurisdiction, as well in place exempt as not exempt, within their dioceses, shall have full power and authority by this Act to reform, correct, and punish by censures of the Church, all and singular persons which shall offend, within any their jurisdictions or dioceses, after the said feast of All Saints next coming, against this Act and statute ; any other law, statute, privilege, liberty, or provision heretofore made, had, or suffered to the contrary notwithstanding.

V. And because there has arisen in the use and exercise of

the aforesaid common service in the church, heretofore set forth, divers doubts for the fashion and manner of the ministration of same, rather by the curiosity of the minister, and mistakers, than of any other worthy cause :

Therefore, as well for the more plain and manifest explanation hereof, as for the more perfection of the said order of common service, in some places where it is necessary to make the same prayers and fashion of service more earnest and fit to stir Christian people to the true honouring of Almighty God, the king's most excellent majesty, with the assent of the Lords and Commons in this present Parliament assembled, and by the authority of the same, has caused the aforesaid order of common service, entitled, The Book of Common Prayer, to be faithfully and godly perused, explained, and made fully perfect, and by the aforesaid authority has annexed and joined it, so explained and perfected, to this present statute : adding also a form and manner of making and consecrating archbishops, bishops, priests, and deacons, to be of like force, authority, and value as the same like aforesaid book, entitled, The Book of Common Prayer, was before, and to be accepted, received, used, and esteemed in like sort and manner, and with the same clauses of provisions and exceptions, to all intents, constructions, and purposes, as by the Act of Parliament made in the second year of the king's majesty's reign was ordained and limited, expressed and appointed for the uniformity of service and administration of the sacraments throughout the realm, upon such several pains as in the said Act of Parliament is expressed.

And the said former Act to stand in full force and strength, to all intents and constructions, and to be applied, practised, and put in use, to and for the establishing of the Book of Common Prayer, now explained and hereunto annexed, and also the said form of making of archbishops, bishops, priests, and deacons hereunto annexed, as it was for the former book.

VI. And by the authority aforesaid it is now further enacted, that if any manner of person or persons inhabiting and being within this realm, or any other the king's majesty's dominions, shall after the said feast of All Saints willingly and wittingly hear and be present at any other manner or form of common prayer, of administration of the sacraments, of making of ministers in the churches, or of any other rites contained in the book annexed to this Act, than is mentioned and set forth in the said book, or that is contrary to the form of sundry provisions and exceptions contained in the aforesaid former statute, and shall be thereof convicted according to the laws of this realm, before the justices of assize,

justices of *oyer* and *terminer*, justices of peace in their sessions,
or any of them, by the verdict of twelve men, or by his or their
own confession or otherwise, shall for the first offence suffer imprisonment for six months, without bail or mainprize ; and for the
second offence, being likewise convicted as is abovesaid, imprisonment for one whole year ; and for the third offence in like manner,
imprisonment during his or their lives.

And for the more knowledge to be given hereof, and better
observation of this law, be it enacted by the authority aforesaid,
that all and singular curates shall, upon one Sunday every quarter
of the year during one whole year next following the aforesaid feast
of All Saints next coming, read this present Act in the church at
the time of the most assembly, and likewise once in every year
following ; at the same time declaring unto the people, by the
authority of the Scripture, how the mercy and goodness of God
has in all ages been showed to His people in their necessities and
extremities, by means of hearty and faithful prayers made to
Almighty God, especially where people be gathered together with
one faith and mind, to offer up their hearts by prayer, as the best
sacrifices that Christian men can yield.

----◆----

163. First Act of Repeal of Mary

(1553. 1 Mary, sess. 2, c. 2.　4 *S. R.* 202.　G. and H. 377–379.)

FORASMUCH as by divers and several Acts hereafter mentioned, as well the divine service and good administration
of the sacraments, as divers other matters of religion, which we
and our forefathers found in this Church of England, to us left by
the authority of the Catholic Church, be partly altered and in some
part taken from us, and in place thereof new things imagined and
set forth by the said Acts, such as a few of singularity have of themselves devised, whereof has ensued amongst us, in very short time,
numbers of diverse and strange opinions and diversities of sects,
and thereby grown great unquietness and much discord, to the
great disturbance of the commonwealth of this realm, and in very
short time like to grow to extreme peril and utter confusion of the
same, unless some remedy be in that behalf provided, which thing
all true, loving, and obedient subjects ought and are bound to
foresee and provide, to the uttermost of their power. In consideration whereof, be it enacted and established by the queen's high-

ness, the Lords spiritual and temporal, and the Commons in this same present Parliament assembled, and by the authority of the same, that an Act made in the Parliament begun at Westminster the fourth day of November in the first year of the reign of the late King Edward VI, and from thence continued to the twenty-fourth day of December then next ensuing, that is to say, in the first session of the same Parliament, entitled, An Act against such Persons as should irreverently speak against the Sacrament of the Body and Blood of Christ, commonly called the Sacrament of the Altar, and for the receiving thereof in both kinds; and also one other Act in the same session, which is entitled, An Act for the Election of Bishops, and what Seals and Styles they and other spiritual Persons exercising Jurisdiction ecclesiastical should use; and also one other Act made in one other session of the said Parliament holden upon prorogation at Westminster the fourth day of November in the second year of the reign of the said late King Edward VI, and there continued and kept to the fourteenth day of March in the third year of the said late king's reign, entitled, An Act for the Uniformity of Service and Administration of the Sacraments throughout the Realm; and also one other Act made in the session last before [named], which is entitled, An Act to take away all positive Laws made against the Marriage of Priests; and also one other Act made in one other session of the said Parliament holden upon prorogation at Westminster the fourth day of November in the third year of the reign of the said late King Edward VI, and there continued and kept to the first day of February in the fourth year of his reign, entitled, An Act for the abolishing and putting away of divers Books and Images; and also one other Act made in the same session last before mentioned, entitled, An Act made for the ordering of the ecclesiastical Ministers; and also one other Act made in one other session of the said Parliament holden upon prorogation at Westminster the twenty-third day of January in the fifth year of the reign of the said late King Edward VI, and there continued and kept till the fifteenth day of April in the sixth year of the reign of the said late king, entitled, An Act for the Uniformity of Common Prayer and the Administration of the Sacraments; and one other Act made in the same last session, entitled, An Act for the Keeping of Holy Days and Fasting Days; and one other Act made in the session last recited, entitled, An Act made for the Declaration of a Statute made for the Marriage of Priests and for the Legitimation of their Children; and every clause, sentence, branch, article, and articles mentioned, expressed, or contained in the said statutes and every of them shall be from henceforth utterly repealed, void, annihilated, and of none effect, to all purposes, constructions, and intents; any thing or things contained or specified in the said statutes or any of them to the contrary in any wise notwithstanding.

II. And be it further enacted by the authority aforesaid, that all such divine service and administration of sacraments as were most commonly used in the realm of England in the last year of the reign of our late sovereign lord King Henry VIII shall be, from and after the twentieth day of December in this present year of our Lord God 1553, used and frequented throughout the whole realm of England and all other the queen's majesty's dominions; and that no other kind nor order of divine service nor administration of sacraments be, after the said twentieth day of December, used or ministered in any other manner, form, or degree within the said realm of England, or other the queen's dominions, than was most commonly used, ministered, and frequented in the said last year of the reign of the said late King Henry VIII.

III. And be it further enacted by the authority aforesaid, that no person shall be impeached or molested in body or goods for using heretofore, or until the said twentieth day of December, the divine service mentioned in the said Acts or any of them, nor for the using of the old divine service and administration of sacraments, in such manner and form as was used in the Church of England before the making of any of the said Acts.

———◆———

164. Act for the Marriage of Queen Mary to Philip of Spain

(1554.   1 Mary, sess. 3., c. 2.   4 S. R. 222.)

WHEREAS most instant suit hath been made to your most excellent Majesty, on the behalf of the most noble and most victorious prince Charles, emperor of Rome, &c., for marriage to be had between your Highness, and his only son and heir the noble prince Philip of Spain, &c.: whereupon to the pleasure of Almighty God, to the comfort of your most noble person, and to the great and singular honour, wealth, benefit and commodity of this your realm of England, and of all us your most humble and obedient subjects of the same, there hath passed and been concluded in two sundry treaties, certain pacts and cove-

nants touching the said marriage, with dependances and circumstances of the same ; and in the one treaty these articles : first, it
is covenanted and agreed that as soon as conveniently may be,
true and perfect marriage, by words of the time present, shall
be contracted, solemnized and consummated in England, between the said most noble prince, and the said most virtuous
lady, the queen ; by force of which marriage so celebrated and
consummated, the said most noble prince Philip shall during
the said marriage have and enjoy jointly together with the said
most gracious queen his wife, the style, honour and kingly name
of the realms and dominions unto the said most noble queen appertaining, and shall aid her Highness, being his wife, in the
happy administration of her Grace's realms and dominions ; the
rights, laws, privileges and customs of the same realms and dominions being nevertheless preserved and maintained : and specially it is provided and covenanted, that the said most noble prince
shall permit and suffer the said most gracious queen his wife, to
have the whole disposition of all the benefices and offices, lands,
revenues and fruits of the said realms and dominions, and that
they shall be bestowed upon such as shall be naturally born in the
same ; and that all the matters of the said realms and dominions
shall be treated and maintained in the same tongues wherein of
old they have been wont to be treated, and by the natural
born of the same realms : it is also covenanted that the same
most noble queen, by virtue of the aforesaid matrimony, shall be
admitted into the society of the realms and dominions of the said
most noble prince, as well such as he hath now presently, as such
other also as during the same matrimony may come hereafter unto
him ; and for her dower, in case that her Highness overlive the
said most noble prince her husband, she shall yearly receive three
score thousand pounds, after the value of forty groats, Flemish
money, to the pound ; the same to be allotted and appointed upon
all the realms, lands and patrimonial dominions, of the said most
victorious lord, the emperor, his father, * * * And lest that among
their children there might arise some strife for the succession,
and thereby disturb the fruit of perpetual concord that is hoped
shall ensue of this matrimony between the realms and dominions
of either party, the said succession shall be ordered in manner
and form following : first, that as touching the right of the
mother's inheritance in the realm of England, and the other
realms and dominions depending of the same, the children as
well males as females that shall be born of this matrimony shall
succeed in them, according to the laws, statutes and customs of

the same : and as touching the lands that the said most noble prince shall leave behind him ; first, there shall be reserved unto his eldest son the lord Charles of Austria, Infante of Spain, and to the children and heirs of him descending, as well females as males, all and singular their rights which to the said prince do either now or hereafter shall belong, and shall at any time by the death either of the noble queen his grandame, or the most victorious emperor Charles the Fifth his father, (which God long defer), be devolved unto him in the realms of Spain, of both the Sicilies, with all their appurtenances, in the dukedom of Milan, and other lands and dominions in Lombardy and Italy, whatsoever name and title they have, which nevertheless shall be burdened and charged with the aforesaid dower of sixty thousand pounds ; in which realms, lands and dominions the children of this present matrimony shall pretend nothing so long as the said lord Charles the Infante, or any issue of his body lawfully begotten, do live : but if it fortune the same lord Charles to die, and the issue of his body to fail, then and in that case the eldest son of this matrimony shall be admitted into the said right, and according to the nature, laws, and customs of the said realms and dominions shall succeed : the same eldest son shall also succeed in all the dukedoms, earldoms, dominions and patrimonial lands belonging unto the said lord the emperor, as well in Burgundy as in the lower Germany * * *   Provided nevertheless and expressly reserved in all and singular the above declared cases of succession, that whatsoever he or she be that shall succeed to them, they shall leave to every of the said realms, lands and dominions whole and entire their privileges, rights and customs, and the same realms and dominions shall administer and cause to be administered by the natural born of the same realms, dominions and lands, and in all things faithfully procure their utility and quiet, and shall rule and nourish them in good justice and peace, according to their statutes and customs : finally, that between the said emperor, the prince and his successors, their realms and dominions whatsoever, and the said most gracious queen and her realms and dominions, there shall be from henceforth an entire and sincere fraternity, unity and most strait confederacy, forever (God willing) happily to endure, so as they shall mutually one of them aid another in all things which to themselves and their honour, and to the conservation of their heirs and successors shall be most agreeable, according to the strength, form and effect of the latter treaty of a strait amity, bearing date at Westminster the year of our Lord God one thousand five hundred forty and two, the declaration of which treaty beareth date at Utrecht the sixteenth day of January in the year of our Lord God one thousand five hundred forty and six.

And in one other treaty these articles following : first, that the said most noble prince shall not promote, admit or receive to any office, administration or benefice in the said realm of England, and the dominions thereunto belonging, any stranger or person not born under the dominion and subjection of the said most noble queen of England : that the said most noble prince shall receive and admit into the service of his household and court gentlemen and yeomen of the same realm of England in a convenient number, and shall esteem, entertain and nourish them as his proper subjects, and shall bring none in his retinue, nor have none with him that will do any displeasure or wrong to the subjects of the said realm ; and if they do, he shall take order to correct them with condign punishment and see them expelled his court : that the said most noble prince shall do nothing whereby anything be innovated in the state and right, either public or private, or in the laws and customs of the said realm of England or the dominions thereunto belonging ; but shall contrary wise, confirm and keep to all estates and orders their rights and privileges : that the said lord prince shall not lead away the aforesaid most noble lady the queen, out of the borders of her Highness' realm, unless she herself desire it, nor carry the children that shall be born of this matrimony out of the same realm of England, but, to the hope of succession to come, shall there suffer them to be nourished and brought up, unless it shall be otherwise thought good by the consent and agreement of the nobility of England ; and in case that no children being left, the said most noble queen do die before him, the said lord prince shall not challenge any right at all in the said kingdom, but without any impediment shall permit the succession thereof to come unto them to whom it shall belong and appertain by the right and laws of the said realm : item, that the said most noble prince shall not bear or carry over out of the aforesaid realm, the jewels and precious things of estimation, neither shall he alienate or do away any whit of the appurtenances of the said realm of England, or suffer any part of them to be usurped by his subjects or any other ; but shall see that all and singular places of the realm, and specially the forts and frontiers of the same, be faithfully kept and preserved to the use and profit of the said realm and by the natural born of the same ; he shall not suffer any ship, guns, ordnances whatsoever of war or defence to be removed or conveyed out of the said realm, but shall con-

trary wise cause them diligently to be kept and renewed when
need requireth, and shall so provide that the same may always be
ready in their strength and force for the defence of the realm:
item, that the realm of England, by occasion of this matrimony,
shall not directly or indirectly be entangled with the war that is
between the most victorious lord the emperor, father unto the
said lord prince, and Henry, the French king, but he the said
lord Philip, as much as shall lie in him, on the behalf of the said
realm of England, shall see the peace between the said realms of
France and England observed, and shall give no cause of any
breach; * * * so it may also please your Majesty for the more
perfect corroboration and strength of the said articles, grants,
pacts and agreements, and to the intent that the same may be
the more inviolably observed and kept, that it may be enacted by
the authority of this present parliament, that all and singular the
said articles, covenants, grants, pacts, treaties and agreements,
had, made and concluded for and concerning the said marriage
between your Highness and the said prince of Spain, and all and
singular the dependances thereof before rehearsed, shall immediately after the said marriage had and solemnized, stand, remain
and abide in perfect force and efficacy, according to the effect,
sense and true meaning of the said treaty.

II. And where among other the articles above remembered, it
is agreed, that the said most noble prince shall, during the said
marriage, have and enjoy jointly together with your Majesty, the
style, honour and kingly name of the said realms and dominions to
your Highness appertaining, and shall also aid your Highness
being his wife in the happy administration of your realms and
dominions, the rights, laws, privileges and customs of the said
realms and dominions being nevertheless reserved and maintained;
and where also it is provided, covenanted and agreed among
other the said articles in the said treaty by and on the behalf of
the said most noble prince, that the said most noble prince shall
permit and suffer your most excellent Majesty to have the whole
disposition of all the benefices and offices, lands, revenues, and
fruits of the said realms and dominions, and that the said most
noble prince shall not do anything whereby the estate and right,
either public or private, or the laws and customs of the said realm
of England, or the dominions thereunto belonging be innovated:
for the more express explanation and declaration of the premises,
we your faithful, loving and obedient subjects, do most humbly
beseech your Highness that it may be provided, enacted and
established by the authority of this present parliament, that your

Majesty as our only queen, shall and may solely and as a sole queen, use, have and enjoy the crown and sovereignty of and over your realms, dominions and subjects, with all the preëminences, prerogatives, dignities, authorities, jurisdictions, honours, castles, manors, lands, tenements and hereditaments belonging to the same, in such sole and only estate and in as large and ample manner and form in all degrees, acts, exercises and conditions, from and after the solemnization of the said marriage, and at all times during the same, which God grant long to continue and endure, as your Highness now hath, useth, exerciseth and enjoyeth the same, and as your Grace hath had, used, exercised and enjoyed, or might have had, used or enjoyed the same before the solemnization of the said marriage; without any right, title, estate, claim or demand to be given, come or grow unto the said most noble prince as tenant by the courtesy of this realm, or in or by any other means by force of the said marriage, of, in and to your said imperial crown, sovereignty, realms, dominions, subjects, pre-eminences, prerogatives, dignities, authorities, jurisdictions, honours, castles, manors, lands, tenements and hereditaments belonging to the same, by any laws, usage or custom whatsoever; the said marriage or any statute, custom, prescription or other thing to the contrary in any wise notwithstanding.

III. And yet nevertheless that it may be enacted, ordained and established by the authority of this present parliament, that all and singular gifts, grants, letters patents, exchanges, confirmations, leases and other writings, which after the said marriage and during the same shall pass and be made of the said benefices, offices, lands, revenues and fruits or any of them, shall be entitled, set forth and made in the names of the said most noble prince and of your most excellent Majesty, whether the said most noble prince shall be present within the said realms and dominions or within any of them, or absent: and the same gifts, grants, letters patents, exchanges, confirmations, leases and other writings, so set forth and made, shall be signed and firmed with the sign manual of your Highness; and the same so signed, and sealed with the great seal of this realm, or with such seal as hath been accustomed, shall be by authority of this present parliament deemed, adjudged, declared and pronounced to be as good, perfect and of like force, strength and effect in the law, to all intents, constructions and purposes, against the said most noble prince, and against your Highness your heirs and successors, as if your excellent Majesty had been at the time of the making thereof sole and unmarried. * * *

IV. And that it may be also further enacted, ordained and

established by the authority aforesaid, that all commissions, instructions, pardons, writs of summons, prorogations or dissolutions of parliaments, royal assents, adjournments of terms, original writs and other process, instruments, licenses, judicial acts and all manner writings, other than the said gifts, grants, letters patents, exchanges, confirmations, leases and other writings concerning or in any wise touching the said benefices, offices, lands, revenues and fruits or any of them, after the said marriage, and during the time of the same, whether the said most noble prince shall be present within the said realms and dominions, or within any of them, or absent, after the signing by your Majesty of the warrants or writings of them heretofore used to be signed, shall pass, be set forth and made from time to time in the names of the said most noble prince, and your most excellent Highness, by such officers and ministers and in such manner, form and order as hath been used and accustomed to pass, be set forth and made in the time or times of your Grace's most noble progenitors or any of them ; and shall be by the authority of this present parliament, of the same and like force, strength and effect in the law to all intents, constructions and purposes, as if your most excellent Majesty were then sole and not married : the said marriage or any law, usage or custom to the contrary in any wise notwithstanding.

*   *   *   *   *   *   *   *   *

---

165. Revival of the Heresy Acts

(1554.   1 & 2 Philip and Mary, c. 6.   4 *S. R.* 244.   G. and H. 384.)

FOR the eschewing and avoiding of errors and heresies, which of late have risen, grown, and much increased within this realm, for that the ordinaries have wanted authority to proceed against those that were infected therewith : be it therefore ordained and enacted by authority of this present Parliament, that the statute made in the fifth year of the reign of King Richard II., concerning the arresting and apprehension of erroneous and heretical preachers, and one other statute made in the second year of the reign of King Henry IV., concerning the repressing of heresies and punishment of heretics, and also one other statute made in the second year of the reign of King Henry V., concerning the suppression of heresy and Lollardy, and every article, branch, and sentence contained in the same three several Acts, and every of them, shall from the twentieth day of January next coming be revived, and be in full force, strength, and effect to all intents, constructions, and purposes for ever.

---

166. Second Act of Repeal of Mary

(1554. 1 & 2 Philip and Mary, c. 8. 4 *S. R.* 246. The whole act reprinted in G. and H. 385–415.)

WHEREAS since the twentieth year of King Henry VIII. of famous memory, father unto your majesty our most natural sovereign and gracious lady and queen, much false and erroneous doctrine has been taught, preached, and written, partly by divers the natural-born subjects of this realm, and partly being brought in hither from sundry other foreign countries, has been sown and spread abroad within the same :

By reason whereof, as well the spiritualty as the temporalty of your highness's realms and dominions have swerved from the obedience of the See Apostolic, and declined from the unity of Christ's Church, and so have continued, until such time as your majesty being first raised up by God, and set in the seat royal over us, and then by His divine and gracious providence knit in marriage with the most noble and virtuous prince the king our sovereign lord your husband, the pope's holiness and the See Apostolic sent hither unto your majesties (as unto persons unde-filed, and by God's goodness preserved from the common infection aforesaid) and to the whole realm, the most reverend father in God, the lord Cardinal Pole, legate *de Latere*, to call us home again into the right way from whence we have all this long while wandered and strayed abroad ;

And we, after sundry long and grievous plagues and calamities, seeing by the goodness of God our own errors, have acknowl-edged the same unto the said most reverend father, and by him have been and are the rather at the contemplation of your majesties received and embraced into the unity and bosom of Christ's Church, and upon our humble submission and promise made for a declaration of our repentance, to repeal and abrogate such Acts and statutes as had been made in Parliament since the said twentieth year of the said King Henry VIII., against the supremacy of the See Apostolic, as in our submission exhibited to

Second Act of Repeal of Mary 291

the said most reverend father in God by your majesties appears :
the tenor whereof ensues :

II. We the Lords spiritual and temporal, and the Commons,
assembled in this present Parliament, representing the whole
body of the realm of England, and the dominions of the same, in
the name of ourselves particularly, and also of the said body
universally, in this our supplication directed to your majesties, with
most humble suit, that it may by your grace's intercession and
mean be exhibited to the most reverend father in God, the lord
Cardinal Pole, legate, sent specially hither from our most holy
father the Pope Julius III and the See Apostolic of Rome, do
declare ourselves very sorry and repentant of the schism and disobedience committed in this realm and dominions aforesaid
against the said See Apostolic, either by making, agreeing, or executing any laws, ordinances, or commandments against the supremacy of the said see, or otherwise doing or speaking, that might
impugn the same : offering ourselves, and promising by this our
supplication, that for a token and knowledge of our said repentance we be and shall be always ready, under and with the
authorities of your majesties, to the uttermost of our powers, to do
that shall lie in us for the abrogation and repealing of the said laws
and ordinances in this present Parliament, as well for ourselves
as for the whole body whom we represent : whereupon we most
humbly desire your majesties, as personages undefiled in the
offence of this body towards the said see, which nevertheless God
by His providence has made subject to you, to set forth this our
most humble suit, that we may obtain from the See Apostolic, by
the said most reverend father, as well particularly and generally,
absolution, release, and discharge from all danger of such censures and sentences, as by the laws of the Church we be fallen
into ; and that we may as children repentant be received into the
bosom and unity of Christ's Church, so as this noble realm, with
all the members thereof, may in this unity and perfect obedience
to the See Apostolic and popes for the time being, serve God and
your majesties, to the furtherance and advancement of His honour
and glory. We are at the intercession of your majesties, by the
authority of our holy father Pope Julius III and of the See Apostolic, assoiled, discharged, and delivered from excommunications,
interdictions, and other censures ecclesiastical, which have hanged
over our heads for our said defaults since the time of the said
schism mentioned in our supplication : it may now like your
majesties, that for the accomplishment of our promise made in the
said supplication, that is, to repeal all laws and statutes made con-

trary to the said supremacy and See Apostolic, during the said schism, the which is to be understood since the twentieth year of the reign of the said late King Henry VIII, and so the said lord legate does accept and recognize the same.

*   *   *   *   *   *   *   *   *

XXV. And where we your most humble subjects, the Lords spiritual and temporal, and Commons, in this present Parliament assembled, have exhibited to your majesties one other supplication in form following: We the Lords spiritual and temporal, and the Commons, in this present Parliament assembled, representing the whole body of this realm, reduced and received by your majesties' intercession to the unity of Christ's Church, and the obedience of the See Apostolic of Rome, and the pope's holiness governing the same, make most humble suit unto your majesties to be likewise means and intercessors, that all occasions of contention, hatred, grudge, suspicion, and trouble, both outwardly and inwardly in men's consciences, which might arise amongst us by reason of disobedience, may by authority of the pope's holiness, and by ministration of the same unto us by the most reverend father in God the lord Cardinal Pole, by dispensation, toleration, or permission respectively, as the case shall require, be abolished and taken away, and by authority sufficient these articles following, and generally all others, when occasion shall so require, may be provided for and confirmed:

XXVI. First, that all bishoprics, cathedral churches, hospitals, colleges, schools, and other such foundations now continuing, made by authority of Parliament, or otherwise established according to the order of the laws of this realm, since the schism, may be confirmed and continued for ever.

XXVII. Item, that marriages made *infra gradus prohibitos consanguinitatis, affinitatis, cognationis spiritualis*, or which might be made void *propter impedimentum publicæ honestatis, justitiæ*, or for any other cause prohibited by the canons only, may be confirmed, and children born of those marriages declared legitimate, so as those marriages were made according to the laws of the realm for the time being, and be not directly against the laws of God, nor in such case as the See Apostolic has not used to dispense withal.

XXVIII. That institutions of benefices, and other promotions ecclesiastical, and dispensations made according to the form of the Act of Parliament, may be likewise confirmed.

XXIX. That all judicial processes made before any ordinaries of this realm, or before any delegates upon any appeals, according to the order of the laws of the realm, may be likewise ratified and confirmed.

XXX. And finally, where certain Acts and statutes have been made in the time of the late schism, concerning the lands and hereditaments of archbishoprics and bishoprics, the suppression and dissolution of monasteries, abbeys, priories, chantries, colleges, and all other the goods and chattels of religious houses; since the which time the right and dominion of certain lands and hereditaments, goods, and chattels, belonging to the same, be dispersed abroad, and come to the hands and possessions of divers and sundry persons, who by gift, purchase, exchange, and other means, according to the order of the laws and statutes of this realm for the time being, have the same : for the avoiding all scruples that might grow by any the occasions aforesaid, or by any other ways or means whatsoever, it may please your majesties to be intercessors and mediators to the said most reverend father Cardinal Pole, that all such causes and quarrels, as by pretence of the said schism, or by any other occasion or mean whatsoever, might be moved by the pope's holiness or See Apostolic, or by any other jurisdiction ecclesiastical, may be utterly removed and taken away ; so as all persons having sufficient conveyance of the said lands and hereditaments, goods, and chattels as is aforesaid, by the common laws, acts, or statutes of this realm, may, without scruple of conscience, enjoy them without impeachment or trouble by pretence of any general council, canons, or ecclesiastical laws, and clear from all dangers of the censures of the Church.

*   *   *   *   *   *   *   *   *

XXXIII. And therefore be it enacted by the authority of this present Parliament, that all and singular articles and clauses contained in the said dispensation, as well touching the establishment of bishoprics and cathedral churches, as also the confirmation of marriages in degrees prohibited by the canons of the Church, the legitimation of children, and the ratification of processes, and of sentences in matters ecclesiastical, touching the invalidity of them for want of jurisdiction, and the institutions and destitutions of and in benefices and promotions ecclesiastical, dispensations and graces given by such order as the public laws of the realm then approved, and all other things before contained in the said letters of dispensation, shall remain and be reputed and taken to all intents and constructions in the laws of this realm, lawful, good, and effectual, to be alleged and pleaded in all courts ecclesiastical and temporal, for good and sufficient matter, either for the plaintiff or defendant, without any allegation or objection to be made against the validity of them, by pretence of any general council, canon, or decree to the contrary made, or to be made, in that behalf.

XXXIV. And whereas divers and sundry late monasteries, priories, commanderies, nunneries, deaneries, prebends, colleges, hospitals, houses of friars, chantries, and other religious and ecclesiastical houses and places, and the manors, granges, messuages, lands, tenements, rectories, tithes, pensions, portions, vicarages, churches, chapels, advowsons, nominations, patronages, annuities, rents, reversions, services, and other possessions and hereditaments to the said late monasteries, priories, nunneries, commanderies, deaneries, chantries, prebends, houses of friars, colleges, hospitals, and other religious and ecclesiastical houses and places, and to sundry archbishoprics and bishoprics, within this realm, late appertaining and belonging, came as well to the hands and possession of the said king of famous memory, Henry VIII, father unto your majesty, our said sovereign lady, by dissolution, gift, grant, surrender, attainder, or otherwise, as also to the hands and possession of divers and sundry other persons and bodies politic and corporate, by sundry means, conveyances, and assurances, according to the order of the laws and statutes of this realm.

XXXV. And where also divers manors, lands, tenements, and hereditaments, parcel of the possession of archbishoprics and bishoprics, and many and sundry late deaneries, colleges, chantries, rectories, prebends, free chapels, guilds and fraternities, manors, houses, granges, lands, tenements, rents, services, and other ecclesiastical possessions and hereditaments, goods and chattels, to the said archbishoprics, bishoprics, deaneries, colleges, chantries, free chapels, rectories, guilds, and fraternities, late appertaining and belonging, or appointed to and for the finding of priests, obits, lights, or other like purpose, came as well to the hands and possession of the late noble king, Edward VI, brother unto your majesty [our] sovereign lady, by virtue of an Act of Parliament thereof made, or otherwise, as also to the hands and possession of divers and sundry other persons and bodies politic and corporate, by sundry means, conveyances, and assurances, according to the order of the laws of this realm ; a great number of which said late monasteries, priories, nunneries, commanderies, deaneries, colleges, hospitals, prebends, chantries, free chapels, guilds, and fraternities, and the manors, granges, messuages, lands, tenements, rents, reversions, services, tithes, pensions, portions, vicarages, churches, chapels, advowsons, nominations, patronages, annuities and hereditaments, goods and chattels, to the said monasteries, priories, nunneries, commanderies, deaneries, colleges, hospitals, chantries, free chapels, guilds, fraternities, and other ecclesiastical houses, archbishoprics, and bishoprics belonging, as well for great sums of money, as for other good and reasonable causes and considerations, have been conveyed and assured to divers the subjects and bodies politic of this realm, as well by the said King Henry VIII, the said King Edward VI, and by your highness our sovereign lady, and jointly by both your majesties, as also by divers the owners of the said ecclesiastical possessions ; which said conveyances and assurances, by their sundry letters patent, and other writings more plainly do and may appear :

Forasmuch as the said most reverend father has also by the said dispensations removed and taken away all matter of impeachment, trouble, and danger, which by occasion of any general council, canon, or decree ecclesiastical, might touch and disquiet the possessions of such goods moveable, lands, tenements, possessions, and hereditaments as were of late belonging to any of the said archbishoprics, bishoprics, monasteries, priories, nunneries, commanderies, deaneries, colleges, chantries, prebends, rectories, hospitals, houses of friars, or other religious and ecclesiastical houses and places, of what nature, name, kind, or quality soever they be of ; yet for that the title of all lands, possessions, and hereditaments, in this your majesties' realm and dominions, is grounded in the laws, statutes, and customs of the same, and by your high jurisdiction, authority royal, and crown imperial, and in your courts only, to be impleaded, ordered, tried, and judged, and none otherwise ; and understanding that the whole, full, and most gracious intents, mind, and determination of your most excellent majesties be, that all and every person and persons, bodies politic and corporate, their heirs, successors, and assigns, and every of them, shall have, keep, retain, and enjoy all and every their estates, rights, possessions, and interests that they, and every of them, now have, or hereafter shall have, of and in all and every the manors, granges, messuages, lands, tenements, tithes, pensions, portions, advowsons, nominations, patronages, annuities, rents, reversions, services, hundreds, wapentakes, liberties, franchises, and other the possessions and hereditaments of the said monasteries, abbeys, priories, nunneries, commanderies, deaneries, colleges, prebends, houses of friars, hospitals, chantries, rectories, vicarages, churches, chapels, archbishoprics, bishoprics, and other religious or ecclesiastical houses or places, or of any of them, within this realm or the dominions of the same, by such laws and statutes as were in force before the first day of this present Parliament, and by other lawful conveyances to them thereof made :

XXXVI. That it may be enacted * * *

* * * * * * * * *

167. The Act of Supremacy

(1559.   1 Elizabeth, c. 1.   4 *S. R.* 350.   The whole act reprinted in G. and H. 442–458.)

MOST humbly beseech your most excellent majesty, your faithful and obedient subjects, the Lords spiritual and temporal, and the Commons, in this your present Parliament assembled, that where in time of the reign of your most dear father, of worthy memory, King Henry VIII, divers good laws and statutes were made and established, as well for the utter extinguishment and putting away of all usurped and foreign powers and authorities out of this your realm, and other your highness's dominions and countries, as also for the restoring and uniting to the imperial crown of this realm the ancient jurisdictions, authorities, superiorities, and pre-eminences to the same of right belonging and appertaining, by reason whereof we, your most humble and obedient subjects, from the five-and-twentieth year of the reign of your said dear father, were continually kept in good order, and were disburdened of divers great and intolerable charges and exactions before that time unlawfully taken and exacted by such foreign power and authority as before that was usurped, until such time as all the said good laws and statutes, by one Act of Parliament made in the first and second years of the reigns of the late King Philip and Queen Mary, your highness's sister, entitled, An Act repealing all statutes, articles, and provisions made against the See Apostolic of Rome since the twentieth year of King Henry VIII, and also for the establishment of all spiritual and ecclesiastical possessions and hereditaments conveyed to the laity, were all clearly repealed and made void, as by the same Act of repeal more at large does and may appear; by reason of which Act of repeal, your said humble subjects were eftsoons brought under an usurped foreign power and authority, and do yet remain in that bondage, to the intolerable charges of your loving subjects, if some redress, by the authority of this your High Court of Parliament, with the assent of your highness, be not had and provided :

II. May it therefore please your highness, for the repressing of the said usurped foreign power and the restoring of the rights, jurisdictions, and pre-eminences appertaining to the imperial crown of this your realm, that it may be enacted by the authority of this present Parliament, that the said Act made in the said first and second years of the reigns of the said late King Philip and Queen Mary, and all and every branches, clauses, and articles therein contained (other than such branches, clauses, and sentences as hereafter shall be excepted) may, from the last day of this session of Parliament, by authority of this present Parliament, be repealed, and shall from thenceforth be utterly void and of none effect.

* * * * * * * * *

XVI. And to the intent that all usurped and foreign power and authority, spiritual and temporal, may for ever be clearly extinguished, and never to be used or obeyed within this realm, or any other your majesty's dominions or countries, may it please your highness that it may be further enacted by the authority aforesaid, that no foreign prince, person, prelate, state, or potentate, spiritual or temporal, shall at any time after the last day of this session of Parliament, use, enjoy, or exercise any manner of power, jurisdiction, superiority, authority, pre-eminence or privilege, spiritual or ecclesiastical, within this realm, or within any other your majesty's dominions or countries that now be, or hereafter shall be, but from thenceforth the same shall be clearly abolished out of this realm, and all other your highness's dominions for ever ; any statute, ordinance, custom, constitutions, or any other matter or cause whatsoever to the contrary in any wise notwithstanding.

XVII. And that also it may likewise please your highness, that it may be established and enacted by the authority aforesaid, that such jurisdictions, privileges, superiorities, and pre-eminences, spiritual and ecclesiastical, as by any spiritual or ecclesiastical power or authority hath heretofore been, or may lawfully be exercised or used for the visitation of the ecclesiastical state and persons, and for reformation, order, and correction of the same, and of all manner of errors, heresies, schisms, abuses, offences, contempts, and enormities, shall for ever, by authority of this present Parliament, be united and annexed to the imperial crown of this realm.

XVIII. And that your highness, your heirs and successors, kings or queens of this realm, shall have full power and authority by virtue of this Act, by letters patent under the great seal of England, to assign, name, and authorize, when and as often as your highness, your heirs or successors, shall think meet and convenient, and for such and so long time as shall please your highness, your heirs or successors, such person or persons being natural-born subjects to your highness, your heirs or successors, as your majesty, your heirs or successors, shall think meet, to exercise, use, occupy, and execute under your highness, your heirs and successors, all manner of jurisdictions, privileges, and pre-eminences, in any wise touching or concerning any spiritual or ecclesiastical jurisdiction, within these your realms of England and Ireland, or any other your highness's dominions or countries; and to visit, reform, redress, order, correct, and amend all such errors, heresies, schisms, abuses, offences, contempts, and enormities whatsoever, which by any manner of spiritual or ecclesiastical power, authority, or jurisdiction, can or may lawfully be reformed, ordered, redressed, corrected, restrained, or amended, to the pleasure of Almighty God, the increase of virtue, and the conservation of the peace and unity of this realm; and that such person or persons so to be named, assigned, authorized, and appointed by your highness, your heirs or successors, after the said letters patent to him or them made and delivered, as is aforesaid, shall have full power and authority, by virtue of this Act, and of the said letters patent, under your highness, your heirs and successors, to exercise, use, and execute all the premises, according to the tenor and effect of the said letters patent; any matter or cause to the contrary in any wise notwithstanding.

XIX. And for the better observation and maintenance of this Act, may it please your highness that it may be further enacted by the authority aforesaid, that all and every archbishop, bishop, and all and every other ecclesiastical person, and other ecclesiastical officer and minister, of what estate, dignity, pre-eminence, or degree soever he or they be or shall be, and all and every temporal judge, justice, mayor, and other lay or temporal officer and minister, and every other person having your highness's fee or wages, within this realm, or any your highness's dominions, shall make, take, and receive a corporal oath upon the evangelist, before such person or persons as shall please your highness, your heirs or successors, under the great seal of England to assign and name, to accept and to take the same according to the tenor and effect hereafter following, that is to say:

'I, *A. B.*, do utterly testify and declare in my conscience, that the queen's highness is the only supreme governor of this realm, and of all other her highness's dominions and countries, as well in all spiritual or ecclesiastical things or causes, as temporal, and that no foreign prince, person, prelate, state or potentate, hath, or ought to have, any jurisdiction, power, superiority, pre-eminence, or authority, ecclesiastical or spiritual, within this realm ; and therefore I do utterly renounce and forsake all foreign jurisdictions, powers, superiorities, and authorities, and do promise that from henceforth I shall bear faith and true allegiance to the queen's highness, her heirs and lawful successors, and to my power shall assist and defend all jurisdictions, pre-eminences, privileges, and authorities granted or belonging to the queen's highness, her heirs and successors, or united and annexed to the imperial crown of this realm. So help me God, and by the contents of this book.'

XX. And that it may be also enacted, that if any such archbishop, bishop, or other ecclesiastical officer or minister, or any of the said temporal judges, justiciaries, or other lay officer or minister, shall peremptorily or obstinately refuse to take or receive the said oath, that then he so refusing shall forfeit and lose, only during his life, all and every ecclesiastical and spiritual promotion, benefice, and office, and every temporal and lay promotion and office, which he has solely at the time of such refusal made ; and that the whole title, interest, and incumbency, in every such promotion, benefice, and other office, as against such person only so refusing, during his life, shall clearly cease and be void, as though the party so refusing were dead.

XXI. And that also all and every such person and persons so refusing to take the said oath, shall immediately after such refusal be from thenceforth, during his life, disabled to retain or exercise any office or other promotion which he, at the time of such refusal, has jointly, or in common, with any other person or persons.

XXII. And that all and every person and persons, that at any time hereafter shall be preferred, promoted, or collated to any archbishopric or bishopric, or to any other spiritual or ecclesiastical benefice, promotion, dignity, office, or ministry, or that shall be by your highness, your heirs or successors, preferred or promoted to any temporal or lay office, ministry, or service within this realm, or in any your highness's dominions, before he or they shall take upon him or them to receive, use, exercise, supply, or occupy any such archbishopric, bishopric, promotion, dignity, office, ministry, or service, shall likewise make, take, and receive the said corporal oath before mentioned, upon the evangelist, before such persons as have or shall have authority to admit any such person to any such office, ministry, or service, or else before such person or persons as by your highness, your heirs or successors, by commission under the great seal of England, shall be named, assigned, or appointed to minister the said oath.

XXIII. And that it may likewise be further enacted by the authority aforesaid, that if any such person or persons, as at any time hereafter shall be promoted, preferred, or collated to any such promotion spiritual or ecclesiastical, benefice, office, or ministry, or that by your highness, your heirs or successors, shall be promoted or preferred to any temporal or lay office, ministry, or service, shall and do peremptorily and obstinately refuse to take the same oath so to him to be offered ; that then he or they so refusing shall presently be judged disabled in the law to receive, take, or have the same promotion spiritual or ecclesiastical, the same temporal office, ministry, or service within this realm, or any other your highness's dominions, to all intents, constructions, and purposes.

XXIV. And that it may be further enacted by the authority aforesaid, that all and every person and persons temporal, suing livery or *ouster le main* out of the hands of your highness, your heirs or successors, before his or their livery or *ouster le main* sued forth and allowed, and every temporal person or persons doing any homage to your highness, your heirs or successors, or that shall be received into service with your highness, your heirs or successors, shall make, take, and receive the said corporal oath before mentioned, before the lord chancellor of England, or the lord keeper of the great seal for the time being, or before such person or persons as by your highness, your heirs or successors, shall be named and appointed to accept or receive the same.

XXV. And that also all and every person and persons taking orders, and all and every other person and persons which shall be promoted or preferred to any degree of learning in any university within this your realm or dominions, before he shall receive or take any such orders, or be preferred to any such degree of learning, shall make, take, and receive the said oath by this Act set forth and declared as is aforesaid, before his or their ordinary, commissary, chancellor or vice-chancellor, or their sufficient deputies in the said university.

XXVI. Provided always, and that it may be further enacted by the authority aforesaid, that if any person, having any estate of inheritance in any temporal office or offices, shall hereafter obstinately and peremptorily refuse to accept and take the said oath as is aforesaid, and after, at any time during his life, shall willingly require to take and receive the said oath, and so do take and accept the same oath before any person or persons that shall have lawful authority to minister the same; that then every such person, immediately after he has so received the same oath, shall be vested, deemed, and judged in like estate and possession of the said office, as he was before the said refusal, and shall and may use and exercise the said office in such manner and form as he should or might have done before such refusal, anything in this Act contained to the contrary in any wise notwithstanding.

XXVII. And for the more sure observation of this Act, and the utter extinguishment of all foreign and usurped power and authority, may it please your highness, that it may be further enacted by the authority aforesaid, that if any person or persons dwelling or inhabiting within this your realm, or in any other your highness's realms or dominions, of what estate, dignity, or degree soever he or they be, after the end of thirty days next after the determination of this session of this present Parliament, shall by writing, printing, teaching, preaching, express words, deed or act, advisedly, maliciously, and directly affirm, hold, stand with, set forth, maintain, or defend the authority, pre-eminence, power or jurisdiction, spiritual or ecclesiastical, of any foreign prince, prelate, person, state, or potentate whatsoever, heretofore claimed, used, or usurped within this realm, or any dominion or country being within or under the power, dominion, or obeisance of your highness; or shall advisedly, maliciously, and directly put in use or execute anything for the extolling, advancement, setting forth, maintenance, or defence of any such pretended or usurped jurisdiction, power, pre-eminence, or authority, or any part thereof; that then every such person and persons so doing and offending, their abettors, aiders, procurers, and counsellors, being thereof lawfully convicted and attainted, according to the due order and course of the common laws of this realm, for his or their first offence shall forfeit and lose unto your highness, your heirs and successors, all his and their goods and chattels, as well real as personal.

XXVIII. And if any such person so convicted or attainted shall not have or be worth of his proper goods and chattels to the value of twenty pounds, at the time of his conviction or attainder, that then every such person so convicted and attainted, over and besides the forfeiture of all his said goods and chattels, shall have and suffer imprisonment, by the space of one whole year, without bail or mainprise.

XXIX. And that also all and every the benefices, prebends, and other ecclesiastical promotions and dignities whatsoever, of every spiritual person so offending, and being attainted, shall immediately after such attainder be utterly void to all intents and purposes, as though the incumbent thereof were dead ; and that the patron and donor of every such benefice, prebend, spiritual promotion and dignity, shall and may lawfully present unto the same, or give the same, in such manner and form as if the said incumbent were dead ; and if any offender or offenders, after such conviction or attainder, do eftsoons commit or do the said offences, or any of them, in manner and form aforesaid, and be thereof duly convicted and attainted, as is aforesaid ; that then every such offender and offenders shall for the same second offence incur into the dangers, penalties, and forfeitures ordained and provided by the statute of Provision and *Præmunire*, made in the sixteenth year of the reign of King Richard II.

XXX. And if any such offender or offenders, at any time after the said second conviction and attainder, do the third time commit and do the said offences, or any of them, in manner and form aforesaid, and be thereof duly convicted and attainted, as is aforesaid ; that then every such offence or offences shall be deemed and adjudged high treason, and that the offender and offenders therein, being thereof lawfully convicted and attainted, according to the laws of this realm, shall suffer pains of death, and other penalties, forfeitures, and losses, as in cases of high treason by the laws of this realm.

*   *   *   *   *   *   *   *   *

———————◆———————

168. The Act of Uniformity

(1559.   1 Elizabeth, c. 2.   4 *S. R.* 355.   The whole act reprinted in G. and H.
459–466.)

WHERE at the death of our late sovereign lord King Edward VI there remained one uniform order of common service and prayer, and of the administration of sacraments, rites, and ceremonies in the Church of England, which was set forth in one book, entitled : The Book of Common Prayer, and Administration of Sacraments, and other rites and ceremonies in the Church of England ; authorized by Act of Parliament holden in the fifth and sixth years of our said late sovereign lord King Edward VI, entitled : An Act for the uniformity of common prayer, and administration of the sacraments; the which was repealed and taken away by Act of Parliament in the first year of the reign of our late sovereign lady Queen Mary, to the great decay of the due honour of God, and discomfort to the professors of the truth of Christ's religion :

II. Be it therefore enacted by the authority of this present Parliament, that the said statute of repeal, and everything therein contained, only concerning the said book, and the service, administration of sacraments, rites, and ceremonies contained or appointed in or by the said book, shall be void and of none effect, from and after the feast of the Nativity of St. John Baptist next coming; and that the said book, with the order of service, and of the administration of sacraments, rites, and ceremonies, with the alterations and additions therein added and appointed by this statute, shall stand and be, from and after the said feast of the Nativity of St. John Baptist, in full force and effect, according to the tenor and effect of this statute; anything in the aforesaid statute of repeal to the contrary notwithstanding.

III. And further be it enacted by the queen's highness, with the assent of the Lords and Commons in this present Parliament assembled, and by the authority of the same, that all and singular ministers in any cathedral or parish church, or other place within this realm of England, Wales, and the marches of the same, or other the queen's dominions, shall from and after the feast of the Nativity of St. John Baptist next coming be bounden to say and use the Matins, Evensong, celebration of the Lord's Supper and administration of each of the sacraments, and all the common and open prayer, in such order and form as is mentioned in the said book, so authorized by Parliament in the said fifth and sixth years of the reign of King Edward VI, with one alteration or addition, of certain lessons to be used on every Sunday in the year, and the form of the Litany altered and corrected, and two sentences only added in the delivery of the sacrament to the communicants, and none other or otherwise.

IV. And that if any manner of parson, vicar, or other whatsoever minister, that ought or should sing or say common prayer mentioned in the said book, or minister the sacraments, from and after the feast of the Nativity of St. John Baptist next coming, refuse to use the said common prayers, or to minister the sacraments in such cathedral or parish church, or other places as he should use to minister the same, in such order and form as they be mentioned and set forth in the said book : or shall wilfully or obstinately standing in the same, use any other rite, ceremony, order, form, or manner of celebrating of the Lord's Supper, openly or privily, or Matins, Evensong, administration of the sacraments, or other open prayers, than is mentioned and set forth in the said book (open prayer in and throughout this Act, is meant that prayer which is for others to come unto, or hear, either in common churches or private chapels or oratories, commonly called the service of the Church), or shall preach, declare, or speak anything in the derogation or depraving of the said book, or anything therein contained, or of any part thereof, and shall be thereof lawfully convicted, according to the laws of this realm, by verdict of twelve men, or by his own confession, or by the notorious evidence of the fact, shall lose and forfeit to the queen's highness, her heirs and successors, for his first offence, the profit of all his spiritual benefices or promotions coming or arising in one whole year next after his conviction ; and also that the person so convicted shall for the same offence suffer imprisonment by the space of six months, without bail or mainprize.

V. And if any such person once convicted of any offence concerning the premises, shall after his first conviction eftsoons offend, and be thereof, in form aforesaid, lawfully convicted, that then the same person shall for his second offence suffer imprisonment by the space of one whole year, and also shall therefor be deprived, *ipso facto*, of all his spiritual promotions ; and that it shall be lawful to all patrons or donors of all and singular the same spiritual promotions, or of any of them, to present or collate to the same, as though the person and persons so offending were dead.

VI. And that if any such person or persons, after he shall be twice convicted in form aforesaid, shall offend against any of the premises the third time, and shall be thereof, in form aforesaid, lawfully convicted, that then the person so offending and convicted the third time, shall be deprived, *ipso facto*, of all his spiritual promotions, and also shall suffer imprisonment during his life.

VII. And if the person that shall offend, and be convicted in form aforesaid, concerning any of the premises, shall not be beneficed, nor have any spiritual promotion, that then the same person so offending and convicted shall for the first offence suffer imprisonment during one whole year next after his said conviction, without bail or mainprize.

VIII. And if any such person, not having any spiritual promotion, after his first conviction shall eftsoons offend in anything concerning the premises, and shall, in form aforesaid, be thereof lawfully convicted, that then the same person shall for his second offence suffer imprisonment during his life.

IX. And it is ordained and enacted by the authority afore-said, that if any person or persons whatsoever, after the said feast of the Nativity of St. John Baptist next coming, shall in any inter-ludes, plays, songs, rhymes, or by other open words, declare or speak anything in the derogation, depraving, or despising of the same book, or of anything therein contained, or any part thereof; or shall, by open fact, deed, or by open threatenings, compel or cause, or otherwise procure or maintain, any parson, vicar, or other minister in any cathedral or parish church, or in chapel, or in any other place, to sing or say any common or open prayer, or to minister any sacrament otherwise, or in any other manner and form, than is mentioned in the said book; or that by any of the said means shall unlawfully interrupt or let any parson, vicar, or other minister in any cathedral or parish church, chapel, or any other place, to sing or say common and open prayer, or to min-ister the sacraments or any of them, in such manner and form as is mentioned in the said book; that then every such person, being thereof lawfully convicted in form abovesaid, shall forfeit to the queen our sovereign lady, her heirs and successors, for the first offence a hundred marks.

X. And if any person or persons, being once convicted of any such offence, eftsoons offend against any of the last recited offences, and shall, in form aforesaid, be thereof lawfully convicted, that then the same person so offending and convicted shall, for the second offence, forfeit to the queen our sovereign lady, her heirs and successors, four hundred marks.

XI. And if any person, after he, in form aforesaid, shall have been twice convicted of any offence concerning any of the last recited offences, shall offend the third time, and be thereof, in form abovesaid, lawfully convicted, that then every person so offending and convicted shall for his third offence forfeit to our sovereign lady the queen all his goods and chattels, and shall suffer imprisonment during his life.

XII. And if any person or persons, that for his first offence con-cerning the premises shall be convicted, in form aforesaid, do not pay the sum to be paid by virtue of his conviction, in such man-ner and form as the same ought to be paid, within six weeks next after his conviction; that then every person so convicted, and so not paying the same, shall for the same first offence, instead of the said sum, suffer imprisonment by the space of six months, without bail or mainprize.

XIII. And if any person or persons, that for his second offence concerning the premises shall be convicted in form aforesaid,

x

do not pay the said sum to be paid by virtue of his conviction and this statute, in such manner and form as the same ought to be paid, within six weeks next after his said second conviction; that then every person so convicted, and not so paying the same, shall, for the same second offence, in the stead of the said sum, suffer imprisonment during twelve months, without bail or mainprize.

XIV. And that from and after the said feast of the Nativity of St. John Baptist next coming, all and every person and persons inhabiting within this realm, or any other the queen's majesty's dominions, shall diligently and faithfully, having no lawful or reasonable excuse to be absent, endeavour themselves to resort to their parish church or chapel accustomed, or upon reasonable let thereof, to some usual place where common prayer and such service of God shall be used in such time of let, upon every Sunday and other days ordained and used to be kept as holy days, and then and there to abide orderly and soberly during the time of the common prayer, preachings, or other service of God there to be used and ministered; upon pain of punishment by the censures of the Church, and also upon pain that every person so offending shall forfeit for every such offence twelve pence, to be levied by the churchwardens of the parish where such offence shall be done, to the use of the poor of the same parish, of the goods, lands, and tenements of such offender, by way of distress.

*   *   *   *   *   *   *   *   *

169. Act of Recognition of the Queen's Title

(1559. 1 Elizabeth, c. 3. Prothero, 21.)

AS there is nothing under God, most dread Sovereign Lady, wherein we your most humble, faithful and obedient subjects, the Lords spiritual and temporal and Commons in this present Parliament assembled, have, may or ought to have more cause to rejoice than in this only, that it hath pleased God of his merciful providence and goodness towards us and this our realm not only to provide but also to preserve and keep for us and our wealths your royal Majesty our most rightful and lawful Sovereign Liege Lady and Queen, most happily to reign over us; for the which we do give and yield unto him from the bottoms of our hearts our humble thanks, lauds and praises; even so there is nothing that we your said subjects for our parties can, may or ought towards your Highness more firmly, entirely and assuredly in the purity of our hearts think or with our mouths declare and confess to be true, than that your Majesty our said Sovereign Lady is, and in very deed and of most mere right ought to be, by the laws of God and the laws and statutes of this realm, our most rightful and lawful Sovereign Liege Lady and Queen ; and that your Highness is rightly, lineally and lawfully descended and come of the blood royal of this realm of England, in and to whose princely person, and the heirs of your body lawfully to be begotten, after you, without all doubt, * * * the imperial and royal estate, place, crown, and dignity of this realm, with all honours * * * and preeminences to the same now belonging and appertaining, are and shall be most fully * * * invested and incorporated * * * as rightfully and lawfully * * * as the same were in the said late King Henry the Eighth or in the late King Edward the Sixth * * * or in the late Queen Mary * * * at any time since the act of parliament made in the thirty-fifth year of the reign of your said most noble father King Henry the Eighth, entitled An Act concerning the establishment of the King's Majesty's succession in the imperial crown of this realm.

*   *   *   *   *   *   *   *   *

IV. And that it may be enacted, That as well this our declaration * * * as also the limitation and declaration of the succession * * * contained in the said Act * * * shall stand the law of this realm for ever.

*   *   *   *   *   *   *   *   *

170. The Treason Act

(1559. 1 Elizabeth, c. 5. Prothero, 23-25.)

* * * BE it enacted * * * that if any person or persons after the first day of May next to come do maliciously, advisedly and directly compass or imagine to deprive the Queen's Majesty * * * from the style, honour and kingly name of the imperial crown of this realm, or from any other the realms and dominions unto our said Sovereign Lady appertaining, or to destroy the Queen's Majesty * * * or to levy war within this realm or within any the marches or dominions to the same belonging

against the Queen's Majesty * * * or to depose the Queen's Majesty * * * from the imperial crown of the realms and dominions aforesaid ; and the same compasses or imaginations or any of them, maliciously, advisedly and directly shall or do utter by open preaching express words or sayings ; or if any person or persons after the said first day of May next coming, shall maliciously, advisedly and directly say * * * or hold opinion, that the Queen's Majesty that now is, during her life, is not or ought not to be Queen of this realm, or after her death that the heirs of her Highness' body, being Kings or Queens of this realm, of right ought not to be Kings or Queens of this realm, or that any other person than the Queen's Highness that now is during her life ought to be King or Queen of this realm * * * ; that then every such offender being thereof duly convicted * * * their abettors and counsellors * * * shall forfeit and lose to the Queen's Highness, her heirs and successors, all their goods and chattels, and the whole issues and profits of their lands, tenements and hereditaments, for term of the life of every such offender or offenders, and also shall suffer during their lives perpetual imprisonment.

II. Provided * * * that every ecclesiastical person being convicted in form aforesaid * * * shall * * * be * * * deprived from all his benefices and promotions spiritual or ecclesiastical. * * *

III. And if any person being hereafter convicted of any the said offences * * * shall * * * eftsoons commit any of the said offences * * * that then every such second offence shall be deemed high treason and the offenders therein, their abettors [&c.] shall be deemed high traitors, and shall suffer pains of death and forfeit all their goods, chattels, lands and tenements to the Queen's Majesty, her heirs and successors. * * *

IV. And be it further enacted * * * That if any person * * * by any writing, printing, overt deed or act * * * do affirm that the Queen's Majesty that now is ought not to have the style, honour, and kingly name of this realm, or that any person other than the Queen's Majesty that now is, ought to have the style, honour, and kingly name of this realm, or that the Queen's Majesty that now is during her life is not or ought not to be Queen of this realm * * * that then every such offence shall be adjudged high treason, and the offender and offenders therein, their abettors [&c.] * * * shall be deemed and adjudged high traitors and shall suffer pains of death and forfeit all their goods [&c.] to the Queen's Majesty. * * *

V. [Saving of titles of strangers.]

VI. Provided * * * that concealment of any high treasons be deemed only misprision of treason and the offenders therein to for-

feit and suffer as in cases of misprision of treason hath heretofore been used. * * *

VII. [Peers to be tried by their peers.]

VIII. And be it further enacted * * * that no person shall be
impeached for any of the offences above-said committed only by
open preaching or words, unless the offender be thereof indicted
within six months. * * *

IX. [Punishment of accessories.]

X. Provided * * * that no person shall be hereafter indicted for
any offence made treason or misprision of treason by this Act, unless
the same offence * * * be proved by the testimony and oath of two
lawful and sufficient witnesses at the time of his indictment ; which
said witnesses also at the time of the arraignment of the party so
indicted (if they be then living) shall be brought forth in person
before the party so arraigned face to face, and there shall avow all
they can say against the said party so indicted, unless the said
party so indicted shall willingly without violence confess the same.

---

171. Grant of Tonnage and Poundage

(1559. 1 Elizabeth, c. 20. Prothero, 26, 27.)

IN their most humble wise show unto your most excellent
Majesty, your poor and obedient subjects and Commons in
this your present Parliament assembled, That where as well your
noble grandfather of worthy memory, King Henry the Seventh
* * * as other your right noble and famous progenitors, kings of
this your realm of England, time out of mind, have had and
enjoyed unto them by authority of Parliament, for the defence of
the same now your realm, and the keeping and safeguard of the
seas for the intercourse of merchandize, safely to come into and
pass out of the same, certain sums of money, named subsidies, of
all manner of goods and merchandize, coming in or going out of
the same your realm ; * * * we your said poor Commons, by the
advice and consent of the Lords spiritual and temporal in this
your present Parliament assembled, and by the authority of the
same, to the intent aforesaid, give and grant to you our supreme
Liege Lady and Sovereign, one subsidy called Tonnage, that is to
say, of every ton of wine * * * that shall or is come into this your
realm, by way of merchandize, the sum of 3s., and so after the
rate, and of every ton of sweet wine as well malvesey as other,

that shall or is come into the same your realm by any merchant
alien, * * * 3s., and so after the rate, over and above the 3s.
afore granted; and of every awm of Rhenish wine coming into
this your realm * * * 12d.: and also one other subsidy called
Poundage, that is to say, of all manner of goods and merchandizes
of every merchant, denizens, and alien, * * * carried out of this
your said realm or brought into the same by way of merchandize,
of the value of every 20s. of the same goods and merchandize,
12d., and so after the rate; and of every 20s. value of tin and
pewter vessel carried out of this your realm by any and every
merchant-alien, 12d. over and above the 12d. aforesaid. * * *

----

172. Establishment of the Court of High Commission

(1559. Prothero, 227–231.)

ELIZABETH by the grace of God [&c.]. To the reverend
father in God Mathew Parker, nominated bishop of Canterbury, and Edmond Grindall, nominated bishop of London, and to
our right trusted and right well-beloved councillors Francis Knowles
our vice-chamberlain, and Ambrose Cave, knights, and to our trusty
and well-beloved Anthony Cooke and Thomas Smyth, knights,
William Bill our almoner, Walter Haddon and Thomas Sackford,
masters of our requests, Rowland Hill and William Chester, knights,
Randoll Cholmely and John Southcote, serjeants at the law, William May, doctor of law, Francis Cave, Richard Gooderick and
Gilbert Gerrard, esquires, Robert Weston and Thomas Huick,
doctors of law, greeting.

[II.] Where at our Parliament holden at Westminster the 25th
day of January and there continued and kept until the eighth of
May then next following, amongst other things, there was two Acts
and Statutes made and established, the one entitled 'An Act for
the uniformity of Common Prayer [&c.],' and the other entitled
'An Act restoring to the Crown the ancient jurisdiction [&c.],' as
by the same several Acts more at large doth appear: and where
divers seditious and slanderous persons do not cease daily to
invent and set forth false rumours, tales, and seditious slanders,
not only against us and the said good laws and statutes, but also
have set forth divers seditious books within this our realm of England, meaning thereby to move and procure strife, division and

dissension amongst our loving and obedient subjects, much to the disquieting of us and our people :

[III.]   Wherefore we, earnestly minding to have the same Acts before mentioned to be duly put in execution, and such persons as shall hereafter offend in anything contrary to the tenor and effect of the said several statutes to be condignly punished, and having especial trust and confidence in your wisdoms and discretions, have authorised, assigned and appointed you to be our commissioners, and by these presents do give our full power and authority to you, or six of you, whereof you, the said Mathew Parker, Edmond Grindall, Thomas Smyth, Walter Haddon, Thomas Sackford, Richard Gooderick and Gilbert Gerrard, to be one, from time to time hereafter, during our pleasure, to enquire as well by the oaths of twelve good and lawful men, as also by witnesses and all other ways and means ye can devise, for all offences, misdoers and misdemeanours done and committed and hereafter to be committed or done contrary to the tenor and effect of the said several acts and statutes and either of them, and also of all and singular heretical opinions, seditious books, contempts, conspiracies, false rumours, tales, seditions, misbehaviours, slanderous words or shewings, published, invented or set forth, or hereafter to be published, invented or set forth by any person or persons against us or contrary or against any the laws or statutes of this our realm, or against the quiet governance and rule of our people and subjects in any county, city, borough or other place or places within this our realm of England, and of all and every the coadjutors, counsellors, comforters, procurers and abettors of every such offender.

[IV.]   And further, we do give power and authority to you or six of you [quorum as before], from time to time hereafter during our pleasure, as well to hear and determine all the premises, as also to enquire, hear and determine all and singular enormities, disturbances and misbehaviours, done and committed or hereafter to be done or committed in any church or chapel, or against any divine service, or the minister or ministers of the same, contrary to the laws and statutes of this realm : and also to enquire of, search out and to order, correct and reform all such persons as hereafter shall or will obstinately absent themselves from church and such divine service as by the laws and statutes of this realm is appointed to be had and used.

[V.]   And also we do give and grant full power and authority unto you and six of you [quorum as before] from time to time and at all times during our pleasure, to visit, reform, redress, order, correct and amend in all places within this our realm of England all such errors, heresies, crimes, abuses, offences, contempts and enormities spiritual and ecclesiastical wheresoever, which by any spiritual or ecclesiastical power, authority or jurisdiction can or may lawfully be reformed, ordered, redressed, corrected, restrained or amended, to the pleasure of Almighty God, the increase of virtue, and the conservation of the peace and unity of this our realm, and according to the authority and power limited, given and appointed by any laws or statutes of this realm.

[VI.] And also that you or six of you [quorum as before] shall likewise have full power and authority from time to time to enquire of and search out all masterless men, quarrellers, vagrant and suspect persons within our city of London, and ten miles compass about the same city, and of all assaults and affrays done and committed within the same city and compass aforesaid.

[VII.] And also we give full power and authority unto you and six of you, as before, summarily to hear and finally determine, according to your discretions and by the laws of this realm, all causes and complaints of all them, which in respect of religion, or for lawful matrimony contracted and allowed by the same, were injuriously deprived, defrauded or spoiled of their lands, goods, possessions, rights, dignities, livings, offices, spiritual or temporal; and them so deprived, as before, to restore into their said livings, and to put them in possession, amoving the usurpers in convenient speed, as it shall seem to your discretions good, by your letters missive or otherwise, all frustratory appellations clearly rejected.

[VIII.] And further, we do give power and authority unto you and six of you [quorum as before], by virtue hereof, not only to hear and determine the same and all other offences and matters before mentioned and rehearsed, but also all other notorious and manifest advoutries, fornications and ecclesiastical crimes and offences with this our realm, according to your wisdoms, consciences and discretions.

[IX.] Willing and commanding you or six of you [quorum as before] from time to time hereafter to use and devise all such politic ways and means for the trial and searching out of all the premises, as by you or six of you, as aforesaid, shall be thought most expedient and necessary; and upon due proof had, and the offence or offences before specified, or any of them, sufficiently proved against any person or persons by confession of the party or by lawful witnesses or by any due mean before you or six of you [quorum as before], that then you or six of you, as aforesaid, shall have full power and authority to award such punishment to every offender by fine, imprisonment or otherwise, by all or any of the ways aforesaid, and to take such order for the redress of the same, as to your wisdoms and discretions [shall be thought meet and convenient].

[X.] [And further we do give full power and authority unto you] or six of you [quorum as before] to call before you or six of you as aforesaid from time to time all and every offender or offenders, and such as [to] you or six of you, as aforesaid, shall seem to be suspect persons in any of the premises; and also all such witnesses as you or six of you, as aforesaid, shall think [meet] to be called before you or six of you as aforesaid and them and every of them to examine upon their corporal oath, for the better trial and opening of the premises or any part thereof.

[XI.] And if you or six of you, as aforesaid, shall find any person or persons obstinate or disobedient either in their [appearance] before you or six of you as aforesaid at your calling or commandment or else not accomplishing or not obeying your order, decrees and commandments in anything touching the premises or any part thereof; that then you, or six of you, as aforesaid, shall have full power and authority to commit the same person or persons so offending to ward, there to remain until he or they shall be by you or six of you, as aforesaid, enlarged and delivered.

[XII.] And further we do give unto you and six of you [quorum as before] full power and authority to take and receive by your discretions of every offender or suspect person to be convented or brought before you a recognizance or recognizances, obligation or obligations to our use, in such sum or sums of money as to you or six of you, as aforesaid, shall seem convenient, as well for their personal appearance before you or six of you, as aforesaid, as also for the performance and accomplishment of your orders and decrees, in case you or six of you, as aforesaid, shall see it so convenient.

[XIII.] And further, our will and pleasure is that you shall appoint our trusty and well-beloved John Skinner to be your register of all your acts, decrees and proceedings by virtue of this commission, and in his default one other sufficient person, and that you or six of you, as aforesaid, shall give such allowance to the same register for his pains and his clerks, to be levied of the fines and other profits that shall rise by force of this commission and your doings in the premises, as to your discretions shall be thought meet.

[XIV.] And further, our will and pleasure is that you or six of you, as aforesaid, shall name and appoint one other sufficient person to gather up and receive all such sums of money as shall be assessed and taxed by you or six of you as aforesaid, for any fine or fines upon any person or persons for their offences : and that you or six of you, as aforesaid, by bill or bills signed with your hands, shall and may assign and appoint as well to the said person for his pains in recovering the said sums, as also to your messengers and attendants upon you for their travail, pains and charges to be sustained for or about the premises or any part thereof, such sums of money for their rewards, as by you or six of you, as aforesaid, shall be thought expedient : willing and commanding you or six of you, as aforesaid, after the time this our commission expired, to certify into our court of exchequer as well the name of the said receiver as also a note of such fines as shall be set or taxed before you ; to the intent that, upon the determination of account of the said receiver, we be assured of that, that to us shall justly appertain : willing and commanding also our auditors and other officers, upon the sight of the said bills signed with the hand of you or six of you, as aforesaid, to make unto the said receiver due allowances according to the said bills upon his accounts.

[XV.] Wherefore we will and command you, our commissioners, with diligence to execute the premises with effect ; any of our laws, statutes, proclamations or other grants, privileges or ordinances, which be or may seem to be contrary to the premises, notwithstanding.

[XVI.] And more, we will and command all and singular justices of the peace, mayors, sheriffs, bailiffs, constables and other our officers, ministers and faithful subjects, to be aiding, helping and assisting, and at your commandment in the due execution hereof, as they tender our pleasure, and will answer to the contrary at their utmost perils.

[XVII.] And we will and grant that these our letters patents shall be a sufficient warrant and discharge for you and every of you against us, our heirs and successors, and all and every other person or persons whatsoever they be, of and for or concerning the premises or any parcel hereof, of or for the execution of this our commission or any part thereof.

Witness the Queen at Westminster, the 19th day of July.

PER IPSAM REGINAM.

173. Ordinance of the Star Chamber for the Censorship of the Press

(1566. Prothero, 168, 169.)

I. THAT no person should print * * * or bring * * * into the realm printed any book against the force and meaning of any ordinance * * * contained in any the statutes or laws of this realm or in any injunctions, letters patents or ordinances set forth by the Queen's authority.

II. That whosoever should offend against the said ordinances should forfeit all such books, and from thenceforth should never exercise * * * the feat of printing ; and to sustain three months' imprisonment.

III. That no person should sell, bind or sew any such books, upon pain to forfeit all such books and for every book 20s.

IV. That all books so forfeited should be brought into Stationers' Hall, * * * and all the books so to be forfeited to be destroyed or made waste paper.

V. That it should be lawful for the wardens of the [Stationers'] Company * * * to make search in all workhouses, shops * * * and other places of printers, booksellers and such as bring books into the realm * * * ; and all books to be found against the said ordinances to seise and carry to the Hall to the uses above said and to bring the persons offending before the Queen's Commissioners in causes ecclesiastical.

VI. Every stationer, printer, bookseller * * * should * * * enter into several recognizances of reasonable sums of money to her Majesty * * * that he should truly observe all the said ordinances * * *

Upon the consideration before expressed and upon the motion of the Commissioners, we of the Privy Council have agreed this to be observed and kept * * * At the Star-Chamber the 29th of June 5, 1566 * * *

N. BACON, C.S.   WINCHESTER.   R. LEICESTER.   E. CLYNTON.
E. ROGERS.   F. KNOLLYS.   AMBR. CAVE.   W. CECYL.

We underwrit think these ordinances meet and necessary to be decreed and observed.

MATTHUE CANTUAR.   AMBR. CAVE.   THO. YALE.
EDM. LONDON.   DAVID LEWIS.   ROB. WESTON.
                                      T. HUYCKE.

174.   Act against bringing Decrees of the Pope into England

(1571.   13 Elizabeth, c. 2.   Prothero, 60–63.)

WHERE in the parliament holden at Westminster, in the fifth year of the reign of our Sovereign Lady the Queen's Majesty that now is, by one Act and Statute then and there made, entitled, An Act for the assurance of the Queen's Majesty's Royal Power [&c.] it is among other things very well ordained and provided, for the abolishing of the usurped power and jurisdiction of the Bishop of Rome * * * That no person shall * * * maintain, defend, or extol the same usurped power, or attribute any manner jurisdiction, authority or preeminence to the same to be used within this realm * * * upon pain to incur the penalties provided by the Statute of Provision and Præmunire * * * : and yet nevertheless, divers seditious and very evil-disposed people * * * minding, as it should seem, very seditiously and unnaturally, not only to bring this realm and the imperial crown thereof (being in very deed of itself most free) into the thraldom and subjection of that foreign, usurped, and unlawful jurisdiction [&c.] claimed by the said see of Rome ; but also to estrange and alienate the minds and hearts of sundry her Majesty's subjects from their dutiful obedience, and to raise and stir sedition and rebellion within this realm * * * have lately procured and obtained to themselves from the said Bishop of Rome and his said see, divers bulls and writings, the effect whereof hath been and is to absolve and reconcile all those that will be contented to forsake their due obedience to our most gracious Sovereign Lady the Queen's Majesty, and to yield and subject themselves to the said feigned, unlawful and usurped authority ; and by colour of the said bulls and writings, the said wicked persons very secretly and most seditiously, in such parts of this realm where the people for want of good instruction are most weak, simple and ignorant, and thereby farthest from the good understanding of their duties towards God and the Queen's Majesty, have by their lewd and subtle practices and persuasions, so far forth wrought, that sundry simple and ignorant persons have been contented to be reconciled to the said usurped authority of the see of Rome, and to take absolution at the hands of the said naughty and subtle practisers, whereby hath grown great disobedience and boldness in many, not only to withdraw and absent themselves from all divine service * * * but also have thought

themselves discharged of all obedience to her Majesty, whereby
most wicked and unnatural rebellion hath ensued, and to the further danger of this realm is hereafter very like to be renewed, if
the ungodly and wicked attempts in that behalf be not by severity
of laws in time restrained and bridled : For remedy and redress
whereof, and to prevent the great mischiefs and inconveniences
that thereby may ensue, be it enacted * * * that if any person,
after the first day of July next coming, shall use or put in use in
any place within this realm * * * any such bull, writing, or instrument * * * of absolution or reconciliation * * * or if any person
after the said first day of July shall take upon him, by colour of
any such bull * * * or authority, to absolve or reconcile any person * * * or if any person within this realm, * * * after the said
first day of July, shall willingly receive any such absolution or
reconciliation ; or else, if any person have obtained since the last
day of the parliament holden in the first year of the Queen's
Majesty's reign, or after the said first day of July shall obtain from
the said Bishop of Rome * * * any manner of bull * * * or instrument * * * or shall publish or by any ways or means put in use
any such bull * * * that then every such act * * * shall be
deemed by the authority of this Act to be high treason, and the
offenders therein, their procurers [&c.] * * * shall be deemed
high traitors to the Queen and the realm ; and being thereof lawfully indicted and attainted according to the course of the laws of
this realm, shall suffer pains of death, and also forfeit all their
lands [&c.] as in cases of high treason by the laws of this realm
ought to be forfeited.

IV. And be it further enacted, that all aiders [&c.] of any the
said offenders, after the committing of any the said acts * * * shall
incur the penalties contained in the Statute of Præmunire * * *

V. Provided always * * * that if any person to whom any
such absolution * * * or instrument as is aforesaid shall, after the
said first day of July, be offered * * * shall conceal the same * * *
and not disclose and signify the same * * * within six weeks then
next following, to some of the Queen's Majesty's Privy Council,
or else to the President or Vice President of the Queen's Majesty's
Council established in the north parts, or in the marches of Wales
* * * that then the same person so concealing * * * the said
offer * * * shall incur the penalty of misprision of high treason.

*   *   *   *   *   *   *   *   *

VII. And be it further enacted, that if any person shall at any
time after the said first day of July bring into this realm of Eng-

land * * * any * * * thing called by the name of an Agnus Dei,
or any crosses, pictures, beads or such-like vain and superstitious
things, from the Bishop or see of Rome, * * * and that if the same
person so bringing in as is aforesaid such Agnus Dei and other like
things, as be before specified, shall deliver * * * the same to any
subject of this realm * * * to be worn or used in any wise : that
then as well the same person so doing, as also every other person
which shall receive the same, to the intent to use or wear the same,
being thereof lawfully convicted and attainted by the order of
the common laws of this realm, shall incur the penalties * * *
ordained by the Statute of Præmunire and Provision * * *

* * * * * * * * *

IX. And be it further enacted, that all persons which at any
time since the beginning of the first year of the Queen's Majesty's
reign have brought * * * into this realm any such bulls [&c.] * * *
and now have any of the same bulls [&c.] in their custody, and
shall within the space of three months next after the end of any
session or dissolution of this present parliament deliver all such
bulls [&c.] * * * to the bishop of the diocese where such absolution hath been given and received * * * and shall publicly before
such bishop confess their offence therein and humbly desire
to be restored * * * to the Church of England, shall be clearly
pardoned and discharged of all offences done in any matter concerning any of the said bulls [&c.] touching such absolution or
reconciliation only ; and that all persons which have received any
absolution from the said Bishop of Rome * * * since the said first
year of the reign of our said Sovereign Lady the Queen, and shall
within the said space of three months next after any session or
dissolution of this present parliament, come before the bishop of
the diocese of such place where such absolution or reconciliation
was had or made, and shall publicly before the same bishop confess
* * * their offence therein, and humbly desire to be restored, and
admitted to the Church of England, shall be clearly pardoned and
discharged of all offences committed in any matter concerning the
said bulls, [&c.] touching only receiving such absolution or reconciliation ; * * *

* * * * * * * *

175. The Oath of a Privy Councillor

(1571. Prothero, 165, 166.)

YOU shall swear to be a true and faithful councillor to the Queen's Majesty as one of her Highness's Privy Council. You shall not know or understand of any manner thing to be attempted, done or spoken against her Majesty's person, honour, crown or dignity royal, but you shall let and withstand the same to the uttermost of your power, and either do or cause it to be forthwith revealed either to her Majesty's self or to the rest of her Privy Council. You shall keep secret all matters committed and revealed to you as her Majesty's councillor or that shall be treated of secretly in council. And if any of the same treaties or counsels shall touch any other of the councillors, you shall not reveal the same to him, but shall keep the same until such time as by the consent of her Majesty or of the rest of the council publication shall be made thereof. You shall not let to give true, plain and faithful counsel at all times, without respect either of the cause or of the person, laying apart all favour, meed, affection and partiality. And you shall to your uttermost bear faith and true allegiance to the Queen's Majesty, her heirs and lawful successors, and shall assist and defend all jurisdictions, preëminences and authorities granted to her Majesty and annexed to her crown, against all foreign princes, persons, prelates or potentates, whether by act of parliament or otherwise. And generally in all things you shall do as a faithful and true councillor ought to do to her Majesty. So help you God and the holy contents of this book.

---

176. Commission for the Manumission of Villeins

(1574. Prothero, 173, 174. Part translated.)

ELIZABETH, by the grace of God, &c., to our right trusty and well-beloved counsellor Sir William Cecil * * * and to our trusty and right well-beloved counsellor Sir Walter Mildmay * * * greeting. Whereas divers and sundry of our poor faithful and loyal subjects, being born bond in blood and regardant to divers and sundry our manors and possessions within our realm of England, have made humble suit unto us to be manumised, enfranchised and made free, with their children and sequels * * * We therefore * * * do name and appoint you two our commissioners * * * and do commit * * * unto you full power to accept * * * to be manumised, enfranchised and made free, such and so many of our bondmen and bondwomen in blood with all their children and sequels, their goods, lands, tenements and hereditaments as are now appertaining or regardant to any of our manors, lands [&c.] within the said several counties of Cornwall, Devon, Somerset and Gloucester, as to you shall seem meet, compounding with them for such reasonable fines or sums of money * * * for the manumission * * * as you and they can agree : * * * the tenor of which said manumissions [&c.] shall be in such order and form as is here in these presents contained * * *

"Elizabeth, by the grace of God [&c.], to all to whom [&c.] greeting. Since from the beginning God created all men free by nature, while afterward the law of nations placed some under the yoke of servitude, we believe it to be pious and acceptable to God and in accordance with Christian charity that those in villeinage to us, our heirs and successors, subject and bound in servitude, should be wholly free.

"Know therefore that we, moved by piety * * * have manumitted and made free, and liberated from every yoke of servitude and servile condition A. B. C. D. &c., and all and every their issue thus begotten and to be begotten in the future and every one of them * * * Also we give and * * * concede to the aforesaid A. B. C. D. &c. messuages, lands [&c.], and also goods, chattels, and whatsoever is owing to them of which they are now seised and possessed * * * to have, to hold, and to enjoy * * * forever * * * without rendering to us thenceforward account of any sort by reason of servitude or servile condition * * * saving to us nevertheless * * * our free-holds and the hereditaments of the customs, lands, and tenements of which they are now seised * * * by copy-hold, and the services, dues [&c.] to be rendered and done for them, as well as the dues and services to be rendered to us as supreme lady of the fief for any free-hold lands [&c.] of which they are now seised."

* * * And our further will and pleasure is * * * that every such bill or warrant * * * so by you subscribed, shall be a sufficient and immediate warrant to the said lord chancellor * * * for the making and passing of every such manumission * * * under our great seal * * * paying only for all manner of fee at the Great Seal 26s. 8d.

Witness ourself at Gorhambury [April 3, a.r. 16]. *Per ipsam reginam.*

177. The Commission of a Justice of the Peace

(1579. Prothero, 144-147. Translated.)

ELIZABETH, by the grace of God * * * etc., to our well-beloved and faithful Edmund, archbishop of Canterbury, etc. and also to our well-beloved Thomas Bromley, knight, lord chancellor, and William, Lord Burghley, treasurer, Thomas Wotton, [and others], greeting.

[I.] Know ye that we have assigned you, jointly and severally, to keep our peace, and also the statutes and ordinances made at Winchester, Northampton, and Westminster for the preservation of the same peace ; and also the ordinances made there and at Cambridge concerning hunters, labourers, artificers, servants, inn-keepers, beggars and vagabonds, and the begging men who call themselves 'travailing men' ; and likewise the statutes and ordinances made at Westminster in the first and second years of the reign of King Henry IV, late king of England, concerning the knights, squires and varlets with liveries bearing the signs of a company or with liveries of cloth or any liveries of any kind whatsoever : and a certain other statute of Henry V, late king etc., concerning counterfeiting, washing, clipping, and other falsifying of the money of our land : and to keep and cause to be kept all other ordinances and statutes made for the good of our peace and the quiet rule and government of our people, in our county of Kent, as well within the liberties as without, according to the force, form, and effect of the same : and to chastise and punish all those found offending against the form of the aforesaid ordinances and statutes, as according to the form of the aforesaid ordinances and statutes ought to be done : and to cause to come before you all those persons who shall threaten any of our people in their persons, or in burning their houses, to find sufficient security to keep the peace and to be of good behaviour towards us and our people, and if they shall refuse to find such security, then to cause them to be kept safe in our prisons until they shall find such security.

[II.] We have also assigned you and every one of you our justices to inquire by the oath of good and lawful men of the county aforesaid, through whom the truth may be better known, of all manner of felonies, trespasses, forestallings, regratings, and extortions in the aforesaid county by whomsoever and howsoever done : and also of all those who have either gone or ridden in

Y

companies with armed force against our peace to the disturbance
of our people : and also of those who have lain in wait to wound
and slay our people ; and also of all those who have used head
coverings and other liveries of a single company, by agreement
or for maintenance, against the prohibition and form of the aforesaid statutes and ordinances made before these times, and of others
using such liveries in the future : and also of inn-keepers and
others who have offended or have attempted to offend in the abuse
of weights and measures and in the sale of victuals ; and also of
any labourers, beggars, artificers, servants, inn-keepers, and vagabonds, and others who have offended or attempted to offend in
the said county against the form of the ordinances and statutes
aforesaid made concerning hunters, labourers [etc.] : and also of
those sheriffs, mayors, bailiffs, stewards, constables, and gaolers
who in the execution of their offices have unlawfully demeaned
themselves according to the form of the aforesaid ordinances and
statutes made against such artificers [etc.] or have been careless,
remiss, or negligent : and of all and singular the articles and circumstances and other premises made against the form of the ordinances and statutes aforesaid.

[III.] And to inspect all indictments whatsoever as well those
made and not yet determined before you or any of you, or before
others, the former guardians of the peace and justices of Edward
IV and Edward V late kings of England, and Richard III late
(de facto and not de jure) king of England, and Henry VII, late
king of England, Henry VIII, Edward VI, and Mary, [etc.]
assigned to hear and to determine such felonies, trespasses, and
misdeeds in the said county, as well as those made before you
and your associates now guardians of our peace, and before our
justices, and not yet determined, and to proceed thereupon and
to make and continue the process against all others who may be
indicted before you or any of you until they be apprehended,
surrender themselves, or be outlawed.

[IV.] We have also assigned you, * * * etc., four, three, and
two of you (of whom we wish you, A, B, C, D, etc. to be one) to
be our justices to punish and chastise according to the law and
custom aforesaid and the form of the ordinances and statutes
aforesaid the aforesaid felonies ; and all and each of the offences
by inn-keepers and others in the abuse of weights and measures
and in the sale of victuals, and by labourers [etc.] against the
form of the ordinances and statutes aforesaid, or in any way in-
fringing them : and to hear and determine the aforesaid extortions
and regratings as well at our suit as at that of any whomsoever

wishing to complain and prosecute in such cases before you on behalf of us and of themselves; and also trespasses and fore-stallings aforesaid and all other things not formally declared to be determined at our suit only: and to hear and determine all other cases which by virtue of the ordinances and statutes aforesaid ought to be investigated and determined by the guardians of our peace and by our justices; and to chastise and punish those labourers, artificers, and servants for their offences by fines, payments, and amercements and in any other way as it was accustomed to be done before the ordinance made concerning the corporal punishment to be given to such labourers [etc.] for their offences; and sheriffs, mayors, bailiffs, stewards, constables, and gaolers, hunters, victualers, inn-keepers, beggars, and vagabonds according to the form of the ordinances and the statutes aforesaid.

[V.] Provided always that if a case of difficulty in determining such extortions, etc., shall happen to come before you, except it be in the presence of one of our justices of the one or the other bench or of our justices of assize in the county aforesaid, as little progress as possible shall be made in your court towards giving judgment.

[VI.] And therefore we command you and every one of you that you diligently concern yourselves with the keeping of the peace, the ordinances, and the statutes aforesaid; and that at certain days and places which you or any of you shall fix for that purpose, you or any of you shall make diligent inquisitions concerning the premises: and that you shall hear and determine all and singular the premises, and perform and fulfil the same in form aforesaid, doing therein that which to justice appertaineth, according to the law and custom of our realm of England: saving to us the amercements and other things to us thereof belonging.

[VII.] And we have commanded our sheriff of Kent that at certain days and places which you or any of you shall make known to him, he shall cause to come before you or any of you such and as many good and lawful men of his bailiwick (as well within the liberties as without) through whom the truth in the premises may be the better known and investigated.

[VIII.] And you the abovementioned Thomas Wotton, shall cause to be brought before you and your said fellows at the said days and places, the writs, precepts, processes, and indictments aforesaid, and you shall inspect them and by a due course determine, as aforesaid.

In witness whereof, &c. Given the sixth day of August, in the twenty-first year of our reign.

178.   The Oath of a Justice of the Peace

(1581.   Prothero, 149, 150.)

YE shall swear that, as justice of the peace in the county of Kent, in all articles in the Queen's Commission to you directed, ye shall do equal right to the poor and to the rich after your cunning, wit and power, and after the laws and customs of the realm and statutes thereof made ; and ye shall not be of counsel with any quarrel hanging before you ; and that ye hold your sessions after the form of statutes thereof made and the issues, fines and amercements that shall happen to be made and all forfeitures which shall fall before you ye shall cause to be entered without any concealment or embezzling and truly send them to the Queen's exchequer.   Ye shall not let for gift or other cause, but well and truly ye shall do your office of justice of the peace in that behalf, and that you take nothing for your office of justice of the peace to be done, but of the Queen, and fees accustomed and costs limited by the statute ; and ye shall not direct nor cause to be directed any warrant (by you to be made) to the parties, but ye shall direct them to the bailiffs of the said county or other the Queen's officers or ministers, or other indifferent persons to do execution thereof.   So help you God and by the contents of this book.

---

179.   Resolutions on the Norfolk Election Case

(1586.   Resolutions of the House of Commons.   Prothero, 130.)

FIRST, That the first writ was duly executed and the election good, and the second election absolutely void.

Secondly, That it was a most perilous precedent that, after two knights of a county were duly elected, any new writ should issue out for a second election without order of the House of Commons itself.

Thirdly, That the discussing and adjudging of this and such like differences only belonged to the said House.

Fourthly, That though the Lord Chancellor and Judges were competent judges in their proper courts, yet they were not in parliament.

Fifthly, That it should be entered in the very journal-book of the House that the said first election was approved to be good, and the said knights then chosen had been received and allowed as members of the House, not out of any respect the said House had or gave to the resolution of the Lord Chancellor and Judges therein passed, but merely by reason of the resolution of the House itself, by which the said election had been approved.

Sixthly and lastly, That there should no message be sent to the Lord Chancellor, not so much as to know what he had done therein, because it was conceived to be a matter derogatory to the power and privilege of the said House.

---

180. The Queen's Message with Regard to Monopolies

(1601. November 25. Message brought to the House of Commons by the Speaker. Prothero, 116, 117.)

IT pleased her Majesty to command me to attend upon her yesterday in the afternoon, from whom I am to deliver unto you all her Majesty's most gracious message, sent by my unworthy self. * * * It pleased her Majesty to say unto me, That if she had an hundred tongues she could not express our hearty good-wills. And further she said, That as she had ever held our good most dear, so the last day of our or her life should witness it ; and that if the least of her subjects were grieved, and herself not touched, she appealed to the throne of Almighty God, how careful she hath been, and will be, to defend her people from all oppressions. She said, That partly by intimation of her council, and partly by divers petitions that have been delivered unto her both going to chapel and also walking abroad, she understood that divers patents, that she had granted, were grievous to her subjects ; and that the substitutes of the patentees had used great oppression. But, she said, she never assented to grant anything which was *malum in se*. And if in the abuse of her grant there be anything evil, which she took knowledge there was, she herself would take present order of reformation thereof. I cannot express unto you the apparent indignation of her Majesty towards these abuses. She said her kingly prerogative was tender ; and therefore desireth us not to speak or doubt of her careful reformation ; for, she said, her commandment given

a little before the late troubles (meaning the Earl of Essex's matters) by the unfortunate event of them was not so hindered, but
that since that time, even in the midst of her most great and
weighty occasions, she thought upon them. And that this should
not suffice, but that further order should be taken presently, and
not *in futuro* (for that also was another word which I take it her
Majesty used), and that some should be presently repealed, some
suspended, and none put in execution but such as should first
have a trial according to the law for the good of the people.
Against the abuses her wrath was so incensed, that she said, that
she neither could nor would suffer such to escape with impunity.
So to my unspeakable comfort she hath made me the messenger
of this her gracious thankfulness and care.

---

181. Act of Recognition of the King's Title

(1604. 1 James I, c. 1. Prothero, 250, 251.)

GREAT and manifold were the benefits, most dread and most
gracious Sovereign, wherewith Almighty God blessed this kingdom and nation by the happy union and conjunction of the two noble
houses of York and Lancaster, thereby preserving this noble realm,
formerly torn and almost wasted with long and miserable dissension and bloody civil war ; but more inestimable and unspeakable
blessings are thereby poured upon us, because there is derived and
grown from and out of that union of those two princely families, a
more famous and greater union, or rather a reuniting, of two mighty,
famous and ancient kingdoms (yet anciently but one) of England
and Scotland, under one imperial crown, in your most royal person * * * We therefore, your most humble and loyal subjects, the
Lords Spiritual and Temporal and the Commons in this present
Parliament assembled, do from the bottom of our hearts yield to
the Divine Majesty all humble thanks and praises, not only for the
said unspeakable and inestimable benefits and blessings above
mentioned, but also that he hath further enriched your Highness
with a most royal progeny, of most rare and excellent gifts and
forwardness, and in his goodness is likely to increase the happy
number of them : and in most humble and lowly manner do beseech your most excellent Majesty, that (as a memorial to all posterities, amongst the records of your High Court of Parliament for
ever to endure, of our loyalty, obedience and hearty and humble

affection), it may be published and declared in this High Court of Parliament, and enacted by authority of the same, That we (being bounden thereunto both by the laws of God and man) do recognize and acknowledge (and thereby express our unspeakable joys) that immediately upon the dissolution and decease of Elizabeth, late Queen of England, the imperial crown of the realm of England, and of all the kingdoms, dominions and rights belonging to the same, did, by inherent birthright and lawful and undoubted succession, descend and come to your most excellent Majesty, as being lineally, justly and lawfully next and sole heir of the blood royal of this realm as is aforesaid ; and that by the goodness of God Almighty and lawful right of descent, under one imperial crown, your Majesty is of the realms and kingdoms of England, Scotland, France and Ireland, the most potent and mighty King * * *

---

182. Commission for Negotiating a Union with Scotland

(1604. 1 James I. c. 2. Prothero, 251, 252.)

WHEREAS his most excellent Majesty hath been pleased, out of his great wisdom and judgment, not only to represent unto us by his own prudent and princely speech on the first day of this Parliament, how much he desired, in regard of his inward and gracious affection to both the famous and ancient realms of England and Scotland, now united in allegiance and loyal subjection in his royal person to his Majesty and his posterities for ever, that by a speedy, mature and sound deliberation such a further union might follow, as should make perfect that mutual love and uniformity of manners and customs which Almighty God in his providence for the strength and safety of both realms hath already so far begun in apparent sight of all the world, but also hath vouchsafed to express many ways how far it is and ever shall be from his royal and sincere care and affection to the subjects of England to alter and innovate the fundamental and ancient laws, privileges and good customs of this kingdom, whereby not only his regal authority but the people's security * * * are preserved * * * : forasmuch as his Majesty's humble, faithful and loving subjects have not only conceived the weight of his Majesty's reasons, but apprehend to their unspeakable joy and comfort his plain * * * intention to seek no other changes, but of such particular, temporary or indifferent man-

ner of statutes and customs as may both prevent and extinguish
all future questions or unhappy accidents, by which the * * *
friendship and quietness between the subjects of both the realms
aforesaid may be completed and confirmed, and also accomplish
that real and effectual union already inherent in his Majesty's royal
blood and person * * *: be it therefore enacted by the King's
most excellent Majesty, by and with the assent and consent of the
Lords Spiritual and Temporal and the Commons in this present
Parliament assembled, and by authority of the same, That Thomas,
Lord Ellesmere, Lord Chancellor of England [and 43 others named],
commissioners selected and nominated by authority of this present Parliament, or any eight or more of the said lords of the said
higher house and any twenty or more of the said knights, citizens
and burgesses of the said house of the commons, shall * * * have
full power * * * before the next session of this Parliament,
to * * * treat and consult with certain selected commissioners
to be nominated and authorized by authority of Parliament of the
realm of Scotland * * * concerning such an union of the said
realms of England and Scotland * * * ; which commissioners of
both the said realms shall * * * reduce their doings and proceedings therein into writings or instruments, * * * that thereupon
such further proceedings may be had as by both the said parliaments shall be thought fit and necessary for the weal and common
good of both the said realms.

———◆———

183. Act in Shirley's Case

(1604. 1 James I. Private Acts c. 9. Prothero, 324, 325.)

HUMBLY pray the Commons of this present parliament that,
whereas Thomas Shirley, knight, which came by your Highness' commandment to this your present parliament, being elected
and returned a burgess for the borough of Steyning in your Highness' county of Sussex, was upon the 15th day of March last past
arrested by the sheriff of London at the suit of one Giles Simpson
first upon an action of debt, and afterwards the same day laid and
detained in execution upon a recognizance, of the nature of the
statute staple, of £3000, in the prison commonly called the
Compter in the Poultry in London, at the suit of the said Simpson,
and from thence by *Habeas Corpus* was removed to your Majesty's
prison of the Fleet, * * * contrary to the liberties, privilege and

freedom accustomed and due to the Commons of your Highness'
parliament, who have ever used to enjoy the freedom of coming
to and returning from the parliament and sitting there without
restraint or molestation, and it concerneth your Commons greatly
to have this freedom and privilege inviolably observed ; yet, to
the end that no person be prejudiced or damnified hereby, May
it please your Highness by the assent of the Lords spiritual and
temporal and Commons in this present parliament assembled, and
by the authority of the same, it may be ordained and enacted,
That the said sheriff of London, the now warden of the Fleet, and
all others that have had the said Thomas in custody since the said
first arrest * * * may not nor shall in any wise be hurt, endamaged
or grieved because of dismissing at large the said Thomas Shirley :
saving always to the said Giles Simpson and other the persons
before said, at whose suit the said Thomas is detained in prison,
their executions and suits at all times after the end of this present
session of parliament to be taken out and prosecuted as if the said
Thomas had never been arrested or taken in execution, and as if
such actions had never been brought or sued against him ; saving
also to your Majesty's said Commons called now to this your parliament, and their successors, their whole liberties, franchises and
privileges in all ample form and manner, as your Highness' said
Commons at any time before this day have had, used and enjoyed
and ought to have, use and enjoy, this present act and petition in
any wise notwithstanding.

---

184. Opinions of the Court of Exchequer in Bates' Case

(1606. 11 State Trials, 30–32. Prothero, 340–342.)

[*Baron Clarke*] * * * It seemeth to me strange that any subjects would contend with the King in this high point of prerogative ; but such is the King's grace that he has showed his intent
to be, that this matter shall be disputed and adjudged by us
according to the ancient law and custom of the realm. * * * As it
is not a kingdom without subjects and government, so he is not a
king without revenues. * * * The revenue of the crown is the
very essential part of the crown, and he who rendeth that from the
King pulleth also his crown from his head, for it cannot be separated from the crown.   And such great prerogatives of the crown,

without which it cannot be, ought not to be disputed; and in these cases of prerogative the judgment shall not be according to the rules of the common law, but according to the precedents of this court, wherein these matters are disputable and determinable. * * *

True it is that the weal of the King is the public weal of the people, and he for his pleasure may afforest the wood of any subject, and he thereby shall be subject to the law of the forest; and he may take the provision of any man by his purveyor for his own use, but at reasonable prices and without abuse, the abuse of which officer hath been restrained by divers statutes; and the King may take wines for his provision, and also timber for his ships, castles or houses in the wood of any man, and this is for public benefit: and the King may alloy or enhance coin at his pleasure, for the plenty of the king is the people's peace. * * *

The Statute of the 45 Edw. III, Cap. 4, which hath been so much urged, that no new imposition shall be imposed upon wool-fells, wool or leather but only the custom and subsidy granted to the King — this extends only to the King himself and shall not bind his successors, for it is a principal part of the Crown of England which the King cannot diminish. And the same King, in the 24th of his reign, granted divers exemptions to certain persons, and because that it was in derogation of his state imperial, he himself recalled and annulled the same * * *

All the ports of the realm belong to the King. * * * The writ of *ne exeat regno* comprehends a prohibition to him to whom it is directed that he shall not go beyond the seas, and this may be directed at the King's pleasure to any man who is his subject; and so consequently may he prohibit all merchants. And as he may prohibit the persons, so may he the goods of any man, viz. that he shall export or import at his pleasure. And if the King may generally inhibit that such goods shall not be imported, then by the same reason may he prohibit them upon condition or *sub modo*, viz. that if they import such goods, that then they shall pay, &c. * * *

[*Chief Baron Fleming.*] The King's power is double, ordinary and absolute, and they have several laws and ends. That of the ordinary is for the profit of particular subjects, for the execution of civil justice, the determining of *meum;* and this is exercised by equity and justice in ordinary courts, and by the civilians is nominated *jus privatum*, and with us common law; and these laws cannot be changed without parliament; and although that their form and course may be changed and interrupted, yet they can never be changed in substance. The absolute power of the King

Opinions of the Court in Bates' Case   331

is not that which is converted or executed to private use, to the
benefit of any particular person, but is only that which is applied
to the general benefit of the people, and is *salus populi;* as the
people is the body, and the King the head ; and this power is
[not] guided by the rules which direct only at the common law,
and is most properly named policy and government ; and as the
constitution of this body varieth with the time, so varieth this
absolute law, according to the wisdom of the King, for the common good ; and these being general rules, and true as they are,
all things done within these rules are lawful. The matter in question is material matter of state, and ought to be ruled by the rules
of policy, and if it be so, the King hath done well to execute his
extraordinary power.

All customs, be they old or new, are no other but the effects and
issues of trades and commerce with foreign nations ; but all commerce and affairs with foreigners, all wars and peace, all acceptance and admitting for current foreign coin, all parties and
treaties whatsoever are made by the absolute power of the King :
and he who hath power of causes hath power also of effects. * * *

It is said that an imposition may not be upon a subject without
parliament. That the King may impose upon a subject, I omit,
for it is not here the question if the King may impose upon the
subject or his goods. But the impost here is not upon a subject,
but here it is upon Bates, as upon a merchant who imports goods
within the land, charged before by the King ; and at the time
when the impost was imposed upon them, they were the goods of
the Venetians and not the goods of a subject, nor within the land ;
* * * and so all the arguments which were made for the subject
fail. * * *

And whereas it is said, that if the King may impose, he may
impose any quantity that he pleases, true it is that this is to be
referred to the wisdom of the King, who guideth all under God by
his wisdom, and this is not to be disputed by a subject ; and many
things are left to his wisdom for the ordering of his power rather
than his power shall be restrained. The King may pardon any
felon : but it may be objected that if he pardoned one felon, he
may pardon all, to the damage of the commonwealth ; and yet
none will doubt but that is left to his wisdom. * * * And the
wisdom and providence of the King is not to be disputed by the
subject ; for by intendment they cannot be severed from his
person, and to argue a *posse ad actum*, to restrain the King and
his power because that by his power he may do ill, is no argument for a subject. * * *

185. The Case of Prohibitions

(1607.   12 Coke's Reports, 63.)

NOTE, upon Sunday the 10th of November in this same term, the king, upon complaint made to him by Bancroft, archbishop of Canterbury, concerning prohibitions, the king was informed, that when the question was made of what matters the ecclesiastical judges have cognizance, either upon the exposition of the statutes concerning tithes, or any other thing ecclesiastical, or upon the statute 1 El. concerning the high commission, or in any other case in which there is not express authority in law, the king himself may decide it in his royal person ; and that the judges are but the delegates of the king, and that the king may take what causes he shall please to determine, from the determination of the judges, and may determine them himself. And the archbishop said, that this was clear in divinity, that such authority belongs to the king by the word of God in the Scripture To which it was answered by me, in the presence, and with the clear consent of all the judges of England, and barons of the exchequer, that the king in his own person cannot adjudge any case, either criminal, as treason, felony, &c. or betwixt party and party, concerning his inheritance, chattels, or goods, &c., but this ought to be determined and adjudged in some court of justice, according to the law and custom of England ; and always judgments are given, *ideo consideratum est per curiam*, so that the court gives the judgment : and the king hath his court, *viz.* in the upper house of parliament, in which he with his lords is the supreme judge over all other judges ; for if error be in the common pleas, that may be reversed in the king's bench : and if the court of king's bench err, that may be reversed in the upper house of parliament, by the king, with the assent of the lords spiritual and temporal, without the commons : and in this respect the king is called the chief justice, 20 H. 7. 7a. by Brudnell : and it appears in our books, that the king may sit in the star-chamber ; but this was to consult with the justices, upon certain questions proposed to them, and not *in judicio :* so in the king's bench he may sit, but the court gives the judgment : and it is commonly said in our books, that the king is always present in court in the judgment of law ; and upon this he cannot be nonsuit : but the judgments are always given *per curiam ;* and the judges are sworn to execute justice according to law and the custom of England.

And it appears by the act of parliament of 2 Ed. 3. cap. 9. [2 Ed. 3. cap. 1.] that neither by the great seal, nor by the little seal, justice shall be delayed ; *ergo*, the king cannot take any cause out of any of his courts, and give judgment upon it himself, but in his own cause he may stay it, as it doth appear 11 H. 4. 8. And the judges informed the king, that no king after the conquest assumed to himself to give any judgment in any cause whatsoever, which concerned the administration of justice within this realm, but these were solely determined in the courts of justice : and the king cannot arrest any man, as the book is in 1 H. 7. 4. for the party cannot have remedy against the king ; so if the king give any judgment, what remedy can the party have. *Vide* 39 Ed. 3. 14. one who had a judgment reversed before the council of state ; it was held utterly void, for that it was not a place where judgment may be reversed. *Vide* 1 H. 7. 4. Hussey, chief justice, who was attorney to Ed. 4., reports that Sir John Markham, chief justice, said to King Ed. 4. that the king cannot arrest a man for suspicion of treason or felony, as others of his lieges may ; for that if it be a wrong to the party grieved, he can have no remedy : and it was greatly marvelled that the archbishop durst inform the king, that such absolute power and authority, as is aforesaid, belonged to the king by the word of God. *Vide* 4 H. 4. cap. 22. which being translated into Latin, the effect is, *judicia in curia regis reddita non nihil annihilentur, sed stet judicium in suo robore quousque per judicium curiæ regis tanquam erroneum, &c. Vide West. 2. cap. 5.   Vide le stat. de Marlbridge, cap. 1.   Provisum est, concordatum, et concessum, quod tam majores quam minores justitiam habeant et recipiant in curia domini regis.   Et vide le stat. de Magna Charta, cap. 29. 25 Ed. 3. cap. 5.* None may be taken by petition or suggestion made to our lord the king or his council, unless by judgment : and 43 Edw. 3. cap. 3. no man shall be put to answer without presentment before the justices, matter of record, or by due process, or by writ original, according to the ancient law of the land : and if anything be done against it, it shall be void in law and held for error. *Vide* 28 Edw. 3. c. 3. 37 Edw. 3. cap. 18. *Vide* 17 R. 2. *ex rotulis parliamenti in Turri, art. 10.* A controversy of land between parties was heard by the king, and sentence given, which was repealed for this, that it did belong to the common law : then the king said, that he thought the law was founded upon reason, and that he and others had reason, as well as the judges : to which it was answered by me, that true it was, that God had endowed his Majesty with excellent science, and great endowments of nature ; but his Majesty was not learned in the laws of his realm of England, and causes which concern the life, or inheritance, or goods, or fortunes of his subjects, are not to be decided by natural reason but by the artificial reason and judgment of law, which law is an act which requires long study and experience, before that a man can attain to the cognizance of it: and that the law was the golden met-wand and measure to try the causes of the subjects; and which protected his Majesty in safety and peace: with which the king was greatly offended, and said, that then he should be under the law, which was treason to affirm, as he said; to whom I said, that Bracton saith, *quod rex non debet esse sub homine, sed sub Deo et lege.*

---

186. Judgment in the Case of the Post-nati, or Calvin's Case

(1608. Judgment of Lord Chancellor Ellesmere. **11 State Trials, 106.** Prothero, 446.)

* * * THUS I have here delivered my concurrence in opinion with my lords the judges, and the reasons that induce and satisfy my conscience that Ro. Calvin, and all the post-nati in Scotland, are in reason and by the common law of England natural-born subjects within the allegiance of the King of England, and enabled to purchase and have freehold and inheritance of lands in England and to bring real actions for the same in England.

---

187. The Case of Proclamations

(1610. 12 Coke's Reports, 74.)

MEMORANDUM, that upon Thursday, *20 Sept. 8 Regis Jacobi,* I was sent for to attend the lord chancellor, lord treasurer, lord privy seal, and the chancellor of the duchy; there being present the attorney, the solicitor, and recorder: and two questions were moved to me by the lord treasurer; the one if the king by his proclamation may prohibit new buildings in and about London &c.; the other, if the king may prohibit the making of starch of wheat; and the lord treasurer said, that these were preferred to the king as grievances, and against the law and justice: and the king hath answered, that he will confer with his privy council, and his judges, and then he will do right to them. To which I answered, that these questions were of great importance. 2. That they concerned the answer of the king to the body, *viz.* to the commons of the house of parliament. 3. That I did not hear of these questions until this morning at nine of the clock : for the grievances were preferred, and the answer made when I was in my circuit. And, lastly, both the proclamations, which now were showed, were promulgated, *anno 5 Jac.*, after my time of attorneyship : and for these reasons I did humble desire them that I might have conference with my brethren the judges about the answer of the king, and then to make an advised answer according to law and reason. To which the lord chancellor said, that every precedent had first a commencement, and that he would advise the judges to maintain the power and prerogative of the king; and in cases in which there is no authority and precedent, to leave it to the king to order in it, according to his wisdom, and for the good of his subjects, or otherwise the king would be no more than the duke of Venice : and that the king was so much restrained in his prerogative, that it was to be feared the bonds would be broken : and the lord privy seal said, that the physician was not always bound to a precedent, but to apply his medicine according to the quality of the disease: and all concluded that it should be necessary at that time to confirm the king's prerogative with our opinions, although that there were not any former precedent or authority in law : for every precedent ought to have a commencement.

To which I answered, that true it is that every precedent hath a commencement ; but when authority and precedent is wanting, there is need of great consideration, before that anything of novelty shall be established, and to provide that this be not against the law of the land : for I said, that the king cannot change any part of the common law, nor create any offence by his proclamation, which was not an offence before, without parliament. But at this time I only desired to have a time of consideration and conference with my brothers, for *deliberandum est diu, quod statuendum est semel;* to which the solicitor said, that divers sentences were given in the star chamber upon the proclamation against building ; and that I myself had given sentence in divers cases for the said proclamation : to which I answered, that precedents were to be seen, and consideration to be had of this upon conference with my brethren, for that *melius est recurrere, quam male currere;* and that indictments conclude, *contra leges et statuta ;* but I never heard an indictment to conclude, *contra regiam proclamationem.*

At last my motion was allowed ; and the lords appointed the two chief justices, chief baron, and baron Altham, to have consideration of it.

Note, the king by his proclamation or other ways cannot change any part of the common law, or statute law, or the customs of the realm, 11 Hen. 4. 37.   Fortescue *De laudibus Angliæ legum,* cap. 9.   18 Edw. 3. 35, 36, &c.   31 Hen. 8. cap. 8. *hic infra :* also the king cannot create any offence by his prohibition or proclamation, which was not an offence before, for that was to change the law, and to make an offence which was not ; for *ubi non est lex, ibi non est transgressio : ergo,* that which cannot be punished without proclamation, cannot be punished with it.   *Vide le stat.* 31 Hen. 8. cap. 8. which act gives more power to the king than he had before, and yet there it is declared that proclamations shall not alter the law, statutes, or customs of the realm, or impeach any in his inheritance, goods, body, life, &c.   But if a man shall be indicted for a contempt against a proclamation, he shall be fined and imprisoned, and so impeached in his body and goods.   *Vide* Fortescue, cap. 9, 18, 34, 36, 37, &c.

But a thing which is punishable by the law, by fine, and imprisonment, if the king prohibit it by his proclamation, before that he will punish it, and so warn his subjects of the peril of it, there if he permit it after, this as a circumstance aggravates the offence ; but he by proclamation cannot make a thing unlawful, which was permitted by the law before : and this was well proved by the ancient and continual forms of indictments ; for all indictments conclude *contra legem et consuetudinem Angliæ,* or *contra leges et statuta,* &c.   But never was seen any indictment to conclude *contra regiam proclamationem.*

So in all cases the king out of his providence, and to prevent dangers, which it will be too late to prevent afterwards, he may prohibit them before, which will aggravate the offence if it be afterwards committed : and as it is a grand prerogative of the king to make proclamation, (for no subject can make it without authority from the king, or lawful custom,) upon pain of fine and imprisonment, as it is held in the 22 Hen. 8. Proclamation B. But we do find divers precedents of proclamations which are utterly against law and reason, and for that void ; for *quæ contra rationem juris introducta sunt non debent trahi in consequentiam.*

An act which was made, by which foreigners were licensed to merchandise within London ; Hen. 4. by proclamation prohibited the execution of it ; and that it should be in suspense *usque ad proximum parliament,* which was against law.   *Vide dors. claus*

8 Hen. 4. Proclamation in London. But 9 Hen. 4. an act of parliament was made, that all the Irish people should depart the realm,
and go into Ireland before the feast of the Nativity of the Blessed
Lady, upon pain of death, which was absolutely *in terrorem*, and
was utterly against the law.

    *   *   *   *   *   *   *   *   *

In the same term it was resolved by the two chief justices, chief
baron and baron Altham, upon conference betwixt the lords of
the privy council and them, that the king by his proclamation
cannot create any offence which was not an offence before, for
then he may alter the law of the land by his proclamation in a
high point; for if he may create an offence where none is, upon
that ensues fine and imprisonment: also the law of England is
divided into three parts, common law, statute law, and custom;
but the king's proclamation is none of them: also *malum aut est
malum in se, aut prohibitum*, that which is against common law is
malum in se, malum prohibitum is such an offence as is prohibited
by act of parliament, and not by proclamation.

Also it was resolved, that the king hath no prerogative, but that
which the law of the land allows him.

Lastly, if the offence be not punishable in the star-chamber,
the prohibition of it by proclamation cannot make it punishable
there: and after this resolution, no proclamation imposing fine
and imprisonment was afterwards made, &c.

---

188. Act against Monopolies

(1624. 21 & 22 James I. c. 3. Prothero, 275–277.)

FORASMUCH as your most excellent Majesty, in your royal
judgment and of your blessed disposition to the weal and
quiet of your subjects, did in the year of our Lord God, 1610,
publish in print to the whole realm and to all posterity, that all
grants of monopolies, and of the benefit of any penal laws, or of
power to dispense with the law, or to compound for the forfeiture,
are contrary to your Majesty's laws; which your Majesty's declaration is truly consonant and agreeable to the ancient and fundamental laws of this your realm: and whereas your Majesty
was further graciously pleased expressly to command, that no
suitor should presume to move your Majesty for matters of that
nature; yet nevertheless, upon misinformations and untrue pre-

z

tences of public good, many such grants have been unduly obtained and unlawfully put in execution, to the great grievance and inconvenience of your Majesty's subjects, contrary to the laws of this your realm and contrary to your Majesty's royal and blessed intention so published as aforesaid : for avoiding whereof and preventing of the like in time to come, may it please your most excellent Majesty * * * that it may be declared and enacted, and be it declared and enacted * * * that all monopolies and all commissions, grants, licences, charters and letters patents * * * to any person, bodies politic or corporate, whatsoever, for the sole buying, selling, making, working or using of anything within this realm or the dominion of Wales, or of any other monopolies, or of power to dispense with any others, or to give licence or toleration to do anything against the tenor of any law or statute, or to give or make any warrant for any such dispensation, licence or toleration, * * * or to agree or compound with any others for any penalty or forfeitures limited by any statute, or of any grant or promise of the benefit of any forfeiture, penalty or sum of money that shall be due by any statute, before judgment thereupon had, and all proclamations, inhibitions, restraints, warrants of assistance, and all other things whatsoever, any way tending to the instituting * * * or countenancing of the same * * * , are altogether contrary to the laws of this realm, and so are and shall be utterly void and of none effect. * * *

II. And be it further enacted, that all monopolies and all such commissions, grants [&c.], and all other things tending as aforesaid * * * ought to be and shall be for ever hereafter * * * tried and determined according to the common laws of this realm, and not otherwise.

*   *   *   *   *   *   *   *   *

V. Provided nevertheless, * * * that any declaration beforementioned shall not extend to any letters patents and grants of privilege for the term of one and twenty years or under, heretofore made of the sole working or making of any manner of new manufacture within this realm to the first and true inventor or inventors of such manufactures, which others at the time of the making of such letters patents and grants did not use, so they be not contrary to the law, nor mischievous to the state by raising of the prices of commodities at home or hurt of trade, or generally inconvenient, but that the same shall be of such force as they were or should be if this Act had not been made. * * *

*   *   *   *   *   *   *   *   *

VI. Provided also, and be it enacted, that any declaration beforementioned shall not extend to any letters patents and grants of privilege for the term of fourteen years or under, hereafter to be made, of the sole working or making of any manner of new manufactures within this realm, to the true and first inventor and inventors of such manufactures * * *

IX. Provided also, * * * that this Act * * * shall not in any wise extend or be prejudicial unto the city of London or to any city, borough or town corporate within this realm, for any grants, charters or letters patents to them * * * granted, or for any customs used by or within any of them, or unto any corporations, companies or fellowships of any art, trade, occupation or mystery, or to any companies or societies of merchants within this realm erected for the maintenance * * * of any trade of merchandise . . .

X.–XIV. [Various special exemptions.]

---

189. The Petition of Right

(1628, June 7.   3 Charles I. c. 1.   5 S. R. 23.   Gardiner, 66–70.)

To the King's Most Excellent Majesty.

HUMBLY show unto our Sovereign Lord the King, the Lords Spiritual and Temporal, and Commons in Parliament assembled, that whereas it is declared and enacted by a statute made in the time of the reign of King Edward the First, commonly called *Statutum de tallagio non concedendo*, that no tallage or aid shall be laid or levied by the King or his heirs in this realm, without the good will and assent of the Archbishops, Bishops, Earls, Barons, Knights, Burgesses, and other the freemen of the commonalty of this realm : and by authority of Parliament holden in the five and twentieth year of the reign of King Edward the Third, it is declared and enacted, that from thenceforth no person shall be compelled to make any loans to the King against his will, because such loans were against reason and the franchise of the land ; and by other laws of this realm it is provided, that none should be charged by any charge or imposition, called a Benevolence, nor by such like charge : by which, the statutes before-mentioned, and other the good laws and statutes of this realm, your subjects have inherited this freedom, that they should not be compelled to contribute to any tax, tallage, aid, or other like charge, not set by common consent in Parliament :

II. Yet nevertheless, of late divers commissions directed to sundry Commissioners in several counties, with instructions, have issued, by means whereof your people have been in divers places assembled, and required to lend certain sums of money unto your Majesty, and many of them upon their refusal so to do, have had an oath administered unto them, not warrantable by the laws or statutes of this realm, and have been constrained to become bound to make appearance and give attendance before your Privy Council, and in other places, and others of them have been therefore imprisoned, confined, and sundry other ways molested and disquieted : and divers other charges have been laid and levied upon your people in several counties, by Lords Lieutenants, Deputy Lieutenants, Commissioners for Musters, Justices of Peace and others, by command or direction from your Majesty or your Privy Council, against the laws and free customs of this realm.

III. And where also by the statute called, 'The Great Charter of the Liberties of England,' it is declared and enacted, that no freeman may be taken or imprisoned or be disseised of his freehold or liberties, or his free customs, or be outlawed or exiled, or in any manner destroyed, but by the lawful judgment of his peers, or by the law of the land :

IV. And in the eight and twentieth year of the reign of King Edward the Third, it was declared and enacted by authority of Parliament, that no man of what estate or condition that he be, should be put out of his lands or tenements, nor taken, nor imprisoned, nor disherited, nor put to death, without being brought to answer by due process of law :

V. Nevertheless, against the tenor of the said statutes, and other the good laws and statutes of your realm, to that end provided, divers of your subjects have of late been imprisoned without any cause showed, and when for their deliverance they were brought before your Justices, by your Majesty's writs of Habeas Corpus, there to undergo and receive as the Court should order, and their keepers commanded to certify the causes of their detainer ; no cause was certified, but that they were detained by your Majesty's special command, signified by the Lords of your Privy Council, and yet were returned back to several prisons, without being charged with anything to which they might make answer according to the law.

VI. And whereas of late great companies of soldiers and mariners have been dispersed into divers counties of the realm, and the inhabitants against their wills have been compelled to receive them into their houses, and there to suffer them to sojourn, against the laws and customs of this realm, and to the great grievance and vexation of the people.

VII. And whereas also by authority of Parliament, in the 25th year of the reign of King Edward the Third, it is declared and enacted, that no man shall be forejudged of life or limb against the form of the Great Charter, and the law of the land; and by the said Great Charter and other the laws and statutes of this your realm, no man ought to be adjudged to death, but by the laws established in this your realm, either by the customs of the same realm or by Acts of Parliament: and whereas no offender of what kind soever is exempted from the proceedings to be used, and punishments to be inflicted by the laws and statutes of this your realm; nevertheless of late divers commissions under your Majesty's Great Seal have issued forth, by which certain persons have been assigned and appointed Commissioners with power and authority to proceed within the land, according to the justice of martial law against such soldiers and mariners, or other dissolute persons joining with them, as should commit any murder, robbery, felony, mutiny, or other outrage or misdemeanour whatsoever, and by such summary course and order, as is agreeable to martial law, and is used in armies in time of war, to proceed to the trial and condemnation of such offenders, and them to cause to be executed and put to death, according to the law martial:

VIII. By pretext whereof, some of your Majesty's subjects have been by some of the said Commissioners put to death, when and where, if by the laws and statutes of the land they had deserved death, by the same laws and statutes also they might, and by no other ought to have been, adjudged and executed:

IX. And also sundry grievous offenders by colour thereof, claiming an exemption, have escaped the punishments due to them by the laws and statutes of this your realm, by reason that divers of your officers and ministers of justice have unjustly refused, or forborne to proceed against such offenders according to the same laws and statutes, upon pretence that the said offenders were punishable only by martial law, and by authority of such commissions as aforesaid; which commissions, and all other of like nature, are wholly and directly contrary to the said laws and statutes of this your realm.

X. They do therefore humbly pray your Most Excellent Majesty, that no man hereafter be compelled to make or yield any gift, loan, benevolence, tax, or such like charge, without common consent by Act of Parliament; and that none be called to make answer, or take such oath, or to give attendance, or be confined, or otherwise molested or disquieted concerning the same, or for refusal thereof; and that no freeman, in any such manner as is before-mentioned, be imprisoned or detained; and that your Majesty will be pleased to remove the said soldiers and mariners, and that your people may not be so burdened in time to come; and that the aforesaid commissions for proceeding by martial law, may be revoked and annulled; and that hereafter no commissions of like nature may issue forth to any person or persons whatsoever, to be executed as aforesaid, lest by colour of them any of your Majesty's subjects be destroyed or put to death, contrary to the laws and franchise of the land.

XI. All which they most humbly pray of your Most Excellent Majesty, as their rights and liberties according to the laws and statutes of this realm: and that your Majesty would also vouchsafe to declare, that the awards, doings, and proceedings to the prejudice of your people, in any of the premises, shall not be drawn hereafter into consequence or example: and that your Majesty would be also graciously pleased, for the further comfort and safety of your people, to declare your royal will and pleasure, that in the things aforesaid all your officers and ministers shall serve you, according to the laws and statutes of this realm, as they tender the honour of your Majesty, and the prosperity of this kingdom.

[Which Petition being read the 2nd of June 1628, the King's answer was thus delivered unto it:

The King willeth that right be done according to the laws and customs of the realm; and that the statutes be put in due execution, that his subjects may have no cause to complain of any wrong or oppressions, contrary to their just rights and liberties, to the preservation whereof he holds himself as well obliged as of his prerogative.

On June 7 the answer was given in the accustomed form, *Soit droit fait comme il est désiré.*]

190. The Remonstrance against Tonnage and Poundage

(1628, June 25.   Rushworth, i. 628.   Gardiner, 70–73.)

MOST Gracious Sovereign, your Majesty's most loyal and dutiful subjects, the Commons in this present Parliament assembled, being in nothing more careful than of the honour and prosperity of your Majesty, and the kingdom, which they know do much depend upon that happy union and relation betwixt your Majesty and your people, do with much sorrow apprehend, that by reason of the incertainty of their continuance together, the unexpected interruptions which have been cast upon them, and the shortness of time in which your Majesty hath determined to end this Session, they cannot bring to maturity and perfection divers businesses of weight, which they have taken into their consideration and resolution, as most important for the common good : amongst other things they have taken into especial care the preparing of a Bill for the granting of your Majesty such a subsidy of Tonnage and Poundage, as might uphold your profit and revenue in as ample a manner as their just care and respect of trade (wherein not only the prosperity, but even the life of the kingdom doth consist) would permit : but being a work which will require much time, and preparation by conference with your Majesty's officers, and with the merchants, not only of London, but of other remote parts, they find it not possible to be accomplished at this time : wherefore considering it will be much more prejudicial to the right of the subject, if your Majesty should continue to receive the same without authority of law, after the determination of a Session, than if there had been a recess by adjournment only, in which case that intended grant would have related to the first day of the Parliament ; and assuring themselves that your Majesty is resolved to observe that your royal answer, which you have lately made to the Petition of Right of both Houses of Parliament ; yet doubting lest your Majesty may be misinformed concerning this particular case, as if you might continue to take those subsidies of Tonnage and Poundage, and other impositions upon merchants, without breaking that answer, they are forced by that duty which they owe to your Majesty, and to those whom they represent, to declare, that there ought not any imposition to be laid upon the goods of merchants, exported or imported, without common consent by Act of Parliament, which is the right and inheritance of your subjects, founded not only upon the most ancient and original constitution of this kingdom, but often confirmed and declared in divers statute laws.

II. And for the better manifestation thereof, may it please your Majesty to understand, that although your royal predecessors the Kings of this realm have often had such subsidies, and impositions granted unto them, upon divers occasions, especially for the guarding of the seas, and safeguard of merchants ; yet the subjects have been ever careful to use such cautions and limitations in those grants, as might prevent any claim to be made, that such subsidies do proceed from duty, and not from the free gift of the subjects : and that they have heretofore used to limit a time in such grants, and for the most part but short, as for a year or two, and if it were continued longer, they have sometimes directed a certain space of cessation, or intermission, that so the right of the subject might be more evident. At other times it hath been granted upon occasion of war, for a certain number of years, with proviso, that if the war were ended in the meantime, then the grant should cease ; and of course it hath been sequestered into the hands of some subjects to be employed for the guarding of the seas. And it is acknowledged by the ordinary answers of your Majesty's predecessors in their assent to the Bills of subsidies of Tonnage and Poundage, that it is of the nature of other subsidies, proceeding from the good will of the subject. Very few of your predecessors had it for life, until the reign of Henry VII, who was so far from conceiving he had any right thereunto, that although he granted commissions for collecting certain duties and customs due by law, yet he made no commissions for receiving the subsidy of Tonnage and Poundage, until the same was granted unto him in Parliament. Since his time all the Kings and Queens of this realm have had the like grants for life by the free love and good will of the subjects. And whensoever the people have been grieved by laying any impositions or other charges upon their goods and merchandises without authority of law (which hath been very seldom), yet upon complaint in Parliament they have been forthwith relieved ; saving in the time of your royal father, who having through ill counsel raised the rates and charges upon merchandises to that height at which they now are, yet he was pleased so far forth to yield to the complaint of his people, as to offer that if the value of those impositions which he had set might be made good unto him, he would bind himself and his heirs by Act of Parliament never to lay any other ; which offer the Commons at that time, in regard of the great burden, did not think fit to yield unto. Nevertheless, your loyal Commons in this Parliament, out of their especial zeal to your service, and especial regard of your pressing occasions, have taken into their consideration, so to frame a grant of subsidy of Tonnage or Poundage to your Majesty, that both you might have been the better enabled for the defence of your realm, and your subjects, by being secure from all undue charges, be the more encouraged cheerfully to proceed in their course of trade; by the increase whereof your Majesty's profit, and likewise the strength of the kingdom would be very much augmented.

III. But not now being able to accomplish this their desire, there is no course left unto them, without manifest breach of their duty, both to your Majesty and their country, save only to make this humble declaration, 'That the receiving of Tonnage and Poundage, and other impositions not granted by Parliament, is a breach of the fundamental liberties of this kingdom, and contrary to your Majesty's royal answer to the said Petition of Right.' And therefore they do most humbly beseech your Majesty to forbear any further receiving of the same, and not to take it in ill part from those of your Majesty's loving subjects, who shall refuse to make payment of any such charges, without warrant of law demanded.

IV. And as by this forbearance, your Most Excellent Majesty shall manifest unto the world your royal justice in the observation of your laws : so they doubt not, but hereafter, at the time appointed for their coming again, they shall have occasion to express their great desire to advance your Majesty's honour and profit.

---

191. The King's Speech proroguing Parliament

(1628, June 26. Rushworth, i. 631. Gardiner, 73, 74.)

IT may seem strange, that I came so suddenly to end this Session; before I give my assent to the Bills, I will tell you the cause, though I must avow, that I owe the account of my actions to God alone. It is known to every one, that a while ago the House of Commons gave me a Remonstrance, how acceptable every man may judge ; and for the merit of it, I will not call that in question, for I am sure no wise man can justify it.

Now since I am truly informed, that a second Remonstrance is preparing for me to take away the profit of my Tonnage and

Poundage, one of the chiefest maintenances of my Crown, by alleging I have given away my right thereto by my answer to your Petition :

This is so prejudicial unto me, that I am forced to end this Session some few hours before I meant, being not willing to receive any more Remonstrances, to which I must give a harsh answer. And since I see that even the House of Commons begins already to make false constructions of what I granted in your Petition, lest it be worse interpreted in the country, I will now make a declaration concerning the true intent thereof :

The profession of both Houses in the time of hammering this Petition, was no ways to trench upon my Prerogative, saying they had neither intention or power to hurt it. Therefore it must needs be conceived that I have granted no new, but only confirmed the ancient liberties of my subjects : yet to show the clearness of my intentions, that I neither repent, nor mean to recede from anything I have promised you, I do here declare myself, that those things which have been done, whereby many have had some cause to expect the liberties of the subjects to be trenched upon, — which indeed was the first and true ground of the Petition, — shall not hereafter be drawn into example for your prejudice, and from time to time ; in the word of a king, ye shall not have the like cause to complain : but as for Tonnage and Poundage, it is a thing I cannot want, and was never intended by you to ask, nor meant by me — I am sure — to grant.

To conclude, I command you all that are here to take notice of what I have spoken at this time, to be the true intent and meaning of what I granted you in your Petition ; but especially, you my Lords the Judges, for to you only under me belongs the interpretation of laws, for none of the Houses of Parliament, either joint or separate, (what new doctrine soever may be raised) have any power either to make or declare a law without my consent.

------◆------

192. Protest of the House of Commons

(162⅝, March 2. Rushworth, i. 660. Gardiner, 82, 83.)

1. WHOSOEVER shall bring in innovation of religion or by favour or countenance seem to extend or introduce Popery or Arminianism, or other opinion disagreeing from the true and orthodox Church, shall be reputed a capital enemy to this Kingdom and Commonwealth.

2. Whosoever shall counsel or advise the taking and levying of the subsidies of Tonnage and Poundage, not being granted by Parliament, or shall be an actor or instrument therein, shall be likewise reputed an innovator in the Government, and a capital enemy to the Kingdom and Commonwealth.

3. If any merchant or person whatsoever shall voluntarily yield, or pay the said subsidies of Tonnage and Poundage, not being granted by Parliament, he shall likewise be reputed a betrayer of the liberties of England, and an enemy to the same.

---

193. First Writ of Ship-money

(1634. Rushworth, ii. 257. Gardiner, 105–108.)

CAROLUS REX, &c.
To the Mayor, commonalty, and citizens of our city of London, and to the sheriffs of the same city, and good men in the said city and in the liberties, and members of the same, greeting : Because we are given to understand that certain thieves, pirates, and robbers of the sea, as well Turks, enemies of the Christian name, as others, being gathered together, wickedly taking by force and spoiling the ships, and goods, and merchandises, not only of our subjects, but also the subjects of our friends in the sea, which hath been accustomed anciently to be defended by the English nation, and the same, at their pleasure, have carried away, delivering the men in the same into miserable captivity : and forasmuch as we see them daily preparing all manner of shipping farther to molest our merchants, and to grieve the kingdom, unless remedy be not sooner applied, and their endeavours be not more manly met withal ; also the dangers considered which, on every side, in these times of war do hang over our heads, that it behoveth us and our subjects to hasten the defence of the sea and kingdom with all expedition or speed that we can ; we willing by the help of God chiefly to provide for the defence of the kingdom, safeguard of the sea, security of our subjects, safe conduct of ships and merchandises to our kingdom of England coming, and from the same kingdom to foreign parts passing ; forasmuch as we, and our progenitors, Kings of England, have been always heretofore masters of the aforesaid sea, and it would be very irksome unto us if that princely honour in our times should be lost or in anything diminished. And although that charge of defence which concerneth

all men ought to be supported by all, as by the laws and customs of the kingdom of England hath been accustomed to be done: notwithstanding we considering that you constituted in the sea-coasts, to whom by sea as well great dangers are imminent, and who by the same do get more plentiful gains for the defence of the sea, and conservation of our princely honour in that behalf, according to the duty of your allegiance against such attempts, are chiefly bound to set to your helping hand; we command firmly, enjoining you the aforesaid Mayor, commonalty and citizens, and sheriffs of the said city, and the good men in the same city and in the liberties, and members of the same, in the faith and allegiance wherein you are bound unto us, and as you do love us and our honour, and under the forfeiture of all which you can forfeit to us, that you cause to be prepared and brought to the port of Portsmouth, before the first day of March now next ensuing, one ship of war of the burden of nine hundred tons, with three hundred and fifty men at the least, as well expert masters, as very able and skilful mariners; one other ship of war of the burden of eight hundred tons, with two hundred and sixty men at the least, as well skilful masters, as very able and expert mariners: four other ships of war, every of them of the burden of five hundred tons, and every of them with two hundred men at the least, as well expert masters, as very able and skilful mariners: and one other ship of war of the burden of three hundred tons, with a hundred and fifty men, as well expert masters, as very able and skilful mariners: and also every of the said ships with ordnance, as well greater as lesser, gunpowder, and spears and weapons, and other necessary arms sufficient for war, and with double tackling, and with victuals, until the said first of March, competent for so many men; and from that time, for twenty-six weeks, at your charges, as well in victuals as men's wages, and other things necessary for war, during that time, upon defence of the sea in our service, in command of the admiral of the sea, to whom we shall commit the custody of the sea, before the aforesaid first day of March, and as he, on our behalf, shall command them to continue; so that they may be there the same day, at the farthest, to go from thence with our ships, and the ships of other faithful subjects, for the safeguard of the sea, and defence of you and yours, and repulse and vanquishing of whomsoever busying themselves to molest or trouble upon the sea our merchants, and other subjects, and faithful people coming into our dominions for cause of merchandise, or from thence returning to their own countries. Also we have assigned you, the aforesaid Mayor and Aldermen of the city aforesaid, or any thirteen, or more of you, within thirteen days after the receipt of this writ, to assess all men in the said city, and in the liberties, and members of the same, and the landholders in the same, not having a ship, or any part of the aforesaid ships, nor serving in the same, to contribute to the expenses, about the necessary provision of the premises; and to assess and lay upon the aforesaid city, with the liberties and members thereof, viz. upon every of them according to their estate and substances, and the portion assessed upon them; and to nominate and appoint collectors in this behalf. Also we have assigned you, the aforesaid Mayor, and also the Sheriffs of the city aforesaid, to levy the portions so as aforesaid assessed upon the aforesaid men and landholders, and every of them in the aforesaid city, with the liberties and members of the same, by distress and other due means; and to commit to prison all those whom you shall find rebellious and contrary in the premises, there to remain until we shall give further order for their delivery. And moreover we command you, that about the premises you dili·gently attend, and do, and execute those things with effect, upon peril that shall fall thereon: but we will not, that under colour of our aforesaid command, more should be levied of the said men than shall suffice for the necessary expenses of the premises; or that any who have levied money for contribution to raise the aforesaid charges, should by him detain the same, or any part thereof; or should presume, by any manner of colour, to appropriate the same to other uses; willing, that if more than may be sufficient shall be collected, the same may be paid out among the contributors, for the rate of the part to them belonging.

Witness myself, at Westminster the twentieth day of October, in the tenth year of our reign.[1]

---

194. The Answer of the Judges in the Matter of Ship-money

(1637, February 7. Rushworth, ii. 355. Gardiner, 108, 109.)

CAROLUS REX
     When the good and safety of the kingdom in general is concerned, and the whole kingdom in danger, whether may not the King, by writ under the Great Seal of England, command all the subjects of our kingdom at their charge to provide and furnish

---

[1] In 1635 the writs were extended to the inland counties.

such a number of ships, with men, victuals, and munition, and for such time as we shall think fit, for the defence and safeguard of the kingdom from such danger and peril, and by law compel the doing thereof, in case of refusal or refractoriness : and whether in such a case is not the King the sole judge both of the danger, and when and how the same is to be prevented and avoided?

May it please your Most Excellent Majesty,

We have, according to your Majesty's command, every man by himself, and all of us together, taken into serious consideration the case and question signed by your Majesty, and inclosed in your royal letter ; and we are of opinion, that when the good and safety of the kingdom in general is concerned, and the kingdom in danger, your Majesty may, by writ under the Great Seal of England, command all your subjects of this your kingdom, at their charge to provide and furnish such a number of ships, with men, victuals, and munition, and for such time as your Majesty shall think fit for the defence and safeguard of this kingdom from such danger and peril : and that by law your Majesty may compel the doing thereof in case of refusal, or refractoriness : and we are also of opinion, that in such case your Majesty is the sole judge both of the danger, and when and how the same is to be prevented and avoided.

John Bramston,	George Croke,
John Finch,	Thomas Trevor,
Humphry Davenport,	George Vernon,
John Denham,	Francis Crawley,
Richard Hutton,	Robert Berkeley,
William Jones,	Richard Weston.

195. The Triennial Act

(164$\frac{0}{1}$, February 15. 16 Charles I. c. 1. 5 *S. R.* 54. Gardiner, 144–155.)

I. WHEREAS by the laws and statutes of this realm the Parliament ought to be holden at least once every year for the redress of grievances, but the appointment of the time and place for the holding thereof hath always belonged, as it ought, to His Majesty and his royal progenitors : and whereas it is by experience found that the not holding of Parliaments accordingly hath produced sundry and great mischiefs and inconveniences to the King's Majesty, the Church and Commonwealth ; for the prevention of the like mischiefs and inconveniences in time to come :

II. Be it enacted by the King's Most Excellent Majesty, with the consent of the Lords spiritual and temporal, and the Commons in this present Parliament assembled, that the said laws and statutes be from henceforth duly kept and observed ; and your Majesty's loyal and obedient subjects, in this present Parliament now assembled, do humbly pray that it be enacted : and be it enacted accordingly, by the authority of this present Parliament, that in case there be not a Parliament summoned by writ under the Great Seal of England, and assembled and held before the 10th of September, which shall be in the third year next after the last day of the last meeting and sitting in this present Parliament, the beginning of the first year to be accounted from the said last day of the last meeting and sitting in Parliament ; and so from time to time, and in all times hereafter, if there shall not be a Parliament assembled and held before the 10th day of September, which shall be in the third year next after the last day of the last meeting and sitting in Parliament before the time assembled and held ; the beginning of the first year to be accounted from the said last day of the last meeting and sitting in Parliament ; that then in every such case as aforesaid, the Parliament shall assemble and be held in the usual place at Westminster, in such manner, and by such means only, as is hereafter in this present Act declared and enacted, and not otherwise, on the second Monday, which shall be in the month of November, then next ensuing. And in case this present Parliament now assembled and held, or any other Parliament which shall at any time hereafter be assembled and held by writ under the Great Seal of England, or in case any Parliament shall be assembled and held by authority of this present Act ; and such Parliaments, or any of them, shall be prorogued, or adjourned, or continued by prorogation or adjournment, until the 10th day of September, which shall be in the third year next after the last day of the last meeting and sitting in Parliament, to be accounted as aforesaid ; that then in every such case, every such Parliament so prorogued or adjourned, or so continued by prorogation or adjournment, as aforesaid, shall from the said 10th day of September be thenceforth clearly and absolutely dissolved, and the Lord Chancellor of England, the Lord Keeper of the Great Seal of England, and every Commissioner and Commissioners for the keeping of the Great Seal of England for the time being, shall within six days after the said 10th day of September, in every such third year as aforesaid, in due form of law and without any further warrant or direction from His Majesty, his heirs or successors, seal, issue forth, and send abroad several and respective writs to the several and respective peers of this realm, commanding every such peer that he personally be at the Parliament to be held at Westminster on the second Monday which shall be in November next following the said 10th day of September, then and there to treat concerning the high and urgent affairs concerning His Majesty, the state and defence of the kingdom and Church of England; and shall also seal and issue forth, and send abroad several and respective writs to the several and respective sheriffs of the several and respective counties, cities and boroughs of England and Wales, and to the Constable of the Castle of Dover, Lord Warden of the Cinque Ports, or his lieutenant for the time being, and to the Mayor and Bailiffs of Berwick upon Tweed, and to all and every other officers and persons to whom writs have used to be directed, for the electing of the knights, citizens, barons and burgesses of and for the said Counties, Cities, Cinque Ports and Boroughs of England and Wales respectively, in the accustomed form, to appear and serve in the Parliament to be held at Westminster on the said second Monday, which shall be in November aforesaid; which said peers, after the said writs received, and which said knights, citizens, barons and burgesses chosen by virtue of the said writs, shall then and there appear and serve in Parliament accordingly. And the said Lord Chancellor, Lord Keeper, Commissioner and Commissioners aforesaid, shall respectively take a solemn oath upon the Holy Evangelists for the due issuing of writs, according to the tenor of this Act, *in hæc verba*, —

'You shall swear that you shall truly and faithfully issue forth, and send abroad all writs of summons to Parliament for both Houses, at such time, and in such manner, as is expressed and enjoined by an Act of Parliament, entitled, "An Act for the preventing of inconveniences happening by the long intermission of Parliaments."'

Which oath is forthwith to be taken by the present Lord Keeper, and to be administered by the Clerk of the Crown to every Lord Chancellor, Lord Keeper, Commissioner and Commissioners aforesaid; and that none of the said officers respectively shall henceforth execute any the said offices before they have taken the said oath. And if the said Lord Chancellor, Lord Keeper, or any of the said Commissioners shall fail, or forbear so to issue out the said writs, according to the true meaning of this Act, then he or they respectively shall, beside the incurring of the grievous sin of perjury, be disabled, and become, by virtue of this Act, incapable, *ipso facto*, to bear his and their said offices respectively; and be further liable to such punishments as shall be inflicted upon him or them by the next, or any other ensuing Parliament. And in case the said Lord Chancellor, Lord Keeper, Commissioner or Commissioners aforesaid, shall not issue forth the said writs as aforesaid : or in case that the Parliament do not assemble and be held at the time and place before appointed, then the Parliament shall assemble and be held in the usual place at Westminster, in such manner, and by such means only, as is hereafter in this present Act declared and enacted, and not otherwise, on the third Monday which shall be in the month of January then next ensuing. And the peers of this realm shall by virtue of this Act be enabled, and are enjoined to meet in the Old Palace of Westminster, in the usual place there, on the third Monday in the said month of November : and they or any twelve or more of them, then and there assembled, shall on or before the last Monday of November next following the tenth day of September aforesaid, by virtue of this Act, without any warrant, issue out writs in the usual form, in the name of the King's Majesty, his heirs or successors, attested under the hands and seals of twelve or more of the said peers, to the several and respective sheriffs * * * for the electing of the knights, * * * to be and appear at the Parliament at Westminster aforesaid, to be held on the third Monday in January then next following : all and every which writs the Clerks of the Petty Bag, and other clerks, to whom the writing of the writs for summons to the Parliament doth and shall belong, or whom the said Lords, or twelve or more of them shall appoint, shall at the command of the said Lords so assembled, or of any twelve or more of them, make and prepare ready for the signature of the said Lords, or any twelve or more of them, under pain of the loss of their places and offices, and of such other punishment as in the next, or any other ensuing Parliament, shall be inflicted on him or them : and it is enacted that the said writs so issued shall be of the same power and force to all intents and purposes, as the writs or summons to Parliament under the Great Seal of England have ever been or ought to be. And all the messengers of the Chamber or others who shall be appointed by the said lords, or any twelve or more, are hereby required faithfully and speedily to deliver the said writs to every person and persons, sheriffs, officers, and others, to whom the same shall be directed : which if the said messengers or any of them shall fail to perform, they shall forfeit their respective places, and incur such other pains and punishments as by that or any other ensuing Parliament shall be imposed on them.

III. And it is also further enacted, that all and every the peers

2 A

of this realm shall make their appearance, and shall assemble on
the said third Monday in January, in such manner, and to such
effect, and with such power, as if they had received every of them
writs of summons to Parliament under the Great Seal of England,
in the usual and accustomed manner.   And in case the said Lords,
or twelve or more of them, shall fail to issue forth such writs, or
that the said writs do not come to the said several Counties, Cities,
Cinque Ports and Boroughs, so that an election be not thereupon
made ; and in case there be not a Parliament assembled and held
before the 23rd day of the said month of January, and so from
time to time, and in all times hereafter, if there shall not be a Parliament assembled and held before the said 23rd day of January,
then in every such case as aforesaid the Parliament shall assemble,
and be held in the usual place at Westminster, in such manner, and
by such means only, as is hereafter in this present Act declared and
enacted, and not otherwise, on the second Tuesday which shall
be in the month of March next after the said 23rd day of January ;
at which Parliament the peers of this realm shall make their appearance, and shall assemble at the time and place aforesaid, and shall
each of them be liable unto such pains and censures for his and
their not appearing and serving then and there in Parliament,
as if he or they had been summoned by writ under the Great Seal
of England, and had not appeared and served ; and to such further pains and censures, as by the rest of the peers in Parliament
assembled they shall be adjudged unto.

IV.   And for the better assembling of the knights, citizens, barons, and burgesses to the said Parliament, as aforesaid, it is further
enacted, that the several and respective sheriffs of the several and
respective Counties, Cities and Boroughs of England and Wales,
and the Chancellors, Masters and Scholars of both and every of
the Universities, and the Mayor and Bailiffs of the borough of
Berwick upon Tweed, shall at the several courts and places to be
held and appointed for their respective Counties, Universities,
Cities and Boroughs, next after the said 23rd day of January, cause
such knight and knights, citizen and citizens, burgess and burgesses of their said Counties, Universities, Cities and Boroughs
respectively, to be chosen by such persons, and in such manner,
as if several and respective writs of summons to Parliament, under
the Great Seal of England, had issued and been awarded.   And
in case any of the several Sheriffs, * * * do not before ten of the
clock in the forenoon of the same day wherein the several and respective courts and places shall be held or appointed for their
several and respective Counties, Universities, Cities and Bor-

oughs as aforesaid, begin and proceed on according to the meaning of this law, in causing elections to be made of such knight and knights, citizen and citizens, burgess and burgesses, of their said Counties, Universities, Cities and Boroughs as aforesaid; then the freeholders of each County, and the Masters and Scholars of every the Universities, and the citizens and others having voices in such election respectively, in each University, City and Borough, that shall be assembled at the said courts or places to be held, or appointed, as aforesaid, shall forthwith, without further warrant or direction, proceed to the election of such knight or knights, citizen or citizens, burgess or burgesses aforesaid, in such manner as is usual in cases of writs of summons issued and awarded.

V. And it is further enacted that the several and respective sheriffs of their several and respective counties, and the Constable of the Castle of Dover, and Lord Warden of the Cinque Ports, or his lieutenant for the time being respectively, shall after the said 23rd day of January, and before the 8th day of February then immediately next ensuing, award and send forth their precepts to the several and respective cities and boroughs within their several counties, and likewise unto the said Cinque Ports respectively, commanding them respectively to make choice of such citizen and citizens, barons, burgess and burgesses, to serve in the said Parliament, at the time and place aforesaid : which said Cities, Cinque Ports and Boroughs respectively, shall before the last day of the said month of February make election of such citizen and citizens, barons, burgess and burgesses, as if writs for summoning of a Parliament, under the Great Seal of England, had issued and been awarded. And in case no such precept shall come unto the said Cities, Cinque Ports and Boroughs respectively, by the time herein limited : or in case any precept shall come, and no election be made thereupon, before the said last day of February, that then the several citizens, burgesses, and other persons that ought to elect and send citizens, barons, and burgesses to the Parliament, shall on the first Tuesday in March then next ensuing the said last day of February make choice of such citizen and citizens, barons, burgess and burgesses, as if a writ of summons under the Great Seal of England had issued and been awarded, and precepts thereupon issued, to such Cities, Cinque Ports and Boroughs : which knights, citizens, barons and burgesses so chosen shall appear and serve in Parliament at the time and place aforesaid, and shall each of them be liable unto such pains and censures for his and their not appearing and serving then and there in Parliament, as if he or they had been elected and chosen by virtue of a writ under the

Great Seal of England, and shall be likewise subject unto such further pains and censures for his and their not appearing and serving then and there in Parliament, as if he or they had been elected and chosen by virtue of a writ under the Great Seal of England, as by the rest of the knights, citizens and burgesses assembled in the Commons House of Parliament, he or they shall be adjudged unto. And the sheriffs and other officers and persons to whom it appertaineth shall make returns, and accept and receive the returns of such elections in like manner as if writs of summons had issued, and been executed, as hath been used and accustomed : and in default of the sheriffs and other officers respectively, in not accepting or making return of such elections, it shall and may be lawful to and for the several freeholders, and other persons that have elected, to make returns of the knights, citizens, barons and burgesses by them elected, which shall be as good and effectual to all intents and purposes as if the sheriff or other officers had received a writ of summons for a Parliament, and had made such returns : and that such elections, precepts and returns shall be had and made at such times, by such persons, and in such manner, as before in this Act is expressed and declared, according to the true intent and meaning of this law ; any writ, proclamation, edict, act, restraint, inhibition, order or warrant to the contrary in any wise notwithstanding. And in case any person or persons shall be so hardy to advise, frame, contrive, serve or put in execution any such writs, proclamation, edict, act, restraint, inhibition, order or warrant thereupon, then he or they so offending shall incur and sustain the pains, penalties and forfeitures limited, ordained and provided in and by the Statute of Provision and Præmunire made in the 16th year of King Richard the Second, and shall from thenceforth be disabled, during his life, to sue and implead any person in any action real or personal, or to make any gift, grant, conveyance, or other disposition of any his lands, tenements, hereditaments, goods or chattels which he hath to his own use, either by act executed in his lifetime, or by his last will, or otherwise, or to take any gift, conveyance, or legacy to his own use : and if any Sheriff, Constable of the Castle of Dover, or Lord Warden of the Cinque Ports, shall not perform his duty enjoined by this Act, then he shall lose and forfeit the sum of £1000, and every County, City, Cinque Port and Borough that shall not make election of their knights, citizens, barons and burgesses, respectively, shall incur the penalties following (that is to say) every County the sum of £1000, and every City, which is no County, £200, and every Cinque Port and Borough the sum of £100 ; all and every of which several forfeitures, and all other forfeitures in this Act mentioned, shall and may be recovered in any of the King's Courts of Record at Westminster, without naming the Christian name and surname of the said Mayor for the time being, by action of debt, bill, plaint or information, wherein no essoine, protection, wager of law, aid, prayer, privilege, injunction, or order of restraint, shall be in any wise prayed, granted or allowed, nor any more 'than one imparlance : and if any person after notice given that the action depending is grounded and prosecuted upon or by virtue of this Statute shall cause or procure any such action to be stayed or delayed before judgment by colour or means of any order, warrant, power or authority, save only of the court wherein such action as aforesaid shall be brought or depending, or after judgment had upon such action, shall cause or procure the execution of, or upon any such judgment, to be stayed or delayed by colour or means of any order, warrant, power or authority, save only by writ of error or attaint, that then the said persons so offending shall incur and sustain all and every the pains, penalties and forfeitures, limited, ordained and provided in and by the said Statute of Provision and Præmunire, made in the 16th of King Richard the Second. And if any Lord Mayor of London shall at any time hereafter commence or prefer any such suit, action or information, and shall happen to die or be removed out of his office before recovery and execution had, that yet no such action, suit or information, sued, commenced or preferred, shall by such displacing or death be abated, discontinued or ended, but that it shall and may be lawful to and for the Lord Mayor of the City of London next succeeding in that office and place, to prosecute, pursue and follow all and every such action, bill, plaint or information for the causes aforesaid, so hanging and depending in such manner and form, and to all intents and purposes, as that Lord Mayor might have done, which first commenced or preferred the same. The fifth part of all and every the forfeitures in this Act mentioned, shall go and be, to, and for the use and behoof of the City of London, and the other four parts and residue to be employed and disposed to, and for such only uses, intents and purposes as by the knights, citizens and burgesses in Parliament assembled, shall be declared, directed and appointed.

Provided that in case the freeholders of any County and inhabitants, or other persons having or claiming power to make election of any knights, citizens, barons or burgesses, shall proceed to making of election of their knights, citizens, barons and burgesses, which election shall afterwards fall out to be adjudged or declared void in law by the House of Commons, by reason of equality of voices or misdemeanour of any person whatsover, then the said County, City, Cinque Port or Borough shall not incur the penalties in this law, so as an election *de facto* be made.

VI. And it is further enacted that no Parliament henceforth to be assembled shall be dissolved or prorogued within fifty days at least after the time appointed for the meeting thereof, unless it be by assent of His Majesty, his heirs or successors, and of both Houses in Parliament assembled ; and that neither the House of Peers nor the House of Commons shall be adjourned within fifty days at least after the meeting thereof, unless it be by the free consent of every the said Houses respectively.

VII. And be it further enacted and declared by authority of this present Parliament, that the Peers to be assembled at any Parliament by virtue of this Act, shall and may from time to time, at any time during such their assembly in Parliament, choose and declare such person to be Speaker for the said Peers as they shall think fit. And likewise that the said knights, citizens and burgesses to be assembled at any Parliament by virtue of this Act, shall and may from time to time, at any time during such their assembly in Parliament, choose and declare one of themselves to be Speaker for the said knights, citizens and burgesses of the House of Commons assembled in the said Parliament as they shall think fit ; which said Speakers, and every of them, as well for the said Peers as for the said House of Commons respectively, shall, by virtue of this Act, be perfect and complete Speakers for the said Houses respectively, and shall have as full and large power, jurisdiction and privileges, to all intents and purposes, as any Speaker or Speakers of either of the said Houses respectively, heretofore have had or enjoyed.

VIII. And it is further enacted and declared, that all Parliaments hereafter to be assembled by authority of this Act and every member thereof shall have and enjoy all rights, privileges, jurisdictions and immunities, as any Parliament summoned by writ under the Great Seal of England, or any member thereof might or ought to have ; and all and every the members that shall be elected and chosen to serve in any Parliament hereafter to be assembled by authority of this Act as aforesaid, shall assemble and meet in the Commons House of Parliament, and shall enter into the same, and have voices in such Parliament before and without the taking of the several oaths of supremacy and allegiance, or either of them, any law or statute to the contrary thereof in any wise notwithstanding.

IX. Provided always, that if the King's Majesty, his heirs or successors, shall at any time during any Parliament hereafter to be assembled by authority of this Act as aforesaid, award or direct any commission or commissions unto any person or persons whatsoever, thereby giving power and authority to him or them to take and receive the oath of supremacy and allegiance, of all or any the members of the Commons House of Parliament, and any the members of that House being duly required thereunto, shall refuse or neglect to take and pronounce the same, that from thenceforth such person so refusing or neglecting shall be deemed no member of that House, nor shall have any voice therein, and shall suffer such pains and penalties as if he had presumed to sit in the same House without election, return or authority.

X. And it is likewise provided and enacted, that this Statute shall be publicly read yearly at every General Sessions of the Peace, to be held next after the Epiphany, and every Assizes then next ensuing by the Clerk of the Peace and Clerk of the Assizes for the time being respectively. And if they or either of them shall neglect or fail to do the same accordingly, then such party so neglecting or failing shall forfeit the sum of one hundred pounds.

XI. And it is lastly provided and enacted, that His Majesty's royal assent to this Bill shall not thereby determine this present Session of Parliament, and that all statutes and Acts of Parliament which are to have continuance unto the end of this present Session, shall be of full force after His Majesty's assent, until this present Session be fully ended and determined ; and if this present Session shall determine by dissolution of this present Parliament, then all the Acts and statutes aforesaid shall be continued until the end of the first Session of the next Parliament.

---

196. The Protestation

(1641, May 3. Rushworth, viii. 735. Gardiner, 155, 156.)

WE the knights, citizens and burgesses of the Commons House in Parliament, finding to the grief of our hearts that the designs of the Priests and Jesuits, and other adherents to the See of Rome, have of late been more boldly and frequently put in practice than formerly, to the undermining and danger of the true reformed Protestant religion in His Majesty's dominions established ; and finding also that there hath been, and having just cause to suspect there still are, even during the sittings in Parliament, endeavours to subvert the fundamental laws of England and Ireland, and to introduce the exercise of an arbitrary and tyrannical government by most pernicious and wicked counsels, practices, plots and conspiracies; and that the long intermission and unhappier breach of Parliaments hath occasioned many illegal taxations, whereby the subjects have been prosecuted and grieved; and that divers innovations and superstitions have been brought into the Church, multitudes driven out of His Majesty's dominions, jealousies raised and fomented between the King and his people, a Popish army levied in Ireland, and two armies brought into the bowels of this kingdom, to the hazard of His Majesty's royal person, the consumption of the revenue of the crown and the treasure of this realm; and lastly, finding the great cause of jealousy, that endeavours have been, and are used, to bring the English army into a misunderstanding of this Parliament, thereby to incline that army by force to bring to pass those wicked counsels; have therefore thought good to join ourselves in a Declaration of our united affections and resolutions and to make this ensuing Protestation: —

I, A. B., do, in the presence of God, promise, vow and protest to maintain and defend, as far as lawfully I may, with my life, power and estate, the true reformed Protestant religion expressed in the doctrine of the Church of England, against all Popery and popish innovation within this realm, contrary to the said doctrine, and according to the duty of my allegiance I will maintain and defend His Majesty's royal person and estate; as also the power and privilege of Parliaments, the lawful rights and liberties of the subjects, and every person that shall make this Protestation in whatsoever he shall do, in the lawful pursuance of the same; and to my power, as far as lawfully I may, I will oppose, and by all good ways and means endeavour to bring to condign punishment all such as shall by force, practice, counsels, plots, conspiracies or otherwise do anything to the contrary in this present Protestation contained: and further, that I shall in all just and honourable ways endeavour to preserve the union and peace betwixt the three kingdoms of England, Scotland and Ireland, and neither for hope, fear or any other respects, shall relinquish this promise, vow and protestation.

197. Act for the Attainder of Strafford

(1641, May 11.   16 Charles I. Private Acts c. 1.   5 *S. R* 177.   Gardiner,
156-158.)

WHEREAS the knights, citizens and burgesses of the House of
Commons in this present Parliament assembled, have, in the
name of themselves and of all the Commons of England, impeached
Thomas, earl of Strafford, of high treason, for endeavouring to subvert the ancient and fundamental laws and government of His
Majesty's realms of England and Ireland, and to introduce an
arbitrary and tyrannical government, against law, in the said kingdoms, and for exercising a tyrannous and exorbitant power over
and against the laws of the said kingdoms, and the liberties, estates
and lives of His Majesty's subjects ; and likewise having by his
own authority commanded the laying and assessing of soldiers
upon His Majesty's subjects in Ireland, against their consents, to
compel them to obey his unlawful summons and orders, made upon
paper petitions in causes between party and party, which accordingly was executed upon divers of His Majesty's subjects in a warlike
manner within the said realm of Ireland ; and in so doing did levy
war against the King's Majesty and his liege-people in that kingdom ; and also for that he, upon the unhappy dissolution of the last
Parliament, did slander the House of Commons to His Majesty:
and did counsel and advise His Majesty that he was loose and
absolved from rules of government ; and that he had an army in
Ireland which he might employ to reduce this kingdom, for which
he deserves to undergo the pains and forfeitures of high treason ;
and the said earl hath also been an incendiary of the wars between
the two kingdoms of England and Scotland, all which offences
have been sufficiently proved against the said earl upon his
impeachment :

Be it therefore enacted by the King's Most Excellent Majesty,
and by the Lords and Commons in this present Parliament assembled, and by the authority of the same, that the said earl of Strafford, for the heinous crimes and offences aforesaid, stand, and be
adjudged and attainted of high treason, and shall suffer such pains
of death, and incur the forfeitures of his goods and chattels, lands,
tenements and hereditaments of any estate of freehold or inheritance in the said kingdoms of England and Ireland, which the
said earl or any other to his use, or in trust for him, have or had,
the day of the first sitting of this Parliament, or at any time since ;

362   English Constitutional Documents

Provided that no judge or judges, justice or justices whatsoever, shall adjudge or interpret any act or thing to be treason, nor hear or determine any treason in any other manner than he or they should or ought to have done before the making of this Act, and as if this Act had never been had or made ; saving always unto all and singular persons, bodies politic and corporate, their heirs and successors, others than the said earl and his heirs, and such as claim from, by, or under him, all such right, title and interest of, in, and to all and singular such of the lands, tenements and hereditaments, as he, they, or any of them had before the first day of this present Parliament, anything herein contained to the contrary notwithstanding ;

Provided that the passing of this present Act, or His Majesty's assent thereunto, shall not be any determination of this present Sessions of Parliament ; but that this present Sessions of Parliament, and all Bills and matters whatsoever depending in Parliament, and not fully enacted or determined, and all statutes and Acts of Parliament which have their continuance until the end of this present Sessions of Parliament, shall remain, continue, and be in full force, as if this Act had not been.

---

198. Act against Dissolving the Long Parliament without its own Consent

(1641, May 11.   16 Charles I. c. 7.   5 *S. R.* 103.   Gardiner, 158, 159.)

WHEREAS great sums of money must of necessity be speedily advanced and provided for the relief of His Majesty's army and people in the northern parts of this realm, and for preventing the imminent danger it is in, and for supply of other His Majesty's present and urgent occasions, which cannot be so timely effected as is requisite without credit for raising the said monies ; which credit cannot be obtained until such obstacles be first removed as are occasioned by fears, jealousies and apprehensions of divers His Majesty's loyal subjects, that this present Parliament may be adjourned, prorogued, or dissolved, before justice shall be duly executed upon delinquents, public grievances redressed, a firm peace between the two nations of England and Scotland concluded, and before sufficient provision be made for the re-payment of the said monies so to be raised ; all which the Commons in this present

Parliament assembled, having duly considered, do therefore most humbly beseech your Majesty that it may be declared and enacted :

And be it declared and enacted by the King, our Sovereign Lord, with the assent of the Lords and Commons in this present Parliament assembled, and by the authority of the same, that this present Parliament now assembled shall not be dissolved unless it be by Act of Parliament to be passed for that purpose ; nor shall be, at any time or times, during the continuance thereof, prorogued or adjourned, unless it be by Act of Parliament to be likewise passed for that purpose ; and that the House of Peers shall not at any time or times during this present Parliament be adjourned, unless it be by themselves or by their own order ; and in like manner, that the House of Commons shall not, at any time or times, during this present Parliament, be adjourned, unless it be by themselves or by their own order ; and that all and every thing or things whatsoever done or to be done for the adjournment, proroguing, or dissolving of this present Parliament, contrary to this Act, shall be utterly void and of none effect.

———◆———

199. Act for the Abolition of the Court of Star Chamber

(1641, July 5. 16 Charles I. c. 10. 5 *S. R.* 110. The whole act reprinted in Gardiner, 179–186.)

WHEREAS by the Great Charter many times confirmed in Parliament, it is enacted that no freeman shall be taken or imprisoned, or disseised of his freehold or liberties or free customs, or be outlawed or exiled or otherwise destroyed, and that the King will not pass upon him or condemn him but by lawful judgment of his peers or by the law of the land ; and by another statute made in the fifth year of the reign of King Edward the Third, it is enacted that no man shall be attached by any accusation nor forejudged of life or limb, nor his lands, tenements, goods nor chattels seised into the King's hands against the form of the Great Charter and the law of the land; and by another statute made in the five-and-twentieth year of the reign of the same King Edward the Third, it is accorded, assented and established, that none shall be taken by petition or suggestion made to the King or to his Council, unless it be by indictment or presentment of good and lawful people of the same neighbourhood where such deeds be done, in due manner or by process made by writ original at the common law, and that none be put out of his franchise or freehold unless he be duly brought in to answer and forejudged of the same by the course of the law, and if anything be done against the same, it shall be redressed and holden for none ; and by another statute made in the eight-and-twentieth year of the reign of the same King Edward the Third, it is amongst other things enacted, that no man of what estate or condition soever he be shall be put out of his lands or tenements, nor taken nor imprisoned nor disinherited without being brought in to answer by due process of law ; and by another statute made in the two-and-fortieth year of the reign of the said King Edward the Third, it is enacted, that no man be put to answer without presentment before Justices or matter of record, or by due process and writ original according to the old law of the land, and if anything be done to the contrary, it shall be void in law and holden for error ; and by another statute made in the six-and-thirtieth year of the same King Edward the Third, it is amongst other things enacted, that all pleas which shall be pleaded in any Courts before any of the King's Justices, or in his other places, or before any of his other ministers, or in the Courts and places of any other Lords within the realm, shall be entered and enrolled in Latin ; and whereas by the statute made in the third year of King Henry the Seventh, power is given to the Chancellor, the Lord Treasurer of England for the time being, and the Keeper of the King's Privy Seal, or two of them, calling unto them a Bishop and a Temporal Lord of the King's most honourable Council, and the two Chief Justices of the King's Bench and Common Pleas for the time being, or other two Justices in their absence, to proceed as in that Act is expressed for the punishment of some particular offences therein mentioned ; and by the statute made in the one-and-twentieth year of King Henry the Eighth, the President of the Council is associated to join with the Lord Chancellor and other Judges in the said statute of the third of Henry the Seventh mentioned : but the said Judges have not kept themselves to the points limited by the said statute, but have undertaken to punish where no law doth warrant, and to make decrees for things having no such authority, and to inflict heavier punishments than by any law is warranted ;

II. Forasmuch as all matters examinable or determinable before the said Judges, or in the Court commonly called the Star Chamber, may have their proper remedy and redress, and their due punishment and correction, by the common law of the land, and in the ordinary course of justice elsewhere ; and forasmuch as the reasons and motives inducing the erection and continuance of that

Court do now cease ; and the proceedings, censures and decrees of that Court have by experience been found to be an intolerable burden to the subjects, and the means to introduce an arbitrary power and government ; and forasmuch as the Council Table hath of late times assumed unto itself a power to intermeddle in civil causes and matters only of private interest between party and party, and have adventured to determine of the estates and liberties of the subject, contrary to the law of the land and the rights and privileges of the subject, by which great and manifold mischiefs and inconveniences have arisen and happened, and much uncertainty by means of such proceedings hath been conceived concerning men's rights and estates : for settling whereof and preventing the like in time to come :

III. Be it ordained and enacted by the authority of this present Parliament, that the said Court commonly called the Star Chamber, and all jurisdiction, power and authority belonging unto or exercised in the same Court, or by any of the Judges, Officers or Ministers thereof, be from the first day of August in the year of our Lord God one thousand six hundred forty and one, clearly and absolutely dissolved, taken away, and determined ; and that from the said first day of August neither the Lord Chancellor or Keeper of the Great Seal of England, the Lord Treasurer of England, the Keeper of the King's Privy Seal, or President of the Council, nor any Bishop, Temporal Lord, Privy Councillor, or Judge, or Justice whatsoever, shall have any power or authority to hear, examine or determine any matter or thing whatsoever in the said Court commonly called the Star Chamber, or to make, pronounce or deliver any judgment, sentence, order or decree, or to do any judicial or ministerial act in the said Court ; and that all and every Act and Acts of Parliament, and all and every article, clause, and sentence in them and every of them, by which any jurisdiction, power or authority is given, limited or appointed unto the said Court, commonly called the Star Chamber, or unto all or any the Judges, Officers or Ministers thereof, or for any proceedings to be had or made in the said Court, or for any matter or thing to be drawn into question, examined or determined there, shall, for so much as concerneth the said Court of Star Chamber, and the power and authority thereby given unto it be, from the said first day of August, repealed and absolutely revoked and made void.

IV. And be it likewise enacted, that the like jurisdiction now used and exercised in the Court before the President and Council in the Marches of Wales ; and also in the Court before the President and Council established in the northern parts; and also in the Court commonly called the Court of the Duchy of Lancaster, held before the Chancellor and Council of that Court; and also in the Court of Exchequer of the County Palatine of Chester, held before the Chamberlain and Council of that Court; the like jurisdiction being exercised there, shall, from the said first day of August one thousand six hundred forty and one, be also repealed and absolutely revoked and made void, any law, prescription, custom or usage; or the said statute made in the third year of King Henry the Seventh; or the statute made in the one-and-twentieth of Henry the Eighth; or any Act or Acts of Parliament heretofore had or made, to the contrary thereof in any wise notwithstanding; and that from henceforth no court, council, or place of judicature shall be erected, ordained, constituted, or appointed within this realm of England or dominion of Wales, which shall have, use or exercise the same or the like jurisdiction, as is or hath been used, practised or exercised in the said Court of Star Chamber.

V. Be it likewise declared and enacted by authority of this present Parliament, that neither His Majesty nor his Privy Council have or ought to have any jurisdiction, power or authority by English bill, petition, articles, libel, or any other arbitrary way whatsoever, to examine or draw into question, determine or dispose of the lands, tenements, hereditaments, goods or chattels of any the subjects of this kingdom, but that the same ought to be tried and determined in the ordinary Courts of Justice and by the ordinary course of the law.

*   *   *   *   *   *   *   *   *

200. Act for the Abolition of the Court of High Commission

(1641, July 5.   16 Charles I. c. 11.   5 *S. R.* 112.   Gardiner, 186–189.)

WHEREAS in the Parliament holden in the first year of the reign of the late Queen Elizabeth, late Queen of England, there was an Act made and established, entitled 'An Act restoring to the Crown the ancient jurisdiction over the State ecclesiastical and spiritual, and abolishing all foreign power repugnant to the same': in which Act, amongst other things, there is contained one clause, branch, article or sentence whereby it was enacted to this effect : namely, that the said late Queen's Highness, her heirs and successors, Kings or Queens of this realm, should have full power and authority by virtue of that Act, by Letters Patents under the Great Seal of England, to assign, name and authorize when and as often as Her Highness, her heirs or successors, should think meet and convenient, and for such and so long time as should please Her Highness, her heirs or successors, such person or persons being natural born subjects to Her Highness, her heirs or successors, as Her Majesty, her heirs or successors, should think meet to exercise, use, occupy and execute under Her Highness, her heirs and successors, all manner of jurisdictions, privileges and preeminences in any wise touching or concerning any spiritual or ecclesiastical jurisdiction within these her realms of England and Ireland, or any other Her Highness's dominions and countries ; and to visit, reform, redress, order, correct and amend all such errors, heresies, schisms, abuses, offences, contempts and enormities whatsoever, which by any manner spiritual or ecclesiastical power, authority or jurisdiction can or may lawfully be reformed, ordered, redressed, corrected, restrained or amended, to the pleasure of Almighty God, the increase of virtue and the conservation of the peace and unity of this realm : and that such person or persons so to be named, assigned, authorized and appointed by Her Highness, her heirs or successors, after the said Letters Patents to him or them made and delivered as aforesaid, should have full power and authority by virtue of that Act and of the said Letters Patents under Her Highness, her heirs or successors, to exercise, use and execute all the premises, according to the tenor and effect of the said Letters Patents, any matter or cause to the contrary in any wise notwithstanding ;

II. And whereas by colour of some words in the aforesaid branch of the said Act, whereby Commissioners are authorized to execute their commission according to the tenor and effect of the King's Letters Patents, and by Letters Patents grounded thereupon, the said Commissioners have, to the great and insufferable wrong and oppression of the King's subjects, used to fine and imprison them, and to exercise other authority not belonging to ecclesiastical jurisdiction restored by that Act, and divers other great mischiefs and inconveniences have also ensued to the King's subjects by occasion of the said branch, and commissions issued thereupon, and the executions thereof : therefore for the repressing and preventing of the aforesaid abuses, mischiefs and inconveniences in time to come :

III. Be it enacted by the King's Most Excellent Majesty and

the Lords and Commons in this present Parliament assembled, and by the authority of the same, that the aforesaid branch, clause, article or sentence contained in the said Act, and every word, matter and thing contained in that branch, clause, article or sentence shall from henceforth be repealed, annulled, revoked, annihilated and utterly made void for ever; anything in the said Act to the contrary in any wise notwithstanding.

IV. And be it also enacted by the authority aforesaid, that no Archbishop, Bishop, nor Vicar General, nor any Chancellor, Official, nor Commissary of any Archbishop, Bishop or Vicar General, nor any ordinary whatsoever, nor any other spiritual or ecclesiastical Judge, Officer or Minister of Justice, nor any other person or persons whatsoever exercising spiritual or ecclesiastical power, authority or jurisdiction by any grant, licence or commission of the King's Majesty, his heirs or successors, or by any power or authority derived from the King, his heirs or successors, or otherwise, shall from and after the first day of August, which shall be in the year of our Lord God one thousand six hundred forty and one, award, impose or inflict any pain, penalty, fine, amercement, imprisonment or other corporal punishment upon any of the King's subjects for any contempt, misdemeanour, crime, offence, matter or thing whatsoever belonging to spiritual or ecclesiastical cognizance or jurisdiction; or shall *ex officio*, or at the instance or promotion of any other person whatsoever, urge, enforce, tender, give or minister unto any churchwarden, sidesman or other person whatsoever any corporal oath, whereby he or she shall or may be charged or obliged to make any presentment of any crime or offence, or to confess or to accuse him or herself of any crime, offence, delinquency or misdemeanour, or any neglect or thing whereby, or by reason whereof, he or she shall or may be liable or exposed to any censure, pain, penalty or punishment whatsoever; upon pain and penalty that every person who shall offend contrary to this statute shall forfeit and pay treble damages to every person thereby grieved, and the sum of £100 to him or them who shall first demand and sue for the same; which said treble damages and sum of £100 shall and may be demanded and recovered by action of debt, bill or plaint in any Court of Record wherein no privilege, essoine, protection or wager of law shall be admitted or allowed to the defendant. And be it further enacted, that every person who shall be once convicted of any act or offence prohibited by this statute, shall for such act or offence be from and after such conviction utterly disabled to be or continue in any office or employment in any Court of Justice whatsoever, or to exercise or execute any power, authority or jurisdiction by force of any Commission or Letters Patents of the King, his heirs or successors.

V. And be it further enacted, that from and after the said first day of August, no new Court shall be erected, ordained or appointed within this realm of England or dominion of Wales, which shall or may have the like power, jurisdiction or authority as the said High Commission Court now hath or pretendeth to have; but that all and every such Letters Patents, Commissions and Grants made or to be made by His Majesty, his heirs or successors, and all powers and authorities granted, or pretended or mentioned to be granted thereby, and all acts, sentences and decrees, to be made by virtue or colour thereof shall be utterly void and of none effect.

——◆——

201. Act Declaring the Illegality of Ship-money

(1641, August 7.   16 Charles I. c. 14.   5 *S. R.* 116.   Gardiner, 189–192.)

WHEREAS divers writs of late time issued under the Great Seal of England, commonly called Ship-writs, for the charging of the Ports, Towns, Cities, Boroughs, and Counties of this realm respectively, to provide and furnish certain ships for His Majesty's service; and whereas upon the execution of the same writs and returns of *certioraries* thereupon made, and the sending the same by *Mittimus* into the Court of Exchequer, process hath been thence made against sundry persons pretended to be charged by way of contribution for the making up of certain sums assessed for the providing of the said ships; and in especial in Easter Term in the thirteenth year of the reign of our Sovereign Lord the King that now is, a Writ of *Scire facias* was awarded out of the Court of Exchequer to the then Sheriff of Buckinghamshire against John Hampden, Esquire, to appear and show cause why he should not be charged with a certain sum so assessed upon him : upon whose appearance and demurrer to the proceedings therein, the Barons of the Exchequer adjourned the same case into the Exchequer Chamber, where it was solemnly argued divers days; and at length it was there agreed by the greater part of all the Justices of the Courts of King's Bench and Common Pleas, and of the Barons of the Exchequer there assembled, that the said John Hampden should be charged with the said sum so as aforesaid assessed on

2 ◢

him; the main grounds and reasons of the said Justices and Barons which so agreed being, that when the good and safety of the kingdom in general is concerned, and the whole kingdom in danger, the King might by writ under the Great Seal of England command all the subjects of this his kingdom at their charge to provide and furnish such number of ships with men, victuals and munition, and for such time as the King should think fit, for the defence and safeguard of the kingdom from such danger and peril, and that by law the King might compel the doing thereof in case of refusal or refractoriness; and that the King is the sole judge both of the danger, and when and how the same is to be prevented and avoided; according to which grounds and reasons all the Justices of the said Courts of King's Bench and Common Pleas, and the said Barons of the Exchequer, having been formerly consulted with by His Majesty's command, had set their hands to an extrajudicial opinion expressed to the same purpose; which opinion with their names thereunto was also by His Majesty's command enrolled in the Courts of Chancery, King's Bench, Common Pleas and Exchequer, and likewise entered among the remembrances of the Court of Star Chamber; and according to the said agreement of the said Justices and Barons, judgment was given by the Barons of the Exchequer, that the said John Hampden should be charged with the said sum so assessed on him: and whereas some other actions and process depend, and have depended, in the said Court of Exchequer and in some other Courts, against other persons for the like kind of charge grounded upon the said writs commonly called Ship-writs; all which writs and proceedings as aforesaid were utterly against the law of the land:

II. Be it therefore declared and enacted by the King's Most Excellent Majesty and the Lords and the Commons in this present Parliament assembled, and by the authority of the same, that the said charge imposed upon the subject for the providing and furnishing of ships, commonly called Ship-money, and the said extrajudicial opinion of the said Justices and Barons, and the said writs, and every of them, and the said agreement or opinion of the greater part of the said Justices and Barons, and the said judgment given against the said John Hampden, were and are contrary to and against the laws and statutes of this realm, the right of property, the liberty of the subjects, former resolutions in Parliament, and the Petition of Right made in the third year of the reign of His Majesty that now is.

III. And it is further declared and enacted by the authority aforesaid, that all and every the particulars prayed or desired in the said Petition of Right shall from henceforth be put in execution accordingly, and shall be firmly and strictly holden and observed as in the same Petition they are prayed and expressed; and that all and every the records and remembrances of all and every the judgment, enrolments, entry, and proceedings as aforesaid, and all and every the proceedings whatsoever, upon or by pretext or colour of any of the said writs commonly called Ship-writs, and all and every the dependents on any of them, shall be deemed and adjudged, to all intents, constructions and purposes, to be utterly void and disannulled; and that all and every the said judgment, enrolments, entries, proceedings and dependents of what kind soever, shall be vacated and cancelled in such manner and form as records use to be that are vacated.

———◆———

202. Act for the Limitation of Forests

(1641, August 7.   16 Charles I. c. 16.   5 *S. R.* 119.   Gardiner, 192–195.)

WHEREAS by Act of Parliament made in the first year of the reign of the late King Edward the Third, it was ordained, that the old perambulation of the forest in the time of King Edward the First should be thenceforth holden in like form as it was then ridden and bounded, and in such places where it was not bounded, the King would that it should be bounded by good men and lawful:

II. And whereas for many ages past certain meets, meers, limits and bounds of the forests have been commonly known and observed in the several Counties, wherein the said forests lie:

III. And whereas of late divers presentments have been made and some judgments given, whereby the meets, meers, limits and bounds of some of the said forests have been variously extended or pretended to extend beyond some of the said meets, meers, limits and bounds so commonly known and formerly observed, to the great grievance and vexation of many persons having lands adjoining to the said meets, meers, limits and bounds so commonly known and formerly observed: and whereas of late time some endeavours or pretences have been to set on foot forests in some parts of this realm and the dominion of Wales, where in truth none have been or ought to be, or at least have not been used of long time: for remedy thereof, may it please your Most

Excellent Majesty that it be declared and enacted by authority of Parliament;

IV. And be it declared and enacted by the King's Most Excellent Majesty and the Lords and Commons in this present Parliament assembled, and by the authority of the same, that from henceforth the meets, meers, limits and bounds of all and every the forests respectively, shall be to all intents and purposes taken, adjudged and deemed to extend no further respectively than the meets, meers, limits and bounds, which in the several Counties respectively wherein the said forests do lie, were commonly known, reputed, used or taken to be the meets, meers, limits and bounds of the said forests respectively in the twentieth year of the reign of our late Sovereign Lord, King James, and not beyond in any wise, any perambulation or perambulations, presentments, extents, surveys, judgments, records, decrees, or other matter or thing whatsoever to the contrary notwithstanding: and that all and every the presentments since the said twentieth year made, and all and every other presentment and presentments, and all and every judgment and award upon or by reason or pretext of any such presentment or presentments, and all and every perambulation and perambulations, surveys, extents, and other act and acts at any time heretofore had or made, by which the meets, meers, limits or bounds of the said forests, or any of them, are or are pretended to be further extended than as aforesaid; and also all and every presentment of any other person or persons at any Justice seat, Swainemote, or Court of Attachments, for or by reason or by colour of any act or acts whatsoever done or committed in any place without or beyond the said meets, meers, limits or bounds respectively, so commonly known, reputed, used, or taken as aforesaid, and all and every fine and fines, and amercement and amercements, upon, by reason or colour of any such presentment or presentments, shall from henceforth be adjudged, deemed, and taken to be utterly void, and of no force or effect; any law, statute record or pretence whatsoever to the contrary notwithstanding.

V. And be it further enacted by the authority aforesaid, that no place or places within this realm of England or dominion of Wales, where no such Justice seat, Swainemote, or Court of Attachment have been held or kept, or where no Verderers have been chosen, or regard made, within the space of sixty years next before the first year of His Majesty's reign that now is, shall be at any time hereafter judged, deemed, or taken to be forest, or within the bounds or meets of the forests; but the same shall be from henceforth for ever hereafter disafforested, and freed, and exempted from the forest laws; any Justice seat, Swainemote, or Court of Attachment held or kept within or for any such place or places at any time or times since the beginning of His Majesty's said reign, or any presentment, enquiry, act, or thing heretofore made, or hereafter to be made or done to the contrary notwithstanding.

VI. Provided also, and be it further enacted by the authority aforesaid, that for the better putting into certainty all and every the meets, meers, bounds and limits of all and every the forests as aforesaid, the Lord Chancellor or Lord Keeper of the Great Seal of England for the time being shall, by virtue of this Act, upon request of any of the Peers of this kingdom, or of the Knights and Burgesses of the Parliament or any of them, grant several commissions under the Great Seal of England to Commissioners to be nominated respectively by the said Peers, Knights and Burgesses, or any of them, to enquire of and find out by inquests of good and lawful men upon oath, and by the oaths of witnesses to be produced at the said inquests, and by all other lawful means, all and every the meers, meets, bounds and limits of the forests respectively, which were commonly known to be their meers, meets, bounds and limits respectively in the said twentieth year of the reign of our late Sovereign Lord, King James; and to return the inquests so taken into the Court of Chancery; and that all and every the Sheriffs and Bailiffs of and in every County wherein any such inquests shall be so to be taken; and all and every the Verderers, Foresters, Rangers, and other officers of the forests respectively, where any such officers be, shall be assistant and attendant to the executions of the said commissions, according as by virtue of the said commissions respectively they shall be commanded; and where no such officers are or where such officers be, if they or any of them shall refuse or neglect such assistance and attendance as aforesaid, then the said Commissioners shall and may proceed without them in the execution of the said commissions.

VII. And be it further enacted by the authority aforesaid, that the forests whereof the meets, meers, limits and bounds shall be so returned and certified by virtue of any the said commissions as aforesaid, from thenceforth shall not extend, nor be extended, nor be deemed, adjudged, or taken to extend any further in any wise than the meets, meers, limits and bounds that shall be so returned and certified; and that all the places and territories that shall be without the meets, meers, limits and bounds so returned and certified, shall be and are hereby declared to be from thenceforth free to all intents and purposes, as if the same had never been forest, or so reputed ; any Act or Acts, matter or thing whatsoever to the contrary thereof notwithstanding.

VIII. Provided, and be it further enacted by the authority aforesaid, that all and every the grounds, territories or places which have been or are disafforested or mentioned to be disafforested in or by any Letters Patents, Charters, or otherwise since the said twentieth year of the reign of our said late Sovereign Lord, King James, shall be excluded and left out of the meets, meers, limits and bounds of the forests which are to be enquired of, returned and certified by virtue of the said commissions, or any of them respectively, and shall be, and hereby are declared and enacted to be utterly disafforested, free, and exempt to all intents and purposes as if the same had never been at all forest, or so reputed ; anything in this present Act contained, or any other Act, matter or thing whatsoever to the contrary in any wise notwithstanding.

IX. Provided nevertheless and be it enacted that the tenants, owners, and occupiers, and every of them of lands and tenements, which shall be excluded and left out of the meets, meers, limits or bounds of the forests to be returned and certified by virtue of any the said commissions, shall or may use and enjoy such common, and other profits and easements within the forest as anciently or accustomarily they have used and enjoyed ; anything in this present Act contained or any Act or Ordinance made in the three-and-thirtieth year of King Edward the First, or any custom or law of the forest, or any other matter or thing to the contrary thereof notwithstanding.

———◆———

203. Act prohibiting the Exaction of Knighthood Fines

(1641, August 10.   16 Charles I. c. 20.   5 S. R. 151.   Gardiner, 196, 197.)

WHEREAS upon pretext of an ancient custom or usage of this realm of England, that men of full age being not Knights, and being seised of lands or rents of the yearly value of forty pounds or more (especially if their seisin had so continued by the space of three years next past), might be compelled by the King's writ to receive, or take upon them, the Order or Dignity of Knighthood, or else to make fine for the discharge or respite of the same, several writs, about the beginning of His Majesty's reign, issued out of the Court of Chancery for proclamations to be made in every

County to that purpose, and for certifying the names of all such persons, and for summoning them personally to appear in the King's presence, before a certain day, to be there ready to receive the said Order or Dignity : upon return of which writs, and transmitting the same with their returns into the Court of Exchequer, and upon other writs for further inquiry of the names of such persons issuing out of the said Court of Exchequer, process by *distringas* was thence made against a very great number of persons, many of which were altogether unfit, in regard either of estate or quality, to receive the said Order or Dignity, and very many were put to grievous fines and other vexations for the same, although in truth it were not sufficiently known how, or in what sort, or where they, or any of them, should, or might have addressed themselves for receiving the said Order or Dignity, and for saving themselves thereby from the said fines, process and vexations : and whereas it is most apparent, that all and every such proceeding, in regard of the matter therein pretended, is altogether useless and unreasonable : may it therefore please your Most Excellent Majesty that it be by authority of Parliament declared and enacted ;

II. And be it declared and enacted by the King's Most Excellent Majesty, and the Lords and Commons in this Parliament assembled, and by the authority of the same, that from henceforth no person or persons of what condition, quality, estate or degree soever, shall at any time be distrained or otherwise compelled by any writ or process of the Court of Chancery or Court of Exchequer, or otherwise by any means whatsoever, to receive or take upon him or them respectively the Order or Dignity of Knighthood, nor shall suffer or undergo any fine, trouble or molestation whatsoever by reason or colour of his or their having not received or taken upon him or them the said Order or Dignity ; and that all and every writ or process whatsoever, and all and every proceeding which shall hereafter be had or made contrary to the intent of this Act, shall be deemed and adjudged to be utterly void ; and that all and every process, proceeding, and charge now depending by reason or colour of the said pretended custom or writs aforesaid, or of any the dependents thereof, shall from henceforth cease, and stand, be and remain discharged and utterly void, any former law or custom, or any pretence of any former law or custom or any other matter whatsoever to the contrary in any wise notwithstanding.

204. The Grand Remonstrance, with the Petition accompanying It

(Presented to Charles I., December 1, 1641.   Rushworth, iv. 438.   The whole
reprinted in Gardiner, 202–232.)

MOST Gracious Sovereign,
    Your Majesty's most humble and faithful subjects the Commons in this present Parliament assembled, do with much thankfulness and joy acknowledge the great mercy and favour of God, in giving your Majesty a safe and peaceable return out of Scotland into your kingdom of England, where the pressing dangers and distempers of the State have caused us with much earnestness to desire the comfort of your gracious presence, and likewise the unity and justice of your royal authority, to give more life and power to the dutiful and loyal counsels and endeavours of your Parliament, for the prevention of that eminent ruin and destruction wherein your kingdoms of England and Scotland are threatened. The duty which we owe to your Majesty and our country, cannot but make us very sensible and apprehensive, that the multiplicity, sharpness and malignity of those evils under which we have now many years suffered, are fomented and cherished by a corrupt and ill-affected party, who amongst other their mischievous devices for the alteration of religion and government, have sought by many false scandals and imputations, cunningly insinuated and dispersed amongst the people, to blemish and disgrace our proceedings in this Parliament, and to get themselves a party and faction amongst your subjects, for the better strengthening themselves in their wicked courses, and hindering those provisions and remedies which might, by the wisdom of your Majesty and counsel of your Parliament, be opposed against them.

    For preventing whereof, and the better information of your Majesty, your Peers and all other your loyal subjects, we have been necessitated to make a declaration of the state of the kingdom, both before and since the assembly of this Parliament, unto this time, which we do humbly present to your Majesty, without the least intention to lay any blemish upon your royal person, but only to represent how your royal authority and trust have been abused, to the great prejudice and danger of your Majesty, and of all your good subjects.

    And because we have reason to believe that those malignant parties, whose proceedings evidently appear to be mainly for the advantage and increase of Popery, is composed, set up, and acted by the subtle practice of the Jesuits and other engineers and factors for Rome, and to the great danger of this kingdom, and most grievous affliction of your loyal subjects, have so far prevailed as to corrupt divers of your Bishops and others in prime places of the Church, and also to bring divers of these instruments to be of your Privy Council, and other employments of trust and nearness about your Majesty, the Prince, and the rest of your royal children.

And by this means have had such an operation in your counsel and the most important affairs and proceedings of your government, that a most dangerous division and chargeable preparation for war betwixt your kingdoms of England and Scotland, the increase of jealousies betwixt your Majesty and your most obedient subjects, the violent distraction and interruption of this Parliament, the insurrection of the Papists in your kingdom of Ireland, and bloody massacre of your people, have been not only endeavoured and attempted, but in a great measure compassed and effected.

For preventing the final accomplishment whereof, your poor subjects are enforced to engage their persons and estates to the maintaining of a very expensive and dangerous war, notwithstanding they have already since the beginning of this Parliament undergone the charge of £150,000 sterling, or thereabouts, for the necessary support and supply of your Majesty in these present and perilous designs. And because all our most faithful endeavours and engagements will be ineffectual for the peace, safety and preservation of your Majesty and your people, if some present, real and effectual course be not taken for suppressing this wicked and malignant party : —

We, your most humble and obedient subjects, do with all faithfulness and humility beseech your Majesty, —

1. That you will be graciously pleased to concur with the humble desires of your people in a parliamentary way, for the preserving the peace and safety of the kingdom from the malicious designs of the Popish party : —

For depriving the Bishops of their votes in Parliament, and abridging their immoderate power usurped over the Clergy, and other your good subjects, which they have perniciously abused to the hazard of religion, and great prejudice and oppression of the laws of the kingdom, and just liberty of your people : —

For the taking away such oppressions in religion, Church government and discipline, as have been brought in and fomented by them · —

For uniting all such your loyal subjects together as join in the same fundamental truths against the Papists, by removing some oppressions and unnecessary ceremonies by which divers weak consciences have been scrupled, and seem to be divided from the rest, and for the due execution of those good laws which have been made for securing the liberty of your subjects.

2. That your Majesty will likewise be pleased to remove from your council all such as persist to favour and promote any of those pressures and corruptions wherewith your people have been grieved, and that for the future your Majesty will vouchsafe to employ such persons in your great and public affairs, and to take such to be near you in places of trust, as your Parliament may have cause to confide in; that in your princely goodness to your people you will reject and refuse all mediation and solicitation to the contrary, how powerful and near soever.

3. That you will be pleased to forbear to alienate any of the forfeited and escheated lands in Ireland which shall accrue to your Crown by reason of this rebellion, that out of them the Crown may be the better supported, and some satisfaction made to your subjects of this kingdom for the great expenses they are like to undergo [in] this war.

Which humble desires of ours being graciously fulfilled by your Majesty, we will, by the blessing and favour of God, most cheerfully undergo the hazard and expenses of this war, and apply ourselves to such other courses and counsels as may support your royal estate with honour and plenty at home, with power and reputation abroad, and by our loyal affections, obedience and service, lay a sure and lasting foundation of the greatness and prosperity of your Majesty, and your royal posterity in future times.

The Grand Remonstrance

* * * * * * * * *

191. For the perfecting of the work begun, and removing all future impediments, we conceive these courses will be very effectual, seeing the religion of the Papists hath such principles as do certainly tend to the destruction and extirpation of all Protestants, when they shall have opportunity to effect it.

192. It is necessary in the first place to keep them in such condition as that they may not be able to do us any hurt, and for avoiding of such connivance and favour as hath heretofore been shown unto them.

193. That His Majesty be pleased to grant a standing Com-

mission to some choice men named in Parliament, who may take notice of their increase, their counsels and proceedings, and use all due means by execution of the laws to prevent all mischievous designs against the peace and safety of this kingdom.

194. Thus some good course be taken to discover the counterfeit and false conformity of Papists to the Church, by colour whereof persons very much disaffected to the true religion have been admitted into place of greatest authority and trust in the kingdom.

195. For the better preservation of the laws and liberties of the kingdom, that all illegal grievances and exactions be presented and punished at the sessions and assizes.

196. And that Judges and Justices be very careful to give this in charge to the grand jury, and both the Sheriff and Justices to be sworn to the due execution of the Petition of Right and other laws.

197. That His Majesty be humbly petitioned by both Houses to employ such counsellors, ambassadors and other ministers, in managing his business at home and abroad, as the Parliament may have cause to confide in, without which we cannot give His Majesty such supplies for support of his own estate, nor such assistance to the Protestant party beyond the sea, as is desired.

198. It may often fall out that the Commons may have just cause to take exceptions at some men for being councillors, and yet not charge those men with crimes, for there be grounds of diffidence which lie not in proof.

199. There are others, which though they may be proved, yet are not legally criminal.

200. To be a known favourer of Papists, or to have been very forward in defending or countenancing some great offenders questioned in Parliament ; or to speak contemptuously of either Houses of Parliament or Parliamentary proceedings.

201. Or such as are factors or agents for any foreign prince of another religion ; such are justly suspected to get councillors' places, or any other of trust concerning public employment for money ; for all these and divers others we may have great reason to be earnest with His Majesty, not to put his great affairs into such hands, though we may be unwilling to proceed against them in any legal way of charge or impeachment.

202. That all Councillors of State may be sworn to observe those laws which concern the subject in his liberty, that they may likewise take an oath not to receive or give reward or pension from any foreign prince, but such as they shall within some reasonable time discover to the Lords of His Majesty's Council.

203. And although they should wickedly forswear themselves, yet it may herein do good to make them known to be false and perjured to those who employ them, and thereby bring them into as little credit with them as with us.

204. That His Majesty may have cause to be in love with good counsel and good men, by showing him in an humble and dutiful manner how full of advantage it would be to himself, to see his own estate settled in a plentiful condition to support his honour; to see his people united in ways of duty to him, and endeavours of the public good; to see happiness, wealth, peace and safety derived to his own kingdom, and procured to his allies, by the influence of his own power and government.

205. The King's Answer to the Petition Accompanying the Grand Remonstrance

(1641, December 23. Rushworth, iv. 452. Gardiner, 233–236.)

WE having received from you, soon after our return out of Scotland, a long petition consisting of many desires of great moment, together with a declaration of a very unusual nature annexed thereunto, we had taken some time to consider of it, as befitted us in a matter of that consequence, being confident that your own reason and regard to us, as well as our express intimation by our comptroller to that purpose, would have restrained you from the publishing of it till such time as you should have received our answer to it; but, much against our expectation, finding the contrary, that the said declaration is already abroad in print, by directions from your House as appears by the printed copy, we must let you know that we are very sensible of the disrespect. Notwithstanding, it is our intention that no failing on your part shall make us fail in ours of giving all due satisfaction to the desires of our people in a parliamentary way; and therefore we send you this answer to your petition, reserving ourself in point of the declaration which we think unparliamentary, and shall take a course to do that which we shall think fit in prudence and honour.

To the petition, we say that although there are divers things in the preamble of it which we are so far from admitting that we profess we cannot at all understand them, as 'of a wicked and malignant party prevalent in the government'; of 'some of that party admitted to our Privy Council and to other employments of trust, and nearest to us and our children'; of 'endeavours to sow among the people false scandals and imputations, to blemish and disgrace the proceedings of the Parliament'; all, or any of them, did we know of, we should be as ready to remedy and punish as you to complain of, so that the prayers of your petition are grounded upon such premises as we must in no wise admit; yet, notwithstanding, we are pleased to give this answer to you.

To the first, concerning religion, consisting of several branches, we say that, for preserving the peace and safety of this kingdom from the design of the Popish party, we have, and will still, concur with all the just desires of our people in a parliamentary way : that, for the depriving of the Bishops of their votes in Parliament, we would have you consider that their right is grounded upon the fundamental law of the kingdom and constitution of Parliament. This we would have you consider; but since you desire our concurrence herein in a parliamentary way, we will give no further answer at this time.

As for the abridging of the inordinate power of the clergy, we conceive that the taking away of the High Commission Court hath well moderated that; but if there continue any usurpations or excesses in their jurisdictions, we therein neither have nor will protect them.

Unto that clause which concerneth corruptions (as you style them) in religion, in Church government, and in discipline, and the removing of such unnecessary ceremonies as weak consciences might check at : that for any illegal innovations which may have crept in, we shall willingly concur in the removal of them : that, if our Parliament shall advise us to call a national synod, which may duly examine such ceremonies as give just cause of offence to any, we shall take it into consideration, and apply ourself to give due satisfaction therein ; but we are very sorry to hear, in such general terms, corruption in religion objected, since we are persuaded in our conscience that no Church can be found upon the earth that professeth the true religion with more purity of doctrine than the Church of England doth, nor where the government and discipline are jointly more beautified and free from superstition ; then as they are here established by law, which, by the grace of God, we will with constancy maintain (while we live) in their purity and glory, not only against all invasions of Popery, but also from the irreverence of those many schismatics and separatists, wherewith of late this kingdom and this city abounds, to the great dishonour and hazard both of Church and State, for the suppression of whom we require your timely aid and active assistance.

To the second prayer of the petition, concerning the removal and choice of councillors, we know not any of our Council to whom the character set forth in the petition can belong : that by those whom we had exposed to trial, we have already given you sufficient testimony that there is no man so near unto us in place or affection, whom we will not leave to the justice of the law, if you shall bring a particular charge and sufficient proofs against him ; and of this we do again assure you, but in the meantime we wish you to forbear such general aspersions as may reflect upon all our Council, since you name none in particular.

That for the choice of our councillors and ministers of state, it were to debar us that natural liberty all freemen have ; and as it is the undoubted right of the Crown of England to call such persons to our secret counsels, to public employment and our particular service as we shall think fit, so we are, and ever shall be, very careful to make election of such persons in those places of trust as shall have given good testimonies of their abilities and integrity, and against whom there can be no just cause of exception whereon reasonably to ground a diffidence ; and to choices of this nature, we assure you that the mediation of the nearest unto us hath always concurred.

To the third prayer of your petition concerning Ireland, we understand your desire of not alienating the forfeited lands thereof, to proceed from much care and love, and likewise that it may be a resolution very fit for us to take ; but whether it be seasonable to declare resolutions of that nature before the events of a war be seen, that we much doubt of.   Howsoever, we cannot but thank you for this care, and your cheerful engagement for the suppression of that rebellion ; upon the speedy effecting whereof, the glory of God in the Protestant profession, the safety of the British there, our honour, and that of the nation, so much depends : all the interests of this kingdom being so involved in that business, we cannot but quicken your affections therein, and shall desire you to frame your counsels, to give such expedition to the work as the nature thereof, and the pressures in point of time require ; and whereof you are put in mind by the daily insolence and increase of those rebels.

For conclusion, your promise to apply yourselves to such courses as may support our royal estate with honour and plenty at home, and with power and reputation abroad, is that which we have ever promised ourself, both from your loyalties and affections, and also for what we have already done, and shall daily go adding unto, for the comfort and happiness of our people.

206. The Clerical Disabilities Act

(164½, February 13. 16 Charles I. c. 27. 5 *S. R.* 158. Gardiner, 241–242. G. and H. 564.)

WHEREAS Bishops and other persons in Holy Orders ought not to be entangled with secular jurisdiction, the office of the ministry being of such great importance that it will take up the whole man ; and for that it is found by long experience that their intermeddling with secular jurisdictions hath occasioned great mischiefs and scandals both to Church and State ; His Majesty, out of his religious care of the Church, and souls of his people, is graciously pleased that it be enacted, and by authority of this present Parliament be it enacted, that no Archbishop or Bishop or other person that now is or hereafter shall be in Holy Orders, shall at any time after the fifteenth day of February, in the year of Our Lord one thousand six hundred forty-one, have any seat or place, suffrage, or voice, or use, or execute any power or authority in the Parliaments of this realm, nor shall be of the Privy Council of His Majesty, his heirs or successors, or Justice of the Peace, of *oyer* and *terminer*, or gaol delivery, or execute any temporal authority by virtue of any commission, but shall be wholly disabled and be incapable to have, receive, use or execute any of the said offices, places, powers, authorities and things aforesaid.

II. And be it further enacted by the authority aforesaid, that all acts from and after the said 15th day of February, which shall be done or executed by any Archbishop or Bishop, or other person whatsoever in Holy Orders, and all and every suffrage or voice given or delivered by them or any of them, or other thing done by them or any of them contrary to the purport and true meaning of this present Act, shall be utterly void to all intents, constructions and purposes.

———◆———

207. The Solemn League and Covenant

(Taken by the House of Commons, September 25, 1643. Rushworth, v. 478. Cobbett's Parliamentary History, iii. 169. Gardiner, 267–271. G. and H. 569–574.)

WE, noblemen, barons, knights, gentlemen, citizens, burgesses, ministers of the Gospel, and commons of all sorts, in the kingdoms of England, Scotland and Ireland, by the providence of God living under one King, and being of one reformed religion; having before our eyes the glory of God, and the advancement of the kingdom of our Lord and Saviour Jesus Christ, the honour and happiness of the King's Majesty and his posterity, and the true public liberty, safety and peace of the kingdoms, wherein every one's private condition is included; and calling to mind the treacherous and bloody plots, conspiracies, attempts and practices of the enemies of God against the true religion and professors thereof in all places, especially in these three kingdoms, ever since the reformation of religion; and how much their rage, power and presumption are of late, and at this time, increased and exercised, whereof the deplorable estate of the Church and kingdom of Ireland, the distressed estate of the Church and kingdom of England, and the dangerous estate of the Church and kingdom of Scotland, are present and public testimonies: we have (now at last) after other means of supplication, remonstrance, protestations and sufferings, for the preservation of ourselves and our religion from utter ruin and destruction, according to the commendable practice of these kingdoms in former times, and the example of God's people in other nations, after mature deliberation, resolved and determined to enter into a mutual and solemn league and covenant, wherein we all subscribe, and each one of us for himself, with our hands lifted up to the most high God, do swear:

I. That we shall sincerely, really and constantly, through the grace of God, endeavour in our several places and callings, the preservation of the reformed religion in the Church of Scotland, in doctrine, worship, discipline and government, against our common enemies; the reformation of religion in the kingdoms of England and Ireland, in doctrine, worship, discipline and government, according to the Word of God, and the example of the best reformed Churches; and we shall endeavour to bring the Churches of God in the three kingdoms to the nearest conjunction and uniformity in religion, confession of faith, form of Church government, directory for worship and catechising, that we, and our posterity after us, may, as brethren, live in faith and love, and the Lord may delight to dwell in the midst of us.

II. That we shall in like manner, without respect of persons, endeavour the extirpation of Popery, Prelacy (that is, Church government by Archbishops, Bishops, their Chancellors and Commissaries, Deans, Deans and Chapters, Archdeacons, and all other ecclesiastical officers depending on that hierarchy), superstition, heresy, schism, profaneness, and whatsoever shall be found to be contrary to sound doctrine and the power of godliness, lest we partake in other men's sins, and thereby be in danger tɔ receive of their plagues ; and that the Lord may be one, and His name one in the three kingdoms.

III. We shall with the same sincerity, reality and constancy, in our several vocations, endeavour with our estates and lives mutually to preserve the rights and privileges of the Parliaments, and the liberties of the kingdoms, and to preserve and defend the King's Majesty's person and authority, in the preservation and defence of the true religion and liberties of the kingdoms, that the world may bear witness with our consciences of our loyalty, and that we have no thoughts or intentions to diminish His Majesty's just power and greatness.

IV. We shall also with all faithfulness endeavour the discovery of all such as have been or shall be incendiaries, malignants or evil instruments, by hindering the reformation of religion, dividing the King from his people, or one of the kingdoms from another, or making any faction or parties amongst the people, contrary to the league and covenant, that they may be brought to public trial and receive condign punishment, as the degree of their offences shall require or deserve, or the supreme judicatories of both kingdoms respectively, or others having power from them for that effect, shall judge convenient.

V. And whereas the happiness of a blessed peace between these kingdoms, denied in former times to our progenitors, is by the good providence of God granted to us, and hath been lately concluded and settled by both Parliaments : we shall each one of us, according to our places and interest, endeavour that they may remain conjoined in a firm peace and union to all posterity, and that justice may be done upon the wilful opposers thereof, in manner expressed in the precedent article.

VI. We shall also, according to our places and callings, in this common cause of religion, liberty and peace of the kingdoms, assist and defend all those that enter into this league and covenant, in the maintaining and pursuing thereof; and shall not suffer ourselves, directly or indirectly, by whatsoever combination, persuasion or terror, to be divided and withdrawn from this blessed union and conjunction, whether to make defection to the contrary part, or give ourselves to a detestable indifferency or neutrality in this cause, which so much concerneth the glory of God, the good of the kingdoms, and the honour of the King ; but shall all the days of our lives zealously and constantly continue therein, against all opposition, and promote the same according to our power, against all lets and impediments whatsoever ; and what we are not able ourselves to suppress or overcome we shall reveal

2 C

and make known, that it may be timely prevented or removed: all which we shall do as in the sight of God.

And because these kingdoms are guilty of many sins and provocations against God, and His Son Jesus Christ, as is too manifest by our present distresses and dangers, the fruits thereof: we profess and declare, before God and the world, our unfeigned desire to be humbled for our own sins, and for the sins of these kingdoms; especially that we have not as we ought valued the inestimable benefit of the Gospel; that we have not laboured for the purity and power thereof; and that we have not endeavoured to receive Christ in our hearts, nor to walk worthy of Him in our lives, which are the causes of other sins and transgressions so much abounding amongst us; and our true and unfeigned purpose, desire and endeavour, for ourselves and all others under our power and charge, both in public and in private, in all duties we owe to God and man, to amend our lives, and each one to go before another in the example of a real reformation, that the Lord may turn away His wrath and heavy indignation, and establish these Churches and kingdoms in truth and peace. And this covenant we make in the presence of Almighty God, the Searcher of all hearts, with a true intention to perform the same, as we shall answer at that Great Day when the secrets of all hearts shall be disclosed: most humbly beseeching the Lord to strengthen us by His Holy Spirit for this end, and to bless our desires and proceedings with such success as may be a deliverance and safety to His people, and encouragement to the Christian Churches groaning under or in danger of the yoke of Antichristian tyranny, to join in the same or like association and covenant, to the glory of God, the enlargement of the kingdom of Jesus Christ, and the peace and tranquillity of Christian kingdoms and commonwealths.

---

208. Ordinance appointing the First Committee of both Kingdoms

(164¾, February 16. Cobbett's Parliamentary History, iii. 248. Gardiner, 271–273.)

WHEREAS, by the covenant and treaty ratified and established between the two kingdoms of England and Scotland, both nations are engaged in one common cause against the enemies of their religion and liberties, and, by the late entrance of the Scottish forces into this kingdom in pursuance hereof, are firmly united in a joint posture of arms for their own necessary defence, and for the attaining of the ends expressed in the covenant and treaty :

And whereas both kingdoms have thought it necessary that they should be joined in their counsels as well as in their forces, and, in pursuance thereof, the Convention of the Estates of Scotland have appointed Committees, residing in Scotland and in the Scottish army, and have sent some of the said Committees as Commissioners for the purposes aforesaid, to repair unto and to reside near the Parliament, who, since their arrival, have presented their commission and powers, with their earnest desire that the Parliament would lay down some speedy and constant way of communicating the desires and joining the counsels of both kingdoms, in pursuance of the covenant, treaty and common interests of His Majesty's dominions.

In consideration hereof, the Lords and Commons do nominate, ordain and appoint Algernon, Earl of Northumberland, Robert, Earl of Essex (Lord General), Robert, Earl of Warwick (Lord Admiral), Edward, Earl of Manchester, William, Viscount Say and Sele, Philip, Lord Wharton, John, Lord Robarts, William Pierpoint, Sir Henry Vane (senior), Sir Philip Stapleton, Sir William Waller, Sir Gilbert Gerrard, Sir William Armyne, Sir Arthur Haslerigg, Sir Henry Vane (junior), John Crewe, Robert Wallop, Oliver St. John (Solicitor-General), Oliver Cromwell, Samuel Browne and John Glynn (Recorder), or any six of them, whereof one Lord and two Commoners, to treat with the Committees and Commissioners appointed by our brethren of Scotland, in such things as shall by them be propounded from and in the name of the kingdom of Scotland, for the ends aforesaid ; as likewise to propound to the Committees and Commissioners of Scotland whatever they shall receive in charge from both Houses, and, from time to time, to advise and consult concerning the same, and report the results to both Houses.

And further power and authority is hereby given to them, or any six of them, whereof one Lord and two Commoners, as a joint Committee with the Committees and Commissioners of Scotland, to advise, consult, order and direct, concerning the carrying on and managing of the war for the best advantage of the three kingdoms, and the keeping a good intelligence between the three kingdoms, their forces, committees and counsels ; and likewise with power to hold good correspondence and intelligence with foreign States ; and further to advise and consult of all things in pursuance of the ends in the covenant and treaty.

Provided always, that nothing in this Ordinance shall authorise
the Committee hereby appointed to advise, treat or consult concerning any cessation of arms or making peace, without express
directions from both Houses of Parliament.

And lastly, the said Committee are to observe such orders and
directions as they, from time to time, shall receive from both
Houses of Parliament; provided also, that this Ordinance shall
continue for three months and no longer.

---◆---

209. The Self-denying Ordinance

1645, April 4.   Rushworth, vi. 16.   Gardiner, 287, 288.)

BE it ordained by the Lords and Commons assembled in Parliament, that all and every of the members of either House of
Parliament shall be, and by authority of this Ordinance are, discharged at the end of forty days after the passing of this Ordinance,
of and from all and every office or command military or civil,
granted or conferred by both or either of the said Houses of this
present Parliament, or by any authority derived from both or
either of them since the 20th day of November, 1640.

And be it further ordained, that all other governors and com-
manders of an island, town, castle or fort, and all other colonels
and officers inferior to colonels in the several armies, not being
members of either of the Houses of Parliament, shall, according to
their respective commissions, continue in their several places and
commands, wherein they were employed and intrusted the 20th
day of March, 1644, as if this Ordinance had not been made.
And that the vice-admiral, rear-admiral, and all other captains and
other inferior officers in the fleet, shall, according to their several
and respective commissions, continue in their several places and
commands, wherein they were employed and entrusted the said
20th day of March, as if this Ordinance had not been made.

Provided always, and it is further ordained and declared, that
during this war, the benefit of all offices, being neither military nor
judicial, hereafter to be granted, or any way to be appointed to
any person or persons by both or either House of Parliament, or
by authority derived from thence, shall go and inure to such public uses as both Houses of Parliament shall appoint.   And the
grantees and persons executing all such offices shall be accountable to the Parliament for all the profits and perquisites thereof,

and shall have no profit out of any such office, other than a competent salary for the execution of the same, in such manner as both Houses of Parliament shall order and ordain.

Provided that this Ordinance shall not extend to take away the power and authority of any Lieutenancy or Deputy-Lieutenancy in the several counties, cities or places, or of any *Custos Rotulorum*, or of any commission for Justice of Peace, or sewers, or any commission of *Oyer* and *Terminer*, or gaol-delivery.

Provided always, and it is hereby declared, that those members of either House who had offices by grant from His Majesty before this Parliament, and were by His Majesty displaced sitting this Parliament, and have since by authority of both Houses been restored, shall not by this Ordinance be discharged from their said offices or profits thereof, but shall enjoy the same ; anything in this Ordinance to the contrary thereof notwithstanding.

---

210. Act erecting a High Court of Justice for the Trial of Charles I

(Passed the Commons, January 6, 164⅞.   Rushworth, viii. 1379.)

WHEREAS it is notorious that Charles Stuart, the now King of England, not content with those many encroachments which his predecessors had made upon the people in their rights and freedoms, hath had a wicked design totally to subvert the ancient and fundamental laws and liberties of this nation, and in their place to introduce an arbitrary and tyrannical government, and that besides all other evil ways and means to bring this design to pass, he hath prosecuted it with fire and sword, levied and maintained a civil war in the land, against the Parliament and kingdom ; whereby the country hath been miserably wasted, the public treasure exhausted, trade decayed, thousands of people murdered, and infinite other mischiefs committed ; for all which high and treasonable offences the said Charles Stuart might long since justly have been brought to exemplary and condign punishment: whereas also the Parliament, well hoping that the restraint and imprisonment of his person, after it had pleased God to deliver him into their hands, would have quieted the distempers of the kingdom, did forbear to proceed judicially against him, but found, by sad experience, that such their remissness served only to encourage him and his accomplices in the continuance of their evil practices, and in raising new commotions, rebellions and invasions : for prevention therefore of the like or greater inconveniences, and to the end no Chief Officer or Magistrate whatsoever may hereafter presume, traitorously and maliciously, to imagine or contrive the enslaving or destroying of the English nation, and to expect impunity for so doing ; be it enacted and ordained by the Commons in Parliament and it is hereby enacted and ordained by the authority thereof, that Thomas, Lord Fairfax, Oliver Cromwell, Henry Ireton [* * * 135 names in all], shall be and are hereby appointed and required to be Commissioners and Judges for the hearing, trying and adjudging of the said Charles Stuart ; and the said Commissioners, or any twenty or more of them, shall be, and are hereby authorised and constituted an High Court of Justice, to meet and sit at such convenient time and place as by the said Commissioners, or the major part of twenty or more of them, under their hands and seals, shall be appointed and notified by public proclamation in the Great Hall or Palace Yard of Westminster ; and to adjourn from time to time, and from place to place, as the said High Court, or the major part thereof meeting, shall hold fit ; and to take order for the charging of him, the said Charles Stuart, with the crimes and treasons above mentioned, and for receiving his personal answer thereunto, and for examination of witnesses upon oath (which the Court hath hereby authority to administer) or otherwise, and taking any other evidence concerning the same ; and thereupon, or in default of such answer, to proceed to final sentence according to justice and the merit of the cause ; and such final sentence to execute, or cause be to executed, speedily and impartially.

And the said Court is hereby authorised and required to appoint and direct all such officers, attendants and other circumstances as they, or the major part of them, shall in any sort judge necessary or useful for the orderly and good managing of the premises. And Thomas, Lord Fairfax, the General, and all officers and soldiers under his command, and all officers of justice, and other well-affected persons, are hereby authorised and required to be aiding and assisting unto the said Court in the due execution of the trust hereby committed. Provided that this Act, and the authority hereby granted, do continue in force for the space of one month from the date of the making hereof, and no longer.

211. Sentence of the High Court of Justice upon Charles I

(164$\frac{8}{9}$, January 27.   Rushworth, viii. 1420.   Gardiner, 377-380.)

WHEREAS the Commons of England assembled in Parliament, have by their late Act entitled ' An Act of the Commons of England, assembled in Parliament, for erecting an High Court of Justice for the trying and judging of Charles Stuart, King of England,' authorised and constituted us an High Court of Justice for the trying and judging of the said Charles Stuart for the crimes and treasons in the said Act mentioned ; by virtue whereof the said Charles Stuart hath been three several times convented before this High Court, where the first day, being Saturday, the 20th of January, instant, in pursuance of the said Act, a charge of high treason and other high crimes was, in the behalf of the people of England, exhibited against him, and read openly unto him, wherein he was charged, that he, the said Charles Stuart, being admitted King of England, and therein trusted with a limited power to govern by, and according to the law of the land, and not otherwise ; and by his trust, oath, and office, being obliged to use the power committed to him for the good and benefit of the people, and for the preservation of their rights and liberties ; yet, nevertheless, out of a wicked design to erect and uphold in himself an unlimited and tyrannical power to rule according to his will, and to overthrow the rights and liberties of the people, and to take away and make void the foundations thereof, and of all redress and remedy of misgovernment, which by the fundamental constitutions of this kingdom were reserved on the people's behalf in the right and power of frequent and successive Parliaments, or national meetings in Council; he, the said Charles Stuart, for accomplishment of such his designs, and for the protecting of himself and his adherents in his and their wicked practices, to the same end hath traitorously and maliciously levied war against the present Parliament and people therein represented, as with the circumstances of time and place is in the said charge more particularly set forth ; and that he hath thereby caused and procured many thousands of the free people of this nation to be slain ; and by divisions, parties, and insurrections within this land, by invasions from foreign parts, endeavoured and procured by him, and by many other evil ways and means, he, the said Charles Stuart, hath not only maintained and carried on the said war both by sea and land, but also hath renewed, or caused to be renewed, the said war against the Parliament and good people of this nation in this present year 1648, in several counties and places in this kingdom in the charge specified ; and that he hath for that purpose given his commission to his son, the Prince, and others, whereby, besides multitudes of other persons, many such as were by the Parliament entrusted and employed for the safety of this nation, being by him or his agents corrupted, to the betraying of their trust, and revolting from the Parliament, have had entertainment and commission for the continuing and renewing of the war and hostility against the said Parliament and people : and that by the said cruel and unnatural war so levied, continued and renewed, much innocent blood of the free people of this nation hath been spilt, many families undone, the public treasure wasted, trade obstructed and miserably decayed, vast expense and damage to the nation incurred, and many parts of the land spoiled, some of them even to desolation ; and that he still continues his commission to his said son, and other rebels and revolters, both English and foreigners, and to the Earl of Ormond, and to the Irish rebels and revolters associated with him, from whom further invasions of this land are threatened by his procurement and on his behalf ; and that all the said wicked designs, wars, and evil practices of him, the said Charles Stuart, were still carried on for the advancement and upholding of the personal interest of will, power, and pretended prerogative to himself and his family, against the public interest, common right, liberty, justice, and peace of the people of this nation : and that he thereby hath been and is the occasioner, author, and continuer of the said unnatural, cruel, and bloody wars, and therein guilty of all the treasons, murders, rapines, burnings, spoils, desolations, damage, and mischief to this nation, acted and committed in the said wars, or occasioned thereby ; whereupon the proceedings and judgment of this Court were prayed against him, as a tyrant, traitor, and murderer, and public enemy to the Commonwealth, as by the said charge more fully appeareth. To which charge, being read unto him as aforesaid, he, the said Charles Stuart, was required to give his answer ; but he refused so to do ; and upon Monday, the 22nd day of January instant, being again brought before this Court, and there required to answer directly to the said charge, he still refused so to do ; whereupon his default and contumacy was entered ; and the next day, being the third time brought before the Court, judgment was then prayed against him on the behalf of the people of England for his contumacy, and for the matters contained against him in the said charge, as taking the same for confessed, in regard of his refusing to answer thereto.   Yet notwithstanding this Court (not willing to take advantage of his contempt) did once more require him to answer to the said charge ; but he again refused so to do ; upon which his several defaults, this Court might justly have proceeded to judgment against him, both for his contumacy and the matters of the charge, taking the same for confessed as aforesaid.

Yet nevertheless this Court, for its own clearer information and further satisfaction, have thought fit to examine witnesses upon oath, and take notice of other evidences, touching the matters contained in the said charge, which accordingly they have done.

Now, therefore, upon serious and mature deliberation of the premises, and consideration had of the notoriety of the matters of fact charged upon him as aforesaid, this Court is in judgment and conscience satisfied that he, the said Charles Stuart, is guilty of levying war against the said Parliament and people, and maintaining and continuing the same ; for which in the said charge he stands accused, and by the general course of his government, counsels, and practices, before and since this Parliament began (which have been and are notorious and public, and the effects whereof remain abundantly upon record) this Court is fully satisfied in their judgments and consciences, that he has been and is guilty of the wicked designs and endeavours in the said charge set forth ; and that the said war hath been levied, maintained, and continued by him as aforesaid, in prosecution, and for accomplishment of the said designs ; and that he hath been and is the occasioner, author, and continuer of the said unnatural, cruel, and bloody wars, and therein guilty of high treason, and of the murders, rapines, burnings, spoils, desolations, damage, and mischief to this nation acted and committed in the said war, and occasioned thereby.   For all which treasons and crimes this Court doth adjudge that he, the said Charles Stuart, as a tyrant, traitor, murderer, and public enemy to the good people of this nation, shall be put to death by the severing of his head from his body.

212. The Death Warrant of Charles I

(164⅘, January 29.   Rushworth, viii. 1426.   Gardiner, 380.)

*At the High Court of Justice for the trying and judging of Charles
Stuart, King of England, Jan. 29, Anno Domini 1648.*

WHEREAS Charles Stuart, King of England, is, and standeth
convicted, attainted, and condemned of high treason, and
other high crimes ; and sentence upon Saturday last was pronounced
against him by this Court, to be put to death by the severing of his
head from his body ; of which sentence, execution yet remaineth to
be done : these are therefore to will and require you to see the said
sentence executed in the open street before Whitehall, upon the
morrow, being the thirtieth day of this instant month of January,
between the hours of ten in the morning and five in the afternoon
of the same day, with full effect.   And for so doing this shall be
your sufficient warrant.   And these are to require all officers, soldiers, and others, the good people of this nation of England, to be
assisting unto you in this service.

To Col. Francis Hacker, Col. Huncks, and Lieut-Col. Phayre,
and to every of them.

Given under our hands and seals.

JOHN BRADSHAW.

THOMAS GREY.

OLIVER CROMWELL.

[* * * 59 names in all.]

---

213. Act appointing a Council of State

(164⅘, February 13, 14.   Cobbett's Parliamentary History, iii. 1288.   Gardiner
381–383.)

BE it ordained and enacted by this present Parliament that Basil,
Earl of Denbigh, Edmund, Earl of Mulgrave [* * * 41
names in all], or any nine of them, shall be a Council of State,
and have hereby power, and are authorised to put in execution
the following instructions.

1. You are hereby authorised and required to oppose and suppress whomsoever shall endeavour or go about to set up or main-

tain the pretended title of Charles Stuart, eldest son to the late King, or any other of the said late King's issue, or claiming under him or them, or the pretended title or claim of any other single person whomsoever to the Crown of England or Ireland, dominion of Wales, or to any of the dominions or territories to them or either of them belonging.

2. You are hereby authorised and empowered to order and direct all the militias and forces both by sea and land of England and Ireland and the dominions to them or either of them belonging, for preserving the peace or safety thereof, and for preventing, resisting, and suppressing all tumults and insurrections that shall happen to rise in them or either of them, or any invasions of them from abroad : and also upon any emergencies to raise and arm such forces as you shall judge necessary for the ends above expressed ; and to give commissions under the seal of the Council to such officers as you shall judge necessary for the leading, conducting and commanding of the said forces ; and for the prosecution and pursuance of these instructions, or of any other instructions you shall receive from the Parliament.

3. You are hereby authorised and required to use all good ways and means for the reducing of Ireland, the isles of Jersey, Guernsey, Scilly, and the Isle of Man, and all other parts and places belonging to the Commonwealth of England, not yet reduced.

4. You shall take care that the stores and magazines of all military provisions both for the land service and for the sea be from time to time well and sufficiently furnished, and that the same be issued as you shall by warrant direct : and you are also from time to time to take care of the repair of the shipping belonging to the Commonwealth, and to build such others as you shall judge necessary for the defence and safety thereof.

5. You are to use all good ways and means for the securing, advancement, and encouragement of the trade of England and Ireland and the dominions to them belonging, and to promote the good of all foreign plantations and factories belonging to this Commonwealth or any of the natives thereof.

6. You shall advise, order, and direct concerning the entertaining, keeping, renewing, or settling of amity and a good correspondency with foreign kingdoms and states, and for preserving the rights of the people of this nation in foreign parts, and composing of their differences there : and you are hereby authorised to send ambassadors, agents, or messengers to any foreign kingdom or state, and to receive ambassadors, agents, or messengers from them for the ends aforesaid.

7. You are to advise and consult of anything concerning the good of this Commonwealth, and report your opinions concerning the same as you find occasion to the Parliament.

8. You are hereby authorised to send for any person or persons whatsoever to advise with them in pursuance of these or any other instructions that shall be given unto you.

9. You have hereby power and are authorised to send for any records, writings, accounts, books, or papers, that you shall think fit for your information in any cause, matter or thing in agitation before you, in pursuance of these or any other instructions that shall be given you by the Parliament.

10. You have hereby power and are authorised in case of danger to the Commonwealth to administer an oath to any person or persons for the discovery of the truth.

11. You are hereby authorised and empowered to send for and imprison or otherwise to secure by taking bond in recognizance any such person or persons as shall be offenders against these or any other instructions which you shall receive from the Parliament; and all such as shall contemn or be refractory to any of your commands, directions, or orders in pursuance of the said instructions.

12. You have hereby power and are authorised to charge the public revenue by warrant under the seal of the Council with such sum or sums of money, from time to time as you shall find necessary, for defraying all charges of foreign negotiations, intelligence, and other incidencies; and for the salary of such subordinate officers and attendants as you shall judge fit to employ, and for the effectual carrying on of the service by these instructions committed to you, or by any other instructions hereafter to be given you from the Parliament.

13. You are also to observe and put in execution such further orders as you shall receive from time to time from the Parliament.

14. The power hereby committed to the Council of State shall continue for the space of one year from the day of passing hereof, unless it be otherwise ordered by the Parliament.

15. You have also hereby power to appoint committees or any person or persons for examinations, receiving of informations, and preparing of business for your debates or resolutions.

16. You are to meet at Derby House at four of the clock this afternoon, and from time to time and from place to place as you shall see cause, and in such manner as you shall think fit for the execution of your instructions.

214. Act abolishing the Office of King

(164⅘, March 17.   Scobell, ii. 7.   Gardiner, 384–387.)

WHEREAS Charles Stuart, late King of England, Ireland, and
the territories and dominions thereunto belonging, hath by
authority derived from Parliament been and is hereby declared to
be justly condemned, adjudged to die, and put to death, for many
treasons, murders, and other heinous offences committed by him,
by which judgment he stood, and is hereby declared to be, attainted
of high treason, whereby his issue and posterity, and all others
pretending title under him, are become incapable of the said
Crown, or of being King or Queen of the said kingdom or
dominions, or either or any of them ; be it therefore enacted and
ordained, and it is enacted, ordained, and declared by this present
Parliament, and by authority thereof, that all the people of England
and Ireland, and the dominions and territories thereunto belonging, of what degree or condition soever, are discharged of all fealty,
homage, and allegiance which is or shall be pretended to be due
unto any of the issue and posterity of the said late King, or any
claiming under him ; and that Charles Stuart, eldest son, and
James, called Duke of York, second son, and all other the issue
and posterity of him the said late King, and all and every person
and persons pretending title from, by, or under him, are and be
disabled to hold or enjoy the said Crown of England and Ireland,
and other the dominions thereunto belonging, or any of them ; or
to have the name, title, style, or dignity of King or Queen of England and Ireland, Prince of Wales, or any of them ; or to have and
enjoy the power and dominion of the said kingdom and dominions,
or any of them, or the honours, manors, lands, tenements, possessions, and hereditaments belonging or appertaining to the said
Crown of England and Ireland, and other the dominions aforesaid,
or to any of them ; or to the Principality of Wales, Duchy of Lancaster or Cornwall, or any or either of them, any law, statute,
ordinance, usage, or custom to the contrary hereof in any wise
notwithstanding.

II. And whereas it is and hath been found by experience, that
the office of a King in this nation and Ireland, and to have the
power thereof in any single person, is unnecessary, burdensome,
and dangerous to the liberty, safety, and public interest of the
people, and that for the most part, use hath been made of the
regal power and prerogative to oppress and impoverish and enslave

the subject; and that usually and naturally any one person in such power makes it his interest to encroach upon the just freedom and liberty of the people, and to promote the setting up of their own will and power above the laws, that so they might enslave these kingdoms to their own lust; be it therefore enacted and ordained by this present Parliament, and by authority of the same, that the office of a King in this nation shall not henceforth reside in or be exercised by any one single person; and that no one person whatsoever shall or may have, or hold the office, style, dignity, power, or authority of King of the said kingdoms and dominions, or any of them, or of the Prince of Wales, any law, statute, usage, or custom to the contrary thereof in any wise notwithstanding.

III. And it is hereby enacted, that if any person or persons shall endeavour to attempt by force of arms or otherwise, or be aiding, assisting, comforting, or abetting unto any person or persons that shall by any ways or means whatsoever endeavour or attempt the reviving or setting up again of any pretended right of the said Charles, eldest son to the said late King, James called Duke of York, or of any other the issue and posterity of the said late King, or of any person or persons claiming under him or them, to the said regal office, style, dignity, or authority, or to be Prince of Wales; or the promoting of any one person whatsoever to the name, style, dignity, power, prerogative, or authority of King of England and Ireland, and dominions aforesaid, or any of them; that then every such offence shall be deemed and adjudged high treason, and the offenders therein, their counsellors, procurers, aiders and abettors, being convicted of the said offence, or any of them, shall be deemed and adjudged traitors against the Parliament and people of England, and shall suffer, lose, and forfeit, and have such like and the same pains, forfeitures, judgments, and execution as is used in case of high treason.

IV. And whereas by the abolition of the kingly office provided for in this Act, a most happy way is made for this nation (if God see it good) to return to its just and ancient right, of being governed by its own Representatives or national meetings in council, from time to time chosen and entrusted for that purpose by the people, it is therefore resolved and declared by the Commons assembled in Parliament, that they will put a period to the sitting of this present Parliament, and dissolve the same so soon, as may possibly stand with the safety of the people that hath betrusted them, and with what is absolutely necessary for the preserving and upholding the Government now settled in the way of a Commonwealth; and that they will carefully provide for the certain choosing, meeting, and sitting of the next and future Representatives, with such other circumstances of freedom in choice and equality in distribution of members to be elected thereunto, as shall most conduce to the lasting freedom and good of this Commonwealth.

V. And it is hereby further enacted and declared, notwithstanding anything contained in this Act, no person or persons of what condition and quality soever, within the commonwealth of England and Ireland, dominion of Wales, the islands of Guernsey and Jersey, and town of Berwick-upon-Tweed, shall be discharged from the obedience and subjection which he and they owe to the Government of this nation, as it is now declared, but all and every of them shall in all things render aud perform the same, as of right is due unto the supreme authority hereby declared to reside in this and the successive Representatives of the people of this nation, and in them only.

----◆----

215. Act abolishing the House of Lords

(164⅘, March 19.   Scobell, ii. 8.   Gardiner, 387, 388.)

THE Commons of England assembled in Parliament, finding by too long experience that the House of Lords is useless and dangerous to the people of England to be continued, have thought fit to ordain and enact, and be it ordained and enacted by this present Parliament, and by the authority of the same, that from henceforth the House of Lords in Parliament shall be and is hereby wholly abolished and taken away; and that the Lords shall not from henceforth meet or sit in the said House called the Lords' House, or in any other house or place whatsoever, as a House of Lords; nor shall sit, vote, advise, adjudge, or determine of any matter or thing whatsoever, as a House of Lords in Parliament: nevertheless it is hereby declared, that neither such Lords as have demeaned themselves with honour, courage, and fidelity to the Commonwealth, nor their posterities who shall continue so, shall be excluded from the public councils of the nation, but shall be admitted thereunto, and have their free vote in Parliament, if they shall be thereunto elected, as other persons of interest elected and qualified thereunto ought to have.

II. And be it further ordained and enacted by the authority aforesaid, that no Peer of this land, not being elected, qualified and sitting in Parliament as aforesaid, shall claim, have, or make use of any privilege of Parliament, either in relation to his person, quality, or estate, any law, usage, or custom to the contrary notwithstanding.

---

216. Act declaring England to be a Commonwealth

(1649, May 19. Scobell, ii. 30. Gardiner, 388.)

BE it declared and enacted by this present Parliament, and by the authority of the same, that the people of England, and of all the dominions and territories thereunto belonging, are and shall be, and are hereby constituted, made, established, and confirmed, to be a Commonwealth and Free State, and shall from henceforth be governed as a Commonwealth and Free State by the supreme authority of this nation, the representatives of the people in Parliament, and by such as they shall appoint and constitute as officers and ministers under them for the good of the people, and that without any King or House of Lords.

---

217. Act declaring what Offences shall be adjudged Treason under the Commonwealth

(1650, July 17. Scobell, ii. 65. Gardiner, 388–391.)

WHEREAS the Parliament hath abolished the kingly office in England and Ireland, and in the dominions and territories thereunto belonging; and having resolved and declared, that the people shall for the future be governed by its own Representatives or national meetings in Council, chosen and entrusted by them for that purpose, hath settled the Government in the way of a Commonwealth and Free State, without King or House of Lords: be it enacted by this present Parliament, and by the authority of the same, that if any person shall maliciously or advisedly publish, by writing, printing, or openly declaring, that the said Government is tyrannical, usurped, or unlawful; or that the Commons in Parliament assembled are not the supreme authority of this nation; or shall plot, contrive, or endeavour to stir up, or raise force against the present Government, or for the subversion or alteration of the same, and shall declare the same by any open deed, that then every such offence shall be taken, deemed, and adjudged by authority of this Parliament to be high treason.

II. And whereas the Keepers of the liberty of England, and the Council of State, constituted, and to be from time to time constituted, by authority of Parliament, are to be under the said representatives in Parliament entrusted for the maintenance of the said Government with several powers and authorities limited, given, and appointed unto them by the Parliament : be it likewise enacted by the authority aforesaid, that if any person shall maliciously and advisedly plot or endeavour the subversion of the said Keepers of the liberty of England, or the Council of State, and the same shall declare by any open deed, or shall move any person or persons for the doing thereof, or stir up the people to rise against them, or either of them, their or either of their authorities, that then every such offence and offences shall be taken, deemed, and declared to be high treason.

III. And whereas the Parliament, for their just and lawful defence, hath raised and levied the army and forces now under the command of Thomas, Lord Fairfax, and are at present necessitated, by reason of the manifold distractions within this Commonwealth, and invasions threatened from abroad, to continue the same, which under God must be the instrumental means of preserving the well-affected people of this nation in peace and safety ; be it further enacted by the authority aforesaid, that if any person, not being an officer, soldier, or member of the army, shall plot, contrive, or endeavour to stir up any mutiny in the said army, or withdraw any soldiers or officers from their obedience to their superior officers, or from the present Government as aforesaid ; or shall procure, invite, aid, or assist any foreigners or strangers to invade England or Ireland ; or shall adhere to any forces raised by the enemies of the Parliament or Commonwealth, or Keepers of the liberty of England ; or if any person shall counterfeit the Great Seal of England, for the time being, used and appointed by authority of Parliament ; that then every such offence and offences shall be taken, deemed, and declared by authority of this Parliament to be high treason, and every such persons shall suffer pains of death ; and also forfeit unto the Keepers of the liberty of England, to and for the use of the Commonwealth, all and singular his and their lands, tenements and hereditaments, goods and chattels, as in case of high treason hath been used by the laws and statutes of this land to be forfeit and lost.

IV. Provided always, that no persons shall be indicted and

2 D

arraigned for any of the offences mentioned in this Act, unless such offenders shall be indicted and prosecuted for the same within one year after the offence committed.

V. And be it further enacted by the authority aforesaid, that if any person shall counterfeit the money of this Commonwealth, or shall bring any false money into this land, counterfeit or other, like to the money of this Commonwealth, knowing the money to be false, to merchandise or make payment, in deceit of the people of this nation ; or if any person shall hereafter falsely forge and counterfeit any such kind of coin of gold or silver, as is not the proper coin of this Commonwealth, and is or shall be current within this nation, by consent of the Parliament, or such as shall be by them authorised thereunto ; or shall bring from the parts beyond the seas into this Commonwealth, or into any the dominions of the same, any such false and counterfeit coin of money, being current within the same, as is above said, knowing the same money to be false and counterfeit, to the intent to utter or make payment with the same within this Commonwealth, by merchandise or otherwise ; or if any person shall impair, diminish, falsify, clip, wash, round or file, scale or lighten, for wicked lucre or gain's sake, any the proper monies or coins of this Commonwealth, or the dominions thereof, or of the monies or coins of any other realm, allowed and suffered to be current within this Commonwealth, or the dominions thereof, that then all and every such offences above-mentioned, shall be and are hereby deemed and adjudged high treason, and the offenders therein, their counsellors, procurers, aiders and abettors, being convicted according to the laws of this nation of any of the said offences, shall be deemed and adjudged traitors against this Commonwealth, and shall suffer and have such pains of death and forfeitures, as in case of high treason is used and ordained.

VI. Provided always, and be it enacted by the authority aforesaid, that this Act touching the monies and coins aforesaid, or anything therein contained, nor any attainder of any person for the same, shall in any wise extend or be judged to make any corruption of blood to any the heir or heirs of any such offender, or to make the wife of any such offender to lose or forfeit her dower, of or in any lands, tenements, or hereditaments, or her title, action, or interest in the same.

218. Declaration by Oliver Cromwell and the Council of Officers after putting an End to the Long Parliament

(1653, April 22. Cobbett's Parliamentary History, iii. 1386. Gardiner, 400-404.)

OUR intention is not to give an account, at this time, of the grounds which first moved us to take up arms, and engage our lives and all that was dear unto us in this cause ; nor to mind, in this declaration, the various dispensations through which Divine Providence hath led us, or the witness the Lord hath borne, and the many signal testimonies of acceptance which He hath given, to the sincere endeavours of His unworthy servants, whilst they were contesting with the many and great difficulties, as well in the wars, as other transactions in the three nations ; being necessitated, for the defence of the same cause they first asserted, to have re-course unto extraordinary actions, the same being evident by former declarations published on that behalf.

After it had pleased God not only to reduce Ireland and give in Scotland, but so marvellously to appear for His people at Worcester, that these nations were reduced to a great degree of peace, and England to perfect quiet, and thereby the Parliament had opportunity to give the people the harvest of all their labour, blood, and treasure, and to settle a due liberty both in reference to civil and spiritual things, whereunto they were obliged by their duty, their engagements, as also the great and wonderful things which God hath wrought for them ; it was matter of much grief to the good and well-affected of the land to observe the little progress which was made therein, who thereupon applied to the army, ex-pecting redress by their means ; notwithstanding which, the army being unwilling to meddle with the civil authority in matters so properly appertaining to it, it was agreed, that his Excellency and officers of the army which were members of Parliament, should be desired to move the Parliament to proceed vigorously in reforming what was amiss in government, and to the settling of the Common-wealth upon a foundation of justice and righteousness ; which hav-ing done, we hoped that the Parliament would seasonably have answered our expectation : but finding, to our grief, delays therein, we renewed our desires in an humble petition to them, which was presented in August last ; and although they at that time, signifying their good acceptance thereof, returned us thanks and referred the particulars thereof to a Committee of the House, yet no considerable effect was produced, nor any such progress made, as might imply their real intentions to accomplish what was petitioned for : but, on the contrary, there more and more appeared amongst them an aversion to the things themselves, with much bitterness and opposition to the people of God, and His spirit acting in them ; which grew so prevalent, that those persons of honour and integrity amongst them, who had eminently appeared for God and the public good, both before and throughout this war, were rendered of no further use in Parliament, than by meeting with a corrupt party to give them countenance to carry on their ends, and for effecting the desire they had of perpetuating themselves in the supreme government, for which purpose the said party long opposed, and frequently declared themselves against having a new Representative : and when they saw themselves necessitated to take that Bill into consideration, they resolved to make use of it to recruit the House with persons of the same spirit and temper, thereby to perpetuate their own sitting ; which intention divers of the activest amongst them did manifest, labouring to persuade others to a consent therein : and the better to effect this, divers petitions, preparing from several counties for the continuance of this Parliament, were encouraged, if not set on foot, by many of them.

For obviating of these evils, the officers of the Army obtained several meetings with some of the Parliament, to consider what fitting means and remedy might be applied to prevent the same : but such endeavours proving altogether ineffectual, it became most evident to the Army, as they doubt not it also is to all considering persons, that this Parliament, through the corruption of some, the jealousy of others, the non-attendance and negligence of many, would never answer those ends which God, His people, and the whole nation expected from them ; but that this cause, which the Lord hath so greatly blessed and borne witness to, must needs languish under their hands, and, by degrees, be wholly lost ; and the lives, liberties, and comforts of His people delivered into their enemies' hands.

All which being sadly and seriously considered by the honest people of this nation, as well as by the Army, and wisdom and direction being sought from the Lord, it seemed to be a duty incumbent upon us, who had seen so much of the power and presence of God going along with us, to consider of some more effectual means to secure the cause which the good people of this

Commonwealth had been so long engaged in, and to establish righteousness and peace in these nations.

And after much debate it was judged necessary, and agreed upon, that the supreme authority should be, by the Parliament, devolved upon known persons, men fearing God, and of approved integrity; and the government of the Commonwealth committed unto them for a time, as the most hopeful way to encourage and countenance all God's people, reform the law, and administer justice impartially; hoping thereby the people might forget Monarchy, and, understanding their true interest in the election of successive Parliaments, may have the government settled upon a true basis, without hazard to this glorious cause, or necessitating to keep up armies for the defence of the same. And being still resolved to use all means possible to avoid extraordinary courses, we prevailed with about twenty members of Parliament to give us a conference, with whom we freely and plainly debated the necessity and justness of our proposals on that behalf; and did evidence that those, and not the Act under their consideration, would most probably bring forth something answerable to that work, the foundation whereof God Himself hath laid, and is now carrying on in the world.

The which, notwithstanding, found no acceptance; but, instead thereof, it was offered, that the way was to continue still this present Parliament, as being that from which we might reasonably expect all good things: and this being vehemently insisted upon, did much confirm us in our apprehensions, that not any love to a Representative, but the making use thereof to recruit, and so perpetuate themselves, was their aim.

They being plainly dealt with about this, and told that neither the nation, the honest interest, nor we ourselves would be deluded by such dealings, they did agree to meet again the next day in the afternoon for mutual satisfaction; it being consented unto by the members present that endeavours should be used that nothing in the mean time should be done in Parliament that might exclude or frustrate the proposals before mentioned.

Notwithstanding this, the next morning the Parliament did make more haste than usual in carrying on their said Act, being helped on therein by some of the persons engaged to us the night before; none of them which were then present endeavouring to oppose the same; and being ready to put the main question for consummating the said Act, whereby our aforesaid proposals would have been rendered void, and the way of bringing them into a fair and full debate in Parliament obstructed; for preventing thereof, and all the sad and evil consequences which must, upon the grounds aforesaid, have ensued ; and whereby, at one blow, the interest of all honest men and of this glorious cause had been in danger to be laid in the dust, and these nations embroiled in new troubles, at a time when our enemies abroad are watching all advantages against us, and some of them actually engaged in war with us, we have been necessitated, though with much reluctancy, to put an end to this Parliament ; which yet we have done, we hope, out of an honest heart, preferring this cause above our names, lives, families, or interests, how dear soever ; with clear intentions and real purposes of heart, to call to the government persons of approved fidelity and honesty ; believing that as no wise men will expect to gather grapes of thorns, so good men will hope, that if persons so qualified be chosen, the fruits of a just and righteous reformation, so long prayed and wished for, will, by the blessing of God, be in due time obtained, to the refreshing of all those good hearts who have been panting after those things.

Much more might have been said, if it had been our desire to justify ourselves by aspersing others, and raking into the misgovernment of affairs ; but we shall conclude with this, that as we have been led by necessity and Providence to act as we have done, even beyond and above our own thoughts and desires, so we shall and do, in that part of this great work which is behind, put ourselves wholly upon the Lord for a blessing ; professing, we look not to stand one day without His support, much less to bring to pass any of the things mentioned and desired, without His assistance ; and therefore do solemnly desire and expect that all men, as they would not provoke the Lord to their own destruction, should wait for such issue as He should bring forth, and to follow their business with peaceable spirits, wherein we promise them protection by His assistance.

And for those who profess their fear and love to the name of God, that seeing in a great measure for their sakes, and for righteousness' sake, we have taken our lives in our hands to do these things, they would be instant with the Lord day and night on our behalfs, that we may obtain grace from Him ; and seeing we have made so often mention of His name, that we may not do the least dishonour thereunto : which indeed would be our confusion, and a stain to the whole profession of Godliness.

We beseech them also to live in all humility, meekness, righteousness, and love one toward another, and towards all men, that so they may put to silence the ignorance of the foolish, who falsely accuse them, and to know that the late great and glorious dispen-

sations, wherein the Lord hath so wonderfully appeared in bring
ing forth these things by the travail and blood of His children,
ought to oblige them so to walk in the wisdom and love of Christ,
as may cause others to honour their holy profession, because they
see Christ to be in them of a truth.

We do further purpose, before it be long, more particularly to
show the grounds of our proceedings, and the reasons of this late
great action and change, which in this we have but hinted at.

And we do lastly declare, that all Judges, Sheriffs, Justices of
the Peace, Mayors, Bailiffs, Committees, and Commissioners, and
all other civil officers and public ministers whatsoever, within this
Commonwealth, or any parts thereof, do proceed in their respective places and offices ; and all persons whatsoever are to give
obedience to them as fully as when Parliament was sitting.

Signed in the name, and by the appointment, of his Excellency
the Lord General and his Council of Officers.

WILL. MALYN, Secretary.

---

219. The Instrument of Government

(1653, December 16. Cobbett's Parliamentary History, iii. 1417. The whole
reprinted in Gardiner, 405-417.)

THE government of the Commonwealth of England, Scotland,
and Ireland, and the dominions thereunto belonging :

I. That the supreme legislative authority of the Commonwealth
of England, Scotland, and Ireland, and the dominions thereunto
belonging, shall be and reside in one person, and the people
assembled in Parliament ; the style of which person shall be the
Lord Protector of the Commonwealth of England, Scotland, and
Ireland.

II. That the exercise of the chief magistracy and the administration of the government over the said countries and the dominions, and the people thereof, shall be in the Lord Protector, assisted
with a council, the number whereof shall not exceed twenty-one,
nor be less than thirteen.

III. That all writs, processes, commissions, patents, grants, and
other things, which now run in the name and style of the Keepers
of the liberty of England by authority of Parliament, shall run in
the name and style of the Lord Protector, from whom, for the
future, shall be derived all magistracy and honours in these three
nations ; and have the power of pardons (except in case of mur·

ders and treason) and benefit of all forfeitures for the public use ; and shall govern the said countries and dominions in all things by the advice of the council, and according to these presents and the laws.

IV. That the Lord Protector, the Parliament sitting, shall dispose and order the militia and forces, both by sea and land, for the peace and good of the three nations, by consent of Parliament ; and that the Lord Protector, with the advice and consent of the major part of the council, shall dispose and order the militia for the ends aforesaid in the intervals of Parliament.

V. That the Lord Protector, by the advice aforesaid, shall direct in all things concerning the keeping and holding of a good correspondency with foreign kings, princes, and states ; and also, with the consent of the major part of the council, have the power of war and peace.

VI. That the laws shall not be altered, suspended, abrogated, or repealed, nor any new law made, nor any tax, charge, or imposition laid upon the people, but by common consent in Parliament, save only as is expressed in the thirtieth article.

VII. That there shall be a Parliament summoned to meet at Westminster upon the third day of September, 1654, and that successively a Parliament shall be summoned once in every third year, to be accounted from the dissolution of the present Parliament.

VIII. That neither the Parliament to be next summoned, nor any successive Parliaments, shall, during the time of five months, to be accounted from the day of their first meeting, be adjourned, prorogued, or dissolved, without their own consent.

IX. That as well the next as all other successive Parliaments, shall be summoned and elected in manner hereafter expressed ; that is to say, the persons to be chosen within England, Wales, the isles of Jersey and Guernsey, and the town of Berwick-upon-Tweed, to sit and serve in Parliament, shall be, and not exceed, the number of four hundred. The persons to be chosen within Scotland, to sit and serve in Parliament, shall be, and not exceed, the number of thirty ; and the persons to be chosen to sit in Parliament for Ireland shall be, and not exceed, the number of thirty.

X. That the persons to be elected to sit in Parliament from time to time, for the several counties of England, Wales, the isles of Jersey and Guernsey, and the town of Berwick-upon-Tweed, and all places within the same respectively, shall be according to the proportions and numbers hereafter expressed : that is to say, [Schedule of constituencies.]

*   *   *   *   *   *   *   *   *

The distribution of the persons to be chosen for Scotland and Ireland, and the several counties, cities, and places therein, shall be according to such proportions and number as shall be agreed upon and declared by the Lord Protector and the major part of the council, before the sending forth writs of summons for the next Parliament.

XI. That the summons to Parliament shall be by writ under the Great Seal of England, directed to the sheriffs of the several and respective counties, with such alteration as may suit with the present government, to be made by the Lord Protector and his council, which the Chancellor, Keeper, or Commissioners of the Great Seal shall seal, issue, and send abroad by warrant from the Lord Protector. If the Lord Protector shall not give warrant for issuing of writs of summons for the next Parliament, before the first of June, 1654, or for the Triennial Parliaments, before the first day of August in every third year, to be accounted as aforesaid ; that then the Chancellor, Keeper, or Commissioners of the Great Seal for the time being, shall, without any warrant or direction, within seven days after the said first day of June, 1654, seal, issue, and send abroad writs of summons (changing therein what is to be changed as aforesaid) to the several and respective Sheriffs of England, Scotland, and Ireland, for summoning the Parliament to meet at Westminster, the third day of September next; and shall likewise, within seven days after the said first day of August, in every third year, to be accounted from the dissolution of the precedent Parliament, seal, issue, and send forth abroad several writs of summons (changing therein what is to be changed) as aforesaid, for summoning the Parliament to meet at Westminster the sixth of November in that third year. That the said several and respective Sheriffs shall, within ten days after the receipt of such writ as aforesaid, cause the same to be proclaimed and published in every market-town within his county upon the market-days thereof, between twelve and three of the clock ; and shall then also publish and declare the certain day of the week and month, for choosing members to serve in Parliament for the body of the said county, according to the tenor of the said writ, which shall be upon Wednesday five weeks after the date of the writ ; and shall likewise declare the place where the election shall be made : for which purpose he shall appoint the most convenient place for the whole county to meet in ; and shall send precepts for elections to be made in all and every city, town, borough, or place within his county, where elections are to be made by virtue of these presents, to the Mayor, Sheriff, or other head officer of such city, town, borough, or place, within three days after the receipt of such writ and writs; which the said Mayors, Sheriffs, and officers respectively are to make publication of, and of the certain day for such elections to be made in the said city, town, or place aforesaid, and to cause elections to be made accordingly.

XII. That at the day and place of elections, the Sheriff of each county, and the said Mayors, Sheriffs, Bailiffs, and other head officers within their cities, towns, boroughs, and places respectively, shall take view of the said elections, and shall make return into the chancery within twenty days after the said elections, of the persons elected by the greater number of electors, under their hands and seals, between him on the one part, and the electors on the other part; wherein shall be contained, that the persons elected shall not have power to alter the government as it is hereby settled in one single person and a Parliament.

XIII. That the Sheriff, who shall wittingly and willingly make any false return, or neglect his duty, shall incur the penalty of 2000 marks of lawful English money; the one moiety to the Lord Protector, and the other moiety to such person as will sue for the same.

XIV. That all and every person and persons, who have aided, advised, assisted, or abetted in any war against the Parliament, since the first day of January, 1641 (unless they have been since in the service of the Parliament, and given signal testimony of their good affection thereunto) shall be disabled and incapable to be elected, or to give any vote in the election of any members to serve in the next Parliament, or in the three succeeding Triennial Parliaments.

XV. That all such, who have advised, assisted, or abetted the rebellion of Ireland, shall be disabled and incapable for ever to be elected, or give any vote in the election of any member to serve in Parliament; as also all such who do or shall profess the Roman Catholic religion.

XVI. That all votes and elections given or made contrary, or not according to these qualifications, shall be null and void; and if any person, who is hereby made incapable, shall give his vote for election of members to serve in Parliament, such person shall lose and forfeit one full year's value of his real estate, and one full third part of his personal estate; one moiety thereof to the Lord Protector, and the other moiety to him or them who shall sue for the same.

XVII. That the persons who shall be elected to serve in Parliament, shall be such (and no other than such) as are persons of known integrity, fearing God, and of good conversation, and being of the age of twenty-one years.

XVIII. That all and every person and persons seised or possessed to his own use, of any estate, real or personal, to the value of £200, and not within the aforesaid exceptions, shall be capable to elect members to serve in Parliament for counties.

XIX. That the Chancellor, Keeper, or Commissioners of the Great Seal, shall be sworn before they enter into their offices, truly and faithfully to issue forth, and send abroad, writs of summons to Parliament, at the times and in the manner before expressed : and in case of neglect or failure to issue and send abroad writs accordingly, he or they shall for every such offence be guilty of high treason, and suffer the pains and penalties thereof.

XX. That in case writs be not issued out, as is before expressed, but that there be a neglect therein, fifteen days after the time wherein the same ought to be issued out by the Chancellor, Keeper, or Commissioners of the Great Seal ; that then the Parliament shall, as often as such failure shall happen, assemble and be held at Westminster, in the usual place, at the times prefixed, in manner and by the means hereafter expressed ; that is to say, that the sheriffs of the several and respective counties, sheriffdoms, cities, boroughs, and places aforesaid, within England, Wales, Scotland, and Ireland, the Chancellor, Masters, and Scholars of the Universities of Oxford and Cambridge, and the Mayor and Bailiffs of the borough of Berwick-upon-Tweed, and other places aforesaid respectively, shall at the several courts and places to be appointed as aforesaid, within thirty days after the said fifteen days, cause such members to be chosen for their said several and respective counties, sheriffdoms, universities, cities, boroughs, and places aforesaid, by such persons, and in such manner, as if several and respective writs of summons to Parliament under the Great Seal had issued and been awarded according to the tenor aforesaid : that if the sheriff, or other persons authorised, shall neglect his or their duty herein, that all and every such sheriff and person authorised as aforesaid, so neglecting his or their duty, shall, for every such offence, be guilty of high treason, and shall suffer the pains and penalties thereof.

XXI. That the clerk, called the clerk of the Commonwealth in Chancery for the time being, and all others, who shall afterwards execute that office, to whom the returns shall be made, shall for the next Parliament, and the two succeeding triennial Parliaments, the next day after such return, certify the names of the several persons so returned, and of the places for which he and they were chosen respectively, unto the Council; who shall peruse the said returns, and examine whether the persons so elected and returned be such as is agreeable to the qualifications, and not disabled to be elected : and that every person and persons being so duly elected, and being approved of by the major part of the Council to be persons not disabled, but qualified as aforesaid, shall be esteemed a member of Parliament, and be admitted to sit in Parliament, and not otherwise.

XXII. That the persons so chosen and assembled in manner aforesaid, or any sixty of them, shall be, and be deemed the Parliament of England, Scotland, and Ireland; and the supreme legislative power to be and reside in the Lord Protector and such Parliament, in manner herein expressed.

XXIII. That the Lord Protector, with the advice of the major part of the Council, shall at any other time than is before expressed, when the necessities of the State shall require it, summon Parliaments in manner before expressed, which shall not be adjourned, prorogued, or dissolved without their own consent, during the first three months of their sitting. And in case of future war with any foreign State, a Parliament shall be forthwith summoned for their advice concerning the same.

XXIV. That all Bills agreed unto by the Parliament, shall be presented to the Lord Protector for his consent; and in case he shall not give his consent thereto within twenty days after they shall be presented to him, or give satisfaction to the Parliament within the time limited, that then, upon declaration of the Parliament that the Lord Protector hath not consented nor given satisfaction, such Bills shall pass into and become laws, although he shall not give his consent thereunto; provided such Bills contain nothing in them contrary to the matters contained in these presents.

XXV. That Henry Lawrence, [* * * 15 names in all] or any seven of them, shall be a Council for the purposes expressed in this writing ; and upon the death or other removal of any of them, the Parliament shall nominate six persons of ability, integrity, and fearing God, for every one that is dead or removed ; out of which the major part of the Council shall elect two, and present them to the Lord Protector, of which he shall elect one ; and in case the Parliament shall not nominate within twenty days after notice given unto them thereof, the major part of the Council shall nominate three as aforesaid to the Lord Protector, who out of them shall supply the vacancy ; and until this choice be made, the remaining part of the Council shall execute as fully in all things, as if their number were full. And in case of corruption, or other miscarriage in any of the Council in their trust, the Parliament shall appoint seven of their number, and the Council six, who, together with the Lord Chancellor, Lord Keeper, or Commissioners of the Great Seal for the time being, shall have power to hear and determine such corruption and miscarriage, and to award and inflict punishment, as the nature of the offence shall deserve, which punishment shall not be pardoned or remitted by the Lord Protector; and, in the interval of Parliament the major part of the Council, with the consent of the Lord Protector, may, for corruption or other miscarriage as aforesaid, suspend any of their number from the exercise of their trust, if they shall find it just, until the matter shall be heard and examined as aforesaid.

XXVI. That the Lord Protector and the major part of the Council aforesaid may, at any time before the meeting of the next Parliament, add to the Council such persons as they shall think fit, provided the number of the Council be not made thereby to exceed twenty-one, and the quorum to be proportioned accordingly by the Lord Protector and the major part of the Council.

XXVII. That a constant yearly revenue shall be raised, settled, and established for maintaining of 10,000 horse and dragoons, and 20,000 foot, in England, Scotland and Ireland, for the defence and security thereof, and also for a convenient number of ships for guarding of the seas; besides £200,000 per annum for defraying the other necessary charges of administration of justice, and other expenses of the Government, which revenue shall be raised by the customs, and such other ways and means as shall be agreed upon by the Lord Protector and the Council, and shall not be taken away or diminished, nor the way agreed upon for raising the same altered, but by the consent of the Lord Protector and the Parliament.

XXVIII. That the said yearly revenue shall be paid into the public treasury, and shall be issued out for the uses aforesaid.

XXIX. That in case there shall not be cause hereafter to keep up so great a defence both at land or sea, but that there be an abatement made thereof, the money which will be saved thereby shall remain in bank for the public service, and not be employed to any other use but by consent of Parliament, or, in the intervals of Parliament, by the Lord Protector and major part of the Council.

XXX. That the raising of money for defraying the charge of the present extraordinary forces, both at sea and land, in respect of the present wars, shall be by consent of Parliament, and not otherwise : save only that the Lord Protector, with the consent of the major part of the Council, for preventing the disorders and dangers which might otherwise fall out both by sea and land, shall have power, until the meeting of the first Parliament, to raise money for the purposes aforesaid ; and also to make laws and ordinances for the peace and welfare of these nations where it shall be necessary, which shall be binding and in force, until order shall be taken in Parliament concerning the same.

XXXI. That the lands, tenements, rents, royalties, jurisdictions and hereditaments which remain yet unsold or undisposed of, by Act or Ordinance of Parliament, belonging to the Commonwealth (except the forests and chases, and the honours and manors belonging to the same ; the lands of the rebels in Ireland, lying in the four counties of Dublin, Cork, Kildare, and Carlow ; the lands forfeited by the people of Scotland in the late wars, and also the lands of Papists and delinquents in England who have not yet compounded), shall be vested in the Lord Protector, to hold, to him and his successors, Lords Protectors of these nations, and shall not be alienated but by consent in Parliament.   And all debts, fines, issues, amercements, penalties and profits, certain and casual, due to the Keepers of the liberties of England by authority of Parliament, shall be due to the Lord Protector, and be payable into his public receipt, and shall be recovered and prosecuted in his name.

XXXII. That the office of Lord Protector over these nations shall be elective and not hereditary ; and upon the death of the Lord Protector, another fit person shall be forthwith elected to succeed him in the Government ; which election shall be by the Council, who, immediately upon the death of the Lord Protector, shall assemble in the Chamber where they usually sit in Council ; and, having given notice to all their members of the cause of their assembling, shall, being thirteen at least present, proceed to the election; and, before they depart the said Chamber, shall elect a fit person to succeed in the Government, and forthwith cause proclamation thereof to be made in all the three nations as shall be requisite ; and the person that they, or the major part of them, shall elect as aforesaid, shall be, and shall be taken to be, Lord Protector over these nations of England, Scotland and Ireland, and the dominions thereto belonging.   Provided that none of the children of the late King, nor any of his line or family, be elected to be Lord Protector or other Chief Magistrate over these nations, or any the dominions thereto belonging.   And until the aforesaid election be past, the Council shall take care of the Government, and administer in all things as fully as the Lord Protector, or the Lord Protector and Council are enabled to do.

XXXIII. That Oliver Cromwell, Captain-General of the forces of England, Scotland and Ireland, shall be, and is hereby declared to be, Lord Protector of the Commonwealth of England, Scotland and Ireland, and the dominions thereto belonging, for his life.

XXXIV. That the Chancellor, Keeper or Commissioners of the Great Seal, the Treasurer, Admiral, Chief Governors of Ireland and Scotland, and the Chief Justices of both the Benches, shall be chosen by the approbation of Parliament; and, in the intervals of Parliament, by the approbation of the major part of the Council, to be afterwards approved by the Parliament.

XXXV. That the Christian religion, as contained in the Scriptures, be held forth and recommended as the public profession of these nations; and that, as soon as may be, a provision, less subject to scruple and contention, and more certain than the present, be made for the encouragement and maintenance of able and painful teachers, for the instructing the people, and for discovery and confutation of error, heresy, and whatever is contrary to sound doctrine; and until such provision be made, the present maintenance shall not be taken away or impeached.

XXXVI. That to the public profession held forth none shall be compelled by penalties or otherwise; but that endeavours be used to win them by sound doctrine and the example of a good conversation.

XXXVII. That such as profess faith in God by Jesus Christ (though differing in judgment from the doctrine, worship or discipline publicly held forth) shall not be restrained from, but shall be protected in, the profession of the faith and exercise of their religion; so as they abuse not this liberty to the civil injury of others and to the actual disturbance of the public peace on their parts: provided this liberty be not extended to Popery or Prelacy, nor to such as, under the profession of Christ, hold forth and practise licentiousness.

XXXVIII. That all laws, statutes and ordinances, and clauses in any law, statute or ordinance to the contrary of the aforesaid liberty, shall be esteemed as null and void.

XXXIX. That the Acts and Ordinances of Parliament made for the sale or other disposition of the lands, rents and hereditaments of the late King, Queen, and Prince, of Archbishops and Bishops, &c., Deans and Chapters, the lands of delinquents and forest-lands, or any of them, or of any other lands, tenements, rents and hereditaments belonging to the Commonwealth, shall nowise be impeached or made invalid, but shall remain good and firm ; and that the securities given by Act and Ordinance of Parliament for any sum or sums of money, by any of the said lands, the excise, or any other public revenue ; and also the securities given by the public faith of the nation, and the engagement of the public faith for satisfaction of debts and damages, shall remain firm and good, and not be made void and invalid upon any pretence whatsoever.

XL. That the Articles given to or made with the enemy, and afterwards confirmed by Parliament, shall be performed and made good to the persons concerned therein ; and that such appeals as were depending in the last Parliament for relief concerning bills of sale of delinquents' estates, may be heard and determined the next Parliament, anything in this writing or otherwise to the contrary notwithstanding.

XLI. That every successive Lord Protector over these nations shall take and subscribe a solemn oath, in the presence of the Council, and such others as they shall call to them, that he will seek the peace, quiet and welfare of these nations, cause law and justice to be equally administered ; and that he will not violate or infringe the matters and things contained in this writing, and in all other things will, to his power and to the best of his understanding, govern these nations according to the laws, statutes and customs thereof.

XLII. That each person of the Council shall, before they enter upon their trust, take and subscribe an oath, that they will be true and faithful in their trust, according to the best of their knowledge ; and that in the election of every successive Lord Protector they shall proceed therein impartially, and do nothing therein for any promise, fear, favour or reward.

———————◆———————

220. An Ordinance by the Protector for the Union of England and Scotland

(1654, April 12.   Scobell, ii. 293.   Gardiner, 418–422.)

HIS Highness the Lord Protector of the Commonwealth of England, Scotland and Ireland, &c., taking into consideration how much it might conduce to the glory of God and the peace and welfare of the people in this whole island, that after all those late unhappy wars and differences, the people of Scotland should be united with the people of England into one Common-wealth and under one Government, and finding that in December, 1651, the Parliament then sitting did send Commissioners into Scotland to invite the people of that nation unto such a happy Union, who proceeded so far therein that the shires and boroughs of Scotland, by their Deputies convened at Dalkeith, and again at Edinburgh, did accept of the said Union, and assent thereunto; for the completing and perfecting of which Union, be it ordained, and it is ordained, by his Highness the Lord Protector of the Commonwealth of England, Scotland and Ireland, and the domin-ions thereto belonging, by and with the advice and consent of his Council, that all the people of Scotland, and of the isles of Orkney and Shetland, and of all the dominions and territories belonging unto Scotland, are and shall be, and are hereby, incorporated into, constituted, established, declared and confirmed one Common-wealth with England; and in every Parliament to be held suc-cessively for the said Commonwealth, thirty persons shall be called from and serve for Scotland.

And for the more effectual preservation of this Union, and the freedom and safety of the people of this Commonwealth so united, be it ordained, and it is ordained by the authority aforesaid, that all the people of Scotland and of the isles of Orkney and Shet-land, and of all the dominions and territories belonging unto Scot-land, of what degree or condition soever, be discharged of all fealty, homage, service and allegiance, which is or shall be pre-tended due unto any of the issue and posterity of Charles Stuart, late King of England and Scotland, or any claiming under him; and that Charles Stuart, eldest son, and James, called Duke of York, second son, and all other the issue and posterity of the said late King, and all and every person and persons pretending title from, by or under him, are and be disabled to hold or enjoy the Crown of Scotland and other the dominions thereunto belong-ing, or any of them; or to have the name, title, style or dignity of King or Queen of Scotland; or to have and enjoy the power and dominion of the said kingdom and dominions, or any of them, or the honours, manors, lands, tenements, possessions and heredita-ments belonging or appertaining to the said Crown of Scotland, or other the dominions aforesaid, or to any of them, any law, statute, usage, ordinance or custom in Scotland to the contrary hereof in any wise notwithstanding.

And it is further ordained by the authority aforesaid, that the said office, style, dignity, power and authority of King of Scotland,

2 E

and all right of the three Estates of Scotland to convocate or assemble in any general Convocation or Parliament, and all conventional and parliamentary authority in Scotland, as formerly established, and all laws, usages and customs, ordaining, constituting or confirming the same, shall be and are hereby and from henceforth abolished and utterly taken away and made null and void.

And that this Union may take its more full effect and intent, be it further ordained by the authority aforesaid, that the Arms of Scotland, viz. a cross, commonly called St. Andrew's Cross, be received into and borne from henceforth in the Arms of this Commonwealth, as a badge of this Union ; and that all the public seals, seals of office, and seals of bodies civil or corporate, in Scotland, which heretofore carried the Arms of the Kings of Scotland, shall from henceforth instead thereof carry the Arms of this Commonwealth.

And be it further ordained by the authority aforesaid, that all customs, excise and other imposts for goods transported from England to Scotland, and from Scotland to England, by sea or land, are and shall be so far taken off and discharged, as that all goods for the future shall pass as free, and with like privileges and with the like charges and burdens from England to Scotland, and from Scotland to England, as goods passing from port to port, or place to place in England ; and that all goods shall and may pass between Scotland and any other part of this Commonwealth or dominions thereof, with the like privileges, freedom, charges and burdens as such goods do or shall pass between England and the said parts and dominions thereof, any law, statute, usage or custom to the contrary thereof in any wise notwithstanding, and that all goods prohibited by any law now in force in England to be transported out of England to any foreign parts, or imported, shall be and hereby are prohibited to be transported or imported by the same law, and upon the same penalties, out of Scotland to any foreign parts aforesaid, or from any foreign parts into Scotland.

And be it further ordained by the authority aforesaid, that all cesses, public impositions and taxations whatsoever, be imposed, taxed and levied from henceforth proportionably from the whole people of this Commonwealth so united.

And further, to the end that all dominion of tenures and superiorities importing servitude and vassalage may likewise be abolished in Scotland, be it further declared and ordained by the authority aforesaid, that all heritors, proprietors and possessors of lands in Scotland, or the dominions thereunto belonging, and their heirs, shall from and after the 12th day of April, in the year of our Lord 1654, hold their respective lands of the respective lord and lords by deed, charter, patent or enfeoffment, to be renewed upon the death of every heritor, proprietor or possessor (as now they do) to his heir or heirs, by and under such yearly rents, boons and annual services as are mentioned or due by any deeds, patents, charters or enfeoffments now in being, of the respective lands therein expressed, or by virtue thereof enjoyed without rendering, doing or performing any other duty, service, vassalage or demand whatsoever, by reason or occasion of the said lands, or any the clauses or covenants in the said deeds, charters, patents or enfeoffments contained, saving what is hereafter, herein and hereby particularly expressed and declared ; that is to say, heriots, where the same are due, fines (certain where the same is already certain, and where the fine is uncertain, reasonable fines) upon the death of the lord, and upon the death or alienation of the tenant, or any of them, where the same have usually been paid, which said fine (not being already certain) shall not at any time exceed one year's value of the lands, and also doing suit and service to such Court and Courts Baron, as shall be constituted in Scotland, in such manner as is ordained by one other Ordinance, entitled, an Ordinance for erecting Courts Baron in Scotland.

And be it ordained by the authority aforesaid, that all and every the heritors, proprietors and possessors aforesaid, and their heirs, are and shall be from henceforth for ever discharged of all fealty, homage, vassalage and servitude, which is or shall be pretended due from them, or any of them, unto any their lords or superiors whatsoever, claiming dominion or jurisdiction over them, by virtue of the said patents, charters, deeds or enfeoffments, and other rights thereof, or of any clauses or conditions therein contained, other than is before declared and ordained. And that all the said superiorities, lordships and jurisdictions (other than as aforesaid) shall be, and are hereby abolished, taken off and discharged ; and that all and every the said deeds, patents, charters and enfeoffments in that behalf be, and are hereby declared, and made so far void and null ; and particularly, that all and every the heritors, and others the persons aforesaid, and their heirs, are and shall be for ever hereafter freed and discharged of, and from, all suits, and appearing at or in any their lords, or superiors courts of justiciary, regality, stewartry, barony, bailiary, heritable sheriffship, heritable admiralty, all which, together with all other offices heritable, or for life, are hereby abolished and taken away ; and that all and every the heritors and persons aforesaid, and their heirs, are and shall be for ever hereafter freed and discharged of and from all military service, and personal attendance upon any their lords or superiors in expeditions or travels, and of all casualties of wards' lands formerly held of the King, or other superiors, and of the marriage, single and double avail thereof, non-entries, compositions for entries, and of all rights and casualties payable, if they be demanded, only or upon the committing of any clauses irritant. And that the said heritors and persons aforesaid be now, and from henceforth, construed, reputed, adjudged and declared free and acquitted thereof, and of and from all and all manner of holding suits, duties, services, personal or real, and demands whatsoever (other than is before declared and ordained), notwithstanding the present tenor of any their deeds, patents, enfeoffments, or any clauses, articles or covenants therein contained or mentioned to the contrary in any wise ; and that in time to come all and every clause, covenant, article, condition, or thing to the contrary hereof, shall be omitted out of all such deeds, patents, charters and enfeoffments.

And be it further ordained, that all forfeitures, escheats, simple or of life, rent bastardy, and last heir, which heretofore escheated, forfeited and fell to the King, lords of regality, or other superiors, shall from henceforth fall, escheat, and forfeit to the Lord Protector of the Commonwealth for the time being.

Passed 12th April, 1654. Confirmed Anno 1656, Cap. 10.

---

221. The Declaration of Breda

(1660, April 4. Cobbett's Parliamentary History, iv. 16. Gardiner, 465–467. G. and H. 585–588.)

CHARLES R.
Charles, by the grace of God, King of England, Scotland, France and Ireland, Defender of the Faith, &c. To all our loving subjects, of what degree or quality soever, greeting.

If the general distraction and confusion which is spread over the whole kingdom, doth not awaken all men to a desire and longing that those wounds, which have so many years together been kept bleeding, may be bound up, all we can say will be to no purpose ; however, after this long silence, we have thought it our duty to declare how much we desire to contribute thereunto ; and that as we can never give over the hope, in good time, to obtain the possession of that right which God and nature hath made our due, so we do make it our daily suit to the Divine Providence, that He will,

in compassion to us and our subjects, after so long misery and sufferings, remit and put us into a quiet and peaceable possession of
that our right, with as little blood and damage to our people as is
possible; nor do we desire more to enjoy what is ours, than that
all our subjects may enjoy what by law is theirs, by a full and entire
administration of justice throughout the land, and by extending
our mercy where it is wanted and deserved.

And to the end that the fear of punishment may not engage any,
conscious to themselves of what is past, to a perseverance in guilt
for the future, by opposing the quiet and happiness of their country, in the restoration of king, peers and people to their just,
ancient and fundamental rights, we do, by these presents, declare,
that we do grant a free and general pardon, which we are ready,
upon demand, to pass under our Great Seal of England, to all our
subjects, of what degree or quality soever, who, within forty days
after the publishing hereof, shall lay hold upon this our grace and
favour, and shall, by any public act, declare their doing so, and
that they return to the loyalty and obedience of good subjects;
excepting only such persons as shall hereafter be excepted by
Parliament, those only to be excepted. Let all our subjects, how
faulty soever, rely upon the word of a King, solemnly given by this
present declaration, that no crime whatsoever, committed against
us or our royal father before the publication of this, shall ever rise
in judgment, or be brought in question, against any of them, to the
least endamagement of them, either in their lives, liberties or
estates, or (as far forth as lies in our power) so much as to the
prejudice of their reputations by any reproach or term of distinc-
tion from the rest of our best subjects; we desiring and ordaining
that henceforth all notes of discord, separation and difference of
parties be utterly abolished among all our subjects, whom we invite
and conjure to a perfect union among themselves, under our protection, for the re-settlement of our just rights and theirs in a
free Parliament, by which, upon the word of a King, we will be
advised.

And because the passion and uncharitableness of the times
have produced several opinions in religion, by which men are
engaged in parties and animosities against each other (which,
when they shall hereafter unite in a freedom of conversation, will
be composed or better understood), we do declare a liberty to
tender consciences, and that no man shall be disquieted or called
in question for differences of opinion in matter of religion, which
do not disturb the peace of the kingdom; and that we shall be
ready to consent to such an Act of Parliament, as, upon mature

deliberation, shall be offered to us, for the full granting that indulgence.

And because, in the continued distractions of so many years, and so many and great revolutions, many grants and purchases of estates have been made to and by many officers, soldiers and others, who are now possessed of the same, and who may be liable to actions at law upon several titles, we are likewise willing that all such differences, and all things relating to such grants, sales and purchases, shall be determined in Parliament, which can best provide for the just satisfaction of all men who are concerned.

And we do further declare, that we will be ready to consent to any Act or Acts of Parliament to the purposes aforesaid, and for the full satisfaction of all arrears due to the officers and soldiers of the army under the command of General Monk; and that they shall be received into our service upon as good pay and conditions as they now enjoy.

> Given under our Sign Manual and Privy Signet, at our Court at Breda, this $\frac{4}{14}$ day of April, 1660, in the twelfth year of our reign.

---

222. Act abolishing Relics of Feudalism and Fixing an Excise

(1660, December 24. 12 Charles II. c. 24. 5 S. R. 259.)

WHEREAS it hath been found by former experience, that the court of wards and liveries, and tenures by knights service either of the king or others, or by knights service *in capite*, or socage *in capite* of the king, and the consequents upon the same, have been much more burdensome, grievous and prejudicial to the kingdom than they have been beneficial to the king; and whereas since the intermission of the said court, which hath been from the four and twentieth day of February, which was in the year of our Lord one thousand six hundred forty and five, many persons have by will and otherwise made disposal of their lands held by knights service, whereupon divers questions might possibly arise unless some seasonable remedy be taken to prevent the same : be it therefore enacted by the king our sovereign lord with the assent of the lords and commons in parliament assembled and by the authority of the same, and it is hereby enacted, that the court of wards and liveries, and all wardships, liveries, primer-seisins and ouster-le-mains, values and forfeitures of marriages, by reason of any tenure of the king's Majesty, or of any other by knights service, and all mean rates, and all other gifts, grants, charges, incident or arising for or by reason of wardships, liveries, primer-seisins or ouster-le-mains, be taken away and discharged, and are hereby enacted to be taken away and discharged, from the said twenty-fourth day of February one thousand six hundred forty-five, any law, statute, custom, or usage to the contrary hereof any wise notwithstanding ; and that all fines for alienations, seizures and pardons for alienations, tenure by homage and all charges incident or arising for or by reason of wardship, livery, primer-seisin or ouster-le-mains or tenure by knights service, scutage and also *aide pur file marrier* and *pur fair fitz chivalier* and all other charges incident thereunto, be likewise taken away and discharged from the said twenty-fourth day of February one thousand six hundred forty and five, any law, statute, custom or usage to the contrary hereof any wise notwithstanding ; and that all tenures by knights service of the king, or of any other person, and by knights service *in capite*, and by socage *in capite* of the king, and the fruits and consequents thereof, happened or which shall or may hereafter happen or arise thereupon or thereby, be taken away and discharged, any law, statute, custom or usage to the contrary hereof any wise notwithstanding ; and all tenures of any honours, manors, lands, tenements or hereditaments of any estate of inheritance at the common law held either of the king or of any other person or persons, bodies politic or corporate, are hereby enacted to be turned into free and common socage to all intents and purposes from the said four and twentieth day of February one thousand six hundred forty-five, and shall be so construed, adjudged and deemed to be from the said twenty-fourth day of February one thousand six hundred forty-five, and forever thereafter turned into free and common socage, any law, statute, custom or usage to the contrary hereof in any wise notwithstanding ;

II. And that the same shall for ever hereafter stand and be discharged of all tenure by homage, scutage, voyages royal and charges for the same, wardships incident to tenure by knights service, and values and forfeitures of marriage, and all other charges incident to tenure by knights service, and of and from *aide pur file marrier* and *aide pur fair fitz chivalier*, any law, statute, custom or usage to the contrary in any wise notwithstanding ; and that all conveyances and devises of any manors, lands, tenements and hereditaments made since the said twenty-fourth of February shall be expounded to be of such effect, as if the same manors, lands, tenements and hereditaments had been then held and continued to be holden in free and common socage only, any law, statute, custom or usage to the contrary hereof in any wise notwithstanding.

III.   And be it further ordained and enacted by authority of this present parliament that one act made in the reign of King Henry the Eighth, entitled An Act for the establishment of the court of the king's wards, and also one act of parliament made in the three and thirtieth year of the reign of the said King Henry the Eighth concerning the officers of the court of wards and liveries, and every clause, article and matter in the said acts contained shall from henceforth be repealed and utterly void.

IV.   And be it further enacted by the authority aforesaid that all tenures hereafter to be created by the king's Majesty, his heirs or successors, upon any gifts or grants of any manors, lands, tenements or hereditaments of any estate of inheritance at the common law shall be in free and common socage, and shall be adjudged to be in free and common socage only, and not by knights service or *in capite*, and shall be discharged of all wardship, value and forfeiture of marriage, livery, primer-seisin, ouster-le-main, *aide pur fair fitz chivalier*, and *pur file marrier*, any law, statute or reservation to the contrary thereof any wise notwithstanding.

*   *   *   *   *   *   *   *   *

VIII.   And be it further enacted by the authority aforesaid, that where any person hath or shall have any child or children under the age of one and twenty years, and not married at the time of his death, that it shall and may be lawful to and for the father of such child or children * * * by his deed executed in his life-time, or by his last will and testament in writing * * * to dispose of the custody and tuition of such child or children, for and during such time as he or they shall respectively remain under the age of one and twenty years, or any lesser time, to any person or persons in possession or remainder, other than popish recusants; * * *

*   *   *   *   *   *   *   *   *

XI.   * * *   That from henceforth no sum or sums of money or other thing shall be taken, raised, taxed, rated, imposed, paid or levied for or in regard of any provision, carriages or purveyance for his Majesty, his heirs or successors.

XII.   And that henceforth no person or persons by any warrant, commission or authority under the great seal or otherwise by colour of buying or making provision or purveyance for his Majesty, or any queen of England for the time being,

or of any the children of any king or queen of England for
the time being, or that shall be, or for his or their or any of their
household, shall take any timber, fuel, cattle, corn, grain, malt,
hay, straw, victual, cart, carriage or other thing whatsoever of any
the subjects of his Majesty, his heirs or successors, without the
free and full consent of the owner or owners thereof had and
obtained without menace or enforcement, nor shall summon, warn,
take, use or require any the said subjects to furnish or find any
horses, oxen or other [cattle], carts, ploughs, wains or other carriages for the use of his Majesty, his heirs or successors, or of any
queen of England, or of any child or children of any the kings or
queens of England for the time being, for the carrying the goods
of his Majesty, his heirs or successors, or the said queens or children or any of them, without such full and free consent as
aforesaid, any law, statute, custom or usage to the contrary notwithstanding.

    *   *   *   *   *   *   *   *   *

XIV. * * * And now to the intent and purpose that his Majesty, his heirs and successors, may receive a full and ample recompense and satisfaction as well for * * * and other the premises
and perquisites incident thereunto ; * * * as also for all and all
manner of purveyance and provisions hereinbefore mentioned,
* * *

 . XV. Be it therefore enacted by the authority aforesaid that there
shall be paid unto the king's Majesty, his heirs and successors for
ever hereafter :

[Then follow clauses fixing the rate of an excise on beer, ale,
cider, perry, metheglin, mead, aqua vitæ or strong-water, coffee,
chocolate, sherbet, tea, the method of raising such excise, and
penalties.]

———◆———

223. Corporation Act

(1661, December 20. 13 Charles II, st. 2., c. 1. 5 *S. R.* 321. The whole
reprinted in G. and H. 594–600.)]

WHEREAS questions are likely to arise concerning the validity
of elections of magistrates and other officers and members in
corporations, as well in respect of removing some as placing others,
during the late troubles, contrary to the true intent and meaning
of their charters and liberties ; and to the end that the succession
in such corporations may be most probably perpetuated in the

hands of persons well affected to His Majesty and the established government, it being too well known that notwithstanding all His Majesty's endeavours and unparalleled indulgence in pardoning all that is past, nevertheless many evil spirits are still working:

II. Wherefore for prevention of the like mischief for the time to come, and for preservation of the public peace both in church and state, be it enacted by the king's most excellent Majesty by and with the advice and consent of the lords spiritual and temporal and commons assembled in Parliament, and by the authority of the same, that commissions shall before the twentieth day of February next be issued forth under the great seal of England unto such persons as His Majesty shall appoint for the executing of the powers and authorities hereinafter expressed, and that all and every the persons to be named commissioners in the said commissions respectively shall by virtue of this act be commissioners respectively for and within the said several cities, corporations and boroughs, and Cinque ports and their members, and other port towns within the kingdom of England, dominion of Wales and town of Berwick upon Tweed, for which they shall be respectively nominated and appointed.

III. And be it further enacted by the authority aforesaid, that no charter of any corporation, cities, towns, boroughs, Cinque ports and their members, and other port towns in England or Wales or town of Berwick upon Tweed shall at any time hereafter be avoided for or by reason of any act or thing done or omitted to be done before the first day of this present parliament.

IV. And be it further enacted by the authority aforesaid, that all persons who upon the four and twentieth day of December one thousand six hundred sixty and one shall be mayors, aldermen, recorders, bailiffs, town-clerks, common council men and other persons then bearing any office or offices of magistracy or places or trusts or other employment relating to or concerning the government of the said respective cities, corporations and boroughs, and Cinque ports and their members, and other port towns shall at any time before the five and twentieth day of March one thousand six hundred sixty and three, when they shall be thereunto required by the said respective commissioners or any three or more of them, take the oaths of allegiance and supremacy, and this oath following:

V. 'I, A. B., do declare and believe, that it is not lawful upon any pretence whatsoever to take arms against the king, and that I do abhor that traitorous position of taking arms by his authority against his person or against those that are commissioned by him: So help me God.'

VI. And also at the same time shall publicly subscribe before the said commissioners or any three of them this following declaration:

'I, A. B., do declare, that I hold that there lies no obligation upon me or any other person from the oath commonly called the Solemn League and Covenant, and that the same was in itself an unlawful oath and imposed upon the subjects of this realm against the known laws and liberties of the kingdom.'

VII. And that all such of the said mayors and other the persons aforesaid by whom the said oaths are to be taken and declarations subscribed as aforesaid, who shall refuse to take and subscribe the same within the time and in manner aforesaid, shall from and immediately after such refusal be by authority of this act (ipso facto) removed and displaced of and from the said offices and places respectively; and the said offices and places from and immediately after such refusal shall be and are hereby declared and adjudged to be void to all intents and purposes, as if the said respective persons so refusing were naturally dead.

*   *   *   *   *   *   *   *   *

XII. Provided also, and be it enacted by the authority aforesaid, that from and after the expiration of the said commissions, no person or persons shall for ever hereafter be placed, elected or chosen in or to any the offices or places aforesaid, that shall not have, within one year next before such election or choice, taken the sacrament of the Lord's Supper, according to the rites of the Church of England; and that every such person and persons so placed, elected or chosen shall likewise take the aforesaid three oaths and subscribe the said declaration, at the same time when the oath for the due execution of the said places and offices respectively shall be administered; and in default hereof every such placing, election and choice is hereby enacted, and declared to be void.

*   *   *   *   *   *   *   *   *

---

224. Last Act of Uniformity

(1662, May 19.   13 & 14 Charles II. c. 4.   5 S. R. 364.   The whole re-printed in G. and H. 600–619.)

WHEREAS in the first year of the late Queen Elizabeth there was one uniform order of common service and prayer and of the administration of sacraments, rites and ceremonies in the Church of England (agreable to the word of God and usage of the primitive church) compiled by the reverend bishops and clergy, set forth in one book, entitled, 'The Book of Common Prayer and Administration of Sacraments and other Rites and Ceremonies in the Church of England,' and enjoined to be used by act of parliament, holden in the said first year of the said late queen, entitled, 'An Act for the Uniformity of Common Prayer and Service in the Church and Administration of the Sacraments,' very comfortable to all good people desirous to live in Christian conversation and most profitable to the estate of this realm, upon the which the mercy, favour and blessing of Almighty God is in no wise so readily and plentifully poured, as by common prayers, due using of the sacraments and often preaching of the gospel with devotion of the hearers ; and yet, this notwithstanding, a great number of people in divers parts of this realm, following their own sensuality and living without knowledge and due fear of God, do wilfully and schismatically abstain and refuse to come to their parish churches and other public places where common prayer, administration of the sacraments and preaching of the word of God is used upon the Sundays and other days ordained and appointed to be kept and observed as holy days ; and whereas by the great and scandalous neglect of ministers in using the said order or liturgy so set forth and enjoined as aforesaid, great mischiefs and inconveniences during the times of the late unhappy troubles have arisen and grown, and many people have been led into factions and schisms, to the great decay and scandal of the reformed religion of the Church of England, and to the hazard of many souls ; for prevention whereof in time to come, for settling the peace of the church and for allaying the present distempers, which the indisposition of the time hath contracted, the king's Majesty, according to his declaration of the five and twentieth of October one thousand six hundred and sixty, granted his commission under the great seal of England to several bishops and other divines to review the Book of Common Prayer, and to prepare such alterations and additions as they thought fit to offer ; and afterwards the convocations of both the provinces of Canterbury and York being by his Majesty called and assembled, and now sitting, his Majesty hath been pleased to authorize and require the presidents of the said convocations, and other the bishops and clergy of the same, to review the said Book of Common Prayer and the book of the form and manner of the making and consecrating of bishops, priests and deacons, and that after mature consideration they should make such additions and alterations in the said books respectively, as to them should seem meet and convenient, and should exhibit and present the same to his

Majesty in writing for his further allowance or confirmation ; since
which time upon full and mature deliberation they, the said presidents, bishops and clergy of both provinces, have accordingly
reviewed the said books and have made some alterations which
they think fit to be inserted to the same, and some additional
prayers to the said Book of Common Prayer to be used upon
proper and emergent occasions, and have exhibited and presented
the same unto his Majesty in writing in one book, entitled, 'The Book
of Common Prayer and Administration of the Sacraments and
other Rites and Ceremonies of the Church according to the Use
of the Church of England, together with the Psalter or Psalms of
David, pointed as they are to be sung or said in Churches, and the
Form and Manner of Making, Ordaining and Consecrating of
Bishops, Priests and Deacons' ; all which his Majesty having duly
considered, hath fully approved and allowed the same, and recommended to this present parliament that the said Books of Common
Prayer, and of the Form of Ordination and Consecration of Bishops,
Priests and Deacons, with the alterations and additions which have
been so made and presented to his Majesty by the said convocations, be the book which shall be appointed to be used by all that
officiate in all cathedral and collegiate churches and chapels, and
in all chapels of colleges and halls in both the universities, and the
colleges of Eton and Winchester, and in all parish churches and
chapels within the kingdom of England, dominion of Wales and
town of Berwick upon Tweed, and by all that make or consecrate
bishops, priests or deacons in any of the said places, under such
sanctions and penalties as the houses of parliament shall think fit :

II. Now in regard that nothing conduceth more to the settling of
the peace of this nation, (which is desired of all good men) nor to
the honour of our religion and the propagation thereof, than an universal agreement in the public worship of Almighty God, and to the
intent that every person within this realm may certainly know the
rule to which he is to conform in public worship and administration of sacraments and other rites and ceremonies of the Church
of England, and the manner how and by whom bishops, priests
and deacons are and ought to be made ordained and consecrated :
be it enacted by the king's most excellent Majesty, by the advice
and with the consent of the lords spiritual and temporal and the
commons in this present parliament assembled, and by the authority of the same, that all and singular ministers in any cathedral,
collegiate or parish church, or chapel, or other place of public worship within this realm of England, dominion of Wales and town of
Berwick upon Tweed shall be bound to say and use the morning

prayer, evening prayer, celebration and administration of both the sacraments, and all other the public and common prayer, in such order and form as is mentioned in the said book annexed and joined to this present act, and entitled, 'The Book of Common Prayer and Administration of the Sacraments and other Rites and Ceremonies of the Church, according to the Use of the Church of England, together with the Psalter or Psalms of David, pointed as they are to be sung or said in Churches, and the Form or Manner of Making, Ordaining and Consecrating of Bishops, Priests and Deacons'; and that the morning and evening prayers therein contained shall upon every Lord's day and upon all other days and occasions and at the times therein appointed, be openly and solemnly read by all and every minister or curate, in every church, chapel or other place of public worship within this realm of England and places aforesaid.

III. And to the end that uniformity in the public worship of God (which is so much desired) may be speedily effected, be it further enacted by the authority aforesaid, that every parson, vicar or other minister whatsoever, who now hath and enjoyeth any ecclesiastical benefice or promotion within this realm of England or places aforesaid, shall in the church, chapel or place of public worship belonging to his said benefice or promotion, upon some Lord's day before the feast of Saint Bartholomew which shall be in the year of our Lord God one thousand six hundred sixty and two, openly, publicly and solemnly read the morning and evening prayer appointed to be read by and according to the said Book of Common Prayer at the times thereby appointed; and after such reading thereof shall openly and publicly before the congregation there assembled declare his unfeigned assent and consent to the use of all things in the said book contained and prescribed, in these words and no other:

IV. I, A. B., do here declare my unfeigned assent and consent to all and everything contained and prescribed in and by the book, entitled, 'The Book of Common Prayer and Administration of the Sacraments and other Rites and Ceremonies of the Church according to the Use of the Church of England, together with the Psalter or Psalms of David, pointed as they are to be sung or said in Churches, and the Form or Manner of Making, Ordaining and Consecrating of Bishops, Priests and Deacons.'

V. And that all and every such person, who shall (without some lawful impediment to be allowed and approved of by the ordinary of the place) neglect or refuse to do the same within the time aforesaid (or in case of such impediment within one month after such impediment removed) shall, ipso facto, be deprived of all his spiritual promotions; and that from thenceforth it shall be lawful to and for all patrons and donors of all and singular the said spiritual promotions or of any of them, according to their respective rights and titles, to present or collate to the same, as though the person or persons so offending or neglecting were dead.

* * * * * * * * *

———◆———

225. First Conventicle Act

(1664, May 17.   16 Charles II. c. 4.   5 *S. R.* 516.)

WHEREAS an act made in the five and thirtieth year of the reign of our late sovereign lady Queen Elizabeth, entitled, An Act to retain the Queen's Majesty's subjects in their due obedience, hath not been put in due execution by reason of some doubt of late made, whether the said act be still in force, although it be very clear and evident, and it is hereby declared, that the said act is still in force and ought to be put in due execution; for providing therefore of further and more speedy remedies against the growing and dangerous practices of seditious sectaries and other disloyal persons, who, under pretence of tender consciences, do at their meetings, contrive insurrections as late experience hath showed; be it enacted by the king's most excellent Majesty by and with the advice and consent of the lords spiritual and temporal, and commons in this present parliament assembled, and by the authority of the same, that if any person of the age of sixteen years or upwards, being a subject of this realm, at any time after the first day of July, which shall be in the year of our Lord one thousand six hundred sixty and four, shall be present at any assembly, conventicle or meeting, under colour or pretence of any exercise of religion in other manner than is allowed by the liturgy or practice of the Church of England, in any place within the kingdom of England, dominion of Wales or town of Berwick-upon-Tweed, at which conventicle, meeting or assembly there shall be five persons or more assembled together over and above those of the same household, then it shall and may be lawful to and for any two justices of the peace of the county, limit, division or liberty wherein the offence aforesaid shall be committed, or for the chief magistrate of the place where such offence aforesaid shall be committed (if it be within a corporation where there are not two justices of the peace), and they are hereby required and enjoined upon proof to them or him respectively made of such offence, either by confession of the party, or oath of witnesses, or notorious evidence of the fact (which oath the said justices of the peace and chief magistrate respectively are hereby empowered and required to administer), to make a record of every such offence and offences under their hands and seals respectively, which record so made as aforesaid shall to all intents and purposes be in law taken and adjudged to be a full and perfect conviction of every such offender for such offence, and thereupon the said justices and chief magistrate respectively shall commit every such offender so convicted as aforesaid to the gaol, or house of correction, there to remain without bail or mainprise for any time not exceeding the space of three months, unless such offender shall pay down to the said justices or chief magistrate such sum of money, not exceeding five pounds, as the justices or chief magistrate (who are hereby thereunto authorized and required) shall fine the said offender at for his or her said offence, which money shall be paid to the church wardens for the relief of the poor of the parish, where such offender did last inhabit.

* * * * * * * * *

III. And be it further enacted by the authority aforesaid, that if any such offender so convicted of a second offence contrary to this act in manner aforesaid shall at any time again commit the like offence contrary to this act, then any two justices of the peace and chief magistrate as aforesaid respectively shall commit every such offender to the gaol or house of correction, there to remain without bail or mainprise, until the next general quarter sessions, assizes, gaol-delivery, great sessions or sitting of any commission of oyer and terminer in the respective county, limit, division or liberty which shall first happen, when and where every such offender shall be proceeded against by indictment for such offence, and shall forthwith be arraigned upon such indictment, and shall then plead the general issue of not guilty and give any special matter in evidence, or confess the indictment, and if such offender proceeded against shall be lawfully convicted of such offence either by confession or verdict, or if such offender shall refuse to plead the general issue or to confess the indictment, then the respective justices of the peace at their general quarter sessions, judges of assize and gaol-delivery at the assizes and gaol delivery, justices of the great sessions at the great sessions and commissioners of oyer and terminer at their sitting, are hereby enabled and required to cause judgment to be entered against such offender, that such offender shall be transported beyond the seas to any of His Majesty's foreign plantations (Virginia and New England only excepted) there to remain seven years.

*   *   *   *   *   *   *   *   *

226. Five Mile Act

(1665, October 31.   17 Charles II. c. 2.   5 *S. R.* 575.   The whole reprinted in G. and H. pp. 620–623.)

*   *   *   *   *   *   *   *   *

III. AND all such person and persons as shall take upon them to preach in any unlawful assembly, conventicle or meeting under colour or pretence of any exercise of religion, contrary to the laws and statutes of this kingdom, shall not at any time from and after the four and twentieth day of March which shall be in this present year of our Lord God one thousand six hundred sixty and five, unless only in passing upon the road, come or be within five miles of any city or town corporate or borough that sends burgesses to the parliament, within His Majesty's kingdom of England, principality of Wales or of the town of Berwick upon Tweed, or within five miles of any parish town or place, wherein he or they have since the act of oblivion been parson, vicar, curate, stipendiary or lecturer, or taken upon them to preach in any unlawful assembly, conventicle or meeting under colour or pretence of any exercise of religion, contrary to the laws and statutes of this kingdom, before he or they have taken and subscribed the oath aforesaid before the justices of peace at their quarter sessions to be holden for the county, riding or division next unto the said corporation, city or borough, parish, place or town, in open court (which said oath the said justices are hereby empowered there to administer), upon forfeiture for every such offence the sum of forty pounds of lawful English money, the one third part thereof to His Majesty and his successors, the other third part to the use of the poor of the parish where the offence shall be committed, and the other third part thereof to such person or persons as shall or will sue for the same by action of debt, plaint, bill or information in any court of record at Westminster, or before any justices of assize, oyer and terminer or gaol delivery, or before any justices of the counties palatine of Chester, Lancaster or Durham, or the justices of the great sessions

2 F

in Wales, or before any justices of peace in their quarter sessions, wherein no essoin, protection or wager of law shall be allowed.

IV. Provided always, and be it further enacted by the authority aforesaid, that it shall not be lawful for any person or persons restrained from coming to any city, town corporate, borough, parish, town or place as aforesaid, or for any other person or persons as shall not first take and subscribe the said oath, and as shall not frequent divine service established by the laws of this kingdom, and carry him or herself reverently, decently and orderly there, to teach any public or private school, or take any boarders or tablers that are taught or instructed by him or herself, or any other, upon pain for every such offence to forfeit the sum of forty pounds, to be recovered and distributed as aforesaid.

*   *   *   *   *   *   *   *   *

227. Charles II's Declaration of Indulgence

(1673, February 1.   Cobbett's Parliamentary History, iv. 515.)

OUR care and endeavours for the preservation of the rights and interests of the Church have been sufficiently manifested to the world by the whole course of our government, since our happy restoration, and by the many and frequent ways of coercion that we have used for reducing all erring or dissenting persons, and for composing the unhappy differences in matters of religion, which we found among our subjects upon our return. But it being evident by the sad experience of twelve years, that there is very little fruit of all those forcible courses, we think ourselves obliged to make use of that supreme power in ecclesiastical matters, which is not only inherent in us but hath been declared and recognized to be so by several statutes and acts of parliament. And therefore we do now accordingly issue out this our royal declaration, as well for the quieting the minds of our good subjects in these points, for inviting strangers in this conjuncture to come and live under us, and for the better encouragement of all to a cheerful following of their trades and callings, from whence we hope, by the blessing of God, to have many good and happy advantages to our government ; as also for preventing for the future the danger that might otherwise arise from private meetings, and seditious conventicles.   And in the first place, we declare our express resolution, meaning, and intention to be, that the Church of England be preserved, and remain entire in its doctrine, discipline, and government, as now it stands established by law : and that this be taken to be, as it is, the basis, rule and standard of the general and public worship of God, and that the orthodox conformable clergy do receive and enjoy the revenues belonging thereunto ; and that no person, though of different opinion and persuasion, shall be exempt from paying his tithes, or other dues whatsoever. And further, we declare, that no person shall be capable of holding any benefice, living, or ecclesiastical dignity or preferment of any kind in this kingdom of England, who is not exactly conformable.   We do in the next place declare our will and pleasure to be, that the execution of all and all manner of penal laws in matters ecclesiastical, against whatsoever sort of non-conformists, or recusants, be immediately suspended, and they are hereby suspended.   And all judges of assize and gaol-delivery, sheriffs, justices of the peace, mayors, bailiffs, and other officers whatsoever, whether ecclesiastical or civil, are to take notice of it, and pay due obedience thereunto.   And that there may be no pretence for any of our subjects to continue their illegal meetings and conventicles, we do declare, that we shall from time to time allow a sufficient number of places, as shall be desired, in all parts of this our kingdom, for the use of such as do not conform to the Church of England, to meet and assemble in, in order to their public worship and devotion ; which places shall be open and free to all persons. But to prevent such disorders and inconveniences as may happen by this our indulgence, if not duly regulated, and that they may be the better protected by the civil magistrate, our express will and pleasure is, that none of our subjects do presume to meet in any place, until such place be allowed, and the teacher of that congregation be approved by us.   And lest any should apprehend, that this restriction should make our said allowance and approbation difficult to be obtained, we do further declare, that this our indulgence, as to the allowance of public places of worship, and approbation of teachers, shall extend to all sorts of non-conformists and recusants, except the recusants of the Roman Catholic religion, to whom we shall no ways allow in public places of worship, but only indulge them their share in the common exemption from the executing the penal laws, and the exercise of their worship in their private houses only.   And if after this our clemency and indulgence, any of our subjects shall presume to abuse this liberty, and shall preach seditiously, or to the derogation of the doctrine, discipline, or government of the established church, or shall meet in places not allowed by us ; we do hereby give them warning, and declare, we will proceed against them with all imaginable severity : and we will let them see, we can be as severe to punish such offenders, when so justly provoked, as we are indulgent to truly tender consciences.

---

228. Test Act

(1673, March 29. 25 Charles II. c. 2. 5 *S. R.* 782. The whole reprinted in G. and H. pp. 632–640.)

FOR preventing dangers which may happen from popish recusants and quieting the minds of His Majesty's good subjects : be it enacted by the king's most excellent Majesty, by and with the advice and consent of the lords spiritual and temporal and the commons in this present parliament assembled, and by authority of the same, that all and every person or persons, as well peers as commoners, that shall bear any office or offices, civil or military, or shall receive any pay, salary, fee or wages by reason of any patent or grant from His Majesty, or shall have command or place of trust from or under His Majesty, or from any of His Majesty's predecessors, or by his or their authority, or by authority derived from him or them, within the realm of England, dominion of Wales or town of Berwick upon Tweed, or in His Majesty's navy, or in the several islands of Jersey and Guernsey, or shall be of the household or in the service or employment of His Majesty, or of His Royal Highness the duke of York, who shall inhabit, reside or be within the city of London or Westminster or within thirty miles distant from the same, on the first day of Easter term that shall be in the year of our Lord, one thousand six hundred seventy-three, or at any time during the said term, all and every the said person and persons shall personally appear before the end of the said term, or of Trinity term next following, in His Majesty's high court of chancery or in His Majesty's court of king's bench, and there in public and open court, between the hours of nine of the clock and twelve in the forenoon, take the several oaths of supremacy and allegiance, which oath of allegiance is contained in the statute made in the third year of King James, by law established, and during the time of the taking thereof by the said person and persons all pleas and proceedings in the said respective courts shall cease ; and that all and every of the said respective persons and officers, not having taken the said oaths in the said respective courts aforesaid, shall on or before the first day of August, one thousand six hundred seventy-three, at the quarter sessions for that county or place where he or they shall be, inhabit or reside on the twentieth day of May, take the said oaths in open court between the said hours of nine and twelve of the clock in the forenoon; and the said respective officers aforesaid shall also receive the sacrament of the Lord's Supper according to the usage of the Church of England, at or before the first day of August, in the year of our Lord one thousand six hundred and seventy-three, in some parish church, upon some Lord's day, commonly called Sunday, immediately after divine service and sermon.

II. And be it further enacted by the authority aforesaid, that all and every person or persons that shall be admitted, entered, placed or taken into any office or offices civil or military, or shall receive any pay, salary, fee or wages by reason of any patent or grant of His Majesty, or shall have command or place of trust from or under His Majesty, his heirs or successors, or by his or their authority, or by authority derived from him or them, within this realm of England, dominion of Wales or town of Berwick upon Tweed, or in His Majesty's navy, or in the several islands of Jersey and Guernsey, or that shall be admitted into any service or employment in His Majesty's or royal highness's household or family after the first day of Easter term aforesaid, and shall inhabit, be, or reside, when he or they is or are so admitted or placed, within the cities of London or Westminster or within thirty miles of the same, shall take the said oaths aforesaid in the said respective court or courts aforesaid, in the next term after such his or their admittance or admittances into the office or offices, employment or employments aforesaid, between the hours aforesaid and no other, and the proceedings to cease as aforesaid; and that all and every such person or persons to be admitted after the first day of Easter term as aforesaid, not having taken the said oaths in the said courts aforesaid, shall at the quarter sessions for that county or place where he or they shall reside, next after such his admittance or admittances into any of the said respective offices or employments aforesaid, take the said several and respective oaths as aforesaid; and all and every such person and persons so to be admitted as aforesaid shall also receive the sacrament of the Lord's Supper, according to the usage of the Church of England, within three months after his or their admittances in, or receiving their said authority and employment, in some public church upon some Lord's day, commonly called Sunday, immediately after divine service and sermon.

III. And every of the said persons in the respective court where he takes the said oaths shall first deliver a certificate of such his receiving the said sacrament as aforesaid, under the hands of the respective minister and churchwarden, and shall then make proof of the truth thereof by two credible witnesses at the least upon oath, all which shall be inquired of and put upon record in the respective courts.

IV. And be it further enacted by the authority aforesaid, that all and every the person or persons aforesaid, that do or shall neglect or refuse to take the said oaths and sacrament in the said courts and places, and at the respective times aforesaid, shall be ipso facto adjudged incapable and disabled in law to all intents and purposes whatsoever to have, occupy or enjoy the said office or offices, employment or employments, or any part of them or any matter or thing aforesaid, or any profit or advantage appertaining to them or any of them, and every such office and place, employment and employments shall be void, and is hereby adjudged void.

V. And be it further enacted, that all and every such person or persons that shall neglect or refuse to take the said oaths or the sacrament as aforesaid, within the times and in the places aforesaid, and in the manner aforesaid, and yet after such neglect or refusal shall execute any of the said offices or employments after the said times expired, wherein he or they ought to have taken the same, and being thereupon lawfully convicted in or upon any information, presentment or indictment in any of the king's courts at Westminster, or at the assizes, every such person and persons shall be disabled from thenceforth to sue or use any action, bill, plaint or information in course of law, or to prosecute any suit in any court of equity, or to be guardian of any child, or executor or administrator of any person, or capable of any legacy or deed of gift, or to bear any office within this realm of England, dominion of Wales or town of Berwick upon Tweed, and shall forfeit the sum of five hundred pounds, to be recovered by him or them that shall sue for the same, to be prosecuted by any action of debt, suit, bill, plaint, or information in any of His Majesty's courts at Westminster, wherein no essoin, protection or wager of law shall lie.

* * * * * * * * *

IX. And be it further enacted by the authority aforesaid, that at the same time when the persons concerned in this act shall take the aforesaid oaths of supremacy and allegiance, they shall likewise make and subscribe this declaration following, under the same penalties and forfeitures as by this act is appointed :

I, A. B., do declare, that I do believe that there is not any transubstantiation in the sacrament of the Lord's Supper, or in the elements of bread and wine, at, or after the consecration thereof by any person whatsoever.

X. Of which subscription there shall be the like register kept as of the taking of the oaths aforesaid.

*   *   *   *   *   *   *   *   *

229. Resolution concerning the Royal Pardon in Bar of Danby's Impeachment

(1679, May 5.   Cobbett's Parliamentary History, iv. 1129.)

THE commons resolved : "That it was the opinion of this house, that the pardon pleaded by the earl of Danby was illegal and void, and ought not to be allowed in bar of the impeachment of the commons of England." After which, Mr. Speaker, with the whole house, went up to the lords' bar, and demanded judgment against the earl in these words :

" My lords ; the knights, citizens and burgesses, in parliament assembled, are come up to demand judgment, in their own names, and the names of all the commons of England, against Thomas, earl of Danby, who stands impeached by them before your lordships of hightreason, and divers high crimes and misdemeanors ; to which he has pleaded a pardon : which pardon the commons conceive to be illegal and void ; and therefore they do demand judgment of your lordships accordingly."

230. Exclusion Bill

(1679, May 15.   Cobbett's Parliamentary History, iv. 1136.)

MAY 15.   The Exclusion Bill was called for and read the first time.   It set forth, after the particulars of the execrable conspiracy : " That the emissaries, priests and agents for the pope had traitorously seduced James, duke of York, presumptive heir to these crowns, to the communion of the church of Rome ; and had induced him to enter into several negotiations with the pope, his cardinals and nuncios, for promoting the Romish church and interest; and by his means and procurement, had advanced the power and greatness of the French king, to the manifest hazard of these kingdoms. That by descent of these crowns upon a papist, and by foreign alliances and assistance, they might be able to succeed in their wicked and villainous designs." Then, after another preamble, they enacted to this effect: 1. "That the said James, duke of York, should be incapable of inheriting the crowns of England, Scotland, and Ireland, with their dependencies; and of enjoying any of the titles, rights, prerogatives and revenues belonging to the said crowns. 2. That in case his majesty should happen to die, or resign his dominions, they should devolve to the person next in succession, in the same manner as if the duke was dead. 3. That all acts of sovereignty and royalty that prince might then happen to perform, were not only declared void, but to be high treason, and punishable as such. 4. That if any one, at any time whatsoever, should endeavour to bring the said duke into any of the fore-mentioned dominions, or correspond with him in order to make him inherit, he should be guilty of high treason. 5. That if the duke himself ever returned into any of these dominions, considering the mischiefs that must ensue, he should be looked upon as guilty of the same offense; and all persons were authorized and required, to seize upon and imprison him; and in case of resistance made by him or his adherents, to subdue them by force of arms."

---

231. Habeas Corpus Act

(1679, May 26. 31 Charles II. c. 2. 5 S. R. 935. Stubbs, Select Charters, 517–521.)

WHEREAS great delays have been used by sheriffs, gaolers and other officers, to whose custody any of the king's subjects have been committed for criminal or supposed criminal matters, in making returns of writs of Habeas Corpus to them directed by standing out an Alias and Pluries Habeas Corpus and sometimes more, and by other shifts to avoid their yielding obedience to such writs, contrary to their duty and the known laws of the land, whereby many of the king's subjects have been and hereafter may be long detained in prison in such cases where by law they are bailable, to their great charge and vexation.

Habeas Corpus Act 441

II. For the prevention whereof and the more speedy relief of all persons imprisoned for any such criminal or supposed criminal matters; be it enacted by the king's most excellent Majesty, by and with the advice and consent of the lords spiritual and temporal and commons in this present parliament assembled, and by the authority thereof, that whensoever any person or persons shall bring any habeas corpus directed unto any sheriff or sheriffs, gaoler, minister or other person whatsoever for any person in his or their custody, and the said writ shall be served upon the said officer or left at the gaol or prison with any of the under officers, under keepers or deputy of the said officers or keepers, that the said officer or officers, his or their under officers, under keepers or deputies shall within three days after the service thereof as aforesaid (unless the commitment aforesaid were for treason or felony, plainly and specially expressed in the warrant of commitment) upon payment or tender of the charges of bringing the said prisoner, to be ascertained by the judge or court that awarded the same and endorsed upon the said writ, not exceeding twelve pence per mile, and upon security given by his own bond to pay the charges of carrying back the prisoner, if he shall be remanded by the court or judge to which he shall be brought according to the true intent of this present act, and that he will not make any escape by the way, make return of such writ; and bring or cause to be brought the body of the party so committed or restrained unto or before the lord chancellor, or lord keeper of the great seal of England, for the time being, or the judges or barons of the said court from whence the said writ shall issue, or unto and before such other person or persons before whom the said writ is made returnable, according to the command thereof; and shall then likewise certify the true causes of his detainer or imprisonment; unless the commitment of the said party be in any place beyond the distance of twenty miles from the place or places where such court or person is or shall be residing, and if beyond the distance of twenty miles and not above one hundred miles then within the space of ten days, and if beyond the distance of one hundred miles then within the space of twenty days after such delivery aforesaid, and not longer.

III. And to the intent that no sheriff, gaoler or other officer may pretend ignorance of the import of any such writ; be it enacted by the authority aforesaid, that all such writs shall be marked in this manner, Per statutum tricesimo primo Caroli Secundi regis, and shall be signed by the person that awards the same; and if any person or persons shall be or stand committed or detained as aforesaid, for any crime, unless for treason or felony plainly expressed in the warrant of commitment, in the vacation time, and out of term, it shall and may be lawful to and for the person or persons so committed or detained (other than persons convict or in execution by legal process) or any one on his or their behalf to appeal or complain to the lord chancellor or lord keeper or any one of His Majesty's justices, either of the one bench or of the other, or the barons of the exchequer of the degree of the coif; and the said lord chancellor, lord keeper, justices or barons or any of them, upon view of the copy or copies of the warrant or warrants of commitment and detainer, or otherwise upon oath made that such copy or copies were denied to be given by such person or persons in whose custody the prisoner or prisoners is or are detained, are hereby authorised and required, upon request made in writing by such person or persons or any on his, her or their behalf, attested and subscribed by two witnesses who were present at the delivery of the same, to award and grant an habeas corpus, under the seal of such court whereof he shall then be one of the judges, to be directed to the officer or officers in whose custody the party so committed or detained shall be, returnable immediate before the said lord chancellor or lord keeper, or such justice, baron or any other justice or baron of the degree of the coif of any of the said courts; and upon service thereof as aforesaid, the officer or officers, his or their under officer or under officers, under keeper or under keepers, or deputy, in whose custody the party is so committed or detained, shall within the times respectively before limited bring such prisoner or prisoners before the said lord chancellor or lord keeper, or such justices, barons or one of them, before whom the said writ is made returnable, and in case of his absence before any other of them, with the return of such writ and the true causes of the commitment and detainer; and thereupon within two days after the party shall be brought before them, the said lord chancellor or lord keeper, or such justice or baron before whom the prisoner shall be brought as aforesaid, shall discharge the said prisoner from his imprisonment, taking his or their recognizance with one or more surety or sureties in any sum according to their discretions, having regard to the quality of the prisoner and nature of the offence, for his or their appearance in the court of king's bench the term following or at the next assizes, sessions or general gaol-delivery of and for such county, city or place where the commitment was, or where the offence was committed, or in such other court where the said offence is properly cognizable, as the case shall require, and then shall certify the said writ with the return thereof and the said recognizance or recognizances into the said court where such appearance is to be made; unless it shall appear unto the said lord chancellor or lord keeper, or justice or justices, or baron or barons, that the party so committed is detained upon a legal process, order or warrant out of some court that hath jurisdiction of criminal matters, or by some warrant signed and sealed with the hand and seal of any of the said justices or barons, or some justice or justices of the peace, for such matters or offences for the which by the law the prisoner is not bailable.

IV. Provided always, and be it enacted, that if any person shall have wilfully neglected by the space of two whole terms after his imprisonment to pray a habeas corpus for his enlargement, such person so wilfully neglecting shall not have any habeas corpus to be granted in vacation time in pursuance of this act.

V. And be it further enacted by the authority aforesaid, that if any officer or officers, his or their under-officer or under-officers, under-keeper or under-keepers, or deputy, shall neglect or refuse to make the returns aforesaid, or to bring the body or bodies of the prisoner or prisoners according to the command of the said writ, within the respective times aforesaid, or upon demand made by the prisoner or person in his behalf shall refuse to deliver, or within the space of six hours after demand shall not deliver, to the person so demanding, a true copy of the warrant or warrants of commitment and detainer of such prisoner, which he and they are hereby required to deliver accordingly; all and every the head gaolers and keepers of such prisons, and such other person in whose custody the prisoner shall be detained, shall for the first offence forfeit to the prisoner or party grieved the sum of one hundred pounds; and for the second offence the sum of two hundred pounds and shall and is hereby made incapable to hold or execute his said office; the said penalties to be recovered by the prisoner or party grieved, his executors or administrators, against such offender, his executors or administrators, by any action of debt, suit, bill, plaint or information, in any of the king's courts at Westminster, wherein no essoin, protection, privilege, injunction, wager of law or stay of prosecution by Non vult ulterius prosequi or otherwise shall be admitted or allowed, or any more than one imparlance; and any recovery or judgment at the suit of any party grieved shall be a sufficient conviction for the first offence; and any after recovery or judgment at the suit of a party grieved for any offence after the first judgment shall be a sufficient conviction to bring the officers or person within the said penalty for the second offence.

VI. And for the prevention of unjust vexation by reiterated commitments for the same offence ; be it enacted by the authority afore-said, that no person or persons, which shall be delivered or set at large upon any habeas corpus, shall at any time hereafter be again imprisoned or committed for the same offence by any person or persons whatsoever, other than by the legal order and process of such court wherein he or they shall be bound by recognizance to appear or other court having jurisdiction of the cause ; and if any other person or persons shall knowingly contrary to this act recom-mit or imprison or knowingly procure or cause to be recommitted or imprisoned for the same offence or pretended offence any person or persons delivered or set at large as aforesaid, or be know-ingly aiding or assisting therein, then he or they shall forfeit to the prisoner or party grieved the sum of five hundred pounds, any colourable pretence or variation in the warrant or warrants of com-mitment notwithstanding, to be recovered as aforesaid.

VII. Provided always, and be it further enacted, that if any per-son or persons shall be committed for high treason or felony, plainly and specially expressed in the warrant of commitment, upon his prayer or petition in open court the first week of the term or first day of the sessions of oyer and terminer or general gaol delivery to be brought to his trial, shall not be indicted sometime in the next term, sessions of oyer and terminer or general gaol delivery after such commitment ; it shall and may be lawful to and for the judges of the court of king's bench and justices of oyer and terminer or general gaol delivery and they are hereby required, upon motion to them made in open court the last day of the term, sessions or gaol delivery, either by the prisoner or any one in his behalf, to set at liberty the prisoner upon bail, unless it appear to the judges and justices upon oath made, that the witnesses for the king could not be produced the same term, sessions or general gaol delivery ; and if any person or persons, committed as aforesaid, upon his prayer or petition in open court the first week of the term or first day of the sessions of oyer and terminer or general gaol delivery to be brought to his trial, shall not be indicted and tried the second term, ses-sions of oyer and terminer or general gaol delivery after his commit-ment, or upon his trial shall be acquitted, he shall be discharged from his imprisonment.

VIII. Provided always, that nothing in this act shall extend to discharge out of prison any person charged in debt or other action or with process in any civil cause, but that after he shall be dis-charged of his imprisonment for such his criminal offence, he shall be kept in custody according to law for such other suit.

IX. Provided always, and be it enacted by the authority aforesaid, that if any person or persons, subjects of this realm, shall be committed to any prison or in custody of any officer or officers whatsoever for any criminal or supposed criminal matter, that the said person shall not be removed from the said prison and custody into the custody of any other officer or officers; unless it be by habeas corpus or some other legal writ, or where the prisoner is delivered to the constable or other inferior officer to carry such prisoner to some common gaol, or where any person is sent by order of any judge of assize or justice of the peace to any common work-house or house of correction, or where the prisoner is removed from one prison or place to another within the same county, in order to his or her trial or discharge in due course of law, or in case of sudden fire or infection or other necessity; and if any person or persons shall after such commitment aforesaid make out and sign or countersign any warrant or warrants for such removal aforesaid, contrary to this act, as well he that makes or signs or countersigns such warrant or warrants as the officer or officers that obey or execute the same shall suffer and incur the pains and forfeitures in this act beforementioned, both for the first and second offence respectively, to be recovered in manner aforesaid by the party grieved.

X. Provided also, and be it further enacted by the authority aforesaid, that it shall and may be lawful to and for any prisoner and prisoners as aforesaid to move and obtain his or their habeas corpus as well out of the high court of chancery or court of exchequer as out of the court of king's bench or common pleas or either of them; and if the said lord chancellor or lord keeper, or any judge or judges, baron or barons for the time being of the degree of the coif, of any of the courts aforesaid, in the vacation time upon view of the copy or copies of the warrant or warrants of commitment or detainer, or upon oath made that such copy or copies were denied as aforesaid, shall deny any writ of habeas corpus by this act required to be granted being moved for as aforesaid, they shall severally forfeit to the prisoner or party grieved the sum of five hundred pounds, to be recovered in manner aforesaid.

XI. And be it enacted and declared by the authority aforesaid, that an habeas corpus according to the true intent and meaning of this act may be directed and run into any county palatine, the Cinque ports, or other privileged places within the kingdom of England, dominion of Wales or town of Berwick upon Tweed, and the islands of Jersey or Guernsey, any law or usage to the contrary notwithstanding.

XII. And for preventing illegal imprisonments in prisons beyond the seas; be it further enacted by the authority aforesaid, that no subject of this realm that now is or hereafter shall be an inhabitant or resident of this kingdom of England, dominion of Wales or town of Berwick upon Tweed shall or may be sent prisoner into Scotland, Ireland, Jersey, Guernsey, Tangier or into any parts, garrisons, islands or places beyond the seas, which are or at any time hereafter shall be within or without the dominions of his majesty, his heirs or successors; and that every such imprisonment is hereby enacted and adjudged to be illegal; and that if any of the said subjects now is or hereafter shall be so imprisoned every such person and persons so imprisoned shall and may for every such imprisonment maintain by virtue of this act an action or actions of false imprisonment in any of his majesty's courts of record against the person or persons by whom he or she shall be so committed, detained, imprisoned, sent prisoner or transported, contrary to the true meaning of this act, and against all or any person or persons that shall frame, contrive, write, seal or countersign any warrant or writing for such commitment, detainer, imprisonment or transportation, or shall be advising, aiding or assisting in the same or any of them; and the plaintiff in every such action shall have judgment to recover his treble costs, besides damages, which damages so to be given shall not be less than five hundred pounds; in which action no delay, stay or stop of proceeding by rule, order or command, nor no injunction, protection or privilege whatsoever, nor any more than one imparlance, shall be allowed, excepting such rule of the court wherein the action shall depend, made in open court, as shall be thought in justice necessary, for special cause to be expressed in the said rule; and the person or persons who shall knowingly frame, contrive, write, seal or countersign any warrant for such commitment, detainer or transportation, or shall so commit, detain, imprison or transport any person or persons, contrary to this act, or be any ways advising, aiding or assisting therein, being lawfully convicted thereof, shall be disabled from thenceforth to bear any office of trust or profit within the said realm of England, dominion of Wales or town of Berwick upon Tweed, or any of the islands, territories or dominions thereunto belonging; and shall incur and sustain the pains, penalties and forfeitures limited, ordained and provided in and by the statute of provision and præmunire, made in the sixteenth year of King Richard the Second; and be incapable of any pardon from the king, his heirs or successors, of the said forfeitures, losses or disabilities, or any of them.

XIII. Provided always, that nothing in this act shall extend to give benefit to any person who shall by contract in writing agree with any merchant or owner of any plantation, or other person whatsoever, to be transported to any parts beyond seas, and receive earnest upon such agreement, although that afterwards such person shall renounce such contract.

XIV. Provided always, and be it enacted, that if any person or persons lawfully convicted of any felony shall in open court pray to be transported beyond the seas, and the court shall think fit to leave him or them in prison for that purpose, such person or persons may be transported into any parts beyond the seas, this act or anything therein contained to the contrary notwithstanding.

XV. Provided also, and be it enacted, that nothing herein contained shall be deemed, construed or taken to extend to the imprisonment of any person before the first day of June one thousand six hundred seventy and nine, or to anything advised, procured or otherwise done relating to such imprisonment, anything herein contained to the contrary notwithstanding.

XVI. Provided also, that if any person or persons at any time resident in this realm shall have committed any capital offence in Scotland or Ireland or any of the islands or foreign plantations of the king, his heirs or successors, where he or she ought to be tried for such offence, such person or persons may be sent to such place there to receive such trial in such manner as the same might have been used before the making of this act, anything herein contained to the contrary notwithstanding.

XVII. Provided also, and be it enacted, that no person or persons shall be sued, impleaded, molested or troubled for any offence against this act, unless the party offending be sued or impleaded for the same within two years at the most after such time wherein the offence shall be committed, in case the party grieved shall not be then in prison ; and if he shall be in prison, then within the space of two years after the decease of the person imprisoned, or his or her delivery out of prison, which shall first happen.

XVIII. And to the intent no person may avoid his trial at the assizes or general gaol delivery by procuring his removal before the assizes, at such time as he cannot be brought back to receive his trial there ; be it enacted, that after the assizes proclaimed for that county where the prisoner is detained, no person shall be removed from the common gaol upon any habeas corpus granted in pursuance of this act, but upon any such habeas corpus shall be brought before the judge of assize in open court, who is thereupon to do what to justice shall appertain.

XIX. Provided nevertheless, that after the assizes are ended any person or persons detained may have his or her habeas corpus according to the direction and intention of this act.

XX. And be it also enacted by the authority aforesaid, that if any information, suit or action shall be brought or exhibited against any person or persons for any offence committed or to be committed against the form of this law, it shall be lawful for such defendants to plead the general issue that they are not guilty, or that they owe nothing, and to give such special matter in evidence to the jury that shall try the same, which matter being pleaded had been good and sufficient matter in law to have discharged the said defendant or defendants against the said information, suit or action, and the said matter shall then be as available to him or them to all intents and purposes, as if he or they had sufficiently pleaded, set forth or alleged the same matter in bar or discharge of such information, suit or action.

XXI. And because many times persons charged with petty treason or felony or as accessories thereunto are committed upon suspicion only, whereupon they are bailable or not according as the circumstances making out that suspicion are more or less weighty, which are best known to the justices of peace that committed the persons, and have the examinations before them, or to other justices of the peace in the county ; be it therefore enacted, that where any person shall appear to be committed by any judge or justice of the peace and charged as accessory before the fact to any petty treason or felony or upon suspicion thereof, or with suspicion of petty treason or felony which petty treason or felony shall be plainly and specially expressed in the warrant of commitment, that such person shall not be removed or bailed by virtue of this act, or in any other manner than they might have been before the making of this act.

------◆------

232. Forfeiture of Charter of London

(1683. 8 State Trials, 1264, 1265.)

Reply of the Lord Chief Justice to the Argument on Behalf of the Corporation

BUT this is one thing, Mr. Pollexfen, that I would say to you upon your argument, what a grievous thing would it be, if so be the being of a corporation might be forfeited or dissolved, because say you, it is possible that all the corporations in England may be dissolved because they may have committed such things that may be forfeitures. We must put the scales equal on both sides. Let us then consider on the other side, whether, if so be that it should be taken for law, that a corporation is indissoluble or cannot be dissolved for any crime whatsoever, then those two things do not follow ; — First, you will shut out the king's Quo Warranto, let him have what reason he can for it, or let them do what they will : and in the next place, you have set up so many independent commonwealths. For if a corporation may do nothing amiss whatsoever, what else does follow, for now I am not upon the point whether this corporation has done any act that is amiss, but considering your argument in general, when you make it a thing of such ill consequence that a corporation should be forfeited by any crime ; but I say now, to put in the other scale the mischiefs that would follow, if so be by law a corporation might not be dissolved for one fault or another : But let them do what they would, it should still remain a corporation. Then it is plain, they are so many commonwealths independent upon the king, and the king's Quo Warranto is quite shut out, that is mighty considerable.

* * * * * * * * *

Judgment

The next term, viz. Trinit. 35 Car. 2. (Chief Justice Saunders dying the day of the judgment given, or the next day after) Mr. justice Jones, justice Raymond, and justice Withens, being in court, justice Jones pronounced the judgment of the court, and justice Raymond and justice Withens affirmed, that chief justice Saunders was of the same opinion with them, and that they all agreed.

1. That a corporation aggregate might be seized. That the statute 28 Ed. 3, cap. 10, is express, that the franchises and liberties of the city, upon such defaults, should be taken into the king's hands. And that bodies politic may offend, and be pardoned, appears by the general article of pardon, 12 Car. 2, whereby corporations are pardoned all crimes and offences. And the act for regulating corporations, 13 Car. 2, which provides that no corporation shall be avoided for anything by them misdone or omitted to be done, shows also that their charters may be avoided for things by them misdone, or omitted to be done.

2. That exacting and taking money by the pretended by-law,

2 G

was extortion, and a forfeiture of the franchise of being a corporation.

3. That the petition was scandalous and libellous, and the making it and publishing it a forfeiture.

4. That the act of the common council was the act of the corporation.

5. That the matter set forth in the record did not excuse or avoid those forfeitures set forth in the replication.

6. That the information was well founded.

And gave judgment, That the franchise should be seized into the king's hands, but the entry thereof respited till the king's pleasure was known in it.   Justice Raymond and justice Withens declare, that they were of the same opinion in *omnibus*.

And accordingly, after entry made by Mr. Attorney, That as to the issue joined to be tried by the country ; as to the claiming to have and constitute sheriffs ; as to the having the mayor and aldermen to be justices of the peace, and to hold sessions, ' quod ipse pro Domino Rege ulterius non vult prosequi ; ' Judgment is entered.

---

233. Hales' Case: The Dispensing Power

(1686.   Chief Justice Herbert.   11 State Trials, 1302.)

Chief Justice. ' In the case of Godwin and Hales, wherein the defendant pleads a dispensation from the king, it is doubted, whether or no the king had such a prerogative?   Truly, upon the argument before us, it appeared as clear a case as ever came before this court : but because men fancy I know not what difficulty, when really there is none, we were willing to give so much countenance to the question in the case, as to take the advice of all the judges in England.   They were all assembled at Serjeant's Inn and this case was put them, and the great case of the sheriffs was put ; whether the dispensation in that case were legal, because upon that depended the execution of all the law of the nation?   And, I must tell you that there were then ten upon the place, that clearly delivered their opinions, that the case of the sheriffs was good law, and that all the attainders grounded upon indictments found by juries returned by such sheriffs, were good, and not erroneous ; and consequently, that men need not have any fears or scruples about that matter.   And in the next place, they did clearly declare, that there was no imaginable difference between that case and this, unless it were, that this were the much clearer case of the two, and liable to the fewer exceptions. My brother Powell said, he was inclined to be of the same opinion, but he would rather have some more time to consider of it; but he has since sent by my brother Holloway to let us know that he does concur with us. To these eleven judges, there is one dissenter, brother Street, who yet continues his opinion, that the king cannot dispense in this case. But that is the opinion of one single judge, against the opinion of eleven : we were satisfied in our own judgments before, and having the concurrence of eleven out of twelve, we think we may very well declare the opinion of the court to be, that the king may dispense in this case ; and the judges go upon these grounds :

'1. That the kings of England are sovereign princes.

'2. That the laws of England are the king's laws.

'3. That therefore, it is an inseparable prerogative in the kings of England, to dispense with penal laws in particular cases, and upon particular necessary reasons.

'4. That of those reasons, and those necessities, the king himself is sole judge : and then, which is consequent upon all,

'5. That this is not a trust invested in, or granted to the king by the people ; but the ancient remains of the sovereign power, and prerogative of the kings of England, which never yet was taken from them, nor can be. And therefore such a dispensation being pleaded by the defendant in this case, and such a dispensation appearing upon record to come, time enough to save him from the forfeiture, judgment ought to be given for the defendant, ' Quod quærens nil capiat per billam.' '

*   *   *   *   *   *   *   *   *

234. James II's Declaration of Indulgence

(1687, April 4. G. and H. 641–644.)

IT having pleased Almighty God not only to bring us to the imperial crown of these kingdoms through the greatest difficulties, but to preserve us by a more than ordinary providence upon the throne of our royal ancestors, there is nothing now that we so earnestly desire as to establish our government on such a foundation as may make our subjects happy, and unite them to us by inclination as well as duty. Which we think can be done by no means so effectually as by granting to them the free exercise of their religion for the time to come, and add that to the perfect enjoyment of their property, which has never been in any case invaded by us since our coming to the crown. Which being the two things men value most, shall ever be preserved in these kingdoms, during our reign over them, as the truest methods of their peace and our glory. We cannot but heartily wish, as it will easily be believed, that all the people of our dominions were members of the Catholic Church; yet we humbly thank Almighty God, it is and has of long time been our constant sense and opinion (which upon divers occasions we have declared) that conscience ought not to be constrained nor people forced in matters of mere religion: it has ever been directly contrary to our inclination, as we think it is to the interest of government, which it destroys by spoiling trade, depopulating countries, and discouraging strangers, and finally, that it never obtained the end for which it was employed. And in this we are the more confirmed by the reflections we have made upon the conduct of the four last reigns. For after all the frequent and pressing endeavours that were used in each of them to reduce this kingdom to an exact conformity in religion, it is visible the success has not answered the design, and that the difficulty is invincible.

We therefore, out of our princely care and affection unto all our loving subjects, that they may live at ease and quiet, and for the increase of trade and encouragement of strangers, have thought fit by virtue of our royal prerogative to issue forth this our declaration of indulgence, making no doubt of the concurrence of our two houses of parliament when we shall think it convenient for them to meet.

In the first place, we do declare that we will protect and maintain our archbishops, bishops, and clergy, and all other our subjects of the Church of England in the free exercise of their religion as by law established, and in the quiet and full enjoyment of all their possessions, without any molestation or disturbance whatsoever.

We do likewise declare, that it is our royal will and pleasure that from henceforth the execution of all and all manner of penal laws in matters ecclesiastical, for not coming to church, or not receiving the Sacrament, or for any other nonconformity to the religion established, or for or by reason of the exercise of religion in any manner whatsoever, be immediately suspended; and the further execution of the said penal laws and every of them is hereby suspended.

And to the end that by the liberty hereby granted the peace and security of our government in the practice thereof may not be endangered, we have thought fit, and do hereby straitly charge and command all our loving subjects, that, as we do freely give them leave to meet and serve God after their own way and manner, be it in private houses or places purposely hired or built for that use, so that they take especial care that nothing be preached or taught amongst them, which may any way tend to alienate the hearts of our people from us or our government; and that their meetings and assemblies be peaceably, openly, and publicly held, and all persons freely admitted to them; and that they do signify and make known to some one or more of the next justices of the peace what place or places they set apart for those uses; and that all our subjects may enjoy such their religious assemblies with greater assurance and protection, we have thought it requisite, and do hereby command, that no disturbance of any kind be made or given unto them, under pain of our displeasure, and to be further proceeded against with the utmost severity.

And forasmuch as we are desirous to have the benefit of the service of all our loving subjects, which by the law of nature is inseparably annexed to and inherent in our royal person, and that none of our subjects may for the future be under any discouragement or disability (who are otherwise well inclined and fit to serve us) by reason of some oaths or tests that have been usually administered on such occasions, we do hereby further declare, that it is our royal will and pleasure that the oaths commonly called ' The oaths of supremacy and allegiance,' and also the several tests and declarations mentioned in the acts of parliament made in the five-and-twentieth and thirtieth years of the reign of our late royal brother, King Charles II, shall not at any time hereafter be required to be taken, declared, or subscribed by any person or persons whatsoever, who is or shall be employed in any office or place of trust, either civil or military, under us or in our government. And we do further declare it to be our pleasure and intention from time to time hereafter, to grant our royal dispensations under our great seal to all our loving subjects so to be employed, who shall not take the said oaths, or subscribe or declare the said tests or declarations in the above-mentioned acts and every of them.

And to the end that all our loving subjects may receive and enjoy the full benefit and advantage of our gracious indulgence hereby intended, and may be acquitted and discharged from all pains, penalties, forfeitures, and disabilities by them or any of them incurred or forfeited, or which they shall or may at any time hereafter be liable to, for or by reason of their nonconformity, or the exercise of their religion, and from all suits, troubles, or disturbances for the same ; we do hereby give our free and ample pardon unto all nonconformists, recusants, and other our loving subjects, for all crimes and things by them committed or done contrary to the penal laws, formerly made relating to religion, and the profession or exercise thereof ; hereby declaring that this our royal pardon and indemnity shall be as good and effectual to all intents and purposes, as if every individual person had been therein particularly named, or had particular pardons under our great seal, which we do likewise declare shall from time to time be granted unto any person or persons desiring the same : willing and requiring our judges, justices, and other officers to take notice of and obey our royal will and pleasure hereinbefore declared.

And although the freedom and assurance we have hereby given in relation to religion and property might be sufficient to remove from the minds of our loving subjects all fears and jealousies in relation to either, yet we have thought fit further to declare that we will maintain them in all their properties and possessions, as well of church and abbey lands, as in any other their lands and properties whatsoever.

Given at our Court at Whitehall the fourth day of April, 1687, in the third year of our reign.

------◆------

235. Confirmation of the Convention Parliament

(168$\frac{8}{9}$, Feb. 20. 1 William and Mary, c. 1. 6 *S. R.* 23.)

FOR preventing all doubts and scruples which may in any wise arise concerning the meeting, sitting and proceeding of this present parliament : be it declared and enacted by the king and queen's most excellent majesties, by and with the advice and consent of the lords spiritual and temporal and commons now assembled, and by authority of the same :

II. That the lords spiritual and temporal and commons convened at Westminster the two and twentieth day of January in the year of our Lord one thousand six hundred eighty eight, and there sitting on the thirteenth day of February following, are the two houses of parliament, and so shall be and are hereby enacted and adjudged to be, to all intents, constructions and purposes whatsoever, notwithstanding any want of writ or writs of summons or any other defect of form or default whatsoever, as if they had been summoned according to the usual form ; and that this present act and all other acts, to which the royal assent shall at any time be given before the next prorogation after the said thirteenth of February shall be understood, taken and adjudged in law to begin and commence upon the said thirteenth of February, on which day their said majesties at the request and by the advice of the lords and commons did accept the crown and royal dignity of king and queen of England, France and Ireland, and the dominions and territories thereunto belonging.

III. And be it further enacted by the authority aforesaid, that the act made in the thirtieth year of King Charles the Second, entitled, An Act for the more effectual preserving the King's Person and Government by disabling of Papists from sitting in either House of Parliament, and all other acts of parliament, as to so much of the said act or acts only as concerns the taking the oaths of supremacy and allegiance or either of them, in the said act or acts respectively mentioned, by any member or members of either house of parliament, with relation to their sitting and voting in parliament, shall be and are hereby repealed to all intents and purposes ; anything in the said recited act or acts to the contrary notwithstanding.

IV. And be it further enacted, that the taking the oaths herein after mentioned and the making, subscribing and repeating the declaration in the said act of the thirtieth year of King Charles the Second mentioned, by every member of either house of this present parliament from and after the first day of March next ensuing, in such manner as the taking the said oaths of allegiance and supremacy and the making, subscribing and repeating the said declaration in the said last mentioned act are required, shall be good and effectual to all intents and purposes, as if the said oaths of allegiance and supremacy had been taken and the said declaration had been made, subscribed and repeated in such manner and at such time as by the said act or acts, or any of them, they are required ; and that in all future parliaments the oaths herein after mentioned and the declaration in the said act made in the thirtieth year of King Charles the Second mentioned, shall be taken, made, subscribed and repeated by every member of either house of parliament within the time, and in the same manner and form, and under the penalties and disabilities, as the said oaths of allegiance and supremacy and the said declaration by the said act of the thirtieth year of King Charles the Second are limited, ordained and appointed to be taken, made, subscribed and repeated, and not at any other time or in any other manner, to enable them to sit and vote in parliament; anything in the said act or acts or any of them to the contrary notwithstanding.

V. And it is hereby further enacted and declared by the authority aforesaid, that the oaths above appointed by this act to be taken in the stead and place of the oaths of allegiance and supremacy, shall be in the words following and no other:

VI. 'I, A. B., do sincerely promise and swear, that I will be faithful and bear true allegiance to their majesties King William and Queen Mary, so help me God.'

VII. 'I, A. B., do swear, that I do from my heart abhor, detest and abjure as impious and heretical, that damnable doctrine and position, that princes excommunicated or deprived by the pope or any authority of the see of Rome may be deposed or murdered by their subjects or any other whatsoever; and I do declare, that no foreign prince, person, prelate, state or potentate hath or ought to have any power, jurisdiction, superiority, preeminence or authority, ecclesiastical or spiritual, within this realm, so help me God.'

VIII. Provided always, and be it declared, that this present parliament may be dissolved after the usual manner, as if the same had been summoned and called by writ.

---

236. The Civil List

(1689, March 20 and April 25. Cobbett's Parliamentary History, v. 193, 235.)

20 MARCH: Resolved, *nemine contradicente*, "That it is the opinion of this committee [of the whole house], that there be a revenue of £ 1,200,000 per annum settled upon their majesties, for the constant necessary charge of supporting the Crown in time of peace." Which was agreed to by the house.

25 April: Resolved, "That, out of the public revenue, for the charge of the civil government (including therein what is to be allowed her royal majesty the queen-regent, the queen-dowager, the prince and princess of Denmark, and the marshal Schomberg) there be allowed the sum of £ 600,000 per annum. And, that £ 700,000 be given towards the occasions and charge of the navy."

237. First Mutiny Act

(1689. 1 William and Mary, c. 5. 6 S. R. 55.)

WHEREAS the raising or keeping a standing army within this kingdom in time of peace, unless it be with consent of parliament, is against law; and whereas it is judged necessary by their majesties and this present parliament that during this time of danger several of the forces which are now on foot should be continued, and others raised, for the safety of the kingdom, for the common defence of the Protestant religion and for the reducing of Ireland;

And whereas no man may be forejudged of life or limb, or subjected to any kind of punishment, by martial law or in any other manner, than by the judgment of his peers and according to the known and established laws of this realm, yet nevertheless it being requisite for retaining such forces as are or shall be raised during this exigence of affairs in their duty, an exact discipline be observed, and that soldiers who shall mutiny or stir up sedition or shall desert their majesties' service be brought to a more exemplary and speedy punishment than the usual forms of law will allow:

II. Be it therefore enacted by the king and queen's most excellent majesties, by and with the advice and consent of the lords spiritual and temporal and commons in this present parliament assembled, and by authority of the same, that, from and after the twelfth day of April in the year of our Lord one thousand six hundred eighty nine, every person being in their majesties' service in the army and being mustered and in pay as an officer or soldier, who shall at any time before the tenth day of November in the year of our Lord one thousand six hundred eighty nine excite, cause or join in any mutiny or sedition in the army, or shall desert their majesties' service in the army, shall suffer death or such other punishment, as by a court martial shall be inflicted.

III. And it is hereby further enacted and declared, that their majesties, or the general of their army for the time being, may by virtue of this act have full power and authority to grant commissions to any lieutenants-general or other officers not under the degree of colonels, from time to time, to call and assemble courts martial for punishing such offences as aforesaid.

IV. And it is hereby further enacted and declared, that no court martial which shall have power to inflict any punishment by virtue of this act for the offences aforesaid shall consist of fewer than thirteen, whereof none to be under the degree of captains.

V. Provided always, that no field officer be tried by other than field officers, and that such court martial shall have power and authority to administer an oath to any witness, in order to the examination or trial of the offences aforesaid.

VI. Provided always, that nothing in this act contained shall extend or be construed to exempt any officer or soldier whatsoever from the ordinary process of law.

VII. Provided always, that this act or anything therein contained shall not extend or be any wise construed to extend to or concern any the militia forces of this kingdom.

VIII. Provided also, that this act shall continue and be in force until the said tenth day of November in the said year of our Lord one thousand six hundred eighty nine, and no longer.

IX. Provided always, and be it enacted, that in all trials of offenders by courts martial to be held by virtue of this act, where the offence may be punished by death, every officer present at such trial before any proceeding be had thereupon shall take an oath upon the evangelists before the court (and the judge advocate or his deputy shall and are hereby respectively authorized to administer the same) in these words that is to say:

"You shall well and truly try and determine according to your evidence the matter now before you between our sovereign lord and lady the king and queen's majesties and the prisoner to be tried. So help you God."

X. And no sentence of death shall be given against any offender in such case by any court martial unless nine of thirteen officers present shall concur therein, and if there be a greater number of officers present then the judgment shall pass by the concurrence of the greater part of them so sworn and not otherwise, and no proceedings, trial or sentence of death shall be had or given against any offender, but between the hours of eight in the morning and one in the afternoon.

238. The Toleration Act

(1689, May 24. 1 William and Mary, c. 18. 6 *S. R.* 74. **The whole**
reprinted in G. and H. 654–664.)

FORASMUCH as some ease to scrupulous consciences in the
exercise of religion may be an effectual means to unite
Their Majesties' Protestant subjects in interest and affection:

II. Be it enacted by the king and queen's most excellent Majesties, by and with the advice and consent of the lords spiritual and
temporal and the commons in this present parliament assembled,
and by the authority of the same, that neither the statute made in
the three and twentieth year of the reign of the late Queen Elizabeth, entitled, An Act to Retain the Queen's Majesty's Subjects in
their due Obedience; nor the statute made in the twenty ninth year
of the said queen, entitled, An Act for the more speedy and due
Execution of certain Branches of the Statute made in the three
and twentieth year of the Queen's Majesty's Reign, viz. the aforesaid act; nor that branch or clause of a statute made in the first
year of the reign of the said queen, entitled, An Act for [the] Uniformity of Common Prayer and Service in the Church and Administration of the Sacraments, whereby all persons having no lawful
or reasonable excuse to be absent are required to resort to their
parish church or chapel or some usual place where the common
prayer shall be used upon pain of punishment by the censures of
the church and also upon pain that every person so offending shall
forfeit for every such offence twelve pence; nor the statute made
in the third year of the reign of the late King James the First,
entitled, An Act for the better Discovering and Repressing Popish
Recusants; nor that other statute made in the same year, entitled,
An Act to Prevent and Avoid Dangers which may grow by Popish
Recusants; nor any other law or statute of this realm made against
papists or popish recusants, except the statute made in the five
and twentieth year of King Charles the Second, entitled, An Act for
Preventing Dangers which may happen from Popish Recusants;
and except also the statute made in the thirtieth year of the said
King Charles the Second, entitled, An Act for the more effectual
preserving the King's Person and Government by disabling
Papists from sitting in either House of Parliament; shall be construed to extend to any person or persons dissenting from the
Church of England, that shall take the oaths mentioned in a statute
made this present parliament, entitled, An Act for removing and

preventing all Questions and Disputes concerning the assembling and sitting of this present Parliament; and shall make and subscribe the declaration mentioned in a statute made in the thirtieth year of King Charles the Second, entitled, An Act to prevent Papists from sitting in either House of Parliament, which oaths and declaration the justices of peace at the general sessions of the peace to be held for the county or place, where such person shall live, are hereby required to tender and administer to such persons as shall offer themselves to take, make and subscribe the same and thereof to keep a register; and likewise none of the persons aforesaid shall give or pay as any fee or reward to any officer or officers belonging to the court aforesaid above the sum of six pence, nor that more than once, for his or their entry of his taking the said oaths, and making and subscribing the said declaration nor above the further sum of six pence for any certificate of the same to be made out and signed by the officer or officers of the said court.

III. And be it further enacted by the authority aforesaid, that all and every person and persons already convicted, or prosecuted in order to conviction, of recusancy by indictment, information, action of debt or otherwise grounded upon the aforesaid statutes or any of them, that shall take the said oaths mentioned in the said statute made this present parliament, and make and subscribe the declaration aforesaid, in the court of exchequer or assizes or general or quarter sessions to be held for the county where such person lives, and to be thence respectively certified into the exchequer, shall be thenceforth exempted and discharged from all the penalties, seizures, forfeitures, judgments and executions incurred by force of any the aforesaid statutes without any composition, fee or further charge whatsoever.

IV. And be it further enacted by the authority aforesaid, that all and every such person and persons that shall as aforesaid take the said oaths, and make and subscribe the declaration aforesaid, shall not be liable to any pains, penalties or forfeitures mentioned in an act made in the five and thirtieth year of the reign of the late Queen Elizabeth, entitled, An Act to retain the Queen's Majesty's Subjects in their due Obedience; nor in an act made the two and twentieth year of the reign of the late King Charles the Second, entitled, An Act to prevent and suppress seditious Conventicles; nor shall any of the said persons be prosecuted in any ecclesiastical court for or by reason of their nonconforming to the Church of England.

V. Provided always, and be it enacted by the authority aforesaid, that if any assembly of persons dissenting from the Church of England shall be had in any place for religious worship with the doors locked, barred or bolted during any time of such meeting together, all and every person or persons that shall come to and be at such meeting shall not receive any benefit from this law, but be liable to all the pains and penalties of all the aforesaid laws recited in this act for such their meeting, notwithstanding his taking the oaths and his making and subscribing the declaration aforesaid.

VI. Provided always, that nothing herein contained shall be construed to exempt any of the persons aforesaid from paying of tithes or other parochial duties or any other duties to the church or minister, nor from any prosecution in any ecclesiastical court or elsewhere for the same.

* * * * * * * * *

VIII. And be it further enacted by the authority aforesaid, that no person dissenting from the Church of England in holy orders or pretended holy orders or pretending to holy orders, nor any preacher or teacher of any congregation of dissenting Protestants, that shall make and subscribe the declaration aforesaid and take the said oaths at the general or quarter sessions of the peace to be held for the county, town, parts or division where such person lives, which court is hereby impowered to administer the same, and shall also declare his approbation of and subscribe the articles of religion mentioned in the statute made in the thirteenth year of the reign of the late Queen Elizabeth, except the thirty-fourth, thirty-fifth and thirty-sixth and these words of the twentieth article, viz. * * * the Church hath power to decree rights or ceremonies, and authority in controversies of faith and yet * * *, shall be liable to any of the pains or penalties mentioned in an act made in the seventeenth year of the reign of King Charles the Second, entitled, An Act for restraining Nonconformists from inhabiting in Corporations; nor the penalties mentioned in the aforesaid act, made in the two and twentieth year of his said late majesty's reign, for or by reason of such persons preaching at any meeting for the exercise of religion, nor to the penalty of one hundred pounds mentioned in an act made in the thirteenth and fourteenth of King Charles the Second, entitled, An Act for the Uniformity of Public Prayers and Administration of Sacraments and other Rites and Ceremonies, and for establishing the Form of making, ordaining and consecrating of Bishops, Priests and Deacons in the Church of England, for officiating in any congregation for the exercise of religion permitted and allowed by this act. * * *

*   *   *   *   *   *   *   *   *

XVI. Provided always, and it is the true intent and meaning of this act, that all the laws made and provided for the frequenting of divine service on the Lord's day, commonly called Sunday, shall be still in force and executed against all persons that offend against the said laws, except such persons come to some congregation or assembly of religious worship allowed or permitted by this act.

XVII. Provided always, and be it further enacted by the authority aforesaid, that neither this act nor any clause, article or thing herein contained shall extend or be construed to extend to give any ease, benefit or advantage to any papist or popish recusant whatsoever, or any person that shall deny in his preaching or writing the doctrine of the Blessed Trinity, as it is declared in the aforesaid articles of religion.

*   *   *   *   *   *   *   *   *

XIX. Provided always, that no congregation or assembly for religious worship shall be permitted or allowed by this act, until the place of such meeting shall be certified to the bishop of the diocese, or to the arch-deacon of that arch-deaconry, or to the justices of the peace at the general or quarter sessions of the peace for the county, city or place in which such meeting shall be held, and registered in the said bishop's or arch-deacon's court respectively, or recorded at the said general or quarter sessions; the register or clerk of the peace whereof respectively is hereby required to register the same, and to give certificate thereof to such person as shall demand the same, for which there shall be no greater fee nor reward taken than the sum of six pence.

239. The Bill of Rights

(1689, December 16. 1 William and Mary, sess. 2, c. 2 (or c. 36). 6 *S. R.* 142. Stubbs, Select Charters, 523–528. G. and H. 645–654.)

WHEREAS the lords spiritual and temporal and commons assembled at Westminster lawfully, fully and freely representing all the estates of the people of this realm, did upon the thirteenth day of February in the year of our Lord one thousand six hundred eighty-eight, present unto Their Majesties, then called and known by the names and style of William and Mary, prince and princess of Orange, being present in their proper persons, a certain declaration in writing made by the said lords and commons in the words following viz. :

Whereas the late king James the Second by the assistance of divers evil counsellors, judges and ministers employed by him did endeavour to subvert and extirpate the Protestant religion and the laws and liberties of this kingdom.

By assuming and exercising a power of dispensing with and suspending of laws, and the execution of laws, without consent of parliament.

By committing and prosecuting divers worthy prelates for humbly petitioning to be excused from concurring to the said assumed power.

By issuing and causing to be executed a commission under the great seal for erecting a court, called the court of commissioners for ecclesiastical causes.

By levying money for and to the use of the crown, by pretence of prerogative, for other time and in other manner than the same was granted by parliament.

By raising and keeping a standing army within this kingdom in time of peace, without consent of parliament, and quartering of soldiers contrary to law.

By causing several good subjects being Protestants to be disarmed, at the same time when papists were both armed and employed, contrary to law.

By violating the freedom of election of members to serve in parliament.

By prosecutions in the court of king's bench for matters and causes cognizable only in parliament, and by divers other arbitrary and illegal courses.

And whereas of late years partial, corrupt and unqualified persons have been returned and served on juries in trials, and particularly divers jurors in trials for high treason, which were not freeholders.

And excessive bail hath been required of persons committed in criminal cases, to elude the benefit of the laws made for the liberty of the subjects.

And excessive fines have been imposed.

And illegal and cruel punishments have been inflicted.

And several grants and promises made of fines and forfeitures before any conviction or judgment against the persons upon whom the same were to be levied.

All which are utterly and directly contrary to the known laws and statutes and freedom of this realm.

And whereas the said late king James the Second having abdicated the government and the throne being thereby vacant, His Highness the prince of Orange (whom it hath pleased Almighty God to make the glorious instrument of delivering this kingdom from popery and arbitrary power) did (by the advice of the lords spiritual and temporal and divers principal persons of the commons) cause letters to be written to the lords spiritual and temporal, being Protestants; and other letters to the several counties, cities, universities, boroughs and Cinque ports for the choosing of such persons to represent them, as were of right to be sent to parliament, to meet and sit at Westminster upon the two and twentieth day of January in this year one thousand six hundred eighty and eight, in order to such an establishment as that their religion, laws and liberties might not again be in danger of being subverted; upon which letters elections having been accordingly made,

And thereupon the said lords spiritual and temporal and commons pursuant to their respective letters and elections being now assembled in a full and free representative of this nation, taking into their most serious consideration the best means for attaining the ends aforesaid, do in the first place (as their ancestors in like case have usually done) for the vindicating and asserting their ancient rights and liberties, declare:

That the pretended power of suspending of laws or the execution of laws by regal authority without consent of parliament is illegal.

That the pretended power of dispensing with laws or the execution of laws by regal authority as it hath been assumed and exercised of late is illegal.

That the commission for erecting the late court of commissioners for ecclesiastical causes and all other commissions and courts of like nature are illegal and pernicious.

That the levying money for or to the use of the crown by pretence of prerogative without grant of parliament for a longer time or in other manner than the same is or shall be granted is illegal.

That it is the right of the subjects to petition the king and all commitments and prosecutions for such petitioning are illegal.

That the raising or keeping a standing army within the kingdom in time of peace unless it be with consent of parliament is against law.

That the subjects which are Protestants may have arms for their defence suitable to their conditions and as allowed by law.

That election of members of parliament ought to be free.

That the freedom of speech and debates or proceedings in parliament ought not to be impeached or questioned in any court or place out of parliament.

That excessive bail ought not to be required nor excessive fines imposed nor cruel and unusual punishments inflicted.

That jurors ought to be duly impanelled and returned and jurors which pass upon men in trials for high treason ought to be freeholders.

That all grants and promises of fines and forfeitures of particular persons before conviction are illegal and void.

And that for redress of all grievances and for the amending, strengthening and preserving of the laws parliaments ought to be held frequently.

And they do claim, demand and insist upon all and singular the premises as their undoubted rights and liberties and that no declarations, judgments, doings or proceedings to the prejudice of the people in any of the said premises ought in any wise to be drawn hereafter into consequence or example. To which demand of their rights they are particularly encouraged by the declaration of His Highness the prince of Orange as being the only means for obtaining a full redress and remedy therein. Having therefore an entire confidence that His said Highness the prince of Orange will perfect the deliverance so far advanced by him, and will still preserve them from the violation of their rights, which they have here asserted, and from all other attempts upon their religion, rights and liberties, the said lords spiritual and temporal and commons assembled at Westminster do resolve, that William and Mary, prince and princess of Orange, be and be declared king and queen of England, France and Ireland and the dominions thereunto belonging, to hold the crown and royal dignity of the said kingdoms and dominions to them the said prince and princess during their lives and the life of the survivor of them; and that the sole and full exercise of the regal power be only in and executed by the said prince of Orange in the names of the said prince and princess during their joint lives; and after their deceases the said crown and royal dignity of the said kingdoms and dominions to be to the heirs of the body of the said princess; and for default of such issue to the princess Anne of Denmark and the heirs of her body; and for default of such issue to the heirs of the body of the said prince of Orange. And the

2 H

lords spiritual and temporal and commons do pray the said prince and princess to accept the same accordingly. And that the oaths hereafter mentioned to be taken by all persons of whom the oaths of allegiance and supremacy might be required by law instead of them; and that the said oaths of allegiance and supremacy be abrogated.

" I, A. B., do sincerely promise and swear, that I will be faithful and bear true allegiance to Their Majesties King William and Queen Mary."

" I, A. B., do swear, that I do from my heart abhor, detest and abjure as impious and heretical this damnable doctrine and position, that princes excommunicated or deprived by the pope or any authority of the see of Rome may be deposed or murdered by their subjects or any other whatsoever. And I do declare that no foreign prince, person, prelate, state or potentate hath or ought to have any jurisdiction, power, superiority, preeminence or authority, ecclesiastical or spiritual, within this realm. So help me God."

Upon which Their said Majesties did accept the crown and royal dignity of the kingdoms of England, France and Ireland and the dominions thereunto belonging, according to the resolution and desire of the said lords and commons, contained in the said declaration. And thereupon Their Majesties were pleased, that the said lords spiritual and temporal and commons being the two houses of parliament should continue to sit, and with Their Majesties' royal concurrence make effectual provision for the settlement of the religion, laws and liberties of this kingdom, so that the same for the future might not be in danger again of being subverted, to which the lords spiritual and temporal and commons did agree and proceed to act accordingly. Now in pursuance of the premises, the lords spiritual and temporal and commons in parliament assembled, for the ratifying, confirming and establishing the said declaration and the articles, clauses, matters and things therein contained, by the force of a law made in due form by authority of parliament, do pray that it may be declared and enacted, that all and singular the rights and liberties asserted and claimed in the said declaration are the true, ancient and indubitable rights and liberties of the people of this kingdom, and so shall be esteemed, allowed, adjudged, deemed and taken to be, and that all and every the particulars aforesaid shall be firmly and strictly holden and observed, as they are expressed in the said declaration; and all officers and ministers whatsoever shall serve Their Majesties and their successors according to the same in all times to come. And the said lords spiritual and temporal and commons, seriously considering how it hath pleased Almighty God in His marvellous providence and merciful goodness to this nation to provide and preserve Their said Majesties' royal persons most happily to reign over us upon the throne of their ancestors, for which they render unto Him from the bottom of their hearts their humblest thanks and praises, do truly, firmly, assuredly and in the sincerity of their hearts think, and do hereby humbly recognize, acknowledge and declare, that King James the Second having abdicated the government and Their Majesties having accepted the crown and royal dignity [as] aforesaid, Their said Majesties did become, were, are and of right ought to be by the laws of this realm our sovereign liege lord and lady, king and queen of England, France and Ireland and the dominions thereunto belonging, in and to whose princely persons the royal state, crown and dignity of the said realms, with all honours, styles, titles, regalities, prerogatives, powers, jurisdictions and authorities to the same belonging and appertaining, are most fully, rightfully and entirely invested and incorporated, united and annexed; and for preventing all questions and divisions in this realm by reason of any pretended titles to the crown and for preserving a certainty in the succession thereof, in and upon which the unity, peace, tranquillity and safety of this nation doth under God wholly consist and depend, the said lords spiritual and temporal and commons do beseech Their Majesties, that it may be enacted, established and declared, that the crown and regal government of the said kingdom and dominions, with all and singular the premises thereunto belonging and appertaining, shall be and continue to Their said Majesties and the survivor of them during their lives and the life of the survivor of them; and that the entire, perfect and full exercise of the regal power and government be only in and executed by His Majesty, in the names of both Their Majesties, during their joint lives; and after their deceases the said crown and premises shall be and remain to the heirs of the body of Her Majesty; and for default of such issue to Her Royal Highness the princess Anne of Denmark and the heirs of her body; and for default of such issue to the heirs of the body of His said Majesty; and thereunto the said lords spiritual and temporal and commons do in the name of all the people aforesaid most humbly and faithfully submit themselves, their heirs and posterities forever; and do faithfully promise that they will stand to, maintain and defend Their said Majesties, and also the limitation and succession of the crown herein specified and contained, to the utmost of their powers with their lives and estates against all persons whatsoever that shall attempt anything to the contrary. And whereas it hath been found by experience, that it is inconsistent with the safety and welfare of this Protestant kingdom to be governed by a popish prince or by any king or queen marrying a papist, the said lords spiritual and temporal and commons do further pray, that it may be enacted, that all and every person and persons that is, are or shall be reconciled to or shall hold communion with the See or Church of Rome, or shall profess the popish religion, or shall marry a papist, shall be excluded and be forever incapable to inherit, possess or enjoy the crown and government of this realm and Ireland and the dominions thereunto belonging, or any part of the same, or to have, use or exercise any regal power, authority or jurisdiction within the same; and in all and every such case or cases the people of these realms shall be and are hereby absolved of their allegiance; and the said crown and government shall from time to time descend to and be enjoyed by such person or persons, being Protestants, as should have inherited and enjoyed the same, in case the said person or persons so reconciled, holding communion, or professing, or marrying, as aforesaid, were naturally dead; and that every king and queen of this realm, who at any time hereafter shall come to and succeed in the imperial crown of this kingdom, shall on the first day of the meeting of the first parliament, next after his or her coming to the crown, sitting in his or her throne in the house of peers, in the presence of the lords and commons therein assembled, or at his or her coronation, before such person or persons who shall administer the coronation oath to him or her at the time of his or her taking the said oath, (which shall first happen), make, subscribe and audibly repeat the declaration mentioned in the statute made in the thirtieth year of the reign of King Charles the Second, entitled, An Act for the more effectual preserving the King's Person and Government by disabling Papists from sitting in either House of Parliament; but if it shall happen that such king or queen upon his or her succession to the crown of this realm shall be under the age of twelve years, then every such king or queen shall make, subscribe and audibly repeat the said declaration at his or her coronation, or the first day of the meeting of the first parliament as aforesaid, which shall first happen after such king or queen shall have attained the said age of twelve years. All which Their Majesties are contented and pleased shall be declared, enacted and established by authority of this present parliament, and shall stand, remain and be the law of this realm forever; and the same are by Their said Majesties, by and with the advice and consent of the lords spiritual and temporal and commons in parliament assembled, and by the authority of the same, declared, enacted and established accordingly.

II. And be it further declared and enacted by the authority aforesaid, that, from and after this present session of parliament, no dispensation by *non obstante* of or to any statute or any part thereof shall be allowed, but that the same shall be held void and of no effect, except a dispensation be allowed of in such statute, and except in such case as shall be specially provided for by one or more bill or bills to be passed during this present session of parliament.

III. Provided that no charter or grant or pardon, granted before the three and twentieth day of October in the year of our Lord one thousand six hundred eighty-nine, shall be any ways impeached or invalidated by this act, but that the same shall be and remain of the same force and effect in law and no other than as if this act had never been made.

---

240. Act Restoring Charter of London

(1690, May 14.   2 William and Mary, c. 8.   6 *S. R.* 171.)

WHEREAS a judgment was given in the court of king's bench in or about Trinity term, in the five and thirtieth year of the reign of the late king Charles the Second, upon an information in the nature of a Quo Warranto, exhibited in the said court against the mayor and commonalty and citizens of the city of London, that the liberty, privilege and franchise of the said mayor and commonalty and citizens, being a body politic and corporate, should be seized into the king's hands as forfeited: and forasmuch as the said judgment and the proceedings thereupon is and were illegal and arbitrary; and for that the restoring of the said mayor and commonalty and citizens to their ancient liberties of which they had been deprived tends very much to the peace and good settlement of this kingdom; be it declared and enacted by the king and queen's most excellent Majesties, by and with the advice and consent of the lords spiritual and temporal and commons in this present parliament assembled and by authority of the same, that the said judgment given in the said court of king's bench, in the said Trinity term, in the five and thirtieth year of the reign of the said king Charles the Second, or in any other term, and all and every other judgment given or recorded in the said court for the seizing into the said late king's hands the liberty, privilege or franchise of the mayor and commonalty and citizens of the city of London of being of themselves a body corporate and politic, by the name of the mayor and commonalty and citizens of the city of London, and by that name to plead and be impleaded and to answer and to be answered, or in what manner or words soever such judgment was entered is, shall be and are hereby reversed, annulled and made void to all intents and purposes whatsoever, and that vacats be entered upon the rolls of the said judgment for the vacating and reversal of the same accordingly.

II. And be it further declared and enacted by the authority aforesaid, that the mayor and commonalty and citizens of the city of London shall and may forever hereafter remain, continue and be, and prescribe to be, a body corporate and politic *in re facto et nomine* by the name of mayor and commonalty and citizens of the city of London, and by that name and all and every other name and names of incorporation, by which they at any time before the said judgment were incorporated, to sue, plead and be impleaded and to answer and to be answered, without any seizure or forejudger of the said franchise, liberty and privilege, or being thereof excluded or ousted, for or upon any pretence of any forfeiture or misdemeanour at any time heretofore or hereafter to be done, committed or suffered; and the said mayor and commonalty and citizens of the said city shall and may, as by law they ought, peaceably have and enjoy all and every their rights, gifts, charters, grants, liberties, privileges, franchises, customs, usages, constitutions, prescriptions, immunities, markets, duties, tolls, lands, tenements, estates and hereditaments whatsoever, which they lawfully had or had lawful right, title or interest of, in or to, at the time of the recording or giving the said judgment or at the time or times of the said pretended forfeitures.

*　*　*　*　*　*　*　*　*

241. The Triennial Act

(1694, December 22.   6 & 7 William and Mary, c. 2.   6 *S. R.* 510.)

WHEREAS by the ancient laws and statutes of this kingdom frequent parliament sought to be held, and whereas frequent and new parliaments tend very much to the happy union and good agreement of the king and people, we Your Majesties' most loyal and obedient subjects, the lords spiritual and temporal and commons in this present parliament assembled, do most humbly beseech Your most excellent Majesties, that it may be declared and enacted in this present parliament, and it is hereby declared and enacted by the king and queen's most excellent Majesties, by and with the advice and consent of the lords spiritual and temporal and commons in this present parliament assembled and by the authority of the same, that from henceforth a parliament shall be holden once in three years at the least.

II.   And be it further enacted by the authority aforesaid, that within three years at the farthest from and after the dissolution of this present parliament, and so from time to time forever hereafter within three years at the farthest from and after the determination of every other parliament, legal writs under the great seal shall be issued by directions of Your Majesties, your heirs and successors, for calling, assembling and holding another new parliament.

III.   And be it further enacted by the authority aforesaid, that from henceforth no parliament whatsoever, that shall at any time hereafter be called, assembled or held, shall have any continuance longer than for three years only at the farthest, to be accounted from the day on which by the writs of summons the said parliament shall be appointed to meet.

IV.   And be it further enacted by the authority aforesaid, that this present parliament shall cease and determine on the first day of November, which shall be in the year of our Lord one thousand six hundred ninety-six, unless Their Majesties shall think fit to dissolve it sooner.

242. Treason Trials Act

(1696.   7 & 8 William III. c. 3.   7 *S. R.* 6.)

WHEREAS nothing is more just and reasonable than that persons prosecuted for high treason and misprision of treason, whereby the liberties, lives, honour, estates, blood and posterity of the subjects may be lost and destroyed, should be justly and equally tried, and that persons accused as offenders therein should not be debarred of all just and equal means for defence of their innocencies in such cases; in order thereunto and for the better regulation of trials of persons prosecuted for high treason and misprision of such treason, be it enacted by the king's most excellent Majesty, by and with the advice and consent of the lords spiritual and temporal and the commons in this present parliament assembled, and by the authority of the same, that from and after the five and twentieth day of March in the year of our Lord one thousand six hundred ninety-six all and every person and persons whatsoever, that shall be accused and indicted for high treason, whereby any corruption of blood may or shall be made to any such offender or offenders or to any the heir or heirs of any such offender or offenders, or for misprision of such treason, shall have a true copy of the whole indictment, but not the names of the witnesses, delivered unto them or any of them five days at the least before he or they shall be tried for the same, whereby to enable them and any of them respectively to advise with counsel thereupon, to plead and make their defence, his or their attorney or attorneys, agent or agents, or any of them requiring the same, and paying the officer his reasonable fees for writing thereof, not exceeding five shillings for the copy of every such indictment; and that every such person so accused and indicted, arraigned or tried for any such treason as aforesaid or for misprision of such treason, from and after the said time, shall be received and admitted to make his and their full defence by counsel learned in the law, and to make any proof that he or they can produce by lawful witness or witnesses, who shall then be upon oath, for his and their just defence in that behalf; and in case any person or persons so accused or indicted shall desire counsel, the court before whom such person or persons shall be tried or some judge of that court shall and hereby is authorized and required immediately, upon his or their request, to assign to such person and persons such and so many counsel, not exceeding two, as the person or persons shall desire, to whom such counsel shall have free access at all seasonable hours; any law or usage to the contrary notwithstanding.

II. And be it further enacted, that from and after the said five and twentieth day of March in the year of our lord one thousand six hundred ninety-six, no person or persons whatsoever shall be indicted, tried or attainted of high treason, whereby any corruption of blood may or shall be made to any such offender or offenders or to any the heir or heirs of any such offender or offenders, or of misprision of such treason, but by and upon the oaths and testimony of two lawful witnesses, either both of them to the same overt act, or one of them to one and another of them to another overt act of the same treason; unless the party indicted and arraigned or tried shall willingly, without violence, in open court confess the same, or shall stand mute or refuse to plead, or in cases of high treason shall peremptorily challenge above the number of thirty-five of the jury; any law, statute or usage to the contrary notwithstanding.

* * * * * * * * *

IV. And be it further enacted and declared by the authority aforesaid, that if two or more distinct treasons of divers heads or kinds shall be alleged in one bill of indictment, one witness produced to prove one of the said treasons, and another witness produced to prove another of the said treasons, shall not be deemed or taken to be two witnesses to the same treason within the meaning of this act.

V. And to the intent that the terror and dread of such criminal accusations may in some reasonable time be removed, be it further enacted by the authority aforesaid, that from and after the said five and twentieth day of March in the year of our Lord one thousand six hundred ninety-six, no person or persons whatsoever shall be indicted, tried or prosecuted for any such treason as aforesaid, or for misprision of such treason, that shall be committed or done within the kingdom of England, dominion of Wales or town of Berwick upon Tweed, after the said five and twentieth day of March in the year of our Lord one thousand six hundred ninety-six, unless the same indictment be found by a grand jury within three years next after the treason or offence done and committed.

VI. And that no person or persons shall be prosecuted for any such treason or misprision of such treason, committed or done or to be committed or done within the kingdom of England, dominion of Wales or town of Berwick upon Tweed before the said five and twentieth day of March, unless he or they shall be indicted thereof within three years after the said five and twentieth day of March; always provided and excepted, that if any person or persons whatsoever shall be guilty of designing, endeavouring or attempting any assassination on the body of the king, by poison or otherwise, such person or persons may be prosecuted at any time, notwithstanding the aforesaid limitation.

VII. And all and every person and persons, who shall be accused, indicted and tried for such treason as aforesaid, or for misprision of such treason, after the said five and twentieth day of March in the year of our Lord one thousand six hundred ninety-six, shall have copies of the panel of the jurors who are to try them, duly returned by the sheriff, and delivered unto them and every of them so accused and indicted respectively, two days at the least before he or they shall be tried for the same; and that all persons so accused and indicted for any such treason as aforesaid shall have the like process of the court, where they shall be tried, to compel their witnesses to appear for them at any such trial or trials, as is usually granted to compel witnesses to appear against them.

VIII. And be it further enacted, that no evidence shall be admitted or given of any overt act, that is not expressly laid in the indictment against any person or persons whatsoever.

*   *   *   *   *   *   *   *   *

X. And whereas by the good laws of this kingdom, in cases of trials of commoners for their lives, a jury of twelve freeholders must all agree in one opinion before they can bring a verdict either for acquittal or condemnation of the prisoner; and whereas upon the trials of peers or peeresses a major vote is sufficient either to acquit or condemn; be it further enacted by the authority aforesaid, that upon the trial of any peer or peeress, either for treason or misprision, all the peers who have a right to sit and vote in parliament shall be duly summoned, twenty days at least before every such trial, to appear at every such trial; and that every peer so summoned and appearing at such trial shall vote in the trial of such peer or peeress so to be tried, every such peer first taking the oaths mentioned in an act of parliament made in the first year of the reign of king William and queen Mary, entitled, An Act for abrogating the Oaths of Supremacy and Allegiance and appointing other Oaths; and also every such peer subscribing and audibly repeating the declaration mentioned in An Act for the more effectual preserving the King's Person and Government by disabling Papists from sitting in either House of Parliament, and made in the thirtieth year of the reign of the late king Charles the Second.

XI. Provided always, that neither this act nor anything therein contained shall any way extend or be construed to extend to any impeachment or other proceedings in parliament in any kind whatsoever.

*   *   *   *   *   *   *   *   *

243. The Act of Settlement.

(1701, June 12. 12 & 13 William III. c. 2. 7 *S. R.* 636. Stubbs, Select Charters, 528–531. G. and H. 664–670.)

WHEREAS in the first year of the reign of Your Majesty and of our late most gracious sovereign lady queen Mary (of blessed memory) an act of parliament was made, entitled, An Act for declaring the Rights and Liberties of the Subject and for settling the Succession of the Crown, wherein it was (amongst other things) enacted, established and declared, that the crown and regal government of the kingdoms of England, France and Ireland, and the dominions thereunto belonging, should be and continue to Your Majesty and the said late queen during the joint lives of Your Majesty and the said queen and to the survivor; and that after the decease of Your Majesty and of the said queen the said crown and regal government should be and remain to the heirs of the body of the said late queen; and for default of such issue to Her Royal Highness the princess Anne of Denmark and the heirs of her body; and for default of such issue to the heirs of the body of Your Majesty. And it was thereby further enacted, that all and every person and persons that then were or afterwards should be reconciled to or should hold communion with the See or Church of Rome, or should profess the popish religion, or marry a papist, should be excluded, and are by that act made forever incapable to inherit, possess or enjoy the crown and government of this realm and Ireland and the dominions thereunto belonging or any part of the same, or to have, use or exercise any regal power, authority or jurisdiction within the same; and in all and every such case and cases the people of these realms shall be and are thereby absolved of their allegiance; and that the said

crown and government shall from time to time descend to and be
enjoyed by such person or persons, being Protestants, as should
have inherited and enjoyed the same, in case the said person or
persons so reconciled, holding communion, professing or marrying as aforesaid, were naturally dead. After the making of which
statute and the settlement therein contained, Your Majesty's good
subjects, who were restored to the full and free possession and
enjoyment of their religion, rights and liberties by the providence of God giving success to Your Majesty's just undertakings
and unwearied endeavours for that purpose, had no greater temporal felicity to hope or wish for, than to see a royal progeny
descending from Your Majesty, to whom (under God) they owe
their tranquillity, and whose ancestors have for many years been
principal assertors of the reformed religion and the liberties of
Europe and from our said most gracious sovereign lady, whose
memory will always be precious to the subjects of these realms;
and it having since pleased Almighty God to take away our said
sovereign lady, and also the most hopeful prince William, duke of
Gloucester, (the only surviving issue of Her Royal Highness the
princess Anne of Denmark), to the unspeakable grief and sorrow
of Your Majesty and your said good subjects, who, under such
losses being sensibly put in mind, that it standeth wholly in the
pleasure of Almighty God to prolong the lives of Your Majesty
and of Her Royal Highness, and to grant to Your Majesty or to
Her Royal Highness such issue as may be inheritable to the crown
and regal government aforesaid, by the respective limitations in
the said recited act contained, do constantly implore the divine
mercy for those blessings; and Your Majesty's said subjects having
daily experience of your royal care and concern for the present
and future welfare of these kingdoms, and particularly recom-
mending from your throne a further provision to be made for
the succession of the crown in the Protestant line, for the happiness of the nation and the security of our religion; and it being
absolutely necessary for the safety, peace and quiet of this realm,
to obviate all doubts and contentions in the same, by reason of
any pretended title to the crown and to maintain a certainty
in the succession thereof, to which your subjects may safely have
recourse for their protection, in case the limitations in the said
just recited act should determine: Therefore for a further provision of the succession of the crown in the Protestant line, we
Your Majesty's most dutiful and loyal subjects, the lords spiritual
and temporal and commons in this present parliament assembled,
do beseech Your Majesty that it may be enacted and declared,

and be it enacted and declared by the king's most excellent Majesty by and with the advice and consent of the lords spiritual and temporal and commons in this present parliament assembled, and by the authority of the same, that the most excellent princess Sophia, electress and duchess dowager of Hanover, daughter of the most excellent princess Elizabeth, late queen of Bohemia, daughter of our late sovereign lord king James the First, of happy memory, be and is hereby declared to be the next in succession in the Protestant line to the imperial crown and dignity of the said realms of England, France and Ireland, with the dominions and territories thereunto belonging, after His Majesty and the princess Anne of Denmark, and in default of issue of the said princess Anne and of His Majesty respectively; and that from and after the deceases of His said Majesty our now sovereign lord and of Her Royal Highness the princess Anne of Denmark, and for default of issue of the said princess Anne and of His Majesty respectively, the crown and regal government of the said kingdoms of England, France and Ireland and of the dominions thereunto belonging, with the royal state and dignity of the said realms and all honours, styles, titles, regalities, prerogatives, powers, jurisdictions and authorities to the same belonging and appertaining, shall be, remain and continue to the said most excellent princess Sophia and the heirs of her body, being Protestants; and thereunto the said lords spiritual and temporal and commons shall and will, in the name of all the people of this realm, most humbly and faithfully submit themselves, their heirs and posterities, and do faithfully promise that after the deceases of His Majesty and Her Royal Highness, and the failure of the heirs of their respective bodies, to stand to, maintain and defend the said princess Sophia and the heirs of her body, being Protestants, according to the limitation and succession of the crown in this act specified and contained, to the utmost of their powers, with their lives and estates, against all persons whatsoever that shall attempt anything to the contrary.

II.   Provided always, and it is hereby enacted, that all and every person and persons, who shall or may take or inherit the said crown, by virtue of the limitation of this present act, and is, are or shall be reconciled to or shall hold communion with the See or Church of Rome, or shall profess the popish religion, or shall marry a papist, shall be subject to such incapacities, as in such case or cases are by the said recited act provided, enacted and established; and that every king and queen of this realm, who shall come to and succeed in the imperial crown of this kingdom by virtue of this act, shall have the coronation oath administered to him, her or them, at their respective coronations, according to the act of parliament made in the first year of the reign of His Majesty and the said late queen Mary, entitled, An Act for establishing the Coronation Oath, and shall make, subscribe and repeat the declaration in the act first above recited, mentioned or referred to, in the manner and form, thereby prescribed.

III. And whereas it is requisite and necessary that some further provision be made for securing our religion, laws and liberties, from and after the death of His Majesty and the princess Anne of Denmark, and in default of issue of the body of the said princess and of His Majesty respectively; be it enacted by the king's most excellent Majesty, by and with the advice and consent of the lords spiritual and temporal and commons in parliament assembled, and by the authority of the same:

That whosoever shall hereafter come to the possession of this crown shall join in communion with the Church of England as by law established.

That in case the crown and imperial dignity of this realm shall hereafter come to any person, not being a native of this kingdom of England, this nation be not obliged to engage in any war for the defence of any dominions or territories which do not belong to the crown of England, without consent of parliament.

That no person who shall hereafter come to the possession of this crown shall go out of the dominions of England, Scotland or Ireland, without consent of parliament.

That from and after the time that the further limitation by this act shall take effect, all matters and things relating to the well governing of this kingdom, which are properly cognizable in the privy council by the laws and customs of this realm, shall be transacted there; and all resolutions taken thereupon shall be signed by such of the privy council as shall advise and consent to the same.

That after the said limitation shall take effect as aforesaid, no person born out of the kingdoms of England, Scotland or Ireland or the dominions thereunto belonging (although he be naturalized or made a denizen, except such as are born of English parents) shall be capable to be of the privy council, or a member of either house of parliament, or to enjoy any office or place of trust, either civil or military, or to have any grant of lands, tenements or hereditaments from the crown to himself or to any other or others in trust for him.

That no person who has an office or place of profit under the king or receives a pension from the crown shall be capable of serving as a member of the house of commons.

That after the said limitation shall take effect as aforesaid, judges commissions be made *quam diu se bene gesserint,* and their salaries ascertained and established, but upon the address of both houses of parliament it may be lawful to remove them.

That no pardon under the great seal of England be pleadable to an impeachment by the commons in parliament.

IV. And whereas the laws of England are the birthright of the people thereof, and all the kings and queens who shall ascend the throne of this realm ought to administer the government of the same according to the said laws, and all their officers and ministers ought to serve them respectively according to the same; the said lords spiritual and temporal and commons do therefore further humbly pray, that all the laws and statutes of this realm for securing the established religion and the rights and liberties of the people thereof, and all other laws and statutes of the same now in force, may be ratified and confirmed, and the same are by His Majesty, by and with the advice and consent of the said lords spiritual and temporal and commons, and by authority of the same, ratified and confirmed accordingly.

----◆----

244. Act of Union with Scotland.

(170⅚, March 6.   5 Anne, c. 8.   8 *S. R.* 566.)

MOST gracious sovereign,
Whereas Articles of Union were agreed on, the twenty-second day of July in the fifth year of Your Majesty's reign, by the commissioners nominated on behalf of the kingdom of England under Your Majesty's great seal of England, bearing date at Westminster the tenth day of April then last past, in pursuance of an act of parliament made in England in the third year of Your Majesty's reign, and the commissioners nominated on the behalf of the kingdom of Scotland under Your Majesty's great seal of Scotland, bearing date the twenty-seventh day of February in the fourth year of Your Majesty's reign, in pursuance of the fourth act of the third session of the present parliament of Scotland, to treat of and concerning an union of the said kingdoms; and whereas an act hath passed in the parliament of Scotland at Edinburgh the sixteenth day of January in the fifth year of Your Majesty's reign, wherein 'tis mentioned, that the estates of parliament considering the said

Articles of Union of the two kingdoms had agreed to and approved of the said Articles of Union, with some additions and explanations, and that Your Majesty, with the advice and consent of the estates of parliament, for establishing the Protestant religion and Presbyterian church government within the kingdom of Scotland, had passed in the same session of parliament an act, entitled, Act for securing of the Protestant Religion and Presbyterian Church Government, which by the tenor thereof was appointed to be inserted in any act ratifying the treaty, and expressly declared to be a fundamental and essential condition of the said treaty or union in all times coming; the tenor of which articles, as ratified and approved of with additions and explanations by the said act of parliament of Scotland, follows:

ARTICLE I

That the two kingdoms of England and Scotland shall upon the first day of May which shall be in the year one thousand seven hundred and seven, and forever after, be united into one kingdom by the name of Great Britain; and that the ensigns armorial of the said United Kingdom be such as Her Majesty shall appoint, and the crosses of St. George and St. Andrew be conjoined in such manner as Her Majesty shall think fit, and used in all flags, banners, standards and ensigns, both at sea and land.

ARTICLE II

That the succession to the monarchy of the United Kingdom of Great Britain and of the dominions thereto belonging after Her most sacred Majesty and in default of issue of Her Majesty be, remain and continue to the most excellent princess Sophia, electress and duchess dowager of Hanover, and the heirs of her body, being Protestants, upon whom the crown of England is settled by an act of parliament made in England in the twelfth year of the reign of His late Majesty king William the Third, entitled, An Act for the further Limitation of the Crown and better securing the Rights and Liberties of the Subject; and that all papists and persons marrying papists shall be excluded from and forever incapable to inherit, possess or enjoy the imperial crown of Great Britain and the dominions thereunto belonging or any part thereof, and in every such case the crown and government shall from time to time descend to and be enjoyed by such person, being a Protestant, as should have inherited and enjoyed the same, in case such papist or person marrying a papist was naturally dead, according to the provision for the descent of the crown of England, made by another act of parliament in England in the first year of the reign of Their late Majesties, king William and queen Mary, entitled, An Act declaring the Rights and Liberties of the Subject and settling the Succession of the Crown.

Article III

That the United Kingdom of Great Britain be represented by one and the same parliament to be styled the Parliament of Great Britain.

Article IV

That all the subjects of the United Kingdom of Great Britain shall from and after the union have full freedom and intercourse of trade and navigation to and from any port or place within the said United Kingdom and the dominions and plantations thereunto belonging; and that there be a communication of all other rights, privileges and advantages, which do or may belong to the subjects of either kingdom, except where it is otherwise expressly agreed in these articles.

* * * * * * * * *

Article XVIII

That the laws concerning regulation of trade, customs and such excises, to which Scotland is by virtue of this treaty to be liable, be the same in Scotland from and after the union as in England; and that all other laws in use within the kingdom of Scotland do after the union and notwithstanding thereof remain in the same force as before, (except such as are contrary to or inconsistent with this treaty), but alterable by the parliament of Great Britain; with this difference betwixt the laws concerning public right, policy and civil government and those which concern private right, that the laws which concern public right, policy and civil government may be made the same throughout the whole United Kingdom, but that no alteration be made in laws which concern private right, except for evident utility of the subjects within Scotland.

Article XIX

That the Court of Session or College of Justice do after the union, and notwithstanding thereof, remain in all time coming within Scotland, as it is now constituted by the laws of that kingdom, * * * and that all inferior courts within the said limits do remain subordinate, as they are now, to the supreme courts of justice within the same, in all time coming; and that no causes in Scotland be cognizable by the courts of chancery, queen's bench, common pleas, or any other court in Westminster Hall; * * *

* * * * * * * * *

ARTICLE XXII

That by virtue of this treaty, of the peers of Scotland at the time of the union sixteen shall be the number to sit and vote in the house of lords, and forty-five the number of the representatives of Scotland in the house of commons of the parliament of Great Britain; and that when Her Majesty, her heirs or successors, shall declare her or their pleasure for holding the first or any subsequent parliament of Great Britain, until the parliament of Great Britain shall make further provision therein, a writ do issue under the great seal of the United Kingdom directed to the privy council of Scotland, commanding them to cause sixteen peers who are to sit in the house of lords to be summoned to parliament, and forty-five members to be elected to sit in the house of commons of the parliament of Great Britain, according to the agreement in this treaty, in such manner as by an act of this present session of the parliament of Scotland is or shall be settled; which act is hereby declared to be as valid as if it were a part of and engrossed in this treaty; and that the names of the persons so summoned and elected shall be returned by the privy council of Scotland into the court from whence the said writ did issue. * * *

* * * * * * * * *

And the tenor of the aforesaid 'Act for securing of the Protestant Religion and Presbyterian Church Government within the Kingdom of Scotland' is as follows:

* * * * * * * * *

* * * And further Her Majesty with advice aforesaid expressly declares and statutes, that none of the subjects of this kingdom shall be liable to, but all and every one of them forever free of any oath, test or subscription within this kingdom, contrary to or inconsistent with the foresaid true Protestant religion and Presbyterian church government, worship and discipline, as above established; and that the same within the bounds of this church and kingdom shall never be imposed upon or required of them in any sort; and lastly, that after the decease of Her present Majesty (whom God long preserve) the sovereign succeeding to her in the royal government of the kingdom of Great Britain shall in all time coming, at his or her accession to the crown, swear and subscribe, that they shall inviolably maintain and preserve the foresaid settlement of the true Protestant religion, with the government, worship, discipline, right and privileges of this church, as above established by the laws of this kingdom, in prosecution of the Claim of Right. * * *

* * * * * * * * *

X. May it therefore please Your most excellent Majesty, that it may be enacted; and be it enacted by the Queen's most excellent Majesty, by and with the advice and consent of the lords spiritual and temporal and commons in this present parliament assembled, and by the authority of the same, that all and every the said Articles of Union as ratified and approved by the said act of parliament of Scotland, as aforesaid, and hereinbefore particularly mentioned and inserted; and also the said act of parliament of Scotland for establishing the Protestant religion and Presbyterian church government within that kingdom, entitled, * * *, and every clause, matter and thing in the said articles and act contained, shall be, and the said articles and acts are hereby forever ratified, approved and confirmed.

* * * * * * * * *

245. The Place Act

(1707. 6 Anne, c. 7. First enacted in 1705, in 4 Anne, c. 8. 8 *S. R.* 742.)

* * * * * * * * *

XXIV. And be it further enacted by the authority aforesaid, that no person who shall have in his own name or in the name of any person or persons in trust for him or for his benefit any new office or place of profit whatsoever under the crown, which at any time since the five and twentieth day of October in the year of our Lord one thousand seven hundred and five have been created or erected, or hereafter shall be created or erected, nor any person who shall be commissioner or sub-commissioner of prizes, secretary or receiver of the prizes, nor any comptroller of the accounts of the army, nor any commissioner of transports, nor any commissioner of the sick and wounded, nor any agent for any regiment, nor any commissioner for any wine licenses, nor any governor [or] deputy governor of any of the plantations, nor any commissioners of the navy employed in any of the out ports, nor any person having any pension from the crown during pleasure, shall be capable of being elected or of sitting or voting as a member of the house of commons in any parliament which shall be hereafter summoned and holden.

XXV. Provided always, that if any person being chosen a member of the house of commons shall accept of any office of profit from the crown, during such time as he shall continue a member, his election shall be and is hereby declared to be void, and a new writ shall issue for a new election, as if such person so accepting was naturally dead; provided nevertheless that such person shall be capable of being again elected, as if his place had not become void as aforesaid.

XXVI. Provided also, and be it enacted, that in order to prevent for the future too great a number of commissioners to be appointed or constituted for the executing of any office, that no greater number of commissioners shall be made or constituted for the execution of any office, than have been employed in the execution of such respective office at some time before the first day of this present parliament.

XXVII. Provided also, that nothing herein contained shall extend or be construed to extend to any member of the house of commons, being an officer in Her Majesty's navy or army, who shall receive any new or other commission in the army or navy respectively.

XXVIII.   And be it further enacted, that if any person hereby disabled, or declared to be incapable to sit or vote in any parliament hereafter to be holden, shall nevertheless be returned as a member to serve for any county, stewartry, city, town or Cinque port in any such parliament, such election and return are hereby enacted and declared to be void to all intents and purposes whatsoever; and if any person disabled or declared incapable by this act to be elected shall after the dissolution or determination of this present parliament presume to sit or vote as a member of the house of commons in any parliament to be hereafter summoned, such person so sitting or voting shall forfeit the sum of five hundred pounds, to be recovered by such person as shall sue for the same in England by action of debt, bill, plaint or information, wherein no essoin, protection or wager of law shall be allowed, and only one imparlance.

XXIX. And be it further enacted and declared, that every person disabled to be elected or to sit or vote in the house of commons of any parliament of England shall be disabled to be elected or to sit or vote in the house of commons of any parliament of Great Britain.

* * * * * * * * *

———◆———

246. The Riot Act

(1715, July 20. 1 George I. stat. 2, c. 5. 13 *S. L.* 142.)

I. WHEREAS of late many rebellious riots and tumults have been in divers parts of this kingdom, to the disturbance of the public peace, and the endangering of His Majesty's person and government, and the same are yet continued and fomented by persons disaffected to His Majesty, presuming so to do, for that the punishments provided by the laws now in being are not adequate to such heinous offences; and by such rioters His Majesty and his administration have been most maliciously and falsely traduced, with an intent to raise divisions, and to alienate the affections of the people from His Majesty: therefore for the preventing and suppressing of such riots and tumults, and for the more speedy and effectual punishing the offenders therein; be it enacted by the king's most excellent Majesty, by and with the advice and consent of the lords spiritual and temporal and of the commons in this present parliament assembled, and by the authority of the same, that if any persons to the number of twelve or more, being unlawfully, riotously, and tumultuously assembled together, to the disturbance of the public peace, at any time after the last day of July in the year of our Lord one thousand seven hundred and fifteen, and being required or commanded by any one or more justice or justices of the peace, or by the sheriff of the county, or his under-sheriff, or by the mayor, bailiff, or bailiffs, or other head-officer, or justice of the peace of any city or town corporate, where such assembly shall be, by proclamation to be made in the king's name, in the form hereinafter directed, to disperse themselves, and peaceably to depart to their habitations, or to their lawful business, shall, to the number of twelve or more, (notwithstanding such proclamation made) unlawfully, riotously and tumultuously remain or continue together by the space of one hour after such command or request made by proclamation, that then such continuing together to the number of twelve or more, after such command or request made by proclamation, shall be adjudged felony without benefit of clergy, and the offenders therein shall be adjudged felons, and shall suffer death as in case of felony without benefit of clergy.

II. And be it further enacted by the authority aforesaid, that the order and form of the proclamation that shall be made by the authority of this act, shall be as hereafter followeth (that is to say) the justice of the peace, or other person authorized by this act to make the said proclamation shall, among the said rioters, or as near to them as he can safely come, with a loud voice command, or cause to be commanded silence to be, while proclamation is making, and after that, shall openly and with loud voice make or cause to be made proclamation in these words, or like in effect:

'Our sovereign lord the king chargeth and commandeth all persons, being assembled, immediately to disperse themselves, and peaceably to depart to their habitations, or to their lawful business, upon the pains contained in the act made in the first year of king George, for preventing tumults and riotous assemblies.

God save the king.'

And every such justice and justices of the peace, sheriff, under-sheriff, mayor, bailiff, and other head officer aforesaid, within the limits of their respective jurisdictions, are hereby authorized, empowered and required, on notice or knowledge of any such unlawful, riotous and tumultuous assembly, to resort to the place where such unlawful, riotous and tumultuous assemblies shall be, of persons to the number of twelve or more, and there to make or cause to be made proclamation in manner aforesaid.

III. And be it further enacted by the authority aforesaid, that if such persons so unlawfully, riotously, and tumultuously assembled, or twelve or more of them, after proclamation made in manner aforesaid, shall continue together and not disperse themselves within one hour, that then it shall and may be lawful to and for every justice of the peace, sheriff, or under-sheriff of the county where such assembly shall be, and also to or for every high or petty constable, and other peace officer within such county, and also to or for every mayor, justice of the peace, sheriff, bailiff, and other head-officer, high or petty constable, and other peace officer of any city or town corporate where such assembly shall be, and to and for such other person and persons as shall be commanded to be assisting unto any such justice of the peace, sheriff or under-sheriff, mayor, bailiff, or other head-officer aforesaid (who are hereby authorized and empowered to command all His Majesty's subjects of age and ability to be assisting to them therein) to seize and apprehend, and they are

hereby required to seize and apprehend such persons so unlawfully, riotously and tumultuously continuing together after proclamation made, as aforesaid, and forthwith to carry the persons
so apprehended before one or more of His Majesty's justices of
the peace of the county or place where such persons shall be so
apprehended, in order to their being proceeded against for such
their offences according to law; and that if the persons so unlawfully, riotously, and tumultuously assembled, or any of them, shall
happen to be killed, maimed or hurt, in the dispersing, seizing
or apprehending, or endeavouring to disperse, seize or apprehend them, by reason of their resisting the persons so dispersing,
seizing or apprehending, or endeavouring to disperse, seize or
apprehend them, that then every such justice of the peace, sheriff,
under-sheriff, mayor, bailiff, head-officer, high or petty constable,
or other peace-officer, or all and singular persons, being aiding
and assisting to them, or any of them, shall be free, discharged
and indemnified, as well against the king's Majesty, his heirs and
successors, as against all and every other person and persons,
of, for, or concerning the killing, maiming, or hurting of any
such person or persons so unlawfully, riotously and tumultuously
assembled, that shall happen to be so killed, maimed or hurt, as
aforesaid.

* * * * * * * * *

---

247. The Septennial Act

(**1716**, April 26. 1 George I. stat. 2, c. 38. 13 *S. L.* 283.)

WHEREAS in and by act of parliament made in the sixth year
of the reign of their late Majesties king William and
queen Mary (of ever blessed memory) entitled, An Act for the
frequent Meeting and Calling of Parliaments: it was among
other things enacted, that from thenceforth no parliament whatsoever, that should at any time then after be called, assembled
or held, should have any continuance longer than for three years
only at the farthest, to be accounted from the day on which by
the writ of summons the said parliament should be appointed to
meet: and whereas it has been found by experience, that the
said clause hath proved very grievous and burdensome, by occa-
sioning much greater and more continued expenses in order to
elections of members to serve in parliament, and more violent

and lasting heats and animosities among the subjects of this realm, than were ever known before the said clause was enacted; and the said provision, if it should continue, may probably at this juncture, when a restless and popish faction are designing and endeavouring to renew the rebellion within this kingdom, and an invasion from abroad, be destructive to the peace and security of the government: be it enacted by the king's most excellent Majesty, by and with the advice and consent of the lords spiritual and temporal, and commons, in parliament assembled, and by the authority of the same, that this present parliament, and all parliaments that shall at any time hereafter be called, assembled or held, shall and may respectively have continuance for seven years, and no longer, to be accounted from the day on which by the writ of summons this present parliament hath been, or any future parliament shall be, appointed to meet, unless this present, or any such parliament hereafter to be summoned, shall be sooner dissolved by His Majesty, his heirs or successors.

———◆———

248. The Peerage Bill

(1719, March 14. Cobbett's Parliamentary History, vii. 592.)

1. THAT in lieu of the 16 elective peers, to sit in this house on the part of Scotland, 25 peers to be declared by his Majesty shall have hereditary seats in parliament and be the peers on the part of the peerage of Scotland.

2. That such 25 peers shall be declared by his Majesty, before the next session of parliament.

3. That 9 of the said 25 shall be appointed by his Majesty to have immediate right to such hereditary seats in parliament, subject to the qualifications requisite by the laws now in being.

4. That none of the remaining 16 so to be declared by his Majesty, or their heirs, shall become sitting peers of the parliament of Great Britain, until after the determination of this present parliament, except such as are of the number of the 16 peers now sitting in parliament on the part of Scotland, and their heirs.

5. That if any of the 25 peers so to be declared by his Majesty, and their heirs shall fail, some one or other of the peers of Scotland shall be appointed by his Majesty, his heirs and successors, to succeed to every such peer so failing; and every peer so

appointed shall be one of the peers on the part of the peerage of Scotland, in the parliament of Great Britain, and so, *toties quoties*, as often as such failure shall happen.

6. That the hereditary right of sitting in parliament, which shall accrue to the 25 peers of Scotland, to be declared by his Majesty, shall be so limited as not to descend to females.

7. That the number of peers of Great Britain, on the part of England, shall not be enlarged, without precedent right, beyond six above what they are at present; but as any of the said present peers, or such six new peers, in case they be created, shall fail, their numbers may be supplied by new creations of commoners of Great Britain, born within the kingdom of Great Britain or Ireland, or any of the dominions thereunto belonging, or born of British parents, and so, *toties quoties*, as often as such failure shall happen.

8. That no person be at any time created by writ, nor any peerage granted by patent, for any longer estate than for the grantee, and the heirs male of his body.

9. That there be not any restraint upon the crown, from creating any of the princes of the blood, peers of Great Britain, with right to sit in parliament.

10. That whenever those lords now sitting in parliament, whose sons have been called by writ, shall die; then it shall be lawful for his Majesty, his heirs and successors, to create a peer to supply the number so lessened.

11. That every creation of a peer hereafter to be made, contrary to these resolutions, shall be null and void to all intents and purposes.

---

249. Use of English Language in the Law Courts made Obligatory

(1731.   4 George II. c. 26.   16 *S. L.* 248.)

WHEREAS many and great mischiefs do frequently happen to the subjects of this kingdom, from the proceedings in courts of justice being in an unknown language, those who are summoned and impleaded having no knowledge or understanding of what is alleged for or against them in the pleadings of their lawyers and attorneys, who use a character not legible to any but persons practising the law: to remedy these great mischiefs, and

to protect the lives and fortunes of the subjects of that part of
Great Britain called England, more effectually than heretofore,
from the peril of being ensnared or brought in danger by forms
and proceedings in courts of justice, in an unknown language,
be it enacted by the king's most excellent Majesty, by and with
the advice and consent of the lords spiritual and temporal and
commons of Great Britain in parliament assembled, and by the
authority of the same, that from and after the twenty-fifth day of
March one thousand seven hundred and thirty-three, all writs,
process and returns thereof, and proceedings thereon, and all
pleadings, rules, orders, indictments, informations, inquisitions,
presentments, verdicts, prohibitions, certificates, and all patents,
charters, pardons, commissions, records, judgments, statutes,
recognizances, bonds, rolls, entries, fines and recoveries, and all
proceedings relating thereunto, and all proceedings of courts leet,
courts baron and customary courts, and all copies thereof, and
all proceedings whatsoever, in any courts of justice within that
part of Great Britain called England, and in the court of exchequer in Scotland, and which concern the law and administration of justice, shall be in the English tongue and language only,
and not in Latin or French, or any other tongue or language
whatsoever, and shall be written in such a common legible hand
and character, as the acts of parliament are usually engrossed in,
and the lines and words of the same to be written at least as close
as the said acts usually are, and not in any hand commonly called
court hand, and in words at length and not abbreviated; any law,
custom or usage heretofore to the contrary thereof notwithstanding: and all and every persons or persons offending against this
act, shall for every such offence forfeit and pay the sum of fifty
pounds to any person who shall sue for the same by action of
debt, bill, plaint or information in any of His Majesty's courts
of record in Westminster Hall, or court of exchequer in Scotland
respectively, wherein no essoin, protection or wager of law, or
more than one imparlance, shall be allowed.

*　　*　　*　　*　　*　　*　　*　　*　　*

250. Judicial Commissions not to cease on the Demise of the Crown

(1760. 1 George III. c. 13. 23 *S. L.* 292.)

* * * BE it enacted by the king's most excellent Majesty, by and with the advice and consent of the lords spiritual and temporal, and commons, in this present parliament assembled, and by the authority of the same, that all persons who were justices of the peace at the time of the demise of His said late Majesty king George the Second, or who shall be justices of the peace at the time of the demise of His present Majesty, or any of his successors, kings or queens of this realm, or shall afterwards be appointed justices of the peace by any commission granted, or which shall be granted, by his said present Majesty, or which, after his demise, shall be granted by any of his successors, kings or queens of this realm, and who shall take the oaths of office of a justice of the peace, for any county, city and county, town and county, riding, or division, before the clerk of the peace of the respective county, city and county, town and county, riding, or division, for which any such justice or justices of the peace shall act, or intend to act, or the deputy of such respective clerk of the peace, and who shall have taken and subscribed at some general or quarter sessions of the peace the said oath, by the said herein before in part recited act, of the eighteenth year of His said late Majesty's reign, directed and required to be there taken and subscribed, shall and may act as a justice of the peace for such county, city and county, town and county, riding, or division, without being obliged to take and subscribe again the said oath, without incurring any penalty or forfeiture, for the not taking and subscribing thereof; the said herein before in part recited act, or any other statute, law, or usage to the contrary thereof in any wise notwithstanding: and that all acts, matters, and things, done or to be done, by all and every such justice and justices, or by authority derived, or to be derived, from him or them, are and shall be deemed and taken to all intents and purposes to be of the same force, effect, and validity, to all intents and purposes, as the same respectively would have been, if such person or persons had taken and subscribed such oath, by the said herein before in part recited act required to be

taken and subscribed, at some general or quarter sessions for such
county, city and county, town and county, riding or division, for
which he or they did or should act, or intend to act.

* * * * * * * * *

———◆———

251. Camden's Decision against General Warrants

(1763.   19 State Trials, 1067.)

* * * HIS lordship then went upon the warrant, which he
declared was a point of the greatest consequence
he had ever met with in his whole practice.   The defendant
claimed a right, under precedents, to force persons' houses,
break open escrutores, seize their papers, etc. upon a general
warrant, where no inventory is made of the things thus taken
away, and where no offenders' names are specified in the warrant, and therefore a discretionary power given to messengers to
search wherever their suspicions may chance to fall.   If such a
power is truly invested in a secretary of state, and he can dele-
gate this power, it certainly may affect the person and property
of every man in this kingdom, and is totally subversive of the
liberty of the subject.

And as for the precedents, will that be esteemed law in a secretary of state which is not law in any other magistrate of this
kingdom?   If they should be found to be legal, they are certainly of the most dangerous consequences; if not legal, must
aggravate damages. * * *

* * * It is my opinion the office precedents, which had been
produced since the Revolution, are no justification of a practice
in itself illegal, and contrary to the fundamental principles of
the constitution; though its having been the constant practice of
the office, might fairly be pleaded in mitigation of damages.

* * * * * * * * *

252. Mansfield's Decision against General Warrants

(1764. 19 State Trials, 1026–1027.)

*   *   *   *   *   *   *   *   *

THE last point is, 'whether this general warrant be good.'

*   *   *   *   *   *   *   *   *

At present — as to the validity of the warrant, upon the single objection of the incertainty of the person, being neither named nor described — the common law, in many cases, gives authority to arrest without warrant; more especially, where taken in the very act: and there are many cases where particular acts of parliament have given authority to apprehend, under general warrants; as in the case of writs of assistance, or warrants to take up loose, idle, and disorderly people.   But here, it is not contended, that the common law gave the officer authority to apprehend; nor that there is any act of parliament which warrants this case.

Therefore it must stand upon principles of common law.

It is not fit, that the receiving or judging of the information should be left to the discretion of the officer.   The magistrate ought to judge; and should give certain directions to the officer. This is so, upon reason and convenience.

Then as to authorities — Hale and all others hold such an uncertain warrant void: and there is no case or book to the contrary.

It is said 'that the usage has been so; and that many such have been issued, since the Revolution, down to this time.'

But a usage, to grow into law, ought to be a general usage, *communiter usitata et approbata;* and which, after a long continuance, it would be mischievous to overturn.

This is the only usage of a particular office, and contrary to the usage of all other justices and conservators of the peace.

There is the less reason for regarding this usage; because the form of the warrant probably took its rise from a positive statute; and the former precedents were inadvertently followed, after that law was expired.

*   *   *   *   *   *   *   *   *

253. Somerset's Case.   Mansfield's Decision

(1771.   20 State Trials, 82.)

* * * THE only question before us is, whether the cause on the return [to a habeas corpus] is sufficient? If it is, the negro must be remanded; if it is not, he must be discharged. Accordingly, the return states, that the slave departed and refused to serve; whereupon he was kept, to be sold abroad. So high an act of dominion must be recognized by the law of the country where it is used. The power of a master over his slave has been extremely different, in different countries. The state of slavery is of such a nature, that it is incapable of being introduced on any reasons, moral or political, but only by positive law, which preserves its force long after the reasons, occasion, and time itself from whence it was created, is erased from memory. It is so odious, that nothing can be suffered to support it, but positive law. Whatever inconveniences, therefore, may follow from the decision, I cannot say this case is allowed or approved by the law of England; and therefore the black must be discharged.

---

254. Dunning's Resolution

(1780, April 6.   Resolution of the House of Commons.   21 Parliamentary History, 347.)

I. "THAT it is the opinion of this committee, that it is necessary to declare, that the influence of the crown has increased, is increasing, and ought to be diminished."

II. "That it is competent to this house, to examine into, and to correct, abuses in the expenditure of the civil list revenues, as well as in every other branch of the public revenue, whenever it shall appear expedient to the wisdom of this house so to do."

255. Dissolution of Parliament does not impair Impeachment.

(1790, December 20.   28 Parliamentary History, 1035.)

MR. BURKE moved: "That it appears that an impeachment by this house, in the name of the commons of Great Britain, in the parliament assembled, and of all the commons of Great Britain, against Warren Hastings, Esq., late governor general of Bengal for sundry high crimes and misdemeanours is now depending." Passed.

———◆———

256. Fox's Libel Act

(1792.   32 George III. c. 60.   37 *S. L.* 627.)

WHEREAS doubts have arisen whether on the trial of an indictment or information for the making or publishing any libel, where an issue or issues are joined between the king and the defendant or defendants, on the plea of not guilty pleaded, it be competent to the jury impanelled to try the same to give their verdict upon the whole matter in issue; be it therefore declared and enacted by the king's most excellent Majesty, by and with the advice and consent of the lords spiritual and temporal, and commons, in this present parliament assembled, and by the authority of the same, that, on every such trial, the jury sworn to try the issue may give a general verdict of guilty or not guilty upon the whole matter put in issue upon such indictment or information; and shall not be required or directed, by the court or judge before whom such indictment or information shall be tried, to find the defendant or defendants guilty, merely on the proof of the publication by such defendant or defendants of the paper charged to be a libel, and of a sense ascribed to the same in such indictment or information.

II.   Provided always, that, on every such trial, the court or judge before whom such indictment or information shall be tried, shall, according to their or his discretion, give their or his opinion and directions to the jury on the matter in issue between the king and the defendant or defendants, in like manner as in other criminal cases.

III. Provided also, that nothing herein contained shall extend, or be construed to extend, to prevent the jury from finding a special verdict, in their discretion, as in other criminal cases.

IV. Provided also, that in case the jury shall find the defendant or defendants guilty, it shall and may be lawful for the said defendant or defendants to move an arrest of judgment, on such ground and in such manner as by law he or they might have done before the passing of this act; anything herein contained to the contrary notwithstanding.

---

257. Suspension of the Writ of Habeas Corpus

(1794. 34 George III. c. 54. 39 S. L. 556.)

WHEREAS a traitorous and detestable conspiracy has been formed for subverting the existing laws and constitution, and for introducing the system of anarchy and confusion which has so fatally prevailed in France: therefore, for the better preservation of His Majesty's sacred person, and for securing the peace and the laws and liberties of this kingdom; be it enacted by the king's most excellent Majesty, by and with the advice and consent of the lords spiritual and temporal, and commons, in this present parliament assembled, and by the authority of the same, that every person or persons that are or shall be in prison within the kingdom of Great Britain at or upon the day on which this act shall receive His Majesty's royal assent, or after, by warrant of His said Majesty's most honourable privy council, signed by six of the said privy council, for high treason, suspicion of high treason, or treasonable practices, or by warrant, signed by any of His Majesty's secretaries of state, for such causes as aforesaid, may be detained in safe custody, without bail or mainprize, until the first day of February one thousand seven hundred and ninety-five; and that no judge or justice of the peace shall bail or try any such person or persons so committed, without order from His said Majesty's privy council, signed by six of the said privy council, till the said first day of February one thousand seven hundred and ninety-five; any law or statute to the contrary notwithstanding.

II. And be it further enacted by the authority aforesaid, that the act made in Scotland in the year of our Lord one thousand seven hundred and one, (entitled, An Act for preventing wrongful Imprisonment, and against undue Delays in Trials), in so far as the same may be construed to relate to cases of treason and suspicion of treason, be suspended until the first day of February one thousand seven hundred and ninety-five, and that until the said day no judge, justice of peace, or other officer of the law in Scotland, shall liberate, try, or admit to bail, any person or persons that is, are, or shall be, in prison within Scotland, for such causes as aforesaid, without order from His said Majesty's privy council, signed by six of the said privy council: provided always, that, from and after the said first day of February one thousand seven hundred and ninety-five, the said persons so committed shall have the benefit and advantage of all laws and statutes in any way relating to or providing for the liberty of the subjects of this realm, and that this present act shall continue until the said first day of February one thousand seven hundred and ninety-five, and no longer.

III.   Provided always, and be it enacted, that nothing in this act shall be construed to extend to invalidate the ancient rights and privileges of parliament, or to the imprisonment or detaining of any member of either house of parliament during the sitting of such parliament, until the matter of which he stands suspected be first communicated to the house of which he is a member, and the consent of the said house obtained for his commitment or detaining.

————◆————

258. Act of Union with Ireland

(1800 July 21.   40 George III. c. 67.   42 *S. L.* 648.)

WHEREAS in pursuance of His Majesty's most gracious recommendation to the two houses of parliament in Great Britain and Ireland respectively to consider of such measures as might best tend to strengthen and consolidate the connection between the two kingdoms, the two houses of the parliament of Great Britain and the two houses of the parliament of Ireland have severally agreed and resolved, that, in order to promote and secure the essential interests of Great Britain and Ireland, and to consolidate the strength, power, and resources of the British Empire, it will be advisable to concur in such measures as may best tend to unite the two kingdoms of Great Britain and Ireland into one kingdom, in such manner and on such terms and conditions, as may be established by the acts of the respective parliaments of Great Britain and Ireland.

And whereas, in furtherance of the said resolution, both houses of the said two parliaments respectively have likewise agreed upon certain articles for effectuating and establishing the said purposes, in the tenor following:

ARTICLE I

That it be the first article of the union of the kingdoms of Great Britain and Ireland, that the said kingdoms of Great Britain and Ireland shall, upon the first day of January which shall be in the year of our Lord one thousand eight hundred and one, and forever after, be united into one kingdom, by the name of The United Kingdom of Great Britain and Ireland; and that the royal title and titles appertaining to the imperial crown of the said united kingdom and its dependencies, and also the ensigns, armorial flags and banners thereof, shall be such as His Majesty, by his royal proclamation under the great seal of the united kingdom, shall be pleased to appoint.

ARTICLE II

That it be the second article of union, that the succession to the imperial crown of the said united kingdom, and of the dominions thereunto belonging, shall continue limited and settled in the same manner as the succession to the imperial crown of the said kingdom of Great Britain and Ireland now stands limited and settled, according to the existing laws, and to the terms of union between England and Scotland.

ARTICLE III

That it be the third article of union, that the said united kingdom be represented in one and the same parliament, to be styled The Parliament of the United Kingdom of Great Britain and Ireland.

ARTICLE IV

That it be the fourth article of union, that four lords spiritual of Ireland by rotation of sessions, and twenty-eight lords temporal of Ireland elected for life by the peers of Ireland, shall be the number to sit and vote on the part of Ireland in the house of lords of the parliament of the united kingdom; and one hundred commoners (two for each county of Ireland, two for the city of Dublin, two for the city of Cork, one for the university of Trinity College, and one for each of the thirty-one most considerable cities, towns, and boroughs), be the number to sit and vote on the part of Ireland in the house of commons of the parliament of the united kingdom:

That such act as shall be passed in the parliament of Ireland previous to the union, to regulate the mode by which the lords spiritual and temporal, and the commons, to serve in the parliament of the united kingdom on the part of Ireland, shall be summoned and returned to the said parliament, shall be considered as forming part of the treaty of union, and shall be incorporated in the acts of the respective parliaments by which the said union shall be ratified and established:

That all questions touching the rotation or election of lords spiritual or temporal of Ireland to sit in the parliament of the united kingdom shall be decided by the house of lords thereof; and wherever, by reason of an equality of votes, in the election of any such lords temporal, a complete election shall not be made according to the true intent of this article, the names of those peers for whom such equality of votes shall be so given, shall be written on pieces of paper of a similar form, and shall be put into a glass, by the clerk of the parliaments at the table of the house of lords whilst the house is sitting; and the peer or peers whose name or names shall be first drawn out by the clerk of the parliaments, shall be deemed the peer or peers elected, as the case may be:

That any person holding any peerage of Ireland now subsisting, or hereafter to be created, shall not thereby be disqualified from being elected to serve if he shall so think fit, or from serving or continuing to serve, if he shall so think fit, for any county, city, or borough of Great Britain, in the house of commons of the united kingdom, unless he shall have been previously elected, as above, to sit in the house of lords of the united kingdom; but that so long as such peer of Ireland shall so continue to be a member of the house of commons, he shall not be entitled to the privilege of peerage, nor be capable of being elected to serve as a peer on the part of Ireland, or of voting at any such election; and that he shall be liable to be sued, indicted, proceeded against, and tried as a commoner, for any offence with which he may be charged.

That it shall be lawful for His Majesty, his heirs and successors, to create peers of that part of the united kingdom called Ireland, and to make promotions in the peerage thereof, after the union; provided that no new creation of any such peers shall take place after the union until three of the peerages of Ireland, which shall have been existing at the time of the union, shall have become extinct; and upon such extinction of three peerages, that it shall be lawful for His Majesty, his heirs and successors, to create one peer of that part of the united kingdom called Ireland; and in like manner so often as three peerages of that part of the united kingdom called Ireland shall become extinct, it shall be lawful for His Majesty, his heirs and successors, to create one other peer of the said part of the united kingdom; and if it shall happen that the peers of that part of the united kingdom called Ireland, shall, by extinction of peerages or otherwise, be reduced to the number of one hundred, exclusive of all such peers of that part of the united kingdom called Ireland, as shall hold any peerage of Great Britain subsisting at the time of the union, or of the united kingdom created since the union, by which such peers shall be entitled to an hereditary seat in the house of lords of the united kingdom, then and in that case it shall and may be lawful for His Majesty, his heirs and successors, to create one peer of that part of the united kingdom called Ireland as often as any one of such one hundred peerages shall fail by extinction, or as often as any one peer of that part of the united kingdom called Ireland shall become entitled, by descent or creation, to an hereditary seat in the house of lords of the united kingdom; it being the true intent and meaning of this article, that at all times after the union it shall and may be lawful for His Majesty, his heirs and successors, to keep up the peerage of that part of the united kingdom called Ireland to the number of one hundred, over and above the number of such of the said peers as shall be entitled, by descent or creation, to an hereditary seat in the house of lords of the united kingdom:

That if any peerage shall at any time be in abeyance, such peerage shall be deemed and taken as an existing peerage; and no peerage shall be deemed extinct, unless on default of claimants to the inheritance of such peerage for the space of one year from the death of the person who shall have been last possessed thereof; and if no claims shall be made to the inheritance of such peerage, in such form and manner as may from time to time be prescribed by the house of lords of the united kingdom, before the expiration of the said period of a year, then and in that case such peerage shall be deemed extinct; provided that nothing herein shall exclude any person from afterwards putting in a claim to the peerage so deemed extinct; and if such claim shall be allowed as valid, by judgment of the house of lords of the united kingdom, reported to His Majesty, such peerage shall be considered as revived; and in case any new creation of a peerage of that part of the united kingdom called Ireland, shall have taken place in the interval, in consequence of the supposed extinction of such peerage, then no new right of creation shall accrue to His Majesty, his heirs or successors, in consequence of the next extinction which shall take place of any peerage of that part of the united kingdom called Ireland:

That all questions touching the election of members to sit on the part of Ireland in the house of commons of the united kingdom shall be heard and decided in the same manner as questions touching such elections in Great Britain now are, or at any time hereafter shall by law be heard and decided; subject nevertheless to such particular regulations in respect of Ireland as, from local circumstances, the parliament of the united kingdom may from time to time deem expedient:

That the qualifications in respect of property of the members elected on the part of Ireland to sit in the house of commons of the united kingdom, shall be respectively the same as are now provided by law in the cases of elections for counties and cities and boroughs respectively in that part of Great Britain called England, unless any other provision shall hereafter be made in that respect by act of parliament of the united kingdom:

That when His Majesty, his heirs or successors, shall declare his, her, or their pleasure for holding the first or any subsequent parliament of the united kingdom, a proclamation shall issue, under the great seal of the united kingdom, to cause the lords spiritual and temporal, and commons, who are to serve in the parliament thereof on the part of Ireland, to be returned in such manner as by any act of this present session of the parliament of Ireland shall be provided; and that the lords spiritual and temporal and commons of Great Britain shall, together with the lords spiritual and temporal and commons so returned as aforesaid on the part of Ireland, constitute the two houses of the parliament of the united kingdom:

That if His Majesty, on or before the first day of January one thousand eight hundred and one, on which day the union is to take place, shall declare, under the great seal of Great Britain, that it is expedient that the lords and commons of the present

parliament of Great Britain should be the members of the respective houses of the first parliament of the united kingdom
on the part of Great Britain, then the said lords and commons
of the present parliament of Great Britain shall accordingly be
the members of the respective houses of the first parliament of
the united kingdom on the part of Great Britain; and they,
together with the lords spiritual and temporal and commons, so
summoned and returned as above on the part of Ireland, shall be
the lords spiritual and temporal and commons of the first parliament of the united kingdom; and such first parliament may (in
that case) if not sooner dissolved, continue to sit so long as the
present parliament of Great Britain may now by law continue to
sit, if not sooner dissolved: provided always, that until an act
shall have passed in the parliament of the united kingdom, providing in what cases persons holding offices or places of profit
under the crown in Ireland shall be incapable of being members
of the house of commons of the parliament of the united kingdom, no greater number of members than twenty, holding such
offices or places, as aforesaid, shall be capable of sitting in the
said house of commons of the parliament of the united kingdom;
and if such a number of members shall be returned to serve in
the said house as to make the whole number of members of the
said house holding such office or place as aforesaid more than
twenty, then and in such case the seats or places of such members as shall have last accepted such offices or places shall be
vacated, at the option of such members, so as to reduce the
number of members holding such offices or places to the number
of twenty; and no person holding any such office or place shall
be capable of being elected or of sitting in the said house,
while there are twenty persons holding such offices or places sitting in the said house; and that every one of the lords of parliament of the united kingdom, and every member of the house of
commons of the united kingdom, in the first and all succeeding
parliaments, shall, until the parliament of the united kingdom
shall otherwise provide, take the oaths, and make and subscribe
the declaration, and take and subscribe the oath now by law
enjoined to be taken, made, and subscribed by the lords and
commons of the parliament of Great Britain:

That the lords of parliament on the part of Ireland, in the
house of lords of the united kingdom, shall at all times have the
same privileges of parliament which shall belong to the lords of
parliament on the part of Great Britain; and the lords spiritual
and temporal respectively on the part of Ireland shall at all times

have the same rights in respect of their sitting and voting upon the trial of peers, as the lords spiritual and temporal respectively on the part of Great Britain; and that all lords spiritual of Ireland shall have rank and precedency next and immediately after the lords spiritual of the same rank and degree of Great Britain, and shall enjoy all privileges as fully as the lords spiritual of Great Britain do now or may hereafter enjoy the same (the right and privilege of sitting in the house of lords, and the privileges depending thereon, and particularly the right of sitting on the trial of peers, excepted); and that the persons holding any temporal peerages of Ireland, existing at the time of the union, shall, from and after the union, have rank and precedency next and immediately after all the persons holding peerages of the like orders and degrees in Great Britain, subsisting at the time of the union; and that all peerages of Ireland created after the union shall have rank and precedency with the peerages of the united kingdom, so created, according to the dates of their creations; and that all peerages both of Great Britain and Ireland, now subsisting or hereafter to be created, shall in all other respects, from the date of the union, be considered as peerages of the united kingdom; and that the peers of Ireland shall, as peers of the united kingdom, be sued and tried as peers, except as aforesaid, and shall enjoy all privileges of peers as fully as the peers of Great Britain; the right and privilege of sitting in the house of lords, and the privileges depending thereon, and the right of sitting on the trial of peers, only excepted:

ARTICLE V

That it be the fifth article of union, that the churches of England and Ireland, as now by law established, be united into one protestant episcopal church, to be called, The United Church of England and Ireland; and that the doctrine, worship, discipline, and government of the said united church shall be, and shall remain in full force forever, as the same are now by law established for the church of England; and that the continuance and preservation of the said united church, as the established church of England and Ireland, shall be deemed and taken to be an essential and fundamental part of the union; and that in like manner the doctrine, worship, discipline, and government of the church of Scotland shall remain and be preserved as the same are now established by law, and by the act for the union of the two kingdoms of England and Scotland.

ARTICLE VI

That it be the sixth article of union, that His Majesty's subjects of Great Britain and Ireland shall, from and after the first day of January one thousand eight hundred and one, be entitled to the same privileges, and be on the same footing, as to encouragements and bounties on the like articles being the growth, produce, or manufacture of either country respectively, and generally in respect of trade and navigation in all ports and places in the united kingdom and its dependencies; and that in all treaties made by His Majesty, his heirs and successors, with any foreign power, His Majesty's subjects of Ireland shall have the same privileges, and be on the same footing, as His Majesty's subjects of Great Britain:

That, from the first day of January one thousand eight hundred and one, all prohibitions and bounties on the export of articles, the growth, produce, or manufacture of either country, to the other, shall cease and determine; and that the said articles shall thenceforth be exported from one country to the other, without duty or bounty on such export:

That all articles, the growth, produce, or manufacture of either country, (not hereinafter enumerated as subject to specific duties,) shall from thenceforth be imported into each country from the other, free from duty, other than such countervailing duties on the several articles enumerated in the schedule number one A. and B. hereunto annexed, as are therein specified, or to such other countervailing duties as shall hereafter be imposed by the parliament of the united kingdom, in the manner hereinafter provided; and that, for the period of twenty years from the union, the articles enumerated in the schedule number two hereunto annexed, shall be subject, on importation into each country from the other, to the duties specified in the said schedule number two; and the woollen manufactures, known by the names of old and new drapery, shall pay, on importation into each country from the other, the duties now payable on importation into Ireland; salt and hops, on importation into Ireland from Great Britain, duties not exceeding those which are now paid on importation into Ireland; and coals, on importation into Ireland from Great Britain, shall be subject to burdens not exceeding those to which they are now subject: * * *

*   *   *   *   *   *   *   *   *

Article VIII

That it be the eighth article of union, that all laws in force at the time of the union, and all the courts of civil and ecclesiastical jurisdiction within the respective kingdoms, shall remain as now by law established within the same, subject only to such alterations and regulations from time to time as circumstances may appear to the parliament of the united kingdom to require; provided that all writs of error and appeals, depending at the time of the union or hereafter to be brought, and which might now be finally decided by the house of lords of either kingdom, shall, from and after the union, be finally decided by the house of lords of the united kingdom; and provided that, from and after the union, there shall remain in Ireland an instance court of admiralty, for the determination of causes, civil and maritime only, and that the appeal from sentences of the said court shall be to His Majesty's delegates in his court of chancery in that part of the united kingdom called Ireland; and that all laws at present in force in either kingdom, which shall be contrary to any of the provisions which may be enacted by any act for carrying these articles into effect, be from and after the union repealed.

And whereas the said articles having, by address of the respective houses of parliament in Great Britain and Ireland, been humbly laid before His Majesty, His Majesty has been graciously pleased to approve the same; and to recommend it to his two houses of parliament in Great Britain and Ireland to consider of such measures as may be necessary for giving effect to the said articles: in order, therefore, to give full effect and validity to the same, be it enacted by the king's most excellent Majesty, by and with the advice and consent of the lords spiritual and temporal, and commons, in this present parliament assembled, and by the authority of the same, that the said foregoing recited articles, each and every of them, according to the true import and tenor thereof, be ratified, confirmed, and approved, and be and they are hereby declared to be the articles of the Union of Great Britain and Ireland, and the same shall be in force and have effect for ever, from the first day of January which shall be in the year of our Lord one thousand eight hundred and one; provided that before that period an act shall have been passed by the parliament of Ireland, for carrying into effect, in the like manner, the said foregoing recited articles.

II. [Clause regulating the election of representative peers and members of the house of commons for Ireland.]

III. And be it enacted, that the great seal of Ireland may, if His Majesty shall so think fit, after the union, be used in like manner as before the union, except where it is otherwise provided by the foregoing articles, within that part of the united kingdom called Ireland; and that His Majesty may, so long as he shall think fit, continue the privy council of Ireland to be his privy council for that part of the united kingdom called Ireland.

———◆———

259. Abolition of the Negro Slave Trade

(1807, March 25. 47 George III. c. 36. 47 *S. L.* 140.)

WHEREAS the two houses of parliament did, by their resolutions of the tenth and twenty-fourth days of July one thousand eight hundred and six, severally resolve, upon certain grounds therein mentioned, that they would, with all practicable expedition, take effectual measures for the abolition of the African slave trade, in such manner, and at such period, as might be deemed advisable; and whereas it is fit upon all and each of the grounds mentioned in the said resolutions, that the same should be forthwith abolished and prohibited, and declared to be unlawful: be it therefore enacted by the king's most excellent Majesty, by and with the advice and consent of the lords spiritual and temporal, and commons, in this present parliament assembled, and by the authority of the same, that from and after the first day of May one thousand eight hundred and seven, the African slave trade, and all and all manner of dealing and trading in the purchase, sale, barter, or transfer of slaves, or of persons intended to be sold, transferred, used, or dealt with as slaves, practised or carried on, in, at, to, or from any part of the coast or countries of Africa, shall be, and the same is hereby utterly abolished, prohibited, and declared to be unlawful; and also that all and all manner of dealing, either by way of purchase, sale, barter, or transfer, or by means of any other contract or agreement whatever, relating to any slaves, or to any persons intended to be used or dealt with as slaves, for the purpose of such slaves or persons being removed or transported either immediately or by transhipment at sea or otherwise, directly or indirectly from

Africa, or from any island, country, territory, or place whatever, in the West Indies, or in any other part of America, not being in the dominion, possession, or occupation of His Majesty, to any other island, country, territory, or place whatever, is hereby in like manner utterly abolished, prohibited, and declared to be unlawful; * * *

---

260. Disfranchisement of Grampound

(1821, June 8.   1 & 2 George IV. c. 47.   59 *S. L.* 103.)

WHEREAS there was the most notorious and general bribery and corruption previous to the election of burgesses to serve in the last parliament for the borough of Grampound, in the county of Cornwall, in order to procure the return of burgesses to serve in parliament for the said borough, and it should therefore be excluded from hereafter returning burgesses to serve in parliament: and whereas it is expedient that two additional knights of the shire should be returned for the county of York to serve in parliament in lieu of two burgesses for the borough of Grampound: may it therefore please Your Majesty that it may be enacted, and be it enacted by the king's most excellent Majesty, by and with the advice and consent of the lords spiritual and temporal, and commons, in this present parliament assembled, and by the authority of the same, that the borough of Grampound, in the county of Cornwall, shall cease to elect and return burgesses to serve in the high court of parliament.

II. And be it further enacted, that if, during the present parliament, the election of the two burgesses now serving therein for the same borough of Grampound or either of them, shall by death or otherwise become void, then and in every such case an additional knight or knights shall be returned to serve in the high court of parliament for the county of York; and that from the end of the present parliament, and at all times thereafter, the said county of York shall return, to serve in the high court of parliament, four knights of the shire instead of two knights of the shire, as the said county has heretofore returned; the said knights respectively to be elected and chosen by virtue of Your Majesty's writ, to be awarded by the lord chancellor or lord keeper of the great seal of that part of the united kingdom called Great Britain for the time being, in that behalf to the sheriff of

the county of York; and the said knights to be elected and returned in the same manner, to all intents and purposes, as knights
have been heretofore returned for the county of York.

*   *   *   *   *   *   *   *   *

261. Repeal of Corporation and Test Acts

(1828, May 9.   9 George IV. c. 17.   65 *S. L.* 22.)

WHEREAS an act was passed in the thirteenth year of the
reign of King Charles the Second, entitled, An Act for the
well governing and regulating of Corporations: and whereas
another act was passed in the twenty-fifth year of the reign of
King Charles the Second, entitled, An Act for preventing Dangers
which may happen from Popish Recusants: and whereas another
act was passed in the sixteenth year of the reign of King George
the Second, entitled, An Act to indemnify Persons who have
omitted to qualify themselves for Offices and Employments within
the Time limited by Law, and for allowing further Time for that
Purpose, and also for amending so much of an Act made in the
twenty-fifth Year of the Reign of King Charles the Second,
entitled, An Act for preventing Dangers which may happen from
Popish Recusants, as related to the Time for receiving the Sacrament of the Lord's Supper now limited by the said Act: and
whereas it is expedient that so much of the said several acts of
parliament as imposes the necessity of taking the sacrament of
the Lord's Supper according to the rites or usage of the Church
of England, for the purposes therein respectively mentioned,
should be repealed; be it therefore enacted by the king's most
excellent Majesty, by and with the advice and consent of the lords
spiritual and temporal, and commons, in this present parliament
assembled, and by the authority of the same, that so much and
such parts of the said several acts passed in the thirteenth and
twenty-fifth years of the reign of King Charles the Second, and of
the said act passed in the sixteenth year of the reign of King
George the Second, as require the person or persons in the said
acts respectively described to take or receive the sacrament of
the Lord's Supper according to the rites or usage of the Church
of England, for the several purposes therein expressed, or to

deliver a certificate or to make proof of the truth of such his or their receiving the said sacrament in manner aforesaid, or as impose upon any such person or persons any penalty, forfeiture, incapacity, or disability whatsoever for or by reason of any neglect or omission to take or receive the said sacrament, within the respective periods and in the manner in the said acts respectively provided in that behalf, shall, from and immediately after the passing of this act, be and the same are hereby repealed.

II. And whereas the Protestant episcopal Church of England and Ireland, and the doctrine, discipline, and government thereof, and the Protestant presbyterian Church of Scotland, and the doctrine, discipline, and government thereof, are by the laws of this realm severally established, permanently and inviolably: and whereas it is just and fitting, that on the repeal of such parts of the said acts as impose the necessity of taking the sacrament of the Lord's Supper according to the rites or usage of the Church of England as a qualification for office, a declaration to the following effect should be substituted in lieu thereof; be it therefore enacted, that every person who shall hereafter be placed, elected, or chosen in or to the office of mayor, alderman, recorder, bailiff, town clerk or common councilman, or in or to any office of magistracy, or place, trust, or employment relating to the government of any city, corporation, borough, or cinque port within England and Wales, or the town of Berwick-upon-Tweed, shall, within one calendar month next before or upon his admission into any of the aforesaid offices or trusts, make and subscribe the declaration following:

' I, A. B., do solemnly and sincerely, in the presence of God, profess, testify, and declare, upon the true faith of a Christian, that I will never exercise any power, authority, or influence which I may possess by virtue of the office of   to injure or weaken the Protestant church as it is by law established in England, or to disturb the said church, or the bishops and clergy of the said church, in the possession of any rights or privileges to which such church, or the said bishops and clergy, are or may be by law entitled.'

*   *   *   *   *   *   *   *   *

262. Catholic Emancipation Act

(1829, April 13.   10 George IV. c. 7.   65 *S. L.* pt. 2, p. 49.)

WHEREAS by various acts of parliament certain restraints and disabilities are imposed on the Roman Catholic subjects of His Majesty, to which other subjects of His Majesty are not liable: and whereas it is expedient that such restraints and disabilities shall be from henceforth discontinued: and whereas by various acts certain oaths and certain declarations, commonly called the declaration against transubstantiation, and the declaration against transubstantiation and the invocation of saints and the sacrifice of the mass, as practised in the Church of Rome, are or may be required to be taken, made, and subscribed by the subjects of His Majesty, as qualifications for sitting and voting in parliament, and for the enjoyment of certain offices, franchises, and civil rights: be it enacted by the king's most excellent Majesty, by and with the advice and consent of the lords spiritual and temporal, and commons, in this present parliament assembled, and by the authority of the same, that from and after the commencement of this act all such parts of the said acts as require the said declarations, or either of them, to be made or subscribed by any of His Majesty's subjects, as a qualification for sitting and voting in parliament, or for the exercise or enjoyment of any office, franchise, or civil right, be and the same are (save as hereinafter provided and excepted) hereby repealed.

II.   And be it enacted, that from and after the commencement of this act it shall be lawful for any person professing the Roman Catholic religion, being a peer, or who shall after the commencement of this act be returned as a member of the house of commons, to sit and vote in either house of parliament respectively, being in all other respects duly qualified to sit and vote therein, upon taking and subscribing the following oath, instead of the oaths of allegiance, supremacy, and abjuration:

'I, A. B., do sincerely promise and swear, that I will be faithful and bear true allegiance to His Majesty King George the Fourth, and will defend him to the utmost of my power against all conspiracies and attempts whatever, which shall be made against his person, crown, or dignity; and I will do my utmost endeavour to disclose and make known to His Majesty, his heirs and successors, all treasons and traitorous conspiracies which may be formed against him or them: and I do faithfully promise to maintain, support, and defend, to the utmost of my power, the succession of the crown, which succession, by an act, entitled, An Act for the further Limitation of the Crown, and better securing the Rights and Liberties of the Subject, is and stands limited to the princess Sophia, electress of Hanover, and the heirs of her body, being Protestants; hereby utterly renouncing and abjuring any obedience or allegiance unto any other person claiming or pretending a right to the crown of this realm: and I do further declare, that it is not an article of my faith, and that I do renounce, reject, and abjure the opinion, that princes excommunicated or deprived by the pope, or any other authority of the see of Rome, may be deposed or murdered by their subjects, or by any person whatsoever: and I do declare, that I do not believe that the pope of Rome, or any other foreign prince, prelate, person, state, or potentate, hath or ought to have any temporal or civil jurisdiction, power, superiority, or preeminence, directly or indirectly, within this realm.   I do swear, that I will defend to the utmost of my power the settlement of property within this realm, as established by the laws: and I do hereby disclaim, disavow, and solemnly abjure any intention to subvert the present church establishment, as settled by law within this realm: and I do solemnly swear, that I will never exercise any privilege to which I am or may become entitled, to disturb or weaken the Protestant religion or Protestant government in the united kingdom: and I do solemnly, in the presence of God, profess, testify, and declare, that I do make this declaration, and every part thereof, in the plain and ordinary sense of the words of this oath, without any evasion, equivocation, or mental reservation whatsoever.

So help me God.'

III. And be it further enacted, that wherever, in the oath here appointed and set forth, the name of His present Majesty is expressed or referred to, the name of the sovereign of this kingdom for the time being, by virtue of the act for the further limitation of the crown and better securing the right and liberties of the subject, shall be substituted from time to time, with proper words of reference thereto.

IV. Provided always, and be it further enacted, that no peer professing the Roman Catholic religion, and no person professing the Roman Catholic religion, who shall be returned a member of the house of commons after the commencement of this act, shall be capable of sitting or voting in either house of parliament respectively, unless he shall first take and subscribe the oath hereinbefore appointed and set forth, before the same persons, at

the same times and places, and in the same manner as the oaths
and the declaration now required by law are respectively directed
to be taken, made, and subscribed; and that any such person
professing the Roman Catholic religion, who shall sit or vote in
either house of parliament, without having first taken and subscribed, in the manner aforesaid, the oath in this act appointed
and set forth, shall be subject to the same penalties, forfeitures,
and disabilities, and the offence of so sitting or voting shall be
followed and attended by and with the same consequences, as
are by law enacted and provided in the case of persons sitting
or voting in either house of parliament respectively, without the
taking, making, and subscribing the oaths and the declaration
now required by law.

V. And be it further enacted, that it shall be lawful for persons professing the Roman Catholic religion to vote at elections
of members to serve in parliament for England and for Ireland,
and also to vote at the elections of representative peers of Scotland and of Ireland, and to be elected such representative peers,
being in all other respects duly qualified, upon taking and subscribing the oath hereinbefore appointed and set forth, instead
of the oaths of allegiance, supremacy, and abjuration, and
instead of the declaration now by law required, and instead also
of such other oath or oaths as are now by law required to be
taken by any of His Majesty's subjects professing the Roman
Catholic religion, and upon taking also such other oath or oaths
as may now be lawfully tendered to any persons offering to vote
at such elections.

VI, VII. [The administration of the oath.]

VIII. [Allowing Roman Catholics to vote and be elected in
Scotland.]

*   *   *   *   *   *   *   *   *

IX. And be it further enacted, that no person in holy orders
in the Church of Rome shall be capable of being elected to serve
in parliament as a member of the house of commons; and if any
such person shall be elected to serve in parliament as aforesaid,
such election shall be void; and if any person, being elected to
serve in parliament as a member of the house of commons, shall,
after his election, take or receive holy orders in the Church of
Rome, the seat of such person shall immediately become void;
and if any such person shall, in any of the cases aforesaid, presume to sit or vote as a member of the house of commons, he
shall be subject to the same penalties, forfeitures, and disabili-

ties as are enacted by an act passed in the forty-first year of the reign of King George the Third, entitled An Act to remove Doubts respecting the Eligibility of Persons in Holy Orders to sit in the House of Commons; and proof of the celebration of any religious service by such person, according to the rites of the Church of Rome, shall be deemed and taken to be *primâ facie* evidence of the fact of such person being in holy orders, within the intent and meaning of this act.

X. And be it enacted, that it shall be lawful for any of His Majesty's subjects professing the Roman Catholic religion to hold, exercise, and enjoy all civil and military offices and places of trust or profit under His Majesty, his heirs or successors, and to exercise any other franchise or civil right, except as hereinafter excepted, upon taking and subscribing, at the times and in the manner hereinafter mentioned, the oath hereinbefore appointed and set forth, instead of the oaths of allegiance, supremacy, and abjuration, and instead of such oath or oaths as are or may be now by law required to be taken for the purpose aforesaid by any of His Majesty's subjects professing the Roman Catholic religion.

XI. Provided always, and be it enacted, that nothing herein contained shall be construed to exempt any person professing the Roman Catholic religion from the necessity of taking any oath or oaths, or making any declaration, not hereinbefore mentioned, which are or may be by law required to be taken or subscribed by any person on his admission into any such office or place of trust or profit as aforesaid.

XII. Provided also, and be it further enacted, that nothing herein contained shall extend or be construed to extend to enable any person or persons professing the Roman Catholic religion to hold or exercise the office of guardians and justices of the united kingdom, or of regent of the united kingdom, under whatever name, style, or title such office may be constituted; nor to enable any person, otherwise than as he is now by law enabled, to hold or enjoy the office of lord high chancellor, lord keeper or lord commissioner of the great seal of Great Britain or Ireland; or the office of lord lieutenant, or lord deputy, or other chief governor or governors of Ireland; or His Majesty's high commissioner to the General Assembly of the Church of Scotland.

* * * * * * * * *

263. Reform Act of 1832

(1832, June 7.   2 William IV, c. 45.)

WHEREAS it is expedient to take effectual measures for correcting divers abuses that have long prevailed in the choice of members to serve in the commons house of parliament, to deprive many inconsiderable places of the right of returning members, to grant such privilege to large, populous, and wealthy towns, to increase the number of knights of the shire, to extend the elective franchise to many of His Majesty's subjects who have not heretofore enjoyed the same, and to diminish the expense of elections: Be it therefore enacted by the king's most excellent Majesty, by and with the advice and consent of the lords spiritual and temporal, and commons, in this present parliament assembled, and by the authority of the same, that each of the boroughs enumerated in the Schedule marked A (56 in all) shall from and after the end of this present parliament cease to return any member or members to serve in parliament.

II. [Boroughs enumerated in Schedule B (30 in all) to return one member only.]
III. [Places named in Schedule C (22 in all) made boroughs to return two members to parliament.]
IV. [Places named in Schedule D (20 in all) made boroughs to return one member to parliament.]
V. [Four boroughs to include adjacent districts.]
VI. [Weymouth and Melcombe Regis to return two members instead of four; Penryn to include Falmouth, and Sandwich to include Deal and Walmer.]
VII. Boundaries to be fixed.]
VIII, IX, X. [Dealing with Wales.]
XI. [Returning officers.]
XII. [Yorkshire to return six members.]
XIII. [Lincolnshire to return four members.]
XIV. [Counties enumerated in Schedule F (25 in all) to return four members.]
XV. [Counties enumerated in Schedule F_2 (7 in all) to return three members, and two members instead of one to be returned by three of the counties in Wales.]
XVI. [Isle of Wight to return one member, apart from Hampshire.]

XVII. [Towns, which are counties of themselves, to be included in adjoining counties.]

XVIII. That no person shall be entitled to vote in the election of a knight or knights of the shire to serve in any future parliament, or in the election of a member or members to serve in any future parliament for any city or town being a county of itself, in respect of any freehold lands or tenements whereof such person may be seised for his own life, or for the life of another, or for any lives whatsoever, except such person shall be in the actual and *bona fide* occupation of such lands or tenements, or except the same shall have come to such person by marriage, marriage settlement, devise, or promotion to any benefice or to any office, or except the same shall be of the clear yearly value of not less than 10 £ above all rents and charges payable out of or in respect of the same; any statute or usage to the contrary notwithstanding: provided always, that nothing in this act contained shall prevent any person now seised for his own life, or for the life of another, or for any lives whatsoever, of any freehold lands or tenements in respect of which he now has, or but for the passing of this act might acquire, the right of voting in such respective elections, from retaining or acquiring, so long as he shall be so seised of the same lands or tenements, such right of voting in respect thereof, if duly registered according to the respective provisions hereinafter contained.

XIX. That every male person of full age, and not subject to any legal incapacity, who shall be seised at law or in equity of any land or tenements of copyhold or any other tenure whatever except freehold, for his own life, or for the life of another, or for any lives whatsoever, or for any larger estate, of the clear yearly value of not less than 10 £ over and above all rents and charges payable out of or in respect of the same, shall be entitled to vote in the election of a knight or knights of the shire to serve in any future parliament for the county, or for the riding, parts, or division of the county, in which such lands or tenements shall be respectively situate.

XX. That every male person of full age, and not subject to any legal incapacity, who shall be entitled, either as lessee or assignee, to any lands or tenements, whether of freehold or of any other tenure whatever, for the unexpired residue, whatever it may be, of any term originally created for a period of not less than sixty years, (whether determinable on a life or lives, or not,) of the clear yearly value of not less than 10 £ over and above all rents and charges payable out of or in respect of the same, or for the unexpired residue, whatever it may be, of any term originally created for a period of not less than twenty years, (whether determinable on a life or lives, or not,) of the clear yearly value of not less than 50 £ over and above all rents and charges payable out of or in respect of the same, or who shall occupy as tenant any lands or tenements for which he shall be *bona fide* liable to a yearly rent of not less than 50 £, shall be entitled to vote in the election of a knight or knights of the shire to serve in any future parliament for the county, or for the riding, parts, or division of the county, in which such lands or tenements shall be respectively situate: provided always, that no person, being only a sub-lessee, or the assignee of any under-lease, shall have a right to vote in such election in respect of any such term of sixty years or twenty years as aforesaid, unless he shall be in the actual occupation of the premises.

XXI. That no public or parliamentary tax, nor any church rate, county rate, or parochial rate, shall be deemed to be any charge payable out of or in respect of any lands or tenements within the meaning of this act.

XXII. That in order to entitle any person to vote in any election of a knight of the shire or other member to serve in any future parliament, in respect of any messuages, lands, or tenements, whether freehold or otherwise, it shall not be necessary that the same shall be assessed to the land tax; any statute to the contrary notwithstanding.

*   *   *   *   *   *   *   *   *

XXVI. That notwithstanding anything hereinbefore contained no person shall be entitled to vote in the election of a knight or knights of the shire to serve in any future parliament unless he shall have been duly registered according to the provisions hereinafter contained; and that no person shall be so registered in any year in respect of his estate or interest in any lands or tenements, as a freeholder, copyholder, customary tenant, or tenant in ancient demesne, unless he shall have been in the actual possession thereof, or in the receipt of the rents and profits thereof for his own use, for six calendar months at least next previous to the last day of July in such year, which said period of six calendar months shall be sufficient, any statute to the contrary notwithstanding; and that no person shall be so registered in any year, in respect of any lands or tenements held by him as such lessee or assignee, or as such occupier and tenant as aforesaid, unless he shall have been in the actual possession thereof, or in

receipt of the rents and profits thereof for his own use, as the
case may require, for twelve calendar months next previous to
the last day of July in such year: provided always, that where
any lands or tenements, which would otherwise entitle the owner,
holder, or occupier thereof to vote in any such election, shall
come to any person, at any time within such respective periods
of six or twelve calendar months, by descent, succession, marriage, marriage settlement, devise, or promotion to any benefice
in a church, or by promotion to any office, such person shall be
entitled in respect thereof to have his name inserted as a voter in
the election of a knight or knights of the shire in the lists then
next to be made, by virtue of this act as hereinafter mentioned,
and, upon his being duly registered according to the provisions
hereinafter contained, to vote in such election.

XXVII. That in every city or borough which shall return a
member or members to serve in any future parliament, every
male person of full age, and not subject to any legal incapacity,
who shall occupy, within such city or borough, or within any
place sharing in the election for such city or borough, as owner
or tenant, any house, warehouse, counting-house, shop, or other
building, being, either separately, or jointly with any land within
such city, borough, or place occupied therewith by him as owner,
or therewith by him as tenant under the same landlord, of the
clear yearly value of not less than 10 £, shall, if duly registered
according to the provisions hereinafter contained, be entitled to
vote in the election of a member or members to serve in any
future parliament for such city or borough: provided always, that
no such person shall be so registered in any year unless he shall
have occupied such premises as aforesaid for twelve calendar
months next previous to the last day of July in such year, nor unless such person, where such premises are situated in any parish
or township in which there shall be a rate for the relief of the
poor, shall have been rated in respect of such premises to all
rates for the relief of the poor in such parish or township, made
during the time of such his occupation so required as aforesaid,
nor unless such person shall have paid, on or before the 20th of
July in such year, all the poor's rates and assessed taxes which
shall have become payable from him in respect of such premises
previously to the 6th of April then next preceding: provided also,
that no such person shall be so registered in any year unless he
shall have resided for six calendar months next previous to the
last day of July in such year within the city or borough, or within
the place sharing in the election for the city or borough, in re-

spect of which city, borough, or place respectively he shall be
entitled to vote, or within seven statute miles thereof or of any
part thereof.

XXVIII. That the premises in respect of the occupation of
which any person shall be entitled to be registered in any year,
and to vote in the election for any city or borough as aforesaid,
shall not be required to be the same premises, but may be different premises occupied in immediate succession by such person
during the twelve calendar months next previous to the last day
of July in such year, such person having paid on or before the
20th of July in such year, all the poor's rates and assessed taxes
which shall previously to the 6th of April then next preceding
have become payable from him in respect of all such premises so
occupied by him in succession.

* * * * * * * * *

XXXVI. That no person shall be entitled to be registered in
any year as a voter in the election of a member or members to
serve in any future parliament for any city or borough who shall
within twelve calendar months next previous to the last day of
July in such year have received parochial relief or other alms,
which by the law of parliament now disqualify from voting in the
election of members to serve in parliament.

XXXVII. That the overseers of the poor of every parish and
township shall, on the 20th day of June in the present and in
every succeeding year, cause to be fixed on or near the doors of
all the churches and chapels within such parish or township, or
if there be no church or chapel therein, then to be fixed in some
public and conspicuous situation within the same respectively, a
notice according to the form numbered 1. in the schedule (H.) to
this act annexed, requiring all persons who may be entitled to
vote in the election of a knight or knights of the shire * * * in
respect of any property situate wholly or in part in such parish or
township, to deliver or transmit to the said overseers on or before
the 20th of July in the present and in every succeeding year a
notice of their claim as such voters, according to the form numbered 2. in the said schedule (H.), or to the like effect: provided
always, that after the formation of the register to be made in
each year, as hereinafter mentioned, no person whose name shall
be upon such register for the time being shall be required thereafter to make any such claim as aforesaid, so long as he shall
retain the same qualification, and continue in the same place of
abode described by such register.

XXXVIII. That the overseer of the poor of every parish and township shall, on or before the last day of July in the present year, make out or cause to be made out, according to the form numbered 3. in the said schedule (H.), an alphabetical list of all persons who shall claim as aforesaid to be inserted in such list as voters in the election of a knight or knights of the shire * * *, in respect of any lands or tenements situate wholly or in part within such parish or township; and that the said overseers shall on or before the last day of July in every succeeding year make out or cause to be made out a like list, containing the names of all persons who shall be upon the register for the time being as such voters, and also the names of all persons who shall claim as aforesaid to be inserted in the last-mentioned list as such voters; and in every list so to be made out by the overseers as aforesaid, the Christian name and surname of every person shall be written at full length, together with the place of his abode, the nature of his qualification, and the local or other description of such lands or tenements, as the same are respectively set forth in his claim to vote, and the name of the occupying tenant, if stated in such claim; and the said overseers, if they shall have reasonable cause to believe that any person so claiming as aforesaid, or whose name shall appear in the register for the time being, is not entitled to vote in the election of a knight or knights of the shire * * *, shall have power to add the words "objected to" opposite the name of every such person on the margin of such list; and the said overseers shall sign such list, and shall cause a sufficient number of copies of such list to be written or printed, and to be fixed on or near the doors of all the churches and chapels within their parish or township, or if there be no church or chapel therein, then to be fixed up in some public and conspicuous situation within the same respectively, on the two Sundays next after such list shall have been made; and the said overseers shall likewise keep a true copy of such list, to be perused by any person, without payment of any fee, at all reasonable hours during the first two weeks after such lists shall have been made; provided always, that every precinct or place, whether extra-parochial or otherwise, which shall have no overseers of the poor, shall for the purpose of making out such list as aforesaid be deemed to be within the parish or township adjoining thereto, such parish or township being situate within the same county, or the same riding, parts, or division of a county, as such precinct or place; and if such precinct or place shall adjoin two or more parishes or townships so situate as aforesaid, it shall be deemed to be within the least populous of such parishes or townships according to the last census for the time being; and the overseers of the poor of every such parish or township shall insert in the list for their respective parish or township the names of all persons who shall claim as aforesaid to be inserted therein as voters. * * *

XXXIX. That every person who shall be upon the register for the time being for any county, or for any riding, parts, or division of a county, or who shall have claimed to be inserted in any list for the then current year of voters * * * may object to any person as not having been entitled on the last day of July then next preceding to have his name inserted in any list of voters * * * so to be made out as aforesaid; and every person so objecting (save and except overseers objecting in the manner hereinbefore mentioned) shall, on or before the 25th of August in the present and in every succeeding year, give or cause to be given a notice in writing according to the form numbered 4. in the said schedule (H.), or to the like effect, to the overseers who shall have made out the list in which the name so objected to shall have been inserted; and the person so objecting shall also, on or before the 25th of August * * * give to the person objected to, or leave at his place of abode as described in such list, or personally deliver to his tenant in occupation of the premises described in such list, a notice in writing according to the form numbered 5. in the said schedule (H.), or to the like effect; and the overseers shall include the names of all persons so objected to in a list according to the form numbered 6. in the said schedule (H.), and shall cause copies of the same to be fixed on or near the doors of all the churches * * * on the two Sundays next preceding the 15th of September in the present and every succeeding year; and the overseers shall likewise keep a copy of the names of all the persons so objected to, to be perused by any person. * * *

XL. That on the 29th of August in the present and in every succeeding year the overseers of every parish and township shall deliver the list of voters so made out as aforesaid, together with a written statement of the number of persons objected to by the overseers and by other persons, to the high constable or high constables of the hundred or other like district in which such parish or township is situate; and such high constable or high constables shall forthwith deliver all such lists, together with such statements as aforesaid, to the clerk of the peace of the county, riding, or parts, who shall forthwith make out an abstract of the number of persons objected to by the overseers and by other persons in each parish or township, and transmit the same to the barrister or barristers appointed as hereinafter mentioned to revise such lists, in order that the said barrister or barristers may fix proper times and places for holding his or their courts for the revision of the said lists.

XLI. That the lord chief justice of the court of king's bench shall, in the month of July or August in the present and in every succeeding year, nominate and appoint for Middlesex, and the senior judge for the time being in the commission of assize for every other county shall, when travelling the summer circuit, * * * nominate and appoint for every such county, or for each of the ridings, parts, or divisions of such county, a barrister or barristers to revise the lists of voters in the election of a knight or knights of the shire; and such barrister or barristers so appointed as aforesaid shall give public notice, as well by advertisement in some of the newspapers circulating within the county, riding, parts, or division, as also by a notice to be fixed in some public and conspicuous situation * * * (* * * to be given three days at the least before the commencement of his or their circuit,) that he or they will make a circuit of the county, riding, parts, or division for which he or they shall be so appointed, and of the several times and places at which he or they will hold courts for that purpose, such times being between the 15th of September inclusive and the 25th of October inclusive in the present and in every succeeding year, and he or they shall hold open courts for that purpose at the times and places so to be announced; and where two or more barristers shall be appointed for the same county, riding, parts, or division, they shall attend at the same places together, but shall sit apart from each other, and hold separate courts at the same time for the despatch of business: provided always, that no member of parliament, nor any person holding any office or place of profit under the crown, shall be appointed such barrister, and that no barristers so appointed as aforesaid shall be eligible to serve in parliament for eighteen months from the time of such his appointment. * * *

XLII. That the clerk of the peace shall at the opening of the first court to be held by every such barrister * * * produce or cause to be produced before him the several lists of voters for such county, riding, parts, or division which shall have been delivered to such clerk of the peace by the high constable as aforesaid; and the overseers of every parish and township who shall have made out the lists of voters shall attend the court to be held by every such barrister at the place appointed for revising the lists relating to such parish or township respectively, and shall also deliver to such barrister a copy of the list of the persons objected to, so made out by them as aforesaid; and the said overseers shall answer upon oath all such questions as such barrister may put to them or any of them touching any matter necessary for revising the lists of voters; and every such barrister shall retain on the lists of voters the names of all persons to whom no objection shall have been made by the overseers, or by any other person, in the manner hereinbefore mentioned; and he shall also retain on the list of voters the name of every person who shall have been objected to by any person other than the overseers, unless the party so objecting shall appear by himself or by some one on his behalf in support of such objection; and where the name of any person inserted in the list of voters shall have been objected to by the overseers, or by any other person in the manner hereinbefore mentioned, and such person so objecting shall appear by himself or by some one on his behalf in support of such objection, every such barrister shall require it to be proved that the person so objected to was entitled on the last day of July then next preceding to have his name inserted in the list of voters in respect of the qualification described in such list; and in case the same shall not be proved to the satisfaction of such barrister, or in case it shall be proved that such person was then incapacitated by any law or statute from voting in the election of members to serve in parliament, such barrister shall expunge the name of every such person from the said lists; and he shall also expunge from the said lists the name of every person who shall be proved to him to be dead; and shall correct any mistake which shall be proved to him to have been made in any of the said lists as to any of the particulars by this act required to be inserted in such lists; and where the Christian name of any person, or his place of abode, or the nature of his qualification, or the local or other description of his property, or the name of the tenant in the occupation thereof, as the same respectively are required to be inserted in any such list, shall be wholly omitted therefrom, such barrister shall expunge the name of every such person from such list, unless the matter or matters so omitted be supplied to the satisfaction of such barrister before he shall have completed the revision of such list, in which case he shall then and there insert the same in such list: provided always, that no person's name shall be expunged from any such list, except in case of his death or of his being objected to on the margin of the list by the overseers as aforesaid, or except in case of any such omission or omissions as hereinbefore last-mentioned, unless such notice as is hereinbefore required in that behalf shall have been given to the overseers, nor unless such notice as is hereinbefore required in that behalf shall have been given to such person, or left at his place of abode, or delivered to his tenant as hereinbefore mentioned.

XLIII. Provided also, that if it shall happen that any person who shall have given to the overseers of any parish or township due notice of his claim to have his name inserted in the list of voters in the election of a knight or knights of the shire, shall have been omitted by such overseers from such list, it shall be lawful for the barrister, upon the revision of such list, to insert therein the name of the person so omitted, in case it shall be proved to the satisfaction of such barrister that such person gave due notice of such his claim to the said overseers, and that he was entitled on the last day of July then next preceding to be inserted in the list of voters in the election of a knight or knights of the shire. * * *

XLIV–LII. [Regulations for registration of voters for boroughs.]

* * * * * * * * *

LVI. That for the purpose of defraying the expenses to be incurred by the overseers of the poor and by the clerk of the peace in carrying into effect the several provisions of this act, so far as relates to the electors for any county, or for any riding, parts, or division of a county, every person, upon giving notice of his claim as such elector to the overseers, as hereinbefore mentioned, shall pay or cause to be paid to the said overseers the sum of 1 s.; and such notice of claim shall not be deemed valid until such sum shall have been paid; and the overseers of each parish or township shall add all monies so received by them to the money collected or to be collected for the relief of the poor in such parish or townships, and such monies so added shall be applicable to the same purposes as monies collected for the relief of the poor; and that for the purpose of defraying the expenses to be incurred by the returning officer of every city and borough, and by the overseers of the several parishes and townships in every city and borough, and place sharing in the election therewith, in carrying into effect the provisions of this act, so far as relates to the electors for such city or borough, every such elector whose name shall be upon the register of voters for such city or borough for the time being shall be liable to the payment of 1 s. annually, which sum shall be levied and collected from each elector in addition to and as a part of the money payable by him as his contribution to the rate for the relief of the poor, and such sum shall be applicable to the same purposes as money collected for the relief of the poor; and that the expenses incurred by the overseers of any parish or township in making out, printing, and publishing the several lists and notices directed by this act, and all other expenses incurred by them in carrying into effect the provisions of this act, shall be defrayed out of the money collected or to be collected for the relief of the poor in such parish or township; and that all expenses incurred by the returning officer of any city or borough in causing the lists of the electors for such city or borough to be copied out and made into a register, and in causing copies of such register to be written or printed, shall be defrayed by the overseers of the poor of the several parishes and townships within such city or borough, or place sharing in the election therewith, out of the money collected or to be collected for the relief of the poor in such parishes and township, in proportion to the number of voters placed on the register of voters for each parish or township; and that all expenses incurred by the clerk of the peace of any county, riding, or parts in causing the lists of the electors for such county, riding, or parts, or for any division of such county, to be copied out and made into a register, and in causing copies of such register to be written or printed, and in otherwise carrying into effect the provisions of this act, shall be defrayed by the treasurer of such county, riding, or parts out of any public money in his hands, and he shall be allowed all such payments in his accounts: provided always, that no expenses incurred by any clerk of the peace under this act shall be so defrayed unless the account shall be laid before the justices of the peace at the next quarter sessions after such expenses shall have been incurred, and allowed by the court.

LVII. That every barrister appointed to revise any list of voters under this act shall be paid at the rate of five guineas for every day that he shall be so employed, over and above his travelling and other expenses; and every such barrister, after the termination of his last sitting, shall lay or cause to be laid before the lords commissioners of His Majesty's treasury for the time being a statement of the number of days during which he shall have been so employed, and an account of the travelling and other expenses incurred by him in respect of such employment; and the said lords commissioners shall make an order for the amount to be paid to such barrister.

* * * * * * * * *

LXII. That at every contested election of a knight or knights to serve in any future parliament for any county, or for any riding, parts, or division of a county, the polling shall commence at nine o'clock in the forenoon of the next day but two after the day fixed for the election, unless such next day but two shall be Saturday or Sunday, and then on the Monday following, at the principal place of election, and also at the several places to be appointed as hereinafter directed for taking polls; and such polling shall continue for two days only, such two days being successive days; (that is to say,) for seven hours on the first day of polling, and for eight hours on the second day of polling; and no poll shall be kept open later than four o'clock in the afternoon of the second day; any statute to the contrary notwithstanding.

LXIII. That the respective counties in England and Wales, and the respective ridings, parts, and divisions of counties, shall be divided into convenient districts for polling, and in each district shall be appointed a convenient place for taking the poll at all elections of a knight or knights of the shire to serve in any future parliament, and such districts and places for taking the poll shall be settled and appointed by the act to be passed in this present parliament for the purpose of settling and describing the divisions of the counties enumerated in the schedule marked (F.) to this act annexed; provided that no county, nor any riding, parts, or division of a county, shall have more than fifteen districts and respective places appointed for taking the poll for such county, riding, parts, or division.

LXIV. That at every contested election for any county, riding, parts, or division of a county, the sheriff, under-sheriff, or sheriff's deputy shall, if required thereto by or on behalf of any candidate, on the day fixed for the election, and if not so required may if it shall appear to him expedient, cause to be erected a reasonable number of booths for taking the poll at the principal place of election, and also at each of the polling places so to be appointed as aforesaid, and shall cause to be affixed on the most conspicuous part of each of the said booths the names of the several parishes, townships, and places for which such booth is respectively allotted; and no person shall be admitted to vote at any such election in respect of any property situate in any parish, township, or place, except at the booth so allotted for such parish, township, or place, and if no booth shall be so allotted for the same, then at any of the booths for the same district; and in case any parish, township, or place shall happen not to be included in any of the districts to be appointed, the votes in respect of property situate in any parish, township, or places omitted shall be taken at the principal place of election for the county, or riding, parts, or division of the county, as the case may be.

* * * * * * * * *

LXXI. That from and after the end of this present parliament all booths erected for the convenience of taking polls shall be erected at the joint and equal expense of the several candidates, and the same shall be erected by contract with the candidates, if they shall think fit to make such contract, or if they shall not make such contract, then the same shall be erected by the sheriff or other returning officer at the expense of the several candidates as aforesaid, subject to such limitation as is hereinafter next mentioned; (that is to say,) that the expense to be incurred for the booth or booths to be erected at the principal place of election * * * or at any of the polling places so to be appointed as aforesaid, shall not exceed the sum of 40 £ in respect of any one such principal place of election or any one such polling place; and that the expense to be incurred for any booth or booths to be erected for any parish, district, or part of any city or borough shall not exceed the sum of 25 £ in respect of any one such parish, district, or part; and that all deputies appointed by the sheriff or other returning officer shall be paid each two guineas by the day, and all clerks employed in taking the poll shall be paid each one guinea by the day, at the expense of the candidates at such election: provided always, that if any person shall be proposed without his consent, then the person so proposing him shall be liable to defray his share of the said expenses in like manner as if he had been a candidate; provided also, that the sheriff or other returning officer may, if he shall think fit, instead of erecting such booth or booths as aforesaid, procure or hire and use any houses or other buildings for the purpose of taking the poll therein, subject always to the same regulations, provisions, liabilities, and limitations of expense as are hereinbefore mentioned with regard to booths for taking the poll.

* * * * * * * * *

LXXVIII. Provided always, that nothing in this act contained shall extend to or in any wise affect the election of members to serve in parliament for the universities of Oxford or Cambridge, or shall entitle any person to vote in the election of members to serve in parliament for the city of Oxford or town of Cambridge in respect of the occupation of any chamber or premises in any of the colleges or halls of the universities of Oxford or Cambridge.

* * * * * * * * *

264. Abolition of Negro Slavery

(1833, August 28. 3 & 4 William IV. c. 73.)

WHEREAS divers Persons are holden in Slavery within divers of His Majesty's Colonies, and it is just and expedient that all such Persons should be manumitted and set free, and that a reasonable Compensation should be made to the Persons hitherto entitled to the Services of such Slaves for the Loss which they will incur by being deprived of their Right to such Services: And whereas it is also expedient that Provision should be made for promoting the Industry and securing the good Conduct of the Persons so to be manumitted, for a limited Period after such their Manumission: And whereas it is necessary that the Laws now in force in the said several Colonies should forthwith be adapted to the new State and Relations of Society therein which will follow upon such general Manumission as aforesaid of the said Slaves; and that, in order to afford the necessary Time for such Adaptation of the said Laws, a short Interval should elapse before such Manumission should take effect: Be it therefore enacted by the King's most Excellent Majesty, by and with the Advice and Consent of the Lords Spiritual and Temporal, and Commons, in this present Parliament assembled, and by the Authority of the same, That from and after the First Day of August One thousand eight hundred and thirty-four all Persons who in conformity with the Laws now in force in the said Colonies respectively shall on or before the First Day of August One thousand eight hundred and thirty-four have been duly registered as Slaves in any such Colony, and who on the said First Day of August One thousand eight hundred and thirty-four shall be actually within any such Colony, and who shall by such Registries appear to be on the said First Day of August One thousand eight hundred and thirty-four of the full Age of Six Years or upwards, shall by force and virtue of this Act, and without the previous Execution of any Indenture of Apprenticeship, or other Deed or Instrument for that Purpose, become and be apprenticed Labourers; provided that, for the Purposes aforesaid, every Slave engaged in his ordinary Occupation on the Seas shall be deemed and taken to be within the Colony to which such Slave shall belong.

II. And be it further enacted, That during the Continuance of the Apprenticeship of any such apprenticed Labourer such Person or Persons shall be entitled to the Services of such apprenticed Labourer as would for the Time being have been entitled to his or her Services as a Slave if this Act had not been made.

III. Provided also, and be it further enacted, That all Slaves who may at any Time previous to the passing of this Act have been brought with the Consent of their Possessors, and all apprenticed Labourers who may hereafter with the like Consent be brought, into any Part of the United Kingdom of Great Britain and Ireland, shall from and after the passing of this Act be absolutely and entirely free to all Intents and Purposes whatsoever.

*   *   *   *   *   *   *   *   *

XXIV. And whereas, towards compensating the Persons at present entitled to the Services of the Slaves to be manumitted and set free by virtue of this Act for the Loss of such Services, His Majesty's most dutiful and loyal Subjects the Commons of Great Britain and Ireland in Parliament assembled have resolved to give and grant to His Majesty the Sum of Twenty Millions Pounds Sterling; be it enacted, That the Lords Commissioners of His Majesty's Treasury of the United Kingdom of Great Britain and Ireland may raise such Sum or Sums of Money as shall be required from Time to Time under the Provisions of this Act, and may grant as the Consideration for such Sum or Sums of Money Redeemable Perpetual Annuities or Annuities for Terms of Years. * * *

*   *   *   *   *   *   *   *   *

XXXIII. And for the Distribution of the said Compensation Fund, and the Apportionment thereof amongst the several Persons who may prefer Claims thereon, be it enacted, That it shall and may be lawful for His Majesty from Time to Time, by a Commission under the Great Seal of the United Kingdom, to constitute and appoint such Persons, not being less than Five, as to His Majesty shall seem meet, to be Commissioners of Arbitration for inquiring into and deciding upon the Claims to Compensation which may be preferred to them under this Act.

*   *   *   *   *   *   *   *   *

XLV. And be it further enacted, That the said Commissioners shall proceed to apportion the said Sum into Nineteen different Shares, which shall be respectively assigned to the several British Colonies or Possessions hereinafter mentioned; (that is to say,) the Bermuda Islands, the Bahama Islands, Jamaica, Honduras, the Virgin Islands, Antigua, Montserrat, Nevis, Saint Christopher's, Dominica, Barbadoes, Grenada, Saint Vincent's, Tobago, Saint Lucia, Trinidad, British Guiana, the Cape of Good Hope, and Mauritius; and in making such Apportionment of the said Funds between the said several Colonies the said Commissioners shall and are hereby required to have regard to the Number of Slaves belonging to or settled in each of such Colonies as the same may appear and are stated according to the latest Returns made in the Office of the Registrar of Slaves in England, appointed in pursuance and under the Authority of an Act passed in the Fifty-ninth Year of His late Majesty King George the Third, intituled An Act for establishing a Registry of Colonial Slaves in Great Britain, and for making further Provision with respect to the Removal of Slaves from British Colonies; and the said Commissioners shall and they are hereby further required, in making such Apportionment as aforesaid, to have regard to the Prices for which, on an Average of Eight Years ending on the Thirty-first Day of December One thousand eight hundred and thirty, Slaves have been sold in each of the Colonies aforesaid respectively, excluding from Consideration any such Sales in which they shall have sufficient Reason to suppose that such Slaves were sold or purchased under any Reservation, or subject to any express or tacit Condition affecting the Price thereof; and the said Commissioners shall then proceed to ascertain, in reference to each Colony, what Amount of Sterling Money will represent the average Value of a Slave therein for the said Period of Eight Years; and the total Number of the Slaves in each Colony being multiplied into the Amount of Sterling Money so representing such average Value as aforesaid of a Slave therein, the Product of such Multiplication shall be ascertained for each such Colony separately; and the said Twenty Millions of Pounds Sterling shall then be assigned to and apportioned amongst the said several Colonies rateably and in proportion to the Product so ascertained for each respectively.

* * * * * * * * *

265. Affirmation allowed instead of Oath

(1833, August 28.   3 & 4 William IV. c. 82.)

WHEREAS there are in various Places in Ireland, and in some Parts of England, and elsewhere, certain Dissenters from the United Church of England and Ireland, and from the Church of Scotland, commonly called Separatists, the Members of which Class or Sect of Dissenters, from conscientious Scruples, refuse to take an Oath in Courts of Justice and other Places, and in consequence thereof are exposed to great Losses and Inconveniences in their Trades and Concerns, and are subject to Fines and to Imprisonment for Contempt of Court, and the Community at large are deprived of the Benefit of their Testimony: And whereas it is therefore expedient that the said Sect called Separatists should be relieved in manner hereinafter mentioned; be it enacted by the King's most Excellent Majesty, by and with the Advice and Consent of the Lords Spiritual and Temporal, and Commons, in this present Parliament assembled, and by the Authority of the same, That every Person for the Time being belonging to the said Sect called Separatists, who shall be required upon any lawful Occasion to take an Oath in any Case where by Law an Oath is or may be required, shall, instead of the usual Form, be permitted to make his or her solemn Affirmation or Declaration in these Words following; videlicet,

'I A. B. do, in the Presence of Almighty God, solemnly, sincerely, and truly affirm and declare that I am a Member of the Religious Sect called Separatists, and that the taking of any Oath is contrary to my Religious Belief, as well as essentially opposed to the Tenets of that Sect; and I do also in the same solemn Manner affirm and declare'

Which said solemn Affirmation or Declaration shall be adjudged and taken, and is hereby enacted and declared to be of the same Force and Effect, to all Intents and Purposes, in all Courts of Justice and other Places whatsoever where by Law an Oath is or may be required, as if such Separatists had taken an Oath in the usual Form.

II.   And be it further enacted, That if any Person making such solemn Affirmation or Declaration shall in fact not be one of the People commonly called Separatists, or shall wilfully, falsely, and corruptly affirm or declare any other Matter or Thing which if the same had been sworn in the usual Form would have amounted to wilful and corrupt Perjury, every such Person so offending shall incur the same Penalties and Forfeitures as by the Laws and Statutes of this Kingdom are or may be enacted or provided against Persons convicted of wilful and corrupt Perjury.

———◆———

266. Jewish Relief Act

(1858, July 23. 21 & 22 Victoria, c. 49.)

BE it enacted by the Queen's most Excellent Majesty, by and with the Advice and Consent of the Lords Spiritual and Temporal, and Commons, in this present Parliament assembled, and by the Authority of the same, as follows:

I. Where it shall appear to either House of Parliament that a Person professing the Jewish Religion, otherwise entitled to sit and vote in such House, is prevented from so sitting and voting by his conscientious Objection to take the Oath which by an Act passed or to be passed in the present Session of Parliament has been or may be substituted for the Oaths of Allegiance, Supremacy, and Abjuration in the Form therein required, such House, if it think fit, may resolve that thenceforth any Person professing the Jewish Religion, in taking the said Oath to entitle him to sit and vote as aforesaid, may omit the Words "and I make this Declaration upon the true Faith of a Christian," and so long as such Resolution shall continue in force the said Oath, when taken and subscribed by any Person professing the Jewish Religion to entitle him to sit and vote in that House of Parliament, may be modified accordingly; and the taking and subscribing by any Person professing the Jewish Religion of the Oath so modified shall, as far as respects the Title to sit and vote in such House, have the same Force and Effect as the taking and subscribing by other Persons of the said Oath in the Form required by the said Act.

II. In all other Cases, except for sitting in Parliament as aforesaid, or in qualifying to exercise the Right of Presentation to any Ecclesiastical Benefice in Scotland, whenever any of Her Majesty's Subjects professing the Jewish Religion shall be required to take the said Oath, the Words "and I make this Declaration upon the true Faith of a Christian" shall be omitted.

III. Nothing herein contained shall extend or be construed

to extend to enable any Person or Persons professing the Jewish
Religion to hold or exercise the Office of Guardians and Justices
of the United Kingdom, or of Regent of the United Kingdom,
under whatever Name, Style, or Title such Office may be constituted, or of Lord High Chancellor, Lord Keeper or Lord Commissioner of the Great Seal of Great Britain or Ireland, or the
Office of Lord Lieutenant or Deputy or other Chief Governor or
Governors of Ireland, or Her Majesty's High Commissioner to
the General Assembly of the Church of Scotland.

IV. Where any Right of Presentation to any Ecclesiastical
Benefice shall belong to any Office in the Gift or Appointment of
Her Majesty, Her Heirs or Successors, and such Office shall be
held by a Person professing the Jewish Religion, the Right of
Presentation shall devolve upon and be exercised by the Archbishop of Canterbury for the Time being; and it shall not be
lawful for any Person professing the Jewish Religion, directly or
indirectly, to advise Her Majesty, Her Heirs or Successors, or
any Person or Persons holding or exercising the Office of Guardians of the United Kingdom, or of Regent of the United Kingdom, under whatever Name, Style, or Title such Office may be
constituted, or the Lord Lieutenant or Lord Deputy, or any other
Chief Governor or Governors of Ireland, touching or concerning
the Appointment to or Disposal of any Office or Preferment in
the United Church of England and Ireland or in the Church of
Scotland; and if such Person shall offend in the Premises he
shall, being thereof convicted by due Course of Law, be deemed
guilty of a high Misdemeanor, and disabled for ever from holding any Office, Civil or Military, under the Crown.

267. Reform Act of 1867

(1867, August 15. 30 & 31 Victoria, c. 102.)

WHEREAS it is expedient to amend the laws relating to the
representation of the people in England and Wales:
Be it enacted by the queen's most excellent Majesty, by and
with the advice and consent of the lords spiritual and temporal,
and commons, in this present parliament assembled, and by the
authority of the same as follows:

1. This act shall be cited for all purposes as "The Representation of the People Act, 1867."

2. This act shall not apply to Scotland or Ireland, nor in any wise affect the election of members to serve in parliament for the universities of Oxford or Cambridge.

PART I

FRANCHISES

3. Every man shall, on and after the year one thousand eight hundred and sixty-eight, be entitled to be registered as a voter, and, when registered, to vote for a member or members to serve in parliament for a borough, who is qualified as follows; (that is to say,)

  1. Is of full age, and not subject to any legal incapacity; and

  2. Is on the last day of July in any year, and has during the whole of the preceding twelve calendar months been, an inhabitant occupier, as owner or tenant, of any dwelling house within the borough; and

  3. Has during the time of such occupation been rated as an ordinary occupier in respect of the premises so occupied by him within the borough to all rates (if any) made for the relief of the poor in respect of such premises; and

  4. Has on or before the twentieth day of July in the same year *bona fide* paid an equal amount in the pound to that payable by other ordinary occupiers in respect of all poor rates that have become payable by him in respect of the said premises up to the preceding fifth day of January:

Provided that no man shall under this section be entitled to be registered as a voter by reason of his being a joint occupier of any dwelling house.

4. Every man shall, in and after the year one thousand eight hundred and sixty-eight, be entitled to be registered as a voter, and, when registered, to vote for a member or members to serve in parliament for a borough, who is qualified as follows; (that is to say,)

  1. Is of full age and not subject to any legal incapacity, and

  2. As a lodger has occupied in the same borough separately and as sole tenant for the twelve months preceding the last day of July in any year the same lodgings, such

lodgings being part of one and the same dwelling house, and of a clear yearly value, if let unfurnished, of ten pounds or upwards; and

3. Has resided in such lodgings for the twelve months immediately preceding the last day of July, and has claimed to be registered as a voter at the next ensuing registration of voters.

5. Every man shall, in and after the year one thousand eight hundred and sixty-eight, be entitled to be registered as a voter, and, when registered, to vote for a member or members to serve in parliament for a county, who is qualified as follows; (that is to say,)

1. Is of full age, and not subject to any legal incapacity, and is seised at law or in equity of any lands or tenements of freehold, copyhold, or any other tenure whatever, for his own life, or for the life of another, or for any lives whatsoever, or for any larger estate of the clear yearly value of not less than five pounds over and above all rents and charges payable out of or in respect of the same, or who is entitled, either as lessee or assignee, to any lands or tenements of freehold or of any other tenure whatever for the unexpired residue, whatever it may be, of any term originally created for a period of not less than sixty years (whether determinable on a life or lives or not), of the clear yearly value of not less than five pounds over and above all rents and charges payable out of or in respect of the same:

Provided that no person shall be registered as a voter under this section unless he has complied with the provisions of the twenty-sixth section of the act of the second year of the reign of His Majesty William the Fourth, Chapter forty-five.

6. Every man shall, in and after the year one thousand eight hundred and sixty-eight, be entitled to be registered as a voter, and, when registered, to vote for a member or members to serve in parliament for a county, who is qualified as follows; (that is to say,)

1. Is of full age, and not subject to any legal incapacity, and

2. Is on the last day of July in any year, and has during the twelve months immediately preceding been, the occupier, as owner or tenant, of lands or tenants within the county of the rateable value of twelve pounds or upwards; and

3. Has during the time of such occupation been rated in respect to the premises so occupied by him to all rates (if any) made for the relief of the poor in respect of the said premises; and

4. Has on or before the twentieth day of July in the same year paid all poor rates that have become payable by him in respect of the said premises up to the preceding fifth day of January.

* * * * * * * * *

PART II

Distribution of Seats

17. From and after the end of this present parliament, no borough which has a less population than ten thousand at the census of one thousand eight hundred and sixty-one shall return more than one member to serve in parliament, such boroughs being enumerated in schedule (A.) [38 in all] to this act annexed.

18. From and after the end of this present parliament, the city of Manchester, and the boroughs of Liverpool, Birmingham, and Leeds, shall each respectively return three members to serve in parliament.

19. Each of the places named in schedule (B.) [10 in all] to this act annexed shall be a borough, and, until otherwise directed by parliament, each such borough shall comprise such places as are specified and described in connection with the name of each such borough in the said schedule (B.); and in all future parliaments the borough of Chelsea, named in the said schedule, shall return two members, and each of the other boroughs named in the said schedule shall return one member to serve in parliament.

20. Registers of voters shall be formed in and after the year one thousand eight hundred and sixty-eight, notwithstanding the continuance of this present parliament, for or in respect of the boroughs constituted by this act, in like manner as if before the passing of this act they respectively had been boroughs returning members to serve in parliament.

21. From and after the end of the present parliament, the boroughs of Merthyr Tydfil and Salford shall each return two members instead of one to serve in future parliaments; and the borough of the Tower Hamlets shall be divided into two divisions, and each division shall in all future parliaments be a separate borough returning two members to serve in parliament.

The said divisions shall be known by the name of the borough of Hackney and the borough of the Tower Hamlets, and, until otherwise directed by parliament, shall comprise the places mentioned in connection with each such borough in schedule (C.) hereto annexed.

22. Registers of voters shall be formed in and after the year one thousand eight hundred and sixty-eight, notwithstanding the continuance of this present parliament, in respect of the said boroughs of Hackney and of the Tower Hamlets constituted under this act in like manner as if such divisions had previously to the passing of this act been separate boroughs returning members to serve in parliament.

23. From and after the end of the present parliament, each county named in the first column of schedule (D.) [8 counties divided into 3 divisions, 4 divisions of counties made in 1832 divided into 2 divisions, and the west riding of Yorkshire divided into 3 divisions] to this act annexed shall be divided into the divisions named in the second column of the said schedule, and, until otherwise directed by parliament, each of such divisions shall consist of the hundreds, lathes, wapentakes, and places mentioned in the third column of the said schedule.

In all future parliaments there shall be two members to serve for each of the divisions specified in the said second column, and such members shall be chosen in the same manner, and by the same description of voters, and in respect of the same rights of voting, as if each such division were a separate county.

All enactments relating to divisions of counties returning members to serve in parliament shall be deemed to apply to the divisions constituted as aforesaid.

Registers of voters shall be formed in and after the year one thousand eight hundred and sixty-eight, notwithstanding the continuance of this present parliament, for or in respect of the divisions of counties constituted by this act, in like manner as if before the passing of this act they had respectively been counties returning members to serve in parliament.

24. In all future parliaments the university of London shall return one member to serve in parliament.

25. Every man whose name is for the time being on the register of graduates constituting the convocation of the university of London shall, if of full age, and not subject to any legal incapacity, be entitled to vote in the election of a member to serve in any future parliament for the said university.

PART III

SUPPLEMENTAL PROVISION .

*   *   *   *   *   *   *   *   *

REGISTRATION OF VOTERS

30. The following regulations shall in and after the year one thousand eight hundred and sixty-eight be observed with respect to the registration of voters:

    1. The overseers of every parish or township shall make out or cause to be made out a list of all persons on whom a right to vote for a county in respect of the occupation of premises is conferred by this act, in the same manner, and subject to the same regulations, as nearly as circumstances admit, in and subject to which the overseers of parishes and townships in boroughs are required by the registration acts to make out or cause to be made out a list of all persons entitled to vote for a member or members for a borough in respect of the occupation of premises of a clear yearly value of no. less than ten pounds:

*   *   *   *   *   *   *   *   *

MISCELLANEOUS

51. Whereas great inconvenience may arise from the enactments now in force limiting the duration of the parliament in being at the demise of the crown: be it therefore enacted, that the parliament in being at any future demise of the crown shall not be determined or dissolved by such demise, but shall continue so long as it would have continued but for such demise, unless it should be sooner prorogued or dissolved by the crown, anything in the act passed in the sixth year of Her late Majesty queen Anne, chapter seven, in any way notwithstanding.

52. Whereas it is expedient to amend the law relating to offices of profit the acceptance of which from the crown vacates the seats of members accepting the same, but does not render them incapable of being reëlected: be it enacted, that where a person has been returned as a member to serve in parliament since the acceptance by him from the crown of any office described in schedule (H.) to this act annexed, the subsequent acceptance by him from the crown of any other office or offices described in such schedule in lieu of and in immediate succession the one to the other shall not vacate his seat.

*   *   *   *   *   *   *   *   *

268. Disestablishment of the Irish Church

(1869, July 26.   32 & 33 Victoria, c. 42.)

WHEREAS it is expedient that the union created by act of parliament between the churches of England and Ireland, as by law established, should be dissolved, and that the Church of Ireland, as so separated, should cease to be established by law, and that after satisfying, so far as possible, upon principles of equality as between the several religious denominations of Ireland, all just and equitable claims, the property of the said Church of Ireland, or the proceeds thereof, should be applied in such manner as parliament shall hereafter direct:

And whereas Her Majesty has been graciously pleased to signify that she has placed at the disposal of parliament her interests in the several archbishoprics, bishoprics, benefices, cathedral preferments, and other ecclesiastical dignities and offices in Ireland:

Be it therefore enacted by the queen's most excellent Majesty, by and with the advice and consent of the lords spiritual and temporal, and commons, in this present parliament assembled, and by the authority of the same, as follows:

1. This act may be cited for all purposes as "The Irish Church Act, 1869."

2. On and after the first day of January one thousand eight hundred and seventy-one the said union created by act of parliament between the Churches of England and Ireland shall be dissolved, and the said Church of Ireland, herein-after referred to as "the said church," shall cease to be established by law.

* * * * * * * * *

269. Education Act

(1870, August 9.   33 & 34 Victoria, c. 75.)

* * * * * * * * *

SUPPLY OF SCHOOLS

5. THERE shall be provided for every school district a sufficient amount of accommodation in public elementary schools (as herein-after defined) available for all the children resident in

such district for whose elementary education efficient and suitable provision is not otherwise made, and where there is an insufficient amount of such accommodation, in this act referred to as "public school accommodation," the deficiency shall be supplied in manner provided by this act.

6. Where the education department, in the manner provided by this act, are satisfied and have given public notice that there is an insufficient amount of such accommodation for any school district, and the deficiency is not supplied as herein-after required, a school board shall be formed for such district and shall supply such deficiency, and in case of default by the school board the education department shall cause the duty of such board to be performed in manner provided by this act.

* * * * * * * * *

MANAGEMENT AND MAINTENANCE OF SCHOOLS BY SCHOOL BOARD

14. Every school provided by a school board shall be conducted under the control and management of such board in accordance with the following regulations:

(1) The school shall be a public elementary school within the meaning of this act:

(2) No religious catechism or religious formulary which is distinctive of any particular denomination shall be taught in the school.

* * * * * * * * *

17. Every child attending a school provided by any school board shall pay such weekly fee as may be prescribed by the school board, with the consent of the education department, but the school board may from time to time, for a renewable period not exceeding six months, remit the whole or any part of such fee in the case of any child when they are of opinion that the parent of such child is unable from poverty to pay the same, but such remission shall not be deemed to be parochial relief given to such parent.

* * * * * * * * *

CONSTITUTION OF SCHOOL BOARDS

29. The school board shall be elected in manner provided by this act, — in a borough by the persons whose names are on the burgess roll of such borough for the time being in force, and in a parish not situate in the metropolis by the ratepayers.

At every such election every voter shall be entitled to a number of votes equal to the number of the members of the school
board to be elected, and may give all such votes to one candidate, or may distribute them among the candidates, as he thinks
fit.

The school board in the metropolis shall be elected in manner
herein-after provided by this act.

30. With respect to the constitution of a school board the following provisions shall have effect:

(1) The school board shall be a body corporate, by the
     name of the school board of the district to which
     they belong, having a perpetual succession and a
     common seal, with power to acquire and hold land
     for the purposes of this act without any license in
     mortmain:

*   *   *   *   *   *   *   *   *

40. Where the education department are of opinion that it
would be expedient to form a school district larger than a
borough or a parish or any school district formed under this act,
they may, except in the metropolis, by order made after such
inquiry and notice as herein-after mentioned, form a united
school district by uniting any two or more adjoining school districts, and upon such union cause a school board to be formed
for such united school district.

*   *   *   *   *   *   *   *   *

———◆———

270. The Ballot Act

(1872, July 18.   35 & 36 Victoria, c. 33.)

WHEREAS it is expedient to amend the law relating to procedure at parliamentary and municipal elections:

Be it enacted by the queen's most excellent Majesty, by and
with the advice and consent of the lords spiritual and temporal,
and commons, in this present parliament assembled, and by the
authority of the same, as follows:

PART I

Parliamentary Elections

PROCEDURE AT ELECTIONS

1. A candidate for election to serve in parliament for a county or borough shall be nominated in writing. The writing shall be subscribed by two registered electors of such county or borough as proposer and seconder, and by eight other registered electors of the same county or borough as assenting to the nomination, and shall be delivered during the time appointed for the election to the returning officer by the candidate himself, or his proposer or seconder.

If at the expiration of one hour after the time appointed for the election no more candidates stand nominated than there are vacancies to be filled up, the returning officer shall forthwith declare the candidates who may stand nominated to be elected, and return their names to the clerk of the crown in chancery; but if at the expiration of such hour more candidates stand nominated than there are vacancies to be filled up, the returning officer shall adjourn the election and shall take a poll in manner in this act mentioned.

A candidate may, during the time appointed for the election, but not afterwards, withdraw from his candidature by giving a notice to that effect, signed by him, to the returning officer: provided that the proposer of a candidate nominated in his absence out of the United Kingdom may withdraw such candidate by a written notice signed by him and delivered to the returning officer, together with a written declaration of such absence of the candidate.

If after the adjournment of an election by the returning officer for the purpose of taking a poll one of the candidates nominated shall die before the poll has commenced, the returning officer shall, upon being satisfied of the fact of such death, countermand notice of the poll, and all the proceedings with reference to the election shall be commenced afresh in all respects as if the writ had been received by the returning officer on the day on which proof was given to him of such death; provided that no fresh nomination shall be necessary in the case of a candidate who stood nominated at the time of the countermand of the poll.

2. In the case of a poll at an election the votes shall be given by ballot. The ballot of each voter shall consist of a paper (in this act called a ballot paper) showing the names and descrip-

tion of the candidates.   Each ballot paper shall have a number printed on the back, and shall have attached a counterfoil with the same number printed on the face.   At the time of voting, the ballot paper shall be marked on both sides with an official mark, and delivered to the voter within the polling station, and the number of such voter on the register of voters shall be marked on the counterfoil, and the voter having secretly marked his vote on the paper, and folded it up so as to conceal his vote, shall place it in a closed box in the presence of the officer presiding at the polling station (in this act called "the presiding officer") after having shown to him the official mark at the back.

Any ballot paper which has not on its back the official mark, or on which votes are given to more candidates than the voter is entitled to vote for, or on which anything, except the said number on the back, is written or marked by which the voter can be identified, shall be void and not counted.

After the close of the poll the ballot boxes shall be sealed up, so as to prevent the introduction of additional ballot papers, and shall be taken charge of by the returning officer, and that officer shall, in the presence of such agents, if any, of the candidates as may be in attendance, open the ballot boxes, and ascertain the result of the poll by counting the votes given to each candidate, and shall forthwith declare to be elected the candidates or candidate to whom the majority of votes have been given, and return their names to the clerk of the crown in chancery.   The decision of the returning officer as to any question arising in respect of any ballot paper shall be final, subject to reversal on petition questioning the election or return.

Where an equality of votes is found to exist between any candidates at an election for a county or borough, and the addition of a vote would entitle any of such candidates to be declared elected, the returning officer, if a registered elector of such county or borough, may give such additional vote, but shall not in any other case be entitled to vote at an election for which he is returning officer.

*   *   *   *   *   *   *   *   *

PART II

Municipal Elections

20.   The poll at every contested municipal election shall, so far as circumstances admit, be conducted in the manner in which the poll is by this act directed to be conducted at a contested

parliamentary election, and, subject to the modifications expressed in the schedules annexed hereto, such provision of this
act and of the said schedules as relate to or are concerned with a
poll at a parliamentary election shall apply to a poll at a contested municipal election: * * *

* * * * * * * * *

---

271. Supreme Court of Judicature Act

(1873, August 5.   36 & 37 Victoria, c. 66.)

WHEREAS it is expedient to constitute a supreme court, and
to make provision for the better administration of justice
in England:

And whereas it is also expedient to alter and amend the law relating to the judicial committee of Her Majesty's privy council:

Be it enacted by the queen's most excellent Majesty, by and
with the advice and consent of the lords spiritual and temporal,
and commons, in this present parliament assembled, and by the
authority of the same, as follows:

PRELIMINARY

1. This act may be cited for all purposes as the "Supreme
Court of Judicature Act, 1873."

2. This act, except any provision thereof which is declared to
take effect on the passing of this act, shall commence and come
into operation on the second day of November, 1874.

PART I

CONSTITUTION AND JUDGES OF SUPREME COURT

3. From and after the time appointed for the commencement
of this act, the several courts herein-after mentioned, (that is
to say,) the high court of chancery of England, the court of
queen's bench, the court of common pleas at Westminster, the
court of exchequer, the high court of admiralty, the court of
probate, the court for divorce and matrimonial causes, and the
London court of bankruptcy, shall be united and consolidated

together, and shall constitute, under and subject to the provisions of this act, one supreme court of judicature in England.

4. The said supreme court shall consist of two permanent
divisions, one of which, under the name of "Her Majesty's High
Court of Justice," shall have and exercise original jurisdiction,
with such appellate jurisdiction from inferior courts as is hereinafter mentioned, and the other of which, under the name of
"Her Majesty's Court of Appeal," shall have and exercise appellate jurisdiction, with such original jurisdiction as herein-after
mentioned as may be incident to the determination of any
appeal.

5. Her Majesty's high court of justice shall be constituted as
follows: — The first judges thereof shall be the lord chancellor,
the lord chief justice of England, the master of the rolls, the
lord chief justice of the common pleas, the lord chief baron of
the exchequer, the several vice-chancellors of the high court of
chancery, the judge of the court of probate and of the court for
divorce and matrimonial causes, the several puisne justices of the
courts of queen's bench and common pleas respectively, the several junior barons of the court of exchequer, and the judge of the
high court of admiralty, except such, if any, of the aforesaid
judges as shall be appointed ordinary judges of the court of appeal.

Subject to the provisions herein-after contained, whenever the
office of a judge of the said high court shall become vacant, a
new judge may be appointed thereto by Her Majesty, by letters
patent. All persons to be hereafter appointed to fill the places
of the lord chief justice of England, the master of the rolls, the
lord chief justice of the common pleas, and the lord chief baron,
and their successors respectively, shall continue to be appointed
to the same respective offices, with the same precedence, and by
the same respective titles, and in the same manner, respectively,
as heretofore. Every judge who shall be appointed to fill the
place of any other judge of the said high court of justice shall be
styled in his appointment "Judge of Her Majesty's High Court
of Justice," and shall be appointed in the same manner in which
the puisne justices and junior barons of the superior courts of
common law have been heretofore appointed: provided always,
that if at the commencement of this act the number of puisne justices and junior barons who shall become judges of the said high
court shall exceed twelve in the whole, no new judge of the said
high court shall be appointed in the place of any such puisne
justice or junior baron who shall die or resign while such whole
number shall exceed twelve, it being intended that the perma-

nent number of judges of the said high court shall not exceed twenty-one.

All the judges of the said court shall have in all respects, save as in this act is otherwise expressly provided, equal power, authority, and jurisdiction; and shall be addressed in the manner which is now customary in addressing the judges of the superior courts of common law.

The lord chief justice of England for the time being shall be president of the said high court of justice in the absence of the lord chancellor.

6. Her Majesty's court of appeal shall be constituted as follows: — There shall be five ex-officio judges thereof, and also so many ordinary judges (not exceeding nine at any one time) as Her Majesty shall from time to time appoint. The ex-officio judges shall be the lord chancellor, the lord chief justice of England, the master of the rolls, the lord chief justice of the common pleas, and the lord chief baron of the exchequer. The first ordinary judges of the said court shall be the existing lords justices of appeal in chancery, the existing salaried judges of the judicial committee of Her Majesty's privy council, appointed under the "Judicial Committee Act, 1871," and such three other persons as Her Majesty may be pleased to appoint by letters patent; such appointment may be made either within one month before or at any time after the day appointed for the commencement of this act, but if made before shall take effect at the commencment of this act.

Besides the said ex-officio judges and ordinary judges, it shall be lawful for Her Majesty (if she shall think fit), from time to time to appoint under her royal sign manual, as additional judges of the court of appeal, any persons who, having held in England the office of a judge of the superior courts of Westminster hereby united and consolidated, or of Her Majesty's supreme court hereby constituted, or in Scotland the office of lord justice general or lord justice clerk, or in Ireland the office of lord chancellor or lord justice of appeal, or in India the office of chief justice of the high court of judicature at Fort William in Bengal, or Madras, or Bombay, shall respectively signify in writing their willingness to serve as such additional judges in the court of appeal. No such additional judge shall be deemed to have undertaken the duty of sitting in the court of appeal when prevented from so doing by attendance in the house of lords, or on the discharge of any other public duty, or by any other reasonable impediment.

The ordinary and additional judges of the court of appeal shall be styled lords justices of appeal. All the judges of the said court shall have, in all respects, save as in this act is otherwise expressly mentioned, equal power, authority, and jurisdiction.

Whenever the office of an ordinary judge of the court of appeal becomes vacant, a new judge may be appointed thereto by Her Majesty by letters patent.

The lord chancellor for the time being shall be president of the court of appeal.

* * * * * * * * *

9. All judges of the high court of justice, and of the court of appeal respectively, shall hold their offices for life, subject to a power of removal by Her Majesty, on an address presented to Her Majesty by both houses of parliament. No judge of either of the said courts shall be capable of being elected to or of sitting in the house of commons. Every judge of either of the said courts (other than the lord chancellor) when he enters on the execution of his office, shall take, in the presence of the lord chancellor, the oath of allegiance, and judicial oath as defined by the Promissory Oaths Act, 1868. The oaths to be taken by the lord chancellor shall be the same as heretofore.

* * * * * * * * *

PART II

JURISDICTION AND LAW

16. The high court of justice shall be a superior court of record, and, subject as in this act mentioned, there shall be transferred to and vested in the said high court of justice the jurisdiction which, at the commencement of this act, was vested in, or capable of being exercised by, all or any of the courts following; (that is to say,)

(1) The high court of chancery, as a common law court as well as a court of equity, including the jurisdiction of the master of the rolls, as a judge or master of the court of chancery, and any jurisdiction exercised by him in relation to the court of chancery as a common law court;

(2) The court of queen's bench;

(3) The court of common pleas at Westminster;

(4) The court of exchequer, as a court of revenue, as well as a common law court;

(5) The high court of admiralty;

    (6) The court of probate;
    (7) The court for divorce and matrimonial causes;
    (8) The London court of bankruptcy;
    (9) The court of common pleas at Lancaster;
  (10) The court of pleas at Durham;
  (11) The courts created by commissions of assize, of oyer
      and terminer, and of jail delivery, or any of such
      commissions:

The jurisdiction by this act transferred to the high court of justice shall include, (subject to the exceptions herein-after contained,) the jurisdiction which, at the commencement of this act, was vested in, or capable of being exercised by, all or any one or more of the judges of the said courts, respectively, sitting in court or chambers, or elsewhere, when acting as judges or a judge, in pursuance of any statute, law, or custom, and all powers given to any such court, or to any such judges or judge, by any statute; and also all ministerial powers, duties, and authorities, incident to any and every part of the jurisdictions so transferred.

  17. There shall not be transferred to or vested in the said high court of justice, by virtue of this act,—

    (1) Any appellate jurisdiction of the court of appeal in
      chancery, or of the same court sitting as a court of
      appeal in bankruptcy:
    (2) Any jurisdiction of the court of appeal in chancery of
      the county palatine of Lancaster:
    (3) Any jurisdiction usually vested in the lord chancellor or
      in the lords justices of appeal in chancery, or either
      of them, in relation to the custody of the persons and
      estates of idiots, lunatics, and persons of unsound
      mind:
    (4) Any jurisdiction vested in the lord chancellor in relation
      to grants of letters patent, or the issue of commissions
      or other writings, to be passed under the great seal of
      the United Kingdom:
    (5) Any jurisdiction exercised by the lord chancellor in
      right of or on behalf of Her Majesty as visitor of any
      college, or of any charitable or other foundation:
    (6) Any jurisdiction of the master of the rolls in relation to
      records in London or elsewhere in England.

  18. The court of appeal established by this act shall be a superior court of record, and there shall be transferred to and vested in such court all jurisdictions and powers of the courts following; (that is to say,)

(1) All jurisdictions and powers of the lord chancellor and of the court of appeal in chancery, in the exercise of his and its appellate jurisdiction, and of the same court as a court of appeal in bankruptcy:

(2) All jurisdiction and powers of the court of appeal in chancery of the county palatine of Lancaster, and all jurisdiction and powers of the chancellor of the duchy and county palatine of Lancaster when sitting alone or apart from the lords justices of appeal in chancery as a judge of re-hearing or appeal from decrees or orders of the court of chancery of the county palatine of Lancaster:

(3) All jurisdiction and powers of the court of the lord warden of the Stannaries assisted by his assessors, including all jurisdiction and powers of the said lord warden when sitting in his capacity of judge:

(4) All jurisdiction and powers of the court of exchequer chamber:

(5) All jurisdiction vested in or capable of being exercised by Her Majesty in council, or the judicial committee of Her Majesty's privy council, upon appeal from any judgment or order of the high court of admiralty, or from any order in lunacy made by the lord chancellor, or any other person having jurisdiction in lunacy.

19. The said court of appeal shall have jurisdiction and power to hear and determine appeals from any judgment or order, save as herein-after mentioned, of Her Majesty's high court of justice, or of any judges or judge thereof, subject to the provisions of this act, and to such rules and orders of court for regulating the terms and conditions on which such appeals shall be allowed, as may be made pursuant to this act.

For all the purposes of and incidental to the hearing and determination of any appeal within its jurisdiction, and the amendment, execution, and enforcement of any judgment or order made on any such appeal, and for the purpose of every other authority expressly given to the court of appeal by this act, the said court of appeal shall have all the power, authority, and jurisdiction by this act vested in the high court of justice.

20. No error or appeal shall be brought from any judgment or order of the high court of justice, or of the court of appeal, nor from any judgment or order, subsequent to the commencement of this act, of the court of chancery of the county palatine of

Lancaster, to the house of lords or to the judicial committee of Her Majesty's privy council; but nothing in this act shall prejudice any right existing at the commencement of this act to prosecute any pending writ of error or appeal, or to bring error or appeal to the house of lords or to Her Majesty in council, or to the judicial committee of the privy council, from any prior judgment or order of any court whose jurisdiction is hereby transferred to the high court of justice or to the court of appeal.

21. It shall be lawful for Her Majesty, if she shall think fit, at any time hereafter by order in council to direct that all appeals and petitions whatsoever to Her Majesty in council which according to the laws now in force ought to be heard by or before the judicial committee of Her Majesty's privy council, shall, from and after a time to be fixed by such order, be referred for hearing to and be heard by Her Majesty's court of appeal; and from and after the time fixed by such order, all such appeals and petitions shall be referred for hearing to and be heard by the said court of appeal accordingly, and shall not be heard by the said judicial committee; and for all the purposes of and incidental to the hearing of such appeals or petitions, and the reports to be made to Her Majesty thereon, and all orders thereon to be afterwards made by Her Majesty in council, and also for all purposes of and incidental to the enforcement of any such orders as may be made by the said court of appeals or by Her Majesty, pursuant to this section (but not for any other purpose), all the power, authority, and jurisdiction now by law vested in the said judicial committee shall be transferred to and vested in the said court of appeal.

The court of appeal, when hearing any appeals in ecclesiastical causes which may be referred to it in manner aforesaid, shall be constituted of such and so many of the judges thereof, and shall be assisted by such assessors being archbishops or bishops of the Church of England, as Her Majesty, by any general rules made with the advice of the judges of the said court, or any five of them (of whom the lord chancellor shall be one), and of the archbishops and bishops who are members of Her Majesty's privy council, or any two of them (and which general rules shall be made by order in council), may think fit to direct: provided that such rules shall be laid before each house of parliament within forty days of the making of the same, if parliament be then sitting, or if not, then within forty days of the commencement of the then next ensuing session; and if an address is presented to Her Majesty by either house of parliament within the next subsequent forty days on which the said house shall have sat, praying that any such rule may be annulled, Her Majesty may thereupon by order in council annul the same; and the rules so annulled shall thenceforth become void and of no effect, but without prejudice to the validity of any proceeding which may in the mean-time have been taken under the same.

22. From and after the commencement of this act the several jurisdictions which by this act are transferred to and vested in the said high court of justice and the said court of appeal respectively shall cease to be exercised, except by the said high court of justice and the said court of appeal respectively, as provided by this act; * * *

* * * * * * * * *

24. [Law and equity to be concurrently administered by both the High Court of Justice and the Court of Appeal.]

* * * * * * * * *

31. For the more convenient dispatch of business in the said high court of justice (but not so as to prevent any judge from sitting whenever required in any divisional court, or for any judge of a different division from his own), there shall be in the said high court five divisions consisting of such number of judges respectively as herein-after mentioned. * * *

The said five divisions shall be called respectively the chancery division, the queen's bench division, the common pleas division, the exchequer division, and the probate, divorce, and admiralty division. * * *

———◆———

272. Appellate Jurisdiction Act

(1876, August 11. 39 & 40 Victoria, c. 59.)

BE it enacted by the Queen's Most Excellent Majesty, by and with the advice and consent of the Lords Spiritual and Temporal, and Commons, in this present Parliament assembled, and by the authority of the same, as follows :

1. This Act may be cited for all purposes as "The Appellate Jurisdiction Act, 1876."

2. This Act shall, except when it is otherwise expressly provided, come into operation on the first day of November, 1876, which day is hereinafter referred to as the commencement of this Act.

3. Subject as in this Act mentioned, an appeal shall lie to the House of Lords from any order or judgment of any of the courts following ; that is to say,

(1) of Her Majesty's Court of Appeal in England ; and

(2) of any Court in Scotland from which error or an appeal at or immediately before the commencement of this Act lay to the House of Lords by common law or by statute ; and

(3) of any Court in Ireland from which error or an appeal at or immediately before the commencement of this Act lay to the House of Lords by common law or by statute.

4. Every appeal shall be brought by way of petition to the House of Lords, praying that the matter of the order or judgment appealed against may be reviewed before Her Majesty the Queen in Her Court of Parliament, in order that the said Court may determine what of right, and according to the law and custom of this realm, ought to be done in the subject-matter of such appeal.

5. An appeal shall not be heard and determined by the House of Lords unless there are present at such hearing and determination not less than three of the following persons, in this Act designated Lords of Appeal ; that is to say,

(1) The Lord Chancellor of Great Britain for the time being ; and

(2) The Lords of Appeal in Ordinary to be appointed as in this Act mentioned ; and

(3) Such Peers of Parliament as are for the time being holding or have held any of the offices in this Act described as high judicial offices.

6. For the purpose of aiding the House of Lords in the hearing and determination of appeals, Her Majesty may, at any time after the passing of this Act, by letters patent appoint two qualified persons to be Lords of Appeal in Ordinary, but such appointment shall not take effect until the commencement of this Act.

A person shall not be qualified to be appointed by Her Majesty a Lord of Appeal in Ordinary unless he has been at or before the time of his appointment the holder for a period of not less than two years of some one or more of the offices in this Act described as high judicial offices, or has been at or before such time as aforesaid, for not less than fifteen years, a practising barrister in England or Ireland, or a practising advocate in Scotland.

Every Lord of Appeal in Ordinary shall hold his office during good behaviour, and shall continue to hold the same notwithstanding the demise of the Crown, but he may be removed from such office on the address of both Houses of Parliament.

There shall be paid to every Lord of Appeal in Ordinary a salary of six thousand pounds a year.

Every Lord of Appeal in Ordinary, unless he is otherwise entitled to sit as a member of the House of Lords, shall by virtue and according to the date of his appointment be entitled during his life to rank as a Baron by such style as Her Majesty may be pleased to appoint, and shall during the time that he continues in his office as a Lord of Appeal in Ordinary, and no longer, be entitled to a writ of summons to attend, and to sit and vote in the House of Lords; his dignity as a Lord of Parliament shall not descend to his heirs.

On any Lord of Appeal in Ordinary vacating his office, by death, resignation, or otherwise, Her Majesty may fill up the vacancy by the appointment of another qualified person.

A Lord of Appeal in Ordinary shall, if a Privy Councillor, be a member of the Judicial Committee of the Privy Council, and, subject to the due performance by a Lord of Appeal in Ordinary of his duties as to the hearing and determining of appeals in the House of Lords, it shall be his duty, being a Privy Councillor, to sit and act as a member of the Judicial Committee of the Privy Council.

*   *   *   *   *   *   *   *   *

---

273. Abolition of Names of King's Bench, Common Pleas, and Exchequer for Divisions of the High Court of Justice

(1877, April 24.   40 Victoria, c. 9.)

*   *   *   *   *   *   *   *   *

4. AND whereas it is expedient that a uniform style should be provided for the ordinary judges of the court of appeal and for the judges of the high court of justice (other than the presidents of divisions): be it enacted, that the ordinary judges of the court of appeal shall be styled Lords Justices of Appeal, and the judges of the high court of justice (other than the presidents of divisions) shall be styled Justices of the High Court.

*   *   *   *   *   *   *   *   *

274. Abolition of Certain Judicial Offices

(1881, August 27.   44 & 45 Victoria, c. 68.)

* * * * * * * * *

2. FROM and after the passing of this act the present and every future Master of the Rolls shall cease to be a judge of Her Majesty's high court of justice, but shall continue by virtue of his office to be a judge of Her Majesty's court of appeal.

* * * * * * * * *

25. Where by any statute any power is given to or any act is required or authorised to be done by the Lord Chief Justice of the Common Pleas and the Lord Chief Baron of the Exchequer, or either of them, either solely or jointly with the Lord Chief Justice of the Queen's Bench or the Lord Chief Justice of England, and either with or without the Lord Chancellor or any judge, officer, or person, such power may henceforth be exercised and such act done by the Lord Chief Justice of England ; and where by any statute the concurrence of the Lord Chief Justice of the Common Pleas, and the Lord Chief Baron of the Exchequer, or either of them, is required for the exercise of any power, or the performance of any act, it shall be sufficient henceforth that the Lord Chief Justice of England shall concur therein.

* * * * * * * * *

———◆———

275. Reform Act of 1884

(1884, December 6.   48 Victoria, c. 3.)

BE it enacted by the queen's most excellent Majesty, by and with the advice and consent of the lords spiritual and temporal, and commons, in this present parliament assembled, and by the authority of the same, as follows :

PRELIMINARY

1. This act my be cited as the Representation of the People Act, 1884.

EXTENSION OF THE HOUSEHOLD AND LODGER FRANCHISE

2. A uniform household franchise and a uniform lodger franchise at elections shall be established in all counties and boroughs throughout the united kingdom, and every man possessed of a household qualification or a lodger qualification shall, if the qualifying premises be situate in a county in England or Scotland, be entitled to be registered as a voter, and when registered to vote at an election for such county, and if the qualifying premises be situate in a county or borough in Ireland, be entitled to be registered as a voter, and when registered to vote at an election for such county or borough.

3. Where a man himself inhabits any dwelling-house by virtue of any office, service, or employment, and the dwelling-house is not inhabited by any person under whom such man serves in such office, service, or employment, he shall be deemed for the purposes of this act and of the representation of the people acts to be an inhabitant occupier of such dwelling-house as a tenant.

* * * * * * * * *

276. Third Redistribution of Parliamentary Seats

(1885, June 25. 48 & 49 Victoria, c. 23.)

BE it enacted by the Queen's Most Excellent Majesty, by and with the advice and consent of the Lords Spiritual and Temporal, and Commons, in this present parliament and by the authority of the same, as follows:

PRELIMINARY

1. This act may be cited as "The Redistribution of Seats Act, 1885."

PART I

REDISTRIBUTION

Boroughs

2. From and after the end of this present parliament the parliamentary boroughs named in the first part of the First Schedule [103 in all] shall cease as boroughs to return any member.

*   *   *   *   *   *   *   *   *

3. [Boroughs of Macclesfield and Sandwich disfranchised for corruption.]

4. From and after the end of this present parliament the City of London shall return two members, and no more, and each of the parliamentary boroughs named in the Second Schedule [39 in all] shall return one member, and no more.

5. [Parliamentary boroughs named in Third Schedule [19 in all] given additional members.]

6. [Towns and places named in the Fourth Schedule [33 in all] made parliamentary boroughs.]

7. [Alterations of boundaries of boroughs.]

8. [Division of boroughs for electoral purposes.]

Counties

9. [Division of counties for electoral purposes into divisions returning one member each — the counties of England and Wales into 244 divisions, the counties of Scotland into 46 divisions, and the counties of Ireland into 85 divisions.]

*   *   *   *   *   *   *   *   *